German Atrocities, 1914

German Atrocities, 1914
A HISTORY OF DENIAL

John Horne and Alan Kramer

Yale University Press
New Haven and London

For information about this and other Yale University Press publications, please contact:
U.S. Office: sales.press@yale.edu   www.yale.edu/yup
Europe Office: sales@yaleup.co.uk   www.yaleup.co.uk

Set in WalbaumMT and Frutiger Condensed by Northern Phototypesetting Co Ltd, Bolton
Printed in Great Britain by Biddles Ltd, Guildford and King's Lynn

Library of Congress Cataloging-in-Publication Data

Horne, John N.
    German atrocities, 1914 : a history of denial / John Horne and Alan Kramer.
    Includes bibliographical references and index.
    ISBN 0–300–08975–9 cloth
        1. World War, 1914–1918—Atrocities. 2. World War, 1914–1918—Germany.
    3. World War, 1914–1918—Belgium. 4. World War, 1914–1918—France.
    5. War crimes. I. Kramer, Alan, 1954– II. Title.
    D626.G3 H67 2001
    940.4′05—dc21   2001026884

A catalogue record for this book is available from the British Library.

10 9 8 7 6 5 4 3 2 1

Contents

Illustrations, maps, figures, and table

Illustrations

Maps

Figures

Table

Preface

In a project lasting several years, which has used archives and libraries in eight countries and produced a number of articles and conference papers in addition to the present book, the authors have placed themselves in the debt of many individuals and institutions for their support.

We would like to acknowledge the consistent help and encouragement of our own university, Trinity College, Dublin, from friends and colleagues in Modern History and other departments, and at an official level the university's commitment to providing the time and funding necessary for research. Such support, while essential, cannot be taken for granted in the current academic climate; it is a pleasure, therefore, to be able to state it as a matter of public record.

Various institutions have provided financial aid. In Trinity College, the Provost's Fund, the Arts and Social Sciences Benefactions Fund, and the Grace Lawless Lee Trust facilitated research trips by both of us. The Grace Lawless Lee Trust also awarded a grant for maps and illustrations. The Royal Irish Academy provided a grant to start the project, and the British Council, Dublin, awarded a research travel grant. The Alexander von Humboldt Foundation, Bonn, provided generous assistance to Alan Kramer to carry out vital research in archives and libraries in Germany (1991–2, 1993, 1994, and 1997) and consult with the colleagues named below. Some of his writing took place at the University of Cape Town, South Africa, thanks to the hospitality of the Department of History and especially Bill Nasson. John Horne received a grant from the Société Belge d'Histoire Militaire and an Irish-Belgian (Francophone community) scholarship for research in Belgium; a French government scholarship (1996); a fellowship at the Institute for Advanced Study, Princeton (1994–5); and a fellowship at the Center for Historical Analysis, Rutgers University, New Jersey, in the same year; and a one-month associate position at the École des Hautes

Études en Sciences Sociales (Centre de Recherches Historiques), Paris, in
1997. We wish to record our gratitude to all these institutions.

We would like to express our appreciation to the archivists and librarians
in the various institutions in which we conducted our research. The good
humour and efficiency of our colleagues in the Library, Trinity College,
Dublin, was unfailing. Also particularly deserving of thanks are the staffs
of the Archives Générales du Royaume, the Bibliothèque Albert Ier, and the
Musée Royal de l'Armée, in Brussels; the Imperial War Museum and the
Public Record Office in London; the Bodleian Library, Department of
Western Manuscripts, Oxford; the Archives Nationales, the Bibliothèque de
Documentation Internationale Contemporaine, the Ministère des Affaires
Étrangères, the Service Historique de l'Armée de Terre, and the Musée
d'Histoire Contemporaine, in Paris; the Archives Départementales of the
Ardennes, Meurthe-et-Moselle, Nord, and Pas-de-Calais; the Bibliothek
für Zeitgeschichte and the Württembergisches Hauptstaatsarchiv,
Stuttgart, the Staats- und Universitätsbibliothek, Hamburg, the Badisches
Generallandesarchiv, Karlsruhe, the Bayerisches Hauptstaatsarchiv-
Militärarchiv, Munich, the Sächsisches Hauptstaatsarchiv, Dresden, the
Politisches Archiv des Auswärtigen Amts, Bonn (now Berlin), the
Bundesarchiv-Militärarchiv, Freiburg, the Bundesarchiv, Koblenz,
the Bundesarchiv and the Bundesarchiv-Militärarchiv, Potsdam, the
Bundesarchiv, Berlin, in Germany; the Centre for the Preservation of
Historical Documentary Collections, Moscow; the Nicholas Murray Butler
Library, Columbia University, New York, the Firestone Library, Princeton
University, the Library of the Institute for Advanced Study, Princeton, and
the National Archives, Washington, D.C.; and the Vatican Archive, Rome.

Many friends and colleagues have helped in a host of ways, from practical assistance to the generous sharing of research leads and information, to
critical discussion of ideas and findings. We cannot name them all, but we
hope they will recognize their contributions and accept our thanks. It would,
however, be invidious not to mention some of those whose help was crucial
at certain stages: the late Fritz Fischer, the late Arnold Sywottek, and
Michael Wildt, Hamburg; Reinhart Koselleck, Bielefeld; Karl Ditt,
Münster; Bernd Weisbrod, Göttingen; Laurent Gervereau, Paris; Rémy
Cazals, Toulouse; Christoph Mueller, Oxford; Irina Renz, Stuttgart; Gay
Conroy and Sarah Smyth, Dublin. Our thanks are also due to Matthew Stout
for the maps, Brendan Dempsey and Brian McGovern for photography.

We would also like to thank the following for their sustained interest and support: Aidan Clarke in Dublin; Trevor Wilson, Adelaide; Jean Stengers, Brussels; Richard Evans, Cambridge; Niall Ferguson, Oxford; Ioannis Sinanaglou, London; Stéphane Audoin-Rouzeau, Annette Becker, Fabienne Bock, and Christophe Prochasson in Paris; Gerhard Hirschfeld, Stuttgart; Gerd Krumeich and Wolfgang Mommsen, Düsseldorf; Jeffrey Herf at Maryland; Omer Bartov and John Chambers at Rutgers; Jay Winter in New York, and Peter Paret at Princeton. The usual disclaimer applies: none of those named bears any responsibility for the arguments advanced below, but we hope that when they read the book they feel their confidence in our project has not been misplaced.

Both authors would like to acknowledge the commitment to this book of Robert Baldock, the copy-editor Ann Bone, and the staff of Yale University Press, and their sheer professionalism in bringing the manuscript to publication.

Finally, the greatest debt of gratitude for each of us is personal. John Horne wishes to acknowledge the unflagging faith in the project of his wife, Michèle Clarke, and the loving forbearance of Alannah and Chloë. Alan Kramer wishes to thank his wife, Renate Ahrens-Kramer, for all her constant support and critical acumen.

Alan Kramer and John Horne
Dublin, November 2000

Abbreviations, technical terms, and place names

Abbreviations in the main text

BDIC	Bibliothèque de Documentation Internationale Contemporaine (Paris)
BEF	British Expeditionary Force
CPI	Committee on Public Information
DDP	Deutsche Demokratische Partei
DVP	Deutsche Volkspartei
DNVP	Deutschnationale Volkspartei
GHQ	Grand Headquarters
IR	Infantry Regiment (including Fusiliers and Grenadiers)
MHC	Musée d'Histoire Contemporaine (Paris)
MP	Member of Parliament
MRA	Musée Royal de l'Armée (Brussels)
NCO	non-commissioned officer
NWAC	National War Aims Committee
OHL	Oberste Heeresleitung (Supreme Army Command)
POB	Parti Ouvrier Belge
POW	prisoner of war
SHA	Service Historique de l'Armée de Terre (Vincennes)
SPD	Sozialdemokratische Partei Deutschlands
TCD	Trinity College, Dublin
UDC	Union of Democratic Control
UGACPE	Union des Grandes Associations contre la Propagande Ennemie
USPD	Unabhängige Sozialdemokratische Partei Deutschlands
WTB	Wolff'sches Telegraphen-Bureau

Technical terms

Infantry regiment (IR) Numbered sequentially in the German army through the Prussian, Württemberg, Baden, and Saxon contingents. Bavarian regiments were numbered separately. 'Fusilier' and 'Grenadier' were honorific titles and implied no difference in function; they have therefore also been abbreviated as 'IR'. Guards regiments have been designated separately. Infantry regiments consisted of three battalions, each of about 1,000 men. The battalion had four companies, and the company three platoons. Jäger battalions consisted of light infantry marksmen.

	The **Landwehr** was the reserve composed of trained former soldiers; the **Landsturm** was a reserve composed of untrained youths and older men not intended for front duty.
Brigade	Consisted of two regiments.
Division	Consisted of two brigades, one-half or one cavalry regiment, one field artillery brigade, and sappers.
Army corps	Consisted of two divisions. Active army corps included foot artillery and an air detachment. Corps had their own general staff. The strength of an army corps of 25 battalions, 8 cavalry squadrons, and 24 field artillery batteries, with auxiliaries, was 41,000.
Army	The largest formation of troops, consisting of several active and reserve army corps. The German land army in 1914 consisted of seven armies on the Western Front, plus the Eighth Army on the Eastern Front, and several smaller formations. Each army had its own general staff.
Oberste Heeresleitung	The army supreme command.

Place names

We have given major places the names in common use in English at the time of the Great War; thus 'Louvain', rather than the Flemish 'Leuven', though we have adopted the modernized spelling of 'Liège', which in 1914 was 'Liége'. Otherwise, we are guided by the name now in common use; we thus use the Flemish name 'Aarschot', rather than 'Aerschot'. The contemporary German place names are used for Alsace and German Lorraine, rather than their current French names, although the latter are also given on first mention.

Introduction

On 4 August 1914, German troops invaded neutral Belgium. Within days, they were rumoured to be committing brutal 'atrocities' against innocent civilians. Comparable tales emerged from Lorraine, 250 kilometres to the south, where German troops simultaneously probed French territory. These stories of 'German atrocities' quickly found their way into the newspapers of the Entente, or Allied powers (Britain, France, and Russia), and their neutral sympathizers. They reached a crescendo as the German invasion swept through Belgium and north-eastern France before being halted at the battle of the Marne in early September. Only in October, when the subsequent German retreat ended in the deadlock of the trenches, did reports of new 'German atrocities' subside.

Accusations of 'atrocities' were not confined to one side. From the outset German soldiers told of 'Belgian atrocities' and 'French atrocities'. According to these accounts, enemy civilians treacherously attacked German troops when they least expected it – by ambush, when they slept, or as they lay wounded. In the most lurid stories, German soldiers were poisoned, blinded, and castrated. These stories, too, found their way quickly into the press and reached civilians at home. Belgian and French 'atrocities' were blamed on civilian irregular soldiers, or guerrillas, who were known as *francs-tireurs* (free-shooters). The term came from the Franco-Prussian War of 1870–1, when volunteer detachments of that name harassed the German armies. The image of the French franc-tireur had lingered in German memory and imagination and re-emerged in 1914 through the belief that enemy civilians were resisting a new German invasion.

It is these incompatible stories of enemy 'atrocities', which amounted to a conflict of mutual denial in which each side rejected the other's accusations, that we seek to explain in this book. In order to do so, we reconstruct as precisely as we can what actually happened during the two and a half months of the invasion in 1914. This is the first step to understanding how contemporaries could have come to such opposed views about it. Part I (chapters 1 and 2) is a history of the invasion constructed from the records of both sides. Yet the heart of the matter is to be found in subjective perceptions. What each side thought was going on — the stories it told — shaped what happened. We therefore have to discover the beliefs, myths, and cultural assumptions that structured the experience of the invasion. Part II (chapters 3 to 5) undertakes this for each side in turn.

The invasion, however, is only half the story. The 'atrocities' question did not disappear once the war of attrition set in. Official reports, newspaper accounts, pamphlets, and cartoons fuelled mutual accusations until by spring 1915, enemy 'atrocities' had become one of the defining issues of the war, for both sides. It was not just a question of the campaigns to win over opinion in neutral countries (America, Italy), important though these were. The 'atrocities' question helped mobilize national opinion behind the war in the main combatant countries by projecting a dehumanized image of the enemy. It is therefore important to understand how the issue was imaginatively and intellectually transformed by the process of cultural mobilization on both sides throughout the conflict. This is the subject of part III (chapters 6 to 8).

Since the 'atrocities' question gave meaning to the war, it also helped shape the peace. The Treaty of Versailles was considered by the Allies to be a moral reckoning and it therefore involved an attempt to try German military figures for 'war crimes' committed during and after the invasion of 1914, foreshadowing the Nuremberg tribunal by a quarter of a century. It has long been forgotten how for much of German opinion throughout the inter-war period the Allied charge of German war crimes stood alongside that of war guilt as the epitome of an unjust peace. But there was soon a reaction in the former Allied countries. Retrospective disillusionment with the war and growing scepticism at war propaganda led to the view that 'German atrocities' were the invention of wartime Allied governments wishing to prolong the slaughter. Yet a minority memory of victimhood and martyrdom during the invasion of 1914 was preserved in France and Belgium, so that 'German atrocities' lay at the heart of irreconcilable memories of the Great War, even after 1945. These conflicting memories are discussed in the last part of the book (chapters 9 and 10).

Despite their importance, the German atrocities of 1914 have not received much attention from historians. A Belgian sociologist writing during the war, Fernand van Langenhove, argued in a remarkable book that the German belief in Belgian francs-tireurs was a 'cycle of legends'.[1] The study had its limitations. It was confined to the Germans, excluding comparable Allied beliefs, and did not explain why German soldiers responded to presumed civilian resistance in the way they did. Nonetheless, van Langenhove's book was considered path-breaking by the young French historian Marc Bloch when, drawing on his own war experience, he wrote in 1921 about myth and rumour in wartime.[2] Bloch reflected on the deeper attitudes and mentalities that shape manifestations of irrationality in moments of crisis or situations of tension. This pointed the way to the history of mentalities later taken up by both Bloch himself and the celebrated review *Annales*. But it was an approach that was not applied to the contemporary period, and the insights of van Langenhove and Bloch about the Great War were forgotten.

Between the wars, historians reflected the prevalent scepticism which saw 'German atrocities' as essentially an Allied fabrication, and thus as part of the broader issue of manipulation by propaganda.[3] This remained the dominant view after the Second World War. It was closely related to the belief that the real message of the Great War was the horror of industrial warfare and nationalist passions, and to the associated conviction that liberal democratic states betrayed their own principles by manipulating opinion in support of the conflict.[4] Only one attempt was made to investigate what actually happened. This was the product of co-operation between Belgian and German historians in the 1950s, and it affirmed that in the case of Louvain, the Belgians had been correct to protest their innocence of any civilian resistance, and that the German official inquiry into Allied atrocity charges, the White Book of 1915, was not reliable.[5]

Only recently has attention begun to focus anew on the 'atrocities'. Lothar Wieland has looked at the role of the issue in Belgian–German relations during and after the war.[6] Michael Jeismann has touched on its place in the construction of antagonistic national identities in France and Germany.[7] Ruth Harris and Stéphane Audoin-Rouzeau have analysed the rapes, real and imagined, committed by Germans during the invasion of 1914.[8] Our own articles have foreshadowed the approach adopted in this book.[9] These studies mark a new departure by their concern with the cultural history of the events they discuss — with the nature of experience and the ways that experience was represented and used. This has been true more generally of the revived interest in the First World War.

The 'atrocities' of 1914, then, are a complex phenomenon. They encompass events that occurred during the German invasion of France and Belgium, the meanings given to those events at the time, the deeper mentalities underlying them, and the way they were later remembered. How contemporaries understood events through collective beliefs and cultural constructions is vital. Yet reconstructing what happened cannot rely solely on this. It is also indispensable to establish who did what to whom, and on what scale. The analysis of subjectivity is central to historical inquiry, but that does not make historical inquiry a purely subjective affair for the historian.

In order to make these distinctions clearer, we have felt justified in calling the events in question German atrocities since in the main this is what they were by reference to the contemporary measure of the 1907 Hague Convention on Land Warfare, which Germany had signed. This meant that for the Allies, German actions constituted war crimes. We have used inverted commas ('German atrocities'), however, when placing the emphasis on a construction of meaning by the Allies which went beyond the categorization of war crimes in order to dehumanize the enemy as part of wartime cultural mobilization. We have not hesitated to refer to 'Belgian' or 'French atrocities' when discussing the comparable German construction of meaning.

Any history of the 'German atrocities' written from a national perspective is doomed to failure, since it could only reflect one dimension of something which, like so much else about the war, transcended frontiers. Apparently self-contained national experiences were in fact components of a larger, international dynamic of the kind which this study seeks to grasp by exploiting archival and published sources from Belgium, Britain, France, and Germany, with selective use of collections in Ireland, Italy, Russia, and the United States of America.

The volume of published sources is enormous. Additionally, the commissions set up by the French and Belgian governments to inquire into German war crimes left large collections of unpublished material which have been almost completely untapped by historians. These, together with the papers and diaries of German officers and soldiers scattered in German archives, have proved vital.[10] The records of the General Staff and of the

Prussian Army were largely destroyed in the Second World War. This makes it hard to write the history of the First and Second Armies, which were entirely Prussian in 1914, and of Prussian units in the other five armies that took part in the invasion of Belgium and France. But documents from the non-Prussian units of the other armies in Dresden, for the Third Army, and in Munich, Stuttgart, Freiburg, and elsewhere relating to the Fourth, Fifth, Sixth, and Seventh Armies, have enabled us to compensate for the loss of Prussian and General Staff records. German army records from the 1914 invasion captured by Soviet forces in 1945 were found in the former KGB archive in Moscow. They filled some crucial gaps, especially concerning events in Dinant, Belgium. The archives of the Vatican and the State Department in Washington, D.C., are rich repositories of claim and counter-claim of enemy atrocities by the warring nations in 1914–15.

What happened during the invasion has been established by using the evidence of the Belgian and French commissions and the extraordinary documentation gathered secretly during the war by two Belgian priests, Jean Schmitz and Norbert Nieuwland.[11] This has been checked and corrected by the use of German sources, primarily the White Book, official war histories, and the unpublished accounts of soldiers. Frequently, the evidence is contradictory, and establishing what happened means analysing the conflicting narratives and adjudicating between them. All the sources mentioned above have been used to explore what contemporaries thought was happening, and why. The depositions made by French and Belgian witnesses to the official inquiries, many of which were not used in the official publications because they were considered untrustworthy, reveal a lot about the attitudes and beliefs of ordinary civilians and soldiers. The same is true of the German contemporary army investigations and post-war inquiries in response to the Allied demands for prosecution of alleged German war criminals. At the level of more codified representations, we have used not only published texts but also images which, especially on the Allied side, provide an elaborate portrait of enemy 'atrocities'.

Overall, we have adopted the approach of a transnational cultural history of the German atrocities of 1914 – 'transnational' because events and perceptions unfolded through interaction between nations in a dynamic that proved more than the sum of its parts. Only such an approach can explain why the issue mesmerized contemporaries and helped shape the meanings and memories of the Great War. Quite apart from the interest of the subject, we hope that our approach will be of wider interest and provoke debate on its applicability to similarly complex and charged issues in recent history.

Part I
Invasion, 1914

1   German invasion, part 1

In August 1914, Germany attacked Belgium with a million men, an invasion force larger than any previously seen. The intention of the General Staff, following the Schlieffen Plan, was to ensure rapid victory in the west by throwing five armies in a massive arc through central and southern Belgium in order to overwhelm the French army from the north and take Paris. Two more armies were to hold the frontier in Alsace-Lorraine against a French invasion of Germany.[1] Time was vital. The German armies had to defeat their enemies in the west before the Russian mobilization was complete so they could join their Austro-Hungarian allies and triumph in the east as well. The planned invasion path in the west was no stranger to war. Overrun by the armies of the French Revolution in 1792–4, Belgium was the site of Napoleon's defeat in 1815. After Belgium achieved independence in 1830, the European powers guaranteed its permanent neutrality in 1839 in order to prevent it being used again as a platform for invasion.

The German armies were to bypass the northern third of Belgium, consisting of a low-lying coastal strip. The First and Second Armies, which formed the right wing of the invasion, were to storm across the densely populated central plain of Limburg, Brabant, and Hainaut provinces to the French border in a matter of days. In the southern third of the country (Namur and Luxembourg provinces) the valleys of the rivers Sambre and Meuse provided access routes to France, although the Ardennes mountains further south were more difficult to cross. Here, the Third and Fourth Armies were to wheel in successively shorter arcs to maintain the invasion front while the Fifth Army drove across the southern tip of Belgium into the Meurthe-et-Moselle in eastern France (map 1).

Before the full invasion could begin, however, the Germans had to force the gate to Belgium. Liège, the most easterly Belgian province, lies adjacent

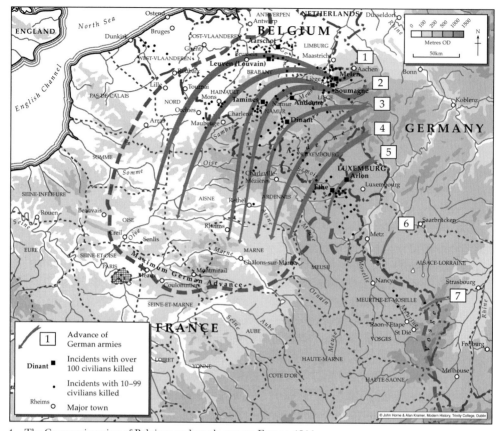

1 The German invasion of Belgium and north-eastern France, 1914

to the German Rhineland. Liège city was the country's largest industrial centre – the 'Birmingham of Belgium'. Strategically it controlled access to both the valley of the Meuse and the central plain. Encircled by modern forts of steel and concrete, it was one of three military complexes (along with Namur and Antwerp) on which the defence of Belgium depended. The German General Staff had provided for a special assault force in order to eliminate Liège in a matter of days. Early on 4 August 1914, under the command of General von Emmich, this force violated Belgian neutrality by crossing the border on a 40-kilometre front between Aachen and Malmédy.[2]

1   The shock of Liège

The Germans reckoned on a Belgian force defending Liège of 6,000 soldiers plus 3,000 members of the Belgian civic guard. Thirty-nine thousand

German troops were deemed sufficient to overcome this resistance.[3] In reality, Belgian soldiers were rushed to defend Liège so that the Germans faced 32,000 enemy troops when the invasion began, the bulk of them in improvised positions between the forts, supported by 150 artillery pieces and 30 machine-guns.[4] The Belgians were in defiant mood, reinforced by King Albert's call for national unity.[5] They knew their army was too small to withstand the German onslaught for long; universal military service had only been introduced in 1913, too late to make maximum use of manpower.[6] Yet Belgians hoped that Germany's breach of the international guarantees of their neutrality would bring rapid assistance from France and Britain. For the first two weeks in August, as the main German invasion force assembled in the Rhineland, the war turned on the fate of Liège.

The Germans converged on Liège in five lines which attacked simultaneously (map 2). The northernmost column, the 34th Mixed Infantry Brigade, struck from Aachen to Visé, with the intention of crossing the river Meuse and attacking the city from the north. The 27th Infantry Brigade moved from the north-east on the fort of Barchon. The 14th Infantry Brigade took the main road from Aachen, traversing a string of villages (Battice, Herve) before assaulting the fort of Fléron which barred entry into Liège from the east. The 11th Infantry Brigade came from Eupen to assault the forts of Chaudfontaine and Embourg, south-east of Liège. The 38th and 43rd Brigades formed the southernmost prong of the attack, moving up from Malmédy to attack the fort of Boncelles, south of Liège.

On 5 and 6 August, the Germans flung themselves at the forts. The bulk of the Belgian defenders were forced to retreat on 6 August, some in disorder, and the city fell on the seventh. But this counted for little since the forts remained intact, and the German onslaught broke down in disarray. On 5 August, for example, the 34th Brigade lost 30 officers and 1,150 men; next day, the 14th Brigade, advancing against fierce artillery and machine-gun fire, lost more than half its men and many of its officers, including the brigade commander and a regimental commander.[7] Five of the six German brigades retreated to their original positions and even beyond, after punishing losses. Faced with the ignominious failure of heroic frontal infantry assaults, on 8 August the Oberste Heeresleitung (OHL – Supreme Army Command) abandoned the tactic and sent in another 60,000 troops as a siege army under General von Einem.[8] Bombardment by heavy artillery now became the decisive tactic. This began in earnest on 10 August, pulverizing the forts one by one until the last surrendered on 16 August, and

LIMBURG
Maastricht
NETHERLANDS
Tongeren
(Tongres)
Lixhe
Berneau
34th
Aachen
Heure-le-
Romain
Haccourt
Visé
Warsage
Gemmenich
Hermée
27th
Lantin
Liers
Milmort
Loncin
Pontisse
Barchon
Blégny-Trembleur
Herstal
Battice
14th
Hollogne
Liège
Evegnée
Wandre
Melen
Herve
Baelen
Retinne
Fléron
Micheroux
Eupen
Flémalle
Romsée
Soumagne
Chaudfontaine
Magnée
11th
Meuse
Olne-St
Hadelin
Soiron
Verviers
Boncelles
Embourg
Vesdre
Esneux
Louveigné
Poulseur
Sprimont
38th
LIEGE
Amblève
Spa
GERMANY
Ourthe
Francorchamps
Malmédy
43rd
Somme-Leuze
Erezée-Briscol
© John Horne & Alan Kramer, Modern History, Trinity College, Dublin
38th
Advance of
German Brigades
Melen
Incidents with over
100 civilians killed
Herve
Incidents with 10–99
civilians killed
Other town or village
Fort
0
100
200
500
1000
Metres OD
10km
N

2 The attack on Liège

eastern Belgium lay open.[9] The cost, however, had been high. Where Schlieffen, in revising his plan in 1912, had allotted just one division to invest Liège and Namur, it took eight divisions to reduce Liège alone and cost the Germans valuable time, as well as some 5,300 casualties.[10]

When the Germans entered Belgium on 4 August, General von Emmich issued a declaration that the Belgians were not considered an enemy and that the Germans merely sought transit, though he warned that in the event of sabotage, the Germans would respond harshly.[11] There was little serious fighting on 4 August. Nonetheless, scattered incidents of aggression against Belgian civilians occurred. When men of the 34th Brigade met resistance from Belgian soldiers in Visé, who fought from houses before blowing up the bridge and then fired on the Germans from the far bank, houses were burned, inhabitants randomly shot at, and two were killed on suspicion of destroying the bridge.[12] That night, soldiers panicked in nearby Berneau, shooting each other and killing 11 of their own men; civilians were blamed and ten were shot down the next day, including a family with five children hiding in a cellar.[13] The inhabitants of Herve and Battice were exposed to random violence by soldiers of the 14th Brigade. The burgomaster (mayor) of Herve, Iserentant, was accused by a German colonel of fomenting civilian resistance and told that: 'Since our entry into this country, our troops have been fired upon [...] The laws of war authorize reprisals; burning, shooting. You will remain our prisoners.'[14]

Such incidents were merely a prelude. The first mass executions of civilians took place on 5 August, and by 8 August nearly 850 civilians had been killed and about 1,300 buildings deliberately burned down.[15] A great deal can be established about these incidents from the witness depositions and reports of the commission of inquiry which the Belgian government set up on 7 August to investigate war crimes, as well as from a variety of sources in German and other archives, and contemporary publications. The same is true for comparable incidents later in the invasion.[16] Although the accounts by German soldiers and Belgian (or French) civilians are often radically different, careful comparison makes it possible to establish what took place, which is what concerns us here, even if explaining why is more difficult. In the case of Liège, it makes sense to consider each of the five lines of attack, from north to south, in turn.

In the north, on the night of 5–6 August, the 34th Brigade succeeded in crossing the Meuse and advanced towards Liège through the villages of Hermée, Milmort, Herstal, and Rhées. It came under heavy bombardment from the fort of Pontisse and intense fire from Belgian infantry ensconced in the industrial outskirts of the city, notably Herstal, which contained the Belgian national arms factory. Units of the brigade were separated from each other and a number of men were captured. A small detachment from Jäger Battalion 7 managed to enter Liège by daybreak, where the population at first greeted them as British soldiers. A fierce Belgian counter-attack inflicted high casualties. Grenadier Regiment 90 shot civilians and Belgian prisoners of war, and set fire to houses, in Herstal. Major-General von Kraewel, commander of the 34th Brigade, ordered a retreat in order to avoid the brigade's 'total annihilation', and he reported that the 'entire population in Liège and the suburbs participated in the fighting'.[17] The retreat caused panic, and the brigade fled in disarray on the morning of 6 August with many soldiers crossing clean into Holland. As others retreated through Hermée, they killed 11 civilians and burned houses, claiming they had been fired on.[18] In Warsage, a village on the east bank which lay in the brigade's rear, 12 hostages were executed. One old man was accused of cutting off the ears and gouging out the eyes of wounded Germans, and bound to the wheel of a wagon.[19]

Early on 7 August, retreating soldiers of Jäger Battalion 7, who had remained near Liège since the night of 5–6 August, collided with the Belgians retiring into the fort of Pontisse. In the ensuing battle in the streets of Herstal, furious Jäger killed more inhabitants, a total of 27 perishing there on the two days. Herstal soon became a notorious case in which official German sources claimed (as Kraewel had) that the population of the working-class district had engaged in mass resistance against the Germans.[20] In all, from 4 to 7 August, the 34th Brigade killed at least 117 civilians.

The civilian death-toll on the invasion path of the 27th Infantry Brigade, attacking from the north-east, was lower, even though the brigade repeatedly failed to take the forts of Barchon and Evegnée on 5–6 August. The commander of Infantry Regiment (IR) 16 decided to withdraw from the regiment's forward base in the village of Blégny-Trembleur to Battice, out of range of the forts' guns. First, however, the population of Blégny was rounded up in the church because there had allegedly been collusion with the fort of Barchon by signalling from the church tower. Belgian nuns who tended the wounded that night in Blégny related the German soldiers' intense distrust of the inhabitants: 'There were some who showed a deep anxiety; they had been told that in Belgium the wounded had their eyes gouged out, were poisoned, were finished off.'[21] The church and many

houses were burned, and 19 people were killed. The brigade took 150 of
Blégny's inhabitants on its retreat to Battice, where it executed 33 of them
on 6 August. The priest and burgomaster were executed on 16 August as
hostages for alleged continued civilian firing.[22]

The 14th Brigade, which launched the attack on the fort of Fléron, east
of Liège, was responsible for some of the worst mass executions of civilians.
When IR 27 and 165 were repulsed on 5 August, they fell back on the
village of Soumagne on which they vented their frustration. They placed
the inhabitants under armed guard in the church. Male victims were
selected and shot in a field in front of women and children. The execution
squad bayoneted the bodies to ensure that no one survived; one injured
victim, covered by corpses, lived to tell his story to the Belgian commission
of inquiry. Over 50 men were killed in this execution, with 118 perishing in
all and over 100 houses destroyed. On this occasion, it was the resistance of
Belgium as a nation which angered the German soldiers, since they report-
edly told the villagers: 'It is your brothers who are firing on us from the fort
of Fléron.'[23] Three hundred to 400 survivors were used as a 'human shield'
by the Germans as they entered Liège on 7 August. Some were kept on the
bridges of the Meuse without food for several days to prevent the Belgian
artillery destroying the crossings.[24]

Similar events marked the 14th Brigade's eventually successful attempt
to penetrate between the forts of Fléron and Evegnée in the night of 5–6
August. Micheroux was burned by IR 27 and 11 inhabitants killed, the
soldiers apparently explaining: 'Belgium will not let us pass.'[25] On 6 August,
houses were burned and 40 civilians killed in Retinne. As at Soumagne, a
'human shield' was driven at bayonet point by the Germans as they fought
towards Liège on 6 August.[26] At Melen, soldiers of IR 165 retreating early
on 6 August roused the inhabitants and shot at least 11 of them.[27] As some
units retreated further to Battice that afternoon, they pillaged and burned
146 houses, farms, and the church, and killed 33 inhabitants.[28] On 8 August,
IR 165 returned to Melen. It took 72 inhabitants, including some from
surrounding villages (such as Herve and Battice), to a meadow, and
executed them collectively. This group included eight women and four girls
under 13 years of age. Much of the village was burned. One witness
recorded that the Germans made children dance in front of the corpses
singing a nursery rhyme, 'Il pleut, il pleut, bergère'. When the burgomaster of Herve, Iserentant, came to identify and bury corpses, he was seized
and shot.[29] The total number of victims in Melen on both days was 108.

In Herve itself on 8 August, the town hall and 300 houses, including farms and dwellings in the countryside, were destroyed, and 38 inhabitants were killed, many gunned down as they fled from burning buildings. One account described the terrifying arrival of the troops, firing thousands of shots and incendiary devices at the houses. 'In a frenzy, the soldiers forced entry into the houses, aiming at the women and children, whose arms were raised, and seizing the men. The sound of explosions mingled with the cries of horror of the women.' It is not clear whether the unit responsible for the massacre at Herve was Reserve IR 39, which arrived that day from Düsseldorf, or a cavalry squadron rebuffed from Fléron.[30] Overall, the fate of the villages along the main Aachen to Liège road, with more than 360 inhabitants killed, was directly linked to the failure of the 14th Brigade to take Fort Fléron, which did not surrender until 13 August.

The advance of the 11th Brigade (IR 20 and Fusilier Regiment 35) from Eupen in the east was associated with the deaths of over 100 inhabitants on 5–6 August. In Olne, the priest and village secretary were shot in the afternoon of 5 August. That night, the Germans tried to penetrate between the forts of Fléron and Chaudfontaine. They suffered heavy losses at the hands of the Belgian infantry and withdrew in panic. Just before midnight, a shell from the fort of Fléron hit the nearby hamlet of Saint-Hadelin, wounding some soldiers, whereupon the local teacher was accused of signalling to the fort and was shot with some of his family. This sparked a wave of killings in which 64 civilians in Olne and Saint-Hadelin perished, with 40 executed in the neighbouring hamlet of Riessonart on 6 August.[31] Fusilier Regiment 35 also burned Romsée and Magnée, between Fléron and Chaudfontaine, on 6 August, killing a number of inhabitants and using the priest of Magnée in an attack on Fléron.[32] The following day, a 'human shield' of 200 civilians from Romsée and Olne was deployed against the forts of Embourg and Chaudfontaine.[33]

In the southernmost advance against the fort of Boncelles by the 38th Brigade (Fusilier Regiments 73 and 74) and the 43rd Brigade (IR 82 and 83), over 100 civilians were killed. On the evening of 5 August, elements of the two brigades gathered for the attack at Poulseur after a long march in torrid heat. As night fell there was a thunderstorm with heavy rain, and some units lost their way in the advance. The vanguard of IR 83 was met with withering fire from the Belgian defence around midnight, but a chaotic assault continued until it was called off around dawn, owing to exhaustion and lack of ammunition. A Belgian counter-attack drove the

German forces into retreat.[34] Throughout the night and following day, German soldiers vented their humiliation and rage on a series of villages – Esneux, Louveigné, Poulseur, and Sprimont. At Louveigné, for example, on 7 August hostages were seized by men of IR 73, 82, and 83, taken before a makeshift court-martial, and told they would be executed since villagers had resisted and had cut off the ears of a major. Shortly after, 17 were shot. Other civilians were killed, the village ransacked (with lorry-loads of booty sent back to Germany), and eventually burned.[35] In Poulseur, sporadic firing at villagers continued throughout the night of 5–6 August, prompted by rumours that German soldiers had been shot in an outlying hamlet. On 6 August, the male inhabitants of Poulseur, and women and children from Chanxe, were used for two days as a 'human shield' on a bridge against the guns of Boncelles, resulting in six deaths.[36]

From 8 August, the suspension of infantry assaults on the Liège forts was accompanied by a lull in violence against civilians. One incident, however, showed that combat was not the only setting in which German soldiers might attack civilians. This occurred on 8 August at Francorchamps, close to the border on the route from Malmédy to Liège. German troops had traversed this village without incident since the beginning of the invasion. On 8 August, a shot rang out on a railway embankment; a fusillade by German soldiers followed, Francorchamps and surrounding villages were burned, and 14 men and women were killed. The Germans claimed they had come under fire from the locals, but the villagers were adamant that the Germans had fired on each other and, their passions fanned by tales of poisoning and mutilation, had wrongly blamed the incident on civilians. The villagers also suggested that the real charge against them was the nation's refusal to allow the German army peaceful passage. When a young tax inspector, whose father had been shot for supposedly putting arsenic in water offered to German soldiers, denied that he had fired on German soldiers from his window, he was told by an officer in French: 'It doesn't matter, at Liège you kill our men. We also have the right to kill you.'[37] Tales of 'Belgian atrocities', plus a refusal to accept the legitimacy of Belgian military resistance, here combined with a single shot of unknown provenance to trigger a massacre 30 kilometres from the nearest fighting by troops who had not yet experienced combat.

The assault on the Liège forts suggests that German troops anticipated civilian resistance from the start and considered this to be wholly against the laws of war and proper military conduct. Many felt national self-defence by the Belgian army to be unjustified. Resentment at the unexpectedly stiff resistance of the forts and the notion that civilians were taking up arms produced a demonized view of the Belgian people. Referring to French guerrilla warfare in 1870, German soldiers assumed that they faced a war conducted by Belgian irregulars (francs-tireurs), which included nocturnal ambush, mutilation, poisoning, and the insurrection of whole districts.

By 8 August, all 13 German infantry regiments involved in the initial attack had engaged in serious violence against civilians. Such violence therefore represented something more than the work of marginal, criminal elements. News of 'Belgian atrocities' soon spread back from Liège to the military build-up area in north-western Germany, where hundreds of thousands of men were crammed into a narrow belt of territory prior to the main invasion. The press in the Rhineland and throughout Germany, from 8 or 9 August, was full of tales of ferocious Belgian civilians preying on the invading Germans.[38] The cumulative effect of this fear is evident in incidents such as those at Francorchamps and possibly Herve, where troops arriving with tales from the build-up area reinforced the sense of menace and provoked incidents which fulfilled their apprehensions.

Nor was this just the perspective of ordinary soldiers. On 8 August, General von Einem wrote to his wife that the Belgian population had 'treacherously' participated in night-time attacks on his troops. Einem related that he had ordered villages where such incidents occurred to be burned and all the inhabitants shot.[39] His immediate superior, General von Bülow, commander of the Second Army, endorsed Einem's measures and accused the Belgian population in a proclamation on 9 August of not appreciating the consequences of violating the 'laws of war' and decreed that villages would be collectively punished for individual crimes by burning, hostage-taking, and heavy fines.[40] On the same day, the Kaiser noted privately that

the population of Belgium [...] behaved in a diabolical, not to say bestial, manner, not one iota better than the Cossacks. They tormented the wounded, beat them to death, killed doctors and medical orderlies, fired secretly [...] on men harmlessly standing in the street – in fact by pre-arranged signal, under leadership [...]

The King of the Belgians has to be notified at once that since his people have placed themselves outside all observance of European customs – from the frontier on, in all the villages, not only in Liège – they will be treated accordingly. Conditions for Belgium will become immensely more difficult.[41]

For their part, the Belgian authorities and civilian witnesses were adamant that no such resistance had taken place. On 5 August, the Minister of the Interior told the population by poster that resistance was only permitted by the army, the Garde Civique, or detachments of volunteers with a distinctive badge, under a responsible officer, and openly carrying arms. Actions by isolated individuals were expressly forbidden, as were the use of poison and killing and wounding by treachery.[42] The point was driven home on 5 August when the Minister reminded the Garde Civique, as it was called up, that it must be organized in military units, carry distinctive signs of identification, and observe the laws of war; otherwise it would expose the whole population to reprisals. In Liège, General Leman, who was directing operations in the city, called for civilians to remain calm, obey the law, and allow the army to fight the war.[43] Nonetheless, the very need to make such declarations shows that the possibility of spontaneous civilian participation in the defence of Liège had occurred to the Belgian authorities.

Liège was the most important zone of contact between German soldiers and enemy civilians in the days before the main German invasion, but it was not the only one. On 2 August, the Germans invaded the Grand Duchy of Luxemburg and began probing French frontier defences in the Meurthe-et-Moselle. From 4 August, the eastern part of Namur and Luxembourg provinces in Belgium and much of the Meurthe-et-Moselle constituted a no-man's-land crossed by patrols from both sides. Further south, the French invaded Upper Alsace from 7 August, reaching Mulhouse before being forced to retreat on 11 August. In all these areas, the Germans claimed they met franc-tireur resistance.

In Belgian Luxembourg, to take just one example in that region, a German patrol entered Arlon (close to the border with the Grand Duchy) on 6 August. As it withdrew, the rear-guard was shot at, apparently from a local café. Fire was returned and a woman killed with a lance. The Belgian authorities, keen to avoid reprisals, arrested the tenant of the café and opened an inquiry. This was continued by German court-martial when the 41st Infantry Brigade occupied the town as its pre-invasion base on 12 August. The tenant was acquitted, but the myth rapidly spread of a young girl who had treacherously shot and wounded a German officer in the back.

Tension was high, and General von der Esch, commander of the 41st Brigade, ordered all firearms confiscated and announced that any hostile action by the inhabitants would be punished by death. Some of the arms collected were sent back to Germany and exhibited as 'weapons used by Belgian francs-tireurs'. The accidental breaking of a field telephone wire by a woman opening her shutters, and the tale that in the night of 12 to 13 August the inhabitants of Arlon had signalled with lights to a neighbouring village, aroused Esch to fury. He razed the village, exacted an indemnity from Arlon, and threatened to execute hostages if there was a further incident. When, on the evening of 13 August, German cavalry claimed to have been fired on, although an NCO of the Landwehr (reserve infantry) insisted that the Germans shot at each other, reprisal was inevitable and a police officer was executed on Esch's orders.[44]

Comparable incidents took place in the northern Meurthe-et-Moselle. The German soldiers who entered Audun-le-Roman on 4 August told the inhabitants that they would be shot and the village razed if they disobeyed orders (map 3).[45] At Joppécourt, a neighbouring village, the Germans discovered a collection of firearms on 7 August, which the mayor had gathered in as a precaution. Taking this as evidence of an intention to resist, they executed him two days later.[46] The village of Affléville was burned and three inhabitants shot on 9 August, on the grounds that it was the villagers (not a French patrol) who had skirmished with the occupying Germans the day before. At Jarny, on 10 August, an Italian (three-quarters of the workers in the Briey iron-ore field were from Italy) shot his dog as an economy measure in conformity with the instructions of the mayor. A German patrol attributed the shot to francs-tireurs, arrested 15 Italians, and executed them.[47] On 11 August, the 23rd Dragoons returned to the village of Bazailles after suffering a setback in a skirmish with French troops. They accused a particular villager of firing on them several days previously, but instead of conducting a court-martial trial, executed him (despite the protest of the priest that the accused had not been in the village at the time of the alleged firing) along with 24 other inhabitants, and burned 45 houses.[48]

In the south-east of the Meurthe-et-Moselle, the German Sixth Army probed French territory although its function was to hold the frontier against French invasion (see map 3). German soldiers arrived in force at Blâmont on 8 August. Immediately, they confiscated all firearms, and ordered the villagers to leave their doors and windows open and the lights on all night. After several days of extreme tension, two civilians were killed,

BELGIUM · LUXEMBURG

Luxemburg

Saint-Pancré · Mont-Saint-Martin
Fresnois-la- · Longwy
Montagne · Longuyon · Chénières
Filières
Bazailles · Audun-le-
Joppécourt · Roman
Mercy-le-Haut · Thionville
Landres
Afflévilie
Rouvres · Briey

Conflans · Jarny
Verdun · Metz

GERMANY

Saar

Saarbrücken

ALSACE-LORRAINE

5

6

Morhange

Pont-à-Mousson
Nomény
Château-Salins
Saarburg

St Mihiel
MEUSE

2

Nancy · Réméréville
Toul · Maixe
MEURTHE-ET-MOSELLE
Lunéville
Gerbéviller · Badonviller · Parux
FRANCE
Baccarat
Raon l'Etape
VOSGES

1

Blâmont
Cirey

Ornain
Meuse

Moselle

Meurthe

© John Horne & Alan Kramer, Modern History, Trinity College, Dublin

N

	Advance of German and French armies	◎ Major town	100 200 500 1000 1500
Nomény ·	Incidents with 10–99 civilians killed	○ Other town or village	Metres OD
		☆ Fortified town	30km

5

3 The Meurthe-et-Moselle

and the German commander put up a poster threatening to raze the village at the least provocation.[49] Nearby Badonviller was occupied by soldiers of four Bavarian infantry regiments on the night of 12 August following a costly action against French light infantry. The villagers were accused of aiding the French soldiers, the village was burned, and three artillery batteries demolished the church tower from which francs-tireurs had supposedly fired. Ten civilians were killed, including the wife of the mayor.[50] Other frontier villages were similarly affected by the fury of German soldiers towards the population.[51]

The case of Alsace and German Lorraine was different in that here the German army was on German territory. Yet it treated the population as uncooperative and unpatriotic, and liable to help the enemy or even engage in armed resistance. Many of the same tales that circulated about Belgian and French civilians mutilating and poisoning German soldiers were also told about Alsace-Lorrainers. When the French briefly invaded Upper Alsace, they were welcomed by some of the population, making it virtually inevitable, given the negative predispositions of the German army, that civilians would be maltreated by the returning Germans, as happened in and around Mulhouse.

According to the testimony of Marcel Schoff, mayor of Pfastatt on the western side of Mulhouse, German troops reoccupying the city on 10 August killed an innkeeper east of Mulhouse at Napoleoninsel (Île Napoléon). They also machine-gunned a crowd of civilians in Mulhouse itself, and set fire to nearby Reiningen (Reiningue) on the pretext that French soldiers had ambushed them, with the result that several inhabitants perished.[52] German sources confirm much of this. General von Huene, commander of the XIVth Army Corps, told headquarters of the Seventh Army (responsible for Alsace) that throughout Upper Alsace the local population had engaged in treacherous, hostile acts against the German troops.[53] Civilians ambushed troops especially when they were offered water to drink; six civilians were caught thus and executed at Napoleoninsel, according to Huene, who issued 'ruthless orders' to the troops to combat the treacherous civilian conduct. There is thus a consensus between French and German sources that the German troops regarded the Alsatian population with deep suspicion, accusing them of firing on them and harbouring French soldiers.

These comparisons show that although the Belgian military defence of Liège may explain the scale of German violence against civilians there, it does not account for the phenomenon. Belief in francs-tireurs was wide-spread, since virtually the same accusations appeared within a few days of each other far away in parts of French Lorraine or German Alsace and, in the earliest cases, before news of 'Belgian atrocities' at Liège could have arrived via military intelligence, rumour, or the press. In France as in Belgium, the authorities and the victims of German 'reprisals' denied the existence of francs-tireurs. The prefect of the Meurthe-et-Moselle, Léon Mirman, was adamant that the German violence was not prompted by civilian resistance.[54] But as in the case of Belgium, the possibility that local inhabitants carried out sabotage or shot at the invaders cannot be excluded.

Characteristic of events in both Belgium and Alsace-Lorraine, however, was the dichotomy between the tiny extent of the alleged resistance, and the nature of the German accusation. Bülow and the Kaiser condemned Belgian civilians on 9 August for nothing less than a popular uprising. Bavarian IR 1 likewise described the civilians in the Meurthe-et-Moselle on 11 August as conducting a 'People's War' (*Volkskrieg*).[55] This was the message of the 'solemn warning' issued on 12 August (published on 14 August) by the German commander-in-chief, Moltke. He accused the Belgian population of illegally participating in fighting and committing 'atrocities' against German soldiers, and threatened that any individual who acted similarly in the future would be 'treated as a franc-tireur and immediately shot according to martial law'.[56] On 18 August, the German government condemned the French for 'organizing a war in which the whole population takes part' and threatened dire consequences if it continued.[57] Even before the main invasion got under way, the notion of mass civilian resistance obsessed the German government and Supreme Command.

2   The First and Second Armies to the French frontier

With the fall of the last forts of Liège, the invasion could proceed. Although skirmishes had taken place between German cavalry patrols and French and Belgian forces further west, serious fighting only began again with the main advance from 18 August. The pace was set by the First and Second Armies as they drove across the Brabant plain and up the valleys of the Meuse and Sambre to the French frontier. Unable to withstand the frontal onslaught, the Belgians skilfully withdrew from their position along the river Gette into the fortified position of Antwerp, as the Germans advanced westward into Hainaut province between 18 and 23 August. From Antwerp, the Belgian army mounted three major counter-attacks against the German flank after the main invasion had moved into France, one on 25–26 August and two later in September.[58] As the German advance followed the line of the Meuse it encountered Belgian forces at the fort system of Namur, the French Fifth Army around Charleroi, and the British Expeditionary Force (BEF) at Mons, the latter having been rushed from the coast to prevent the German flood-tide from engulfing the Allies (map 1 above).

The main German advance marked a new phase in violence towards civilians, characterized by the widespread fear of enemy civilians seen in the first phase combined with a pattern of apparently predetermined measures to deal with francs-tireurs. Several cases in Liège province exhibited these features. The first systematic destruction of a Belgian town occurred at Visé, on 16–18 August, and was accompanied by civilian deportations to Germany. Since Visé had been occupied since 4 August, all arms had long been seized; every house had been searched and patrols circulated each night, firing in the air in order to terrify the inhabitants.[59] New troops, the Königsberg Pioneers, arrived on 15 August.[60] That evening, after heavy drinking, they shot at each other and rampaged through the town shouting 'Man hat geschossen!' ('We have been shot at!'), burning, pillaging, and shooting.[61] A Dutch journalist, Mokveld, who witnessed the events, wrote: 'The most tipsy began to shoot at doors and windows simultaneously in various parts of town, which made the people in the houses scream, and this excited the mad drunken soldiers all the more. They forced their way into several houses knocking down the frightened inhabitants when these tried to stop them.'[62] The following day, women and children were driven into Holland while 631 citizens were deported to Germany.[63] From 16 to 18 August, the town was completely pillaged, 600 houses were burned, and 23 inhabitants were killed.

A similar incident took place at Tongeren. On the evening of 18 August, German troops in transit shot 12 civilians. What actually happened can be deduced from two competing narratives. The Germans claimed they had come under attack from the Garde Civique. General von der Marwitz reported in a letter to his wife that there had been a small battle in which 'many civilians' took part and were therefore executed; he 'tamed' the town by disarming the Garde Civique and deporting them.[64] In reality, the population of 10,000 was expelled for the night and three days later 51 members of the Garde Civique were indeed deported to Cologne.[65] The German story was a cover for a serious lapse of discipline. Belgian sources suggest there was a drunken brawl between soldiers on 18 August, during which shots were fired. The inhabitants were blamed and randomly fired on, houses were burned, and the town was pillaged, before the First Army command issued an apology and set up an inquiry.[66] Tongeren had been occupied since 9 August, and it is unthinkable that the Garde Civique were still in possession of their weapons and unlikely that any other group of citizens suddenly rose against the Germans.

In the city of Liège, too, the occupants had long been warned of the consequences of resistance, hostages had been seized, and any weapons had undoubtedly been confiscated.[67] The resultant fear on the part of the inhabitants made resistance highly unlikely. But a pattern of random German shooting at houses soon emerged, caused by the soldiers' nervousness or drunkenness, or both. In the night of 19–20 August, Reserve IR 13 and 57 unleashed a sudden fusillade, pillaging and burning four houses on the accusation that civilians had fired. However, the houses were empty. The following night, a series of such incidents took place, the most important being that at the Place de l'Université and Place Cockerill. Drunken soldiers of IR 39 fired from a club where they were lodged. In fact, all the surrounding buildings from which the Germans claimed shots had come were occupied by German troops.[68] Over 60 civilians were shot in this and related incidents and 38 houses pillaged and burned. A gun bombarded the Quai de la Meuse on the left bank from across the river, and German soldiers harassed the city's firemen.[69]

The Germans blamed Russian-Jewish students, who had a library in the Place de l'Université, for the main incident. But the library was locked and empty at the time. Possibly, as Somville suggested, the Germans selected the students as scapegoats.[70] Some 400 Russian-Jewish students and other citizens of Liège were deported and held in the prison camp at Munster.[71] The German-Jewish community was disquieted by the army allegations. The German Foreign Ministry was also aware that the allegation was false, but took no steps to have the students released.[72] The incidents in Visé, Tongeren, and Liège city all confirmed the lesson of Francorchamps that violence against civilians need not be combat-related.

As the First and Second Armies moved west, nervous volatility on the part of the troops and a policy of draconian repression of perceived civilian resistance became widespread. Advancing on the river Gette, German soldiers burned villages and shot civilians in a series of clashes with Belgian forces, at Attenrode-Wever, Molenstede, Schaffen, and elsewhere (map 4).[73] At Schaffen, German cavalry patrols had been rebuffed several times by Belgian soldiers hidden in houses and the church tower before IR 49 burned their way into the village on the morning of 18 August. The Germans were convinced that it was the inhabitants who had opposed them, with the priest acting as ringleader.[74] One German soldier noted in his diary that 50 civilians were executed for resisting with a machine-gun from the church tower.[75] The inhabitants insisted that only regular Belgian soldiers had been involved and that the priest had exhorted the villagers to stay calm and welcome the Germans. In fact, even in German sources there is evidence that the locality was defended by a company of Belgian cyclist-riflemen, against overwhelming German superiority. But the explanations were of no avail. The priest barely escaped with his life, having been beaten and insulted, while 23 inhabitants, including several women, were shot, and much of the village was razed.[76]

The most serious incident linked to the Belgian army's retreat from the Gette occurred the following day in Aarschot, less than 20 kilometres beyond Schaffen. There were two distinct outbreaks of violence. Early on 19 August, the German 8th Brigade (IR 49 and 140) attacked two Belgian regiments acting as rear-guard in the small Brabant town. Despite heavy losses, the Belgians held up the advance for two hours.[77] Over 20 captured Belgian soldiers were shot and thrown into the river Demer.[78] The German troops transferred their anger towards the civilians: people were ejected from their houses, and many were accused of firing on the Germans, including monks from the monastery of the Sacred Heart Order. Six civilians were shot. There is some evidence, albeit of dubious quality, that they had resisted. The burgomaster, Jozef Tielemans, was then forced to make threatening declarations to the townsfolk on behalf of the Germans, and the male inhabitants were rounded up and searched before being dismissed.[79]

Far greater violence towards civilians was triggered later that day by a sudden outbreak of shooting at 7 pm in which the 8th Brigade commander, Colonel Stenger, was killed. The Germans claimed that he was shot from behind by the burgomaster's son and that a rising of francs-tireurs had taken place. Both charges were denied by the Belgians, although they agreed that Stenger was killed when standing on a first-floor balcony in

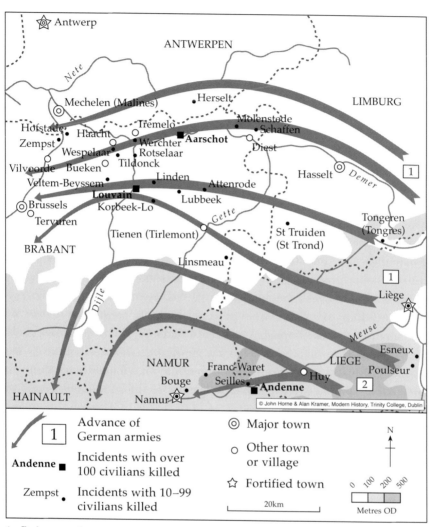

4   Brabant province

Map labels

Antwerp

ANTWERPEN

Nete

Mechelen (Malines) ·Herselt LIMBURG

Hofstade· ·Trémelo ·Molenstode
Zempst· Haacht ·Schaffen
Wespelaar· ·Werchter **Aarschot** ·Diest
Vilvoorde· Bueken ·Rotselaar Hasselt *Demer* ⬜1
Veltem-Beyssem· Tildonck ·Linden ·Attenrode
⊚Brussels **Louvain** ■ Lubbeek
  Korbeek-Lo *Gette* Tongeren
  ○Tervuren (Tongres)

BRABANT Tienen (Tirlemont)○ St Truiden
  ·Linsmeau (St Trond)

  ⬜1
  Dijle Liège☆

  Meuse
  Esneux·
  NAMUR Franc-Waret· LIEGE Poulseur
  Bouge· Seilles· ○Huy ⬜2
HAINAULT Namur☆ ■**Andenne**

© John Horne & Alan Kramer, Modern History, Trinity College, Dublin

Legend

↝ ⬜1 Advance of German armies

Andenne ■ Incidents with over 100 civilians killed

Zempst · Incidents with 10–99 civilians killed

⊚ Major town

○ Other town or village

☆ Fortified town

N

0 100 200 500
Metres OD

20km

Tielemans's house on the main square. Two Belgian witnesses rejected the charge against the Tielemans family. Tuerlinckx, a printer whose workshop was on the square, asserted that a fusillade broke out at 6 pm (7 pm German time), before Stenger was shot. Asking an officer what the cause was, he was told: 'Die Franzosen sind da' ('The French have arrived'). He then saw three officers appear on the Tielemans' balcony, one of whom fell. Madame Tielemans, whose testimony was taken in Holland later in 1914, swore that she and her husband had been out when the fusillade began, and took refuge in the cellar with her son, having seen the officers on the balcony.[80]

The precise cause of Stenger's death is impossible to establish, but the burgomaster's son can be ruled out on forensic grounds. When the Prussian War Ministry investigated the events at Aarschot, it heard Captain Folz, quartermaster of IR 49, cite the autopsy carried out by the surgeon of IR 140 to the effect that Stenger had been struck by a bullet which ricocheted into the house from a hard object outside. This was confirmed by a post-war Belgian autopsy which found that Stenger had been shot laterally through the chest from the front, so that shooting from behind or below (by Tielemans' son) was impossible.[81] The eventual official German report duly played down the role of the Tielemans family. Folz, however, claimed that the bullet which had struck Stenger came from an old muzzle-loading gun and that a house search revealed 40 armed civilians, among them two priests.[82] Although it is conceivable, if unlikely, that Colonel Stenger was shot by an individual inhabitant of Aarschot, the German investigation missed the opportunity to prove its case. It did not cite the military autopsy, nor did it produce the bullet, or any suspects. Captain Karge, the military police commander responsible for searching houses and arresting inhabitants, did not claim to have found any armed civilians. Moreover, both Belgian and German evidence confirmed that a thorough search for weapons had taken place before the evening, by which time some 10,000 soldiers had crowded into Aarschot. A 'franc-tireur' rising was thus the least likely explanation.[83]

The true cause of the wild shooting was panic by nervous German soldiers. Folz, in his testimony, unwittingly painted a scene of hysteria. Initially, shooting seemed to be coming from the north-west entrance to the town and some units reported that they had come under fire from attacking Belgian troops. Folz pursued an imaginary Belgian battalion for three kilometres with a machine-gun company. When he returned to the town, he saw German troops returning fire, having been shot at from the houses with rifles and machine-guns: 'I saw several men wounded by these shots; bullets whistled about my head, too.' But Folz was ambiguous as to who exactly had done the firing. Colonel Jenrich, commander of IR 140, described how he had to stop the shooting by German soldiers in the central square, revealing that this was panic-driven.[84] Captain Karge identified the house whence the first shot seemed to have come, describing spurts of dust or smoke rising from the roof-edge. These were most likely caused by bullets striking the masonry or window lintels.[85] In the circumstances, it is virtually certain that Colonel Stenger was killed by his own men.

Once started, however, the German fusillade resulted in a hunt for francs-tireurs. Most male citizens were rounded up. One group was taken to a field near a house from which francs-tireurs had supposedly shot, where Karge ordered their execution; 76 were immediately killed in groups of three, the scene illuminated by flames from the house, which had been set on fire.[86] Another group including burgomaster Tielemans was held throughout the night. At dawn, according to a survivor, Achille Claes, German officers approached the group, whereupon Tielemans declared the Germans' behaviour in Aarschot was inexplicable in view of their peaceful reception. Claes himself called out that Tielemans was an honourable man who had done his utmost to ensure that the inhabitants remained calm. One officer replied that an inquiry would be held; but another ordered the execution of Tielemans, his brother, and his son, and one in three of the others. Corroboration came from Colonel Jenrich who told the Prussian War Ministry inquiry that 'the burgomaster, his son, the burgomaster's brother, and every third man were executed.'[87]

Burning and looting, which had begun before the death of Stenger, continued throughout the night.[88] The German army imposed a reign of terror until the return of the Belgian army in a short-lived counter-attack on 9 September. The inhabitants were interned in the church for several days and nights while the town was systematically pillaged.[89] Thirty men were deported to Liège on 23 August, and on 28 August 1,000 inhabitants (including the old, infirm, and children) were expelled to Louvain where they were shot at on arrival, some being killed and wounded, and the rest imprisoned overnight, without food.[90] Sent back to Aarschot on 29 August, the men and women were separated, and on 6 September, 400 men under 45 years of age were deported to Germany in cattle wagons. Amongst the latter were the monks of the Sacred Heart Order, together with other clerics, who were accused of being francs-tireurs.[91] As at Schaffen, the parish priest had supposedly allowed firing from the church tower.[92] In all, 156 civilians perished at Aarschot during the period 19 August to 6 September 1914.[93]

Further south, forces of the Second and Third Armies moved up the Meuse valley towards Namur, the second fort complex blocking the German advance (map 5). Fifteen kilometres east of Namur are the towns of Andenne and Seilles, on opposite sides of the river. On 19 August, the advance guard of the Guards Reserve Corps (Guards Reserve Dragoon Regiment, Guards Reserve Rifle Battalion, and two companies of Pioneer Battalion 28) reached Andenne, on the south bank, only to find that the bridge had been destroyed by retreating Belgian troops. Later that day, German forces also moved into Seilles on the north bank. Throughout the night of 19–20 August, more German troops arrived, especially in Andenne, awaiting the construction of a pontoon bridge by the pioneers before crossing to continue the advance on Namur. The bridge was completed late in the afternoon of 20 August, and the German soldiers began to cross *en masse*. Suddenly, at 7 pm (German time), German soldiers began firing wildly at civilians in Seilles. The fusillade spread to Andenne and went on all night, culminating in a mass execution which made Andenne-Seilles one of the principal incidents of German violence against civilians during the invasion.[94]

Although the massacre of the inhabitants began well over 24 hours after the German arrival in Andenne, the intervening period had been tense. On 19 August, two German cavalry patrols near Andenne were fired on by the detachments of the Belgian 8th Line Regiment, according to the post-war Belgian inquiry, and a German officer's arm was shattered. German accounts, especially an inquiry conducted by the Reich Supreme Court in 1920, confirm the incidents (including the officer's broken arm) but show that the Germans believed they had been ambushed by francs-tireurs, and that the inhabitants had been responsible for destroying the bridge. Later on 19 August, the rebuff of the first German cavalry patrol into Seilles by a Belgian rear-guard, resulting in German fatalities, was likewise attributed to the inhabitants.[95] Not surprisingly, the Germans were hostile towards the population. The burgomaster of Andenne, Dr Camus, and the priest were taken hostage, although later released, and several houses were burned down.

Contemporary Belgian and German accounts of what triggered the massacre are difficult to reconcile. Numerous Belgian (and some German)

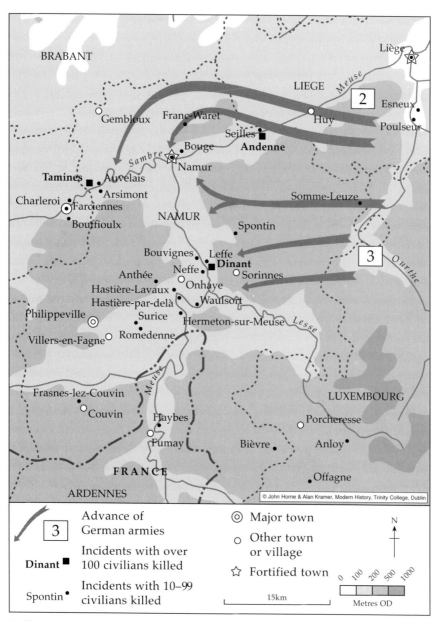

BRABANT

LIÈGE

Liège

LIEGE

2

Esneux

Gembloux

Franc-Waret

Huy

Poulseur

Seilles

Andenne

Meuse

Bouge

Sambre

Namur

Tamines

Auvelais

NAMUR

Somme-Leuze

Charleroi

Farciennes

Arsimont

3

Ourthe

Bouffioulx

Spontin

Bouvignes

Leffe

Dinant

Anthée

Neffe

Sorinnes

Onhaye

Hastière-Lavaux

Hermeton-sur-Meuse

Lesse

Hastière-par-delà

Waulsort

Philippeville

Surice

Villers-en-Fagne

Romedenne

Meuse

LUXEMBOURG

Frasnes-lez-Couvin

Couvin

Haybes

Porcheresse

Bièvre

Anloy

Fumay

FRANCE

Offagne

ARDENNES

© John Horne & Alan Kramer, Modern History, Trinity College, Dublin

Advance of German armies	⊚ Major town	N
Dinant ■ Incidents with over 100 civilians killed	○ Other town or village	
Spontin • Incidents with 10–99 civilians killed	☆ Fortified town	0 100 200 500 1000
	15km	Metres OD

5   Namur province

witnesses concurred that a detonation in Seilles, of unknown origin, unleashed the German shooting. Many Belgians also attributed the fusillade to drink or to a 'friendly fire' incident. Seilles was a depot for wines and liquor brought down the Meuse by barge from France; its priest, among others, testified that German officers and soldiers 'got drunk [in the afternoon of 20 August] in the numerous cafés of the neighbourhood'.[96] German soldiers, by contrast, swore that they had come under fire from francs-tireurs. The 1st Guards Reserve Division reported that it had been fired at by civilians in houses at Seilles as it crossed the Meuse, resulting in 35 casualties, including five men killed.[97] A Guards lieutenant described in a letter to his wife the next day the 'not very pleasant crossing of the Meuse at Andenne', during which 'we shot several farmhouses into flames, whose inhabitants were firing at us. After crossing the river we came under heavy rifle fire from the houses [...] Those shooting were also francs-tireurs. They shot at us like madmen, but without causing serious damage.'[98]

Although individual acts of defiance cannot be ruled out, the thesis of concerted civilian resistance is implausible, given the warning of the fate of suspected resisters at Liège, and especially since the burgomaster had confiscated civilian arms before the arrival of the Germans. Belgian witnesses' belief that nervous and intoxicated German soldiers mistook unidentified firing for the franc-tireur rising of their imagination is corroborated by the depositions of former German soldiers to the Reich Supreme Court investigation in 1920.

At about 6 pm on 20 August, a small detachment of pioneers and military police rode through Seilles to inspect a tunnel west of the town, which the Belgian 8th Line Regiment had destroyed the previous day. Reaching the outskirts of Seilles it was fired on from farmhouses by unidentified enemies.[99] The source of the shooting may have been other German soldiers. It equally may have been a Belgian rear-guard left near Seilles to hamper the German crossing; as the war diary of the 1st Pioneer Company admitted, it was not possible to see where the firing came from. While the houses were being searched, chaotic shooting spread throughout Seilles: 'This firing by our own troops [in Seilles] undoubtedly caused a large part of the casualties.'[100] The shooting rapidly spread to soldiers in Andenne. The loud detonation which was taken by so many to have started the incident was the German artillery firing.

Belgian witnesses were thus entirely correct to report a 'veritable panic among the troops in Andenne'.[101] Throughout the night of 20–21 August, soldiers roamed the streets on both sides of the river, breaking into houses and killing civilians. In Seilles, 43 inhabitants were killed and 150 houses were burned.[102] In Andenne, burgomaster Camus was sought out in his home and hacked to death with an axe. Soon after the initial fusillade, a group of 17 civilians was arrested and 13 (including girls, women, and a baby) were shot and bayoneted. German soldiers frequently shot at each other and civilian witnesses saw the bodies of German soldiers in the streets the following morning.[103] From about 4 am on 21 August, the repression became more systematic as German soldiers began dragging civilians from their homes. In many cases they were killed on the spot.

German sources corroborate the testimony of Belgian survivors on this escalation of the massacre. At 4 am on 21 August, majors Bronsart von Schellendorf, commander of Guards Reserve Rifle Battalion, and Scheunemann, commander of the Pioneers, issued an order approved by brigade commander Colonel von Below to search the town for weapons. Although in 1920 the two officers claimed that the order prescribed the death penalty only for civilians found in possession of weapons and ammunition, Captain Wabnitz, commander of 2nd Company Pioneer Battalion 28, distinctly recalled that Bronsart and Scheunemann told the company commanders that 'all men capable of bearing arms were to be executed on the spot' and that they wanted 'an example to be made' of the town. Moreover, as Wabnitz pointed out, the order was capable of being interpreted by every soldier as a licence to execute any civilian. Bayonets were to be used where possible, indicating that the commanders feared that shooting would unleash yet more panic firing by troops.[104] Although Bronsart, Scheunemann, and others claimed to have seen fighting by civilians, several German witnesses (Wabnitz, Rifleman Worms) were adamant there had been none. Sergeant Woite, of the Guards Reserve Rifle Battalion, was in the thick of the house search but found no armed inhabitants. He confirmed to the post-war German inquiry that he had participated in storming a house in which a man was arrested and shot although he was unarmed; he saw several other unarmed men being killed. During the house-to-house search 20 people were killed by the enraged troops. Of the men arrested, 110 were sentenced to death by the court-martial and executed.[105] The total of 130 civilian dead in this phase of the massacre roughly tallies with Belgian estimates of 150.

By daybreak on 20 August, the Germans had rounded up 800 people in the central Place des Tilleuls. During the forced march to the square a ten-year-old child was bayoneted in the back; a 14-year-old was shot four times because he had remained in bed, and he died a few hours later. In one house seven members of a family were executed in their cellar. According to one report, a girl of 20 was raped and mutilated.[106] A priest was bound, tortured, and left to die. Events in the square were directed by Captain Junge, from a hastily constructed rostrum, in conjunction with Major Bronsart von Schellendorf.[107] Women and children were separated from the men; those considered suspect had a white cross marked on their backs. When a German national, Eva Comes, who had been on holiday in Andenne and had been caught in the round-up, taxed Junge with the arbitrariness of the procedure, he rejoined that he did not have time to find those responsible and that the innocent must pay for the guilty. Clearly, he considered that none were really innocent since they had fired on 'his' soldiers after being incited to do so by the 'chief priest'. Comes denied that the priest had preached resistance the previous Sunday, as she had been at the service; civilian firearms had long been deposited in the town hall and the inhabitants had been warned against resistance with posters still on display.[108] Junge, however, took the deposit of arms to be evidence of the franc-tireur plot which was to become the staple German interpretation of events at Andenne.

At that point, the body of a German NCO was carried on to the Place des Tilleuls, accompanied by a group of civilians under armed guard. The NCO, according to a Belgian witness, had been accidentally killed by a shot from a rifle with which a German soldier was battering down a door in the rue d'Horseilles; the civilians were local residents who had been arrested as francs-tireurs. The incident fed Junge's conviction that there had been a civilian uprising.[109] Three of the group from the rue d'Horseilles were taken at random and shot in front of the crowd (two dying) and the remaining 25 men were conducted to the river bank and executed.[110] The others marked as 'suspects' on the Place des Tilleuls were also shot here and at other points near the square and by the river.[111] Men were selected for execution because their hands were dirty or tobacco-stained; impatient to carry out the executions, some soldiers bayoneted the men in front of their wives.[112]

About 10 am, a German officer (probably Junge) designated a new burgomaster, De Jaer, and forced him to announce that all male inhabitants were hostages and that two would be executed for each further shooting at German soldiers; a notice to this effect was displayed for the following ten days.[113] Shortly after this, the women on the Place des Tilleuls were ordered to return home and bury their dead. In all 262 civilians perished in Andenne-Seilles.

Several German soldiers were sickened by the proceedings. Sergeant Woite felt in 1920 that the arbitrary executions had been unjustified since they punished the innocent.[114] Captain Wabnitz absented himself from the 'terrible trial'. The advocate Monjoie, with whom he was billeted, later recounted that Wabnitz, when asked who had ordered the executions, said that it was Colonel Scheunemann, who had been ten years with the army in the Cameroons. Monjoie replied that 'he treated us as negroes!', and Wabnitz rejoined: 'Yes, monsieur, like semi-negroes; I do not like that, that is no longer war.'[115]

Later, on Saturday 28 August, a new town commander, Captain Becker, proclaimed the army's belief in the peaceful intentions of most inhabitants, promised an inquiry into any future incidents, and announced a festival of reconciliation to which the religious and municipal authorities were 'invited' that evening. This macabre event, which consisted of a banquet to the sound of a military band on (of all places) the Place des Tilleuls, indicates that doubts had surfaced as to the reality of the franc-tireur plot.[116] According to several witnesses, Lieutenant Backhaus of IR 83 began an inquiry as early as 22 August, and admitted the possibility that the entire matter had been a 'friendly-fire' incident.[117] The senior officers ordering this inquiry and Becker, as the new town commander, must have felt that since no plotters were found and the 'court-martial' of the night of 20–21 August bore no resemblance to due legal process, some gesture of reconciliation was required.

Fury at francs-tireurs was widespread in the invaded areas, but like a brush-fire its effects were uneven as it skipped some centres while igniting others, and left potential disasters unkindled or quickly dowsed. In the latter category were Namur with its ring of forts, which the Germans feared might be a second Liège, and Brussels (map 4 above).

Namur surrendered after only two days, on 23 August, but some of the forts in the western sector held out until 25 August, so that initially tension remained high.[118] German soldiers used a human shield on entering Namur, including two priests who were killed in the battle.[119] On 24 August, the municipal and military authorities both issued posters warning the population of the consequences of resistance. That same evening, isolated shots on the outskirts of the city provoked a panic by German soldiers who killed 30 civilians and destroyed 110 buildings, including the town hall and much of the Grand' Place. The shooting only ended after the bishop, Thomas Heylen, and town commander, Major-General von Below, persuaded the men to stop. Belgian witness evidence suggests that German soldiers believed the town to be riddled with francs-tireurs and disguised Belgian and French soldiers. Four hundred hostages were rounded up in a riding-school early on 25 August and repeatedly threatened. One German officer told them in halting French:

> Our soldiers have been fired on. We are going to act as we did at Andenne. Andenne [is] finished. At Andenne, the inhabitants tried to poison our soldiers, fired on our soldiers [...] More than 500 shot. You too, you are going to be shot because you've fired on our soldiers right near here, in the Grand' Place. You Belgians have also cut off our soldiers' noses, ears, eyes and fingers. For that, you will be shot.

In fact, the hostages were released that evening. Namur thus narrowly escaped a much higher death toll.[120]

Unlike Namur, Brussels was an 'open city'. Controlling no strategic artery like the Meuse–Sambre river system, its defence did not figure in Belgian military plans. The burgomaster, Adolphe Max, forbade resistance in a poster of 12 August, a warning that he subsequently repeated, and gathered in civilian firearms.[121] In fact, both Max and Lieutenant-General Clooten, commander of the Garde Civique in Brabant, seemed determined to preserve the capital's 'honour' by ordering the Garde Civique to fight. Trenches were dug and companies mustered in the parks around the city. On 19 August, 24 hours before the German entry into Brussels, on a 'day of terrible tension', Brand Whitlock, the American ambassador, and his Spanish counterpart, who were fully informed about German brutality towards civilians in Liège province, pleaded with Max not to jeopardize the artistic heritage of the capital or the lives of its inhabitants by a futile gesture. When the city was occupied the following day by what Whitlock described as 'a mighty grey, grim horde, a thing of steel, that came thundering on with shrill fifes and throbbing drums [...], nervous horses and lumbering guns and wild songs', the Garde Civique had vanished, and no random shots triggered massacres or destruction.[122]

The Garde Civique did figure, however, in the incident which occurred on 22 August at Tamines. As the First and Second Armies drove south-west past Namur and Brussels through the industrial district of Charleroi and

Mons, they met the first real opposition from French and British forces. Conducted skilfully through villages and suburbs still full of civilians, this resistance fanned the German fear of francs-tireurs and resulted in numerous incidents entailing widespread destruction and massacre (map 5 above).[123]

The dearth of German source material rules out close study of Tamines. French and Belgian evidence suggests that as the German Second Army descended on the Sambre between Namur and Charleroi, it was met with harassing tactics by the French forces covering the bridges (barricades, trenches, and enfilading fire from houses), and responded with ferocity against civilians.[124] Tamines and several neighbouring villages on the Sambre were defended by the French 19th Infantry Division. Local inhabitants naturally welcomed French aid, but subsequently denied any involvement in the fighting. Human shields were used by German troops to take the villages of Arsimont and Auvelais on 21 August, and massacres followed.[125] At Tamines, German patrols in the morning of 21 August were ambushed by French soldiers and a score of artillerymen from the Charleroi Garde Civique. The population responded with cries of 'Vive la Belgique! Vive la France!', and the Germans may well have gained the impression that it was participating in the fighting.[126] However, when the main German force arrived, it was clear the resistance came from French soldiers (IR 70) who eventually withdrew to the steep south bank of the Sambre.[127] From there, they maintained accurate fire against repeated assaults by the Germans, who did not finally dislodge them until early on 22 August.

The effective French defence, and German belief in civilian collusion laid the basis for what followed. Violence towards civilians accompanied the fighting; a human shield was used in one assault and house-burning and executions occurred throughout the afternoon and night of 21 August.[128] German recrimination smouldered long after the fighting had stopped and erupted in a massacre on the evening of 22 August. From late afternoon of 21 August, much of the population of Tamines was rounded up in the church. Fragments of conversation with the guards indicated that they were convinced the civilians, led by priests, had participated *en masse* in the fighting. Twenty-four hours later, the church was full to bursting, the atmosphere made more stifling by the heat of the surrounding houses in flames. Belgian witnesses claimed that Protestant soldiers of IR 77 (from Hanover) mocked their Catholic piety and practices.[129]

Around 7 pm (Belgian time), the men were ordered out of the church and driven by furious soldiers who beat and insulted them to the Place Saint-Martin, on the banks of the Sambre. The priest was the object of particular derision. An unknown officer on horseback accused the men of being francs-tireurs and forced them to shout 'Vive l'Allemagne!'[130] They were then executed by rifle and machine-gun fire in a chaotic manner. Some escaped by jumping into the river, while others survived by shamming death among the heaped dead. Many German soldiers fired too high or too low, and an officer had to complete the execution by machine-gun. Other soldiers, by contrast, were only too willing to finish off the killing with bayonet and rifle butt.[131] A total of 383 citizens of Tamines were killed, including approximately 269 in the mass execution, making it the second most important incident of the invasion. The fact that German official publications ignored Tamines suggests that the government did not contest the basic facts and probably considered the army's behaviour there indefensible.[132]

3   The destruction of Louvain

One last mass reprisal against alleged francs-tireurs occurred on the right of the German army in Belgium in an incident which by contrast with Tamines achieved worldwide notoriety. In Louvain, the famous university town east of Brussels, 248 citizens were killed and one-sixth of the buildings were destroyed (see map 4 above), including the university library with its collection of early books and medieval manuscripts.[133] None of this happened, however, before 25 August. Louvain was an open city when the German troops entered on 19 August, the last Belgian troops having left that morning. The Garde Civique had been disbanded and its weapons transferred to Antwerp. All necessary measures had been taken to warn the inhabitants against protesting or shooting at the German soldiers. As elsewhere, weapons had been confiscated and posters warned the people not to take up arms, reminders being issued daily in the newspapers and by the clergy.[134] Louvain was a genteel city, inhabited by wealthy retired people, academics, priests, monks, and nuns. At first, the rumours of massacres in Liège and Aarschot were not believed, but as refugees began to arrive, telling stories of atrocities, fear took over. This intensified as the Belgian army withdrew; people fled on the last trains for Brussels and Antwerp, shopkeepers closed their shutters, and Belgian flags were removed from the streets. German troops marched in with bands playing and singing 'Die Wacht am Rhein' to find a subdued population. A proclamation was posted which threatened that if a single weapon were found, '[the owner] will be executed without mercy [...] the inhabitants of the neighbouring villages will be expelled, and the villages and towns themselves will be destroyed and burned.'[135]

For the next six days, the people of Louvain lived in an atmosphere of intimidation. There was a strict curfew after 8 pm; house doors had to be kept open at night and windows lit. Every day, hostages were taken to guarantee the conduct of the citizens. New troop arrivals increased the concentration of soldiers in Louvain to at least 15,000.[136] From 19 to 22 August Louvain was even the headquarters of the First Army, a sure sign there was little security risk for the Germans.[137] All remained calm until the evening of 25 August. Suddenly, the alarm sounded (variously recorded as at 5.30, 6.00 or 7.00 pm). For a while there was silence. Then shooting broke out at 8 pm, according to both Belgian and German accounts. This sparked a fusillade all over the town, with soldiers breaking into houses and firing down into the streets. Men were dragged out of the houses in front of their terrified families; some were beaten and shot immediately, others were taken to the railway station. Hubert David-Fischbach, for example, a man of 83, who had had German officers quartered in his house, was tied up and made to watch his house burn, beaten with bayonets, and finally shot. Others were killed during the night as they fled from their burning houses.[138]

Not only houses, but the commercial boulevards and the historic centre were deliberately burned down. At about 11.30 pm, German soldiers broke into the university library and, using petrol and inflammable tablets, set it on fire, subsequently preventing anyone from attempting to extinguish the blaze. As the rector of the university, Monsignor Paulin Ladeuze, remarked in a private report to the Vatican in 1915, only arson could account for the fact that 'in nine or ten hours, all that remained of this enormous building and the 300,000 volumes it contained were four walls and ashes.'[139] Other university buildings perished, as did the collegiate church of St Peter.[140] The Germans later made much of the fact that they saved the gothic town hall; but this was because it served as German headquarters and billeted many officers. The intention was clearly to destroy the most important parts of the town.[141]

Shooting and arson continued throughout 26 August, with civilians fired on as soon as they showed themselves in the street or at a window. On 27

August, the town commander, Major von Manteuffel, announced that Louvain was to be bombarded, and some 10,000 people – old, young, and infirm – were expelled. The threat of bombardment was not carried out but the town continued to burn until the following day. Overall, some 2,000 buildings were destroyed between 25 and 28 August. On 28 August, shooting broke out once more, centred on the station, with soldiers alleging civilians were firing.[142] It was at this point that the column of refugees expelled from Aarschot reached Louvain and was fired upon. In fact, few Louvain citizens remained in the town, most having been expelled to the surrounding district where they were maltreated and marched around by the troops for days. Many were deported in cattle wagons to Germany; apparently 1,500 Louvain citizens, including over 100 women and children, were detained under harsh conditions at Munster army camp until January 1915.[143]

The events at Louvain closely matched the pattern established at Visé and repeated elsewhere, but on a much greater scale. There is considerable evidence of mutual killing by German soldiers.[144] Ladeuze and Simon Deploige, rector of the theology faculty, both saw German soldiers firing on each other and were told the same by many others.[145] Everything points to a major panic, therefore, in which the German soldiers ran riot. Yet the unfolding incident also exhibited a policy of systematic punishment. Arson, executions, expulsion of the inhabitants, and the deportation of supposed ringleaders to Germany, had become the standard military tactic which was applied in a particularly severe fashion in Louvain.

Perhaps a key to understanding the severity of the German response is the way Louvain embodied the German soldiers' fear of the Belgian clergy as ringleaders of the 'People's War'. For Louvain was a major religious centre and its university a Catholic institution; it included Belgium's leading theology faculty, the Institut Supérieur de Philosophie. The town normally sheltered Belgian and foreign clerical students (though most were on vacation in August), as well as religious orders. There is ample evidence that the clergy were singled out for German hostility before the massacre. L. H. Grondijs, a retired Dutch professor who was a friend of Ladeuze and who witnessed the events while staying in Louvain, noted that during the day of 25 August German officers were telling anyone who would listen that the 'priests, from the pulpit, had excited the population against the enemy'. Ladeuze recorded that a priest who knew German and who was used as a hostage by German soldiers between St Trond and

Louvain heard 'every insult' hurled at the 'Pfaffen-Universität' (*Pfaffen* was a term of abuse for Catholic priests), whose students had supposedly fired on German soldiers.[146]

Once the panic began, the clergy and professors attracted particular violence. Ladeuze surmised that the soldiers who set fire to the library less than four hours after the shooting began mistakenly thought that it was the 'university', which is how it was referred to in tourist guides to Louvain, whereas the university in reality was spread throughout the town. Other university institutes were nonetheless burned along with the homes of 22 professors, which destroyed their private libraries and research material.[147]

During the expulsion of the population on 27 August, about 400 priests and clerical academics (including Ladeuze) were separated from other civilians and placed in a field near Tervueren, on the outskirts of Brussels, where they were searched for weapons. One young Jesuit, Father Dupierreux, was discovered to have a notebook in which he had written his private thoughts on the events of the previous days. These were read out in French and then German: 'Decidedly, I do not like the Germans. In my youth, I learned that centuries ago it was the barbarians who burned unfortified towns, pillaged houses, and assassinated innocent townsfolk. The Germans have done exactly the same thing. I was told that long ago Omar burned the library of Alexandria; the Germans have done the same thing at Louvain. This people can be proud of its *Kultur* [...]', at which point, after being given a moment for confession, he was executed.[148] For the next 24 hours, many of the clerics, including Ladeuze and the rector of the Jesuits in Louvain, were marched about to copious insults from officers and soldiers. They were suddenly released on orders from the commandant of Brussels, General von Lüttwitz, with whom Grondijs, Brand Whitlock, and possibly others had interceded. When Ladeuze met Lüttwitz on 30 August, the latter made it clear that he believed civilians had shot at German soldiers in Louvain. But he expressed his regret for the burning of the library and promised to protect the university from further damage, indicating his scepticism vis-à-vis the anti-Catholic hysteria of many of his troops.[149]

Despite later Belgian accusations, there is no serious evidence that the German actions in Louvain were premeditated. Manteuffel, the town commander, and many of the German troops believed there was a franc-tireur insurrection, and this soon became the standard German view.[150] If the events had been planned by the Germans, they got badly out of hand, for the soldiers in their panic inflicted considerable damage on each other, whereas the number of German troops in Louvain was quite adequate to deal with any real civilian uprising.

In reality, the proximate cause of the German behaviour was anxiety aroused by military events. The First Army, with its main forces now 70 to 80 kilometres distant on the French border, had good reason to fear that a counter-attack by the 100,000-strong Belgian army at Antwerp would endanger its overextended supply and communication lines. This explains the nervousness of the troops and their commanders in Louvain, aware of their numerical inferiority.[151] The Belgian army launched just such a counter-attack on the German flank on 25–26 August. Marching south from Antwerp on a broad front, Belgian divisions broke through German lines at several points, including the immediate vicinity of Louvain, where the sound of battle could be heard all day and where rumours flew about that (variously) the Belgians, the British, or the French would soon arrive. Towards nightfall, the Belgians forced a German column back to Tildonk, only eight kilometres from Louvain, and the Belgian cavalry drove several German companies back from Werchter. It was these German units which retreated into Louvain, and were almost certainly responsible for the panic firing, perhaps triggered by an accidental shot, perhaps unleashed because in the twilight they were held to be advancing enemy. This converted widespread fear into fury that the citizens of Louvain had apparently launched an uprising co-ordinated with the counter-attack. The military context also explains a broader pattern of brutality to civilians in the villages surrounding Louvain.[152]

4   The Third Army and Dinant

The Third Army (from Saxony), commanded by General von Hausen, was ordered forward on 18 August across the middle of Namur province. It met no serious resistance until it reached the Meuse which ran from south to north across the line of advance. Dinant, with 7,000 inhabitants, was the second largest town in Namur province and it constituted the strategic key to crossing the river. Already on 15 August, an advance German raid tried to secure the bridge but was repulsed by a French force defending the town. When the Third Army arrived, it encountered the French Fifth Army, which covered the triangle of territory between the Sambre, the Meuse, and the French frontier (map 5 above). The Fifth Army was vastly outnumbered since, together with the small BEF, it faced the combined weight of the three armies of the German right and centre. Joffre, the French commander-in-chief, was reluctant to recognize that the bulk of the German invasion was coming through Belgium and he only began to shift the weight of the French forces northwards from Lorraine after the Germans took Dinant. Thus on 23 August, a single French division (the 51st Reserve) faced three German army corps along a 30-kilometre front on the Meuse; at Dinant French IR 273 confronted the entire the German XIIth Army Corps.

As elsewhere, however, inferior numbers were no impediment to a fighting withdrawal that caused the Germans damage and delay. In Dinant, the French were aided by the terrain. The Meuse at this point runs between a steep escarpment to the east, and a west bank studded with hedges and woods. The town in 1914 consisted of a ribbon of streets winding nearly four kilometres along the eastern bank, but only a few hundred metres wide, with a high rock cliff behind it. This was pierced by three roads and one narrow path leading from the plateau beyond, and it was down these routes that any attack from the east had to come. The sparsely settled west bank offered good cover. The French had destroyed all the bridges across the Meuse on 22 August, except those at Bouvignes, Dinant, and Hastière, which they had fortified at both ends, so it was here that the French defence concentrated.[153]

The assault by the XIIth Army Corps on Dinant resulted in the largest single instance of violence towards civilians during the invasion, with a total of 674 dead (nearly 10 per cent of the population) and most of the town destroyed. Rich surviving records of the Saxon army, in addition to intensive contemporary Belgian and German investigations, allow a particularly full reconstruction of the events.[154]

According to the memoirs of its commander, the Third Army was primed with stories of treacherous Belgian civilians while still assembling in west Germany, and had gained the impression that 'the population, excited by the chauvinist press, the clergy, and the government, was acting on instructions given in advance. One could not [...] hesitate for a single instant to deal with this situation by the most serious and rigorous measures.'[155] As the army crossed into eastern Belgium, it wreaked havoc in villages that were far removed from any fighting (Somme-Leuze, Erezée, Champlon, and Hargimont), with hostages taken, civilians shot, houses burned, and notables deported.[156] Cavalry patrols in the countryside around Dinant told the artillery on 21 August that the civilians shot at them from houses and barns, and sent signals to the French artillery across the Meuse, giving away the German positions.[157]

Even more revealing of the outlook of the German soldiers was the episode of a motorized German raid on Dinant in the night of 21–22 August. A mixed battalion of riflemen and pioneers descended the route from Ciney, the middle road into Dinant, which became the rue Saint-Jacques in the town (map 6).[158] Seven civilians were killed and 15 to 20 houses were set on fire with incendiary bombs. Whereas German official accounts presented the incursion as a 'reconnaissance in force' and the participants later swore that they had been ambushed by civilians, the attack seemed so inexplicable to the inhabitants of Dinant that, according to the town's leading legal officer, state prosecutor Maurice Tschoffen, it was discounted as the escapade of drunken soldiers.[159] In reality, it was symptomatic of the reckless bravado of the XIIth Army Corps, its assumption that the population would fight with the French, and its predisposition to punish the inhabitants.

A battalion combat report showed that the raid (ordered at brigade level) was absurdly ambitious, having as its aim: 'to seize Dinant, [...], expel the defenders, and destroy the town as far as possible.'[160] This was confirmed by one of the soldiers, Rasch, who described in a letter to his parents how the men knew that Dinant was defended by a strong detachment of French troops, but had been given orders to 'kill everyone and wipe off the map one part on the left bank [sic, in fact right bank] of the Meuse!!! It was a tremendously ('kolossal') honourable task and if successful, it would be famous for all time.' As the mixed battalion crept down the rue Saint-Jacques at the dead of night, all was quiet. Seeing a light in a café, they threw in a hand-grenade, whereupon 'indescribably' heavy fire was unleashed 'from every window' in the houses. This caused what Rasch frankly called a 'panic', as the Germans ran for their lives. His company suffered eight killed, and the captain was seriously wounded; in total, the raid cost 19 dead and 117 wounded.[161] The advance guard of the battalion reached the Meuse. Finding it suspicious that gas lamps were burning, they extinguished them, and decided to search houses. Then they were fired on from all sides.[162]

The alleged use of revolvers and shotguns was taken by German soldiers to mean civilian participation. Self-defence by civilians is a possibility, though the inhabitants never admitted to this at any stage during the battle

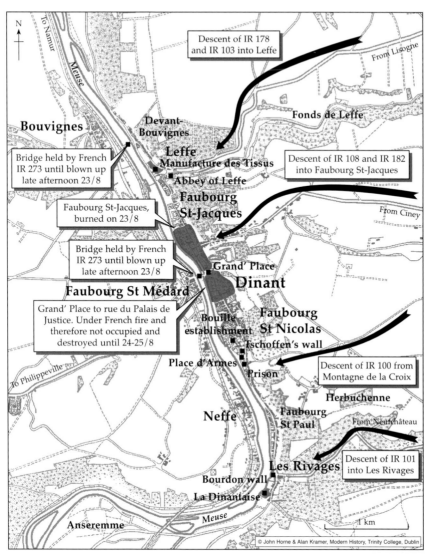

Descent of IR 178 and IR 103 into Leffe

Descent of IR 108 and IR 182 into Faubourg St-Jacques

Bridge held by French IR 273 until blown up late afternoon 23/8

Faubourg St-Jacques, burned on 23/8

Bridge held by French IR 273 until blown up late afternoon 23/8

Grand' Place to rue du Palais de Justice. Under French fire and therefore not occupied and destroyed until 24-25/8

Descent of IR 100 from Montagne de la Croix

Descent of IR 101 into Les Rivages

To Namur

Meuse

From Lisogne

Bouvignes

Devant-Bouvignes

Fonds de Leffe

Leffe

Manufacture des Tissus

Abbey of Leffe

Faubourg St-Jacques

From Ciney

Faubourg St Médard

Grand' Place

Dinant

Faubourg St Nicolas

Bouille establishment

Tschoffen's wall

To Philippeville

Place d'Armes

Prison

Herbuchenne

Neffe

Faubourg St Paul

From Neufchâteau

Les Rivages

Bourdon wall

La Dinantaise

Anseremme

Meuse

1 km

© John Horne & Alan Kramer, Modern History, Trinity College, Dublin

6 Dinant

for Dinant. In the panic in the rue Saint-Jacques, however, German soldiers may well have shot each other. Moreover, as the raiders knew, French soldiers still held the bridge over the Meuse and patrolled the town. They may have fired on the Germans in the rue Saint-Jacques, and it was almost certainly they who shot at the group that reached the river. In the dark, the Germans with their flaming torches were visible to the French but would not have been able to see who was firing, 'especially not the machine-guns'.[163] However, the Germans' impression of Dinant as a nest of francs-tireurs was confirmed by the experience of the abortive raid.

When the main assault took place on Dinant and neighbouring villages, the inhabitants were therefore seen to be just as much the enemy as the French. What ensued was no military panic (as at Louvain) but rather the systematic, premeditated elimination of presumed civilian resistance. Under cover of an artillery bombardment, which forced the inhabitants to shelter in their cellars, four German columns advanced into the city early on 23 August. The northernmost force came down into the industrial suburb of Leffe and the hamlet of Devant-Bouvignes (map 6 above). Two columns descended from the plateau into the centre of the town, one down the rue Saint-Jacques, the other down the steep lane that led to the Faubourg Saint-Nicolas and the Place d'Armes. The last column came along the road from Neufchâteau into the southern suburb of Les Rivages. The French occupied the west bank of the Meuse for most of the day, firing at the exposed Germans as they entered the town and bombarding them with artillery. They blew up the bridge at Bouvignes in mid-afternoon.[164] Initially, they held both ends of the main Dinant bridge, and may even have had forward defences in the town centre. They repulsed an attack early in the day and only blew the bridge up during the afternoon.[165] By early evening, the French had slipped away in the direction of the border.[166] But for most of the day, the Germans were rebuffed and subjected to intense fire from the west bank.

Leffe was dominated by an abbey and a large cloth factory. When the soldiers of IR 178 and IR 103 entered it early on 23 August, they were convinced they faced heavy civilian resistance as well as shooting and artillery fire from the French at Bouvignes, on the opposite bank. Paul Zschocke, NCO in IR 103, was ordered by his company commander to search a steep river-bank for franc-tireurs and 'to shoot everyone we found there'. Three civilians were killed, two of them by Zschocke, who freely admitted that he did not know if they had fired or were even carrying weapons; they had fled at the sight of the soldiers and tried to hide in a stream.[167] The 3rd company of IR 178 was sent in to purge Leffe of 'francs-tireurs' who had allegedly directed devastating fire at the soldiers from a saw-mill.[168] Corporal Franz Stiebing described the action:

> We pushed on house by house, under fire from almost every building, and we arrested the male inhabitants, who almost all carried weapons. They were summarily executed in the street. Only children under 15, old people, and women were spared. During this we were fired on from the nearby hills at a distance of 150 to 200 metres. I did not see if anyone from my battalion was killed or injured in this street-fighting. But I saw the corpses of at least 180 francs-tireurs – only francs-tireurs were executed – lying in the streets. Near a saw-mill I saw another 30 to 35 corpses. I was later told that the francs-tireurs had assembled in masses in the saw-mill.[169]

Many of the inhabitants were dragged from their houses by the German soldiers and taken to the abbey church, or themselves sought refuge there. At about 10 am, 43 men were taken out of the church and executed. The monks were accused of firing on the Germans and fined 15,000 francs. The women and children were held prisoner in the abbey for a number of days.[170] Another part of the population hid in the cellars of the woollen factory, including the manager, Rémy Himmer, and his family. Here, at 5 pm, they gave themselves up to stupefied German soldiers who were still firing on the French. The women and children were taken to the abbey while Himmer and 31 workers were shot.[171] Late in the evening, the factory buildings were burned down.

IR 108 and 182, with the 12th and 48th artillery, followed the route of the ill-fated raid of 21 August down the rue Saint-Jacques into the town centre, just north of the bridge.[172] Here they came under withering fire from the French defenders. Throughout the day, German soldiers killed male civilians. In one collective execution at 5.30 pm, 27 men who had taken refuge in a bar were executed by a squad of IR 108 in the rue des Tanneries.[173] From 4 pm the troops built street barricades from looted furniture; soldiers from IR 182 seized one young man on suspicion of firing on them, although they found no weapon, and tied him to a barricade as a human shield. Coming under artillery fire from their own side at 6 pm, they shot the young man and retreated.[174] The Germans burned much of the district, and by late afternoon the whole area was a sea of flames.[175] Taking Leffe and the Saint-Jacques district together, 312 inhabitants were killed by German soldiers on 23 August.[176]

Just south of the town centre, the 100th Grenadiers descended a narrow path from the heights above Dinant into the Faubourg Saint-Nicolas, coming under heavy fire from the French.[177] Their suspicion of the inhabitants was immediately evident, as state prosecutor Tschoffen witnessed: 'They marched in two columns down the deserted street, those on the right aiming their rifles at the houses on the left, and inversely, all with their fingers on the trigger and ready to fire. At each door a group stopped and riddled the houses, especially the windows, with bullets [...] I know that the soldiers threw many bombs into the cellars.'[178] In order to cross the Place d'Armes, the square at the heart of the district which was open to the river and thus to French fire, the Germans seized a human shield of several civilians. As at Leffe, the inhabitants were forced from their houses and rounded up, in this case in the Bouille iron-working establishment and in the town prison, which stood on the Place d'Armes. Tschoffen testified that the soldiers saw the civilians as collectively culpable for the supposed actions of the francs-tireurs. This mentality is illustrated by the incident in the early afternoon in which German soldiers on the heights above the town fired on civilians in the prison courtyard, until frantic signalling from the soldiers in the prison got them to stop. The mere appearance of the townspeople suggested francs-tireurs.[179]

Late in the afternoon, German anger with the inhabitants reached its climax. Nineteen men were taken from the large group of civilians in the ironworks and shot. The remainder of the group were led back towards the Place d'Armes, being made to cry 'Long live Germany! Long live the Kaiser!' Men and youths were separated from their families. Having been told that they had fired on German soldiers and were to receive exemplary punishment, they were lined up against the garden wall in front of prosecutor Tschoffen's house, and executed by a detachment of the 100th Grenadiers. The order for the execution was given by the commander of the first battalion of the regiment, and 137 civilians perished in what became known as the 'Tschoffen wall' massacre.

The extraordinary testimony that Major von Loeben, who commanded the execution squad, later gave to a German inquiry shows how hearsay and an officer's word sufficed to condemn people to death. It should be noted how often the words 'I was told' and 'assumed' are used.

all of the assumptions and rumors seem to argue against premeditation

I was told there was also shotgun fire. The quarter was divided into districts and the companies searched for franc-tireurs and weapons. The prison, too, was searched and the prison officers disarmed. Quite a number of revolvers and other weapons emerged. My company was installed by a garden wall near the prison and thus did not suffer from the franc-tireur shooting. But I was told that my regiment continually came under fire here and there from the houses. Finally [commander of 1st Battalion, Lt-Col.] Count Kielmannsegg decided to make an example and ordered me to have a large number of men of military age shot. The men were taken partly from the prison, partly they were brought in groups. I assumed they were people who had been firing or had otherwise behaved in a hostile manner towards our troops. The people were arranged in several ranks by the garden wall. Women, children, and older men were excluded. It was two detachments, each under the command of a lieutenant (one of them was v. Ehrenthal) which carried out the executions. I had some difficulty separating the women and children. One woman clung to her husband and wanted to be shot together with him. I therefore decided to let her go free, together with her husband. One man had a child of about five in his arms, which was not his own, according to his own words. The child was taken away from him and sent to the women. The man was shot with the rest. Several salvos were fired. Whether some were merely wounded I do not know, since we had to resume our march. I certainly know that no women or children were killed at this place. But if women or children had hidden behind the garden wall, it is very possible they were hit by bullets passing through it [...] I told Mme Bozet [?] that a comrade of mine, Captain Legler, had been shot at by a civilian. I probably also said that a young girl had taken part in the shooting at German troops. That is what soldiers told me.

Signed under oath Loeben.[180]

The survivors of this execution provided evidence on which the account in the Belgian Second Commission report is based, and it matches Loeben's affidavit in every respect.[181] Thus the Tschoffen wall massacre was not committed to punish alleged francs-tireurs. The soldiers knew the victims, as individuals, were 'innocent'; but they perceived the civilians as collectively culpable for the supposed actions of the francs-tireurs. When people asked the guards why they had been assembled in the Bouille establishment, the reply was: 'Some said it was for our own safety. Others said we were to be executed for shooting. Protests and denials. Response: "All for one! This is war." But who had fired? "Many civilians, among them a girl of 13 who shot at a major."[182] By an ironic twist, the Tschoffen wall shooting may have prevented another massacre, underlining how arbitrary the proceedings were. Prosecutor Tschoffen was with the detainees in the prison; he testified that the threat of executions grew in the late afternoon until at 6 pm the men were separated from the women and children and lined up in the prison yard. At that moment, sustained firing broke out near the prison, spreading confusion, and the men rejoined their families. The firing in question was the massacre taking place outside Tschoffen's own house.[183]

The 101st Grenadiers and the 3rd company of Pioneers entered Les Rivages, at the southern edge of Dinant, in mid-afternoon. Their mission was to construct a pontoon bridge over the Meuse. Since the right bank becomes a narrow defile at this point between the escarpment and the river, with barely room for the road and a single line of habitations, this district was particularly exposed to French fire. Nonetheless, on arriving the Germans had an hour or so of relative peace. The houses were searched for arms, hostages rounded up, and the engineers succeeded in constructing 40 metres of the pontoon bridge. At around 5 pm, a number of the men working on the bridge were killed by sustained fire, which the German soldiers later claimed came from francs-tireurs on both sides of the river, but which the Belgian civilians attributed to French soldiers on the west bank.[184] Flat water concentrating sound, the river created the impression that distant firing was close at hand, a misperception that was reinforced by the sheer rock wall behind Les Rivages which distorted echoes and made it hard to know where the sound came from. This phenomenon was generally true of the Meuse valley at Dinant. French bullets echoing and ricocheting off the cliff at Les Rivages certainly contributed to the Germans' impression of being attacked from the rear, though several German witnesses accepted that the French were 'also' firing from the opposite bank.[185]

Bourdon, a magistrate who lived locally, was sent to the west bank to warn the 'francs-tireurs' that if the firing continued, the hostages would be executed. He returned (being shot in the leg by the Germans on the way) to report that only French soldiers were firing. When further shots rang out, a large group of civilians were lined up against the wall of Bourdon's house, and executed. More than half of the 77 killed were women and children: 38 women and girls, and 15 children under 14, of whom seven were babies;

seven of the men were over 70 years old.[186] Bourdon and his family, except his 15-year-old son Félix, perished. When the 101st Grenadiers reached the west bank, they continued the killing in the village of Neffe, 86 of whose inhabitants died. Twenty-three were found hiding under a railway viaduct, where they were shot, and 43 were transported to the right bank and executed at the Bourdon wall.[187]

The records of the post-war Reich Supreme Court investigation now make it possible to establish how the mass execution at Les Rivages came about and who was responsible. In 1922, the Belgian government announced the intention to prosecute Colonel Meister, commander of IR 101, for ordering the execution. But as far as can be ascertained, Meister was not present, for the French attack on the pontoon bridge occurred while he was making his way to Les Rivages from Dinant, and wild firing by his own men (which he was unable to stop) forced him to take cover.[188] The first soldiers of IR 101 to arrive in Les Rivages had already arrested a large group of inhabitants before the firing started, apparently without having harmed them, but at the sound of gunfire, Major Schlick arrived, 'his face contorted with rage'. It was Schlick who gave the order to kill the civilians. The troops, who had been with the hostages from the start, knew they could not have been firing. Moreover, all the soldiers could see that the hostages included many women and children.[189] Schlick himself admitted that as he arrived at Les Rivages he *assumed* the captive civilians had been arrested because they were guilty of firing, and he therefore gave the order to execute them without consulting Colonel Meister. Captain d'Elsa intervened and tried to prevent the execution, but to no avail. Schlick also admitted that he later ordered his men to shoot civilians lying on the ground who were 'apparently not yet dead, [. . .] so to speak as mercy killing'.[190] Schlick was not acting without authority, however. Several hours earlier, about midday, a lieutenant had reported to the commander of 45th Brigade, Major-General Lucius, that his battalion was in combat with civilians, and had been given the order to continue the fighting against the 'illegal behaviour' of the population of Dinant.[191]

In the days after 23 August, the scene in Dinant resembled something out of a medieval depiction of hell. Inhabitants were still being hunted down and shot on 24 August. Houses were ablaze for days, lighting up the countryside at night. The stench polluted the air, above all because of the heaps of corpses decomposing in the hot sun.[192] The district immediately south of the bridge, which had escaped unscathed on 23 August (including the post office, main banks, and a convent), was systematically burned down. Dinant was comprehensively looted. Troops completed the devastation by destroying all Dinant's public and historic buildings, including the collegial church and the town hall with its archives and art treasures.[193] Over 400 citizens of Dinant and neighbouring villages were deported to Germany and interned in a camp in Kassel, until November.[194]

Dinant was the epicentre of wider violence against civilians on 23 August along the entire front of the Third Army's assault on the Meuse. The bridges were flash-points. When IR 178 crossed over to Bouvignes, north of Dinant, it killed 31 villagers. South of Dinant, a furious battle raged all day as IR 104 and 133 tried to force the Meuse against stiff resistance from the French at Hastière-par-delà and Hastière-Lavaux (map 5 above). The villagers were caught in the middle, accused by the Germans of aiding the French, and 19 inhabitants of Hastière-par-delà were killed (including two ten-year old boys) and the village razed.[195] The Third Army left a swathe of destruction as it fanned out from the Meuse towards the French border, executing civilians and razing villages at Surice, Romedenne, and elsewhere.[196]

Incidents also occurred in the rear of the German advance although no enemy was present and fighting had completely ceased. In the most notorious case, at Spontin (near Third Army headquarters at Ciney), a sudden fusillade in the early hours of 23 August, which was almost certainly a friendly-fire incident, caused the death of a major and two soldiers. German troops were convinced of the guilt of the villagers. One Captain Heinzmann, Reserve Infantry Regiment 101, wrote that the major and other soldiers were killed by local people armed with shotguns. German artillery shot the village into flames, after which IR 103 arrested and executed those found with weapons that should have been turned in. The victims included the priest, the burgomaster, and, according to Heinzmann, a doctor who had fired from a house marked with the Red Cross.[197] Belgian sources confirm that the burgomaster and the priest were executed, 131 out of 161 houses and the medieval church were razed, and 44 citizens were killed.[198]

The initial outburst of fury against Belgian civilians by German troops at Liège was not purely spontaneous. Similar manifestations by soldiers as far away as Alsace-Lorraine show that the phenomenon was related to more than German frustration at being held up by the Belgian forts. The rapidity with which orders for ruthless 'reprisals' were issued, and France and Belgium accused of waging a 'People's War', shows that the soldiers' mentalities and expectations were shared, even endorsed, by the most senior levels of army and government.

In the second phase of the invasion, after the fall of Liège, the readiness to execute civilians arose partly from these underlying assumptions, but now also from superior orders. Cold-blooded measures of 'reprisal' and deterrence became more frequent, although panics and 'friendly fire' were often still the immediate cause. Even though the documentation does not always allow the precise triggering incident to be reconstructed, the general precondition for the outbreak of violence against civilians was the soldiers' ubiquitous fear of treacherous civilian resistance, a fear now magnified and officially disseminated throughout the army. Dinant marked the culminating point because it was no longer a question of reaction, but of pre-emptive action. Along the Meuse and the path to the French frontier, the Third Army took on two enemies, French soldiers and the francs-tireurs of its imagination.

Do they prove that Dinant in fact was pre-emptive?

2   German invasion, part 2

The period from the onset of the general advance on 18 August until the German invasion force left Belgian soil ten days later constituted the most intense phase of violence against civilians. As in the first phase, German belief in francs-tireurs was manifest in every part of the combat zone. When the Fourth and Fifth Armies, the left wing of the invasion force, battled through the wooded hills of the Belgian Ardennes into France, they acted in the same fashion as the armies to the north. This proved equally true of the Sixth and Seventh Armies as they repulsed the French invasion of German Lorraine and moved into the southern Meurthe-et-Moselle and the Vosges.

1   The battle of the Ardennes

The Ardennes saw the largest battle in the invasion of Belgium. The French war plan (Plan XVII) called for the main French offensive to be launched into German Lorraine. This was to be supported by a flanking advance further north into the supposedly empty Ardennes by the French Third and Fourth Armies. In reality, this placed them on a collision course with the German Fourth and Fifth Armies. On 21 August the French Third and Fourth Armies took the offensive along a front from Longwy to Mézières northward and met the Germans, to mutual surprise, on 22–23 August, in the battle of the Ardennes (map 7). In a series of encounters from Anloy and Neufchâteau in the north to Rossignol in the valley of the Semois, and to Virton, Ethe, and Baranzy near the French border, there were heavy losses on both sides.[1] The French armies were so badly mauled they had to retreat across the frontier. The German armies followed slowly into the French

Map labels (clockwise / by region):

Erezée-Briscol

Bouvignes NAMUR **Dinant**

Neffe

Hastière-Lavaux

Waulsort

Hastière-par-delà **BELGIUM** Ourthe

Meuse Lesse

[3]

[4]

[4]

Porcheresse Maissin Anloy **LUXEMBOURG** GRAND DUCHY OF LUXEM-BURG

Bièvre

Paliseul A

Offagne *Forest of Luchy*

Bertrix Neufchâteau

Ardennes

Forest of Neufchâteau

[5]

Herbeumont Semois

Rossignol Houdemont

Izel Tintigny

Sedan Pin **Arlon**

Bazeilles Saint Vincent Bellefontaine

Saint-Léger

FRANCE Robelmont **Ethe** Bleid Mussy-la-Ville

Margny Musson

ARDENNES Meuse Virton Baranzy

Montmédy Latour Goméry Longwy

Ruette [3]

MEUSE [3]

© John Horne & Alan Kramer, Modern History, Trinity College, Dublin

Legend:

[5] Advance of German and French armies

◎ Major town

○ Other town or village

☆ Fortified town

Arlon ■ Incidents with over 100 civilians killed

Anloy • Incidents with 10–99 civilians killed

N

20km

100 200 500 1000

Metres OD

7 Luxembourg province

départements of the Ardennes, Meuse, and Meurthe-et-Moselle. Between 21 and 26 August, the German Fourth and Fifth Armies killed about 1,000 civilians in Luxembourg and the borderlands of the Meurthe-et-Moselle and French Ardennes.[2]

Anloy and Neufchâteau saw heavy fighting on 22 August at the point of furthest advance by the French Fourth Army against the German Fourth Army. When the French tried to take Anloy, with severe losses on both sides, the exasperated Germans, according to Belgian sources, accused the villagers of firing and hunted them down while setting fire to their houses. The Germans also seized 170 civilians as a human shield and, having temporarily been driven out by French artillery fire, killed more inhabitants on their return during the night. According to the primary school teacher, German soldiers accused his pupils of cutting off German soldiers' fingers in order to steal rings, while the priest was alleged to have signalled to the French by ringing the church bell. Portraits of King Albert and Queen Elisabeth were vandalized. In all, 49 civilians perished.[3] Neufchâteau had been occupied by both French and German advance units, with the Germans shooting some inhabitants and seizing hostages, before the battle of 22 August, when the Germans held the town against fierce French attack. As in Anloy, the Germans accused the inhabitants of taking part in the battle, killed 17 of them, and threatened that if 'civilians or francs-tireurs' fired again, they would be hanged or shot and their houses razed.[4]

Further south, the French and German Fourth Armies clashed along the river Semois. In a day-long battle at Rossignol on 22 August, the German 12th Division and 3rd Cavalry Division finally took the village from the French 3rd Colonial Division in heavy fighting. At Tintigny, a hamlet that lay in the German rear, a German soldier had been shot in the morning of 22 August, almost certainly by a French patrol or mobilized Belgian foresters; the Germans claimed the inhabitants were responsible and began maltreating them. As exhausted and wounded German soldiers fell back on Tintigny, civilians were gunned down in the streets or burned alive in their houses. A group of notables was taken hostage and later joined by a large number of villagers on the edge of the town. Here, they were interrogated by a German officer. One of the hostages, a retired notary, Lefèvre, offered his entire fortune to save the lives of the group. But the officer cried in French: 'Too late, you will all be shot', while soldiers made menacing gestures of execution. Late in the afternoon, the menfolk were separated and marched beyond a neighbouring village, where 40 were killed.

Another group of inhabitants was marched towards the battle, four being shot at the sound of gunfire with the accusation that civilians were resisting. The survivors were brought back to the schoolhouse in Tintigny that night and the men were used as a human shield against French artillery the following day. In all, 63 inhabitants of Tintigny were killed and the village was largely destroyed.[5]

The conviction that villagers had helped the French spread to German troops moving up in the wake of the battle. On 24 August, inhabitants were shot and large numbers of houses destroyed in the surrounding villages of Izel, Pin, and Houdemont. Arlon became the centre of more organized repression. As noted, the town was an important German military base from 12 August in which courts-martial tried civilians for franc-tireur activities; on 23 August, for example, ten civilians were executed, including two from Tintigny.[6] On 26 August, however, 122 civilians were killed *en masse* without any pretence of a court-martial in a cold-blooded execution whose origins are to be found in the battle of Rossignol four days before.[7]

When the 12th Division had finally taken Rossignol on the evening of 22 August, capturing 2,600 French soldiers and three generals, they rounded up the inhabitants and kept them in the church until the morning of 24 August.[8] On 23 August, the Germans sought an excuse to maltreat the civilians, and staged incidents so that they could accuse the inhabitants of shooting at them. A number of houses were set on fire and several villagers killed. On 25 August, according to Belgian accounts, 108 civilians from Rossignol and 14 from elsewhere were taken to Arlon.[9] They were handed over to the Landsturm Battalion Gotha, commanded by Major von Hedemann. The following morning, Hedemann obtained the agreement of his commander, Colonel von Thessmar, in the Grand Duchy of Luxemburg, for the executions. According to evidence provided by Abbé Peiffer in Arlon and four citizens in the Grand Duchy, Thessmar was seated on the terrace of the Café du Commerce, Place d'Armes.[10] An orderly informed him that 120 francs-tireurs had been brought to Arlon. Thessmar enquired if there were carriages at Arlon, presumably for onward transport to Germany, and being told there were not instructed some to be requested from Trier. Then, changing his mind, he had the orderly recalled, told him he need not put himself to so much trouble for a bunch of francs-tireurs ('was machen Sie so viele Geschichten?'), and ordered them shot instead.[11] All 122 (including one female) were killed in groups of ten by firing squads. The last victims had to climb on the mound of their predecessors to be dispatched.[12]

The essential details in this major massacre are corroborated by an internal German investigation, to which Hedemann stated in March 1915 that 'one hundred francs-tireurs and one woman' were handed over to his battalion by an officer with the words: 'All these people shot at German soldiers in the area of Rossignol and Ethe and are to be executed; the woman put out the eyes of a wounded officer.' Hedemann confirmed that Thessmar was called by telephone and agreed to the execution.[13] It was then announced to the assembled prisoners in German and French, three times, that they were accused of having shot at and murdered German troops. Whoever felt they were innocent or had anything to say should step forward. If no one had anything to say then they would be condemned to death and summarily executed. No one stepped forward, so Hedemann concluded they all felt guilty.

The mass execution left such an impression that German officers were still talking about it two months later. One officer in a supply column told the Württemberg medical officer Professor von Pezold that he had heard that the franc-tireur fighting in Arlon was so heavy that after it 123 inhabitants were shot dead in groups of ten:

> They were then dragged by the legs and thrown on to a pile, and the corporals shot with their revolvers all those who had not been killed by the infantry. The whole execution was witnessed by the pastor, a woman and two young girls. They were the last to be shot, for they had put out the eyes of wounded soldiers.[14]

In fact, there were no girls; the female victim was a 41-year-old woman.

In the extreme south of Luxembourg province, along the French frontier, the German Fifth Army and the French Third Army collided in the vicinity of Ethe-Latour and Baranzy-Musson on 22 August. Ethe and the neighbouring hamlet of Goméry had been the site of skirmishes between German and French patrols nine days earlier, and were already identified by the Germans as a nest of francs-tireurs.[15] On 21 August, the German 10th Division occupied Ethe. But the following day, in hard fighting with high casualties, it was driven from most of the village by the French 7th Division, whose main base was in Goméry, before the overextended French left both villages that evening and slipped away towards France. Already, during the afternoon's combat, German soldiers in Belmont, a part of Ethe that remained under their control, killed up to 60 wounded French soldiers and 23 civilians. This, and the 'rage' of the soldiers noted by some Belgian witnesses, suggests that enemy soldiers and civilians were considered to be complicit in illegitimate resistance – the French guilty of using Belgian aid, the Belgians guilty of helping French soldiers – a view which helps explain the events of the next day.[16]

German troops occupied Ethe and Goméry early on 23 August. They entered Ethe shooting on all sides, set fire to houses, and marshalled Belgian civilians and numerous French wounded and stretcher-bearers into a column. The column was then marched in the direction of Goméry, and when shots rang out (possibly from a French rear-guard hidden in a chicory factory), the Germans turned on the column, killing 13 civilians and an unknown number of French prisoners. A further 18 men from the column were shot in a collective execution.[17] The violence in Ethe was undoubtedly reinforced by events in Goméry. Hundreds of French wounded soldiers and medical personnel had been left in various buildings, notably the château of Baron Gerlach de Goméry, which had served as the main first-aid centre during the battle, and a house in which a French army doctor, Sedillot, had set up a dressing station. When the Germans entered Goméry, according to Sedillot, they suddenly became highly agitated. They claimed that they had been shot at from a first-aid station flying the Red Cross flag. This was denied by all the surviving French and Belgian witnesses. But in the massacre that followed, 150 wounded French soldiers died at the hands of IR 47.[18]

The known events in Goméry bore a strange resemblance to the account of Ethe given by the commander of the German forces responsible for the killings in both villages. Major-General von der Horst of the 20th Infantry Brigade (IR 47 and 50) related that on entering Ethe, he ordered several inhabitants, 'who were wearing the Red Cross armband apparently without any right', to act as a human shield for troops searching the houses for French soldiers. A sudden attack was launched on the brigade staff, apparently from 'all the houses [...] the church, and also from the houses marked with the Red Cross flag'. For General von der Horst there was no doubt that the medical personnel and the civilian population in Ethe were participating in a well-planned ambush: 'I ordered the captured civilians and French soldiers, in total about one hundred men, to be shot on the spot, and the village to be burned down.' It is possible that von der Horst retrospectively conflated Ethe and Goméry.[19] Equally possibly, German soldiers from the same units made the same accusation in the two villages on the same morning. Either way, the powerful symbolism of Red Cross facilities is clear. These supposed oases of impartial humanitarian activity under the Geneva Convention were seen by the Germans as potential sources of treachery and danger, leading to massacres of soldiers and civilians in both places.

In Ethe, the violence intensified over the following 24 hours. Two further collective executions occurred during the day, and most of the village was set on fire, as the 10th Division continued to pass through en route for France. Finally, the entire population was expelled. The men were separated and sent to nearby Latour while the women and children returned, some 600 of them spending the night in the primary school. The following day, 24 August, in a nightmare of contradictory orders by the Germans, a column of civilians from Ethe was set to work clearing the battlefield of corpses before being led in the direction of Latour, where they met some of their men, who had been sent to Latour the previous day, returning with more inhabitants of that village, likewise ordered to clear the battlefield. As the two columns merged, they were suddenly charged by German cavalry, who attacked them with lances and revolvers in what seems more like a revenge killing than an execution. A total of 96 civilians died, 25 in the column from Ethe and 71 from Latour.[20] Another group of civilians discovered hiding in cellars in Ethe on 24 August was taken to the same vicinity and 46 men were executed.[21] In all, the 20th Infantry Brigade (IR 47 and 50), IR 46, and associated units, killed 218 inhabitants of Ethe on 22–24 August, including 30 children aged between two and 17 and 45 people over 60, in addition to an unknown number of captured French soldiers.[22]

The now familiar pattern of German soldiers expecting francs-tireurs, killing civilians while fighting the French, and terrorizing settlements in the rear of military operations, was replicated elsewhere in southern Belgian Luxembourg. As the German XIIIth (Württemberg) Army Corps drove south towards the French fortified town of Longwy, fierce fighting broke out on the Belgian side of the border on 22 August, at Baranzy and Musson. In early morning fog there were incidents of 'friendly fire', apparently on both sides, which fed the Germans' belief in treacherous civilian resistance. Almost as soon as the battle began, troops of IR 125 burned down 86 (out of 106) houses in Baranzy and killed 27 villagers. Mussy, in the rear of the German attack, was also destroyed with 13 villagers dying during the day.[23] Colonel Ebbinghaus, commander of IR 125, recorded that there had been 'franc-tireur' fighting in Baranzy and also a machine-gun in the church tower. Machine-guns were heavy items used by specialized units and unlikely to have been in the possession of irregulars; it is far more probable that if there was a machine-gun, it belonged to French troops.[24] Two hundred and eight inhabitants of Baranzy and nearby Musson were deported to Germany.

2   The Germans in the Meurthe-et-Moselle

As the Fifth Army (especially the XIIIth Army Corps) pursued the retreating French across the northern Meurthe-et-Moselle, in French Lorraine, the preoccupation with francs-tireurs continued unabated (map 3, p. 21). When IR 121 and 122 fought their way on 21 August into Mont-Saint-Martin, practically a northern suburb of Longwy, the German soldiers shot down or burned to death 16 inhabitants, including two children of ten and four years.[25] The next day, IR 121 shot six people in Gorcy, apparently in reprisal for a rear-guard action by French soldiers.[26] On 21–22 August, 13 civilians were killed in Audun-le-Roman, and 388 houses (of 400) destroyed by fire. According to the primary school teacher, the German soldiers fired 'without any motive', there was one rape, and the village was looted.[27] Other villages suffered the same fate.[28]

On 23 August, the Germans accused the inhabitants of Fresnois-la-Montagne − including the priest − of firing on them. The inhabitants denied the charge, pointing out that the priest was away with the army. Fifty-one civilians were killed. Among those attacked was a column of women and children whom the teacher was trying to lead to safety. The French official commission maintained on the basis of civilian witness identification that IR 121, 122, 124, and 125 were responsible.[29] Infantry Regiment 125 had indeed just arrived from Baranzy, and although it was later denied that orders were given to set fire to Fresnois or to execute inhabitants, the contemporary war diary of Captain Fauser, commander of the 7th Company, tells a different story.[30] Fauser reported that his men came under 'heavy franc-tireur fire' and were therefore ordered to 'attack Fresnois, round up the francs-tireurs and kill them.'[31] Moreover, since the artillery was also deployed, this must have been a superior order, probably issued by Lieutenant-General Wilhelm von Urach, commander of the 26th Infantry Division.

German soldiers also entered nearby Longuyon on 23 August. The troops (IR 122, 125, and 156) took 18 notables hostage.[32] Early next day, widespread pillaging began.[33] At the sound of French artillery fire around 5 am, the Germans began to burn the town down, using incendiary pastilles and petrol. Some inhabitants were asphyxiated in their cellars, while others were shot down as they fled into the countryside.[34] The Germans claimed that 'the civilians remaining in the town were francs-tireurs.'[35] Twenty-one boys between 16 and 18 years were ordered to bury the dead and, this done, were themselves executed. A refugee priest in Longuyon, Abbé Braux, the priest of Longuyon, and his assistant, were executed together on the railway bridge on the morning of 27 August. The total death-toll was considered incomplete by the French Commission, even in 1919, owing to the dispersion of much of the population. Sixty was given as a conservative estimate.

The diaries of Major-General von Ebbinghaus and Lieutenant Roth corroborate the French record on Longuyon. Ebbinghaus, commander of IR 125, recorded that the regiment was fired on from the houses, and also by French artillery.[36] While there was only hearsay evidence of heavy fighting with francs-tireurs, Ebbinghaus and Roth provide direct proof of plunder, theft of wine, and drunkenness. The jagged nerves of the men and a breakdown in discipline led to panic firing, in which one soldier was killed; Ebbinghaus had great difficulty in stopping it. Lieutenant Roth confirmed that two abbés were arrested on suspicion of abetting the francs-tireurs, although, as Roth noted, they had been conspicuous in tending the wounded. They were shot on 27 August after a search of their premises had revealed a false beard and pistols hidden in a sofa. The same day three alleged francs-tireurs and a group of ten French soldiers who had surrendered in a wood east of Longuyon were executed by the railway line.[37] There was no evidence of real civilian resistance, such as people caught firing weapons. In fact, it seems that the municipal authorities had done what they could to prevent it. On 28 August the deputy mayor was arrested because weapons and ammunition were found in the town hall.[38]

The swathe of destruction cut by the Württemberg soldiers of the XIIIth Army Corps through the northern Meurthe-et-Moselle was matched by the Sixth Army's campaign in the south of the département. The role assigned to the Sixth Army was to contain the French invasion of German Lorraine. Towards the middle of August, the French First Army regained the border villages in the south-eastern Meurthe-et-Moselle (including Badonviller and Blâmont) prior to advancing on Saarburg with the ultimate goal of taking Lower Alsace. The French Second Army advanced north-east from Nancy crossing the border in the direction of Saarbrücken (map 3, p. 21).

The German Sixth and Seventh Armies retreated respectively behind the rivers Saar and Breusch (Bruche). On 19 August the French First Army reached beyond Saarburg, over 15 kilometres into Germany, while the Second Army advanced as far as Morhange, 20 kilometres inside the frontier. Crown Prince Rupprecht, commander of the Sixth Army, and Heeringen, commander of the Seventh Army, urgently sought permission to attack the French. The OHL warned against this for fear of compromising the two armies' defensive function, but the advice was ignored. From 20 August, a German counter-offensive broke the French XVth and XVIth Army Corps and forced the French back to the line of the Meurthe. This was a dramatic collapse of the French forces; but the rout was stemmed and a reconstituted Second Army held the fortified zone around Nancy and inflicted a powerful counter-blow which halted the German advance northwest of Lunéville on 25 August. Nancy remained in French hands for the remainder of the war. Nonetheless, within four days of 20 August, the XXIst Army Corps and the Bavarian IInd Army Corps of the German Sixth Army found themselves in control of a large salient in the central and southeastern Meurthe-et-Moselle.[39] Accusations of civilian resistance flared anew and civilians were massacred, notably at Nomény, Gerbéviller, and Lunéville.

At Nomény (near the frontier north of Nancy), there was a history of tension between German soldiers and the inhabitants before the battle, which was fought on 20 August.[40] On 14 August the Germans, awaiting the initial French offensive, shot a 17-year-old farm boy who had hesitated when questioned on the whereabouts of the enemy.[41] The German occupiers then withdrew and were replaced by the French. When they returned to attack Nomény on 20 August, Bavarian IR 2 and 4, fortified with tales of mutilation perpetrated on the German wounded, behaved with extreme hostility towards the civilians.[42]

French IR 277 fought a delaying action at the bridge over the Seille, and as the Germans advanced in serried ranks they were mown down by enfilading fire from a field next to the bridge.[43] But the French were outnumbered and almost without artillery support. They withdrew in the early evening of 20 August towards Nancy, leaving the Germans in possession of the village, although they continued to send in patrols during the night.[44] French sources portray the conduct of the Bavarians towards the inhabitants as characterized by rage and unprovoked brutality. One witness noted: 'The German soldiers were in a state of extreme excitation. Their eyes were bloodshot. They said they had been told that the French had torn out the eyes of their wounded.'[45] During the night, much of the village was burned and many civilians were killed as they fled. In one of the worst such incidents, a house in which people had taken refuge was set on fire and soldiers shot those attempting to leave. Virginie Maire saw her husband, son, and eight-year-old daughter killed in this manner, along with another man, his children, and three others.[46] The following day, the inhabitants of Nomény were expelled amid more accusations of mutilation. Barbe Conrad, who spoke German, was told on asking why Nomény had been razed that: 'We were ordered to do it. There can be no mercy because the French are no longer taking prisoners; they are gouging out the eyes of our wounded and cutting off their members one after the other. If it wasn't true, our leaders wouldn't have affirmed it.'[47] Overall, 55 residents of Nomény were killed – 46 shot, seven suffocated in cellars, and two dying of their wounds.[48]

The official Bavarian history contradicts the French accounts only in claiming that the villagers had engaged in illegal resistance and in justifying their legitimate punishment. When Bavarian IR 4 approached Nomény it came under heavy fire from 'enemies who were at first invisible', hidden in houses. The Bavarians accused the French of having left behind small units of sharpshooters to attack the Germans 'treacherously', and claimed that the inhabitants also participated in the fighting. The commander of the 8th Bavarian Infantry Brigade, Major-General Riedl, saw how 'all kinds of weapons' were used to fire on the Bavarians from the windows, and saw one inhabitant throw away his shotgun. 'Even if it was soldiers who conducted the ambush, misusing civilian clothing,' he stated, 'the measures of defence taken by the 4th Bavarian Infantry Regiment are completely justified. Inhabitants caught with weapons in their hands were subject to the death penalty.' Because there was still firing from the houses ('despite the most drastic and ruthless measures'), Major-General Riedl decided to withdraw his troops from the town and shell it into flames as retribution, in a move approved by Major-General Bausch, commander of the 33rd Reserve Division.[49]

In fact, Bausch may have explicitly ordered IR 8 to help IR 4 by burning Nomény, shooting all male inhabitants, and expelling the women in the direction of France. This order was apparently found by a French journalist, Antoine Redier, who published a book denouncing German crimes during the invasion. Redier provided no source, nor did the French official report mention it.[50] But the Bavarian official history certainly stated that

Major-General Bausch ordered the 3rd Battalion of Bavarian IR 8 to expel the population from Nomény towards the enemy, and systematically set fire to the town.[51] Corroboration comes from the war diary of a soldier of the same regiment, Fischer, who stated that his commander issued an order at 5 pm on 20 August to shoot all the male inhabitants of Nomény and destroy the village completely. Fischer went on to describe forcing entry into the houses, shooting inhabitants, burning the village, and the 'terrible picture' of the women and children herded together to be 'expelled to France'.[52]

The Bavarian official history provided no evidence of civilian resistance at Nomény. The mayor, Chardin, had called a meeting of the council on 3 August which decided to have all firearms handed in.[53] The obvious source of the shooting encountered by the Bavarians was French IR 277, relieved late in the afternoon of 20 August by IR 325. As elsewhere in August 1914, spontaneous defence of their homes by civilians cannot be ruled out. But instead of conducting a judicial investigation, the Germans punished the entire population.

The circumstances in Gerbéviller, a sizeable village south-east of Nancy, were almost identical to those of Nomény.[54] On 24 August, 60 men of the 2nd Battalion, Chasseurs-à-pied, and some members of the 19th Dragoons, tenaciously defended the bridge over the Mortagne, inflicting serious casualties on the German advance guard, consisting of units of IR 60 and 166 (31st Division, XXIst Army Corps).[55] As German troops entered Gerbéviller at about 5 pm on 24 August, they seized civilians from a reduced population, many having fled. Two collective executions occurred – at La Prêle, where 15 corpses were discovered, and at Haut-de-Vourmont, where ten corpses were disinterred, nine of them probably inhabitants of Badonviller (retaken by the Germans the day before) and brought to Gerbéviller before being killed.[56] Gerbéviller was pillaged and burned from 24 to 27 August.[57] The best estimate is that overall 60 inhabitants died.[58]

The Bavarian official history makes no reference to the civilians killed at Gerbéviller, or to civilian resistance. This is astonishing, for the troops claimed that civilians were responsible for the losses they sustained.[59] Major von Xylander recorded that the Bavarian 2nd Jäger Battalion encountered stiff resistance from the local population as well as from regular French troops.[60] There is, in fact, some French evidence that there was firing by civilians at Gerbéviller. An unwritten, oral account has survived among the citizens, as an alternative narrative, that civilians in the rue de la Vacherie, flanking the German approach to the bridge, shot at the German troops and killed a major.[61] The official commission and French published works denied all such resistance. This unique paradox of official French denial and official German ignorance of civilian resistance is best resolved by concluding that while some individual citizens may have participated in resistance, the Germans failed to find sufficient evidence; moreover, it was clearly regular French army resistance that provoked the German soldiers to take indiscriminate revenge on the inhabitants. According to Sister Julie, the 'heroine of Gerbéviller' (who, with nuns of her order, kept a first-aid station going throughout the occupation), the Germans were furious that a handful of French soldiers had held up two German regiments — but disguised this with accusations of civilian resistance.[62] Joseph Peck, a Düsseldorf locksmith and former soldier in IR 174 who testified for the French in September 1921, recalled encountering IR 166 which claimed to have lost a patrolling soldier to civilians. In consequence, the commander of the 31st Infantry Division, Major-General von Behr, ordered the destruction of Gerbéviller. Peck also recounted how his regimental commander forced a woman and her small child to remain in a burning building.[63]

The incident at Lunéville, on 25 August, was of a rather different kind.[64] The town, south-east of Nancy, was captured after a fierce, day-long battle on 22 August, an advance-guard of the XXIst Army Corps entering late in the evening.[65] From the start there was widespread pillage, but at first no overt violence towards civilians. On 24 August Major Bertold Schenk von Stauffenberg ordered his troops to stop plundering.[66] Late that night, the Bavarian 5th Reserve Division reached Lunéville, already crowded with other troops. On 25 August, the town was the main base for an unsuccessful attempt by the Bavarians to drive through the French fortified line only a few kilometres to the west against devastating artillery fire and without adequate support from German guns. The Bavarian 5th Reserve Division was repulsed with heavy losses and retreated into Lunéville, having run out of ammunition and abandoned its artillery. The Bavarian 6th Infantry Division was likewise forced to retreat in disarray.[67]

At 4.30 pm, according to French accounts, German soldiers fanned through the streets of Lunéville accusing the inhabitants of firing on their wounded and supply columns.[68] The Germans shot wildly into shops and dwellings and at individuals in the street. Major Schenk von Stauffenberg, for example, was convinced that as the Bavarian Cavalry Division retreated into the town, civilians fired on it from the roofs. Schenk ordered his men to return fire and search the houses. He took 60 civilians hostage and used them as human shields to stop the firing. Two civilians were discovered who 'were said to have been shooting' and who were carrying cartridges.[69] All the civilian witnesses, including the mayor, Keller, categorically denied there had been civilian resistance.[70]

German records suggest the cause of the executions was panic. Lunéville was a major military transit point. Chaos reigned, and the alleged ambush (possibly a French patrol or German soldiers in the town firing on their retreating comrades) produced hysteria. 'Mindless fear was the result', recorded the Bavarian official history. 'Vehicles rushed in every direction, while their guards returned the fire without any plan.'[71] Some officers admitted the panic, at least in the privacy of their diaries. Captain von Beckh (Bavarian IR 14) saw Prussian and Bavarian troops disobey the orders and threats of their officers and retreat in disorder.[72] But most German soldiers were convinced that organized civilian resistance had taken place.[73] Indeed, the diary of cavalry officer Major Fleischmann suggests that a mass execution loomed in the evening of 25 August, as German troops anticipated a major civilian uprising. The Bavarian Cavalry Division was given the order to 'shoot down everyone found with arms', and, to Fleischmann's dismay, it prepared to 'commit [a] bloodbath among the inhabitants', a group of women and children already having been rounded up.[74]

Lunéville experienced a similar combination of military and psychological factors to that in Louvain. Demoralized troops retreated into a town full of exhausted, nervous men of many different units. In both cases, the soldiers were utterly convinced the civilian population had launched an uprising to support the enemy's military offensive, and prepared to carry out a mass execution. Why the order was rescinded in Lunéville, and a massacre on the scale of Louvain avoided, is not known. As it was, 19 civilians were killed in response to the imagined attacks, and 70 houses burned down.

do general patterns emerge in the interpretation of atrocities — other than German fear

3   To the Marne and back: September–October 1914

Similar violence and destruction occurred when the German invasion force moved into other frontier départements of France in the last week of August. Units of the First Army in pursuit of the retreating BEF through the Nord, for example, apparently shot down civilians in Quérénaing near Valenciennes, on 25 August, though details remain sketchy.[75] Sixth Army troops, striking from the Meurthe-et-Moselle into the neighbouring Meuse, ran into a rear-guard of the French Third Army at Rouvres, near the town of Étain, on 24 August. When they took the village, having first bombarded it, they accused the inhabitants of firing at them, burned most of the 150 buildings, and massacred residents; 47 civilians died or disappeared.[76]

Events in the département of the Ardennes, which was crossed by the German Third and Fourth Armies (map 1, p. 10), could barely be investigated by the French commission, since the Ardennes remained under German occupation for the entire war. But during the inter-war period the work of a local primary school teacher, Émile Marlier, compensated for official neglect and, together with German sources, allows the events to be reconstructed.[77] As the Third Army fought its way up the Meuse in the centre and west of the département, only a few days after the destruction of Dinant, it massacred civilians and burned a string of villages, claiming in each case that it had been attacked by francs-tireurs. As elsewhere, 'friendly fire' incidents and skilful French rear-guard actions provoked claims of popular resistance.[78]

Haybes, just inside France, was the scene of the most serious massacre, with 61 victims. On 24 August, an advance German patrol was fired on by French soldiers, who had blown up the bridge before hiding on the west bank of the Meuse, opposite the village. Mobilized forest guards hidden in Haybes may also have conducted an ambush. The invaders immediately assumed they were confronted by francs-tireurs.[79] Furious, they informed the mayor that the village would be bombarded, despite his protestation that all firearms had long been gathered in. The panic-stricken population sought refuge in cellars, in a nearby slate quarry, or in flight. As German soldiers of IR 133 and 179 (40th Division) poured into Haybes, engaging in a fierce battle with the French on the far shore of the river, they burned down 596 out of 623 houses.[80] One soldier of IR 133 recorded: 'Haybes. Here we first came into battle. The 2nd Battalion into the village, the houses searched, plundered, and wherever shots were fired, burned down.'[81] Some civilians forced by the heat and smoke from their cellars were interned in a nearby château, some were killed, and others used as a human shield as the Germans tried to throw up a temporary bridge.[82]

At dawn on 25 August, according to the priest of Haybes, Abbé Hubert, a French raid crossed the Meuse and ambushed German soldiers in the streets before withdrawing. This fuelled German belief that the inhabitants were shooting at them. Major Rothlaufs, Machine-Gun Company 179, claimed his men were fired on by both regular troops and civilians, including women, and that men had put on women's clothing. He also claimed to have found three francs-tireurs hiding in a brickworks, though he provided no evidence.[83] The killing and destruction of the village reached a paroxysm on 26 August. On that day, inhabitants were shot in the streets and 17 men, women, and children who had taken refuge in the slate quarry were executed.[84] In a curious finale, the same day saw Abbé Hubert tried before a court-martial on the charge of encouraging francs-tireurs, only to find himself pardoned by a German general on condition that he placed posters forbidding resistance.[85] Comparable incidents to Haybes occurred as the Third Army moved south, at neighbouring Fumay, Maubert-Fontaine, Saulces-Monclin, Rethel, and Perthes.[86] The same was true of the Fourth Army in the eastern Ardennes, notably at Margny (42 civilian victims) and Sedan with its suburb of Givonne (23 dead), both on 25 August.[87]

The Ardennes, however, marked a shift in the pattern of German violence towards civilians that was to become ever more apparent. The exodus of civilians which had gradually built up ahead of the German invasion of Belgium became such a flood in France that it hampered military operations. By early September, hundreds of thousands of Belgian and French refugees were falling back into the interior.[88] Increasingly, German forces discovered half-empty towns and villages, in which only the elderly and infirm or those who refused to abandon their property remained. Additionally, France, like Germany but unlike Belgium, was a nation with well-established universal military service. In wartime, the calling up of reserves and territorial troops meant that a large proportion of able-bodied adult men aged 20 to 45 was enrolled in the army. The process occurred in stages, but by late August 1914 most eligible men under the age of 40 had departed.[89] Young men, prime suspects as francs-tireurs, were simply scarcer on the German invasion path in France.

Thus, as the Third Army moved south through the Ardennes, destruction and looting continued unabated but the civilian death-rate declined. In Rocroi, only some 50 inhabitants were left when the Germans arrived, though two were killed after an officer claimed he had been fired upon.[90] In Saulces-Monclin, where French colonial soldiers fought a rear-guard action, IR 102 claimed francs-tireurs had resisted and killed 14 inhabitants on 30 August. But much of the population had already fled.[91] When units of the Third Army took Rethel, the principal town of the southern Ardennes, on 30 August, only 100 or so old people remained following an official evacuation. The following day, a number of fires, fanned by the wind, incinerated the town. French and Germans blamed each other. But the same fate awaited the suburb of Sault-lès-Rethel on 31 August, which was set on fire by IR 178 (responsible for the massacre at Leffe) after a panic in which it was alleged that the population was firing on them. In the two incidents, 15 civilians were shot or perished in the flames, a total that would surely have been higher had most of the population still been there.[92]

In the first few days of September, the German advance broadened through the départements of the Aisne, Marne and Meuse, and into the Oise and Seine-et-Marne, north-east of Paris. At their point of furthest penetration, between Chantilly and Meaux, the Germans were barely 40 kilometres from the capital. On 6 September, the French and their British allies counter-attacked against the overstretched German right. They forced the German First and Second Armies to retreat north-eastwards, recrossing the Marne and Aisne rivers. By mid-September, the Germans had dug in along the line Noyon-Verdun, starting a line of trenches which reached south-eastwards to the Swiss border (map 1, p. 10).[93] This phase was marked by continued German aggression towards civilians, but with lower fatalities, accompanied by destruction of property and systematic pillage.

Two incidents were reminiscent of earlier massacres. Units of the German First Army, probably the 4th Division, immediately accused the inhabitants of firing when they entered Senlis on 2 September. No evidence of resistance was produced, but a private French enquiry revealed that some of the citizens may have told the Germans that there were no French soldiers present, not knowing about the rear-guard of French Moroccan troops that was responsible for the shooting.[94] Inhabitants were seized as a human shield, and several were shot immediately. The mayor, Eugène Odent, was given a summary court-martial before being executed. The sentence, according to French sources, stated that: 'By superior order, every town or village where a civilian attack has been carried out on our troops must be reduced to ashes; the population is responsible and the inhabitants must be brought before our troops for immediate execution. Senlis, being in this position, must suffer the consequences.'[95] Twenty-one residents died, and 105 buildings were destroyed, before the Germans departed on 5 September. Retreating German soldiers claimed to have been fired upon also in Bignicourt-sur-Saulz on 6 September, which they burned down, causing the death of 12 civilians.[96]

More typically, however, violence towards civilians after the battle of the Marne resulted in individual killings but not massacres. The lack of German documentation on most of these incidents makes it hard to establish the immediate cause with certainty, although the common denominator was the widespread fear of enemy civilians and franc-tireur resistance. To give but a few examples, German troops at Marfaux, in the Marne, accused the population of helping French troops and lined them up against a wall on 4 September. Although dissuaded from carrying out the execution, the Germans destroyed the village.[97] Raon-l'Étape and Saint-Dié, in the Vosges (at the southern end of the German advance), were terrorized during their brief occupations by the German Seventh Army; the inhabitants of both towns were accused of resisting, many houses were burned down, but the civilian death-toll was low, because the bulk of the population had fled.[98] Réméréville, east of Nancy, was likewise destroyed on 6–7 September on the charge that the priest had signalled to French troops from the church tower; but only a few remaining elderly inhabitants were killed.[99]

Even where it did not lead to death, violence was omnipresent. The French Commission drew attention to the high level of rape. This will be considered later, as part of the civilian experience of the invasion. For the moment, it may be noted that while there was no official toleration of rape by the German army, and rape thus was not part of a reprisal policy against supposed francs-tireurs, sexual menace was ubiquitous in the violence of the German invasion.[100]

Also widespread was the use of civilians as human shields and their deportation to Germany. Time and again, German soldiers forced French civilians to precede them into battle, for example at Senlis, or at Néry (Oise), where soldiers of the German First Army used the director of a sugar-beet refinery, his family, and workforce as a shield when attacking the BEF on 1 September.[101] Towards the end of September, during the pursuit of the Germans, a French soldier recounted how he had seen the enemy firing on French trenches protected by 'a cordon of old people, women, and children taken from the inhabitants of the district. They were shooting over the heads of these unfortunate people, and we naturally couldn't shoot back.'[102] At Saint-Dié, on 27 August, the Germans used four hostages as a human shield while advancing on the elite French Chasseurs-Alpins. Two were killed and two wounded. When a self-justifying account was published in a Munich paper by one of the officers involved, corroborating the French version of events, this incident was picked up by international opinion and became notorious.[103]

Deportation, by the time France was reached, had become extensive, and in the chaos of vast troop movements the vicissitudes of the deportees could be extreme. A column of 1,000 French prisoners of war and 35 civilians stopped on 16 September at Frasnes-lez-Couvin, just inside Namur province, en route to Germany. Thirty-four of the civilians, from Montmirail, Meaux, Châlons-sur-Marne, and Rheims, were taken to a quarry and executed. The Germans claimed that they were guilty of spying, robbing soldiers who had fallen on the battlefield, and trying to burn a hospital with German wounded. Proceedings before the execution were witnessed by Countess de Villermont, with whom the responsible German officers were lodged. Her view was that the executed were nearly all old, infirm, or exhausted, and were killed because they impeded the progress of the column. There were indeed a number of elderly victims in the list established subsequently. One civilian, a retired teacher, escaped by hiding among the military prisoners, and later testified to the cruel treatment of the civilian prisoners, and to the fact that all claimed to have been wrongly arrested and absurdly accused. A German officer, on being told the civilians were 'francs-tireurs, spies, etc.', had organized the execution.[104]

This incident was exceptional in its outcome but not in its evidence of German harshness towards deported civilians. By February 1915, some 10,000 French civilians deported during and immediately after the invasion had been repatriated from Germany, where they had been held in poor conditions in 31 camps across the country. Thirteen to fourteen thousand Belgian civilians were deported in the same period. The French Commission devoted an entire report to the subject, concluding that many deportees had been arrested on the 'false pretext' of civilian resistance, while others had been given no explanation.[105] Precisely because many active adults, especially men, had fled the German advance, the deportees were disproportionately composed of women, children, the elderly, and the infirm.

From mid-September, each side tried to turn the other's flank in the northward movement that ended on the coast inside Belgium. Meanwhile, the Germans decided to eliminate the Belgian menace to their rear by taking Antwerp (map 1, p. 10). The siege began on 26 September as artillery opened fire on the city and also bombarded the nearby cathedral city of Malines (Mechelen). With British aid, the Belgian army resisted at Antwerp until 8 October, but the government withdrew to Ostend and eventually Le Havre in France. The army slipped away and joined the Allied forces on the coastal strip in Flanders. The gap soon closed along the line of the river Ijzer, as both sides pushed through to the sea. Initially, the Allies faced the Germans on the east bank of the Ijzer. On 16 October the Germans launched an attack that forced French and Belgian troops back on Diksmuide, and after three weeks under enormous pressure, the Allies left the devastated town and retreated to the west bank. The Belgians opened the dyke gates, and the flood-plain of the Ijzer filled, turning the river into an impregnable obstacle protecting the Allied left for the rest of the war. The Germans lost some 10,000 dead in the battle of Diksmuide.[106] This final phase of mobile warfare produced an epilogue to the German army's violence against enemy civilians.

Before the Belgian retreat from Antwerp, at least 60 people were killed in several incidents in East Flanders, including 13 in a collective execution on 4 September at Lebbeke and 20 at Aalst on 27 September, arising from a skirmish between German troops and a Belgian patrol from Antwerp.[107] More serious were the eight incidents closely linked with the battle of Diksmuide in which 161 civilians were killed at the villages of Beerst, Vladslo, Roeselare, Staden, Ledegem, Handzame, Zarren, and Esen, within the space of three days from 19 to 21 October. Villages fiercely defended by French troops were accused of franc-tireur resistance, and the inhabitants shot or used as human shields. Roeselare, south-east of Diksmuide, had been briefly occupied by the Germans on 15 October, when all civilian arms (which had been collected in the prison) were removed or destroyed. The French reoccupied the town, and fought from the houses when the Germans attacked again on 19 October. As the Germans retook Roeselare in the early afternoon, they used a human shield of the inhabitants. Claiming that civilians had fired on them, they burned about 250 buildings, pillaged the town, and either shot or burned 31 people. One witness described how 40 or 50 villagers were rounded up in a field and told by a German officer 'who was fuming with rage' that they were enemies who deserved to suffer, before four men were selected and executed. A much larger human shield of about 150 inhabitants was used later the same day as the Germans attacked nearby Staden, where more civilians (including the curate) were summarily shot.[108]

At Ledegem, on 19 October, the local notables were taken hostage and (according to their own account) informed by an officer of IR 242 that 34 houses had been burned down and 18 civilians slaughtered because two little girls had fired on the German soldiers outside the village; two eight-year-old girls (and a woman) were indeed among the civilian victims. In the final incident, at Esen on 21 October, the inhabitants were accused of signalling to the French during a hard-fought battle for the village; furious German troops dragged terrified residents out of their cellars and three sheltering in a brasserie, and killed them. Forty-seven villagers died and 275 were deported.[109] The invasion ended, as it had begun, with German soldiers raging at the presumed treachery of enemy civilians.

4 The pattern of German military violence towards civilians

German military violence towards Belgian and French civilians in 1914 can be summarized statistically by taking all the incidents in which ten or more civilians were killed ('major incidents') and examining them for ten variables: date; locality; Belgian province or French département; civilians killed; buildings destroyed; whether the incident was related to combat; panic by German troops; human shields; deportation of civilians; and the German units responsible. The resulting database in appendix 1 is derived from the French Commission and Belgian Second Commission, corrected and supplemented by German and other sources.

In these 129 major incidents during the invasion (101 in Belgium and 28 in France) 5,146 civilians were killed – 4,421 in Belgium and 725 in France.[110] The importance of Belgium is clear, but it did not define the phenomenon. The Meurthe-et-Moselle with 17 major incidents and 409 civilian dead was comparable to a Belgian province (e.g. Brabant with 15 incidents and 618 dead, or Hainaut with 12 incidents and 309 dead). Not Belgians but civilians were the potential enemy in German eyes.

To calculate the overall civilian death-toll, 'minor' incidents of between one and nine deaths must be added to major incidents. In the case of Belgium there were 383 minor incidents, resulting in the deaths of a further 1,100 civilians, giving a total of 5,521.[111] The same calculation is more difficult for France, owing to the gaps in the official commission's investigation of areas that remained under German occupation. But by applying the same ratio of deaths in minor to major incidents as in Belgium (1:4), a French total of 906 may be assumed. The resulting total death-toll of Belgian and French civilians deliberately killed by the German army during the invasion is therefore 6,427.

The sheer number of incidents (major and minor) which led to deaths – 90 in Brabant, 100 in Namur, 484 for Belgium as a whole – indicates the extent of violence. Along with innumerable encounters of a less fatal nature, it helps explain the size of the refugee exodus. There can have been few civilians in the path of the invasion who had not heard of people being killed in a familiar locality.

The other violence committed against the person was rape. Rapes occurred quite widely, but calculation of the total number is impossible given the difficulty of recording this crime. For this reason, rape is not included in the statistical analysis of major incidents.

German military conduct towards civilians essentially conformed to a pattern. This emerges from the major incidents (see figure 1). Eighty-four (65 per cent) were directly related to combat. Whether the Germans genuinely believed the civilians to have participated in battle or whether this claim was merely a cover for some other motive (frustration at setbacks, revenge for high German casualties), the civilians' fate was closely linked to battle. In 29 cases (22 per cent) the incident was either caused or exacerbated by a 'panic' – that is, an uncontrollable and hysterical response by the German troops, which the command only mastered with some difficulty. Panics contributed to some of the most serious incidents (Warsage, Visé,

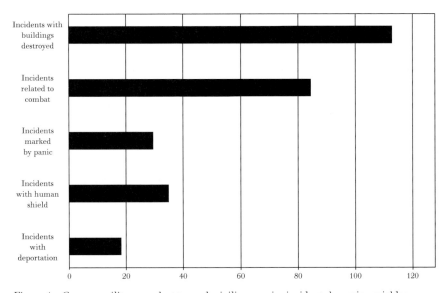

Figure 1   German military conduct towards civilians: major incidents by main variables

Aarschot, Andenne, Louvain, Lunéville), and in 19 out of 29 cases were not connected with battle.

The geography of the incidents shows that violence against enemy civilians was endemic throughout the German army. As noted, virtually every regiment in the initial assault force at Liège was involved in such brutality. During the main invasion between 18 and 31 August, the various armies manifested broadly similar levels of violence towards civilians, allowing for the differences in distance travelled. The First and Second Armies were responsible for 40 major incidents with 1,862 civilian deaths.[112] The Third Army accounted for 16, resulting in 1,005 deaths.[113] The Fourth and Fifth Armies were involved in 26 incidents with 991 civilian dead. During the Marne campaign in France, violence against civilians spanned all the départements crossed by the invasion force. Some German units participated in several cases. IR 165, for example, was active in seven major incidents at Liège. Infantry Regiment 83, involved in the massacre of Andenne-Seilles on 19–20 August, had probably helped burn houses and shoot hostages at Louveigné, near Liège, on 7 August. IR 178, which burned down Rethel, had been chiefly responsible for the massacres at Leffe (Dinant) a week earlier. More striking, however, is the spread of units concerned. Over 150 regiments out of some 300 are known to have participated in major incidents, and many more in minor ones.

The deliberate destruction of buildings featured in almost every incident. During the attack on Liège, at least 1,289 houses and public buildings were deliberately burned down, blown up, or bombarded by artillery in response to the supposed resistance of francs-tireurs. During the invasion as a whole, 113 out of 129 major incidents were accompanied by such devastation, giving a minimum total (since the figures are not known in several cases) of 14,101 buildings destroyed. Similar destruction occurred in many other instances, including those with no deaths, so that the overall total is much higher. A figure of 15,000 to 20,000 buildings deliberately destroyed is a conservative estimate. Fire was the preferred method, and civilian witnesses frequently commented on the Germans' use of inflammable pastilles and petrol pumps, as well as more primitive means.[114] Arson was thus a structural element of German violence towards enemy populations.

Starting with the assault on Liège, human shields were used in 32 cases (25 per cent) during the invasion. It proves that for whatever motive (punishment, revenge, or tactical efficacy), the Germans from start to finish used civilians for cover when attacking and that this measure was not the result of maverick orders. Hostage-taking and deportation were equally integral to German behaviour. But whereas hostage-taking occurred from the outset, deportation was unknown before the destruction of Visé, on 16 August. Thereafter, civilians were deported to Germany in 18 major incidents (14 per cent). Deportation took time and resources to organize, although the German army camps vacated by the invasion provided ready-made prisons.

Analysis of the major incidents also reveals the outlook of the German military towards civilians. As the sources of both sides agree, German troops blamed virtually every one of the major incidents on francs-tireurs. If they had been correct in this, there would have been a 'People's War' throughout Belgium and north-eastern France on such a scale and with such consistency that it would have constituted a major historical event leaving a real trace in French and Belgian collective memory. Although some scattered, individual acts of resistance certainly occurred, there is no evidence for a phenomenon of this kind. Nor was it inherently likely. In the Franco-Prussian War and on the eastern front during the Second World War, irregular and partisan warfare only emerged once the invasion had come to a standstill or after serious disruption of the defending army. In 1914 it was alleged to have started at once on the outbreak of a war that had taken Europe by surprise. Organized civilian resistance on a scale commensurate with German reactions in August 1914 is an historical impossibility.

It can thus be concluded that the substantive phenomenon was German *belief* in a People's War, which constituted a massive case of collective self-suggestion, probably unparalleled in a modern army. A million men were swept by a delusion which mistook the fantasy of the franc-tireur war for reality. The German atrocities were the symptomatic result of the mobilizing power of the fantasy.

How and why such collective self-suggestion began and developed is the subject of chapters 3 and 4. But an important feature of its evolution is revealed by the chronology of the major incidents (see figure 2). Twenty-one cases arose from the initial fighting at Liège (until 8 August) and three from that in the Meurthe-et-Moselle before 12 August – accounting for 729 civilian deaths (14 per cent of the total). Then came a pause, with only isolated incidents, notably the destruction of Visé, before the onset of the main invasion. Between 18 and 31 August, however, 87 major incidents (two-thirds of the total) occurred while the German armies crossed Belgium and the frontier départements of France. While many of the initial incidents displayed spontaneous rage by German soldiers, an increasing number were carried out in cold blood, indicating that a policy

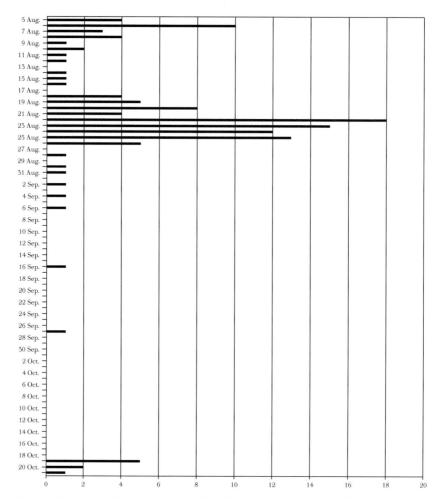

Figure 2   German military conduct towards civilians: major incidents per day,
August–October 1914

of repression had been consciously adopted by the German command. From
the beginning of September, fatalities declined, though not necessarily
other manifestations of violence towards civilians, until the brief resur-
gence of major incidents in West Flanders in mid-October.

5   Comparisons

An important question remains to be answered before the mental worlds of
the German soldiers and French and Belgian civilians in 1914 can be exam-

ined. Did other armies during the early part of the war commit comparable violence against civilians, or was German behaviour in the west unique? There are four potential comparisons: first, the Russian invasion of East Prussia in August–early September 1914; second, the subsequent German invasion of the north-western fringe of the Russian Empire (Poland and Lithuania); third, the Russian invasion of Galicia and the Bukovina, in Austria-Hungary, in autumn 1914, followed by the Russian retreat in spring and summer 1915; and finally, the failed Austro-Hungarian invasions of Serbia in August–September and November 1914. Next to the German invasion of Belgium and France, these invasions produced the main occasions for violence between soldiers and enemy civilians.[115]

Lurid atrocity tales emerged in all four theatres of war which told not only of widespread pillage, physical destruction, and rape by invading soldiers but of mutilation and murder by civilians as well. The army and public in Germany were stunned by the rapid Russian mobilization and invasion of East Prussia. 'The Cossacks are coming' was the catchword of widespread panic, motivating the German Social Democrats to vote for war credits and impelling a large part of the East Prussian population to flee. By mid-August 1914, stories circulated in the German army, and then in Germany at large, of women being raped, mutilated, or murdered by Russian troops.[116] In Galicia and the Bukovina, from autumn 1914 to summer 1915, stories abounded of rape and brutality by Russian troops, especially Cossacks, and of pogroms against the Jewish population. In Serbia and Bosnia, Serb civilians were held to be mutilating captured Austro-Hungarian soldiers, and Austro-Hungarians to be raping Serb women and decimating whole villages. Intense images of enemy atrociousness accompanied the invasions in eastern Europe as in the west.

Evidence of real civilian resistance and military brutality, however, varied considerably. The German government, in a report published in March 1915, charged the Russians with practising 'indisputably barbarous' methods of warfare in East Prussia, including the spoliation of towns and villages, the murder of 'thousands' (including young men of military service age), mass deportation, rape, and mutilation.[117] But such accusations must be treated with caution. Although in some cases corroborated details were given, in many the evidence was weak; for example, no Russian army units were named. This makes the report's estimate that only 101 civilians were killed during the invasion of East Prussia, in a campaign of the same duration as that of Belgium and the Marne, all the more remarkable. There were two 'major incidents', as defined above, at Santoppen, where 19 civilians were executed on 28 August, and at Christiankehmen on 11 September, with 14 civilian fatalities.[118]

A more nuanced account emerges from an unpublished collection of reports and diary extracts made with the intention of writing a history of East Prussia during the war. This reveals a varied pattern of Russian army conduct, and also helps explain the motivation for violence. Certainly the Russian troops often had to requisition supplies and this, as elsewhere, led to plunder and destruction, and sometimes casual violence against civilians. The Russians claimed that they had been fired upon in a number of localities, such as Jusmen (Pillkallen district) on 9 August, where Russian cavalry shot six inhabitants, or Neidenberg on 22 August.[119] According to a report to the Ministry of the Interior by the provincial governor of Gumbinnen, where a major battle was fought, there had been

> numerous cases in which the enemy has burned down farmhouses used by German patrols as shelter and from which they had fired. In most cases the Russians then accused German civilians of unauthorized use of weapons in order to justify their incendiarism. The arson committed in the villages Groß and Klein Daguthelen and Bartschkühnen on 17 August had its origins in this cause.[120]

The Russians thus appear to have shared the German idea of the illegitimacy of civilian participation in combat. In fact, the evidence for such resistance on any serious scale is even weaker for East Prussia than for Belgium and northern France. But the Russians seldom intentionally killed civilians in response. Even where there was a civilian militia which they considered illegal, reprisals against civilians did not ensue. Although much remains to be established about the East Prussian campaign, systematic violence against German civilians was not a major constituent of Russian behaviour, even though the same potential for it existed as in the German army's invasion of France and Belgium.

By and large the Russian troops in East Prussia respected international law and the laws of war, as a commission of the Reich Office for Internal Affairs concluded after the recovery of East Prussia. It reported that 'Russian atrocities have [...] turned out to have been grossly exaggerated.' The commission has found that the descriptions of Russian cruelties and the reported devastation of the country are based on falsehood. It is reported that the Russian troops have behaved correctly everywhere towards the inhabitants. If individual towns and villages were burned down, this occurred almost without exception during artillery battles, in some cases also because German patrols fired from houses and the Russians assumed that the civilian inhabitants were involved in the shooting.[121]

This view was shared by no less a person than Erich Ludendorff, who after playing a leading role in the assault on Liège city, was given command with Hindenburg of the East Prussian campaign and masterminded the victory of Tannenberg (26 to 31 August). Ludendorff wrote in 1919 that he had been appalled by the Belgian francs-tireurs and the way in which 'the Belgian government had systematically organized civilian warfare', whereas by contrast he found that 'many of the Russian troops behaved in exemplary manner in East Prussia.' He attributed the 'harshness and terror' that undoubtedly did take place to Cossack indiscipline rather than to military policy.[122] For all the destruction caused by the invasion, the 'harrowing' of East Prussia by the Russians appears to be a myth.[123]

The German invasion of western Poland from 1914, and subsequently of Lithuania and Courland, was the first stage of what became a vast experiment in the conquest and administration of eastern Europe by the German army.[124] The Russians, like the Germans, accused the enemy of brutality, and a semi-official Russian report published in January 1915 charged the Germans with numerous atrocities. But these mostly concerned alleged crimes against wounded or captured Russian soldiers and some civilian resistance during the East Prussian campaign. In August 1914, German troops laid waste two towns just over the border in Russian Poland, Kalisz (in Lodz province) and Czestochowa (in Silesia).[125] In scenes comparable to Belgium, German soldiers shot civilians and seized hostages in reprisal for what they took to be civilian resistance, although the Russian reports suggested that 'friendly fire' was the real explanation. In both cases, material damage was considerable, including the desecration of the icon of the virgin of Czestochowa, a shrine of national importance to Catholic Poles. But such cases were exceptional.

The German invasion of the north-western territories of the Russian

Empire was accompanied by the same harsh attitude to presumed civilian resistance as in western Europe.[126] But there is little evidence to suggest either that such resistance occurred on a significant scale or that the Germans fantasized that it did. The Russian army showed itself to be more brutal, in fact, by conducting a scorched-earth policy as it withdrew before the German advance into Lithuania and western Poland. This included the compulsory withdrawal of suspect non-Russian elements of the population and all men of military service age.[127] Such a massive upheaval doubtless left little local inclination for resistance to the Germans; indeed, in the case of Warsaw, the population (and especially the Jews) generally welcomed the arrival of the German army. The good conduct of the troops helped reinforce this favourable attitude.[128] As for German perceptions, belief in a new franc-tireur war may have been curtailed by the fact that invasion in the east came later than in the west, at a time when the army and government were grappling with the international repercussions of the earlier 'German atrocities'. Certainly the memoirs of the German commanders involved in the east contain no reference to such a phenomenon. On the contrary, Ludendorff remarked that the inhabitants of the western part of Russian Poland in late autumn 1914 'gave us no trouble'.[129] Later, resistance developed and the Germans responded harshly; but this had more to do with the occupation than the invasion.[130]

In Galicia and the Bukovina mutual exaggeration also characterized Austrian and Russian claims of atrocities against enemy civilians. The Russian report of January 1915 accused the Austrians as well as the Germans of brutality; but since the Austro-Hungarian forces were retreating, not advancing, they could be charged with little in relation to enemy civilians. By contrast, the successful Russian invasion of Austrian territory which brought an ethnically heterogeneous population in Galicia and the Bukovina under Russian control allowed the Dual Monarchy to level its own atrocity charges. An official Austrian report, published in January 1915 and updated with supplements, provides a basis for assessing this Russian violence against civilians.[131]

At first, the pattern of Russian military conduct was similar to that in East Prussia. Some units were disciplined, others engaged in disorderly brutal treatment of civilians. Antisemitism was an unmistakable feature. In the Bukovina, the Jews of the main city, Czernowitz, were initially left in peace, though in smaller centres they were subjected to rape, plunder, and deportation.[132] Later, the Jews of Czernowitz were penalized and five Jews were killed in nearby Sadagóra for resisting plundering.[153] Further violence against Jews and Romanians occurred during a second invasion of the Bukovina in early 1915.[154] Galicia also experienced antisemitic brutality, with a Cossack pogrom in Lemberg claiming the lives of 20 Jews in November 1914.[155]

The issue of civilian resistance emerged in the form of the Polish legions, the Sokol (Falcons), which fought in Galicia against the Russians. The Austro-Hungarian Foreign Ministry protested to the neutral countries that the supreme commander of the Russian army ordered his troops not to recognize the Sokol as combatants but to punish them with the full force of military law. The Austrians explained that the Sokol not only conformed to international law but were an integral part of the Austro-Hungarian army. The irony of this protest escaped the governments of the Central Powers.[156]

If we take the Austrian reports at face value, it is clear that the Russian soldiers invading Galicia and the Bukovina lived off the land, wilfully destroyed property, and engaged in sporadic violence towards civilians, including rape. The Cossacks especially were responsible for brutal antisemitism. However, the total number of civilians killed from August 1914 to May 1915, according to the Austrian reports, was 69.

The dramatic change occurred when the Russians retreated in the face of the combined Austro-German offensive in the late spring and summer of 1915. As in Lithuania and western Poland, the Russian High Command emulated the scorched-earth policy of 1812 and added to this the persecution of the civilian population. The victims were suspect elements of the minority populations of the Russian Empire which straddled the western frontier – in other words, Russian subjects as much as enemy civilians. Deportations became the systematic policy of the Russian army. In the disorder of retreat, discipline frequently broke down, and Poles, Ukrainians, Ruthenes, Germans, and especially Jews were exposed to maltreatment.[157]

The Austrian reports noted this change. For example, 17,000 Jewish citizens of Przemysl were deported to Lemberg, and there was massive theft of property.[158] The 'Savage Division', commanded by the Tsar's brother Michael Alexandrowicz, pillaged and burned Jewish property and synagogues in Horodenka, in May 1915, forced Jews to confess to arson, and hanged six of them.[159] Using one of the rare pieces of corroboration from a Russian source, the Austro-Hungarian publication pointed out that the Russian army was also persecuting its own population. A report by a Colonel Sasonow condemned the pillaging by the Cossacks, who 'disgrace the Russian name not only in Galicia, but also in the whole world, and now they repeat the pillaging and rapes among the peaceful inhabitants, among Russian subjects!' Sasonow called on officers to punish such deeds.[140]

The devastation caused by the Russian retreat of 1915 was probably greater than anything experienced by civilians in France and Belgium. Although an overall death-toll is hard to establish, at least 300,000 Lithuanians, 250,000 Latvians, 350,000 Jews, and 743,000 Poles were deported to the Russian interior.[141] But it was also a different phenomenon – a combination of chaos and the persecution of the imagined 'enemy within'. The crisis of 1915 reactivated deep hostilities to the minorities within the Russian Empire which had lain barely dormant since the 1905 Revolution, triggering a wave of antisemitism and more general paranoia. Among the Russian elites and the nationalist right there was an obsession with spies and traitors which focused on ethnic identities.[142] In effect, military setback metamorphosed the fragile process of domestic mobilization for war in the Russian Empire into a violent but uncoordinated attempt to suppress or isolate reputedly anti-national elements.

Here, there is a parallel with the Turkish campaign against the Armenians in 1915. Although officially orchestrated, more coherent, and far more lethal than that against civilians in Russia, the violence of the Young Turks targeted a domestic group which also straddled a frontier (with Russia), whose distinct ethnic, linguistic, and religious identity had been accentuated by wartime mobilization, and which had been transformed into an internal enemy by invasion and the menace of defeat – from the Russians in the Caucasus and the Allied landing at Gallipoli. The result was a controlled explosion of violence by the regime against its own subjects producing a genocide in which between 800,000 and 1.2 million Armenians died. On a scale bearing no comparison with the killing of civilians in the invasion of France and Belgium, it was, even more than the Russian pogroms, a different phenomenon.[143]

The two Austro-Hungarian invasions of Serbia, by contrast, are more directly comparable with the German invasion in the west. In mid-August 1914, Austrian forces under General Potiorek launched an undermanned attack on western Serbia from Bosnia, which was soon pushed back, while the Austrians concentrated on the Galician front. In November–December, Potiorek received reinforcements and renewed the campaign, only to be comprehensively defeated and forced to retreat across the Danube. The Serb army was only expelled from its own territory by a combined German,

Austro-Hungarian, and Bulgarian offensive a year later, in October–December 1915.[144] These campaigns generated mutual accusations of inhumane military conduct. The Austrians claimed that Bosnian Serb civilians attacked Austro-Hungarian troops, especially during the retreat of September 1914.[145] The Austrians also alleged widespread civilian opposition to both invasions in Serbia itself. It is unclear whether this actually occurred, although it may have. But genuine confusion may also have arisen from the fact that older segments of the Serbian call-up did not have proper uniforms and may have been taken for partisans.[146]

Whatever the degree of provocation from Serb civilians, the two Austro-Hungarian invasions of Serbia in 1914 were accompanied by harsh action against villagers, including women and children. Austrian military commanders considered the Serb population to be abetting the Serb army in almost identical ways to those alleged by the Germans in Belgium and France (sabotage, signalling, etc.). After visiting the region, the British academic, R. W. Seton-Watson, estimated that at least 2,000 civilians had been slaughtered by Hungarian regiments in north-western Serbia in September 1914 'under circumstances of the most revolting cruelty'. A Swiss academic who conducted an investigation on behalf of the Serb government arrived at a total of 1,253 civilians killed by the invading armies, and 554 missing, though a more recent estimate is lower.[147] Subsequently, in the campaign of late 1915, there were mutual accusations of outrages by Serb and Bulgarian forces of the kind that had marked the Balkan Wars – and shocked European opinion – in 1912–13.[148]

The First World War is not usually thought of as one marked by conflict between enemy soldiers and civilians, in contrast to the wars which succeeded it (the Second World War and wars of decolonization) or some of those which preceded it (the Balkan Wars, the Franco-Prussian War, the American Civil War). This view is broadly justified. The superiority of defensive firepower which kept the principal antagonists locked in trench warfare for four years restricted conflict between civilians and soldiers. This is truer of the Western than the Eastern Fronts but even the latter were marked by long periods of immobility in between phases of rapid movement.

Nonetheless, there were periods of interaction between soldiers and enemy civilians, most notably during the invasions and mobile warfare of 1914–15, and they brought the issue of civilian resistance and military repression to prominence. In reality, while isolated civilian acts of resistance may have occurred on all fronts, there is little evidence of any concerted action unless in the form of militias or auxiliary forces, such as the older cohorts of the Serbian army or the Polish Sokol. The Balkans, where the boundary between war and communitarian violence was the most blurred, may well have come the closest to armed civilian resistance. Elsewhere, there is little evidence of it during invasions that were conducted and opposed by national armies.

Many factors common to the different invasions produced military violence against civilians. The necessity of requisitioning by armies living off the land led almost everywhere to theft and looting. Reports of rape are pervasive, suggesting that the weakening of normal, civil codes of conduct and the violence of war encouraged this form of violation. But differences between the invasions are also clear. The most devastating violence unleashed against civilians, during the Russian retreat of 1915 and the simultaneous Turkish genocide of the Armenians, was a largely (though not entirely) domestic affair, driven above all by internal political tensions. What distinguished the German violence towards French and Belgian civilians from military violence to *enemy* civilians on other fronts, and especially from Russian behaviour in the invasion of East Prussia and Galicia, was the omnipresent belief in the franc-tireur and a concerted military response which carried hostility to civilians to every corner of the invasion zone.

Part II
War of illusions?
'Francs-tireurs' and
'German atrocities', 1914

3   The German army and the myth of the francs-tireurs, 1914

In order to explain how the franc-tireur delusion emerged, what sustained it, and why the German army responded as it did, the subjective experience of German soldiers must be reconstructed. The same approach is required if we are to understand how the civilian victims and Allied opinion and governments perceived German behaviour. This chapter will analyse the nature of the franc-tireur delusion. Chapter 4 will discuss the cultural assumptions and mentalities that underlay it and determined the German military response. Chapter 5 will consider how these events were perceived in the first three months of the war in Belgium, France, and Britain. The same German and Allied sources used to establish what happened during the invasion allow this subjective dimension to be explored. In addition to letters and diaries, published and unpublished, the official wartime inquiries on both sides provide rich evidence on contemporary beliefs, illusions, and myths.

1   Concepts and precedents

To discuss the franc-tireur delusion, it is important to establish the concepts that might be helpful in understanding it. The starting-point is the remarkable study written in 1915–16 by Fernand van Langenhove, referred to in the introduction.[1] Van Langenhove, a young sociologist who before the war had been a member of the Solvay Institute in Brussels, was preoccupied by the delusion itself rather than by the German army's response to it. The central intellectual task that he set himself was to explain how German soldiers collectively came to believe in something that did not exist. Deliberately confining himself to German sources in order to avoid the charge of contamination by Allied propaganda, he exploited internal contradictions in the German evidence as well as the sceptical inquiries undertaken by the Socialist and Catholic press in Germany.[2]

Van Langenhove achieved his aim in three ways. First, he established that the core of the collective delusion consisted not merely of false rumours and tales about Belgian civilian resistance but of a number of legends that codified the delusion as a 'myth-cycle' and provided much of its contagious energy. He defined a myth or legend as 'localized, individualized stories which even if differing from historical truth, are nonetheless objects of collective belief'.[3] Typical of such myths was the ambush by a band of francs-tireurs, or the machine-gun mounted in a church tower, or the priest inciting his flock to resistance. Van Langenhove considered the myths a cycle by virtue of their internal unity, consisting of a relatively small number of motifs that were endlessly repeated in differing variants. The 'myth-cycle' reduced a mass of strange experiences and inexplicable events to a conspiracy – that of the premeditated People's War. Legends, in van Langenhove's sense, are different from the archetypal stories that structure permanent belief-systems or literary works. In fact, the absence of a central person or event of the kind around which the more conventional legend revolves makes 'complex' a better term than 'cycle'. Nonetheless, ephemeral legends share the metaphoric nature of the archetypal sort. As exemplary tales, whatever their factual value, they embody truths of perception, making the impenetrable clear and restoring a sense of control to the believer.

Second, van Langenhove drew on some early experimental work in social psychology on the role of distorted witness evidence in the creation of legends. More recent psychological literature has underlined how unreliable eye-witness testimony often is, and how the distortion is likely to increase in the case of traumatized participants – which is what many German soldiers in 1914 undoubtedly were – to the point that some memory, especially if recorded much later, may be largely or entirely invented.[4] Since witness memory may serve to justify the actions of a participant and restore a sense of narrative control to overwhelming events, it is often highly biased.[5] This is not to deny the factual value of witness testimony, especially where it can be cross-checked with different sources. But other, contemporary accounts of the same type may validate the distorted memory of an individual. The trauma of German soldiers snatched from civilian life and invading unknown territory with its attendant terrors was, according to van Langenhove, the source for the distorted memories and false rumours which turned into the self-reinforcing myth-complex of the franc-tireur war.[6] Yet van Langenhove stressed the sincerity of the false belief which spread from the army to much of Germany.

While van Langenhove considered the myth-complex ephemeral, he also insisted that its imaginary content could not be invented on the spur of the moment. This constituted the third element of his explanation. 'Preconceived ideas' charged with emotional and historical significance were activated by the trauma of the invasion and supplied the mythic content – notably through the memory of the French francs-tireurs in 1870. Van Langenhove sketched the cultural mentalities that predefined the franc-tireur in Germany between 1870 and 1914.[7] This idea was reformulated by Marc Bloch in his endorsement of van Langenhove's book shortly after the First World War when he stated that 'a false rumour is always born of collective representations which predate its own birth.' In other words, a transient phenomenon of mass self-suggestion interacts with a more permanent substratum of attitudes and beliefs which shape the content of the former and provide much of its force. This theme fascinated the young Frenchman, sensing his vocation as a historian of 'mentalities'.[8] The conclusion to be drawn from this aspect of van Langenhove's analysis is that the collective delusion of the German army in 1914 must be related to its broader cultural context.

Although a virtuoso performance under wartime conditions, van Langenhove's account ignored much. The temporal and spatial dimensions of the phenomenon were not defined. Close demonstration of the relationship between the circumstances of the invasion and the illusion of a franc-tireur war was not possible since van Langenhove could not use the archival sources that are now available. Manipulation by the army command or propagandists (though not entirely ignored) was played down in favour of the real belief in the franc-tireur myth. The harsh German response to the myth was barely touched on. Moreover, van Langenhove did not extend his investigation to the Allied camp. Yet his book remains a vital guide to the franc-tireur myth-complex as well as a pioneering study of mass delusion.

Other episodes of collective delusion in history reinforce van Langenhove's central points and yield additional insights. Social scientists have attested to the importance of the phenomenon in the developed world – mass literacy and bureaucratic rationality notwithstanding.[9] By and large, historians have not focused on the twentieth century when studying collective delusions, which they have deemed to be more characteristic of earlier societies, an assumption which is surely mistaken. Historical attention has concentrated more on the religious turmoil of the sixteenth and seventeenth centuries (including the obsession with witchcraft) and on the myth-complexes of the eighteenth and nineteenth centuries.[10] Studies from these periods have much to offer contemporary historians. Particularly suggestive is the pioneering book by Georges Lefebvre, *The Great Fear of 1789: Rural Panic in Revolutionary France* (1932).[11]

Lefebvre's subject was the belief that in the summer of 1789 bands of brigands, in league with the aristocracy and foreign monarchs, were invading the French countryside to commit murder and mayhem, and overthrow the National Assembly and Revolution. Conventional historiography had accepted the counter-revolutionary conspiracy as reality or, in the counter-revolutionary tradition, had blamed a revolutionary plot to arm the people by manipulating the fear of brigands. Lefebvre demonstrated that neither view was credible. In reality, the 'aristocrat-brigand' was a delusion, but one so widely believed in that it became a force in its own right.[12] As Lefebvre pointed out, the episode was not historically unique. Wars and revolutions favour such apocalyptic 'fears' and although apparently unfamiliar with van Langenhove and the case of 1914, he referred to a string of such episodes. These included the 'Irish night' in 1688 when rumours spread that 'hordes of wild fanatical Irish' supporting James II had invaded England following the monarch's abdication. Another was the panic triggered in Normandy during the 1848 Revolution by the belief that Communist insurrectionaries from Paris were invading the countryside to divide up the land. 'When an assembly, an army or an entire population sits waiting for the arrival of some enemy,' Lefebvre observed, 'it would be very unusual if this enemy were not actually sighted.'[13] This was the key to Lefebvre's interpretation. What characterized 'fears' such as that of 1789 was the total conviction, or 'autosuggestion' (Lefebvre's term), that the delusional event *was* happening.[14]

For Lefebvre, fear is a powerful generator of rumour and false tales, and in a particularly concentrated form it can produce a collective delusion such as the Great Fear, which exploded in a short period of two and a half weeks (20 July to 6 August) and affected much of France. The parallel with 1914 seems apt. The scale of the franc-tireur delusion was at least as great, affecting a million men in the German armies and spreading through German society, and its central period of propagation was of similar duration – about two weeks. Fear was indeed the driving emotion – the ubiquitous fear of the treacherous civilian. All this justifies applying Lefebvre's concept of a 'Great Fear' to the German army as it invaded Belgium and France.

Perhaps reflecting his vocation as a social historian, Lefebvre, unlike van Langenhove, did not explore the cultural content of the delusion – its language and imagery. However, he emphasized the central role played by conspiracy. The imaginary plot by Parisian counter-revolutionaries converted a general fear of brigands into the politicized Great Fear, reducing the myriad threats surrounding the Revolution to a single enemy. Lefebvre also insisted that all the elements of the delusion were pre-existent. In these respects, he confirms van Langenhove on the imaginary content of 'fears'.

It was precisely as a social historian, however, that Lefebvre made his most sophisticated contribution by establishing how the Great Fear originated and was disseminated. He identified in detail the 'panics' which, in a climate of acute anxiety where 'a sound, a light, a shadow is enough to start an alarm', triggered the outbreak of five distinct currents of fear.[15] He described how 'fear engendered fear' and how it provoked a countervailing popular mobilization, as the church bell sounded in alarm, and thousands of armed men assembled spontaneously.[16] Although dissemination was primarily oral, Lefebvre identified the importance of mail, the press, and printed posters as well as the government, which endorsed the delusion with its authority.

This suggests by way of comparison that in 1914 the available means of communication, or 'relays', were as important as the internal dynamic of the collective delusion in propagating the franc-tireur fear, and helped determine its extent. Van Langenhove had pointed out that verbal networks of rumour, gossip, and story-telling were vital not only within the army but between the army and the home population, and also that belief in the *Franktireurkrieg* was reinforced by the press and the authorities. Lefebvre concluded his study by remarking that although ephemeral, the Great Fear affected the history of the French Revolution both by the response it provoked (the arming of the people in 1789 being a forerunner of the full revolutionary mobilization of 1792–4) and by the legacy of narrative interpretations that it left to both revolutionaries and counter-revolutionaries.[17] In 1914, the collective delusion of a People's War likewise resulted in a German response which gave it enduring significance for both sides.

2   The myth-complex of the 'franc-tireur war'

The Great Fear that swept the German army in 1914 was thus one manifestation of a phenomenon that can occur at moments of collective anxiety
or exaltation. The central legend – that of francs-tireurs resisting German
soldiers – was the most protean. Like the brigands of 1789, it provided a
portmanteau image that could account for any unexplained firing and
convert harmless civilians into an embodiment of the German fear. This
became apparent immediately the German strike-force approached Liège.
A German soldier recorded in his diary that the troops occupying Berneau
on the night of 4–5 August had been fired on by the inhabitants as they
peaceably drew water.[18] Similarly in the Meurthe-et-Moselle in the first
days of the war, ordinary civilians were randomly transformed into treacherous resisters. This was true of the Italian workers at Jarny shooting their
dogs on orders from the local authorities, and of the local garde-champêtre
(village guard) at Fillières, who happened to be returning one of his sister-
in-law's children to her house when the Germans accused him of firing at
them. The mayor and priest, already taken hostage, claimed that a German
soldier had discharged his rifle accidentally, but the garde-champêtre was
executed.[19] Whether it was an isolated shot or a hail of rifle-fire from the
roofs and windows of houses, the mythic perpetrator was the franc-tireur,
an apparently innocuous adult male civilian resisting the German invasion
by treacherous means.

Drawing on the memory of 1870, the franc-tireur was assumed not
merely to indulge in reckless rage but to wage guerrilla warfare, harassing
the enemy at his most vulnerable. He struck in the dark, as the Germans set
up camp or slept, and attacked supply-lines and communications in their
rear. He specialized in ambush, as claimed in countless villages across the
invasion zone, and in sudden, concerted uprisings in apparently pacified
localities, such as Aarschot or Louvain. The term 'franc-tireur' was used
virtually from the outset. The Chief of Staff of the VIIIth Army Corps
(Fourth Army), Colonel August von Cramon, heard on 6 August that a lieutenant of the Hussars and several of his patrol had been 'shot from behind
by francs-tireurs', whereupon a village was burned down.[20] The press used
the term widely from 9 August, prompted by a report issued by the semi-
official news agency, the Wolff'sches Telegraphen-Bureau (WTB).[21] What
franc-tireur meant was spelt out by Moltke in his 'Warning' issued on 12
August.

[From] now on every non-uniformed person, if he is not designated as being justified in participating in fighting by clearly recognizable insignia, is to be treated as someone standing outside international law, if he takes part in the fighting, interferes with German communications with the rear, cuts telegraph lines, causes explosions, in short participates in any way in the act of war without permission. He will be treated as a franc-tireur and immediately shot according to martial law.[22]

By October 1914, 'franc-tireur' was a term familiar throughout Germany as applied to enemy civilians and, by extension, any treacherous behaviour.[23]

The franc-tireur inverted the self-image of the German military. His mode of war was the opposite of that which the Germans believed they were practising, conducted in the open by a professionally officered national army. His hallmarks were disguise, secrecy, and cunning. 'Treacherous' (*heimtück- isch*) was one of the commonest epithets applied to him. As noted, this was the term used by von Einem when describing the barbarity of supposed civilian resistance at Liège. The franc-tireur perpetrated *Greueltaten* ('atroc- ities'), and *Grausamkeit* ('cruelty'), both terms signifying that legal and moral norms had been transgressed. In effect, he was a criminal.

The contrast with the law-abiding German soldier extends even to the way modern societies organized for war. Given the assumption of universal military service, any adult male not in the army was a potential franc- tireur. The latter represented the unfulfilled potential of the nation-in- arms, but in an aberrant form. He was particularly likely to be found in Belgium, which did not have full conscription. A French journalist, Pierre Mille, who managed to get to Antwerp in mid-August, observed that:

The [Belgian] countryside is not empty of men as in France or Germany. No industry has stopped, nor has work in the fields. During the fierce fighting around Diest and Haelen [on the river Gette], this extraordinary spectacle occurred: hardly had the enemy been put to flight than the peasants were seen reappearing with their teams of horses and their mechanical harvesters. They cut their wheat, bound it, and returned peaceably to their farms.[24]

The omnipresence of men who were not soldiers, and the very normality of their occupations, turned Belgium for the Germans into a reservoir of potential guerrilla fighters.

Since the franc-tireur encapsulated the hidden menace of ordinary life, his fundamental characteristic was invisibility. Time and again, he was described as firing from hiding. Wilhelm Nau, of IR 76 from Hamburg, recalled that he and his fellow-soldiers were told en route for Belgium before 8 August that: 'We were not to expect to meet the enemy in honest battle; the enemy hides behind the hedges in the clothes of the peaceful civilian. Horror stories and rumours are being told.'[25] Nau's unit spent its first night in Belgium in the open rather than in tents because of their fear of attack. Woods, hedges, and houses were the deceptive exteriors that hid the menace. A German artist-soldier recorded in his war diary near Andenne, on 19 August:

> Our cavalry patrols, we hear, are being shot at in the villages again and again. Several poor fellows have already lost their lives. Disgraceful! An honest bullet in honest battle – yes, then one has shed one's blood for the Fatherland. But to be shot from ambush, from the window of a house, the gun-barrel hidden behind flower-pots, no, that is not a nice soldierly death.[26]

Such a scene was portrayed in the painting 'A Victim of the Francs-tireurs' reproduced by an illustrated journal. It showed a patrol surprised in a sunny village street by a franc-tireur ambush. One man falls but only the flashes of rifle-fire at the windows indicate where the shooting is coming from (illustration 1). The same fear of the invisible enemy emerged in a collection of 78 German letters captured by the French before about 22 August, mainly from Bavarian soldiers in Lorraine. These revealed how the soldiers feared French civilians more than troops, since they were not in uniform, fired on the Germans from houses, mutilated the wounded, and killed sleeping soldiers.[27]

The invisibility of the franc-tireur was fundamental to the myth. Faceless, the franc-tireur was inhuman and yet potentially he was any of the passive or benign visages encountered in the course of the invasion. The contrast was expressed by one *Lüttichstürmer* (stormer of Liège) in the heroic tale of his unit's retreat to a village, early in the morning after being repulsed with two casualties in a nocturnal attack on one of the forts. The villagers had treated the soldiers hospitably the previous day.

1   An imagined attack by francs-tireurs

Now's the good part. We were just about to rest when we were suddenly fired on from each house [...] Each male inhabitant of the village was arrested. Then our artillery was brought into action and shot the whole place into flames. I can tell you, [it's not easy] when you go through something like this – to go through the burning village and simply shoot down everyone. But the people have only themselves to blame, for during the day they were hospitable and in the night they shot at us.[28]

The supposed kindness of the inhabitants followed by a 'deceitful' attack was a common stereotype. The 'attack' takes place after a real setback, the soldiers are exhausted, the attackers cannot be identified, and no villagers bearing weapons are found. Yet because the firing came from 'every house', the villagers are made to incarnate the faceless francs-tireurs. The official German report on Andenne came to the same conclusion:

The inhabitants of Andenne received the passing troops in an apparently friendly manner; they gave them water, and the soldiers believed that in the quiet of the evening they would be able to pass peaceably through

Andenne [...] But scarcely had the head of the marching column arrived at the bridge over the Meuse, when the peaceful picture presented by the town suddenly changed, and the inhabitants showed their true character, a thing which unfortunately occurred only too often in Belgium. This time their deeds were truly devilish.[29]

The question of uniforms and disguises, of fighting under false colours, gave a further twist to this theme. As Moltke indicated in his 'Warning', the franc-tireur was charged with refusing to wear a uniform or any distinguishing mark. Disguise compounded the offence. Francs-tireurs supposedly abused the cover of the Red Cross and thus betrayed the humanitarian status of medical facilities under the Geneva and Hague Conventions. This belief caused the massacre of Belgian civilians and wounded French soldiers at Ethe and Goméry on 23 August.[30] It was portrayed by a drawing of Fritz Erler, in the modernist periodical, *Jugend*, which showed a brutal peasant sporting a Red Cross armband and holding the severed head of a uniformed German soldier (illustration 2). The caption read: 'The Franctireur. The Geneva Cross is the finest modern means of waging war!' In several cases, too, imagined resistance was imputed to French or Belgian troops, stranded or deliberately remaining behind, who took off their uniforms and ambushed the Germans in civilian disguise. In the case of Louvain, the garrison commander, Major von Manteuffel, told the Dutch journalist, Mokveld, that Belgian soldiers in civilian clothes had remained secreted in the town after its capture on 19 August and had attacked the Germans in the rear when they were fighting off the Belgian attack from Antwerp, a story he later retracted.[31] General Max von Boehn, commander of IXth Reserve Army Corps, who returned to Louvain from the fighting late in the evening of 25 August, claimed that: 'A large number of the civilians who took part in the rising and were shot, were ascertained to be soldiers.'[32] This was untrue; none of those shot was a serving soldier. Soldiers in civilian disguise were also accused of fomenting resistance in Aarschot, No600ény, and Andenne.[33] At Senlis, in early September, when a German-speaking inhabitant begged for the lives of the townspeople by arguing that they had been forbidden to participate in fighting, his German interlocutors instead blamed the firing on French soldiers 'who then put on civilian clothes in order to save themselves'.[34]

The invisibility of the franc-tireur made the moment of his unmasking dramatic. This, too, was portrayed in *Jugend*, in a painting by the Munich

2　The decapitation of a German soldier by a franc-tireur by Fritz Erler

artist, Max Feldbauer, of 'franc-tireur prisoners', in clogs and with brutal faces, surrounded by uniformed soldiers (illustration 3). Summary trials or condemnations could be used to unmask the culprit before the assembled German soldiers, as with a café proprietor, Foëll, executed before German troops in Blâmont after a 15-minute harangue by the German comman- der.[35] At Tamines, a German officer on horseback informed the victims, and thus the German soldiers, that they were francs-tireurs before they were shot. Patently innocuous civilians could be transformed in the imagination of nervous soldiers into a deadly threat. A cavalry captain related to an army doctor how one day he arrived in a village where all the inhabitants had been ordered to hand in their weapons. An old man who arrived late with his useless rifle was about to be shot for bearing a weapon, but the captain prevented the execution.[36] At Jarny in the Meurthe-et-Moselle, a M. Collignon, obeying orders to turn in his rifle at the town hall, was actually killed by German soldiers on 10 August.[37] Yet frustration with the difficulty of finding real faces for mythic crimes was commoner. It helps explain the German readiness to execute civilians indiscriminately and the anger shown on these occasions; few could be proved guilty, but all were poten- tially so.

It was the collective resistance of the franc-tireurs, however, which made them truly fearful. They appeared in two contrasting images. One was the anarchic fury associated with the mob or with political or religious fanati- cism, which was spontaneous and could erupt anywhere at any time. The other was the concerted *levée en masse* which the Belgian and French governments stood accused of organizing. In the episodes involving a major panic both images appeared. The delusion of a civil insurrection produced its own response, turning the streets of the occupied town into a bedlam of rifle-fire, burning buildings, and exploding shells – reinforcing the delu- sion. The chaos was portrayed vividly in contemporary German illustra- tions such as that of fighting in Louvain in the leading art magazine, *Die Kunst*, in 1915 (illustration 4). But the chaos was made intelligible, if more terrifying, by the belief that it was prepared by the authorities and operated according to a design.

The Germans believed in planned uprisings at Andenne, Aarschot, Louvain, Lunéville, Longuyon, and elsewhere. At Andenne, the chiming of a church bell was taken to be the signal. An officer with the First Guards Reserve Regiment testified that 'it was reported to us that a document had been found [...] showing the attack of the civil population to have been

3   A painting of franc-tireur prisoners by the Munich artist Max Feldbauer (September 1914): 'Bring all the scoundrels here – bullets are too good for them, a cattle-rope will do well enough.'

4   The People's War in Louvain as imagined by a German artist

minutely planned, with a fixed hour for its commencement. Shortly before the prearranged time all the inhabitants, who had met us with such friendliness in the streets, locked themselves in, and at the given minute fire was opened upon us.'[58] At Aarschot, Captain Karge, the military police commander who was a key perpetrator of the mass execution, unconsciously demonstrated in his subsequent testimony to the Ministry of War the conspiracy theory behind the franc-tireur complex. He recounted that several stories were circulating before the massacre: first, that the Belgian government and the King had committed every Belgian man to 'do as much harm as possible to the German army'; second, that Belgian soldiers had been sent in civilian clothing to lead the insurrection; and third, that a notice had been found attached to a church door announcing that Belgians were obliged to kill every captured German officer. Finally, the 'seminary teacher' from Aarschot, who under threat of the death penalty had 'revealed' the 'organization' behind the attack on the German troops, told Karge that the Garde Civique had received the order to damage the German army in every possible way.[59] Given such tales, the outbreak of shooting by German soldiers at each other confirmed the thesis of a planned uprising and justified the draconian repression that followed.

Proof that the Belgians had planned insurrection was found by the Germans in the firearms collected by the municipal authorities to prevent spontaneous shooting.[40] Commonplace, too, was misunderstanding about the role of the Garde Civique, whose barracks and armaments, and even actual presence (as at Tongeren and Tamines), fuelled assumptions about premeditated resistance. Mayors were frequent targets for German anger because they were assumed to have directed the actions of their citizens. This explains the fate of Tielemans at Aarschot and Camus at Andenne, for example, and the harrowing experience of the mayor of Badonviller, Joseph-Edmond Benoît, who was awarded the Légion d'honneur for his composure in the face of troops who killed his wife and accused the villagers of planned resistance.[41]

The People's War thesis thus linked any apparent resistance to the illegal and dishonest intentions of the government. In the case of Belgium it turned the entire society, which should in the German view have allowed free passage, into an enemy. It was a conspiracy theory which concentrated the Germans' fear of the civilian population into one overriding accusation. To borrow Lefebvre's formulation, it 'synthesized the causes of their insecurity' and produced a vision of the enemy which allowed for a violent discharge of fear.

The myth-complex of the franc-tireur war contained more specific legends. Most striking were tales which recounted Catholic priests in Belgium, France, and Alsace-Lorraine inciting their flocks into armed resistance. The German authorities came to admit that such tales had little validity.[42] Yet the legend was potent because it distilled a particular version of the People's War – a Catholic population capable of fanatical violence and an authoritarian priesthood able to manipulate it at will. German diarists frequently recorded their hostility to Catholics and pathological fear of priests. A Hamburg soldier described his first Belgian priest as: '*monsieur le curé*, this sinister figure of Belgium.'[43]

The myth formed during the first phase of the invasion. The priests of Olne and Forêt, near Liège, were killed on 5 and 6 August and the church tower of Visé, supposedly used for signalling to the fort of Pontisse, was burned on 10 August.[44] By the time the general advance began, priests were taken to be ringleaders of resistance. General von Beseler wrote to his wife on 16 August: '[The Belgians] do not behave like a civilized people, but a band of robbers – a pretty result of the priests' domination of Belgium (*Pfaffenherrschaft*).'[45] The mainly Protestant First Army maltreated and executed clergy west of the Gette, accusing them of organizing firing and communicating with the enemy from their church towers. The priest of Schaffen barely escaped with his life after being beaten and mocked by furious German soldiers, while the priest at Aarschot was forced to hide.[46] The priest of Gelrode (adjacent to Aarschot) was believed to have orchestrated resistance during the night of 19–20 August. In reality, nervous sentries of IR 49 fired on each other, but the priest was executed with some of his parishioners.[47] Desecration occurred frequently. On his second day in Belgium, a Catholic Polish-German soldier, Wladyslaus Ossowski, in IR 34 from Stettin, witnessed not only the killing of old people and arbitrary arrest of a priest but also the image of the Virgin Mary being mocked and thrown to the ground by his mainly Protestant comrades.[48] It was not only Belgian victims or disaffected German Catholics who commented on the widespread anti-Catholicism. The Dutch academic, Grondijs, noted at Aarschot that 'most of the houses are destroyed. The soldiers above all attacked the statues of the Catholic cult', a view confirmed by an Australian journalist, Louise Mack, who got into the town and saw altars, confessionals, and wooden statues of saints destroyed in the church.[49]

Soldiers of the Second Army executed the priest of Tamines for supposedly machine-gunning them from the church tower and ridiculed the Catholic practices of the inhabitants, while the destruction of Louvain by units of the same army owed much to the city's notoriety as the educational hub of Belgian Catholicism. Reserve Captain Rump from Hamburg, reaching Louvain 24 hours after the massacre began, saw the evening sky lit up by the burning town. He was told how under the leadership of the *Pfaffen*, hordes of Belgians had attacked the Germans, 'slit the throats of 60 ill soldiers, castrated them and committed other infamies'. The result was the order to raze Louvain to the ground.[50] Later, describing how comrades from Hamburg were killed in the battle for Dendermonde on 4 September, he commented that: 'These people cannot give up their infamous franc-tireur habits. The priests are the worst, for they are better educated and usually they are the seducers.'[51]

Like the regiments of the First and Second Armies, those of the Saxon Third Army were predominantly Protestant and markedly anti-Catholic. This was less evident at Dinant than Louvain, although the Germans accused the monks of the Abbey of Leffe of resisting them and some soldiers paraded mockingly in looted vestments.[52] The massacre at Spontin, close to Third Army headquarters, on 23 August, included the execution of the priest, and the rumour soon spread to Germany (published by the National Liberal *Kölnische Zeitung*) that he had preached armed resistance.[53] When IR 104 and 133 took Hastière-par-delà, south of Dinant, razing the village and shooting 19 inhabitants, they desecrated the church, and the priest was shot by soldiers of IR 106 in neighbouring Hermeton-sur-Meuse.[54] The hunt for priests continued as the XIIth Army Corps moved into the French Ardennes. Abbé Hubert was blamed for the imagined resistance of Haybes. The war diary of an officer of IR 178 recorded the killing of the priest of Villers-en-Fagne, on the Belgian side of the frontier. The same regiment vainly sought the curé of Marlemont-la-Guinguette for signalling to the French with lights from the church tower and executed a priest in Sault-lès-Rethel during the panic of 31 August.[55]

The Fourth Army was equally affected. Chief of Staff, VIIIth Army Corps, Colonel August von Cramon was convinced that the Belgian population was 'very hostile' and the 'noble clergy' were setting a bad example: 'Bells were rung to warn of our arrival, and often there were machine-guns emplaced in the church towers; is it any wonder that several gentlemen of the cloth have had to pay with their lives?'[56] To cite but two examples, the priest of Anloy was accused of ringing his bell precisely 13 times as a signal to the French during the battle of the Ardennes, while the inhabitants of Bertrix were taxed with firing on the XVIIIth Army Corps from their church tower.[57]

The Württemberg regiments in the Fifth Army, which took the northern Meurthe-et-Moselle, also believed that priests organized resistance at Fresnois-la-Montagne and Longuyon. The same was often true even of Catholic soldiers. Landsturm Battalion Neuss from the Rhineland played a central role in the events at Louvain.[58] In the case of mainly Catholic Bavarian and Baden regiments in the Sixth and Seventh Armies, the myth arose from suspicion of francophile priests in Alsace and German Lorraine who were in the forefront of the movement in favour of autonomy for the provinces, and from the help they received from priests on the French side of the frontier. In German Lorraine, 19 priests of the diocese of Metz were jailed on charges of treason, and others were seized when the Germans invaded the Vosges and Meurthe-et-Moselle.[59] The case of Abbé Émile Wetterlé, an Alsatian Reichstag deputy who took refuge in France, notoriously confirmed these suspicions.[60] The Bavarian Major Joseph Fleischmann considered the priests of Lorraine to be spies who had 'without a doubt passed on information to the French about the arrival and deployment of our troops'.[61] Such views help explain why several of the 11 priests killed in the Meurthe-et-Moselle were executed by Bavarians, including Abbé Vouaux at Jarny on 26 August.[62] The Bishop of Nancy noted that Catholic soldiers shared the German hatred of enemy Catholic priests.[63] Feelings of national betrayal outweighed confessional solidarity.

The myth of the resistant priest continued inside France. Abbé Fossin, who was the parish priest of Varreddes (Seine-et-Marne), was accused of signalling to French troops from his church tower. Despite his protestation that at the age of 76 he was physically incapable of climbing the tower and had in reality turned his church into a first-aid station, he was severely beaten and humiliated before being condemned by a hastily convened court-martial. He was never seen again.[64] Another elderly priest, Abbé Oudin of Sompuis (Marne), was likewise accused of signalling to the French when the cable of the electric bell in the presbytery was mistaken for a telephone line. Although the Germans recognized their error, discovery of a letter from the priest's brother, a retired army captain, was enough for Oudin to be arrested on 7 September and severely maltreated. He died during deportation.[65]

Fear of the person was transposed onto his setting so that the church and its tower aroused particular suspicion as the site of deadly machine-guns and of communication with the enemy – by flag, bell, telephone, or the new and mysterious wireless radio.[66] Monasteries and convents seemed to Protestant soldiers even stranger and more dangerous places than churches. One wounded officer, Lieutenant Reichel, IR 177, heard in Leffe on 24 August that 80 civilians, among them a priest and a monk, had been discovered in a tunnel in the abbey, and all but the monk executed.[67] A variant of the tale soon found its way, via a returning nurse, into a Berlin newspaper, according to which the bodies of 50 murdered German soldiers were found in the cellar of a convent in Louvain.[68] In Aarschot, the monastery of the Order of the Sacred Heart was the object of continued suspicion, despite operating as a first-aid station. On 25 August, the monks were accused of being francs-tireurs and were deported to Germany with other clerics from the town.[69] The numerous religious orders at Louvain were the target of German fury. A senior Capuchin monk related the suspicion they encountered, especially when wearing the Red Cross armband. On 28 August, he was stopped by a group of drunken German soldiers who claimed: 'Everyone fired at us, priests, women, the Red Cross [...] The monks also fired. We had to defend ourselves.'[70] The stand-in for the Vatican nuncio in Brussels intervened vigorously to protect the religious orders in Louvain, including the Jesuits who were accused of contacting the enemy by radio.[71] Faced with the intensity of anti-Catholic mythology in places such as Aarschot and Louvain, the Dutch witness, Grondijs, felt that 'one might take it to be a religious war!'[72]

Altogether weaker was the myth of working-class insurrection, despite the invasion of the industrial districts of Liège and Charleroi. The only distinct narrative this generated was that of a proletarian rising at Herstal on 6–7 August. As noted, the commander of the 34th Brigade reported that resistance by the 'entire population of Liège and the suburbs' forced him to order a precipitate retreat early on 6 August, and clashes occurred in the streets of Herstal the following morning between German stragglers and Belgian troops.[73] The evening edition of the Amsterdam *De Telegraaf*, on 7 August, published a sensational account of women, old people, and children who repulsed the invaders, firing from every house and pouring boiling oil on the Uhlans (as mounted German lancers were called).[74] This account was reproduced in the Belgian and international press as an example of the heroic defence of Liège, before the Belgians issued a disclaimer stating that the original Dutch account was a gross exaggeration.[75] Naturally, the German press ignored this and recycled the Dutch story as Belgian self-incrimination for civilian resistance.[76]

Since Herstal was the site of a branch of the Belgian national arms factory, it is possible that some inhabitants may have taken up the defence of their town, though given the battle raging between the Germans and the troops of General Leman between the Liège forts, its significance can only have been marginal. The system of outworking by which rifles were manu-factured led to stores of bolts and barrels being discovered in houses in Herstal and other villages around Liège, contributing to the impression of a planned insurrection. But rather than representing reality, it is far more likely that the account in *De Telegraaf* (which came from a journalist in Maastricht, on the Dutch side of the frontier) reflected the distorted memo-ries of soldiers of Grenadier Regiment 90 and Jäger Battalion 7, many of whom, as we have seen, fled from Herstal as far as Holland. Two Jäger held captive by the Dutch in Maastricht reported to German military authori-ties that when they entered Liège on 6 August, they were repulsed by 'civil-ians' firing in the streets, and after retiring into the fields, they were attacked on three sides. They then sought refuge next to a mill in an unnamed location between Liège and Hermée (which may have been Herstal), where they were shot at by Belgian troops and citizens from the roofs, before they were 'almost wiped out', a few men eventually escaping to Holland.[77] Such witness-participants were at best disoriented and pro-bably traumatized. The narrative of treacherous civilians helped excuse rout and capture. In some cases, it extended to women pouring boiling tar, and it was these tales that Dutch journalists picked up and probably further exaggerated for newspapers avid for copy on the war. A leading German apologist for the army's behaviour in the 1920s, Bernhard Schwertfeger, conceded privately that the story of women and children fighting and pouring boiling oil at Herstal was fantasy.[78]

Once in circulation, the legend of the working-class insurrection at Herstal took on a life of its own. The *Frankfurter Zeitung* carried an article in mid-August 1914 entitled 'The Devils of the Liège Basin', explaining that this area had risen against the German troops because it was a centre of arms production whose working class was characterized by drunkenness, violence, and anarchism and was accustomed to carrying out class warfare with bombs and revolvers. Coarse barbarians, the diabolical hordes of the 1913 general strike (for universal male suffrage), now shot at the German wounded and stabbed the defenceless in the back.[79] A Hamburg newspaper cited an officer home on leave who described the 'atrocities' (*Scheußlichkeiten*) suffered by the Germans at Liège, adding: 'Many girls and women, trained in the use of firearms because many of them work in the local arms factories, participated in the fighting. If they were caught, they were disposed of in short order.'[80] A German novelist and Landwehr captain, Paul Oskar Höcker, whose job included 'purging' the countryside between Liège and the German border to make it safe, recounted in his memoirs how shocked he was to discover weapons parts in the houses, a search by his company confiscating enough to produce 20,000 rifles. Höcker therefore assumed that the francs-tireurs would be drawn from the '*canaille*' (rabble) of Liège, and feared being shot at from every house. He also mistook the working-class passion for pigeon-racing as evidence of espionage.[81] Herstal thus recast the fear of proletarian insurrection in military form as a legend redolent of the Paris Commune – which had been marked by street-fighting and mythic women arsonists, the *pétroleuses*. However, it found little wider application.

Women and children participating in fighting, however, were part of a much broader mythic theme. The treachery that was intrinsic to the franc-tireur, normally imagined as an adult male, became all the greater when his age and especially gender were inverted. The conventionally most inno-cent person, a child and particularly a girl, became the most dangerous assailant because the most unexpected. Women and children, accused of barbaric conduct from the outset, were killed in several incidents at Liège, including the collective execution carried out by IR 165 at Melen on 6 August.[82] Fragments of soldiers' accounts hint at the legends that circulated. One man from IR 165 testified to the official German inquiry that while he was marching through a village 'lying west of Herve', which was quite possibly Melen, he 'noticed that some girls of eight or ten years of age, armed with sharp instruments, were busying themselves with the German wounded. I subsequently ascertained that, from the most severely wounded, the lobes and the upper parts of their ears had been cut off.'[83] This was echoed by an officer's account of the fighting at Liège published by the *Hamburgischer Correspondent*, which referred to 'the eleven-year old girl who had put out the eyes of a sleeping soldier with knitting needles'.[84] No Belgian girl was ever arrested and tried for such an act; the different versions of the tale originating in one locality suggest a legend which, like the boiling oil in Herstal, was a collective fantasy of traumatized German soldiers.

Variants on this legend occurred throughout the invasion. In Luxembourg province, the incident at the Café Turc in Arlon, in which a young woman was wounded by a German lance on 6 August, rapidly spawned the reverse legend of the girl who fired on German soldiers from shelter. A Lieutenant Glückmann recorded in his diary that a *Strafexpedition* (punishment expedition) was sent to Arlon on 12 August 'because a soldier had been stabbed to death by a 16-year-old girl [...] Booty: many weapons, 100,000 francs.'[85] At Ethe, 20 kilometres from Arlon, two young girls were held to have fired on a German patrol on 13 August, although an inquiry demonstrated that one had been in Arlon at the time and the other, the daughter of the burgomaster, was only three years old.[86] It was also rumoured that two of the civilians executed *en masse* at Arlon on 26 August were young girls guilty of blinding German soldiers.[87]

At Dinant, women and children were frequently accused of participating in the fighting on 23 August; soldiers of Grenadier Regiment 100 were told by their captain that the captain of the 1st company had been wounded by a girl of 14 years.[88] The myth of women and children pouring boiling oil on German troops in Herstal resurfaced in Louvain.[89] As noted, one of the last incidents, at Ledegem in West Flanders on 19 October, involved the tale that two little girls had fired on IR 242, and a woman and two eight-year-old girls were among the 18 inhabitants killed.[90]

The assassination of Colonel Stenger at Aarschot by the young son of Burgomaster Tielemans furnished another myth with wide currency in the German army. According to Godefroid Kurth, emeritus professor of history at the university of Liège, who made an investigation in Aarschot in 1915:

> Via the press, the legend of Aarschot passed into the trenches; the entire German army related it with horror; ten days after the event, soldiers billeted in my house [in Liège] informed me about it: they took it as gospel truth. Even today, it is taken as law; it has already passed into popular books and in the future it will, like Tilly's burning of Magdeburg [in the Thirty Years' War], be one of those Protestant dogmas that it takes centuries to extirpate from history.[91]

The tale was translated into a female variant. The troops who destroyed Haybes held that a 15-year old girl of the village had killed one of their senior officers. On the following day, 26 August, the same myth contributed to the execution by machine-gun of 38 civilians at Surice (Namur province), some 20 kilometres away.[92] Women and children thus symbolized the intrinsic treachery of the enemy civilian in its most extreme form, and served to warn German troops against trusting any inhabitants of invaded territory.

Finally, the *Franktireurkrieg* operated at a more atavistic level with tales of blinding, mutilation, and poisoning. These drew on a fascination with bodily violation which Marc Bloch felt to be a permanent cultural substratum – 'these themes which the human imagination [...] has ceaselessly recycled since the dawn of time'.[93] Like the other myths, they emerged at the precise moment that the strike-force attacking Liège was rebuffed at the forts. In addition to the tales of girls blinding German soldiers at Melen, the massacre at Warsage (34th Brigade) on 6 August was accompanied by accusations of eyes being gouged out and ears lopped off. The nuns at Blégny noted on 5–6 August that the men repulsed at the Fort of Barchon believed German soldiers were being blinded and given poisoned water. The execution of 17 civilians at Louveigné on 7 August (38th and 43rd Brigades) was linked to the accusation that a major's ears had been cut off. The killings at Francorchamps the following day were accompanied by claims of poisoning and mutilation.[94] Mokveld, the correspondent for the Dutch paper *De Tijd*, who chronicled the emergence of the franc-tireur myth-complex around Liège at first hand, commented that:

> The mad fury [responsible for the collective delusion about the francs-tireurs] was also intensified considerably by the accusations about gruesome mutilations committed on German soldiers by Belgians who were said to have cut off the noses, ears, genitals and so on of their enemies. These rumours were so persistent that in the end it was generally believed in neutral countries that these things had happened frequently.[95]

Such tales surfaced at every point of the invasion. In the Meurthe-et-Moselle, the regimental diary of Bavarian IR 1 recorded that by 11 August, the soldiers were 'outraged' at reports of mutilation, and the two primary school teachers of Avricourt related that on 12 August, a Bavarian officer billeted with them considered that 'the French were barbaric [and] that they cut off the ears of [German] soldiers'.[96] One of the motives for the massacre at Noménywas the alleged mutilation and blinding of wounded German soldiers, while inhabitants of Gerbéviller and nearby Réméréville reported suspicious German soldiers who made them taste drinking water.[97] Even the official German *White Book*, whose evidence was carefully selected for its apparent credibility, retailed over a dozen examples of the myth – one German soldier disembowelled and another castrated at Louvain; one castrated, another with his eyes gouged out, and a third with his throat slit at Dinant; tales from RIR 203 and 204 of exhausted stragglers mutilated by Belgian villagers on the road to Diksmuide in mid-October (these regiments carried out the massacres at Esen and Zarren); and so on.[98]

The most significant incident directly attributable to alleged civilian mutilation of German soldiers occurred at Orchies, in the département of the Nord, during the 'race for the sea'.[99] Orchies was on the fluid northern edge of the invasion, though essentially in the German sphere, and both French and German wounded remained there after fighting on 24 August. On 22 September, a detachment of French troops suddenly arrived in the town. The following day, a German convoy of seven ambulances (but according to the French, not carrying Red Cross markings) was sent by the German commander at Valenciennes to recover the German wounded. The Germans shot and killed a French sentry, but were fired on in turn, losing eight dead. Next day, 400 men of Landwehr IR 35 attacked Orchies. French and British soldiers beat them off, but withdrew later on 24 September and the mayor evacuated the town, leaving only a score of elderly inhabitants. When a punishment expedition of the First Battalion of the Bavarian Pioneer Regiment arrived on 25 September, it found (according to its senior medical officers) the mutilated bodies of 21 soldiers.[100] The town was burned, four old people and one young woman who had returned for a calf perishing in the flames. The German accusation was not that living, but dead, soldiers had been mutilated. The medical evidence which the German government published to prove 'French atrocities' may have been compatible with small-arms and shrapnel fire, but the corpses were buried without an autopsy. The medical officers, however, concluded that the injuries proved the 'bestial barbarity of the people of the district', and the commander at Valenciennes issued a poster which combined all the elements of the story into a comprehensive denunciation of the townspeople:

I have unfortunately been forced to apply the severest measures decreed by the laws of war against the town of Orchies. In this locality doctors and medical personnel were attacked and killed and a score of German soldiers were assassinated. The worst atrocities were committed in an unbelievable manner (ears cut off, eyes torn out, and other bestial acts of the same kind).[101]

However protean, the franc-tireur myth-complex had an imaginative unity. The central motif of the treacherous adult male portrayed the reverse of an honest military opponent; in a further inversion images of priests, women, and children heightened the sense of transgression and threat. These myths structured the Great Fear that swept the German armies in the west. As a reductive allegory for the dangers faced by German soldiers, it worked with a terrible simplicity. Although extended equally to French civilians, it had the particular advantage of placing the Belgians, who were not generally perceived as a potential enemy in pre-war Germany, on the same footing as the French, who were. But perhaps the deepest and most paradoxical function was that which emerged through the atavistic fascination with mutilation and poisoning. The *Franktireurkrieg* transformed the French and Belgian victims of German military violence into the imaginary perpetrators of truly atrocious acts, thus making victims of the invaders and legitimizing the invasion.

3   The military situation and the franc-tireur fear

How, in terms other than its own mythic structure, can the origin and spread of the franc-tireur complex be explained? Since it derived from multiple misunderstandings of what was really happening, it follows that the circumstances of the invasion must have shaped the delusion, even if, as van Langenhove and Lefebvre both noted, a collective delusion is also driven by its internal dynamic, usually fear.

As shown, the initial belief in franc-tireur resistance, and the violence against civilians in which it resulted, were essentially autonomous, occurring among German soldiers and junior officers in battle or on patrol before being endorsed at senior levels and becoming more systematic. Yet the fact that such beliefs manifested themselves simultaneously along a front of more than 300 kilometres demonstrates that they were in the minds of German soldiers as they went to war. Too little is known about the instructions given to the Liège strike-force or initial patrols further south to establish how explicitly the danger of civilian resistance was addressed. But what took form as a false belief on enemy territory must have been a strong presumption in the pre-war thinking of the German army, in ways that will be discussed in the next chapter.

The franc-tireur belief was linked to the outbreak of war in another way.

It was one expression of a broader anxiety about the enemy which emerged in all the belligerent societies, although this anxiety usually failed to acquire the independence and motivating force characteristic of a collective delusion. Lurid tales and false rumours flourished in the form of xenophobia and spy mania as public opinion fluctuated between confidence in national success and anxiety at possible invasion and defeat.[102]

Often, enemy citizens, departing diplomats, and later the first prisoners of war, drew hostility as symbols or surrogates of the national foe. Indeed, both sides used such incidents to bolster the charges of enemy brutality and emphasize their own fairness and restraint. The French, British, and Russians all claimed that their nationals had been attacked as they left Germany. The Germans and Austrians likewise maintained that their nationals had been victimized in enemy countries on the outbreak of war. Accounts of sadistic attacks on German civilians in Brussels and Antwerp (including murder in the latter) enjoyed wide acceptance. The Belgian government was so alarmed that it commissioned an inquiry. This concluded that apart from the short ultimatum given to leave Belgium, neither the authorities nor the population had been guilty of violence against the expelled Germans, a finding confirmed after investigation by the German Foreign Ministry.[103]

With military mobilization, each country became obsessed by the internal enemy perfidiously delivering it into the hands of the foe. Anxiety and anger were discharged onto mythic figures and innocent bystanders. In Belgium, France, and Britain, as in Germany, marginal and vulnerable people – the itinerant pedlar, the foreign resident, the tourist with a camera (war coincided with the holiday season) – were seized as spies.[104] Shops and businesses with enemy-sounding names were attacked. German establishments (including the mistakenly targeted Swiss Maggi food company) were assaulted in Paris and elsewhere in France in early August.[105] Angry crowds vandalized German businesses in Brussels and Antwerp on the evening of 5 August. The lawlessness in the capital was soon curbed, but it was replaced by the 'hunt for the imaginary German', as *Le Soir* put it.[106] In England, German shops and bakeries were attacked in London and Yorkshire.[107] Rumours circulating in Germany in the first days of the war included those of French saboteurs shot while attempting to place bombs in railway tunnels and cars carrying gold destined for Russia. Stories of French aircraft bombing Nuremberg and incursion into German territory were used by the Foreign Ministry to justify the declaration of war on France.[108]

Fantasies of mutilation and poisoning were woven into these visions of the enemy within. In Brussels, tales that the city's water had been poisoned by German agents (or Uhlans, in another variant) forced officials to taste water publicly at street corners in order to demonstrate their absurdity. In Britain, a journalist on *The Times* wrote in his diary on 11 August 1914 that 'rumour has begun to flap her wings [...] It is said that German purveyors of food are putting slow poison in their commodities. And as for the barbers [...] you run the risk of having your throat cut by them instead of your hair.'[109] In south-central France, the story that foreigners were distributing poisoned cakes or sweets to children ran through three départements.[110]

Tales of espionage, sabotage, and occult death had obvious affinities with the idea of enemy 'atrocity'. Popular anxiety was expressed in the figures of the spy and saboteur during the first days of the war because they were the harbingers of invasion. Hostility to spies and 'enemy aliens' continued throughout the conflict, but once real invasions occurred anxiety focused directly on the demonized image of the enemy soldier, as in the terror at 'Cossack atrocities' that spread through East Prussia.[111] In the case of the German invasion of Belgium, the false news of maltreatment of German civilians in Antwerp and Brussels was unlikely to have caused the violence against Belgian civilians by German soldiers since newspapers were not initially available and the reports appeared when Liège was already under attack. Rather, the rapidity with which the invasion of Belgium followed the outbreak of war elided the visions of the internal and external enemy, so that poisoning and mutilation symbolized the 'treachery' of Belgian resistance, and those supposedly fomenting it became traitors in their own land.

Although German soldiers were predisposed to find enemy civilians dangerous, military circumstances in August–October 1914 played a vital role in defining the franc-tireur myth-complex. The crucial factors were the kind of warfare being fought and the conditions encountered during the invasion. If these were determined by the Schlieffen Plan, the German General Staff's image of war in 1914 was in turn dominated by the 'Cannae' concept. Around 1900, Schlieffen began to study the battle of Cannae of 216 BC, in which the Carthaginians under Hannibal defeated a Roman force almost twice their size through a battle of envelopment and annihilation.[112] This idea provided the key to the Plan of 1905 which was designed to en-circle and destroy the French in a decisive battle. The hope in German mili-tary circles at the beginning of August 1914 was that Liège would fall quickly and that France would be knocked out of the war in three to six weeks.[113]

In reality, the German plan was seriously flawed. Faith in a war of annihilation (*Vernichtungskrieg*) and in the superior fighting qualities of the German soldier glossed over the required expansion of the army, which was short of at least six army corps in 1914.[114] Additionally, Moltke underestimated the strength of the Liège fort system and the Belgian army's capacity for resistance. Yet Schlieffen's strategy needed the German invasion force to cover a lot of territory rapidly in order to annihilate the French. Anything that restricted speed and movement threatened the plan and the subsequent redeployment of the victorious armies against the Russians. Little wonder that the local commanders and the OHL were under great psychological pressure. The slightest delay threatened the technical precision and timetable laid down by the all-important railway staff for the march towards the grand battle.[115]

Frustration and tension as the shortcomings of the Schlieffen Plan were exposed found an easy scapegoat in the supposed People's War. The shock and embarrassment felt at the humiliating rebuff from the forts of Liège directly engendered the collective delusion of the francs-tireurs among the troops. The institutional memory of the army, as recorded by the official history of the war, also used the francs-tireurs as one explanation for the setback.[116] The scapegoat mechanism is evident in General von Einem, commander of the siege-force sent in after 8 August, who (as we have seen) told his wife about the 'cruel manner' of fighting by the inhabitants which he held partly responsible for the high casualties. Einem confessed in his private diary, but not to his wife, that the severe losses had occurred because 'the troops advanced recklessly and also they often shot at each other' – in other words, because of the time constraints of the Schlieffen Plan.[117] Einem's view was confirmed by Emmich, commander of the initial strike-force, who was faced with a rash of undisciplined firing by troops who had been led to expect only weak resistance at Liège. Emmich had to issue an order on 5 August stating that during darkness, rifles were to be kept unloaded; firing was only to be allowed by officers: 'The outrageous and nervous shooting at one's own troops is a crime.'[118]

Cavalry General von der Marwitz was similarly frustrated. The cavalry was supposed to make the offensive sweep through Belgium before the decisive battles in France. After Liège, it was to 'ride straight through to Brussels', yet on 18 August Marwitz was still only 75 kilometres from the

German border. On 19 August, he expected a major battle (on the Gette) 'if the Belgians stand their ground', but they preferred tactical retreat and defensive skirmishes.[119] Marwitz considered this kind of warfare 'mean': unseen barbed-wire fences tripped up the horses, and the cavalry presented an easy target for the defenders. Many horses were killed, causing unexpected logistical problems. Time and again, clashes between German cavalry and Belgian patrols or rear-guards provoked retaliation against 'francs-tireurs', i.e. uninvolved villagers.

The sheer speed necessitated by the Schlieffen Plan made the troops vulnerable to disorientation. The slightest unfamiliar noise or inexplicable occurrence produced acute nervousness and called for explanation which, in view of the warnings about enemy civilians, easily took the form of mythic francs-tireurs. Punishing daily marches on the right and centre of the invasion force, often in oppressive heat, led to exhaustion which heightened the general nervousness. Some of the troops involved in the events at Louvain, for example, had been woken at 3.30 am on 25 August and marched some 36 kilometres from Landen.[120] The men attacking Dinant on 23 August in some cases had been marching up to 60 or 70 kilometres daily since 18 August. Field kitchens failed to keep up, and soldiers, forced to live off the land, had increased opportunities for aggression towards civilians.[121]

The kind of warfare practised by the Belgian army in its skilful fighting withdrawal, and also by the French army and the BEF as they retired towards the Marne, compounded enemy confusion. Where the Germans expected to mount offensives against fixed positions, they encountered barricades, ambushes, and enfilading fire from houses. Where they sought to close with the enemy, they were constantly frustrated by its disengagement and retreat, covered by rear-guards. In a word, the enemy refused to stand and fight as the Schlieffen Plan required, but rather inflicted painful losses before slipping away. Time and again, whether the Allied troops responsible were Belgian, French, or British, the Germans blamed such tactics on chimerical francs-tireurs, and reacted accordingly.

Thus, in the Meurthe-et-Moselle, the Germans accused civilians of aiding French troops, as at Nomény and Gerbéviller. Likewise, at Schaffen, Aarschot, and other villages in Brabant, the First and Second Armies blamed inhabitants for the actions of highly mobile Belgian troops. General Beseler wrote from Aarschot on 20 August that: 'The town has been half burned down and terribly treated. The inhabitants turned out to be very hostile yesterday and have been very severely punished. Many poor innocents have also had to suffer! This kind of warfare, forced upon us by criminal fools, is horrifying. If only they saw reason.'[122] Even the landscape appeared to conspire with the defenders. General von Einem commented in his diary that: 'The roads are bordered with thick hedges, because there is mainly cattle farming here, and because the region is very hilly the roads lead through many gorges. These characteristics have lent encouragement to the popular war which has been so fateful for the Belgian people.'[123] The devastating rifle-fire of long-service professional British soldiers at Mons, in Hainaut province, contributed to a rash of brutal German reprisals against civilians, including 66 killed at Quarégnon.[124] The same type of rear-guard action conducted by colonial French troops resulted in violence against civilians in early September at Senlis.

Whether German soldiers on occasions attacked civilians in revenge for a kind of warfare they knew to be conducted by enemy soldiers, or whether they were always persuaded that francs-tireurs were the authors, is difficult to determine. Clearly, the collective delusion was widespread. But in the Belgian case, where any resistance was considered to be unnecessary if not illegal, the distinction between soldiers and civilians was more blurred in German eyes. Ultimately, German military doctrine predefined its enemy. Any combat with the Belgians, who could potentially jeopardize the main goal, was construed in the worst possible light. French (and British) harassing tactics were equally objectionable, but confronting the French in battle was the point of the plan, so that when the decisive battle began to take shape in the first week of September on French soil, and Allied resistance stiffened, Moltke was at last fighting the battle he (and Schlieffen) had sought. The franc-tireur complex became less necessary as an expression of the frustrations caused by the Schlieffen Plan.

Other military factors added to the franc-tireur myth-complex. Although before 1914 general staffs had generally recognized the expanded destructiveness of modern firepower, they had not found adequate ways of countering the advantage which it conferred on the defender. Despite the well-publicized experiences of the South African and Russo-Japanese wars and the prediction of military stalemate with enormous losses by the independent Polish analyst, Ivan Bloch, military strategy had not adjusted to the new reality. Between the prevailing doctrine of the offensive and the reality of a battlefield determined by defensive technology − the machine-gun, heavy artillery, and barbed wire − lay a contradiction that was central to the First World War, with the deadlock of trench warfare as the logical outcome.[125] In fact, the initial mobile warfare exhibited the same discrepancy and the same huge casualties, demonstrated by the costly *Handstreich* against Liège. The long march to the Marne was an apprenticeship in modern firepower. Once again, belief in the franc-tireur war helped the Germans to fill the gulf between expectation and reality.

High-velocity rifle-fire contributed to this misunderstanding. An assailant shooting from over a kilometre away was often unseen, allowing the recipient free rein in imagining his identity. Quite apart from distortions produced by cliffs and water (as at Dinant), the noise from the shot could also be misleading. As Ernst Mach demonstrated in the 1880s, the report of the percussion travelled more slowly than the bullet, but the latter carried with it a sound caused by the compression of air at the tip and a slight thinning of air at the base. Hearing this noise almost simultaneously with the arrival of the projectile could make distant firing seem close. German soldiers constantly testified that they were fired on from short range during the invasion and blamed this on anyone who happened to be close by – usually inhabitants.[126] High explosives, which were capable of stripping a body of its clothes, and shrapnel, which mutilated faces and limbs, were also misinterpreted as the work of vicious civilians, as probably happened at Orchies.

Pillage was the natural consequence of armies outstripping their supply trains. It occurred throughout the invasion, and was not confined to the German forces. Yet in their case, it allowed soldiers to vent their frustration and aggression on civilians who were considered complicit in resistance and who thus deserved their fate. Wojcieck Jacobson, the Polish medical officer in IR 49 (First Army), described how his regiment systematically pillaged near-empty villages between Liège and Brussels and destroyed what could not be taken: 'We requisition in every house along the route. If the door is closed, we break it down. Everything the soldier finds that is edible, he consumes, then he breaks and demolishes the mirrors and furniture. Often whole rows of houses are burned down.'[127] The reputation of the German army was felt to be at stake by some of the more old-fashioned officers. In Château-Thierry (southern Aisne) on 4 September 1914, General von Einem recorded seeing broken windows, shops raided, and their contents thrown about: 'not a pretty sight'. He encountered men from IR 56 and 57 taking possession of 'quite unnecessary objects'. The men were arrested, and von Einem 'had serious words with General Schwarte'.[128]

Looting was part of a larger problem of indiscipline which beset the invasion force. This contrasts with the view which, at the time and subsequently, saw the German Army as the epitome of military order and efficiency.[129] Indiscipline was most obviously apparent in incidents of 'friendly fire', which were readily blamed on enemy civilians. As noted, both the commanders at Liège, Emmich and Einem, considered this to be a serious factor in the failure of the assaults on the forts. The judgement was supported by Major-General von Hülsen who confessed that German soldiers were the 'main cause' of the shooting in the forest near the fort of Boncelles during the attack carried out by the 38th and 43rd Brigades on the night of 5–6 August, which led to the massacre of civilians at Esneux, Louveigné, and Poulseur.[130] Friendly fire played a key role in many major panics during the invasion, as well as in a host of minor incidents, and fed the illusion of franc-tireur resistance.

A Württemberg medical officer, Dr Flammer, recorded a typical incident at Baranzy (Belgian Luxembourg) in his diary. Twenty-seven villagers had been killed as francs-tireurs, and much of the village destroyed, after German forces had shot at each other in fog during the battle of Baranzy-Musson. Three days later, on 25 August, German soldiers fired a salvo of shots during the burial of officers who had died in the battle. This led to further shooting near a field hospital, whose personnel thought the enemy were attacking. Flammer and his men seized their weapons, and the hospital guards started firing in the direction they thought the shots had come from. Heightening the panic a cyclist arrived, reporting that on the road from Signeulx he had been shot at 25 times. Patrols, however, found no sign of the enemy. Assistance was requested from the command post in Signeulx, which sent out a unit to shoot a suspicious-looking farmhouse into flames. When it arrived in Baranzy, general merriment and drinking of wine ensued in relief.[131] This was the type of hysterical panic in reaction to friendly fire that operated on a greater scale in major panics such as those at Andenne, Aarschot, Lunéville, and above all Louvain.

Another incident was no less revealing for taking place in German territory. A Bavarian sergeant recorded that on 20 August in the village of Freiburg, near St Johann von Bassel, Alsace, exhausted soldiers returning to their bivouac in the dark heard a shot, which occasioned wild shooting in all directions. The sergeant and his lieutenant were forced to take cover while they whistled with all their strength to stop the fusillade. Meanwhile, another company took them to be the enemy, and there were many casualties.

I do not know exactly how many losses our company suffered, but the 1st company lost six men and a horse. Next morning the word was put around that the civilian population of Freiburg had been shooting, so we had to search the whole village for weapons. No proof could be found, and I do not believe the story. I presume that it was the overexcited nerves of some of the men which was the cause.[132]

Suspicion of the francophile tendencies of the population was sufficient to transform them into traitorous guerrilla fighters.

A remarkable German document found by Belgian civilians and smuggled to the government-in-exile provides insight into a friendly-fire incident which might have produced a major panic and civilian massacre had discipline not been restored in time. On 24 August at Huy, a town midway between Liège and Namur, the inhabitants were forced out of their houses, 28 of which were burned down, and one man was hanged for possession of a revolver. German soldiers claimed that they had been fired upon. But a written copy of an order by Major von Bassewitz to the troops in Huy, found in a nearby meadow, revealed the true origin of the incident to be German friendly fire induced by fear of francs-tireurs.

Last night shots were fired. It has not been proved that the citizens of the town still have weapons in their possession. Nor has it been proved that the population took part in the firing. On the contrary, the impression is unavoidable that German soldiers, under the influence of alcohol, in quite incomprehensible fear of enemy attack, opened fire. The conduct of the soldiers last night, with few exceptions, has made a completely shameful impression. It is most regrettable when officers or NCOs set fire to houses and incite the men to burn and pillage by their conduct without permission or order of the most superior officer ... No shooting in the town is to be allowed without officers' orders. The wretched attitude of the men has resulted in one NCO and one soldier being injured by German bullets.[133]

The consumption of alcohol which, according to Bassewitz, contributed to the panic at Huy, aggravated the indiscipline of German soldiers and their propensity to blame their own anxieties on francs-tireurs. Drunkenness helped produce panics such as those at Andenne and Louvain which occurred late in the day when soldiers had been relaxing. German soldiers by and large came from a beer-drinking culture, but in Belgium

death on 8 August for shooting German soldiers near Visé.[144] At Neuviller, near Badonviller, on the night of 11–12 August, Bavarian IR 1 came under fire and arrested several inhabitants in whose possession revolvers were found.[145] On 20 August at Evelette, near Andenne, three civilians shot at baggage-troops according to a German diarist. The troops returned fire, wounding one of the 'francs-tireurs'. All three protested their innocence. But a rifle was found next to the wounded man, and they were taken before a court-martial. The diarist did not record their fate, but Belgian sources, though denying resistance, reveal that the wounded man was hanged from a lamppost.[146] Sergeant Langenhan, IR 102, was certain he was fired at on the road between Dinant and Houx on 24 August 1914. He and his men shot and injured a man running towards the Meuse. Near where he fell a revolver was found which had been fired. The civilian, aged 35 to 50, was killed. The same witness saw at least six men and a woman firing from a churchyard and the church tower on 26 August. The woman was injured, and a hunting rifle was found next to her. A soldier from 6th company, IR 102, finished her off with a shot. The men were not found. The church and the entire village were then burned down.[147]

A revealing sequence of events is that at Baranzy in southern Luxembourg province. On 16 August, a small German cavalry patrol was ambushed there, with one Uhlan killed and another wounded and captured, by mobilized French customs officers according to one account.[148] This is possible: customs officers became military personnel in war and Baranzy was on the French border. But the truth may have been the version that emerged from the German inquiry conducted among the 208 inhabitants deported to Magdeburg after the executions on 22–23 August. Four of the prisoners were tax officials, who confessed to taking part in an attack on an Uhlan patrol; in Baranzy they killed one Uhlan, wounded another, and captured an officer. 'All the tax officials hid their weapons in their houses, as they themselves admit, although the mayor had demanded the handing over of weapons. Moreover they had put on civilian clothing.'[149] This last sentence provides the key: the tax officials were probably members of the Garde Civique, as befitted their station as civil servants. In uniform, they ambushed the Uhlans on 16 August. Faced with overwhelming German force (four regiments) five days later, the small Garde Civique unit disbanded and concealed its weapons. Nonetheless, this remains conjecture, for the German inquiry did not mention the Garde Civique.

Incidents such as these are enough to suggest that there were scattered cases of civilians firing. Forensic evidence would be useful in establishing its extent. Yet autopsies were rarely carried out, and in the case of Aarschot, undermined the official case on Colonel Stenger's assassination. If German soldiers were killed or wounded by shotguns, this would indicate that the cause was civilian, not military, fire. A post-war publication tried to establish the incidence of such cases, but apart from the difficulty of distinguishing between the effects of shotguns and splintering from small-arms or artillery fire, it could only report 128 dead or wounded.[150] Legal evidence would also help. Yet the official German publications produced no such material or even the name of a single alleged franc-tireur. The Foreign Ministry prepared a statistical analysis which recorded that in 1914 francs-tireurs had caused 2,656 casualties in Belgium, with 536 officers and men killed.[151] But no evidence was adduced and the analysis was never published. The figure may equally be read as the cost of incidents blamed on francs-tireurs whatever their real cause. German records are thus of limited help in measuring local civilian fighting, while they provide overwhelming proof that organized resistance along the lines of 1870, let alone a state-sponsored *levée en masse*, was a delusion.

The case of Baranzy, however, suggests one further military factor that fostered the franc-tireur myth-complex, namely the Garde Civique. Belgium's small standing army was supplemented by a system which combined something of the modern reserve with the nineteenth-century bourgeois militia, and the even older tradition of the municipal guard. The Garde Civique had two elements, 'active' and 'non-active'. The organization was 'active' in towns with over 10,000 inhabitants and in fortified places. Here, it served a double function as a prestigious institution dominated by middle-class volunteers (it was often an essential stepping-stone in a civil service career), and as a reserve of the standing army. Illustration 5 shows the uniformed Garde Civique of Arlon. The active Garde Civique was organized in sections of infantry, artillery, cavalry, etc., and in wartime operated under military command as part of the army. In 1913, it had 46,000 members.[152]

The Garde Civique was 'non-active' in smaller towns, villages, and the countryside. Here, it was a paper organization. In theory it comprised all men between 20 and 40 and could be mobilized by the Ministry of the Interior in an emergency to support the gendarmerie in maintaining order.

La garde civique active d'Arlon, seule force armée belge du Luxembourg devant la Caserne, août 1914

5   The active Garde Civique of Arlon, August 1914

In reality, since only those who could afford to buy their uniforms were obliged to serve, it too was largely middle-class. On 5 August 1914, about 100,000 men of the non-active Garde Civique were called up by royal decree. Whereas the active Garde Civique fully expected to play a military role, the non-active Garde Civique was assigned to security duties. Yet for several reasons, both bodies were liable to be taken by German soldiers for francs-tireurs.

The rush of volunteers to join the Garde Civique in August 1914 was a powerful expression of Belgian national sentiment, but it overwhelmed the government.[153] In Liège, according to *L'Étoile Belge* there were more than 1,000 applicants per day.[154] The frequently reported shortages of tunics, armbands, and national cockades, which were the identifying garb of the non-active Garde Civique, and the difficulty of procuring sufficient weapons, are clear evidence of this popular self-mobilization. Individuals and some newspapers called for a *levée en masse*.[155] On 4 August, for example, *Le Soir* printed one of 'hundreds' of letters it had received as evidence of the 'national enthusiasm', by a former NCO who longed for francs-tireurs on the model of 1870 in France.[156] *L'Express* of Liège carried an appeal on 5 August under the heading 'Francs-tireurs': 'Walloon Cocks, 50 to 60 years old, are required to form a corps of independent francs-tireurs.'[157]

Although the Belgians had failed by a technical oversight formally to mobilize the active Garde Civique, they communicated its uniforms and distinguishing signs to the German government on 8 August. In any event, the latter knew perfectly well that the Garde Civique formed part of Belgian defence plans. According to the Hague Convention on Land Warfare of 1907, it was also legitimate for the non-active Garde Civique to participate in fighting (although this was not its prescribed role) provided that it bore its weapons openly, was properly commanded, and carried a distinguishing mark, which did not need to be a full uniform. However, the two sides understood militia-style organizations differently. For reasons to be discussed in the next chapter, the German Army was deeply opposed to any quasi-civilian involvement in warfare. Recognition of the Garde Civique was also made difficult by the variable uniforms of the active units and the civilian appearance of the blue tunic and hats worn by the non-active element. Illustration 6 is a rare photograph of a 'non-active' Garde Civique in August 1914, showing how rudimentary the uniforms were and how improvised the weapons.

German troops encountered the active Garde Civique in combat. The civic guards of Liège and Verviers fought under General Leman and indeed were the first to sight the approaching German troops in the night of 5–6 August.[158] Gardes Civiques also fought at Tongeren and elsewhere, and guarded the main river approaches (as at Tamines).[159] Even in open combat, the active Garde Civique was often considered illegitimate by the Germans or simply not distinguished from the civilian population. The Garde Civique briefly defended St Truiden (St Trond), 35 kilometres beyond Liège, against General von der Marwitz's cavalry on 9 August, since the Belgian Army had pulled back to the river Gette. The Germans were furious at the resistance, and at a possible incident in which the Garde Civique mistakenly fired on a group of Germans with a white flag coming to negotiate the town's surrender. When the town fell, the invaders killed 17 inhabitants, and forced the Garde Civique to parade unarmed under threat of the town's destruction before deporting its members.[160] As noted, Marwitz also blamed the Garde Civique in Tongeren for a serious fusillade between German troops on 18 August, and likewise deported its members. This happened at Louvain, too, where the men of the Garde Civique were the first to be deported even though they had been demobilized before the Germans arrived.

The combat role of the non-active Garde Civique is more difficult to assess. It, too, was most likely to occur in the first phase of the invasion,

6 The 'non-active' Garde Civique, August 1914

when the phenomenon of Belgian popular self-mobilization against the invader was at its height and before the ferocity of German reactions was apparent. Initially there was confusion as to whether the non-active Garde Civique was part of the military effort or merely an auxiliary police force, and this may have encouraged local action. However, the more restrictive view speedily won out. The government's circulars of 4 and 5 August spelt out the legal constraints and obligations attached to popular participation in resisting the invasion, including that by the Garde Civique, and the press backed this up. On 7 August, *Le XXe Siècle* felt compelled to remind its readers that: 'Any murder or any attack carried out by individual citizens would lead the German officers *to have innocent victims executed* in the villages where such acts might have been committed.' The military authorities had the sole right of command; the role of civilians was to aid them in every way, but not to engage in fighting, which would be considered acts of banditry.[161] On 8 August *Le Pays Wallon* (Charleroi) and *L'Ami de l'ordre* (Namur) warned civilians not to act in a hostile manner against the enemy troops.[162]

Tielemans, the burgomaster of Aarschot, placarded the walls of the town on 10 August with a reminder that in some villages the citizens had fired at the enemy, calling forth drastic reprisals, and stating that only the army had the right to take up arms against the enemy.[163] The government renewed its warning to the civilian population on 16 August, following it up by large advertisements in the newspapers on 20 August.[164] On 15 August the Ministry of War announced that the non-active Gardes Civiques would not be utilized on combat service but restricted to police duties.[165] This, and corresponding instructions issued by the provincial governors, put an end to its military deployment, and the Garde Civique in the main was quickly disbanded, with some elements being absorbed into the military.[166]

The significance of the Garde Civique should not be exaggerated. It played at most a marginal role in the fighting. It contributed to the German conviction of a franc-tireur war, in that the Germans reconstrued it as francs-tireurs: they were reluctant to recognize the combatant status of the active Garde Civique and took the scattered attacks by units of the non-active Garde Civique – if these occurred – as banditry. Furthermore, after 18 August the Garde Civique was largely disbanded and so could not have occasioned violence against Belgian civilians when this reached its peak during the main invasion. Even during the initial phase, the importance of the Garde Civique is relativized by the example of France. The French also provided for a local security force in time of war, the *gardes civils*, which at the beginning of August 1914 carried out functions similar to those prescribed for the non-active Garde Civique. Admittedly, universal military service enrolled most younger Frenchmen in the army. But in a border region such as the Meurthe-et-Moselle, there was a possibility for the *gardes civils* to clash with German patrols.[167] Neither the Germans nor the French claimed any such occurrence, yet this did not impede the development of a full-blown franc-tireur complex among the German troops. There could be no clearer proof that, whatever was claimed in Germany subsequently, the Garde Civique did not account for German belief in mass civilian resistance during the invasion.

4   The internal dynamic of the franc-tireur fear

Neither predispositions nor military circumstances in 1914 suffice to explain the extraordinary mobilizing force of the franc-tireur myth complex which was driven by a self-reinforcing dynamic. How did this dynamic develop? The myths swiftly spread by rumour and hearsay in the field, were relayed along the routes between the invasion front and the rear, and were embellished from unit to unit. Railway junctions, border crossings, and supply dumps all favoured their dissemination. The outcome amounted to a particularly virulent case of the false rumours that abounded in all belligerent countries at the start of the war.[168]

The franc-tireur myths began in the Liège strike-force, in Marwitz's cavalry corps, in the troops based in the Duchy of Luxemburg, and among those in Alsace-Lorraine who probed into the Meurthe-et-Moselle and repelled the French invasion of Upper Alsace. The long strip of territory from the Rhineland to German Lorraine acted as a hothouse, propagating the complex among the vast influx of soldiers prior to the main invasion. The tales of wounded soldiers from Liège, and the insatiable demand for news, provided fertile soil for this process. The District President of Aachen asked the government on 6 August to deport all Belgians resident there, for 'since the news from Belgium about the hostile behaviour of the population towards our troops, even towards the injured, has come in, anger at Belgium is growing here.'[169] Colonel von Cramon heard while stationed in Luxemburg prior to the invasion that 'the French are very cruel towards the wounded: they stab them.'[170] There were many reports of the enemy perpetrating cruelties, 'which of course increases the rage of our men'.[171] His diction signifies these 'reports' were hearsay, without official standing. As noted, the incidents at Francorchamps and possibly Herve on 8 August were the result of fresh soldiers ready to see francs-tireurs everywhere. The arrival of the 60,000 strong siege-force at Liège from that date, and the onset of the main invasion ten days later, unleashed the fervid imaginings which had built up inside Germany.

The main invasion did not merely disseminate the franc-tireur myths, however, but like a supercharger, added massive power to the complex. It amounted to what for Lefebvre was the defining moment of the Great Fear of 1789, when fear spread fear in a self-reinforcing spiral. As German troops embarked on the invasion, the host of military circumstances already identified was transformed into the belief in a People's War. The resort to violent repression provided confirmation of the myth's apparent truth: burning houses, civilian corpses, and columns of deportees were all so much tangible evidence of the francs-tireurs. The onset of combat and the trauma of firepower often formed the critical moment when the tales became real, and the soldier believed himself to be confronted personally by civilian treachery.

The proliferation of the franc-tireur fear during the ten days it took the invasion force to cross Belgium and the frontier region of France is conveyed by an anonymous Saxon officer of IR 178, who gave a virtual anatomy of the process in his diary, later found by the French. On 8 August, before leaving Germany, the regiment was already being told of the treachery of Belgian civilians towards German soldiers when they were at rest. Nonetheless, crossing into Belgium, the author felt that the population were amicable, with an old woman saying: 'You are not barbarians; you have spared our crops.' By the night of 22–23 August, however, the regiment was near the Meuse and the atmosphere was tense. The diarist noted a house on fire 'doubtless to betray our position', and the following day he was convinced that stiff opposition encountered at Leffe came from francs-tireurs ('we shot all the people who had fired on our men, 16 at a time'). Between Dinant and the frontier, there were tales of civilians resisting or signalling to the French in nearly every village. Civilians were taken hostage, and, as noted, Villers-en-Fagne was burned and civilians shot for having supposedly signalled from the church tower. Approaching the frontier on 26 August, the officer recorded that there were no stragglers 'for fear of francs-tireurs'. He admitted that the first village in the French Ardennes (Gué d'Hossus) was burned down because of an accidental shot by a German soldier. After the burning of Rethel ('frightening but beautiful'), which he attributed to the French, accounts of open combat predominated and there were no further references to francs-tireurs.[172]

Another way of understanding the franc-tireur dynamic is by the emotions which drove it. Fear predominated. Yet fear bred anger. German troops became 'outraged' while still on German soil by tales of civilian resistance. A sergeant in Bavarian Reserve IR 1 recorded the connection between these emotions. While still in German Lorraine on 13 August, he heard that two German units had almost been wiped out in a heavy battle on the frontier. He and his comrades doubted this but not the accompanying story about 'the treason of a priest who had rung bells', the church tower from which unsuspecting German soldiers were attacked with a machine-gun, and the civilians who engaged in fighting: 'Our soldiers were seized with a great rage.'[173] Anger thus discharged extreme emotions of fear resulting from the trauma or even anticipation of battle by being projected onto the chimerical franc-tireur. Civilians in certain circumstances became a scapegoat for the violence of war.

This helps explain the crucial role of panics. These were a simultaneous explosion of anxiety and rage so disorderly that military discipline broke down. Bavarian Infantry Captain von Beckh, who had repeatedly had to warn his men against firing on each other, described how one NCO had 'tears of rage in his eyes' as he retreated in the general panic following the battle of Nancy on 25 August. It was this double impetus of fear and fury that gave rise immediately afterward to the massacre at Lunéville.[174] Actual combat (as at Louvain, Longuyon, and Lunéville) was not necessary. Imaginary combat, as at Aarschot, sufficed to trigger the crisis of discipline, which local commanders had to validate and exorcize through 'reprisals' in order to regain control. The emotional shock of the major panics remained long afterwards, feeding the memory and fostering the myth-complex of the francs-tireurs. The Dutch correspondent, Mokveld, following his investigations at Liège, Visé, and Louvain, commented that:

> These stories [of civilian resistance] emanated from the officers and permeated the rank and file; and the men grew fearfully angry with the Belgians, whom they cursed and abused. It also made the soldiers terribly afraid of francs-tireurs, and I noticed many a time that some loud sound [...] made a whole troop of soldiers jump up, lay hold of their rifles, and hide themselves in an absolute 'blue funk'. The mere noise made them curse and rage and talk of nothing but burning houses.[175]

Mokveld's observation about officers raises an important question – the role of the military command in the proliferation of the franc-tireur myth-complex.[176] The complex was generated essentially from below during the first phase of the invasion, by soldiers in the field, although it is likely that prior warning made them receptive. We have argued that during the main invasion, the part played by the military command became much more pronounced. Protests to the French and Belgian governments, warnings to the invaded populations, orders on how to deal with civilian resistance, and draconian 'punishment' in cases such as Andenne and Tamines, all endorsed the ordinary soldiers' belief in francs-tireurs. The political and military apparatus of the state encouraged the collective delusion of the People's War. Many senior officers clearly believed the essence of the myth-complex, if not every detail. For example, when General von Boehn told an American war correspondent that he saw civilians using machine-guns at Louvain and warned that 'whenever civilians fire upon our troops we will teach them a lasting lesson', there is no reason to suppose that he was deliberately lying.[177]

Yet it is also possible that the franc-tireur war was used manipulatively to ready men for combat. In the case of the Third Army, as we have noted, franc-tireur resistance was anticipated and prepared for. In 1915, a French officer, Lieutenant Loustalot, conducted a remarkable inquiry into the mental and psychological state of 414 officers and men of the XIIth Army Corps who had participated in the attack on Dinant, and who were now prisoners of war in France. This revealed much about how the command structure promoted the franc-tireur mythology. In most cases the German soldiers held the common view that anyone firing at them in Belgium must be civilians and therefore francs-tireurs. Yet almost all those Loustalot interrogated told him that their own experience contradicted this view:

> The population displayed an extremely correct attitude, 'irreproachable', as one of them said, at the start almost friendly. They declared that only towards the end, as from 22 August, as they advanced towards Dinant, and above all after the massacres at Dinant, did they find civilians who were overexcited and openly hostile.[178]

Loustalot argued that the key factor in turning peaceable civilians into fantasy francs-tireurs was manipulation by officers who told the troops that Belgian civilians shot at the Germans, mutilated the wounded, tortured them, cut off their ears, and so forth.[179] 'The alleged hostility of the inhabitants, from the start, was nothing but a pretext destined to mask the worst outrages, coldly conceived and ferociously executed.'[180] The stories of civilian attacks were 'fables', some resulting from rumours, some propagated by the soldiers, most deliberately created by the military command in order to sow terror among the Belgians out of revenge for opposing the plan to invade France. One soldier stated that from the moment of arrival on Belgian territory the commanders warned the men to be on their guard, for the preceding troops had been fired on by the citizens. However, as far as he knew, 'not one civilian ever attacked us.'[181]

The military commanders even staged a scene which, if true, is a classic of manipulation. According to the evidence of two men from different regiments, a car was driven past a large formation of soldiers. At the centre of the formation, a colonel opened the car door, and presented two women dressed as German nuns, who were said to have been odiously mutilated because of their nationality. They showed their wrists covered in bandages. Exploiting the emotions produced by the claim that the nuns' hands had been severed, the colonel warned his men about the brutal people of the country they were about to cross, exhorting them to vengeance.[182]

Loustalot's inquiry suggests that the XIIth Army Corps was so determined not to fall victim to civilian resistance that it systematically prepared an outlook favourable to pre-emptive violence against the population. The question of the German military response to presumed civilian resistance is examined in the next chapter. It is enough here to note that in the case of the Third Army, the myth of the Belgian People's War was inculcated by the officers in their men. The same may have been true more widely.

Although the myth of the franc-tireur began in the army, it extended to the home front. In the build-up to the main invasion, soldiers' tales circulated among civilians and soldiers in the Rhineland and Alsace-Lorraine and were amplified by the press in cities such as Cologne, Metz, and Strasbourg. Two Cologne newspapers, the *Kölnische Zeitung* and the Catholic *Kölnische Volkszeitung*, played a particularly important role, reporting the stories of wounded men who returned from the assault on Liège. Retrospectively the *Kölnische Volkszeitung* became worried by the anti-Catholic tone of the 'Belgian atrocity' stories, and looked critically at how civilians had spread atrocity tales or even helped create them:

> I observed as a silent onlooker on the benches of the boulevards [wrote a reporter] how curious people, men and women, interrogated the wounded, [...] suggesting the answers to their own questions concerning the war's battles, casualties, and atrocities; how they interpreted silence as an affirmative reply and how they looked for confirmation of ever more frightful things. I am convinced that a little later, they repeated the conversation further on, adding that they had heard it all recounted by someone who had been present as his own personal experience.[185]

Such 'witness' accounts were spread by the press, including the *Kölnische Volkszeitung*. The paper had run a series of reports starting on 6 August on the cruelties perpetrated on German civilians in Belgium, especially the 'atrocities' at Antwerp.[184] By 12 August, it was publishing accounts of the franc-tireur war, such as a letter from a soldier to his parents relaying rumours of night attacks by Belgian peasants.[185]

The generally pro-government *Kölnische Zeitung* also retailed atrocity stories though in a less sensationalist manner. After reporting the false tales of maltreated civilians in Antwerp from 6 to 8 August, it switched to

German soldiers on 9 August with a front-page report entitled 'Foul deeds of the Belgian population. Belgian atrocities'. This explained that Germans had been the victims of cruelties and mutilation such as only seen 'in combat with Negroes' in South-West Africa, and had been obliged to burn down houses and entire villages. Other reports in the same issue spoke of Belgian civilians shooting at soldiers from ambush, mutilating the wounded, murdering sleeping soldiers, disregarding Red Cross markings, etc.[186] On 11 August, the paper published an account based on the letters of a soldier who was involved in the rebuffed attack on Liège early in the morning of 6 August. The author described how civilians fired at the troops from the houses, and he himself joined in killing five civilians on 5 August.[187]

The initial press stories thus emanated from the tales of the soldiers themselves, refracted through local hearsay and uncritical journalism. None were inspired by the government. While the military authorities had total control over news reports from the front, in other respects German newspapers were not mouthpieces of official policy. Indeed, by comparison with the Rhineland press, the semi-official *Norddeutsche Allgemeine Zeitung* initially published few allegations of atrocities against German civilians.[188]

Subsequently, the German press gave wide publicity to the official thesis of a People's War, starting with the WTB statement of 9 August. Under the headline 'Franktireurkrieg' this accused the population around Liège of participating in the fighting, firing on troops from behind, and attacking doctors. The French border population was accused of ambushing German patrols. The statement suggested that the franc-tireur war had been prepared in France and Belgium; if this were to be confirmed by the repetition of such events, 'then our enemies have only themselves to blame if the war is waged on the guilty civilian population, too, with ruthless severity. German troops, who are used to maintaining discipline and to wage war only against the armed forces of the enemy state, can hardly be blamed if they give no quarter in justified self-defence.'[189] On 11 August, the Social Democrat national daily, *Vorwärts*, published a communiqué by the Quartermaster-General, von Stein, under the title 'Details of the capture of Liège', according to which the German troops were held up not by the Belgian army, which 'fought badly', but by the nature of the terrain and the 'treacherous participation of the entire population, even the women, in the fighting'. The German press thus endorsed and publicized the General

Staff and Foreign Ministry thesis of an illegitimate People's War waged against the German Army in France and Belgium.

Parallel with this, the press continued to disseminate the franc-tireur myth-complex in a non-official and localized way. Published soldiers' letters became a minor journalistic genre in 1914 and spawned anthologies in book form.[190] The *Leipziger Neueste Nachrichten* published an account of the incidents at Schaffen and nearby Diest, which had the priest of Schaffen executed for firing from the church tower together with four francs-tireurs, and Belgian soldiers escaping from the church at Diest through a secret tunnel.[191] The press also did not shrink from detailing the harsh reprisals being carried out for franc-tireur activity, as this extract from an officer's letter shows, published in the *Deutsche Tageszeitung*:

> We have to shoot practically every town and village to smithereens, as we did yesterday, for civilians, above all women, shoot at the troops as they march past. Yesterday civilians shot at the infantry from the church tower in X. and wiped out half a company of brave soldiers. The civilians were fetched down and executed and the village was shot in flames. A woman chopped off the head of an injured Uhlan. She was caught and had to carry the head to Y., where she was killed. My great men are full of courage. They are ardent for vengeance. They protect their officers, and whenever they catch francs-tireurs etc., they string them up from the roadside trees.[192]

In effect, the press multiplied the audience reached by the franc-tireur myth-complex. Lefebvre showed for the late eighteenth century how the printed word could significantly accelerate and extend the transmission of the Great Fear. How much more was this the case with the popular press in an age of near total literacy. German papers, local and national, acted as an enormous multiplier of the conviction that the German armies faced sustained civilian resistance, spreading it to the entire country in a matter of days. The consequences of this were twofold. First, while newspaper accounts did not create the franc-tireur myth, they were able to reinforce the soldiers' belief in the phenomenon during the main invasion.[193] It was not always easy for the invasion force to receive letters and newspapers. But the men constantly moving up to the front and the endless arrival of supply columns from Germany brought the home-front accounts and official reports of francs-tireurs to the soldiers already in the field. Second, newspapers, along with the return of wounded soldiers to hospitals across Germany, ensured that during the invasion, the franc-tireur myth became a commonplace of the home front as well as the army.

The franc-tireur was thus added by way of the invasion to the spy, saboteur, and Cossack as one of the signifiers of the enemy for Germany. The critical article in the *Kölnische Volkszeitung* to which we have already referred considered that by mid-September exaggerated tales of the People's War had reached the furthest corners of German society. Van Langenhove felt this to be the 'final stage of their elaboration and the completion of their diffusion. They spread equally to the depths of the towns and the most remote countryside, to educated circles and to the popular classes.'[194] Cheap postcards and prints popularized the image of the evil franc-tireur. Quality magazines and middle-class periodicals expatiated on the theory and iniquity of the People's War. The illustrated weekly *Die Gartenlaube* ('The Garden Bower'), for example, published an article in early September on 'Franktireure'. The author demonstrated the accepted wisdom in Germany that civilian resisters forfeited their rights and deserved harsh punishment. He defined two types of francs-tireurs in the Franco-Prussian War: those organized into regular units, and civilians who participated in fighting in a 'disloyal way'. The former was an open and 'loyal' fighter, the latter a cowardly murderer who deserved the 'harshest and most terrifying penalties, such as execution of the culprits and burning of their houses'. The author concluded that the prevalence of universal military service in Europe made any kind of irregular warfare redundant.[195]

The franc-tireur myth was reinforced by fictional accounts. The *Illustrirte Zeitung* carried a novella in late August 1914 about a franc-tireur attack in the Franco-Prussian War which contained many elements of the current mythology:[196] two cavalry officers are welcomed by a Marquis to spend the night in his château, they are given a good meal and good wine, the seductive Marquise makes advances to the first-person narrator, and at the moment of greatest erotic tension there is a well-planned franc-tireur attack. The village and the château are burned down, and no prisoners are taken, for 'it was no honest war in this night, but the struggle of wild animals for life and death.'

A final proof of the strength of the franc-tireur dynamic comes from its influence on the strategic calculations of the military command. The German race towards the English Channel in September 1914 was held up, among other reasons, by the delayed arrival of the Bavarian troops. Because of the perceived danger of saboteurs and francs-tireurs in Belgium, trains stopped at every signal and drivers had to change points themselves. General Krafft von Dellmensingen, Chief of Staff of the Sixth Army, noted after the Marne that the prospects for Germany were uninviting, for the Entente had access to colonies and world markets while Germany was cut off from world trade, with a hostile Belgium in the rear: 'On the front we cannot allow anything to happen, otherwise we will have a popular uprising in the rear, cutting our lines, and it will not be easy to suppress it.'[197] The franc-tireur therefore signalled the potential danger for Germany of extended occupation of enemy territory when the Schlieffen Plan had failed and a long war loomed.

The myth of the francs-tireurs amounted to a unified complex, which operated in three dimensions. First, a set of fictional representations of the enemy crystallized in the first few days of war from the anxiety and shock provoked by the first engagements. The resulting false rumours and tales furnished the content of the myth-complex, portraying the enemy as the exact opposite of the German soldier and the qualities he embodied. The myth content could not survive, however, without reinforcement from the circumstances of the invasion, which provided the second dimension. The Schlieffen Plan, the traumatic experience of modern firepower, and the exhaustion and nervousness of troops in a hostile land, were among the factors that fed the myth — whose reductivist logic made francs-tireurs a scapegoat for the soldiers' own anxieties and shaky discipline. A third dimension was the energy supplied by the collective delusion itself. This provided the inner dynamic of the myth-complex. As Lefebvre pointed out for the comparable phenomenon in 1789, the defining feature of the franc-tireur fear of 1914 was its capacity to convince large numbers of people that something which was an illusion was actually happening. Of course, there were sceptics. But enough soldiers and decision-makers were convinced, or found it useful to be convinced, for the delusion to affect the entire command structure of the most powerful army in Europe. This dynamic, moreover, extended beyond the military domain and made the franc-tireur mythology one expression of the larger war trauma of German society.

The evolution of the phenomenon is explained by the interaction of all three dimensions. It is possible that the internal dynamic of the myth-complex weakened after the paroxysm of the ten or twelve days after 18 August, as some officers and men grew more sceptical of false rumours and fear of civilians became less contagious. Yet the nature of the fighting also changed, with the confrontation on the Marne and subsequent German retreat. So, too, did the character of the civilian population encountered by German troops, which contained fewer adult males. The net effect was a change in the tempo and intensity of the franc-tireur myth-complex in September. Yet the change should not be exaggerated. The factors which produced the delusion that the French and Belgian populations had risen *en masse* against the invasion in August remained powerful enough to sustain it throughout the entire invasion zone until the end of mobile warfare in October.

4   Memories, mentalities, and the German response to the 'franc-tireur war'

The power and coherence of a myth-complex like that of the *Franktireurkrieg* in 1914 depended on the longer-term mentalities that furnished its imagery and language as much as on the immediate circumstances that gave rise to it. The same is true of the nature of the German army's harsh response to the franc-tireur war, which had its roots in the army's pre-war mentalities, doctrines, and socialization, and ultimately in the dominant political culture of the *Kaiserreich*.

1   Memories of 1870 and the laws of war

The memory of the Franco-Prussian War was formative for the German military down to 1914. Not only had the war given birth to the new nation-state and consolidated the army's prestige in a conservative political system, it also served as a model of what modern warfare conducted by a professionally officered army entailed. If proud regimental identities and strategic lessons for the future were nourished by the memory of 1870 and embodied in the teachings of the General Staff, the *levée en masse* decreed by the new French Republican government (above all the guerrilla warfare conducted by francs-tireurs) was the unacceptable alter ego of the nation in arms. What should be more natural than to assume that since the enemy in 1914 was the same (plus French-dominated Belgium), the war might be fought in a similar manner?

Even before the final surrender of the armies of the French Empire at Metz in October 1870, irregular units, raised as a temporary expedient, had begun harassing the German invaders. The military effort of the new Republic was ideologically inspired by the French Revolution. The term by which the irregulars became known, francs-tireurs, went back to 1792, when a succession of irregular forces and volunteer levies (also known as *corps francs*) had been raised to supplement the army in the opening campaign of the revolutionary wars.[1] The Convention's declaration in 1793 of a compulsory *levée en masse* amounted to the first, hesitant attempt to introduce the principle of universal military service as the corollary of democratic citizenship. The spirit of the volunteer – the self-motivated citizen defending nation and Revolution – remained central to the idealized mythology of the French *levée en masse*.[2] In early November 1870, the Republican government of national defence under Gambetta directly invoked this Revolutionary precedent and decreed a *levée en masse* as the basis of the Republican army. Existing franc-tireur formations and national guard units were incorporated into the new army.[3] The centrality of the citizen volunteer to this new *levée en masse* (which the Republic was in no position to enforce) was symbolized by Garibaldi, hero of Italian unification, who commanded a unit fighting for the French Republic in 1870 and appealed to 'volunteers' and 'francs-tireurs' to constitute the 'Armed Nation'.[4]

Despite the gulf between rhetoric and reality, a feeling of national and Republican identity undoubtedly emerged.[5] Consequently, the Prussians were confronted by a second phase of the war from October 1870 to January 1871 during which, in addition to the siege of Paris, they faced a Republican army in the field and met considerable resistance from irregulars and francs-tireurs. In total, there were 300 franc-tireur units, with some 57,600 members.[6] To defeat this 'People's War', Moltke ordered drastic measures of repression. Civilian resisters and the francs-tireurs were considered to be illegal and 'treacherous', although the regular armies levied by the Republic were given legal recognition.

Moltke issued instructions to safeguard the railways which included 'harsh reprisals against those villages near which any kind of disturbance of rail transport occurred'; in cases of frequent disturbance the mayor or other local notables were to be placed as hostages on the locomotives.[7] Where civilians actively resisted, contributions were to be exacted from the community, and in the case of large-scale participation the entire village was to be destroyed.[8] Such orders gave rise to widespread random violence against uninvolved civilians. On the Loire, collective reprisals for franc-tireur action became commonplace. On the night of 7–8 October, for example, the town of Ablis, near Orléans, was razed and its male inhabitants killed in reprisal for an attack by irregulars. At Varice, also near

Orléans, ten francs-tireurs were shot when they surrendered after engaging the First Bavarian Corps for three hours.[9] In one of the worst incidents, at Fontenoy-sur-Moselle on 22 January 1871, 400 francs-tireurs wearing rudimentary uniforms attacked a German infantry post, whereupon outraged men of Prussian IR 57 burned the village as they retook it, bayoneting the inhabitants and throwing them into the flames. Moltke ordered Landwehr battalions to carry out executions at Fontenoy, and that 10 million francs be exacted from the nearby town of Toul.[10]

This behaviour by the German armies (Bavarian as well as Prussian) was at one level an operational response to irregular warfare. Although only about 1,000 soldiers were lost to francs-tireurs, perhaps a quarter of the German troops in France were deployed in protecting the communications lines on which the irregulars preyed.[11] But it was also a political response to the Republican phase of the war, which both Moltke and Bismarck found deeply distasteful. In their eyes, the Republic refused to accept the defeat of Napoleon III's armies in conventional battle, encouraged a treacherous style of combat reminiscent of the revolutions of 1848, including ambush, street-fighting, and barricades, and so created a new and negative image of the enemy as an insurrectionary civilian.[12] Such warfare seemed to be inspired by the very essence of Republicanism. Moltke summed up these objections in a letter in late October 1870:

> The [Republican] government still tries [...] to rouse the unfortunate population of the provinces to a new resistance, to put down which will entail the destruction of whole towns. Then, too, the nagging of the francs-tireurs has to be paid for by bloody reprisals, and the character of the war becomes ever more vindictive. It is bad enough that armies sometimes have to butcher one another; there is no necessity for setting whole nations against each other – that is not progress, but rather a return to barbarism. How little can even the *levée en masse* of a nation, even so brave a one as this, do against a never so small but well-trained division of troops! Our liberals, who preach the arming of the people, should see its success in this campaign.[13]

Bismarck also condemned insurrectionary warfare. 'Our men are quick at shooting, but not at executing', he complained, demanding that all villages where there was 'treason' should be burned down and all the men hanged.[14] This view of civilian involvement in combat and the appropriate military response became dominant in German military thinking between 1870 and 1914. As the military theorist, Julius von Hartmann, summed it up: 'Where the People's War breaks out, terrorism becomes a principle of military necessity.'[15]

In military circles, the memory of the francs-tireurs and the Republican war of 1870 was transmitted across the intervening period in a variety of ways. Personal experience was one. Senior commanders in their sixties and seventies in 1914 had served as young officers in 1870–1. The commander of the Third Army in August 1914, Colonel-General von Hausen, for example, frequently recollected his own experiences in the Franco-Prussian War.[16] Colmar von der Goltz, born 1843, who was named governor-general of Belgium by the Kaiser in August 1914 and participated in the fighting at the front, had served as a staff officer in the Franco-Prussian war.[17] General von Einem, Minister of War from 1898 to 1909, successor of Hausen in September 1914 as commander of the Third Army, had won the Iron Cross as a 17-year-old lieutenant in the Franco-Prussian War, in which he was active in combating francs-tireurs.[18] General von Emmich, born in 1848, served in the army from 1866 and also won the Iron Cross in the war of 1870–1.[19]

More important than biographical continuity was the resonance of such recollections within the institutional memory of the army and officer training schools. It is not possible here to reconstruct the oral story-telling and reminiscences with which young recruits and cadets were instructed and entertained.[20] But something can be gleaned from the memoirs, histories, and works on military doctrine written by soldiers, many of which enjoyed broad public recognition. Moltke remained a towering influence on the German General Staff long after his death in 1891, not least on his nephew, Moltke the younger, Chief of Staff until the debacle of the Marne. Moltke the elder's history of the Franco-Prussian War and his published correspondence covering the period were widely read. He placed great emphasis on the resistance of francs-tireurs both in the east and on the Loire.[21] Moltke also tended to devalue the regular Republican army while exaggerating the role of the francs-tireurs, as in the advance of the Prussian forces on Orléans, in December 1870, which was hindered by the hostile population sniping at cavalry patrols.[22] This tendency to contrast the fanaticism of self-recruited irregulars with the inefficiency of professional French soldiers left its mark on German responses in 1914.

General Hans von Kretschman's war letters from 1870–1, which by 1911 were on their twelfth edition, provide another example of the detestation of the franc-tireur by the German officer corps. Among them was this letter to his wife:

> You are wrong about the francs-tireurs. In international law only he has the right to be treated according to the customs of war who acts according to the customs of war. If I hide behind a tree, in civilian clothing, shoot dead an officer passing by, hide the shotgun, and then come out of the woods as if nothing had happened, then I am no soldier, but a murderer. The francs-tireurs are associations of men not in uniform, who have come together on their own account to organize treacherous murder.[23]

As early as August 1870 Kretschman described how the activities of civilian resisters necessitated harsh reprisals, including the razing of villages from which they fired.[24]

One of the most revealing and influential military writers between the two wars was Colmar von der Goltz, who served in both. At the time, he wrote to his mother describing how the new French government had fomented insurrection: 'The poor people! ... [The francs-tireurs] shoot at our soldiers with old shotguns to defend their villages. They don't do any damage. But they are ruthlessly executed if they are caught gun in hand.' He also reflected on the devastating consequences of the war, remarking to his wife: 'Who would have thought this war would last so long? It has become a People's War, and its end cannot be forecast even today. But it is rapidly destroying the country.'[25] Yet in 1877, Goltz published a book on Gambetta's armies which hazarded the argument that if ever Germany were to suffer a defeat such as that of the French at Sedan, it would need to find an equivalent to the French Republican leader and his policies. Von der Goltz's reflections were not popular and he found himself transferred to a small garrison in Thuringia.[26] The German army's opinion of the *levée en masse* was characterized rather by loathing of irregular and insurrectionary combat which menaced the conventional understanding of warfare as a professional activity. This was the view that Goltz took in his semi-official work which was immensely influential among junior officers, *The Nation in Arms*, first published in 1883.[27] As military governor of Belgium, von der Goltz approved of deterrence against insurrectionary warfare, remarking on 18 September 1914 that the reason why Brussels was so safe and quiet, despite the relative weakness of the German garrison, was the shock the population had felt at the destruction of Louvain.[28]

The issues posed by the Franco-Prussian War emerged in another domain, that of international law on war. The view expressed on the German side in 1870 that if the *levée en masse* was legal but reprehensible, guerrilla warfare was illegal and immoral, presupposed legal as well as moral norms. In the wake of the American Civil War and the Franco-Prussian War, the rather indeterminate nature of international law on war as a whole was defined more tightly in a series of international conferences, notably at Brussels in 1874 and The Hague in 1899 and 1907. These meetings, and the fruit they bore in the Hague Conventions of 1899 and 1907, represented a major attempt to codify war and, in line with late nineteenth-century humanitarian sensibilities, make it less barbarous.[29] Although a huge range of topics was covered, like a leitmotiv through the discussions on the conduct of war ran the determination of the politically conservative great powers, Russia and Germany, to proscribe or at least restrict the *levée en masse* and irregular warfare that had characterized the French Republican effort in 1870. Ranged against them were the small powers without a large standing army (The Netherlands, Switzerland, and Belgium), backed by Britain, which pressed with equal determination to have the *levée en masse* officially recognized.[30]

The only prior guidance on this issue came from the American Civil War, which saw the first code of military conduct governing relations between soldiers and civilians (the Lieber Code). This authorized properly constituted *corps francs* to resist an invasion though not to contest an occupation. At Brussels, the Russian delegation tried to ban any volunteer force or militia not subject to national military command and place the obligation on the invaded population to 'act in conformity with the laws and usages of war, so as to prevent the struggle becoming cruel and barbarous'. The smaller powers, which wanted to keep the option of a *levée en masse* in case of invasion by the armies of large nations based on universal conscription, objected, and succeeded in having an article passed at Brussels which was later incorporated into the Hague Conventions of 1899 and 1907, stating: 'The population of a non-occupied territory who, on the approach of the enemy, of their own accord take up arms to resist the invading troops, without having time to organize themselves [...] shall be considered as belligerents, if they respect the laws and customs of war.'[31]

At the Hague conference in 1899, the Belgian delegate, Beernaert, with British and Swiss support, endorsed the right of popular resistance, expressing the logic of the *levée en masse*: 'If warfare is reserved exclusively for states and if the citizens are mere spectators, does one not thus lame the force of resistance, does one not thus deprive patriotism of its effectiveness? Is it not the first duty of the citizen to defend his fatherland?'[32] The Germans and Russians voiced strong criticism, arguing that popular uprisings were generally unsuccessful and provoked barbarous warfare. Colonel Gross von Schwarzhoff, the German delegate, considered the aim of the whole exercise to ensure that 'the population shall remain peaceful'. Against the right of civilians to resist, he pitted the rights of the invading soldiers to secure their rear and enjoy peace after open combat. 'Since we are speaking of humanity,' he stated, 'it is time to remember that soldiers are also men, and have a right to be treated with humanity. Soldiers who, exhausted [...] after a long march or a battle, come to rest in a village have a right to be sure that the peaceful inhabitants shall not change suddenly into furious enemies.' If civilians resisted, Schwarzhoff maintained, they forfeited any claim to be treated as combatants according to the laws of war. He declared that the Brussels provision endorsed at The Hague, by which a population openly resisting invasion might enjoy combatant status, marked the extreme limit of the German concessions.[33]

Faced with deadlock, and despite moral support from the French and Belgians, the Swiss and British withdrew their resolutions.[34] In 1907, the German delegation tried to strengthen its position by requiring irregular forces to communicate their uniforms or distinctive signs to potential enemy powers in advance, again to curb a spontaneous *levée en masse*, but on strenuous French objection the proposal fell. Hence, the 1899 definition of combatant status remained more or less intact as Article 2 of 'Hague Convention IV Respecting the Laws and Customs of War on Land', although the Germans managed to get amendments accepted stating that irregular forces had to bear arms openly. According to Article 1, militia and volunteer corps had to be under responsible command, have a distinct emblem, carry arms openly, and observe the laws of war. Article 2 repeated the provision of the 1899 Convention providing for the right to a spontaneous *levée en masse* in the case of an invasion. Further articles of Hague Convention IV forbade pillage, punishment of innocent individuals (and by implication hostage-taking and human shields), and the deliberate destruction of historic buildings and cultural monuments (see appendix 2).

The international debate thus turned on the irreconcilable differences between potential invaders with large armies and smaller powers reliant on an improvised *levée en masse* for resisting aggression. Yet the memory of franc-tireur warfare of 1870–1 is not sufficient to explain the quasi-allergic overreaction of the German army to the idea of popular war. For the

Germans (and possibly the Russians) there was a deeper connection between war and politics. The condemnation of the 'People's War' involved suppressing one strand of German historical memory in favour of another. There was nothing intrinsic to militias or improvised civilian involvement in warfare that linked these exclusively to revolutionary and democratic forms of politics, as in the French *levée en masse*. During the Napoleonic wars, the French were resisted by traditionalist guerrilla fighters in the Austrian Tyrol, southern Italy, and Spain. More importantly, Prussia, reeling under the annihilation of its army by Napoleon at Jena in 1806, had to embark on a sweeping programme of civil and military reform which included a variant of the *levée en masse*, for which none other than Clausewitz called. Planned in secret since 1807, the new military organization sprang into being in 1813 with the Prussian campaign against the French following Napoleon's defeat in Russia.[35]

The war effort declared by Friedrich-Wilhelm III had several elements, including regularly established volunteer units and a militia (the Landwehr) attached to the army. However, the King also called for a *Volkskrieg*, or popular insurrection, against the French, conducted by the Landsturm, or local defence force. This was tantamount to guerrilla warfare. Apart from armbands for captains and lieutenants there were no uniforms, for these 'would make the *Landstürmer* recognizable', nor were there flags or prescribed weapons.[36]

Even at the time this was controversial. The conservative elites were sceptical as to the legality and desirability of such a *Volkskrieg*. Conventional military success made the *Volkskrieg* unnecessary, and the declaration was withdrawn. The Landsturm became little more than a paper organization.[37] Once the reaction set in after 1815, it was reorganized as the reserve of the Landwehr and the two bodies were brought under permanent military control, diluting their civilian character. Nonetheless, the revival of the demand for a civilian militia by the left in the 1848 Revolution and the humiliation suffered by Friedrich-Wilhelm IV and his army in that year were a trauma with long-term consequences for the German military. The absorption of the Landwehr into the standing army and the elimination of its civilian character were central to the larger political crisis that Bismarck resolved through the reunification of Germany by military means, culminating in the Franco-Prussian war.[38]

Thus, the question of civilian participation in warfare was largely solved through an army based on short-term universal military service but firmly under the control of the professional officer corps – the army as 'school of the nation'. The alternative models evoked dangerous political ideologies, such as Republicanism and revolution. What remained was a deep suspicion in the new *Kaiserreich* of anything associated with popular war, as von der Goltz discovered with his book on Gambetta. The *Volkskrieg* was a skeleton in the German army's cupboard, of which the ideas defended by the smaller powers in the Hague conferences were an uncomfortable reminder.

The question remained of how the German army would accommodate itself to the dominant trend in international law. Signatories were required to publish Hague Convention IV on Land Warfare officially (in Germany's case, in the Reich gazette in 1910) and inform their armies on the conventions.[39] An early answer came with the publication by the War Historical Department of the General Staff in 1902 (after the first Hague conference) of the *Kriegsbrauch im Landkriege*, known in English as the *German War Book*.[40] The *War Book* recognized on the one hand that a 'limitation in the use of certain methods of war and a total renunciation of the use of others' was advisable: 'Chivalrous feelings, Christian thought, higher civilization and, by no means least of all, the recognition of one's own advantage, have led to a voluntary and self-imposed limitation, the necessity of which is today tacitly recognized by all States and their armies.' On the other hand, it claimed that most attempts during the nineteenth century to codify warfare had 'completely failed'. The implication was that the German army should rely not on written international agreements, but reciprocity and custom. In fact, the Prussian General Staff felt the codification of the principles of humanity in warfare conflicted with its own concept of war:

But since the tendency of thought of the last century was dominated essentially by humanitarian considerations which not infrequently degenerated into sentimentality and flabby emotion there have not been wanting attempts to influence the development of the usages of war in a way which was in fundamental contradiction with the nature of war and its object.[41]

The German officer therefore had to 'guard himself against excessive humanitarian notions', and to learn that 'certain severities are indispensable to war, nay more, that the only true humanity very often lies in a ruthless application of them.'[42]

The *War Book* was particularly concerned with the issue of combatant status. It quoted from a German regulation in the war of 1870–1 which made prisoner of war status conditional on proof of identity as an enemy soldier. Although it conceded something to the trend in international law by omitting the need for public authorization of irregular units, it insisted that the latter must be openly recognizable as a military force. When discussing the francs-tireurs of the Franco-Prussian war, the *War Book* described the absence of the red armlet or the concealing of weapons as 'offences'.[43] In other words, shots fired by irregular troops from ambush would disqualify them as legitimate combatants. Since this was the prevailing view of German military law, it is no wonder that in 1914 unidentified shots were so often attributed to concealed weapons which, by definition, came from illegal francs-tireurs. John H. Morgan, professor of constitutional law at the university of London, who published the *Kriegsbrauch* in English in 1915, concluded that it flatly contradicted Article 2 of Hague Convention IV on Land Warfare. After the First World War, German apologists minimized the importance of the *Kriegsbrauch*, portraying it as an unofficial publication with a low circulation.[44] However, this was not the view held before the war. One of Germany's leading international lawyers, Christian Meurer, stated in 1907 that it was an authoritative statement of the laws of war by the body responsible for conduct in war; he also regretted that it did not integrate the Hague Convention.[45]

The issuing of the *Felddienstordnung* (field service regulations) in 1908, after the second Hague conference, demonstrated conclusively that the German army had no intention of accepting the provisions of Convention IV in spirit or in letter.[46] Not only did they receive no mention (although reference was made to the Geneva Convention of 1906), but the *Felddienstordnung* stated that preventive security measures were justified against possible attack by enemy civilians, including 'threatening the inhabitants with penalties, arresting hostages, lighting the streets with torches or lights in the windows, keeping the houses open, etc.'[47]

In effect, the right of civilians to resist was denied by the General Staff, despite German endorsement of Hague Convention IV. True, the latter was attached as an appendix to the *Felddienstordnung* in 1911.[48] But since the text of 1908 was not altered, it is hardly surprising that the conduct of German troops and their officers in 1914 showed little respect for anything resembling an insurrectionary *levée en masse*. On the contrary, German officers were trained to expect civilian resistance in a coming war and treat it as criminal. Major Georg von Mücke, who had attended the War Academy in Berlin from 1912 to 1914, the elite officer college from which the top graduates joined the General Staff, confirmed this.[49] In several different classes – Russian language, tactics, and strategy – the question of how to treat enemy troops was discussed. It was stressed that an enemy who carried weapons openly, wore recognizable insignia, and respected the customs of war (as specified by Article 1 of Hague Convention IV) was to be recognized as a combatant. Germany's own railway protection force, which wore civilian clothing but also insignia recognizable at a distance, and carried its weapons openly, was taken as an example. However, the War Academy also taught that Article 2 of the Convention 'did not comply with the German viewpoint, since it opened the door to franc-tireur war and permits the most impudent evasion of the previous article'.[50] In other words, the German army selectively interpreted the clauses of the Hague Convention to suit its own doctrine on civilian involvement.

Pre-war German military manuals confirm this picture. The expectation was that the opposing army would be encountered in open countryside or forests, because towns and villages offered little protection against modern artillery and infantry.[51] A manual on how to command an army corps, published in 1910, assumed that the enemy population would participate in fighting and rise up in insurrection in towns.[52] All its set tasks were drawn from the Franco-Prussian War, but based in the imaginary present, using modern weapons and communications (e.g. radio, bicycles, motor vehicles, and improved railways). The population in Alsace-Lorraine was held to be hostile, and the army was expected to clear everything out of its way, 'whether enemy troops or inhabitants' with 'maximum energy'.[53] Other tasks imagined the inhabitants shooting at the troops at Bensdorf, for which houses were burned down and hostages taken. The population of Saarburg, German Lorraine, it was imagined, would rise up against German rule as the French army approached.[54]

General Friedrich von Bernhardi, one of the authors of the *Felddienstordnung* and later notorious as the author of the bellicose *Deutschland und der nächste Krieg* (*Germany and the Next War*), also wrote an official manual on cavalry tactics and training.[55] In this, he instructed the cavalry to expect hostile acts by civilians in enemy territory, including ambushes, and warned them they would confront *Freischaren* (literally freeshooters, a synonym for francs-tireurs).[56]

A manual on tactics made similar use of examples from the Franco-Prussian War to illustrate the dangers posed by francs-tireurs and the need for ruthless measures.[57] Neither this nor another manual for the use of officers in training recruits made mention of the Hague Conventions, the latter manual stating bluntly: 'Francs-tireurs are strung up on the next best tree without further ado.'[58]

The same points are tellingly illustrated by a French language textbook for German officers of 1906, which provided the useful French sentence: 'Francs-tireurs are placed outside the law and shot when they are captured.' The manual even suggested (also in French): 'Since several assassinations have been committed by francs-tireurs who are hidden in the nearby woods, I order as follows: "1. Every individual encountered in the interior of the forests and woods will be considered a franc-tireur and treated accordingly."'[59] A copy of this or a similar phrase-book appears to have been found by the French in the possession of a captured German NCO in 1914–15.[60] Another handbook for young officers to prepare them for entrance to the War Academy included among the French texts to be translated an extract from a French elementary school textbook: a 'patriotic' tale from the Franco-Prussian War about a woman who takes revenge on the Germans, killing four Uhlans, because her father, husband, and son had all been executed as francs-tireurs.[61]

The opinion of senior military figures confirms that the hostility to insurrectionary and irregular warfare formulated in official military doctrine expressed deeply held beliefs. Colmar von der Goltz dismissed the 1907 Hague Convention as hypocrisy, since the signatory nations 'behave as if they were serious about the silly negotiations and agreements, while each is aware that they have no intention of sticking to them'. The international aspirations to peace were simply evidence of these nations' moral and military decay.[62] The veneration afforded to General von Schlieffen as architect of the invasion plan of 1914 made his thoughts on civilian resistance authoritative. In late 1912, shortly before his death, Schlieffen emphasized to his successors the importance of the Landwehr and Landsturm, which were to follow the active formations because 'the whole of the enemy's country behind the fighting forces would remain in rebellion and a state of war.'[63]

On the eve of the Great War the journal published by the General Staff summed up the German army's doctrine on insurrectionary warfare by recalling the francs-tireurs of 1870–1. It portrayed them as the antithesis of the German soldier, for they frequently had a criminal attitude, insulted and even attacked their officers, and carried out robbery, theft and murder. Their value in regular combat was low, for they ran away after the first shots were fired. The author conceded, however, that they found support everywhere, were useful in reconnaissance, sabotage, and ambushing weak German forces, and he expressed fear of their mobility and flexibility.[64] He cited Moltke's speech to the Reichstag of 1874 on the francs-tireurs, saying that their activities 'lent our warfare a harshness which we regret, but could not alter'.[65] The readers of the journal – the German officer corps – were thus reminded that the francs-tireurs' illegality was beyond question.

The memory of 1870 of course extended far beyond the army. In addition to memoirs and military theory, fictional accounts of the Franco-Prussian War constituted a flourishing popular genre which also preserved and transmitted the francs-tireurs as symbols of French treachery.[66] At the time of the war, the popular author, Friedrich Gerstäcker, devoted an entire novel to the topic, *Die Franctireurs*.[67] The book included many of the essential elements of the stereotype of 1870–1, including the indiscipline, colourful uniforms, cowardly ambushes, and illegitimacy, and hence justified executions of captured francs-tireurs. In another story, Gerstäcker described a series of incidents in the village of Courcelles in which civilians, egged on by their priests, ambushed soldiers and mutilated the wounded and dying. The punishments were described with obvious relish: one old woman was beaten and kicked to death, and another dragged behind a cart until dead. 'This seems to have been a salutary shock to the population, for no more of such horrible deeds have occurred in the last few weeks.'[68] The moral was clear: French civilians could be expected to act treacherously, and the only effective answer was brutal revenge.

The franc-tireur of 1870 was still a familiar stereotype four decades later. In 1912 another popular author, Walter Bloem, published a novel under the title *Volk wider Volk* ('People against People'), set in the Franco-Prussian War. In it he described an encounter with francs-tireurs.

The francs-tireurs ran for their lives … Then one of them stumbled [… and] a second later Georg's black horse shot past the body on the ground – only a swipe of his sword hit the raised arm, behind which was an ugly face with a staring expression of fury and fear of death … It was a woman […] Now all three were tied together with a strap, the young lady and the two pests; then they had to run along at a fast trot, tongues hanging out, if they did not want to be dragged to death … And the

Uhlans were not sparing with thumps, kicks, blows to the neck with the lance-shaft ... the woman also got her share... One had long since forgotten how to distinguish between human beings and animals ... a captured enemy was no more than a wild, vicious beast ...[69]

Another novel published in 1906 under the title '1906: The Collapse of the Old World' described a future war between Britain and Germany in which the German invasion of Belgium faced a socialist insurrection by the workers of Charleroi.[70]

None of this is meant to suggest that German memory of the war of 1870–1 or German views on the kind of warfare deemed legitimate were monolithic. The popularity of the journal *Simplicissimus*, renowned for its satires of the military, or the anti-militarist campaigns of the Social Democratic Party, suffice to show that there were many critical views of German 'militarism' inside Germany.[71] Indeed, public outrage at the army's harsh conduct towards civilians in Alsace in 1913, in the Zabern affair, which isolated the army and the government, demonstrated the divisiveness of this issue.[72] The urban proletariat expressed scant respect for the military and criticized the government's aggressive foreign policy.[73] Nevertheless, certain stereotypes of the enemy civilian and illegitimate warfare, reaching back to the franc-tireur episode of 1870, were present not just within the army but more broadly. In the circumstances of a new war, they could rapidly resurface to define the enemy anew.

2   German nationalism: externalizing the enemy within

Anticipation of civilian resistance was not the only factor that predisposed the German military to a collective delusion in 1914. Broader mentalities and specific ideologies encouraged this receptivity. By 'mentalities' we mean cultural values and beliefs such as religious affiliation, regional feeling, or attitudes to violence, which were rarely expressed systematically or formally.[74] These occupied one end of a spectrum at the other end of which stood more explicit political ideologies such as nationalism or Social Darwinism. Both types of cultural construct helped infuse the figure of the enemy franc-tireur with beliefs drawn from pre-war German society.

In a mass army of conscripts, reservists, and career soldiers, the variety of cultural traditions and political views was huge. The values of the officer corps, however, were those which dominated. Reflecting the nature of the state, they were broadly authoritarian and nationalist, although not aligned with the views of any one party. While Social Democratic and pacifist views could not be totally excluded from the army, they were banned in published form and their influence was restricted. The outlook governing military behaviour towards enemy civilians was formed both by the officer corps' memory of the Franco-Prussian War and by a militarist nationalism which stressed the role of war and the importance of military preparation. This nationalism derived not merely from aristocratic Prussian conservatism but from a self-confident middle class which fashioned a new German identity through the *Kaiserreich*. Militarist nationalism had considerable mobilizing capacity in domestic politics. It was exclusive in its vision of the nation (with Socialists and Catholics presented as anti-national minorities), and was influenced by Social Darwinism and Pan-Germanism.[75]

Social Darwinism – the application of Darwin's theories of evolution and natural selection to human society and international relations – was not the sole property of the right-wing nor always embraced by the latter. It could be used to argue that war was negative selection, the elimination of the fittest. Yet it remained powerfully attractive to those who sought to justify war.[76] The Social Darwinism which coloured the outlook of the officer corps was associated with the views held by the Pan-German movement, which wielded an influence far greater than suggested by its relatively small membership. According to Roger Chickering, Pan-Germanism consisted of a closed world-view split between fearful images of the enemy on the one hand, and a glorification of 'Germanness' on the other.[77] The paranoid kernel of this world-view was an elevated ideal of the collective German self and a rejection of all the negative elements of German society, such as 'anti-national' minorities, which were projected onto an image of the enemy to be combated and persecuted.[78] The enemy was both internal, ever ready to betray the nation, and external, threatening Germany with 'encirclement'. Fear of 'encirclement' gripped not only Pan-Germans and the right-wing opposition but also key decision-makers before 1914.[79] In many ways, the Pan-Germans anticipated the polarized outlook produced more generally by the war, which linked the internal and external enemy. War was the obvious medium of international politics for Pan-Germanism because it promised to purge domestic as well as international society in a Darwinian struggle.

Bernhardi illustrates the force of such assumptions. As noted, he had considerable influence in the officer corps; and although he was not yet a

Pan-German when he wrote *Germany and the Next War*, he proclaimed that the German people was 'justified in competing for domination of the earth', and asserted that 'strength is the highest right and the legal dispute will be decided by the measure of strength, war, which always decides biologically, and therefore fairly.' Bernhardi's bellicose Social Darwinism, his predictions of a three-front war against France, Britain, and Russia, and his demands for a forward colonial policy and rapid rearmament, corresponded fully with the programme of the Pan-Germans, as their newspaper acknowledged.[80] Similar ideas were advanced by Heinrich Claß, chairman of the Pan-German League, in his book *Wenn ich der Kaiser wär* ('If I were the Kaiser'), published in 1912. Claß demanded the formation of a greater Germanic Reich, abolition of the elected Reichstag, and a renewed anti-Socialist law. In common with Bernhardi, he proclaimed the intention in a coming war to impose a crushing defeat on France, to annihilate it.[81]

By 1913, despite government disapproval of such unrestrained bellicosity, militarist nationalism exercised considerable influence, especially in the army. Appreciative responses to 'If I were the Kaiser' came from officers of all ranks.[82] The Pan-German League's members were drawn principally from the educated middle class and local Protestant elites, including the officer corps in garrison towns.[83] Several prominent members were retired officers who were recalled to active service in 1914 and occupied responsible positions in the invasion of Belgium: von der Goltz, Litzmann, and August Keim, who founded the Army League in 1912.[84] The Army League, essentially a front organization of the Pan-German League, proved highly attractive among regimental officers; in some units, the entire body of officers joined, and it was well connected with the General Staff via Ludendorff. The Crown Prince, who commanded the Fifth Army in the war, sympathized openly with both the Pan-German and Army Leagues.[85] Von der Goltz, whose book *The Nation in Arms* was imbued with the ideas of Social Darwinism and cultural pessimism, founded the Young Germany Union (Jungdeutschlandbund) in 1911, which was based on the 'military idea' and by May 1914 had no fewer than 750,000 members – a quarter of German males aged between 14 and 20.[86] Social Darwinism was also shared by the ex-servicemen's associations, many of whose members were reservists.[87]

During the 1914 invasion militarist nationalism helped fuel German anger at Belgian military resistance and belief in a 'franc-tireur war'. The burgomaster of Warsage, Fléchet, who was fluent in German, was told by one officer on 6–7 August: 'All these little countries have to be made to disappear.'[88] German sources confirm that many German officers, senior and junior, were fond of repeating Social Darwinist clichés about Belgium. General Hans von Beseler, commander of the IIIrd Reserve Corps (First Army) wrote from a village near Louvain to his wife on 23 August 1914: 'I do not like this people; they are mainly Flemings, but they give one the impression of being a race which has been kept down, and they are also worth less than the Germans in physical terms.'[89] For Beseler, the 'despicable Belgians' were evidently some kind of savage, immature people which if 'treated with understanding' would one day 'come to trust us'.[90] He envisaged a long, colonial-type occupation with a German civilizing mission. Constantin Baron von Gebsattel, retired general and member of the Pan-German League executive, wrote to Claß on hearing rumours of 'Belgian atrocities' during the invasion:

> According to the report of a medical officer with the troops, the Belgian people has committed atrocities against German soldiers, especially the wounded, such as are found otherwise only among the hordes of inferior races, and which will serve to strike this people from the ranks of the civilized nations [...] The German people can trust its army and the army commanders to take the appropriate measures to suppress such barbarities [...] The Belgians rank with the Herero well below the level of the Hottentots![91]

While Belgium was regarded as intrinsically inferior to Germany, France, a powerful enemy, was considered to have lost in the Darwinian struggle for survival. As an old Württemberg medical doctor said to three captured French military doctors during their journey to Basle under the protection of the Red Cross: 'You are degenerates.'[92] Even before the war, this was a common idea in the right-wing press, which regarded France as 'sick and bad': 'The evil is in the race. It is a dying people', as one newspaper wrote in February 1914.[93] Such views were mirrored by the underestimation of the fighting capacity of the French army as from the 1890s, as exemplified by the Schlieffen Plan.[94] The reverse side of Social Darwinism was pessimism at Germany's own capacity to survive the life struggle. Moltke the younger was no Pan-German but his thinking expressed this fear. In calling for expansion of the army in 1911, he argued that war in Europe was not merely inevitable, but also a test for the survival of Germanic culture.[95]

In 1914, militarist nationalism projected the minority identities of the internal enemy onto the external enemy. Francs-tireurs were pictured as Catholics, proletarians, and Alsace-Lorrainers, each of them considered to be an anti-national minority within Germany. Anti-Catholicism was undoubtedly the most important of these negative identities. It should be understood in the context of the *Kulturkampf*, the political campaign conducted by Bismarck with liberal support against German Catholicism in the 1870s. There was a persistent memory of this campaign, in which Catholics were perceived as an internal threat to the cohesion of the Reich, loyal not to the new nation-state but to a shadowy foreign power. Anti-Catholicism was not only right-wing, but also drew on liberal Protestantism and Social Democratic anticlericalism. For many of its exponents, it was a progressive ideology.[96]

In the wake of the *Kulturkampf*, a new type of Protestant pressure group politics emerged, of which the Evangelischer Bund zur Wahrung der deutsch-protestantischen Interessen (Evangelical League for the Protection of German-Protestant Interests) was the prime representative. Founded in 1886, and convinced of the identity between the German nation and Protestantism, it campaigned against ultramontanism and Catholic demands for parity. This brought it into conflict with the government, which had to co-operate with the Catholic Centre Party. Yet the League's phenomenal growth made it a huge middle-class organization with half a million members by the eve of the Great War. In 1906, it was joined by the 'Anti-Ultramontane Reich League', which had strong support, especially from students. Taken with the fact that the Young Liberals were even more anticlerical than their elders, this indicates that anti-Catholicism was a growing force in the pre-war decade, precisely in the social and age groups from which the active and reserve officers were drawn.[97]

This half-hidden *Kulturkampf* re-emerged with the outbreak of war in 1914. The press, as we have seen, gave prominence to the role of Catholic priests in the People's War. The *Hannoverscher Courier*, for example, carried a report on 13 August which laid responsibility for the 'atrocities' perpetrated on wounded German soldiers on the 'ultramontanist government' of 'Christian Belgium', with its 70,000 priests. The Belgians were bloodthirsty beasts who attacked German soldiers, mutilating and murdering in a manner reminiscent of St Bartholomew's Night (a reference to the infamous Parisian massacre of Protestants by Catholics in 1572). *Germania*, the Catholic daily newspaper, attacked the *Hannoverscher Courier* for its 'cheeky and unscrupulous sectarian agitation', appealing to the anti-Catholic instincts of its readers.[98] Yet such anti-Catholicism was expressed by the Kaiser and his immediate entourage. The court preacher, Goens, military chaplain of the Guards, conducted a service on 13 September 1914 which portrayed the war as a German Protestant crusade, and which Admiral von Müller, Chief of the Naval Cabinet, disparagingly summarized: 'We were fighting for Protestantism and we were the Chosen People, archangel Michael etc. Entirely the Kaiser's style.'[99] The Kaiser himself made no secret of his anti-Catholicism. The Bavarian military attaché at Grand Headquarters recorded that Wilhelm 'cursed the French and Belgian "*Pfaffen*" who incited the people to violence, gouged out the eyes of the wounded and engaged actively in the fighting'.[100] In an inchoate and largely unofficial way, domestic anti-Catholicism was thus externalized in the construction of the menacing enemy civilian.

Another internal 'enemy of the Reich', Social Democracy, was likewise projected outwards in 1914. The memory of the Franco-Prussian War in the German army was bound up with that of the Paris Commune which was the defining example of the horrors of revolutionary warfare.[101] The German army projected this spectre onto the rise of socialism as a mass force at home, against which it was assigned a counter-revolutionary role. As the secret General Staff instructions for 'Fighting in Insurgent Cities' (1907) stated, there would be no negotiations; it would be 'a life-or-death struggle, or subjugation at the mercy or disfavour of the victor'. If a crowd of people did not disperse after being warned, troops were to fire directly into the assembly, even if the people were unarmed. 'Ringleaders' would be executed summarily, as would anyone caught bearing arms.[102] The instructions were still in force on the eve of the Great War.[103]

The expectation of proletarian resistance influenced the invasion and occupation of Belgium. The myth of the proletarian defence of Herstal is one example. More generally, Moltke anticipated that the Belgian working class would pose a constant danger to the communications of the German army. He demanded the expulsion of a section of the 'revolutionary and poor' working-class population from Liège and Charleroi to Antwerp, where it would be 'left to the Royal Belgian government to provision these masses'.[104] In this form, nothing came of the planned expulsion; the deportation of some 120,000 workers to other parts of Belgium and Germany later in the war was for economic exploitation, not fear of insurgency.[105] In early November 1914, however, the first conference of the German military governors of Belgium still anticipated unrest, especially in the cities, with harsh measures envisaged which were similar to those already taken against the 'francs-tireurs'.[106]

In reality, there was no armed proletarian resistance to the invasion and no proletarian insurrection during the occupation. The path of the German invasion cut through many rural areas, villages, and small towns, where Catholicism and its symbols predominated – priests, churches, roadside calvaries. Where it crossed industrial districts (Liège, Charleroi, the northern Meurthe-et-Moselle), the fear of proletarian insurrection, though present, was not the main motivator of violence against civilians. The Belgian labour and socialist movement (the Parti Ouvrier Belge) turned out to be a less visible or plausible conspiratorial enemy than Catholicism. Nor could it be credited with running the country, and thus planning a People's War, unlike the Catholic Party which had dominated Belgian politics since the early 1880s.

National minorities – the Poles, Danes, and Alsace-Lorrainers – were even more directly linked with the external enemy in 1914 owing to the charge of dual national allegiance. This was especially true of Alsace-Lorrainers, who were regarded by the German army as pro-French and liable to engage in franc-tireur resistance. Hence the same myth-complex arose here as on the invasion path in Belgium and France, with civilians accused of firing at their own army and supporting the French. Consequently, German civilians in Alsace-Lorraine were the victims of German violence in several cases in August and September, such as that noted at Mulhouse.

Relations between Alsace-Lorraine and the *Kaiserreich* had been modified in the years preceding the war. Limited home rule was granted in 1911 and the substantial francophile elements of the population increasingly demanded cultural and political autonomy rather than outright rejection of the annexation of 1871.[107] Yet reconciliation remained superficial, and was offset by the distrust and authoritarianism of the German officer corps in the two provinces which displayed its contempt for the *Wackes* (the derogatory term for Alsatians) in the notorious Zabern affair of 1913.[108] War polarized allegiances. Nationalist hopes that the mobilization would weld Alsace-Lorraine more firmly to Germany proved illusory. Enthusiasm for the war was mainly limited to recent German settlers, and more than twice as many Alsatians enlisted in the French army as volunteered (rather than being conscripted) in the German army.[109] Many Alsace-Lorrainers favoured the

Allies, but were obliged to serve in the German forces. German nationalist and military suspicions, exaggerated in peacetime, turned Alsace-Lorrainers into potential traitors, even insurrectionaries, with the war.[110]

Thus a Württemberg officer found that the population in Lower Alsace was 'undoubtedly francophile'. He wrote: 'Infantry tell of horrible cruelties inflicted on the [German] wounded. One of them was said to have had his eyes gouged out and [another] soldier's heart had been cut out. Disgraceful beasts.'[111] Lieutenant-Colonel von Gleich, commander of the 25th (Württemberg) Dragoon Regiment, noted that the people in Saaraltdorf (German Lorraine) were hostile to Germany. The *'Wackes'* were all untrustworthy: not only did they show no enthusiasm, but also put up passive resistance at every step. The mayor, who allegedly had been a franc-tireur in the Franco-Prussian War, was suspected of sabotage.[112] The hostility of the population in Aspach (Lorraine) and their refusal to speak German made the troops nervous and afraid that the meals served to them had been poisoned.[113] In numerous cases, civilians were punished for their supposed disloyalty even if there were no massacres such as those which occurred in Belgium and the French border départements. The men of Hampont, Lorraine, were arrested after Bavarian troops claimed they had been fired on from the windows, even though a French patrol sighted there was probably responsible for the shooting.[114]

Catholic priests, suspected of supporting French irredentism in Alsace-Lorraine, were targeted even by mainly Catholic German regiments. At Sennheim (Cernay) the mayor and priest, along with notables from nearby villages, were arrested for sympathizing with the French, beaten and marched through the streets, and told they would die if any more French soldiers were found in the village.[115] The people of Dalheim (Dalhain), near Château-Salins in German Lorraine, were accused of welcoming the French during their brief invasion and firing on German troops. In revenge a priest was shot, the village burned down, and the population deported.[116] In St Moritz near Schlettstadt (Sélestat), in Alsace, in the night of 18–19 August, Bavarian troops, convinced that the villagers had fired on them, ordered the inhabitants out of their houses with their hands up, and shot down many of those fleeing in terror as their houses were burned.[117] The Catholic priest narrowly escaped with his life, after being threatened by drunken soldiers.[118] An investigation carried out by a tribunal of the XVth Army Corps concluded that it was not the inhabitants of St Moritz who fired on the troops, but French soldiers.[119]

In reality, there was no sabotage of the mobilization in Alsace-Lorraine, nor was there evidence of guerrilla resistance by the population. On the contrary, German military inquiries concluded that mistaken identity or friendly fire caused the incidents alleged by the army.[120]

For German militarist nationalism with its paranoid world-view, war offered the opportunity to solve these problems of internal unity by externalizing the domestic enemy as part of the 'ring of enemies'. Of course, hostility to domestic minorities was not part of the official *Burgfrieden*, or political truce, in August 1914, and in fact it troubled the political establishment which sought to foster national unity. Anger against the internal enemy, however, was part of the uncontrollable outburst of feelings unleashed by the war which provided an important ingredient of the collective delusion of the franc-tireur war.

3   The German way of war? Responding to the 'franc-tireur war'

The pre-war doctrines and mentalities discussed above only partly explain the German army's harsh response to the franc-tireur war. The crucial question is whether there was not only a set of predispositions, but a prepared, coherent German response in 1914. Was there a 'German way of war', as the Allies alleged?

Legal preparations would be one indication. The Imperial Ordinance on Extraordinary Military Criminal Justice Proceedings against Foreigners and Prisoners of War (1899) was republished in 1911, and again on 2 August 1914 in the German army gazette. The important second paragraph stipulated that on entering enemy territory, a proclamation should be made that 'all persons, including civil servants of the enemy government, who do not belong to the enemy army and who endeavour to assist the enemy power or cause damage to the German forces or their allies, will incur the death penalty.' Clearly, this was addressed not so much to foreigners as to German officers, who were empowered to execute any suspect enemy civilians. There was a well-defined legal procedure. The court was to be composed of officers, and there had to be a written record. The defendant had a right to be represented, and if he spoke no German, or no member of the court spoke the foreign language, to an interpreter. The judgment was to be confirmed by a commanding officer. However, all the apparent safeguards in the procedure could be short-circuited: paragraph 18 stated that if civilians were caught red-handed engaging in treasonable acts, summary justice could be dispensed, 'according to the customs of war'.[121]

Elements of these regulations are apparent in the first few days of the invasion – e.g. von Emmich's poster of 4 August warning the Belgian people not to resist the passage of the German army, or court-martial trials of supposed francs-tireurs. From the start, however, violence against civilians in retaliation for the alleged crimes of unidentified individuals developed in a manner quite at variance with the military justice code. Initially, this divergence was ordered or sanctioned by relatively junior officers such as battalion commanders, even if the presence of senior commanders during the assault on Liège suggests higher approval.

Within days, however, senior commanders formally endorsed violence against civilians. We have seen that on 8 August, General von Einem gave orders to the second wave of troops moving on Liège to burn down villages and shoot all the inhabitants if they met with 'treacherous' civilian attacks, an order endorsed and extended by the commander of the Second Army, General von Bülow. By the time the main invasion began, widespread repression of imagined civilian resistance was ordered at senior levels. Evidence for this is particularly clear in the case of the Third Army's attack on the Meuse around Dinant.

The two army corps charged with this operation issued pre-invasion orders which prescribed the intimidation and repression of civilians. The XIXth Army Corps declared on 14 August that 'the franc-tireur nuisance reported on from everywhere is to be suppressed right from the start with the most drastic means.' These included extensive hostage-taking.[122] The following day, the XIIth Army Corps issued a general order which specified that civilians who failed to turn in firearms, who were caught with weapons in their hands, or who tried to sabotage the German advance were to be shot, and that: 'Where the culprits cannot be found [...] hostages and also villages will be held liable with life and property for the damage.'[123] These two similar orders at army corps level suggest that the Third Army commander, Hausen, who was deeply concerned by news of the supposed franc-tireur war, had issued a prior order stipulating harsh measures against civilians, the record of which has not survived.[124]

Evidence for the transmission of the order down the command hierarchy is plentiful. The 40th Infantry Division (XIXth Army Corps) repeated the corps order almost verbatim.[125] Foot Artillery Battalion 58 stated bluntly:

'We enter Belgian territory tomorrow. One cannot be drastic enough with francs-tireurs.'[126]

These commands were applied by the two corps in the assault on and around Dinant. According to Belgian sources, villagers east of Dinant were told by German soldiers before 23 August of the impending destruction of the town.[127] The intention was made known to the troops at the latest on 21 August.[128] The war diary of IR 108 for the day of the attack suggests that some modification may have been made to the XIIth Army Corps order of 15 August: 'Each house is to be individually purged. Spare only women and children, do not burn houses.'[129] But this change was not communicated clearly to the troops, who targeted women and children in their rampage and caused a general conflagration. As one man from IR 103 told Lieutenant Loustalot's enquiry in 1915:

> From the first houses [in Dinant] our troops came under fire, mainly from a convent flying the Red Cross flag. The order was given by the Brigade [sic] General von Hausen not to spare anyone. After this order we penetrated into the houses, and 90 persons were massacred, including women and some children [...] Many prisoners were taken, and the men were taken to a barracks by the banks of the Meuse. Many of them were executed: I estimate about 110.
>
> With my own eyes I saw a group of eight men execute six or seven men [...] There would no doubt have been many more executions if an order from the general commanding the army corps had not arrived to stop the executions.[130]

It was in fact General d'Elsa, commander of the XIIth Army Corps, who sought to stop the dynamic of destruction he had helped to start with his order of 15 August.

A soldier from IR 108, Grimmer, confirmed that civilians were massacred indiscriminately in response to an order originating well up the command hierarchy:

> We were given the order to kill all civilians shooting at us, but in reality the men of my regiment and I myself fired at all civilians we found in the houses from which we suspected there had been shots fired; in that way we killed women and even children. We did not do it light-heartedly, but we had received orders from our superior officers to act in

this way, and not one single soldier in the active army would know to disobey an order from the senior command. My company did not kill more than about 30 civilians in the conditions I have just described.[131]

Many soldiers stated to Loustalot that an order was given simply to massacre civilians, not only those caught resisting or suspected of being francs-tireurs. One man accurately identified it as an army corps order, and another said that it was given to all the companies in his regiment.[132] A soldier in IR 100 stated it was part of the pre-war preparations of the army to 'treat civilians without pity'.[133]

The scarcity of evidence (especially for the Prussian First and Second Armies) makes it impossible to establish whether such senior orders were issued elsewhere. Panic-induced incidents, such as Aarschot, Lunéville, and Louvain, did not have the same chain of causality as the premeditated destruction of Dinant. Yet the similarity across all seven armies of the reaction to incidents not originating in panic suggests that orders like those of the Third Army may have been issued more widely. Indeed, it is highly likely that Moltke's 'warning' of 12 August was paralleled by an OHL order made around the same date which has not survived, and which was translated by the army and corps commanders into instructions to all ranks to expect francs-tireurs, treat civilian resisters as criminals deserving the death penalty, and carry out reprisals.

Readiness to punish criminalized enemy civilians with extreme severity certainly became dominant at the highest level of the army. The Bavarian military attaché at the GHQ in Koblenz noted in his diary on 18 August 1914 that he had encountered a group of French civilians (possibly Alsatians, he thought), and including three priests (*Pfaffen*), who had been caught with weapons in their hands. He deplored the fact that they were being 'done the honour' of being sent to Germany, proposing a more summary solution: 'A cattle-rope around the neck and a kick in the behind would also do the trick and send this rabble to hell, where they belong; and it'll cost the state neither powder nor lead.'[134] (Cf. illustration 3 above.)

This reaction was reflected in official military policy. Falkenhayn, Prussian Minister of War, observed in a decree of 26 August 1914 that deporting francs-tireurs to Germany was an onerous burden on the army and no solution to the problem. He pointed out that anyone 'regardless of age and sex' who was not a combatant under Article 1 of Hague Convention IV (duly constituted militias and volunteer corps) could, if caught red-handed resisting the invaders, be dealt with summarily, in accordance with the military justice code.[135] In the absence of any reference to Article 2 of Hague Convention IV, on the right of populations to resist invasion, this was tantamount to an invitation to liquidate civilian resisters on the spot. In fact, court-martial trials against alleged francs-tireurs took place in relatively few instances and summary executions were the rule. The 24 hours between the imprisonment of people in Tamines and the mass execution on 21–22 August, for example, were not used to conduct a court-martial hearing. By the end of August, not just local practice but policy in the German army had been radicalized in response to the franc-tireur myth-complex, and the military justice system for enemy civilians largely suspended.

Did this amount to a deliberate strategy of deterrence by terror? Evidence in favour of this view comes from the practice of warning the Belgian and French populations by poster of the fate that awaited them if they resisted, with examples increasingly given of reprisals which had taken place. The exemplary use of violence became widespread during the main invasion. As it entered Belgium, the 6th Reserve Division issued a poster in German, French, and Flemish, threatening the population with the death penalty:

> All inhabitants of the country who shoot at our soldiers or who in any way take part in the fighting, or who, without belonging to the organized army, try to damage our troops, help the Belgian troops or their allies, are guilty of committing acts likely to damage the life or health of our soldiers [...] Whoever is found with weapons will incur a severe penalty, in serious cases the death penalty. Places where the inhabitants commit hostile acts against our troops will be burned down [...] The above-mentioned penalties will be applied with full severity and mercilessly.[136]

On 22 August, after the mass executions in Andenne, Bülow put up posters in Liège to say the same fate was in store for its inhabitants if they attacked German troops.[137] His statement that Andenne had been entirely destroyed by fire was an exaggeration designed to intimidate.[138]

The most powerful piece of evidence for the deterrence argument is Moltke's order to the armies on the western front of 27 August 1914, in which he outlined the forces the enemies were likely to deploy in the near future, among which were 'franc-tireur bands'. He instructed the cavalry divisions to be accompanied by Jäger and infantry 'in order rapidly to break the resistance of francs-tireurs and inhabitants'. The memory of 1870 haunting him, he added: 'Only with energetic measures against the population can a popular uprising [*Volksaufstand*] be nipped in the bud.'[139] Yet the date of this order is all-important. By 27 August, the great majority of the major incidents had already taken place. The 'deterrence' argument was here a retrospective rationalization. The threat or example of violence against civilians was undoubtedly used by the German army to try and curb the imagined franc-tireur war and to prevent its escalation. Deterrence, however, rarely caused the incidents, which were always rooted in the delusion that concerted civilian resistance was taking place. It was at most one element of a rather chaotic reaction by the German command to the powerful dynamic of the franc-tireur complex, and not a coherent pre-emptive policy.

The question of deportation supports this conclusion. Those sent to Germany were rarely put on trial as francs-tireurs, the Aachen court-martial on 8 August being an apparent exception. Court-martial trials were probably the original intention, but Falkenhayn's directive of 26 August soon intervened. In fact, we do not know whether deportations were intended as a measure of security, punishment, or deterrence. The holding of at least 10,000 French civilians and at least 13,000 Belgians in poor conditions in camps across Germany served all three functions in 1914. The importance of security is revealed by Bavarian General Konrad Krafft von Dellmensingen, Chief of General Staff of the Sixth Army, in mid-September. Since he considered the franc-tireur war to be over, expelling the population capable of bearing arms as a measure to protect the German rear now seemed to him an 'unnecessary hardship'.[140] However, since many of the deportees were women, children, and the infirm, the motivation cannot have been purely security, but must also have been collective punishment for alleged resistance. Yet the deportation of local notables, such as burgomasters and priests, points to deterrence, since the aim was to deprive the resistance of its assumed leaders. Deportation developed as a localized response with mixed motives, rather than as a preventive strategy, although its scale and penal spirit distinguished it from the internment of 'enemy aliens' practised by all belligerent nations in 1914.[141]

The military response to the 'franc-tireur war' was not predetermined by a set of orders which anticipated a civilian uprising. The General Staff and troop commanders undoubtedly discussed the eventuality of civilian resistance. But no record has been found of orders issued prior to the war. Indeed, the Bavarian Chief of General Staff, Dellmensingen, retrospectively criticized German war planning for having ignored the issue, which he argued 'should have been tackled much more energetically during our preparations for war, on the basis of our experiences in 1870'. Instead, because of Schlieffen there had been a concentration exclusively on military operations in the first 40 days of mobilization.[142] The implication of this comment is that the military response to the 'franc-tireur war' was a largely improvised affair.

Yet contemporaries in the Allied camp were not mistaken in seeing a pattern in the German violence. This arose from the military doctrines and operational assumptions, and also the underlying mentalities and ideologies, which produced the collective delusion of civilian resistance in the first place. It was this cultural and political predisposition that carried not just ordinary soldiers but the entire military command rapidly beyond its own legal code and even contemporary moral norms of acceptable violence against civilians.

Most obviously, the memory of the Franco-Prussian war in the German officer corps offered a host of precedents for how to deal with irregular warfare. The army response to the Hague Convention on Land Warfare presumed that German military precedent constituted the 'customs of war' which overrode Article 2 of Hague IV on the right of a population to resist invasion. Hence reprisals of the kind ordered by Moltke the elder in 1870 – collective executions, arson, hostage-taking, and expulsions – remained the standard policy (illustration 7). Fines exacted on the village or town deemed guilty of resistance, for example, were a practice of 1870 renewed on a wide scale in 1914. The German officer corps needed to do no more than consult its own past in response to its collective fantasy in 1914.

There were other influences, too. One of the most intriguing is the colonial domain in which Germany, like other European powers, fought brutal campaigns in the quarter-century before 1914. The assumptions of the military and the conservative establishment about empire cannot be dismissed as exceptional: the European dimension was not far from their minds. Not for nothing did the government, the Conservatives, and National Liberals defend colonial policy against fierce criticism from the Social Democrats, Left Liberals, and the Centre Party over the army's war against the Herero people in South-West Africa in 1904–7. After their defeat the Herero were driven into a waterless desert, where at least 50,000

7 Incendiarism as the norm. The inscription states that this house (inhabited by Dutch
people) should be spared

men, women, and children perished. This was an intentional policy of annihilation, planned by the General Staff: Schlieffen was in daily contact by
telegram with the colonial army and approved its measures. At the end he
congratulated Lieutenant-General von Trotha, the commander of the colonial force, on exterminating almost the entire people.[143] Defending colonial
policy in the Reichstag in 1906, the Free Conservative deputy Wilhelm von
Kardorff compared the harsh measures taken against the natives with the
executions of French civilians in 1870–1 for having collaborated with the
francs-tireurs. According to Kardorff the natives had no place in Germany's
civilizing mission: 'The earth is not here to be inhabited by cannibals.'[144]
Although it is hard to establish precise causal connections, colonial warfare
was a link in the transmission of ideas between the Franco-Prussian War
and 1914. The colonial experience gave German politicians greater
freedom for experimentation in political and military conduct, and lowered
the threshold to violence against European civilians ten years later.[145]

Most important of all, however, were the consequences of the doctrine of
the 'war of annihilation' (*Vernichtungskrieg*) on which the strategic thinking of the General Staff was founded. War planning was radically transformed in the half-century between 1870 and 1914. Prussian military
history – and indeed the history of all successful commanders from antiq-
uity to Napoleon – was narrowed down to a story of 'total war by battles of
annihilation'.[146] When Clausewitz wrote his seminal work, *On War*, in the
aftermath of the Revolutionary and Napoleonic wars, he described the
dynamic of escalation whereby, in theory at least, each side used more
extreme means to defeat its enemy in an 'absolute' victory. In reality, he
argued, the political purpose of war, and the social conditions of the societies waging it, limited how it was fought.[147] After 1870, when Clausewitz's
influence reached its zenith, he was misinterpreted as the theorist of
extreme measures, including inhumanity, in pursuit of total victory. War, in
other words, was now seen to possess its own logic to the exclusion of the
conditioning political factors on which Clausewitz had insisted. Military
bureaucracies across Europe looked to Clausewitz as the theorist of the short
war based on a concentration of forces with maximum efficiency in order
to achieve decisive victory.[148]

The German General Staff attached special importance to his thinking
as an endorsement of the triumph of 1870 and the basis of future strategy.
Potentially, however, Clausewitz's process of escalation ran counter to the
decisive offensive by turning war into a struggle of attrition entailing

economic or popular mobilization which would lead to what von der Goltz called 'general devastation and pauperization'.[149] Apprehension of this threat explains the German officer corps' continued awareness of the war of the francs-tireurs in 1870, and the dangers of popular involvement in combat. Yet by and large, it was assumed (even by von der Goltz) that decisive victory could be achieved before war reached these extremes. Hence, dealing harshly but effectively with civilian resistance was intrinsic to the German military's understanding of the offensive, since it allowed the war to be concluded more speedily. Crushing guerrilla warfare was one means of limiting war, and preventing its escalation. Paradoxically, it could be viewed as a form of restraint, which is exactly how it was presented by the *German War Book* of 1902. If there was a 'German way of war', it consisted in this readiness to take ruthless measures against civilians with the aim of keeping warfare in what, for the German officer corps, were deemed to be acceptable bounds. Wilhelm von Stumm, the Foreign Ministry's representative at Grand Headquarters, was asked by the liberal newspaper editor, Theodor Wolff, in early 1915 for his opinion on the alleged German atrocities. Stumm replied that some of the reports were true, 'but the military could not be restrained; quoting Clausewitz, they said the cruellest war was the most humane [...] The franc-tireur shooting in the Belgian villages', he added, 'was, incidentally, really terrible.'[150]

Brutal and arbitrary repression of enemy civilians was by no means universally accepted in the German army in 1914. The myth-complex of the 'franc-tireur war' encountered scepticism, while officers and soldiers refused on occasions to apply draconian punishments or subverted them, like the soldiers who aimed to miss in the massacre at Tamines, or Captain Wabnitz and others at Andenne. Three examples illustrate doubt, and even dissidence.

General Götz von Olenhusen, commander of the 40th Division south of Dinant, voiced strong disapproval of his troops in his order of the day on 26 August 1914. He first congratulated his division on their successes, which showed that the warlike spirit was still alive, but went on:

It pains me all the more to be forced to observe that discipline among the ranks has disappeared to an ominous degree. Pillage and disregard of private property have been recorded not only in single cases: almost all parts of the division in their totality have been guilty of this reprehensible conduct. Using the excuse of searching for weapons or foraging, troops have soiled and laid waste to the homes and farms of the inhabitants in an outright *barbaric* manner, with the result that the houses are even quite unsuitable as billets. Arson, ordered at random by unauthorized men without any kind of order, is on the agenda. The good name of the German army has already been seriously imperilled in front of the world by this disorderliness, and the Fatherland will learn of it, with indignation and shame, through the press of the entire world. This outrageous state of affairs has to be ended immediately!

Olenhusen went on to order that officers were to restore local order and control requisitioning, and that punitive arson could only be ordered by the most senior officer present. 'Drastic' sanctions were threatened for renewed indiscipline.[151] Although Olenhusen's comments were directed ostensibly at the plunder and wanton destruction of property, the vehemence of the protest, above all the word 'barbaric', suggests condemnation of the killing of defenceless civilians. He was profoundly shaken at the transgression of moral as well as legal norms by his troops in an uncontrollable dynamic of violence against civilians which went beyond what could be justified as the punishment of francs-tireurs.

A Württemberg medical officer, Professor von Pezold, who served with the XIIIth Army Corps (Fifth Army) in southern Luxembourg and French Lorraine, kept a diary throughout the campaign. On 15 August he recorded the 'painful news' that a medical colleague, Dr Stamer (of the Uhlans), had been 'ambushed while riding behind the squadron and shot dead by a Lorraine local inhabitant'.[152] In fact, as an internal army investigation established, Stamer was shot not by francs-tireurs but by French army snipers on bicycles.[153] Pezold became increasingly sceptical about franc-tireur stories. He noted on 14 September 1914: 'We wanted to move into a farmhouse 3 km outside Rémonville but the local commander [Captain Ruthardt, IR 127] warned us away because our retreat had given courage everywhere to the francs-tireurs. In Varennes, Ruthardt said, the Crown Prince had just had seven people hanged. Nevertheless medical NCO Steinthal [...] rode up there and prepared an excellent billet for us.'[154] When Pezold was told the 'news' that there was a wounded soldier in the Katharinenhospital in Stuttgart whose eyes had been put out by the French, he refused to believe it. The story-teller later confessed that 'the whole affair was a fabrication; a letter from his father-in-law had told the [original] story and the latter had now retracted it.'[155] In mid-November, presumably in approval, Pezold recorded the comments of an equally sceptical fellow-officer who said that 'the pharisaic tone of the German newspapers made him sick and the Russian depredations can hardly have been any worse than those committed by our soldiers.' The officer went on to observe that 'many sins had been committed when villages were set on fire because of shooting from the houses by isolated French soldiers and then even the women and children became the victims of the firing of our infantry against the will of the senior commanders.'[156]

One final testimony, written some 13 years later, conveys the trauma and guilt of an ordinary German soldier, Paul Reime, who witnessed the massacre at Les Rivages, in Dinant. Reime described marching on a hot afternoon down a steep incline into the town, a 'descent into hell', past burning houses and glowing rubble. The bridge-building company was already at work, and his group was carrying the first boat to the water when they encountered a group of civilians who had been hiding by the bank. The civilians, caught between river, rock wall, and soldiers, unavailingly tried to escape.

> Trembling they submit to their fate and apparently expect to be killed by our bayonets. But we make an effort to reassure them. Captain d'Elsa, whom we call, assures them in French that they have nothing to fear. Pitiable to see how the torment they have suffered turns into a kind of paroxysm, as the people (women, children, old people) throw themselves at our feet and try to kiss our hands, weeping and laughing [...] What follows proceeds with the speed and inexorability of a catastrophe:

> The people have been brought back up to the road. At the sight of the companies which have halted there they are seized with fear. They are searched, without anything suspicious being found; they are to be taken behind the line, but – the poor souls! – it does not come to that. A machine-gun firing from the opposite bank causes the most appalling confusion. The sound of the shots echoes a hundredfold as they strike the rock wall. Whoever has not heard the initial 'tactac' from over there believes that the shooting comes from an ambush. Suddenly the word 'francs-tireurs' is shouted wildly, men point up the rock face and seize their rifles, and start a senseless fusillade. The firing is only ended gradually with the order 'cease fire!'

> Meanwhile, I did not let the people out of my sight. They shudder when they heard the word 'franc-tireur'. But does that prove their bad

conscience? Is it not more likely that they have a sense of foreboding of the vengeance that destroyed them?

Reime recounted how Major Schlick ordered the execution, and how Captain d'Elsa (son of the commander of the XIIth Army Corps) attempted unsuccessfully to prevent it. As Reime and his comrades began to cross the Meuse in a boat, the first salvo rang out.

> I turn to look: a terrible sight! A block of humans writhing, trembling, falling … the cries of women and children … the second salvo … a convulsion of bodies on the ground in wild confusion. I see people still alive who crawl behind the dying, and I turn away …

That night, as the company bivouac on the opposite bank, they realize that the 35 French infantry soldiers and two officers they have captured were the 'francs-tireurs'. Reime continued:

> Our 'executioners' arrive, grim, silent. One of them, a reserve, bursts into tears[…]
> We are sitting with Tennhardt on a bed of straw, shivering, and unable to sleep.
> 'Why', T. asks me, 'didn't we punch the major [i.e. Schlick] in the face?' and adds, 'because we are cowards.'
> 'No', I say, 'because we do not know each other, we don't trust each other … because we do not have an organization of resistance against this organization of murder.'[157]

The moral of anti-militarist solidarity was probably a post-war addition; but the course of events is corroborated by other documents, and Reime's distress was certainly shared by other German soldiers. A reserve lieutenant, Hahn, begged his company commander not to put him in charge of a group of civilian hostages, because he had witnessed the shooting of a group of civilians, the sight of which was 'too horrible'. This was almost certainly the execution at Les Rivages. The company commander insisted, and so long as the hostages were guarded by Hahn they were in safe hands.[158]

Despite differences of rank and experience, Olenhusen, Pezold, Reime, and others all felt guilt by association for the transgression of moral boundaries. It is impossible to say how widespread such feelings were; they may have been as common as the belief in francs-tireurs and the legitimacy of harsh reprisals. But it was difficult to make the alternative view prevail. Olenhusen addressed one reason – the collective fury of soldiers barely under discipline. Reime hinted at another – the authority of the military hierarchy and the impetus of a smoothly functioning machine of destruction.

Contradictory explanations (margin note)

Brutality and inhumanity characterized the response to the 'franc-tireur war' because these reflected the prevailing doctrine of the German military on civilian involvement in warfare. But other traditions – the humanitarianism of some of the educated bourgeoisie, the anti-militarism and internationalism of the labour movement, different religious beliefs – were by no means negligible. Radical nationalism and militarism were not the preferred ideology of the majority of Germans in 1914. It was the liberal press, in fact, which enjoyed the greatest circulation, and the public sphere was characterized by pluralism in which criticism of authority was commonplace.[159] Guilt on the part of some soldiers and growing scepticism towards the franc-tireur myth-complex in the Catholic, Socialist, and liberal press, confirm the influence of other Germanies which tempered the fantasy of the enemy as an evil civilian and rejected the world-view of militarist nationalism.

5   Allied opinion and 'German atrocities', August–October 1914

From August to October 1914, what the Germans justified as 'legitimate reprisals' against 'Belgian' and 'French atrocities' came to be seen by Belgian, French, and British opinion as the exact opposite – German 'terror' and 'frightfulness'. The most widely used term, 'German atrocities' or 'atrocités allemandes', accused not just individual perpetrators but the German army and even the German people as a whole of committing moral outrages. This radically different view of the matter was shaped by cultural values, political views, and historical memories particular to the Allied countries. Understanding how German reactions to the 'franc-tireur war' were interpreted as 'German atrocities' means reconstructing the experience of the invaded populations in 1914 and the terms in which that experience was expressed.

1   Refugees, soldiers, and the Allied invasion 'fear' of 1914

Accusations of enemy atrociousness spread unevenly during the first two weeks of the war. Not surprisingly they appeared earliest in France. On 7 August, a French communiqué condemned the execution of two boys, for warning gendarmes of the arrival of German cavalry, as a crime which would 'arouse the profound indignation of the entire civilized world'.[1] The burning of Affléville and the execution of three of its inhabitants on 9 August were termed an 'atrocity' by both the moderate *Le Temps* and the more nationalist *Le Matin*.[2] By the middle of the month, the word was being applied to the news filtering out of Belgium. *Le Temps* used it in the account of 'the assassination of Warsage', given by the burgomaster Fléchet to Dutch journalists in Maastricht, as did *Le Matin* for a story of the murder of several civilians in Linsmeau (Brabant province), after a German officer was killed in combat.[3] The harsh German treatment of the population in southern Alsace was characterized by a communiqué as 'acts of unspeakable savagery'.[4]

It was the news about Liège and the Meurthe-et-Moselle, however, followed by the incidents accompanying the main German invasion, that confirmed the vocabulary of moral denunciation. On 17 August, *Le Temps* gleaned from German prisoners their intense fear of being poisoned or shot by francs-tireurs, and concluded that the Germans were systematically brutal because they suffered a collective delusion: 'It seems that the Germans are 40 years behind the times. They are proceeding as in 1870 with an infantile and barbaric imagination. They see francs-tireurs every-where and still cannot believe that we have a regular army.'[5] The press gave prominent coverage to the report written by Léon Mirman, the prefect of the Meurthe-et-Moselle, on the 'acts of revolting savagery' committed by the Germans in Badonviller, Parux, Blâmont and elsewhere. The violence in Lorraine was confirmed by the discovery of German soldiers' letters recounting the shooting of civilians.[6]

The government issued a series of protests to the signatories of the Hague Conventions. On 16 August, the first of these accused the Germans of systematically violating the Convention on Land Warfare by killing French wounded and prisoners and 'burning villages, massacring inhabi-tants, and making women and children walk before them'. It invited the 'civilized powers' to condemn such criminal acts by the light of a 'universal conscience'. The French issued ten more such protest notes before the end of the month.[7] On 20 August 1914, the Ministers of War and the Interior accused the Germans of systematic barbarism towards women, children, the old, and wounded soldiers, and they instructed the prefects and local officials to list German war crimes so that 'the army, or even the population, of a country which is henceforth struck from the ranks of civilized peoples' could be brought to justice.[8]

In Belgium, the Minister of Justice, Henri Carton de Wiart, established a commission on 7 August to collect evidence of enemy violations of the 'rights of people and the duty of humanity' which called for the 'reproba-tion of the civilized world'.[9] Yet the press seemed initially hesitant to endorse such claims. On 8 August, for example, the Brussels daily paper *Le Soir* dismissed a false rumour that the Germans had committed a full-scale massacre at Visé on 4 August, as did the London *Times*.[10] The refugees' tales gained credence, however, through the authority of Dutch journalists who interviewed escapees from Mouland, Visé, Warsage, and Berneau, and visited some of the villages concerned. The article in *Le Soir* on 11 August, 'The Barbarians', expressed the emergent sense of outrage.

> Retracing my steps [recounted a Dutch journalist] I saw a picture whose horror was inconceivable. [The Germans] had acted like barbarians in the villages around Visé. In one farm which I saw, all the inhabitants had been massacred, except a young girl and a dog which guarded the corpses while howling mournfully. As for the young girl, she wandered through the orchards, quite mad. Lord knows what moral and physical torture she had suffered.[11]

Official condemnation by the Belgian Commission of German violence against civilians and their property came on 14 August; from then on the category of *atrocités allemandes* was firmly established.[12] 'German atrocities are beyond counting', declared *Le Soir* on 15 August: 'the civilian population is massacred, the inhabitants are killed, women and children are brutalized in the most odious fashion, crops and dwellings are burned.' On 25 August, the Belgian authorities sent their first note of protest about the conduct of the German army to Allied and neutral governments. It excused in advance any evidence of isolated resistance that might emerge from 'the legitimate overexcitement provoked in the Belgian population by the cruelties committed by the German soldiers'; but the principal point was a ringing rejection of German allegations of mass, organized resistance, and a condemnation of German 'reprisals'.[13]

In the British case, lack of direct involvement in the early fighting and a tight news blackout resulted in 'atrocities' being ignored until the third week of the war. *The Times* continued to report German accusations of a Belgian *Franktireurkrieg* and even the aggressively patriotic and sensationalist *Daily Mail* made little of the 'atrocity' issue at this stage. But by the onset of the main German advance, the major British dailies had war correspondents operating out of the coastal Belgian cities and the language of 'atrocity' became commonplace. By 31 August, a typical story in the *Daily Mail* carried the headline: 'Holocaust of Louvain — Terrible Tales of Massacre'.

Despite different starting-points, by the end of August 'German atrocities' were presented in the same terms by the governments and mainstream press of all three countries. An identical message was carried by the full-page drawings in the British satirical magazine *Punch* on 26 August, and the French weekly *L'Illustration* three days later (illustrations 8 and 9). Both showed a brutal German soldier, presiding over the burning ruins of a Belgian village and astride the corpses of those most symbolic victims, a woman and a child. 'The Triumph of German "Culture"', stated *Punch* laconically, while *L'Illustration* asked: 'How can such spectacles be presented to the world, in 1914, by a people who pretended only yesterday to the glory of being in the front rank of civilized countries?'

If this view had been merely official discourse, it is unlikely that it would have resonated as it did in Allied opinion. The potency of the 'atrocities' issue came from the impact of the main German invasion on ordinary soldiers and civilians in Belgium, France, and Britain. Diplomatic neutrality and the absence of recent invasion may explain an initial unwillingness by Belgian opinion to credit the stream of press reports about German violence in Liège province. Before the German onslaught of 18 August, villagers along the Belgian defensive line on the river Gette displayed uncertainty. According to one Belgian soldier, 'fearful women asked the soldiers if it was true that the Germans were burning, pillaging, and massacring everything in their path. For sinister rumours were beginning to circulate. It was said that around Barchon, Evegnée, Chaudfontaine, the enemy had shot the defenceless inhabitants, burned the villages and committed ferocious cruelties.'[14] Another soldier recounted how reluctant he had been to credit the newspaper tales until he saw the aftermath of a German raid, in which a farmer had been clubbed to death. 'It was no longer the clear, dry account of the newspapers, one of these atrocity stories that I had still refused entirely to believe the day before [...] It was the body of a poor, tall old man whose head the bandits had stoved in an hour earlier.'[15] For some, the 'atrocity' tales remained hard to accept. As we have seen, on 21 August, inhabitants of Tamines innocently shouted encouragement to the Franco-Belgian forces repulsing German patrols, thereby contributing to the myth of civilian resistance, while many inhabitants of Dinant attributed the violent German incursion into the district of the rue Saint-Jacques that same night to drunkenness rather than systematic atrocities.

Innocence evaporated in the face of the major incidents at Andenne, Tamines, Dinant, Louvain, and elsewhere, from 18 to 31 August. Tales ran ahead of the German advance. On the northern flank of the invasion, a

THE TRIUMPH OF "CULTURE."

8 'The Triumph of "Culture"', *Punch*, August 1914

civilian population which the Germans deliberately drove into the country-side at Aarschot, Louvain, and elsewhere sought shelter on the coastal strip still under Belgian control or in Holland. By 20 August, over 20,000 refugees from Liège, Tirlemont, and Brussels crowded into Ghent; the columns of fleeing civilians, pushing carts piled with belongings, grew longer over the following week.[16] It was not just the invasion but the growing credibility of stories of German brutality that provoked a mass exodus by the fourth week of August, which spread the belief in enemy atrocities.

9   'Their way of waging war'. *L'Illustration*, August 1914

In France, border populations with long memories of 'Prussian' invasion believed tales of German cruelty more readily. This was nowhere truer than in Lorraine, divided between France and Germany in 1871 and the theatre of subsequent war scares. As recently as November 1912, at the height of the Balkan crisis, a mistaken order triggered local mobilization. Men left for their military depots, and the population of Nancy and surrounding communes believed itself to be on the brink of hostilities, before the mobilization was countermanded.[17] Not surprisingly, in August 1914 popular opinion was quick to react to incidents in the villages of the border region, and the prefects of the Meuse and the Meurthe-et-Moselle commented on local outrage at German behaviour.[18]

On 21 August, news of the destruction of Nomény the day before changed the atmosphere in Nancy. Prefect Mirman in the Meurthe-et-Moselle reported: 'From the morning, the [mood of the] town was shaken violently. It was learned that the Germans were arriving in the north and the east, in the north via Nomény, where they were committing atrocities (murder, fire, rape) and whence part of the terrified population had taken refuge in Nancy.'[19] The local paper, *L'Est républicain*, reinforced the 'atrocity' terror even as it sought to allay it: 'The news which the poor people of Nomény, chased out of their town by the Germans who sacked and burned it, have spread through the streets of Nancy has disturbed the inhabitants. One would be disturbed by much less, for our enemy respects no law and appears to delight in ruins and murder. But the people of Lorraine will quickly rediscover their *sang-froid* which is the most manly form of courage.'[20] Despite the efforts of the prefect and the military to calm the 'panic' and divert the refugees away from Nancy, the exodus redoubled as the main German invasion swept through the northern Meurthe-et-Moselle and into the Meuse.[21] Refugees in Verdun (Meuse) spread news of German actions in the Meurthe-et-Moselle, where 'all is robbery, pillage and burning.'[22]

Events in Lorraine were not exceptional but part of a broader reaction throughout the area exposed to the German invasion. Of some 17 départements directly or indirectly involved, prefects' reports survive for 13. In eight of these départements, the reports mention 'fear' or 'panic' linked to rumours of 'atrocities' (Nord, Pas-de-Calais, Seine-Inférieure, Seine-et-Marne, Aube, Meuse, Meurthe-et-Moselle, and Vosges). Evidence already considered shows that similar tales certainly affected the Ardennes. It can thus be concluded that a specific invasion 'fear', driven by tales of 'German atrocities', affected the entire north-east of France as well as Belgium during the last ten days of August and at least the first week of September (map 8). In the Nord, the fall of Brussels on 20 August immediately increased tension. Belgian refugees passing through Avesnes, in the German First Army's line of attack, so alarmed the local population that many, especially women, joined the exodus. Displaced Belgians depressed morale in Dunkirk, though it lay well north of the German advance.[23] By 27 August, tales of 'the carnage of Dinant and the horrors of Louvain' spread panic in Lille and two days later the prefect requested local officials to try to halt the exodus which, as in the Meuse, was hindering Allied military action.[24] The exodus was cumulative; inhabitants of the Nord were held

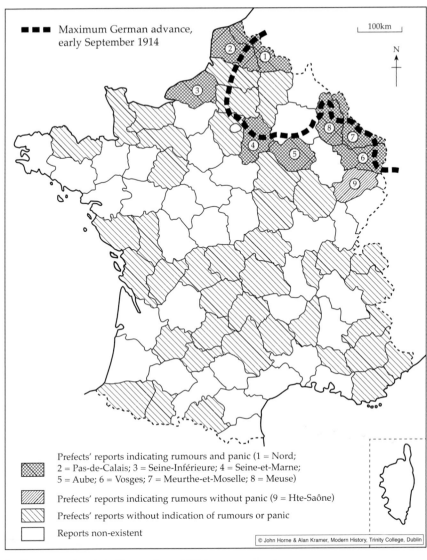

8   Rumour and panic in France, August 1914

responsible for unsettling opinion in the neighbouring Pas-de-Calais with the 'most fantastic stories'.[25]

The Vosges, south of the main invasion, was adjacent to southern Alsace, while its north-eastern corner was briefly occupied by the Germans. The prefect noted that by 19 August, fear of German reprisals was causing Alsatian civilians to leave ahead of the French army's withdrawal, and by 27 August, the border population near Saint-Dié in the north-east had fled: 'It is very difficult to calm the emotions aroused by the long lines of women, children and old people, some on foot, others in carts, coming from communes where fighting is going on. These people exaggerate events, talk about bombardments and fires, and sow panic all around them.'[26]

The incremental effect of these fears drove out local inhabitants ahead of the German advance down to the battle of the Marne. The prefect of the Seine-et-Marne, close to Paris, spoke of a panic on 30 August–1 September, pointing the finger at 'newspaper articles which have harped so much on the atrocities committed by the enemy troops'. In the Aube, on 8 September, the prefect told Paris that 'the unfortunate emigrants coming from the Ardennes and the Marne [directly to the north] are spreading terror in the communes through which they pass by the stories they tell of their misfortune.'[27] A penumbra of 'atrocity' fear edged beyond the départements directly touched by the German invasion. In the Seine-Inférieure, for example, newspaper atrocity tales and refugees from the Nord provoked flight from 24 August.[28] The Haute-Saône, by contrast, on the rim of the German advance in Lorraine and the Vosges, was slightly affected by 'several pedlars of alarmist stories' but experienced neither panic nor flight.[29]

This fear and the exodus in the north-east are distinguished from the mood in France more generally. During the last ten days of August, trains bore refugees and wounded soldiers to the remotest regions, disseminating the essential content of 'German atrocity' stories to the country as a whole. The prefect of a south-eastern department, the Ain, for example, reported on 22 August that a captain of French IR 97, who had been injured in the fighting in southern Alsace, was retailing stories of the Germans finishing off French wounded soldiers and gouging out their eyes. His colleague in the Tarn-et-Garonne, in far south-western France, ordered a police inquiry four days later following the 'revolting details of acts of (enemy) savagery' told to him by wounded soldiers.[30] In western Normandy, shocked refugees arriving from Lorraine included one girl who claimed to have witnessed were repeatedly mentioned at recruiting meetings in September 1914. At one of these, a Belgian senator was followed by a British MP who translated the Belgian experience into local terms: 'If the German troops were to land at Bognor, [the audience] would see women and children flocking into Chichester, driven before these Uhlans, wounded men shot as they ran into the streets, women bayoneted and outraged. That was the outlook if a raid took place upon the sacred soil of our shores.'[42]

2   Allied narratives of victimhood

What types of incident constituted 'German atrocities' for Allied refugee and soldier witnesses? It is not easy to be precise. The original material collected by the British inquiry, the Bryce Committee, has not survived, while that received by the Belgian Commission was random, owing to the circumstances of the invasion. The evidence of the French inquiry was dispersed; some statements made by Belgian soldiers and civilians in France were sent to the Belgian Commission, some made by French witnesses were published in the French reports, but many French and Belgian statements remained unused, filed under the rubric of the judicial district where they were gathered. Exceptionally, in the case of western Normandy (Caen), a summary list of all depositions allows the number of different types of 'atrocity' and hence their relative importance to be established for a total of 284 incidents reported by Belgian and French refugees and soldiers in the region and referring to the entire invasion (table 1).[45] There is no reason to suppose that this is not broadly representative of witness perceptions of 'German atrocities' more generally in France, Belgium, and Britain.

Overall, 69 per cent of the 284 incidents concerned German violence against civilians. Included in this category were individual or collective executions, which made up 32 per cent of the total; 15 per cent dealt with German soldiers firing at civilians or otherwise physically threatening them. Six per cent accused the Germans of using human shields in combat, 4 per cent of mutilating civilians, and 2 per cent of rape, though by reason of contemporary attitudes rapes were underreported. Only one deposition concerned the taking of hostages, but many hostages and all deportees were unable to flee, so this category was also underrepresented. Thus, a majority of the cases (59 per cent) concerned violence against people. Ten per cent concerned crimes against property as separate occurrences, with 6 and 4 per cent respectively for arson and pillage. But since virtually all the accounts of executions and intimidation included these, some two-thirds of the total cases in reality involved arson and pillage. As for alleged crimes against Allied soldiers (30 per cent of the total), the killing or maiming of the captured and wounded accounted for 11 per cent of the overall total, the use of soft-nosed or exploding bullets for 11 per cent, and deliberate firing on hospitals and first-aid stations accounted for 8 per cent.

Table 1 Reported incidents of 'German atrocities' (Caen judicial district)

Category of 'German atrocity'	Number	Percentage
Crimes against civilians		
Execution of civilians	92	32
Firing on or menacing civilians	43	15
Mutilation	10	4
Rape	7	2
Human shields	17	6
Hostages	1	0
Arson	16	6
Pillage	10	4
(Subtotal)	(196)	(69)
Crimes against soldiers		
Killing, wounding prisoners	32	11
Dumdum bullets	30	11
Hospitals etc. attacked	22	8
(Subtotal)	(84)	(30)
Other	4	1
TOTAL:	284	100

Equally important is why the incidents thus categorized were seen by contemporaries as a single entity – 'German atrocities' – and why they were so shocking. The dominant theme of witness statements gathered in France, Belgium, and Britain was the sense of violation, individual and collective. This did not stem just from the destructiveness of battle, or casual enemy violence against civilians, but from the particular attitude of German soldiers to the invaded populations, which confounded Allied presuppositions of warfare in Europe.

Civilians endlessly related their sense of the total vulnerability of their bodies and homes – the physical self and its most intimate sphere. The

the priest) massacred, was appalled by the evidence of deliberate profanation.

> Everything in the church had been desecrated. Horses had been brought in and the holy vestments had been torn and scattered. [The Germans] used these for wiping themselves after satisfying their needs. The reliquaries had been broken and the relics scattered. Among these were the relics of the Virgin of Cologne which had escaped the French Revolution. The soldiers had tried unsuccessfully to smash the tabernacle with their rifle butts, but the high altar and another altar had been broken up.[53]

The sense of total vulnerability on the part of civilians was intensified by two features of German behaviour. On the one hand, German violence towards civilians appeared to be random. On the other hand, once set in motion, it often seemed to proceed systematically according to a plan. Civilians testified to the host of ways in which they felt victims of random violence. Since German actions were motivated by the belief that the army had faced civilian hostility, the 'reprisals' were driven by high emotion which was volatile and unpredictable. Time and again, witnesses refer to the fury with which the soldiers committed their 'atrocities'. 'In their rage they sacked and fired the village', recounted a French customs officer who saw the Germans enter Haybes on 24 August, '[and] soon everything was reduced to ashes and the terrified population fled into the woods and slate quarries.'[54] One survivor of the shooting of 118 inhabitants in Soumagne on 5 August showed a witness the wounds he received when German soldiers who had dispatched the dying kept stabbing the dead in their frenzy, including the corpse under which he was hiding.[55]

With relations between soldiers and civilians balanced on a knife-edge, violence could be started by almost anything. Attempts to intervene by gesture and word might go either way. A hotel proprietor at Villeneuve-la-Lionne (Marne) finally lost her temper with the invaders' incessant demands and told the 'Prussian soldiers' that they could at least respect the little that remained to her – only to see her establishment set on fire.[56] Others tried to explain misunderstandings, disavow accusations, or simply beg for mercy. In Andenne, Eva Comes, the German woman who had been staying in the town, accused Captain Junge of arbitrariness as he presided over the massacre from the Place des Tilleuls without any mitigating effect.[57] At Surice (Namur province), where the Germans believed a 16-

year-old girl had shot an officer, women and children wept and begged mercy for their menfolk, and a German soldier broke down and shared their distress. But they were powerless to influence an 'impassive officer, who turned on his heels and actively prepared the execution' – by machine-gun.[58] It is not surprising that civilians who anticipated that accident or appearance might place them in a compromising position fled in advance of the Germans' arrival. The mayor of Atton (Meurthe-et-Moselle) left because French troops retaking the village killed one German soldier and captured seven who had been sleeping in his stable, and if the Germans returned, 'my goose was cooked.'[59]

Yet the fury might as easily switch direction, leaving a house or village untouched or defusing a potential massacre. A woman of Aarschot described this extreme unpredictability. She gave food and drink to 55 or 60 Uhlans and in consequence was left in peace. But the neighbouring houses were suspected of harbouring Belgian soldiers. 'Fifty rifles were ready to fire on the four houses. I begged [the Germans] in Flemish and French to leave them, which they did and on our door and the others' they wrote "good people, spare them fire."'[60] An inhabitant of Azy (Seine-et-Marne) felt the town had been saved from systematic pillage because several inhabitants knew German and understood what the soldiers needed.[61] On an altogether different scale, Thomas Heylen, the Bishop of Namur, intervened directly with Major-General von Below, as we have seen, and almost certainly prevented a bloodbath in the city.[62]

Whether violence occurred thus seemed random. How the violence unfolded, however, appeared to be anything but accidental. Rounding up the inhabitants in the public square or church, separating men and boys from the women, children and old, proceeding to collective executions and deportations, trailing the inhabitants for days on a forced march, or exposing them to fire as a human shield – all suggested a predetermined policy. The intentions of the Germans were made quite explicit by the notices which warned the population of indiscriminate reprisals in the event of hostile acts and the seizure of local notables as hostages. They indicated, too, that such measures reflected high military policy and not just vagaries of mood among the NCOs and junior officers with whom most civilians came into contact.[63] Details of the invasion appeared to support this picture of a policy of terror. German soldiers sometimes engaged in mock executions, using symbolic violence to make their power of life and death humiliatingly clear.

From the outset, Allied governments accused the Germans of committing 'atrocities' against their soldiers. The third French report claimed an 'immense number' of accounts of German soldiers summarily dispatching prisoners and wounded, and deliberately bombarding Red Cross establishments.[70] The unpublished depositions in the commission's archive support this claim (with 30 per cent of the Caen list concerning alleged crimes against Allied soldiers). Some of these accounts mentioned the mutilation of wounded soldiers – with eyes gouged out, limbs amputated, and even castration. The bayonet (serrated or normal) achieved a mythic symbolism as the instrument of mutilation and dispatch. It was rumoured, for instance, that up to 60 French wounded had been 'skewered' to the hilt on their own bayonets by the Germans after the battle of the Marne.[71] The soldiers interviewed by Professor Morgan for the Home Office reported cases of Germans mutilating British wounded.[72] Combat allows acts of sadism, but there is no corroborating witness or medical evidence for such stories, as the French official report admitted.[73] It seems more likely that they were a delusion of warfare, and above all of the trauma produced by being wounded.

The majority of the Allied soldiers' accounts, however, were more straightforward. They were typically survivor or witness narratives of wounded men lying on the battlefield who were shot at close range with rifle or revolver, stabbed with bayonets, or whose skulls were smashed with rifle butt and axe. Often the German soldiers were further accused of stripping the dead and dying of their possessions. For example, Jules Malgouverné, a corporal in French IR 146, claimed that while hidden behind a pile of rocks after the battle of Morhange in German Lorraine, on 20 August, he had 'easily distinguished the gesture of the Germans who struck the unfortunate wounded with their bayonets or their rifle butts [...] There is no doubt that they were finishing off the wounded.'[74] Jean-Baptiste Raymond (IR 338) was wounded at the battle of Bapaume in September 1914, where he saw 'German officers and soldiers finish off the wounded with rifles and revolvers [...] I saw the Germans search numerous wounded and I was robbed myself of about 15 francs.'[75] There are comparable accounts of the killing of prisoners. The most notorious concerned the order issued by Major-General Stenger to the German 58th Brigade (Sixth Army) not to take prisoners in Lorraine. The order was issued verbally on 21 August and renewed in writing on 26 August; the French had corroborating evidence from German soldiers in captivity and from an Alsatian medical officer serving in IR 112, Dr Henri Zimmerman, who managed to smuggle out a copy of the order via his brother-in-law to the French embassy in Berne.[76]

By their volume (numbering hundreds), their independent corroboration, and confirmation from German sources, as in the Stenger case, these reports suggest that French and British soldiers were not mistaken in what they saw. A significant number of Allied wounded and some prisoners were shot by the Germans during the period of mobile warfare, though statistical precision is impossible. Various explanations can be advanced for this behaviour. It might be accounted for by the trauma of modern firepower, to which soldiers in various armies responded by maltreating their opponents. Or it might be explained by strategic and cultural factors – the German army fighting a ruthless war on a tight timetable, which made enemy prisoners and wounded an encumbrance. The most infamous massacre of French wounded, however, that of Goméry in Belgium on 23 August, resulted from the German myth-complex about civilian resistance, since the Germans maintained that francs-tireurs and French soldiers had fired from the first-aid station.[77] But whatever the cause, Allied military witnesses explained such incidents as German brutality. The enemy seemed ready to kill those whom by the laws of war, common decency, and self-interest they should have protected; the violence of war and the violence of the enemy were indistinguishable.

The point is underpinned by the question of 'illegal' ammunition (i.e. the use of exploding or soft-nosed bullets). Numerous depositions (11 per cent of the Caen list) declared that particular wounds received in battle could only have come from the deliberate enemy use of dumdum bullets, and this accusation was made formally by the French and Belgian official reports.[78] The reality was more complex. The Germans almost certainly used lead-nosed bullets to some degree, but this was a matter of confusion rather than policy. A prisoner from IR 19, interrogated in November 1914, rejected as an 'infamous lie' the notion that Germans used 'dumdums'. But he explained that soft-nosed bullets used for shooting practice, to avoid splintering the target, had on occasion been issued for combat. The German army, like others, ran short of munitions in 1914. The OHL responded to the French accusation with an order for all soldiers to be checked to ensure that no such bullets were carried.[79] Another explanation of the infamous dumdum emerged from the scepticism of some French military doctors, who noted that modern bullets fired from close range or ricocheting into noise, was also shot.[86] In such instances, rape became the most extreme violation of the domestic interior.

In other cases, rape accompanied pillage or mass murder and was intended as part of a multiple violation. Mathilde B., for example, described how the Germans terrorized the inhabitants of Creue (Meuse), on 17 September, with chaotic pillaging and attempted rape. The invading soldiers stripped her home bare of food, wine, and other supplies while threatening her with bayonets, and trampled on her husband's clothes and smashed the furniture. They also

> chased after women with knives in their hands in order to rape them; I saw one, armed with a knife and unbuttoned, trying to rape Madame Denise Q. who managed to escape by calling for help. Another cornered Madame G. against a pile of hay in an attic, but as he let her go for a moment while he put down his revolver, she jumped out of a window and fled to a neighbour's, where she remained hidden in a cellar for two days.[87]

Some of the major massacres may have been accompanied by mass rapes which barely figured in the official reports. After the Belgian Commission visited Aarschot (briefly under Belgian control in mid-September 1914), it referred obliquely to the raping of women and girls but admitted that 'on this particular point, the inquiry ran into great difficulties, since those indicated as the victims, along with their families, generally opposed a total muteness to all questions.'[88] In fact, the commission heard from two Belgian soldiers who had accompanied it into Aarschot and talked to the mainly female population which remained:

> More than 20 of them told us that the Germans forced their way into their houses, locking their husbands on the upper floor or in the church; they then seized the women, making them sleep with them, for several days in succession; certain women were forced to cohabit with German soldiers for more than a fortnight. A young girl of about 16 years told our whole company, while weeping, that 18 Germans had successively raped her and that every day they recommenced.[89]

The French reports made little reference to rapes at Nomény and Gerbéviller. They left unpublished the depositions of an artillery officer who had been told appalling tales of the rape and humiliation of women in Nomény, and of an infantryman who related that the women of Gerbéviller told him: 'all the women of this locality had been violated by German soldiers belonging to the Bavarian IR 23 or 17.'[90]

Rape demonstrated in the starkest possible way that the relationship between invader and invaded was also one of gender. If male civilians were more likely to be shot, only girls and women (as far as we know) were raped, so that the invader's absolute power to violate the body was expressed in different, gendered ways.[91] This had consequences for the experience of rape. Although it was usually perpetrated in semi-secret, there were occasions on which the desire to humiliate and punish was expressed publicly. Some gang rapes took place, and the presence of the husband, parents, or children during rape was a double humiliation. Jules Laurent, a 65-year-old grocer at Magnières (Meurthe-et-Moselle), recounted that a soldier armed with a rifle raped a 12-year-old girl who had sought refuge in his house. 'The soldier was so threatening that I dared not intervene.'[92] At Connigis (Aisne), a woman was raped at gunpoint in the presence of her mother-in-law, her father-in-law being held by another soldier just outside the door.[93]

Rape before a captive audience indicates that the invasion as a gendered process was not a two-, but a three-way relationship – between perpetrator, victim, and the victim's male compatriots. The distinction is clear in the witness statements, as Ruth Harris has pointed out.[94] Silence and shame ruled the responses of raped women, whose accounts are terse and often evade the brutal heart of the matter. 'One of [the soldiers] pushed me over, pulled up my skirt, and ...' tailed off one 71-year-old victim of the collective rape of women who had taken refuge in a cellar at Louppy-le-Château (Meuse), while another added, after describing how a German soldier forced her to lie on the ground, 'I've no need to tell you the rest, you can easily guess it.' A 13-year-old girl, raped on the same occasion, simply stated that her under-garment 'filled with blood'.[95] By contrast, French and Belgian men (civilians and soldiers) often gave lurid accounts of the rape and mutilation of women and girls. These tales, which were almost totally ignored by the published reports, suggest that rape was a male fantasy that symbolized their impotence in the face of the invader.

Of course, men's accounts may have accurately reported levels of degradation and violence, including sadism and murder, which the victims' depositions ignored. A French sergeant who patrolled north of Dinant along the Meuse, from 16 to 19 August, is entirely plausible when he recounts generated by the experience of terror during the invasion, or whether they were part of the imagined memory through which the retrospective narrative was constructed, is more difficult to say. Sufficient early accounts of myths exist to suggest that these were usually generated by the experience itself, though they certainly grew in the telling.[105] What is beyond doubt is their importance for the emergence of 'German atrocities' as a mental category. The myths of the invaded had a thematic unity comparable to those of the invaders. While German soldiers vented their fear of those whom they dominated through myths of the hidden, treacherous civilian, Allied soldiers and civilians expressed their sense of being dominated through myths of direct and brutal mutilation. The fantasies so far noted were essentially masculine – advancing Germans maiming helpless Allied soldiers or raping and mutilating defenceless women. But the commonest myth of all was one that expressed a shared sense of violation: that of the baby or child whose hand had been severed by a Teutonic brute.[106]

Visions of 'severed hands' occurred throughout the civilian exodus of 1914. To quote only a few of many, Marguerite Maumert, a refugee from Mézières (Ardennes), met a little girl in the course of her flight '[whose] hands were enveloped in bandages', and of whom other people said that she was the victim of mutilation by the Germans.[107] Lucienne Boulanger, wife of a metallurgical worker from Charleville, found herself at Beugnies (Nord), at her parents' home, when the invasion occurred. On 24 August, she noticed a young boy whose hand had been severed at the wrist in a column of Belgian refugees passing through the village. 'He wore a dressing, nonetheless it was perfectly clear to me that he no longer had his hand.'[108] Marie Derumez recounted how in the neighbouring Pas-de-Calais, between Lens and Béthune, the gendarmes captured half a dozen German soldiers who, on being searched, turned out to have the severed hands of babies in their greatcoat pockets ('two hands were found on one Prussian').[109] A Belgian aircraft mechanic from Brussels, Egide Jossaert, claimed that he had seen a 12-year-old boy south of Charleroi whose hands had been amputated by Germans, who 'were supposed to have said' that it was to prevent him bearing arms against them in the future.[110]

Paris was alive with such tales. Joseph Bauduin, a refugee from Fumay (near Haybes, in the Ardennes) who reached the Gare de l'Est on 26 August, noticed a young woman followed by a five-year-old boy whose right hand was bound. 'This woman told me along with other persons', Bauduin continued, 'that she was in her house near Sedan when German soldiers came in and, without the least provocation, shot her husband in front of her and her child while others cut three fingers off the child's right hand with their sabres.'[111] A Paris policeman unconsciously indicated how suggestible opinion in the capital had become at the height of the German advance when in a statement made on 8 September he recounted what, a week earlier, he had been told by an acquaintance, René Pascal, who was a commercial traveller: 'We were talking about the atrocities committed by the German troops in Belgium. At a certain point, M. Pascal said to me: "Yesterday, I saw a little Belgian girl, aged six; she was with one of her relatives who is a butcher established on the rue de Flandre; when the German soldiers arrived in her village, they cut off her two hands, at the wrists, with a hatchet."'[112] Other witnesses indicated how the rumours of mutilation continued to circulate for several months throughout the occupied regions. A French customs officer at Vireux (Ardennes), who escaped to unoccupied France after nine months in invaded territory, declared that 'as far as atrocities which the Germans are supposed to have committed are concerned, I have frequently heard reference to them. In particular, I was told that they had cut off children's arms and women's breasts, but as I was not a witness to any deed of this kind, I don't think I can say more on the subject.'[113]

In the case of Dinant, it is possible to reconstruct how a tale of severed hands functioned as a symbol of terror. One current of opinion in Dinant, as we have seen, remained sceptical about 'German atrocities' after the brief German raid into the Saint-Jacques district on the night of 21–22 August. But some of the population fled, encountering French IR 43 the following day. A sergeant recalled that 'these people were in a state of extreme terror' as they described how the yelling Germans had killed women and children. As noted, seven civilians were indeed killed, including women and children. But in the account of another sergeant of IR 43, the civilians' terror was turned into a tale of mutilation. 'I heard several inhabitants tell our officers', he stated, 'that the Germans had taken a very young infant, cut off its feet and hands, and given it back thus mutilated to its mother.'[114] There is no evidence for mutilation in Dinant. The myth was a condensed representation of the fugitives' fear as well as an account of what had precipitated their flight.

An important variant of the 'severed hands' theme, in which German soldiers stole women's rings (with their matrimonial associations) by lopping off their hands, linked children and women as victims. Auguste Portefaix, a corporal in French Colonial IR 1 near Charleroi in August, soldiers drunk with beer and spirits, hallucinating with the terror which makes all their commanders tremble [...], began to kill each other on the night of 25–26 August.'[123]

In the absence of an overall account, witnesses from both sides were important because they particularized the phenomenon. War diaries found on German soldiers were released to the press. Both *Le Temps* and the London *Times* quoted (among others) the officer diarist who chronicled IR 178's bloody 'reprisals' against francs-tireurs as it crossed Belgium, noting that it was 'like the Thirty Years' War. Murder and burning.'[124] Testimony by Belgian and French civilians was of course more widely cited. *Le Temps*, for example, published a gripping account of No}ény by a Mademoiselle Jacquemot, borrowed from *L'Est républicain*, and *Le Matin* carried witness accounts of Louvain and Charleroi, the former from Belgian refugees camped in the Winter Circus in Paris.[125] Such statements were presented as unmediated testimonies to the reality of the events they recounted, as if they spoke for themselves.[126]

In reality, of course, the newspapers added powerful editorial rhetoric. This was the second factor at work in the journalistic construction of the 'German atrocities', and arguably it was the most important. For incomplete information was no bar to absolute moral judgement, and the press helped develop a public discourse on 'German atrocities' that portrayed these as emblematic of the larger issues at stake in the war. Fine distinctions were not made. Despite evidence of a collective German delusion about civilian resistance, the press preferred explanations of German behaviour in terms of history and national character. Roland de Marès, editor of the oldest Brussels liberal daily, *L'Indépendance belge*, witnessed the exodus from the capital before reaching Paris, where he wrote a series of columns for *Le Temps*. He explained the Germans' franc-tireur claim as a cynical cover for a long-planned 'war of extermination'.[127]

In fact, 'German atrocities' supplied an editorial yardstick of good and evil. As early as 4 August 1914 *Le Matin* had begun to present the war as the conflict between 'civilization' and 'barbarism'.[128] The brutal invader was generalized as the German army or nation or individualized as the Kaiser, or the Crown Prince. 'William the Ravager' was the caption of a composite photo in *Le Matin*, showing the Kaiser in a spiked helmet surrounded by the devastation of Louvain, Malines, Senlis, Liège, Visé, and Antwerp, while a cartoon in *La Guerre sociale* portrayed a cart creaking under the weight of booty and pulled by soldiers, with 'Crown Prince Removals' marked on its side.[129] The Allied countries were portrayed as victims of German aggression, and observing civilized norms of warfare. The treatment of wounded and prisoners underlined the same simple dichotomy, the compassion of the Allies being contrasted with enemy callousness. 'Dedicated to the Barbarians' was the title of a photo in *Excelsior*, showing two Belgian nurses bandaging the arm of a German prisoner, in what became a mini-genre.[130]

It would be surprising if the editorial morality tale of 'German atrocities' ignored the mythic dimension of the witness reports. It is possible that journalists fabricated 'atrocity' stories, although the evidence for this seems slight. One example may be the story attributed to an official communiqué and reproduced on 18 August about the little boy who, playfully aiming his wooden rifle at a German column, was summarily executed. Apart from naming the village of Magny where it supposedly occurred, the tale was unencumbered with facts and soon disappeared.[131] But by 20 August it appeared as a front page cartoon in *La Guerre sociale*, and as a free-standing image of German brutality (sometimes accompanied by a poem) it enjoyed considerable success on postcards and in illustrated journals (illustration 10).[132] More typically, however, newspapers uncritically derived their myths from refugees and soldiers. This is demonstrated by the transition of the 'severed hands' from witness myth to newspaper report.

The Agence Havas picked up the story from refugees at Ostend in late August of an old woman in Liège who had her hand cut off as she extended it in farewell to the departing German soldiers who had been billeted on her. The story was published by the *Daily Chronicle* from which *Le Matin* copied it a day later. It already suggested that the Germans (as barbarians) did not understand elementary hospitality, but it remained unembellished.[133] The myth quickly revealed its protean character, however, as it was used by the French and British press to demonize the enemy. An editorial in *Le Matin* on 20 September concerned the supposed discovery of two hands (one of a woman, the other of a young girl) in the pockets of two wounded Germans, and elaborated a double message from the tale. Not only did the brutal amputation with a saw-toothed bayonet for the theft of rings condemn the 'wretched soldiers of William II' but it also revealed the sinister intentions of 'the Pan-German professors' to 'exterminate the French race in order to seize its territory'. This spiralling editorial investment of the myth is entirely typical. Nonetheless, it should not be supposed that the serious press embraced such fantasies. Neither *Le Temps* nor *The*

10   The boy with the wooden gun. French postcard, 1914

Times ran 'severed hands' stories, and L.-L. Klotz, the minister responsible for censorship in France, later recalled that he intervened in order to suppress a story in *Le Figaro* in which two eminent scientists had supposedly seen 100 children whose hands had been cut off by the Germans.[154] It was in the undergrowth of the popular and sensationalist press that the myth flourished – and also in cartoons.

As with the boy and the wooden gun, the journalistic myth of the 'severed hands' probably achieved its greatest impact in graphic form. The

— « ... T'as peur, Tropmann ?...
— Non ! mais avant de mourir, j'aurais
voulu voir Carcassonne ! »

A. Willette
1914

11   Severed hands: a German soldier caught stealing rings (French cartoon, October 1914)

conventions of the political cartoon may explain why this and other myths were more acceptable as an illustration, ambiguously understood as either literal or symbolic, than as a news story. The *Bulletin des Armées de la République*, which reached every French military unit, did not mention 'severed hands' in its detailed coverage of 'German atrocities' from August to December 1914. Yet in late October, it published a cartoon on the theme (by Adolphe Willette) as an autonomous symbol that required no contextual comment (illustration 11). Four Allied soldiers confront a very unmilitary-looking enemy prisoner from whose pockets spill severed hands and stolen rings. Condemned to die, he replies (when asked) that he is not afraid but would have liked to see Carcassonne, that is, to have reached the south of France. The Allies (a Scot, as the most identifiable British soldier, a Belgian civic guard, and ironically a Senegalese, conventionally seen as the 'savage') are the accusatory voice of 'civilization', with the French infantryman naturally its spokesman. The motif of the 'severed hands' had become an allegory of the invasion, the enemy, and the war.

A flood of similar caricatures appeared in the first year of the war. Poulbot, well known for his sentimental images of children, showed an

12 Severed hands: the child as symbolic victim. Poulbot, 'It's her hand' (1915)

infant martyr, a little girl with her wrist bandaged, kneeling at the tomb of her own hand! (illustration 12). A further cartoon by Willette evoked the bad conscience of the German soldier on returning home as he recalled the dismembered infants of the invasion, a theme echoed in a different register by Ibels in the waking dream of the Kaiser, who stares at a mutely imploring army of handless children (illustration 13). The systematic pillaging of the invaded regions was condemned by Hermann-Paul with a drawing of a soldier, in the process of emptying a house, who asks his officer if he should 'also pack the hands of the little girl' (illustration 14). In parallel with these images in established journals came a profusion of much cruder picture postcards, in which 'severed hands' were equally important. The theft of rings was illustrated by a primitive postcard of October 1914, 'Their war trophy' (illustration 15).[155]

Like the soldiers and civilians in the invasion zone, the French (and British) press grounded its perception of 'German atrocities' in actual occurrences. The reports of massacres, incendiarism, human shields,

3　Severed hands: the Kaiser's guilt. French cartoon, 1915

pillage, and even the killing of Allied wounded and prisoners did not have
to be invented. Witness evidence, military reports, and journalists' investigations provided a mass of fragments from which some larger picture could
be built, though it remained incomplete during the invasion period. Yet the
meanings which the press gave events were passionate and partisan.
Detached and sceptical analysis would have countered the tendency, but the
press was caught in a powerfully conformist tide of national solidarity. Its
language, and even more its iconography, were charged with moral outrage
and hatred and it was this, rather than any fabrication or distortion of the
major incidents, which shaped the terms in which it understood the
'German atrocities'. The myths which it trawled from the rich imagery of
terrified soldiers and refugees were an allegorical distillation of the broader
message, rather than deliberate or even guileless misinformation, though
both of these occurred. Press representations of 'German atrocities' spoke to
real events, but did so in the language of vilification.

14   Severed hands: German pillage ('Should I also pack up the hands of
the little girl, Sir?'). French cartoon, 1915

5   Memories, mentalities, and the construction of 'German atrocities'

The hold of 'German atrocities' over Allied opinion is explained not only by
the events to which they referred but also by deeper mentalities and traditions through which they were expressed. Neither the content nor the
vocabulary of national antagonism was new. Both had developed against a
background of rising international tension, and this explains why the
language of 'atrociousness' emerged fully fledged within a few days of the
outbreak of war. The Franco-Prussian War left an enduring legacy in
France. In 1870, the trauma of invasion and the Republican mobilization
for war were seen as the defence of 'civilization' against 'barbarism'. If the
attempted *levée en masse* by the French Republic turned France into

Oct. 1914
O'Gery

Leurs trophé   de guerre
Une main afec des bagues, ça
faut mieux qu'un trapeau.

15   Severed hands: German triumph ('Their war trophy'). French postcard, 1914

Germany's arch-enemy, the German invaders were accused by the French of committing outrages – 'German atrocities' – in combating the francs-tireurs. French military organization between 1870 and 1914 in no sense relied on irregular volunteers, but on the full implementation of universal military service in a national army (for which the example of the *levée en masse* of 1793 provided an ideological justification).[136] Nonetheless, the polarized language inherited from the war of 1870–1 lived on, not least in memoirs and fiction (such as stories and novels by Alphonse Daudet and Émile Zola) which celebrated the heroic franc-tireur or civilian resisting Prussian tyranny.[137]

The dichotomy between French 'civilization' and German 'barbarism' also fitted the universal claims of French Republicanism, deriving from the Enlightenment and the Revolution, which were reinforced by the war of 1870 and given institutional and ideological expression by the new regime. Between 1870 and the First World War, 'civilization' in a universal sense was increasingly contrasted with the German concept of *Kultur* ('culture') which emphasized linguistic and cultural particularity. The new nationalist right which developed from the late 1880s had a quite different concept of French 'civilization', viewing it as everything which made France particular and unique; but this was premised on the difference, and potential barbarism, of other 'races'. These linguistic tensions between 'civilization', 'culture', and 'barbarism' were thus present in pre-war language. They were exacerbated by the Moroccan crises in 1905 and 1911, which renewed the sense of German threat in what was increasingly seen as a contest between fundamental value systems.[138]

In the British case, the antagonism with Germany was more recent, dating from the 1880s, and especially from the early 1900s. The German naval challenge increased anxiety about the health and vitality of British society and 'civilization' already aroused by the South African War. It revived long-standing British fears of invasion from the continent as well as concern at a naval threat to the Empire.[139] None of this meant that Germany was portrayed one-dimensionally as the national enemy in either Britain or France before 1914. Multiple Germanies were perceived to exist by different currents of opinion in both countries. But the language of polarization was at work. The second Moroccan crisis rehearsed and refined the language of national enmity, with the picture of the Germans as half buffoons, half brutal menace a commonplace of the British and French coverage of events in 1911–12.

Belgium might seem to be a contrasting case. The Francophile tendencies of the pre-war elites of both language communities, as well as of the
Walloon population as a whole, did not imply Germanophobia. The preservation of neutrality in a more tense international climate lay at the heart of
the robust Belgian sense of identity. This was enhanced in the pre-war years
by the current of 'new nationalism' within government, and the belated
introduction of universal military service in 1913. It was the shock and
anger produced by the threat to this Belgian identity, not pre-existing
antipathy, that more than anything else created a vocabulary of national
antagonism in Belgium in August 1914 that was almost identical to those
of its new allies. 'Are you resolved to defend the sacred patrimony of our
ancestors?' demanded King Albert of parliament, on 4 August, referring to
the state's foundation in 1830.[140]

Pre-war attitudes to the international law of war also shaped the Allied
construction of 'German atrocities'. The humanitarian impulse to codify
war in the later nineteenth century sprang from belief in a European civilization based on moral progress, the rule of law, and peace, which was well
represented in all the powers that found themselves at war in 1914. True,
the principles of 'civilized' conduct in warfare were flouted frequently
between 1870 and 1914, but this was usually in what were perceived as
'uncivilized' or at best 'semi-civilized' armies or theatres of war, such as the
colonies or the Balkans. Only six months before the European war, for
example, the Carnegie Commission published a comprehensive report
condemning atrocities in the Balkan wars of 1912–13 which shocked
German as well as French and British opinion, and were widely held to
indicate the uncivilized status of the societies concerned.[141] For contemporaries, it was by no means self-evident in 1914 that 'civilized' belligerents
which had signed the Hague Conventions would contravene the 'laws of
war'.

In Germany, as we have seen, the army and nationalist circles were in
reality deeply sceptical of both the Hague position on civilian involvement
in warfare and the general possibility of moderating military violence by
international law. Such views were not unknown elsewhere, but the
governments, armies, and intellectual establishments of France, Britain,
and Belgium seem to have taken the Hague Convention IV on Land
Warfare very seriously, as evidenced by the incorporation of its provisions in
the French and British military manuals.[142] The Belgian government made
copious reference to it in the instructions issued from 4 August which were

designed to avoid undisciplined civilian resistance.[143] French government officials were equally well informed, and referred to the Convention when anticipating a German invasion of the frontier departments and making provision for local *gardes civils*.[144]

Belief in the Hague Conventions not only made 'German atrocities' in 1914 genuinely shocking, but also turned them into war crimes. The German army appeared to repudiate its own legal obligations by engaging in the 'barbaric' warfare so recently decried by German opinion. *Le Temps* commented ironically on the fact that 'at the moment of the Balkan War the German press indignantly denounced the excesses of the soldiery in Macedonia' and that 'committees were set up in Germany to protest in the name of civilization against the finishing off of the wounded, the assassination of civilians, the burning of several villages and the forced exodus of the population.'[145] In late October 1914, Louis Renault, professor of law at the Sorbonne and the chief French legal adviser at the 1907 Hague Conference, delivered the annual public address at the Institut de France before a huge audience on the subject of 'War and human rights in the twentieth century'. He rehearsed the classic texts codifying war, culminating in the 1907 Hague Convention on Land Warfare, before concluding that 'so many eminent men were convinced, like me, that we had helped civilization make serious progress. The disappointment is too cruel [...]'[146]

Ordinary opinion was undoubtedly less concerned with international law. Yet the sense that an invading army had no right to target innocent civilians and their property was strong. Although the restrained language of the civilian depositions to the official commissions did not favour invective, the vocabulary of outrage, where it broke through, resembled that of government and press: 'I consider that the conduct of the Germans in our canton was that of bandits and robbers rather than soldiers,' stated several inhabitants of Rebais (Marne), while other witnesses condemned the Germans who pillaged their property or murdered their menfolk as 'barbarians'.[147] Official or demotic, the conclusion was the same – the Germans had placed themselves beyond the law and reverted to 'barbarism'.

The shock of invasion ensured that the pre-war vocabulary and imagery of national antagonism, with its simple contrasts, assumed a particularly reductivist form in France and Britain. Central to this was a linguistic reconfiguration which allowed Germans to be portrayed in the most negative light. 'Civilization', in its commonest French and British usages, had a double reverse side. As a term purporting to describe human evolution, its natural opposite was 'barbarism' or 'savagery'. Barbarism was defined historically as the primitive past from which 'civilization' had emerged, and geographically, as those regions of the earth which 'civilization' had not yet transformed. Yet as we have seen, in a more technical sense, and before the war not in a necessarily antagonistic one, the universalizing idea of 'civilization' was also contrasted with the particularist German concept of 'culture'. With the war, these two opposites merged and German 'Kultur' (as it was mockingly spelt) became the very essence of 'barbarism'.

This linguistic adjustment meant that history and geography could be used to depict the Germans as barbarians in newspapers, cartoons, and ordinary language. History pointed to the barbarian invasions of the Roman Empire with which mass primary school education had familiarized most soldiers and civilians by 1914. 'Vandals', 'Huns', and the image of the barbarian hordes descending on 'civilization' saturated the representation of the 'atrocity' issue, as with the ludicrous figure of the German 'vandal' taken from Hansi's popular cartoon history of Alsace (illustration 16), or the sinister figure of the Kaiser as the 'modern Attila' (illustration 17). The theme of the barbarian invasions also helps explain the impact of Louvain and Rheims, which provided graphic symbols of the Germans as the new barbarians, who committed what amounted to cultural atrocities.

The invention of national traditions in the nineteenth century included the redefinition of major historical and architectural monuments as sites of memory which helped constitute the nation. Their destruction by the enemy was taken to be a deliberate attack on national identity, and was forbidden by Articles 27 and 56 of Hague Convention IV (see appendix 2). In the case of Rheims, German forces, after withdrawing from the town following the battle of the Marne, bombarded the cathedral on 17–19 September, alleging that the French artillery were shooting from its towers. Much of the medieval statuary and stained glass was destroyed in the ensuing fire, although the reduction of the fabric to a mere shell only occurred after prolonged trench warfare. The French denied they had used the cathedral for military purposes, claiming their nearest batteries were 1,200 metres distant; the Red Cross flag was flown from its towers and like many churches, it was used as a first-aid station. There may have been genuine confusion over the military role of the cathedral. Yet given the place of church towers in the collective delusion of the People's War – and Rheims cathedral had the biggest towers encountered during the invasion

16   The Germans as vandals (wartime postcard from Hansi's *History of Alsace*)

– the Germans may have responded as they did elsewhere by deliberately destroying them with artillery fire. Certainly, before leaving Rheims on 12 September, they had seized 81 hostages and threatened to burn the town down at the first sign of resistance.[148]

From the Allied point of view, the destruction of historic monuments was the ultimate proof of barbarism. 'The town of Louvain [...], which was the intellectual metropolis of the Low Countries since the fifteenth century, is

SON RÊVE : ÊTRE L'ATTILA DES TEMPS MODERNES
L' HERBE NE REPOUSSE JAMAIS SOUS LES PAS DE MON CHEVAL !...

17   The Kaiser as Attila the Hun (French postcard, 1914–15)

today nothing but a heap of cinders', declared the Belgian government. Rheims, in addition to being one of France's most glorious cathedrals, was the deeply historic and symbolic place at which the coronation of the French monarchs had taken place, and where Jeanne d'Arc, after raising the English siege of Orléans, had led the young Dauphin in triumph to be crowned Charles VII. The French government communiqué on Rheims protested:

> So disappears, in the twentieth century, due to German troops acting against the international agreements signed by their government, in the

18   German 'Kultur' and the destruction of Rheims cathedral
(French postcard, 1914–15)

course of a war which France neither declared nor provoked, [...] a monument so sacred that in the course of innumerable previous wars and many invasions it has been respected by the armies of all countries, even in the darkest periods of the Middle Ages.[149]

French postcards portrayed German 'Kultur' stalking past the ruins of Rheims (illustration 18) and the Kaiser as the 'King of the Vandals', chained before a crucified Rheims cathedral and an avenging Jeanne d'Arc (illustration 19).

19   The coronation of the Kaiser as 'King of the Vandals' (French
postcard, 1914–15)

No less effective for portraying enemy barbarism was the ironic inversion
of the relationship between contemporary 'savages' and cultured Germans.
Two French postcards illustrate the transposition, with a native American
in one, holding a grotesque shield and a serrated spear, commenting to a
German soldier with his saw-toothed bayonet: 'You are even more savage
than me.' In another, which conflated the bombarding of churches with the
'wooden rifle' myth, the supercilious monocled officer and the bestial
soldier were unambiguously designated 'savages' (illustration 20). The
colonial theme supplied a highly charged and complex repertory for this
process, given the pre-war accusations against various powers of imperialist
'atrocities' and the legacy of guilt in different European countries. French

20   'Savages'. The German military as seen by a French
cartoonist. Postcard, 1914

cartoonists used the wide-eyed amazement of 'savages' and cannibals at
German military behaviour to underscore the inversion, as shown by the
inclusion of the Senegalese soldier in the Allied contingent confronting the
German soldier with his collection of amputated hands (illustration 11).
Another cartoon in the *Bulletin des Armées de la République* made the
same point, with two cannibals reading the European papers and commenting: 'Germans used to treat us as savages! … We little lambs alongside
them!'

Yet the colonial theme was not just a matter of representation; it intruded into the substance of the 'atrocity' question. As we have seen, the treatment of Africans in colonial wars probably influenced German military doctrine on how to deal with civilian resistance, and at Andenne, the lawyer Monjoie protested that Major Scheunemann, who ordered the executions and who had spent ten years in the Cameroons, 'treated us as negroes'.[150] The Germans reversed the terms of the argument by maintaining that the use in the European theatre of colonial troops who were by definition 'savages' offended against civilized norms. They developed counter-accusations focusing on the ferocity of 'coloured troops' in the French and British armies and on their supposed mutilation of the enemy.[151] The most powerful image, the myth of the 'severed hands', which was Belgian in origin and had no precursor in 1870–1, almost certainly drew its content from the international scandal which engulfed the Belgian Congo Company from 1903 to 1908, and which included the sensational charge that the company's officials had punitively cut off the hands of indentured Congolese workers, including children. Among the international outpouring of condemnation, the leading pre-war French satirical journal, *L'Assiette au beurre*, devoted an entire issue in 1908 to the 'severed hands' of the Congo (illustration 21). What an ironic reversal, then, that Belgian colonial brutality (and Belgian guilt) should supply the dominant motif of victimhood for Belgium in 1914.[152]

A further reservoir of collective representation for 'German atrocities' was provided by criminality. Belgian and French civilians experienced the invasion as a violation not only of person and property but of the legal order protecting these. All the German actions against civilians – murder, rape, arson, armed robbery, or simple pilfering – were offences under domestic criminal (and indeed military) law. But what was individual, deviant, and punishable in peacetime became collective, flagrant, and officially condoned by the enemy in wartime. The invasion was thus seen as an act of mass criminality, and ordinary German soldiers, or symbolically the Kaiser, as the worst of felons. In France, assassination and armed robbery evoked the notorious pre-war Bonnot gang of motorized bank robbers, and according to *Le Charivari*, the 'soubriquet of Kaiser-Bonnot (was) given at the beginning of the war to the biggest criminal who has ever reigned over a people'.[153] To many, the invasion appeared to overturn public order and respect for property, and it is no semantic accident that when witnesses and journalists described the invader, they constantly used the terms 'assassins',

21   The origin of the 'severed hands'? Belgian atrocities in the Congo as seen by *L'Assiette au Beurre* (Paris) 1908

'criminals', 'brigands', 'bandits', and even 'thugs', or *apaches* – the word for street gangs from half-developed suburban Paris that preyed on the richer districts.

Perhaps the deepest cultural references feeding the Allied understanding of 'German atrocities' were those attached to violence itself. The invasion, after all, was an act of unparalleled violence. The vocabulary and imagery of violence available to make sense of it was by definition unmatched to the task. Only slowly did languages develop which were adequate to the events and to the kind of warfare so dramatically revealed in 1914. In some respects, the growing humanitarian impulse to codify war was part of a broader sensibility that emerged in nineteenth-century Europe which sought to mask and control naked violence, as evidenced by the emergence of more humane and less public forms of capital punishment and the decline in violent sports.[154] Much energy was spent on civilizing the expression of violence, and this made the shock of 1914 all the greater.[155]

The perennial fascination with mutilation and violation noted by Marc Bloch had hardly been eliminated from peacetime society. It had, however, been channelled into the growing interest in deviant criminality and even, one historian has argued, in sado-masochistic pornography. The appeal of both took many forms, including the obsession of the sensationalist press with violent crime.[156] The very deviance and marginality which made violence and pornography unrespectable also made them attractive. Precisely because they were not the norm, they provided extreme words and images which could be used both in the public arena (e.g. applied to domestic political enemies) and for private fantasy. Rape, murder, mutilation, and pain occupied a central place. From this viewpoint, Jack the Ripper or his late nineteenth-century French equivalent, Jacques Vacher, expressed the fascination with extreme violence, including dismemberment, which civilized norms of behaviour had by no means succeeded in eliminating.[157] When real violence intruded on a massive scale in 1914, condensed and highly charged forms of representation were needed to describe it. Rape, brutal murder, and above all mutilation fulfilled this need, whether as collective myth or media image.

None of these cultural references, and the language and collective representations they supplied, operated independently of experience. In constructing 'German atrocities', Allied opinion was reacting to German methods of warfare. Although there were similarities with the German franc-tireur myth-complex, there was also a fundamental difference: 'German atrocities' were not only a means of designating the enemy, they also attempted to find a language for the realities of the German invasion.

Part III
War of words, 1914–1918: German atrocities and the meanings of war

German form of warfare consisting of 'systematic' violence against civilians and captured or wounded Allied soldiers.[4] The commission accompanied the Belgian government to Le Havre. Only there could it piece together the experience of the inhabitants of Namur and Luxembourg provinces, who had fled to France.[5] A detailed itemization of the initial atrocities in Liège province did not appear until May 1915, and the final report on the invasion, concerning Hainaut province, was published only in October 1915. By that stage, the overall magnitude of the 'German atrocities' was clear, and the Belgian government information service in Le Havre (the Bureau Documentaire Belge) quoted a broadly correct figure of 6,000 Belgian civilian victims.[6]

Unlike the Belgian Commission, the French inquiry could visit the site of the alleged crimes. The original ministerial investigation ordered on 20 August 1914 was turned into a semi-judicial inquiry, under Georges Payelle, the president of the Cour des Comptes (Audit Office), whose first report used on-the-spot investigations of areas freed by the Germans as they retreated from the Marne. But refugees and convalescing soldiers were soon scattered throughout France, and Briand, the Minister of Justice – as we have seen – placed the entire judicial apparatus at the disposal of the commission for gathering their evidence.[7] The difficulties of conducting investigations by roving commissions throughout the liberated areas and sifting the mass of material from the rest of the country explains the slow pace of publication, with the first report not appearing (despite press criticism) until early January 1915.[8] Continued government anxiety about a renewed invasion fear may have added to the delay.[9]

When it came, however, the first French report made a profound impression at home and abroad. It took the form of a 45-page brochure covering the départements wholly or partly freed from German control. It detailed collective executions (especially in the Meurthe-et-Moselle), rapes, individual acts of brutality, and the full panoply of arson and pillage. Edited testimony was added in the full version (over 250 pages), but it was the short version that was published in many newspapers, sold in differently priced editions, and circulated internationally in translation.[10] *Le Temps* considered that the report placed the Kaiser and his army before the 'tribunal of universal conscience'.[11]

British opinion, including that in the highest political circles, was impressed by the French document. Successive Belgian reports had already been received by the Foreign Office and published in the British press.[12] But the measured tone and seemingly irrefutable evidence of German 'frightfulness' in the French report, including its sober yet explicit recital of rapes, generated even greater anger. The press magnate Lord Riddell discussed it with Lloyd George (then Chancellor of the Exchequer) in mid-January 1915. According to Riddell, '[the report] contains most obscene and dreadful details. [Lloyd George] said that it should be published verbatim.'[13] In fact, the *Daily Chronicle* published two editions of the report, an official translation following in 1916, and it was widely summarized in the press.[14] Subsequent French (and Belgian) reports received less attention in Britain, doubtless because of the intense publicity generated in the late spring of 1915 by the report of Britain's own investigation, the Bryce Committee.

Given the importance of Belgium in justifying British entry into the war, the British government had just as much reason to condemn German atrocities as the nations directly exposed to them. In September 1914, the Prime Minister, Asquith, who publicly condemned the 'blind, barbarian vengeance' of the sack of Louvain, instructed the Home Secretary (Sir Reginald McKenna) and the Attorney-General (Sir John Simon) to collect evidence on the 'accusations of inhumanity and outrage' made against German soldiers.[15] More than 1,200 depositions were taken in the autumn of 1914, mainly among the Belgian refugees in Britain, by a team operating under the authority of the Director of Public Prosecutions.[16] The Home Office also participated in the separate investigation carried out by the Belgian official commission in Britain and almost certainly used the same network of contacts (established through the Belgian Relief Committee) for its own inquiry.[17] As in France and Belgium, Allied soldiers were an important source of evidence, and the Home Office sent Professor J. H. Morgan to France from November 1914 to March 1915 to interview British soldiers.[18]

The initial format of the inquiry suggested a quasi-judicial motivation – that of establishing breaches of the laws of war.[19] However, in mid-December 1914, the government shifted the focus by appointing a small committee of non-governmental legal experts and intellectuals to advise the government on the evidence already collected on 'outrages alleged to have been committed by German troops [...], cases of alleged maltreatment of civilians in the invaded territories, and breaches of the laws and established usages of war'.[20] The motivation of Asquith and the cabinet is not entirely clear. The battle for neutral opinion was vital, especially in the USA. But the British government may also have wanted to restrain the more lurid allegations about German behaviour which might weaken the moral advantage which the German invasion of Belgium had given the Allies.[21]

Viscount James Bryce had impeccable credentials for presiding over the reoriented British inquiry. He was an academic historian, lawyer, and educationalist who had studied at Heidelberg as well as Oxford, and was sympathetic to German culture (he held honorary doctorates from two German universities and was a member of the German order Pour le Mérite). After a political career as a Liberal MP and cabinet minister, he was a highly successful non-career ambassador to the United States from 1907 to 1913 and served as a delegate to the International Court at The Hague. He became an ardent advocate of the League of Nations during the war.[22] The Bryce Committee's report, published in early May 1915, has been criticized for falling well short of the standards of an impartial legal investigation and contributing to the distorted propaganda on 'German atrocities', especially through lurid accounts of rape and mutilation. Bryce's credentials are seen to have made the deception all the more effective, while the report's enormous success has cast additional doubt on the purity of Bryce's motives.[23] It was translated into more than 30 languages and widely circulated by British propaganda services, especially in the USA.[24] The question of how the 'atrocities' issue was seen in neutral countries will be returned to later. But the nature of the Bryce Report, like that of the Belgian and French reports, goes to the heart of the Allied official construction of 'German atrocities'.

The Bryce Committee issued two publications – a 61-page report, its argument backed up with copious quotations from witness depositions, and a longer appendix which cited more witness evidence at greater length.[25] The report was divided into two parts, the first describing instances of German brutality to civilians, the second being a typology of the 'outrages' committed.[26]

The report refers to 'outrages' in 38 places in Belgium. Twenty-one of these were 'major' incidents as defined in chapter 2 above. Comparison between Bryce and the major incidents which we have established in appendix 1 (below) shows that the Bryce Report was geographically out of balance, dealing mainly with Liège and Brabant provinces. There was only cursory mention of Namur province (Andenne, Tamines, and Dinant). Coverage of Hainaut was confined to the Charleroi district, and Luxembourg was ignored. This reflects the geographical origins of most of the refugees in Britain. Nonetheless, granted its uneven coverage, the Bryce

Report's narratives of individual incidents essentially match those in appendix 1. Sometimes, the Bryce account exaggerates numbers – with 400 instead of 262 killed at Andenne, for example. Yet for Tamines, Dinant and Aarschot, Bryce gave lower figures than the real total, and overall, the committee underestimated the death and destruction caused by the invaders. Its explanations of the bigger incidents were broadly correct, such as German fury at being held up by the forts of Liège, and confusion in the face of Belgian counter-attack as the cause of Louvain.

The typology of acts which the report established certainly reflected the balance of the witness evidence since it closely resembles the main categories of material gathered in France, as reconstructed in chapter 5 (table 1). It has already been noted that the Belgian, French, and British commissions dealt with comparable evidence drawn from civilian refugees and Allied and German soldiers, though in the case of Bryce, the original depositions have disappeared.[27] The Bryce Report emphasized a systematic German policy of terrorization of the civilian population. It highlighted hostage-taking, human shields, collective executions, punitive arson and other acts which, it is now clear, indeed took place. Contrary to the hitherto accepted view, material of a sexual or prurient nature did not dominate the report, at least quantitatively. Taking all 38 incidents, rapes were mentioned in connection with four of them (10.5 per cent), the killing of children in three, and mutilation in six (16 per cent). The section on 'the treatment of women and children' in the thematic part of the report represented a little over five out of 50 pages. Yet even this weighting of the sexual and the sadistic would be unwarranted if the evidence used was suspect. Precisely because rape, mutilation and the slaughter of children all carried a powerful symbolic charge, there was an obvious danger (acknowledged by the Bryce Committee) of witness distortion that might be passed on to investigators.

The section of the Bryce Report dealing with the 'treatment of women and children' was due essentially to one of its members, the historian and Vice-Chancellor of Sheffield University, H. A. L. Fisher. Many of the Bryce Report's accounts of rape are plausible, given the difficulty of obtaining corroborated evidence; however, no attempt was made to claim that they were part of military policy, and it was admitted that some rapes had been punished by the German military authorities.[28] Mutilation and the murder of children are more problematic. Many accounts of mutilation in Bryce relate to the fury of the German rear-guard at the Belgian counter-attack on 25 August, resulting in brutal retribution on the villages in the triangle formed by Vilvoorde, Mechelen (Malines) and Rotselaar. Here, the first and second Belgian committees' reports and unpublished Belgian depositions provide some corresponding evidence. They support, for example, the Bryce Report's account of charred and mutilated civilian corpses found after German soldiers were driven from the villages of Zempst and Hofstade.[29] Other cases are less clear. There is nothing to say whether the woman recorded by the post-war Belgian report as killed in Eppeghem was the bayoneted pregnant woman mentioned by the Bryce Report – though in this case other details tally.[30] The Bryce witnesses at Elewyt told of a naked female corpse and a mutilated man's body tied to a ring in the wall of a house. The Belgian post-war report states that as well as deportations and house-burning, there were four rapes in Elewyt and five male civilians were killed, including one after torture.[31]

Yet comparison with the death lists published in the post-war Belgian Commission's reports indicates that some of the witness evidence cited by Bryce on the fate of women and children was fantasy. In reality adult males were the chief victims. Where the second Belgian report records ten dead for Hofstade, with one woman, Bryce records 12, five of them women, three of them boys under 16 years, and five of them mutilated. At Weerde, one person died according to the post-war report, yet the Bryce Committee has four men shot down and two children bayoneted.[32] Women's corpses seen in Malines and Hofstade with breasts amputated fit the category of male hysteria discussed in chapter 5, and indeed, the evidence of mutilation and sadistic killing comes disproportionately from Belgian soldiers involved in the counter-offensive of late August.

Despite the double filter of the Home Office investigators and the committee itself, myth and hysteria coloured many of the witness statements used. The cumulative effect of the extracts published in the separate appendix to the report was one of random and widespread German sadism, especially towards women and children, which exceeded any possible reality. The Bryce Report slid from the factual into the symbolic. The process is epitomized by the most charged symbol of all – severed hands. The report noted that the severing of hands was 'alleged' to have occurred and a number of depositions to this effect were published in the appendix. The possibility that the tales were witness fantasy was ignored. Rational explanations were offered instead (the sweeping sabres of charging cavalry, the theft of rings). Yet Bryce never endorsed these stories as fact, thus achieving maximum benefit from what remained merely a suggestion.[33]

However, the Bryce Committee was more balanced in explaining German military behaviour than the French report. Both commissions rejected German claims of massive civilian resistance. The Bryce Report accepted the possibility of scattered local hostility, but pointed out that no proof of francs-tireurs had been presented by the Germans. Yet where the French report condemned the German argument as a cynical cover for military terror, Bryce (like the Belgian wartime commission) accurately identified the genesis of the German belief in the mythology and hysteria of the invading army, although it suggested that 'this attitude of mind may have been fostered by the German authorities before the troops passed the frontier.'[34]

The French report blamed German society as a whole, claiming that 'the German mentality [has shown] an astonishing regression since 1870,' but the Bryce Report was more sophisticated.[35] It refused to blame the German people ('whoever has travelled among the German peasantry knows that they are as kindly and good-natured as any people in Europe') and asserted that no comparable charges were levelled against them in 1870. Significantly, Bryce withdrew his introduction to the book in which J. H. Morgan presented his inquiry among British soldiers when Morgan, who was not a member of the committee, called for reprisals against German non-combatants in a letter to *The Times*.[36] The real culprit for the Bryce Committee was not the German nation but the German officer corps, and the 'ruling caste' from which it sprang. Militarism was to blame.

This last point provides the key to understanding the motivation of the Bryce Committee, which was chaired and largely staffed by Liberal sympathizers. Both Lord Bryce and the Attorney-General, Sir John Simon, who defined the committee's brief, had opposed British involvement in the war until the invasion of Belgium converted it into a moral crusade in defence of small nations.[37] Even then, Bryce and other committee members shared a wider Liberal reluctance to endorse atrocity tales, for these resurrected memories of British atrocity-mongering during the South African War and were seen as the preserve of Tories and the jingoist press, notably Northcliffe's *Daily Mail*.[38] Asquith, for example, wrote in a private letter at the end of August that 'there are horrible stories of the Germans killing [the wounded], which one prefers not to believe. The burning of Louvain is the worst thing they have yet done. It reminds one of the Thirty Years' War [...] and the achievements of Tilly and Wallenstein.' Two days later, when

Armies that it would be necessary to respond to the Belgian accusations. The investigation was to have a judicial character, and include the following points:

1. Are there any examples of weapons not being carried openly, of friendly reception being given to the troops, followed by sudden treacherous assault?
2. Can it be proved that the Belgian government provided the civilian population with weapons and called on them to use weapons?
3. Details of cases of cruelties perpetrated by the civilian population against Germans, especially the wounded and medical personnel.
4. Precise establishment of the circumstances at the root of the punishment of the city of Louvain.[48]

The intention was clearly to substantiate the charge of an organized Belgian *Volkskrieg* already made by the German government. By 16 September 1914, the Foreign Ministry, together with the Deputy War Ministry and Deputy General Staff in Berlin, had produced a seven-page internal document which anticipated the argument and the title of the White Book, published eventually in May 1915.[49] In order to use this in propaganda at home and abroad, in a revealing admission the Foreign Ministry requested Grand Headquarters to gather supporting evidence, especially concerning the 'cruelties of Belgian irregulars against our wounded men, for which we have not found any evidence here'. The War Ministry agreed to appoint court-martial officials in Berlin, Liège, and Allenstein (East Prussia) to take sworn statements from soldiers on the events. These reports were to be published as separate White Books.[50]

Progress was not rapid enough to keep up with international pressure. In the winter of 1914–15, the Allied and neutral press focused on the destruction of Dinant. Already in mid-November, the Prussian Ministry of War had told the XIIth Army Corps that the Foreign Ministry intended to collect material under oath on the violations of international law committed against German troops as they took the town.[51] In December 1914, a highly critical eye-witness report by a Dutch dentist resident in Dinant, Staller, appeared in newspapers across neutral Europe. Staller reported both on the German raid on the night of 21 August, in which he considered civilian firing unlikely given that the municipal authorities had called in all arms, and the massacres of 23 August. He firmly rejected the German claim that the inhabitants had put up any resistance to the main German assault and pointed out that the Germans had suffered many casualties at the hands of French soldiers firing across the Meuse into Dinant. He was himself among those imprisoned in the abbey at Leffe for three days, who included women and children, and who were virtually deprived of food and drink, and subjected to terrifying treatment by officers in the form of mock executions. He helped disinter and rebury the civilians executed at Leffe, the Tschoffen wall in Dinant, and Anseremme. Staller stated that only 300 of the 1,500 houses in Dinant were left standing, concluding that: 'A village on the side of a volcano could not have been more completely, more terribly annihilated.'[52] Although he felt frustration that world opinion seemed unaware of what had happened, the publicity achieved by his own account, along with the Belgian official report on the town's destruction, published in mid-January 1915, made a German response imperative.

In the first half of January 1915, the Foreign Ministry reinforced pressure on the army to supply material for an early defence of German behaviour.[53] In mid-February 1915, the XIIth Army Corps was still appealing for witness statements from its soldiers, 'especially with regard to the participation of the inhabitants of Dinant and the counter-measures thus necessitated, including the shooting of inhabitants and the burning of houses'. Particular attention was to be paid in the depositions to 'injuries caused by shotguns, maltreatment of German wounded, and participation in the fighting by Belgian women and youths'.[54]

Tensions between the Foreign Ministry and the War Ministry were hardly surprising. Editorial work on the White Book appears to have been done in both departments. Scheüch, War Minister at Grand Headquarters, for example, recommended cutting the discussion of Article 2 of the Hague Convention on Land Warfare, and avoiding a detailed legal treatment, for this would only offer advantages to the enemy.[55] Under-Secretary of State at the Foreign Ministry, Arthur Zimmermann, took the opposite view. He informed GHQ that the discussion of the Hague Convention was to be maintained, since it was essential for use in neutral countries. Making the document 'shorter and more decisive' was possible only on the basis of new documentary evidence, which, despite requests, the army had still not supplied. Zimmermann reiterated how urgent it was to make a publication available soon, especially to the neutrals.[56] But the Foreign Ministry also refused to publish the White Book until the War Ministry Investigation Department had supplied the necessary information on Dinant. As a senior legal expert in the Foreign Ministry, Bruno Wedding, argued in late spring 1915: 'Dinant is by far the most prominent issue being discussed in the neutral press, and if we publish a memorandum on Belgium and exclude Dinant, then the answer will undoubtedly be that our defence is worthless for by ignoring Dinant we admit that the Belgian case is justified.'[57]

In gathering evidence that would vindicate Germany, the military authorities were brought face to face with the original franc-tireur delusion. Unlike the Allies, the Germans were in a position to interrogate enemy witnesses (i.e. French and Belgian civilians); failure to do this would undoubtedly attract attention. Additionally, the current of scepticism with regard to the *Franktireurkrieg* which emerged in the German army during the invasion was bound to find its way into the witness evidence. Documenting the thesis of a People's War against the German army would not be easy.

When it finally appeared in May 1915, the German report was defiantly unapologetic. Published by the Foreign Ministry and known abroad as the White Book (from the custom of referring to the various governments' wartime diplomatic publications by the colour of their cover), it bore the official title of *Die völkerrechtswidrige Führung des belgischen Volkskriegs* ('Human Rights Breaches in the Conduct of the Belgian People's War').[58] This robustly summarized the central argument that the German army had been the victim of premeditated Belgian atrocities on a massive scale. The report consisted of a brief introductory essay stating this thesis ('the Belgian civil population of every grade, age and sex took part with the greatest bitterness and fury in the fights against the German troops'), followed by extracts of witness evidence, for the most part taken on oath.[59] The first section of these was drawn from the whole invasion zone and painted a picture of typical franc-tireur activity, from treacherous ambushes to sadistic brutality, including mutilation. There followed four appendices, each consisting of a report signed by Bauer and Wagner for the Ministry of War's investigation department into the cases of Aarschot, Andenne, Dinant, and Louvain.

The report on Louvain (dated 10 April 1915) illustrates the fundamental difficulties faced by the authors of the White Book. When the young German academic, Peter Schöller, examined it in the 1950s on behalf of a joint commission of Belgian and German historians, he discovered an earlier printed version of Bauer and Wagner's report on Louvain, dated 15 January 1915.[60] Comparing the two texts, Schöller discovered that half the witness statements had been dropped from the final version in order to illustrate the central contention of a premeditated civilian uprising.[61]

All the testimony from German soldiers pointing to panic was suppressed, including that of one witness who had initially been convinced that he was advancing to meet an assault by British troops from Antwerp. Five Belgian civilians' testimony quoted in the original version was likewise cut, including that of the Louvain police commissioner, Gilbert, who had stated his conviction that German troops in Louvain had fired on their own men returning from combat against the Belgian counter-offensive. Other witness statements in the final version had been edited in order to change their meaning. A sentence was eliminated from the account of a German lieutenant, Telemann, who remained under cover in a café when the firing started, in which he stated that he 'had no desire to be shot at by [his] own men'.[62] Also dropped was the evidence of priests who challenged the statement of a German medical officer, Berghausen, to the effect that Belgian hostages had admitted that civilians fired on German soldiers. Yet much of the evidence which remained was either hearsay or cast further doubt on the official thesis. Thus, many witnesses agreed that as soon as the shooting began, soldiers who were billeted throughout Louvain ran to their windows and began firing down into the streets, apparently confirming to those below that the civilians were shooting. Overall, Schöller judged that the military witnesses were collectively much less sure about the thesis of a franc-tireur rising than the White Book asserted, that the psychological state of the soldiers made their testimony unreliable, and that much evidence had been tampered with. The purpose of the account of Louvain finally published by the White Book, Schöller concluded, was not to establish the truth but to counter Belgian accusations.

The discovery of substantial fragments of the original War Ministry investigation into Dinant allows a comparable analysis.[63] Louvain and Dinant together account for two-thirds of the White Book. Unsurprisingly, most of the interrogations confirmed the War Ministry's thesis, for the evidence was submitted by men who were aware of international interest and who had been told what answers the investigation wanted to produce. Many of the witnesses stated that civilians had engaged in shooting, although testimony that civilians were caught with weapons was rare; more usually it was by hearsay or inference.

Contrary or uncertain evidence was suppressed either by simple omission or by heavy editing. The testimony of Major von Loeben, for example, who commanded the firing squad at the Tschoffen wall, was deleted from the published version, almost certainly because he admitted that he had only hearsay evidence that civilians had fired and stated that Lieutenant-Colonel Count Kielmannsegg, who ordered the execution, was not punishing francs-tireurs but executing 'a large number of men of military age' by way of example.[64] Loeben's evidence was corroborated by another witness, Lieutenant von Haugk, who also remained uncited in the White Book.[65] By contrast, Kielmannsegg, whose testimony was used in the White Book, claimed that the 100 men killed in the mass execution were 'guilty' of franc-tireur warfare.[66] On the events at Leffe, there are several significant differences between the statements given by Corporal Franz Stiebing, IR 178, to the War Ministry investigation, and the one printed in the White Book. The latter omitted Stiebing's references to the summary execution of 30 to 34 men in a factory, and of 25 more francs-tireurs late in the evening, mentioning instead only the corpses of the francs-tireurs.[67] In his testimony of 5 February, Stiebing stated that his company entered the houses and arrested the male inhabitants, 'who *almost* all bore weapons', and summarily executed them in the street. In the White Book, this became 'all the male inhabitants [...] were armed and were firing', and were therefore shot in combat.[68] The White Book also suppressed Stiebing's admission that no one in his battalion was injured or killed in the fighting for Leffe, that a previous description which he had given of the fighting was 'very embellished', especially in relation to the casualties suffered by his regiment, and that he saw at least 180 corpses of executed francs-tireurs.[69]

Some testimony was suppressed because it revealed too much of the truth. Captain Hans Hauth told the court-martial investigators he knew nothing of any women or children participating in the fighting in and around Dinant, nor of German wounded soldiers being mutilated by Belgian women or children. He recalled that at the Bourdon wall Major Schlick gave the order to shoot two groups of civilians as a measure to stop others firing from the houses. Among the victims were women and children, including a baby. Hauth himself gave two women 'who still showed some signs of life' the coup de grâce.[70]

Other testimony could, where needed, be invented. When Zimmermann of the Foreign Ministry noted that the material finally submitted by the War Ministry in April 1915 contained no definitive statement that the fighting civilians did not wear military insignia, he asked von Stumm (Director of the Political Department attached to GHQ) to obtain an official statement from the General Command of the XIIth Army Corps as soon as possible.[71] Three sentences to this effect were inserted into depositions.[72] Yet in the case of what should have been a crucial statement, the military inquiry remained empty-handed. Repeated requests were made for a statement by the commander of the XIIth Army Corps, General d'Elsa. As we have seen, d'Elsa sought in vain to countermand his own advance instructions to suppress civilian resistance at Dinant, and his son was an appalled spectator of the massacre at the Bourdon wall. General d'Elsa never submitted his report.[73]

A number of Belgian witnesses were interviewed concerning the events of Dinant, but none of their testimony was cited in the White Book.[74] One woman, Madame Poucelet, had described to German investigators how her husband was killed in front of her and their seven children at Leffe. The XIIth Army Corps was asked in a circular: 'Who can provide evidence on this, or rectify the description?' The answer was silence.[75]

In fact, the German authorities had been in close contact with a key Belgian witness, Maurice Tschoffen, who was deported with many of his townsmen to Kassel, before returning to Dinant in the winter of 1914–15. He was not interviewed as a witness (though he provided detailed reports for the Belgian official commission). But he claimed to have been told by the camp commander at Kassel that 'the military authorities in Berlin are now convinced that no one [i.e. no civilian] fired at Dinant', a view repeated to him on his return by General von Longchamp, the German military governor of Namur. Longchamp additionally exonerated the monks of Leffe of all charges of resistance.[76]

What remained, once the contrary evidence was discarded, were numerous statements by German soldiers, some hearsay, others eye-witness, which testified that the civilian population, including women and children, had poured murderous fire onto the Germans, with those executed being 'persons who had been caught with weapons in their hands'.[77] The depositions by men of IR 178 portrayed a house-by-house battle to seize Leffe against sinister civilians armed with Browning pistols or hunting rifles who fought from barricaded buildings and picked off straggling Germans. Little mention was made of the sustained shooting at Leffe by French soldiers barely 200 metres away across the Meuse, although one company commander admitted this, and added: 'The reports of firing in the streets of terraced houses in Leffe were continuous, and one could not always tell whence the shots came. Without doubt they were pistol-shots discharged from cellars and attics ...'[78] There was an illuminating contradiction concerning the role of the French army. It was wrongly asserted that the French had abandoned Dinant on 17 August, which reflected the urgently felt need to replace the memory of real military resistance with imagined civilian resistance.[79] In effect, the military inquiry concentrated exclusively on unreliable evidence from German soldiers in a state of collective self-suggestion, from which the Foreign Ministry turned Dinant into a major episode of the Belgian People's War.

Overall, the White Book was selective in what it chose to defend. It had nothing to say about the second largest massacre of Belgian civilians, at Tamines. Although various soldiers mentioned fighting against civilians in Tintigny and Rossignol, the mass execution of civilians from Rossignol at Arlon was ignored.[80] In late September or October 1914, a German officer from Arlon conducted an investigation in Ethe, and was disconcerted to hear the flat denial by the burgomaster, Christophe Baulard, that there had been any francs-tireurs.[81] The omission of Spontin, given the publicity accorded by the German press at the time to the alleged role of its priest in fomenting civilian resistance, was another retreat.

Moreover, the two appendices dealing with Aarschot and Andenne were extremely thin, with barely a handful of witness statements each. This suggests either that the military authorities decided to concentrate on the cases attracting most international attention, or that they were unable to find apparently convincing statements of the kind left in abundance by the experiences of Louvain and Dinant. Equally striking was the absence of civilian evidence, except for a number of brief Belgian statements on Andenne which failed, however, to endorse the German thesis of a civilian insurrection. Yet this was not for want of trying. The Germans interviewed civilians throughout Belgium and in the camps in Germany. One Belgian, Gustave Somville, who conducted his own clandestine inquiry in Liège province in the winter of 1914–15 before escaping to publish it from Britain, recorded that the Germans interrogated civilians from villages such as Melen, Hermée, Visé, and Blégny in January–February 1915, with the first question in the latter case being: 'Did you see the francs-tireurs whose aggression so exasperated our troops?'[82] Any damning evidence by Belgian civilians would certainly have been used; its absence from the White Book can only mean that the civilian depositions failed to confirm the official German interpretation of events.[83]

The White Book also ignored German scepticism concerning the most lurid aspects of the franc-tireur fear. German Catholics were disturbed by the anti-Catholic tenor of many 'Belgian atrocity' stories, and Social Democrats expressed disbelief at tales of enemy sadism. As will be shown below, when these doubts were raised with the military authorities, the War Ministry Investigation Department replied by endorsing such scepticism. Doctors searched German hospitals for evidence of blinded and mutilated soldiers, without success. But none of these doubts appeared in the White Book, which maintained depositions recording acts of mutilation.[84]

Although there were numerous references to resistance by priests, the original anti-clerical hysteria was considerably toned down.[85] This shift reflected the policy adopted in December 1914 by the new military governor of Belgium, General von Bissing, of seeking the collaboration of the Belgian hierarchy in order to 'pacify' Belgian opinion and reconcile the country to its absorption in a greater Germany, a policy pursued with the help of Cardinal von Hartmann of Cologne.[86] On 22 January 1915, Bauer and Wagner sent a memorandum to the Chancellor, Bethmann Hollweg, which exonerated the bishops and the bulk of the clergy from blame for civilian resistance, limiting the accusations in this regard to 16 specific cases in Belgium and three in France.[87]

The Belgian government therefore emerged even more clearly as the principal culprit for the People's War, although only two documents were cited alleging this idea, both on hearsay evidence. The Garde Civique acquired an important supporting role. The White Book ignored the copious evidence presented by the Belgians that their government had consistently warned against civilian resistance and ensured that the use of the Garde Civique conformed to the 1907 Hague Convention. The case of Aarschot illustrates the logic of the German emphasis on planned resistance. The original narrative turned on the assassination of Colonel Stenger by the son of burgomaster Tielemans. In the White Book, the role of the burgomaster and his family was transformed: they had co-ordinated an armed uprising by the population and Garde Civique, in the course of which Stenger died.[88] The crime thus became collective, providing stronger justification for killing over 150 civilians.

Does this mean that the White Book was a cover-up? In one sense, it was. The official German thesis of a People's War in Belgium encountered rising international disbelief. Serious doubts were beginning to emerge even inside the government. In late September 1914, the Chief of the Naval

Cabinet and Bethmann Hollweg discussed the 'thriving atrocity propaganda spread by our enemies (cutting of children's hands, etc.)', which both men agreed would ideally be vetted by the International Court in The Hague. But the Chancellor later revealed that von Jagow, the Foreign Minister, had scotched the notion 'because we already have too much on our conscience' – an extraordinary statement, if true.[89] The War Minister at Grand Headquarters, Scheüch, made the remarkable admission that he was doubtful about the success of the White Book, but felt the investigation should nevertheless continue, for 'no means should be left untried in order to protect the honour of our army from defamatory attacks.'[90] Bethmann Hollweg himself visited Louvain in November 1914 where he inspected the ruined library, apologized for the conduct of the German troops, and promised that a proper inquiry would be carried out when the dust of battle had settled.[91] In February 1915 Theodor Wolff, the liberal editor of the *Berliner Tageblatt*, challenged Bethmann Hollweg in private to admit that the German army had committed atrocities. Bethmann replied, 'Yes, it cannot be denied.'[92]

What had therefore happened between September 1914 and May 1915 was that Germany's civilian and military authorities agreed on a policy of denial. By a conspiracy of silence and misinformation they sought to protect the 'honour' of the army. Although leading political and military figures accepted that the German army had been guilty of crimes (both in the sense of international law, and of an international moral code), the government decided the best form of defence was attack.

Yet in another sense, the White Book was much more than a 'cover-up' of some other, secretly admitted 'truth'. When figures like Manteuffel, the commander at Louvain, swore that they personally had seen the furious civilians, and when the most senior commanders – Kluck, Bülow, Hausen, the Crown Prince, and Ludendorff – maintained in memoirs written during or shortly after the war that their armies had faced heavy civilian resistance, it must be assumed that many in army and government circles continued to believe in the reality of the *Franktireurkrieg*. The original myth-complex of 1914 gave this belief its inner strength. The belief amounted to a case of unconscious denial, and it was fixed in more permanent ideological form by the broader justification of the war as one of defence against encirclement by a hostile and uncomprehending world. Given the belief of so many in the reality of the Franco-Belgian People's

War, and German dismissal of the Hague Convention as irrelevant, Allied accusations of 'German atrocities' seemed cynical and deeply offensive.

3 The Belgian riposte: the 'Grey Book' and Fernand van Langenhove

Continued German belief in the franc-tireur war presented a problem for the Allied response to the White Book, in what amounted to the last round in the battle of official reports. H. A. L. Fisher triumphantly noted that the Germans seemed to prove all the Bryce Report's charges by failing to repudiate the accusation of widespread brutality towards civilians.[93] Sir Claude Schuster, who was involved in the dissemination of the Bryce Report, wrote: 'The more we examine the [White] book the more thankful we are for the best piece of propaganda on our side that has yet been published.'[94] But this was to misunderstand the German case, which took 'legitimate reprisals' so much for granted that they scarcely required comment. For them, treacherous civilian resistance constituted the real crime. While the Allies might contend that this had not occurred, they still faced the irreducible core of apparently credible witness statements in the White Book which maintained that the streets of Belgian towns and villages had teemed with treacherous francs-tireurs.

The response of the Belgian government-in-exile therefore took two forms. The official commission immediately set to work producing a meticulous and densely argued refutation of the White Book, over 500 pages long, which was published 11 months later in April 1916. Known as the *Livre gris* ('Grey Book'), it consisted of a long rebuttal of the White Book's central arguments about the Belgian government's preparation of a People's War and the role of the Garde Civique.[95] It also criticized each of the White Book's appendices on Aarschot, Andenne, Dinant, and Louvain and, drawing on the material accumulated for the Belgian reports, provided opposed interpretations and evidence, including full civilian death lists. A summary of the *Livre gris* was written by Fernand Passelecq, the Brussels lawyer who ran the Belgian propaganda bureau (the Bureau Documentaire Belge) in Le Havre.[96]

In a confidential lecture given shortly after the war to the staff of the German Foreign Ministry, the military historian, Colonel Bernhard test not just of which side made its case better, but of which held the higher moral ground.

Some neutral countries were particularly important. The USA was the most powerful nation outside the European diplomatic system. Italy was the only major European power hesitating to enter the war. Switzerland, with a German majority and French and Italian minorities, was a nation which internalized the passions of the war while remaining deeply committed to neutrality. In these countries especially, the warring states mounted major campaigns to influence opinion. Each side assumed the other's propaganda was far better organized than its own. In reality, many of the belligerent powers had agencies operating before the war in support of their diplomatic and commercial efforts, but all were forced to expand and improvise their propaganda in neutral countries once war broke out.

The Belgians sent missions to protest at the violation of Belgian neutrality and 'German atrocities' not only in Washington but also in Italy, Switzerland, and elsewhere. In January 1915, the Belgian campaign moved onto a more permanent footing with the establishment of the Bureau Documentaire.[104] The British government created a secretive organization for propaganda in foreign countries, especially the USA, in early September 1914, under the Liberal politician, Charles Masterman. Wellington House, as it became known, was responsible for the translation and dissemination of the Bryce Report in spring 1915.[105] In France, the Ministry of Foreign Affairs worked to influence neutral opinion, partly by fostering various private or semi-official bodies emanating from different milieux within France (Catholic, Socialist, intellectual), but also by publishing a substantial documentary compilation, *Germany's Violations of the Laws of War, 1914–1915*.[106] In Germany a host of private organizations sprang up to promote the national cause abroad, alongside the diplomatic service and competing state agencies, which in October 1914 were reorganized under one umbrella, the Central Office for Foreign Service (Zentralstelle für Auslandsdienst), attached to the Foreign Ministry.[107]

All these agencies used persuasive techniques, including not only reports, press communiqués, and other official publications, but also covert action. The British proved particularly adept in the USA at disguising official lobbying as disinterested individual action, while the Germans favoured the secret purchase of newspapers. Yet to see the battle for neutral opinion only, or even essentially, as an exercise in manipulation, with the issues merely tools of political leverage, is to misunderstand it.

Neutral opinion was not a blank slate on which the most effective belligerents could simply write their message. It responded on its own account to the events in Europe, which the neutral press sought to investigate and interpret. Nor was neutral opinion uniform; some elements sympathized more with one camp than the other. In Switzerland, the division was naturally by language community. In Italy, democratic interventionists favoured the Allies and conservatives the Central Powers, even if the majority was largely indifferent. In the USA, the bulk of opinion was uncommitted. But significant sympathy for the Allies was evident among the east coast elites, while the sizeable German-American community (and some Irish-Americans) tended to favour Germany. The 'atrocities' issue, incorporated into national politics in the neutral countries, helped define attitudes to the war.

American opinion can be used to illustrate this process. In August 1914, American war correspondents sought to exploit their neutral status by gaining access to the fighting in Belgium and France and providing independent accounts for their newspapers, which were otherwise dependent on censored stories from the belligerent powers.[108] The 'atrocities' issue soon divided the American reporters. One group mirrored the Allied press in its interpretations. E. Alexander Powell, for example, writing for the *New York World*, visited Aarschot and Louvain within days of their destruction. He uncritically relayed certain myths, such as mass rape in Aarschot and the mutilation of civilians, but he also stressed the scale and devastation of the German destruction and deduced accurately that panicking German soldiers firing on each other had triggered the sack of Louvain.[109] The doyen of American war correspondents, Richard Harding Davis, was likewise appalled by the destruction of Louvain, of which he was a passing witness. He, too, picked up various myths, but unlike Powell, he failed to grasp the importance of German panic. His sensationalist report portrayed Louvain as destroyed by order of the high command in reprisal for supposed sniper attacks.[110]

Other American reporters, however, found no evidence of 'German atrocities' in Belgium. Typical of this group are Irvin S. Cobb, writing for the Philadelphia press, and James O'Donnell Bennett of the *Chicago Daily Tribune*. Cobb, who spent two weeks with the German army in August, concluded that '80 per cent' of the stories of German atrocities were 'absolutely untrue', even though recounted in good faith by traumatized refugees or German soldiers, that 10 per cent were grossly exaggerated, and 10 per cent 'approximately correct'.[111] But Cobb also averred without proof neutrality. It received accurate reports on the 'atrocities' question from Brand Whitlock, the American ambassador in Brussels, who told it that while there had been some exaggeration in the press accounts of 'the excesses' committed by the German army in Belgium, 'they are in spirit true.'[123] While the American government decided that it had no duty under the 1907 Hague conventions to condemn Germany, public opinion was drawn into the issues involved in the conflict, producing deep divisions.[124] These were exacerbated by the competing belligerent campaigns but were rooted ultimately in ethnic and political identities within America and in the long-term shift in attitudes towards Germany. The question of the 'German atrocities' acted as a magnifying glass, focusing these separate antagonisms. It undoubtedly redounded more to the Allies' than to Germany's advantage – even before the sinking of the *Lusitania* in May 1915 with the loss of 1,200 lives (some of them American) brought the issue of the rules of war uncomfortably close to home.

The battle for neutral opinion was also more than mere manipulation by the belligerent powers, for many of those conducting it evidently believed in some notion of international moral standards against which military and diplomatic behaviour might be judged. Again, the American case illustrates the point. The British campaign in the USA was commonly interpreted after 1918 as a triumph of duplicity, largely because of its covert nature.[125] As a judgement on the means employed, this is well founded. The Foreign Office and the British Embassy in Washington campaigned to disseminate the Bryce Report as widely as possible. Given the importance of the battle for neutral opinion, it is unlikely they would have done anything less with an official parliamentary paper on such a vital subject. But there is no evidence that Foreign Office officials, some of whom had been critical of exaggerated anti-German propaganda in the press, saw the judgements in the Bryce Report as distorted or manipulative. Bryce himself had opposed a British campaign in the USA on the 'atrocities' issue in September 1914 on the grounds that German conduct in the invasion made the case perfectly: 'All that is needed is an abundant supply of facts [...] as to the origin of the war, the facts, stripped of incredibilities and exaggerations, of the harsh and violent conduct of the German troops in Belgium and their breaches of international law [...]'[126]

Timing helped the reception of the report, since it was released a week after the sinking of the *Lusitania*, with which, as a Wellington House survey reported, most American newspaper editorials closely related the

'German atrocities' in Belgium.[127] American press coverage of stories of rapes and mutilation may have been influenced by the contaminated witness evidence in the Bryce Report. But mutilation myths were already part of the American war correspondents' own reporting. The demonization of Germany sprang from American internalization of the conflict over the meaning of the war, and the Bryce Report achieved its great impact because it blamed militarism, a negative concept among Americans, for German behaviour.

Responses to the 'atrocities' issue were similarly shaped in other neutral states by domestic political factors, and events, as much as by propaganda campaigns. In Italy, three deputies were the principal agents of the Belgian mission – the Liberal Georges Lorand of Virton, Jules Destrée, the Socialist representative of Charleroi, and Auguste Mélot, the Catholic deputy for Namur.[128] They combed Italy, addressing meetings and distributing publicity on the violation of Belgian neutrality and on 'German atrocities'. Destrée specialized in Socialist and free-thinking circles, while Mélot operated in Catholic milieux, but war crimes were central to their speeches and literature, as they were to the Belgian propaganda committee established in Rome by November 1914.[129] Destrée described how in dealing with the 'atrocities' at meetings, he would simply read out extracts from the official reports, 'documents consisting not of accusations or witness statements, relating particular isolated acts of atrocity, but proclamations drawn up by the German officers themselves, and particularly revealing about their methods. These samples of barbary and despotism revolt a people like the Italians which has conserved its sense of justice and liberty.'[130] The Belgian campaign in Italy had the urgent motive of securing Italian entry into the war – it was enthusiastically backed by the British and French governments for that reason. But it was also one of deep conviction by men expelled from their constituencies and country by the invasion, and this reinforced its credibility in pro-Allied interventionist milieux.

Ultimately, events made the Allied campaigners plausible. Their weight was reinforced by the fact that neutral opinion was not totally dependent on Allied news but received its information through myriad channels, including its own witnesses and reporters. Accounts of massacres were bad enough for the Germans, but worse still was the news of the devastation of historic buildings and works of art. The State Department in Washington served as an international barometer of plunging German prestige. Architects, artists, and literary figures in the United States, Britain, and elsewhere published by the semi-official *Norddeutsche Allgemeine Zeitung* and disseminated by the WTB. Thus, in September 1914, German representatives in neutral and friendly states were circulated with the statement by the five American journalists exonerating the German army from atrocity charges.[144] The following January, the Foreign Ministry tried to counter Staller's damaging account of the destruction of Dinant by sending a five-page exculpation to German embassies in nine neutral countries.[145] Individually authored rejoinders to the Allied accusations were also published with official backing. When Émile Waxweiler, leading the Belgian campaign in Switzerland in 1914–15, accused Germany of violating Belgian neutrality and exposed the franc-tireur war as a myth in a book translated into German, it prompted a response from Richard Graßhoff, who worked in the War Ministry Investigation Department, which was quickly translated into French and English.[146] In highly emotive language, Graßhoff repeated the story of women pouring boiling oil on soldiers, and claimed the Belgian civilian population was incited to commit horrific crimes on German soldiers by intellectuals and the press. Even the Belgian government's official statements warning civilians not to engage in fighting and delineating the duties of the civic guard were reinterpreted as coded calls for a civilian uprising, with the civic guard playing a leading part.[147]

German self-defence against Allied atrocities charges faced the fundamental difficulty that the severity of the German response could not be disguised. The difficulties posed by the first French report on German war crimes illustrate the problem. On 11 January 1915, the WTB broadcast the Foreign Ministry's rejection of the short version of the French report, published two days earlier.[148] It accused the French of wilfully creating the impression of premeditated German brutality by making unfounded accusations. The German rejoinder claimed that the German army had merely imposed strict observance of the laws of war, and it promised a detailed response in due course. But the Germans felt confident enough to reject immediately the French account of the incident at Lunéville, on 25 August 1914, with a counter-accusation that civilians had treacherously attacked the military hospital, necessitating reprisals. As noted, the incident, which came after three days' peaceful occupation of the town, was the result of a German panic. But the Foreign Ministry's plausible alternative interpretation could not disguise the incident's outcome – the slaughter of 19 inhabitants and the destruction of 70 buildings.[149] Perhaps not surprisingly, no detailed German answer to the wider charges made by the French Commission's reports ever emerged.

The second tactic was to deflect attention from the *Franktireurkrieg* by focusing on different kinds of Allied atrocity. As early as 10 October 1914, a short collection of reports was published concerning alleged French attacks on medical facilities and the mutilation and murder of German prisoners in breach of the 1906 Geneva Convention.[150] Among the incidents cited was Orchies which the Germans destroyed, after the population had fled, in reprisal for the alleged mutilation of German soldiers. In July 1915, the Foreign Ministry also condemned the British and French governments for using 'coloured troops' in the European theatre of war. This issue undoubtedly tapped into strong German feelings. Already in 1870, the Prussians had protested at the French use of North African soldiers as inherently barbaric.[151] While the Foreign Ministry accepted that there was nothing in international law to forbid the use of disciplined native troops under European officers, it accused the British and French colonial soldiers of committing revolting atrocities, and especially of lopping off German heads and ears as souvenirs and gouging out the eyes of the living. Evidence was supplied concerning 16 allegations. Much of this amounted to a variant of the mutilation mythology that flourished on both sides. Several allegations (e.g. one group rape of German women being deported from France) may have been founded on facts, but they were too limited in number and evidence to influence neutral or enemy opinion.[152]

More promising was the counter-accusation that the French and British had allied themselves with the barbaric Russians who were incapable of fighting by civilized norms. In a variety of ways, Russia was the Achilles heel of Franco-British claims to be waging a morally righteous war, given the nature of its government, its pre-war record of political repression and pogroms, and the reputation of the Cossacks as brutal and undisciplined soldiers. But at least down to the great retreat of mid-1915, neither the German nor the Austrian government could produce evidence of Russian brutality against enemy civilians remotely matching that alleged by the Allies against Germany.

The naval war also gave the Germans some opportunities to rebut Allied condemnation of the use of U-boats against civilian shipping or neutral vessels. Perhaps the most famous case arose with the *Baralong* incident, when a British auxiliary cruiser, disguised as a merchant ship and flying the American flag, hunted down and destroyed a German submarine in August

7   Communities of truth and the 'atrocities' question

The battle of official reports showed that the 'atrocities' issue in 1914 amounted to more than the propaganda by which it has usually been explained. This chapter and the next will argue that while the struggle lasted, the war of words over 'atrocities' is better understood as one of the frameworks of meaning by which contemporaries sought to grasp the significance of the conflict.

This is not to say that the emphasis on propaganda is entirely misplaced. There is no doubt that enemy 'atrocities' were used to achieve ulterior political goals; the campaigns fought by both sides in neutral countries demonstrate this. But events played a shaping role, and real conflicts of value and interpretation were at issue. These were related to the broader mobilization which swept up individuals and redefined their standpoints in ways of which they were often unaware. As the Bryce Report showed, this was more important than the conscious manipulation of 'truth' in determining views on the war.

Indeed, a genuine belief persisted that the meaning of the war could be judged by some absolute standard of truth even as the shared assumptions on which this depended disintegrated. It was particularly evident in those groups and identities which adhered to a supranational value system and belonged to networks transcending national boundaries. Socialists, Catholics, and intellectuals, in their different ways, all participated in such communities of truth, and they naturally assumed that the conflicting official narratives of the 'atrocity' issue could, and should, be resolved in one, accurate account.

1   Socialists

Socialists were especially resistant to 'atrocity' tales which conjured up the pre-war jingoism they had so frequently denounced. By and large, they avoided the use of atrocity myths to demonize the enemy and even cautioned against them. This was certainly the case with the German Social Democratic Party (SPD). A leading SPD regional paper, the *Hamburger Echo*, called several times for humanity in warfare even while repeating stories of atrocities perpetrated on German civilians and soldiers.[1] It qualified its reproduction of Moltke's 'Warning' to France and Belgium by arguing that even if the declaration was 'fully justified by international law, which forbade popular war', summary justice would sully German culture. 'We are convinced that each of our soldiers would rather risk his life ten times in open fighting than take part once in the execution of a defenceless person standing in front of him.'[2]

The national SPD daily, *Vorwärts*, was overtly sceptical about the most lurid claims of Belgian atrocities. On 24 August, it noted that the news about enemy 'atrocities', which it regarded as frequently exaggerated, had led in some quarters to the call for 'medieval barbarity' in revenge, notably from those sections of the population which liked to think of themselves as representing German *Kultur*. Throughout autumn 1914, *Vorwärts* punched holes in the franc-tireur myth by demanding evidence. On 22 October it claimed that the stories of cigarettes and cigars filled with gunpowder and sold to German soldiers, which had been reported in the *Berliner Tageblatt*, were nothing but figments of the imagination. It considered, moreover, that the tales still sweeping Germany of francs-tireurs who gouged out the eyes of German soldiers were also the work of rumour-mongers. It pointed out that no such story had been confirmed, that the Catholic *Kölnische Volkszeitung* had established that there were no soldiers in Aachen hospitals suffering from such injuries, and that the Socialist deputy, Karl Liebknecht, had received a letter saying the same from the director of the hospital in Berlin-Lichtenberg. Finally, *Vorwärts* reminded its readers that foreign newspapers were publishing almost identical reports about German soldiers committing alleged atrocities.[3] The conservative Prussian Minister of the Interior, Friedrich Wilhelm von Loebell, complained to Bethmann

German units. But Noske and Koester remained loyal to the German army's interpretation of a civilian uprising, even defending the execution of 'innocent' civilians in Louvain and Dinant together with the 'guilty'. This was clearly compensated for in their minds by the soldiers' courageous actions in saving the Town Hall and works of art from St Peter's Church.[10]

Little wonder, then, that when Koester and Noske turned up in army uniform at the Brussels Maison du Peuple (trade union headquarters), and proposed that Belgian organized labour should collaborate in the enemy occupation, their erstwhile Belgian comrades denounced both the invasion and the 'atrocities' to their faces. The German Social Democrats justified the former and refused to accept that the latter had occurred. They referred instead to the *Franktireurkrieg* and (as one Belgian witness put it) claimed that the German army could not have carried out any atrocities since it was composed 'of the elite of the German population [...], and what is more, half of the troops belonged to the Social Democrats'.[11]

The left-wing Social Democratic deputy, Karl Liebknecht, went to Belgium at the beginning of September 1914, to find news of his brother-in-law, one of the Russian-Jewish students at Liège. He visited Liège, Andenne, Namur, and Brussels, and at one point intervened to prevent the execution of some Belgian peasants accused of being francs-tireurs. In Brussels, he told Belgian Socialists that most Germans believed a fiercely clerical Belgium had risen against the German troops at the instigation of the Catholic priesthood, but made it clear that he, unlike Koester and Noske, regarded the People's War as a myth. Even so, the charge that German soldiers had committed atrocities seemed to disorient him.[12]

Little by little, guarded criticism of German military behaviour during the invasion emerged in the SPD. Criticism was naturally strongest among the minority that was beginning to oppose the party's support for the war. Bernstein stated that he would not have voted for war credits in the Reichstag on 4 August 1914 if he had known 'how cruelly our side would conduct the war'.[13] Ledebour protested at Hindenburg's threat to burn down three villages in occupied Russia for every one burned by the Russians in East Prussia. Kurt Eisner attacked both the military for its brutal treatment of Belgian and French civilians and the SPD executive for not protesting against the 'monstrosities of German warfare'.[14] 'I am not sentimental [...],' Eisner declared, 'but this German system (not the barbarities of individuals) has created an unprecedented war terrorism, which does not even serve a *military* purpose, but will be our *political* ruin.'[15]

Yet the pro-war majority leadership of the SPD refused to concede the Belgian case on 'German atrocities'. The party secretary, Philip Scheidemann, attacked Émile Vandervelde, the leader of the Belgian Workers' Party (POB), for compromising his role as president of the executive bureau of the Second International by entering government upon the German invasion. Vandervelde retorted that the German violation of Belgian neutrality and the 'atrocities' committed against civilians made it the duty of Socialists everywhere to work for Germany's total defeat. 'Our Maisons du Peuple at Tamines, Auvelais, [and] Louvain have been burned, our deputies, our local councillors, like others, have been taken hostage', he protested, and he condemned the SPD for not treating the 'atrocity' charges seriously enough to mount their own investigation.[16] In 1917, the POB continued to castigate Germany for the atrocities of 1914, as well as the violations of Belgian neutrality and the rigours of the occupation, and refused to meet the SPD until it repudiated the German government's actions. The conflict was irreconcilable. Not only was there no internal or international Socialist commission of inquiry, but the bitterness provoked by the issue helps explain why the Second International (whose executive bureau remained predominantly Belgian) was so reluctant to convene an international Socialist gathering during the war.[17]

2   Catholics

Catholics in Belgium, France, and Germany were also riven by the 'atrocities' issue. The divisions were complicated by the Vatican's position as an authority with universal spiritual claims which had to tread a relativized path on temporal matters, since it could not afford to alienate any of its divided flock.[18]

The Vatican was left in no doubt as to the nature of events during the German invasion of Belgium. The primate of Belgium, Cardinal Désiré Mercier, learned of the destruction of Louvain and the bombardment of his own seat of Mechelen (Malines) when he was in Rome, in late August, for the conclave to elect the successor to Pius X.[19] Although the papal nuncio, Giovanni Tacci, left Belgium with the government, an official of the Brussels nunciature, Emanuele de Sarzana, took over as chargé d'affaires and reported to Rome throughout the invasion, until the Vatican allowed Tacci to return to Brussels in early December.[20] Sarzana interceded on

Under the redoubtable figure of Cardinal Mercier, the Belgian bishops emerged as the single most important voice of resistance to German domination, and their primary task in 1914–15 was repudiating the German interpretation of the invasion. The German church, for its part, faced conflicting pressures. Cardinal Hartmann, Archbishop of Cologne and the most important Catholic prelate in Prussia, initially believed the rumours of 'Belgian atrocities' committed against German soldiers and wrote to Gasparri in mid-August 1914 asking for the Pope to remind the Belgian population of their obligation to act as Christians towards their enemy.[30] But Hartmann became concerned at the anti-Catholic tone of these 'Belgian atrocities' stories, fearing that they would undermine the position of Catholics in Germany, and by late autumn he was mediating between the military government in Brussels and the Belgian church. His actions converged with Bissing's idea of using the support of the Belgian hierarchy to 'pacify' Belgium, and the upshot was the more conciliatory statement of January 1915, already referred to, which excused the Belgian church from collective responsibility for the 'People's War'.

The Belgian hierarchy, however, would not accept its own exculpation at the price of compromising the innocence of the Belgian people. It is this which explains the tenor of Cardinal Mercier's pastoral letter of Christmas 1914, 'Patriotism and Endurance', and the response it provoked. After his return from Rome, Mercier had written to Benedict XV confirming the reality of German brutality towards Belgian civilians, and describing the misery and ruins in the most severely affected part of his diocese. Referring bluntly to Belgian incomprehension of the Vatican's silence, Mercier requested 'a word of sympathy and consolation' to the Belgian people, clergy, and the exiled royal family.[31] Benedict XV replied in early December with a sybilline apostolic blessing, which recognized Belgian suffering but refrained from condemning German actions and praised Cardinal Hartmann's efforts on behalf of innocent Belgian priests deported to Germany. It urged that nothing should be done that might lengthen or extend the war.[32] Gasparri wrote at the same time to Tacci, underlining the policy of *imparzialità*.[33] Meanwhile, a conciliatory advance to the Belgian clergy made in early December by the military governor, General Bissing, including the release of the interned Belgian priests, was rejected by Cardinal Mercier.[34] Mercier insisted that the German army's 'atrocities' during the invasion could not be forgotten by the Belgian people. Bissing refused point-blank to discuss the matter.[35] But as Mercier wrote to Hartmann:

I have been unable to establish one single act of savagery inflicted by a Belgian civilian on a German soldier, while, on the other hand, I am aware of hundreds of acts of cruelty 'clashing with all the laws of civilization' committed by German soldiers on innocent Belgians. Your Eminence will understand that patriotism and justice impose upon me the duty to go on protesting against these crimes until they have been punished, and I add that if you were in possession of all the evidence that I have gathered, your own sense of righteousness would compel you to unite your protest with ours.[36]

It was in response to this triple refusal to acknowledge the 'German atrocities' – by Rome, the German church, and the German military government – that Mercier wrote his pastoral letter. In it, he described the destruction wrought by the Germans, in almost identical terms to those used in his private letter to Benedict XV, referring to Aarschot, Louvain, Andenne, Dinant, and Tamines. He reiterated that several hundred innocent people had been executed, though he underestimated the true figure, and added that at least 43 members of the clergy had been killed. Mercier saw the calumny against Belgium as one of the country's heaviest tribulations; he roundly rejected the legality of the German occupation and called on his flock to withhold their recognition.[37]

For the Germans, this dangerously combined resurgent Catholicism with Belgian patriotism. Mercier's pastoral letter outraged Bissing, who sought unsuccessfully to prevent it being read in Belgian churches, provoking confrontations which rapidly reached the press in Allied and neutral countries.[38] He gave orders for the arrest of Mercier, but his chief political adviser, Baron von der Lancken, persuaded him to consult the Chancellor, who counselled caution. Bethmann Hollweg feared that repression would make a martyr of Mercier, possibly lead to a popular uprising against a weak occupation army, and revive a *Kulturkampf* which would undermine the *Burgfrieden*. A more indirect solution was sought, via the Vatican, where the Prussian envoy demanded papal intervention to discipline the Cardinal.[39] The Belgian community in Rome increased the pressure on the Vatican by commemorating the 43 priests killed by German troops, in a ceremony on 22 January 1915.[40] The same day, Benedict XV made a small departure from the policy of *imparzialità* by condemning breaches of law in the war, mentioning Belgium as a victim though not Germany as a perpetrator.[41] But the Pope restored the balance by sending a sinuous letter to Mercier next day congratulating him on 'calming' Belgian opinion while stating that 'there is nothing further to be done.'[42]

Yet the Belgian bishops found it impossible to abandon the 'atrocities' issue so long as the Germans maintained their official explanation. In particular, the Bishop of Namur, Thomas Heylen, whose diocese also included Luxembourg province, insistently rejected the German thesis. Already on 12 September 1914 he had protested to the German military governor of Namur at the accusations levelled against Belgian priests by the Kaiser in his telegram to Woodrow Wilson. In February 1915, Heylen issued a Lenten letter which addressed the lingering trauma left by the invasion, although the harshest judgements against the Germans were toned down at the insistence of the German governor of Namur.[43] But the January 1915 note from the Prussian War Ministry, which excused the Belgian church from collective responsibility for the 'People's War', brought a riposte from Heylen as soon as he learned of its existence two months later through the Dutch press. Heylen's reply, sent to the military government in Brussels and to the Vatican in mid-April 1915, explicitly rejected the charge of a war of francs-tireurs. Indeed, although Heylen observed that isolated acts of resistance by Belgian civilians would have been perfectly comprehensible, he insisted that none had been recorded, let alone proved by the Germans. There had been a mass delusion on the Germans' part, 'a legend, a calumny and an invention', resulting from the prior conviction of the invading army that it would meet armed groups of francs-tireurs on the model of 1870.[44] As Heylen pointed out, the population in several villages had been 'exterminated' simply because it was rumoured that a major had been killed or a young girl had tried to assassinate an officer. Nothing justified the disproportionate collective violence deliberately unleashed in what the inhabitants of his diocese considered 'a monstrous war conducted not against soldiers but against civilians'.[45] Heylen concluded his angry indictment by appealing to the 'impartiality and justice of honest consciences and the neutral nations' to set the record straight.

When the German White Book was published in May 1915, Heylen extended his rebuttal of the German charges concerning Namur and Luxembourg provinces. The secretary of the diocese, Canon Jean Schmitz, visited the parishes and interviewed witnesses, allowing a point-by-point rejection of the German case, especially on Dinant.[46] The collective delusion driving German actions during the invasion was identified in psychological terms as 'hysteria' and 'mass psychosis'.[47] Heylen's repudiation of the

White Book was written in the form of an open letter to Bissing and published without German permission in November 1915, together with a shorter rebuttal by the Bishop of Liège.[48] The German occupation administration rejected the two bishops' claims.[49]

The culmination of the battle within the Catholic church came in the winter of 1915–16. Exasperated at the obdurate defence of the 'People's War' thesis by the Germans and the moral neutrality of the Vatican, the Belgian bishops issued a collective letter to their German and Austrian colleagues, calling for a Belgian-German Catholic commission to investigate the atrocities issue, which was published clandestinely inside Belgium (in French and Flemish) and abroad in November 1915.[50] In condemning the German church for its support of the German official line, the Belgian bishops engaged in a larger battle between Allied and German Catholic opinion. In April 1915, a French Catholic propaganda committee, established under the double patronage of the archdiocese of Paris and the French Foreign Ministry, and headed by Alfred Baudrillart, had published a book, *La Guerre allemande et le catholicisme* ('The German War and Catholicism'), which attacked the German church and defended the Allies in terms of Catholic doctrine.[51] At the heart of the book lay the charge of 'German atrocities'.[52] Archbishops Hartmann of Cologne and Bettinger of Munich complained indignantly to the Kaiser at the French 'libels' and also to the Pope in a memorandum, which was published in the *Kölnische Volkszeitung* on 17 June 1915.[53]

A more sustained German response was required, however, and Matthias Erzberger, the Catholic political leader who also directed Germany's foreign propaganda effort, established a committee of German Catholics to respond to the French accusations. On Vatican insistence, a university theologian, A. J. Rosenberg from Paderborn, was placed in charge in order to keep the hierarchy out of the fray.[54] The resulting book dismissed the French charge that Germany had deliberately conducted a religious war against French and Belgian Catholics. It pointed out that no regiments in the German army were exclusively Protestant and referred to the Belgian bishops' co-operation with the German military authorities in establishing that tales of Belgian nuns raped by German soldiers were myths. It rebutted the charge of 'atrocities' committed by German soldiers by reaffirming the franc-tireur thesis, for which it drew heavily on the White Book.[55]

The collective letter of the Belgian bishops was in part a response to Rosenberg's book which, it was reasonably assumed, spoke for German

Catholicism as a whole.[56] The letter was also designed to state the Belgian church's case as strongly as possible to the Vatican. Its publication coincided with a visit by Cardinal Mercier to the Holy See to which he had been summoned at the request of the German government.[57] By this stage, the Vatican had at its disposal an abundance of private intelligence on what had occurred during the invasion, especially in Louvain. It had received extensive eye-witness reports from Ladeuze, rector of the university, and from Simon Deploige, head of the Institute of Philosophy.[58] Benedict XV, in a spirit of charity and reconciliation, had supported a premature and rapidly abandoned scheme to reconstitute the university library.[59] But the Vatican refused to compromise its policy of *imparzialità*, and although Mercier and Heylen spent January and February 1916 in Rome, they failed in their aim of obtaining a letter from the Pope condemning Germany.[60]

The Belgian bishops' letter therefore stood as the definitive statement of the Belgian church on the issue of the 'German atrocities'. In itself, the idea of a Belgian-German commission was not new. Mercier and Heylen had both suggested it to the German military authorities earlier in 1915.[61] But this was the first proposal for a purely Catholic tribunal. Reproducing Hague Convention IV on Land Warfare and reasserting the non-existence of a 'People's War', the letter called for a tribunal composed of equal numbers of Belgian and German bishops, with an independent arbitrator nominated by neutral bishops. The Belgian bishops counted on theological doctrine and the international structures of the church to arrive at the 'truth'. 'We bishops [...]', the Belgian letter concluded, 'have a moral duty, and therefore a religious one, which takes precedence over all others, that of searching out and proclaiming the truth.'[62] Cardinal Mercier and his colleagues appealed to their German confrères to facilitate the kind of inquiry which, unlike those conducted by the German military, would allow Belgian witnesses to speak freely. They were in no doubt that the outcome would compel the German bishops to admit their error and restore the honour of the Belgian church and nation.

The idea was foredoomed. Neither the German Catholic church nor the Vatican had the remotest interest in opening the question, still less the German government. National Catholic communities dug in along the same battle lines of interpretation as the official reports, and the Vatican sought to impose its policy of impartiality by papal authority. On 14 January 1916, Gasparri informed the nuncio in Munich that 'these polemics between members of the two Catholic hierarchies displease the

Holy Father', and a few days later he let the German hierarchy know that Benedict XV opposed any response to the collective letter of the Belgian bishops.[63] A reply had been drafted by Hartmann, and approved by the Prussian bishops, which rejected the Belgian suggestion of a neutral tribunal, citing impracticability and the Belgian bishops' closed mind on the issue.[64] However, this was not sent, and the terms of the conflict remained unchanged for the remainder of the war.

In reality, many German Catholics harboured deep reservations and privately accepted something close to the Belgian bishops' view of the conduct of the army during the invasion. Cardinal Hartmann, army chaplains in Belgium and northern France, and important lay Catholics were certainly aware of what had happened. Erzberger, for example, admitted: 'It has been proved beyond doubt, including by the testimony of German officers, that there have been cases of gross pillage, that many houses were set on fire without due cause, and that many Belgians were executed, without a judgment or without their guilt being shown. In addition, hostages have been treated very harshly [...].'[65] Erzberger added that he had received a memorandum from German-Belgian Catholics, averring that 'German soldiers were prejudiced against the clergy. Whenever German troops entered a place they took the priest hostage, churches were set on fire.'[66]

Bishop Faulhaber of Speyer, who later became Archbishop of Munich, responded to one of the contributors to a German Catholic publication rebutting French 'atrocity' accusations by suggesting that 'the historical clarification of the events in Belgium is not yet complete. According to the latest documents more blame is to be attached to the German side than we originally believed. What if 43 innocent priests really were shot and those kneeling down to give the last anointment to soldiers were held to be gouging out eyes?'[67]

Faulhaber was almost certainly referring to a devastating private admission of German guilt submitted by Bissing to the War Ministry on 28 February 1915.[68] Although the Belgian hierarchy and priests had been exonerated from collective responsibility for resisting the invasion in January 1915, Bissing went further by admitting the gratuitous violence of German soldiers towards Belgian clerics. He described the torture and killing of the priest at Spontin, whose resistance had been maintained in the January 1915 report. He referred to the arrest and maltreatment of clerics from Louvain, and the execution of the Jesuit novice, Dupierreux, at Tervuren. He also reported the harrowing account given personally to him by the apparently 'trustworthy' priest of Schaffen of his narrow escape from death at the hands of German soldiers for supposedly fomenting civilian resistance.[69] Above all, Bissing confirmed that his own list of executed Belgian clerics matched the 47 names submitted to him by the Belgian bishops.

No doubt Erzberger and the German Catholic hierarchy were reluctant to publicize the truth about the Belgian clergy out of loyalty to national unity. Yet they were also concerned at the uncontrolled anti-Catholicism in Germany that was part of the collective emotions unleashed by the war. As Cardinal Hartmann complained to the papal nuncio, Andreas Frühwirth, there was a veritable flood of anti-Catholic articles in the German press and he wrote to Mühlberg, Prussian envoy at the Vatican, expressing his concern on 22 September 1914 that national enthusiasm for the war would suffer serious damage as a result.[70] The military and civil authorities were no less concerned by popular anti-Catholicism. The Deputy General Staff of the army sent strict instructions to all Deputy General Commands (which controlled civilian life in the German regions), warning that the 'inner unity of the German people' was to be maintained by ensuring that anti-Catholic remarks did not appear in print. For there had recently been 'unconfirmed rumours about the participation of Catholic clergy in committing atrocities in Belgium, which have sometimes been linked with hateful commentaries on the Catholic clergy in general'.[71]

Reinforcing national unity while defusing popular anti-Catholicism placed German Catholics in a particularly delicate position, however, since it was a short step from exposing the myth of Belgian clerical resistance to accusing the German army, implicitly at least, of 'atrocities'. Hence the public silence on 'German atrocities' of leading Catholics who were convinced that Belgian clerics, if not the Belgian population, had been unjustly accused. The ambivalence of German Catholic attitudes to the 'atrocity' question emerges clearly in the brochure entitled *Der Lügengeist im Völkerkrieg* ('Falsehood in the War of the Peoples'), published in January 1915 by the Jesuit priest Bernhard Duhr. Duhr defended the French and Belgian clergy against the charge of orchestrating resistance and committing cruelties on the German troops.[72] No doubt in order to make his argument palatable to the military authorities, he also denied that German soldiers had committed atrocities on Belgian priests. But despite the fact that Duhr had been supported in his research by military authorities, including the military government in Belgium and the War Ministry, his brochure came under attack in the German press. Duhr asked the Bavarian War Ministry whether to withdraw the book from the market, 'in the interest of the fatherland', but the ministry recommended only that Duhr should ensure the brochure was not sold abroad in enemy or neutral countries. This was impossible to enforce, and on 20 November 1915 the Bavarian War Ministry prohibited further sales – although this did not prevent van Langenhove using the brochure as a key text in writing his study of the German atrocity myth-complex.[73]

Duhr's brochure was based on investigations carried out by the Catholic priests' association, Pax, in Cologne. Pax had established the mythic status of many of the tales of 'atrocities' committed against German soldiers by Belgian clerics. But it soon found it had to deny the logical inference that if accusations against priests were inventions, so probably were those against Belgian civilians as a whole – which turned German military reprisals into war crimes. The organization stated weakly that: 'The conduct of the civilian population, which according to statements of the German troops has waged the franc-tireur war against them, has not at all been the subject of the *Pax-Informationen*, for it is not its task.'[74] Atrocities committed by German soldiers were a 'truth' that German Catholics found as hard to embrace as did German Social Democrats. The 'atrocities' issue thus reinforced the national orientation of Catholicism in the belligerent countries and showed how difficult it was for the church to achieve consensus on the 'truth' of what had happened, let alone reconciliation between co-religionists.

3   Intellectuals

The 'international republic of letters' formed a third group whose values, activities, and cosmopolitan links intrinsically favoured an investigation of enemy 'atrocities' transcending national perspectives. In particular, university-trained academics, rooted in the methods of internationally verifiable empirical research, might appear to have been well placed to withstand the pressures of national mobilization and arrive at some measure of objective 'truth'. Yet the countervailing pressures were enormous, since intellectuals were at the forefront of that same mobilization. Many writers, artists, academics, scientists, and literary figures in the belligerent countries saw the war as a cultural conflict and themselves as combatants. If governments welcomed and channelled their enrolment, they scarcely had to solicit what was spontaneous and self-motivated.

There were a number of reasons for this involvement. Since intellectuals and artists had helped shape the political identities and sense of nationhood that were now threatened by the enemy, it was logical that they should step forward and define the conflict in these same terms. For the more conventional, the war restored them to the centre of the national community after years of apparent menace by philistinism, decadence, or the forces of modernism. Others found in the action and emotional engagement of wartime the longed-for antidote to the banality of ordinary life in urban industrial society. Yet others, who were too old or infirm to fight, took up the pen or brush from guilt at inaction and with the desire to be useful. Almost all were drawn into a vortex of emotions – love of country and hatred of the enemy – which submerged norms of academic objectivity, critical dispassion, and artistic independence.[75]

Yet against these common features must be set certain national differences. The fact that the war was defined as a contest of values meant that contrasting ideologies were at stake between the different belligerent states. While each country justified the war by a variety of ideas converging from often conflicting domestic traditions, the overall tenor of its national position assumed a distinctive character. Thus, in the French case, the support of Catholic and nationalist intellectuals for the *Union sacrée* could not disguise the fact that mainstream Republicanism (rallying the left and the labour movement) supplied the predominant language. It portrayed the war as the defence not just of the fatherland, but also of the universal values associated with the French Revolution.[76] Likewise in Britain, the Liberal Party's crusade for international law and the defence of small nations provided the essential definition of the national cause more broadly.[77] For the western Allies, including Belgium, the conflict was seen as one in defence of established norms of civilized behaviour which were rooted in liberal democratic ideals.

In Germany, conservative and modernizing intellectuals alike considered the war to be a defining moment for German national identity – expressed by the 'ideas of 1914' which were held to be of equivalent importance to 1789 for France. German intellectuals commonly rejected French political democracy and British commercial society. Against western models of liberalism, they argued that the spiritual values associated with German *Kultur* provided a superior ideal of freedom. The pamphlet by the noted sociologist, Werner Sombart, entitled *Händler und Helden* ('Merchants and Heroes'), which celebrated the warrior idealism of German spirituality over crass British materialism and hypocrisy, was only the most famous expression of convictions held by German intellectuals of different political persuasions.[78] Many considered the 'ideas of 1914' to be the values through which Europe as a whole could be remade under German inspiration and best defended against the threat of barbarism from the east.[79] Because of the intellectuals' image of Germany as the land of *Kultur*, it was a particular shock for them when the Germans were traduced as 'barbarians'. The conflict between 'civilization' and '*Kultur*' was thus no mere caricature. It reflected a real ideological antagonism between Germany and its enemies in the west.

These intellectual positions were rapidly established through a battle of manifestos. But as with governments and the press, events were critical. The language may have been preformed, but the issues over which it unfolded were specific, unpredicted, and highly charged. Initially, these issues were the outbreak of war and the violation of Belgian neutrality. On 20 August, a group of eminent German academics and artists renounced their honorary awards from British universities and scholarly bodies, declaring that Britain had engineered the war in order to crush Germany as a world power and to undermine its 'cultural achievements'.[80] Within a month, they were answered by 52 leading English authors, ranging in politics from Kipling's Tory imperialism to the liberalism of H. G. Wells, discreetly co-ordinated by the government. They published a 'Declaration' in *The Times* which accused Germany of being the aggressor and 'trying by brute force to impose its culture on other nations'.[81] A publication by the Oxford History School in September, *Why We Are at War: Great Britain's Case*, and an exchange of manifestos by leading German and British Protestant theologians, renewed accusations of broken trust and fellowship.[82]

The issue of 'atrocities' fed a powerful draught of oxygen to this intellectual conflagration. In particular, the destruction of Louvain library and the shelling of Rheims cathedral exposed German artistic and intellectual circles to further obloquy. Starting with the Société des Artistes Français, which in mid-September banned Germans from displaying works in its famous salon, French artistic and academic institutions expelled and boycotted German colleagues and stripped them of pre-war honours in protest at 'the systematic vandalism by Germany [which] has aroused indignation throughout the world'.[83] Nor was it just a question of the Allied countries. In Italy and the USA, 'cultural atrocities' aroused strong hostility from intellectuals.[84] The reaction in Germany was an urgent counter-mobilization in order to win back neutral opinion. This resulted in an 'Appeal to the World of Culture!' signed by 93 of Germany's leading intellectuals and artists which was published in and outside Germany on 1–4 October 1914.[85]

The 'Appeal to the World of Culture!' originated in two initiatives, by Ludwig Fulda, one of Germany's most popular authors, and by Hermann Sudermann, also a writer, on 10 and 11 September. They suggested a declaration condemning the 'atrocities' being committed by Germany's enemies. At the same time – significantly, just after the defeat on the Marne – the Foreign Ministry and the Navy Intelligence Bureau (an important centre of propaganda) were coming to realize that Allied condemnation of German methods of warfare needed vigorous repudiation. At a meeting held in the Navy Ministry on 13 September, Fulda and Sudermann proposed a survey of hospitals to find evidence of Germans suffering from enemy atrocities.[86] However, the chief of the Navy Intelligence Bureau doubted whether such lurid atrocities had ever been committed against German troops, and the text drafted by Fulda and Sudermann over the following days with the assistance of Georg Reicke (the liberal, democratic mayor of Berlin) switched from attacking enemy atrocities to defending Germany against Allied charges.[87]

The essence of the Appeal was contained in six short paragraphs, each headed by a ringing rejection of Allied claims that Germany had started the war, violated Belgian neutrality, and fought in a barbarous manner, as exemplified by the case of Louvain:

> It is not true that Germany is guilty in having brought about the war [...];
> It is not true that we wantonly violated Belgian neutrality [...];
> It is not true that the life or property of a single Belgian citizen has been infringed by our soldiers, except where such an attack was dictated by the bitter necessity of self-defence [...];
> It is not true that our soldiers have brutally devastated Louvain [...];
> It is not true that our warfare flouts international law [...];
> It is not true that the war against our so-called militarism is not a war against our culture [...]

The last point was aimed at those in the Allied countries who (like Bryce) sought to differentiate traditional German culture and idealism from the army and the Prussian elites. The entire Appeal ended by unequivocally identifying German culture with the army: 'Without German militarism German culture would long since have been erased from the earth [...] *The German army and the German people are one.*'

The signatories of the Appeal included some of the most internationally renowned names in German art and scholarship. Ernst Haeckel, the eminent professor of zoology at Jena and popularizer of Darwin's theories of evolution, and Rudolf Eucken, philosopher and Nobel laureate for literature in 1908, had already signed the first declaration, of 20 August, as had the composer Engelbert Humperdinck and the painter, Max Liebermann. Paul Ehrlich was Nobel laureate in 1908 for his research in immunology and had developed Salvarsan to treat syphilis. August von Wassermann, bacteriologist and immunologist, was director of the Kaiser-Wilhelm-Institut in Berlin-Dahlem. Emil von Behring received the Nobel prize in 1901 for his research on diphtheria.[88] Fritz Haber, the pioneering chemist who helped invent the process of the fixation of atmospheric nitrogen, and who during the war worked on the poison gas programme, was co-founder of the Kaiser-Wilhelm-Institut. Karl Lamprecht and Eduard Meyer were two of Germany's most distinguished historians, Gerhart Hauptmann the most notable German playwright of the time.

Overall, the Appeal reflected a broad spectrum of academic and artistic opinion, liberal as well as conservative.[89] It is true that most of the 93 signatories of the Appeal gave their assent on the basis of a two-line telegram signed by Fulda and eight other notable figures which invited them to support a declaration condemning the 'lying attacks against the German troops' – without knowing either the text or the role of the Navy and Foreign Ministries in its genesis.[90] But this makes the document all the more revealing not only of the uncritical self-mobilization of German intellectuals behind the national cause but also of their readiness to believe that the treatment of Belgian civilians was a case of legitimate self-defence. The signature by 4,000 university teachers of a declaration of solidarity with the army on 16 October, which had been initiated by the renowned classical philologist Ulrich von Wilamowitz-Moellendorf, and actively supported by the Foreign Ministry, confirmed the solid backing of the German professoriate for the invasion of Belgium and France.[91]

Sceptical voices emerged nevertheless. Given that the Appeal made claims which should have been doubted by any historian trained in the Rankean school (with its emphasis on proof from primary documents) or by any scientist applying the canons of scientific method, it is not surprising that some signatories and other German intellectuals soon signalled their unease. On 7 October 1914, Eduard Meyer wrote to Theodor Wiegand (archaeologist and fellow signatory) that he did not believe the Appeal would 'help much for we affirm things in it about which *we* cannot know or attest anything, except that *we* believe *our* authorities etc. about Louvain, the manner of warfare, the intentions to breach Belgian neutrality by England and France [...]; this cannot convince the cool judge.'[92] Another sceptic was Georg Friedrich Nicolai, professor of medicine at Berlin University. He had refused to sign the Appeal and instead persuaded some colleagues (including Albert Einstein and the Berlin astronomy professor, Wilhelm Foerster, who was one of the 93) to support an 'Appeal to the Europeans' in protest against German nationalism.[93] Ten of the 93 signatories of the Appeal subsequently withdrew their support on the grounds that they had not known its true content – among them Foerster and the economist Lujo Brentano.[94] In 1919, Brentano wrote to his colleague, Charles Gide, professor of economics at the Sorbonne, that he had heard in January 1916 from 'absolutely trustworthy persons of certain actions which individual German troop units were guilty of committing at the start of the war' which made him 'bitterly regret' signing the Appeal.[95]

Theodor Wolff, editor of the *Berliner Tageblatt*, displayed his usual acuteness. On 8 October he wrote in his diary: 'Of course, all such proclamations and declarations will be ineffective and will only achieve the opposite of their intended aim [...] Unnecessary acts of violence, pointless shootings of hostages, etc., have occurred, far too many villages have been razed, and there has also been no lack of misappropriation of private property.'[96] Despite censorship, Wolff published several articles in the *Berliner Tageblatt* criticizing both appeals for their arrogant tone and expressing his doubts as to their efficacy.[97]

The principal target of the appeals was the academics, artists, and intellectuals of neutral countries, to whom the documents were sent before being released in Germany.[98] But the declarations were immediately passed on to the Allied nations, where they were denounced. German members of French professional bodies were expelled at an accelerated tempo. The Société des Auteurs et Compositeurs Dramatiques, for example, stripped

Humperdinck, Gerhart Hauptmann, Siegfried Wagner, and Sudermann of their membership for signing the Appeal, and the Académie des Inscriptions et Belles-Lettres removed Wilamowitz-Moellendorf on the same grounds.[99] At the end of October, the Académie Française formally repudiated the 'Appeal to the World of Culture!', stating: 'In the name of French civilization and human civilization, [the Academy] condemns the violators of Belgian neutrality, the murderers of women and children, the savage destroyers of the noble monuments of the past, the arsonists of Louvain University and Rheims cathedral [...]'[100] The Académie des Sciences joined with the other academies of the Institut de France on 4 November when it protested against the claim of the 4,000 German university professors that 'the salvation of European civilization lies in the victory of German militarism in solidarity with German culture.'[101] On 8 November, French university professors attacked the declaration with a manifesto addressed to their colleagues in neutral countries. Although the French academics proclaimed their continuing attachment to the educational ideals associated with the Germany of Leibniz, Kant, and Goethe, they needed to do no more than repeat the German professors' association of German culture with German militarism to claim that the war and the brutality of the invasion were due as much to the former as the latter.[102]

British academic and artistic institutions were somewhat less zealous in stripping Germans of their membership and honours, for the Royal Society and the British Academy (under the presidency of Lord Bryce) rejected this path.[103] However, the two German declarations were repudiated as categorically as in France. On 21 October 1914, *The Times* published a Reply to the 'Appeal to the World of Culture!' which was signed by well over 100 leading academics and a scattering of artists and musicians. Though acknowledging the ties of 'comradeship, of respect, and of affection' which had long linked British academics with German colleagues and institutions, the Reply blamed writers such as Nietzsche, Treitschke, Bülow, and Bernhardi for fostering expansionist violence. It held Germany solely responsible for the outbreak of the war and contended that German armies alone had deliberately destroyed cultural monuments. Summarizing the liberal paradigm, the Reply concluded that Germany stood 'revealed as the common enemy of Europe and of all people which respect the Law of Nations'.[104]

Following hard on the news of Louvain and Rheims, the 'Appeal to the World of Culture!' significantly added to Germany's public relations difficulties in neutral countries. Sudermann himself, when travelling to

Switzerland on behalf of the Foreign Ministry, found that the Appeal had had a 'disastrous effect', and in early December he asked the Foreign Ministry if it could be withdrawn.[105] Similarly in the United States, the Appeal added to the discomfiture of pro-German and German-American intellectuals. Despite the fact that Germany had deeply influenced the professionalization of American universities, academics, like elite opinion more generally, inclined to the Allies, even if they kept their distance from the European War.[106] Defence of the German cause came from a minority of professors, most notably Hugo Münsterberg at Harvard. In his book, *The War and America*, published in the late autumn of 1914, Münsterberg portrayed a pacific Germany forced into war by the jealous aggression of Russia and Britain, and he dismissed the tales of 'German atrocities', somewhat contradictorily, as both deliberate British falsification and the hallucinations of traumatized witnesses.[107] George Viereck enthusiastically endorsed Münsterberg's case in *The Fatherland* and reproduced the 'Appeal to the World of Culture!'[108]

The president of the Carnegie Institute, S. H. Church, however, rebutted the Appeal with a public letter to the Berlin sculptor, Fritz Schaper, who had sent him the document. Church argued that Germany had incontrovertibly started the war, violated Belgian neutrality, and committed 'atrocities'. He drew on the Kaiser's telegram to Wilson as proof of the destruction of Louvain, but defended the right of Belgian civilians to resist the invader without incurring the annihilation of whole towns, just as Mexicans had recently fired on American forces 'restoring order' in Vera Cruz. Succumbing nevertheless to the mutilation myth, he added the tale sent home by an American Red Cross nurse in Belgium of how a young boy shooting at German soldiers had had his hands cut off.[109] Reeling off the standard litany of intellectual deviants who had corrupted the admirable traditions of German culture (Nietzsche, Treitschke, Bernhardi), Church proffered the German-American community as evidence that German culture and influence did not need to be associated with expansionist nationalism.

Church's rejection of the Appeal was the most formal American response. But the perception that the luminaries of German culture and academia had been compromised by their uncritical endorsement of the government and army was widely shared. The Columbia historian James Harvey Robinson dismissed the Appeal as a 'pitifully feeble manifesto', while the philosopher Arthur O. Lovejoy felt that it demonstrated the intellectual failure of professional academics at a critical point in German history.[110]

The intellectual battle over the 'atrocities' by no means ended with the German failure to conquer neutral opinion with the 'Appeal to the World of Culture!'. The Allies took the offensive in order to drive home what they considered to be the 'truth' of the German army's conduct in France and Belgium. The Bryce Committee, for example, had a strong academic component (including the historian and Vice-Chancellor of Sheffield University, H. A. L. Fisher), and its stance of intellectual impartiality contributed to its success. In France, leading Republican intellectuals established a Comité d'Études et de Documents sur la Guerre in October 1914 which secured the government's support for a series of brochures. These, according to the committee's secretary, the sociologist Émile Durkheim, were to be sent 'to the neutral countries where they might neutralize, as far as possible, Germany's audaciously lying propaganda'.[111] The president of the committee was Ernest Lavisse, doyen of French historians and director of the elite École Normale Supérieure in Paris, who had experienced the German invasion of 1870–1 in his native département of the Aisne and had studied in Germany. Opening the first semester of the war at the Sorbonne, on 5 November 1914, Lavisse had flayed Germany for its arrogance in destroying Louvain library and Rheims cathedral and accused it of massacring women, children, and wounded French soldiers.[112] The other members of the committee were all leading Paris academics closely connected with Lavisse, while its archivist and guiding editorial spirit was the celebrated librarian of the École Normale Supérieure, Lucien Herr. In every sense, the committee was the voice of the Republican academic elite mobilizing itself for war.

The atrocity issue was central to the committee's brochures. Overall, the Germans were accused of corrupting what Durkheim called the 'humanitarian morality of the Christianized west' by a Nietzschean drive for world dominance.[113] The atrocities for Durkheim were the expression of 'a completely organized system, deeply rooted in the public mentality, and working automatically', with the result that men who had imbibed this 'pathological' attitude were entirely unconscious of the gravity of their behaviour. This general analysis was repeated by Lavisse and the German specialist, Charles Andler, and in a book edited by Lavisse which presented the committee's findings to a French audience.[114]

The most controversial use of the 'atrocities' issue by the committee, however, came with two brochures written by Joseph Bédier, philologist and professor of medieval French at the Collège de France. The war diaries taken from dead or captured German soldiers by the Allied armies during the invasion seemed to supply evidence by the perpetrators of their actions and motivation. As such, they were manna to the Allies, and after some extracts had been used in the press in late autumn 1914 French military intelligence gave Bédier exclusive access to the diaries in its possession. In early 1915 he produced his two brochures, *Les Crimes allemands d'après des témoignages allemands* and *Comment l'Allemagne essaye de justifier ses crimes*, the second addressing the fierce German rejoinders to the first.[115]

Since the originals of the war diaries have disappeared, it is impossible to say how selective Bédier was in his use of them. But he drew on nearly 50 diaries in order to provide evidence of 36 incidents. Unlike Bryce, he avoided the topic of overtly sexual and sadistic crime. The incidents cited involved brutality towards civilians, killing of Allied wounded and prisoners, pillage, and arson. Although Bédier could have corroborated these from other sources, such as the Belgian official reports, he chose to adopt the approach of his discipline and deduce both what had happened and what had motivated the German soldiers by a process of exegesis of German sources. Bédier's brochures were fiercely contested in what turned into a battle between philologists. The German respondents were former colleagues or teachers of Bédier, for, like many academics in Allied countries, he had served his apprenticeship at prestigious German universities.[116]

Possessing only Bédier's edited texts and commentary, the German academics (and some neutrals sympathetic to them) sought to turn Bédier's methods against him and draw the opposite conclusion. In general, they were unconvincing when seeking to contest the account of what had happened. Bédier's diary extracts spoke clearly of the executions of Schaffen, the burning of villages around Dinant, Stenger's order, and so on. But Bédier placed the worst possible construction on German motives, ignoring the evidence that the German troops had suffered a collective self-delusion, and asserting reductionist cultural theories to explain the 'atrocities'. An expert on the *Chanson de Roland* (in between writing the two brochures, he composed a show entitled *Chivalry* for the Comédie Française), Bédier contrasted German behaviour with his own vision of French military conduct rooted in medieval ideals. Bédier's German opponents attacked him for slipshod textual analysis, justified the events recorded by the diarists (when these were irrefutable) by military necessity against francs-tireurs, and pilloried his interpretations as fantasies in the worst traditions of French literary licentiousness, from Rabelais to Zola.

Yet, though the battle of interpretation turned on opposed values and perceptions, the evidence of the captured diaries was hard to explain away. Virtually no German commentators claimed they were forgeries.

German intellectuals thus found themselves defending the same delusion as the German government – that the German army really had faced a *Franktireurkrieg* – as well as the legal and moral principles behind the German army's response. Allied intellectuals, however exaggerated their interpretations, had a simpler task because the evidence made it easier. The point can be demonstrated by looking at intellectual dissidence on the two sides. As we have seen, the two German declarations were almost as counter-productive domestically as internationally. Both were rapidly discredited among important segments of German intellectual opinion because the 'People's War' accusation was unverifiable, while what was defended had far exceeded severe military sanctions.

Intellectual doubt on the 'atrocities' issue also emerged in Britain and France. But it was different and, above all, more limited than in Germany. Scepticism arose most easily over mythic representations of 'German atrocities', such as Belgian children with severed hands. André Gide, for example, who was engaged in charitable work for the Belgian government in Paris, discounted lurid tales of mutilation from his personal experience.[117] But the evidence of widespread maltreatment of civilians and the punitive destruction of property, let alone the apparently incontrovertible reality of the destruction of Louvain library and Rheims cathedral, were less easily dismissed. The most outspokenly sceptical writer in Britain during the first year of the war was George Bernard Shaw. He was not only scornful of tales of German barbarity ('We have some Belgian wounded in the neighbourhood,' he told a correspondent in December 1914; 'they keep up their spirits by telling lies for which there is an unlimited demand'), but also shrugged off more solidly documented happenings as the brutality not of the enemy but of war. 'The truth about war is always bad enough,' he wrote to another friend, 'but there really isn't a solitary scrap of evidence that the Germans, apart from their obsolete usage of hostage shooting, are behaving worse than we should behave in their circumstances.'[118]

Shaw vented his dissidence in an incandescent essay, 'Common Sense about the War', published in autumn 1914, which told the British with typically Shavian paradox that they were fighting the right war for the wrong reasons. Shaw denied the Allies any moral superiority unless they used the war to build a new democratic and Socialist world order as its outcome. He 'atrocities', including Louvain. Massart received only one reply, from Ernst Haeckel, who refused the suggestion on the ground that such 'well-intentioned' proposals were simply impractical.[129]

Socialists, Catholics, and intellectuals do not exhaust the list of those who claimed some special basis on which to resolve the conflict between the warring camps over the 'atrocities' question.[130] But they show clearly how international communities of truth had been ruptured by the war, and especially by the process of cultural mobilization. Consequently, no mechanism existed for investigating the fraught issue of enemy 'atrocities'. This was not because such mechanisms were unthinkable. The Commission for Relief in Belgium, which assured that country's provisioning by neutral powers from late 1914, showed them to be perfectly practicable where consensus existed between the warring parties. But where the definition of the enemy was concerned, consensus was the first casualty of the conflict.

draw
strength of nationalism : Germans, Frenchmen,
power   etc. first, all else
                                  second...

8   Wartime culture and enemy atrocities

'Enemy atrocities' continued to resonate long after the end of mobile warfare in 1914. The memory of invasion remained a compelling source of meaning for a war bogged down in military stalemate. This was especially true of the Allied countries which had experienced invasion directly, and even of Britain. The war was also presented to the German public as defensive, but the reality was that Germany occupied enemy territory and, after the brief Russian invasion of East Prussia, fought beyond its own borders. Consequently, it was less easy for 'atrocities' to continue to symbolize the war, although naval warfare and the British blockade provided a substitute.

The persistence of the atrocity question beyond 1914, however, is not explained only by differences in the experience of invasion. Atrocity accusations were central to the 'war cultures' which emerged in 1914–15 in all the belligerent societies. If their content differed, the form and function of the war cultures displayed common features.[1] War cultures operated everywhere at overlapping levels – elite, traditional, and commercial. Government and other official bodies played an important role in stimulating the war cultures in order to consolidate national unity, including measures of control and censorship. Yet more important was the 'self-mobilization' in support of the national cause by private and semi-official organizations, the market, and individuals – as already seen in the case of the Socialists, Catholics, and intellectuals.[2] Perhaps the most important function of the war cultures was to polarize collective identities between the positive, communal identity of each nation (and its allies) and the demonized enemy.[3] This occurred almost instantaneously in August 1914, contributing to the accusation of enemy atrocities in the first place. But atrocity and invasion narratives continued to provide key motifs around which the figure of the enemy was elaborated.

[handwritten marginal note:] indeed, polarization of enemies, allies — identification of enemy — occurred preceded war itself — Germanophobia in England.

24   Naval atrocities – the *Lusitania* (recruiting poster, 1915)

German government to issue a declaration that were the German armed forces to reach Ireland, they would not be coming as invaders and destroyers, but as liberators.[11]

Much of the Allied reference to 'atrocities', however, was not directed to a particular goal. It assumed an extraordinary variety of forms, from official reports and academic publications to the press, postcards, and films, and it was marked by a broad range of tone, from the restrained to the sensational. The sober end of the spectrum repeated the argument that Germany had flouted the norms of civilized behaviour and international law, warranting criminal proceedings as part of the peace settlement. This view was widely publicized by lawyers and academics, such as the professor of law at Limoges University who told a public meeting that Germany deserved to be tried for war crimes 'in the name of the human conscience'.[12] The professor of law at the University of Montpellier and J. H. Morgan at London University made the same point in published rebuttals of the German White Book.[13] There is no mistaking the sense of contemporary shock at the idea of the Germans as lawbreakers, which was echoed by numerous cheap editions and anthologies of the official reports.

At the other end of the spectrum, the sensationalist press and popular books, as well as cartoons and postcards, portrayed a dehumanized enemy. Prints and postcards demonized Germans as evil incarnate, given to the most atrocious crimes. In one among many possible examples, a 12-year-old boy, René Santo, son of an extreme French nationalist, produced caricatures of German atrocities in a spidery, infantile hand which only made the brutality of the imaginary crimes the more shocking, as in his religious parody, 'The Monstrous Triptych' (illustration 25).[14] But lurid descriptions of 'German atrocities' were by no means the preserve of marginal or ephemeral publications. A 'quality' journal such as *The Field*, a distinctly upper-class British magazine, ran exaggerated tales with venomous comment which its editor, Sir Theodore Cook, distilled into books with alliterative titles such as *Kaiser, Krupp and Kultur* or *Kultur and Catastrophe*.[15]

Taken as a whole, the literature and imagery of 'atrocity' in the Allied countries provided a condensed representation of the enemy. The fact that it drew on actual events and real moral and political concerns explains much of its resilience. Yet within the war culture, the enemy was almost by definition 'atrocious'. Since this conviction arose as much by 'self-mobilization' from below as by manipulation from above, enemy 'atrocities' gained a strong grip on the wartime imagination in virtually every belligerent country. The logic of this polarized representation meant that the enemy could escape its condition as a dehumanized perpetrator of atrocities only by admitting its guilt – in short, by cultural and ideological surrender. Self-justification and counter-accusations merely confirmed the original charges in the eyes of those who had made them. Conversely, any mitigation of judgment on enemy 'atrocities' risked undermining the enemy's demonic nature, and the moral absolutism of the accusers' own cause. Locked into this representational antagonism, it was hard for observers to

25　A child's vision of 'German atrocities'. 'The monstrous triptych' (René Santo)

analyse actual atrocities dispassionately, as the Bryce Committee's susceptibility to exaggerated witness evidence demonstrated.

As a framework for interpreting the war, the Allied construction of 'German atrocities' grew to encompass enemy behaviour which bore little relationship to the events of 1914. Unrestricted U-boat warfare against the British naval blockade provided a further chapter of German 'frightfulness'. The right of the British to blockade neutral shipping and the morality of reducing the enemy by civilian starvation were both questionable. Nevertheless, German retaliation against merchant shipping was deemed an 'atrocity', epitomized by the sinking of the *Lusitania*, which loomed large in British perceptions.[16] For the French and Belgians, the harshness of German occupation policies (with economic exploitation and the forced deportation of labour – including women and girls) further confirmed the image of systematic German brutality in representational terms set by the invasion of 1914.[17] The polemical function of the charge of German 'atrociousness' is nowhere more evident than in the distorted Allied perspective on the Armenian genocide, conducted by Germany's Turkish ally in 1915. As discussed in chapter 2, this was by far the worst case of violence against civilians during the war, on a wholly different scale to the invasions of 1914.

But since the perpetrators were a junior partner of Germany, the genocide was given a minor place in Allied accusations, even though none other than Lord Bryce espoused the Armenian cause.[18] 'Atrociousness' denoted the importance of the enemy, not the crime.

The extraordinary celebrity achieved during the war by the Dutch cartoonist Louis Raemaekers shows better than anything how, by addressing real issues through the imagery of national enmity, 'German atrocities' occupied a central place in the war cultures of Allied countries. Raemaekers was the most famous of a number of neutral 'witnesses' whose independent status made their published condemnation of German conduct during the invasion particularly telling for Allied opinion.[19] Born of a German mother, Raemaekers was a middle-aged painter who, shortly before the war, had discovered his real strength as a cartoonist. His life was transformed, however, by the experience of the invasion, which he encountered both through the flood of Belgian refugees into Holland and by a visit he made to Belgian territory. Within months, the cartoons that he produced for the Amsterdam *Telegraaf* condemning the invasion, and especially 'German atrocities', were being reproduced internationally, and at German prompting he was unsuccessfully prosecuted by the government for jeopardizing Dutch neutrality.

Raemaekers' international fame was consolidated with his arrival in London in December 1915, where an exhibition of his work was organized by the Fine Arts Society. Although the public had been saturated with 'German atrocities', *The Times* claimed that 'this neutral is the only genius produced by the war.'[20] A mass public agreed. For over four months, the exhibition was swamped by visitors, before touring the major British cities. Raemaekers was lionized by London society. He was presented to Asquith, who felt that Raemaekers gave 'form and colour to the menace which the Allies are averting from the liberty, the civilisation and the humanity of the future. He shows us our enemies as they appear to the unbiased eyes of a neutral [...]'.[21] In February 1916, Raemaekers met with the same rapturous response in Paris, being received at the Sorbonne and awarded the Légion d'honneur.[22] But the real mechanisms of his success lay in the mass dissemination of his images by books, lantern slides, millions of postcards, and syndication in the world's newspapers, especially in the USA. Wellington House and the British propaganda effort played a key role in this process; Raemaekers became the single most influential figure in projecting the Allied vision of the German enemy to home audiences and to the rest of the world.

26   Louis Raemaekers, 'Seduction'

Although Raemaekers produced more than 500 cartoons during the war, the essence of his vision was expressed by the book associated with his London exhibition, *The Great War: A Neutral's Indictment*.[23] The book defined the Allies and Germany in terms of the prevailing dichotomy between 'civilization' and 'Kultur'/barbarism. Many of its cartoons derided the Kaiser, other German leaders, or the nation as a whole. Demonizing the enemy was explicit in the cartoon of 'Satan's Partner', in which the devil selects as his accomplice General von Bernhardi, whose *Germany and the Next War* (1912) was widely taken by Allied opinion to voice the beliefs of the German military. The positive pole consisted of reassuring images of the moral force and military fortitude of the Allies. But 27 of the 100 cartoons contained in the book dealt directly with 'German atrocities'. One

27   Louis Raemaekers, 'The Shields of Rösselaere' (*sic*)

cartoon portrayed nurse Edith Cavell's execution (condemned in Britain and the USA as an outrage), while eight dealt with naval atrocities, centred on the sinking of the *Lusitania*. Eighteen of the atrocity cartoons concerned the invasion of Belgium, the original inspiration for Raemaekers' vision of the war. These were also among the most widely reproduced of Raemaekers' images.

Unlike the other cartoons, which were often heavily symbolic, those of the 'atrocities' in Belgium mainly took the form of sketches of supposed events.[24] Sometimes the events were generic, such as rape or pillage at the hands of stereotypical German soldiers (the brutish private, the supercilious and sadistic officer), as in 'Seduction' (illustration 26). But others dealt with specific incidents, such as that on 19–20 October at Roeselare (West Flanders), which German troops captured with the help of a human shield.

28   Louis Raemaekers, 'The Massacre of the Innocents' (Dinant)

Thirty-one civilians were shot or burned and around 250 buildings destroyed (illustration 27).[25] Likewise, the 'Massacre of the Innocents' pictured one of the collective executions in Dinant, with brutal German soldiers restraining anguished women and girls while their menfolk are being executed (illustration 28). 'The Hostages' portrayed the seizure of burgomaster Tielemans and his son at Aarschot (illustration 29). Other cartoons sought to convey the scale of the devastation visited on Belgium, as in the crude cartoon, 'Kreuzland, Kreuzland über Alles', which showed an immeasurable throng of bereft children asking 'Where are our fathers?'

29   Louis Raemaekers, 'The Hostages' (Aarschot)

It was these dramatic images of German 'frightfulness' in action that made Raemaekers' reputation, which waned subsequently with the war culture that had created it. In a backhanded tribute to his influence, the German government attacked him to the end. In Switzerland, the German ambassador initiated a lawsuit early in 1918 over an exhibition of Raemaekers' prints in Geneva. The defence argued that Raemaekers' vision of Germany was true, including the question of brutality towards civilians, and Bédier's pamphlets and the 1907 Hague Convention on Land Warfare were cited as evidence. The ambassador lost the action.[26]

2   War cultures and national martyrdom

Defining the enemy as the perpetrator of 'atrocities' was one source of the issue's potency. Another was identifying the victims with the nation. The 'atrocities' permitted a sense of national victimhood to be derived from the fate of individual people and places in three ways. First was the exposure of women, children and families to the brutality of the invader. Second was the destruction of localities. Third was the need for remembrance of the invasion while the war was still in progress. All three dimensions provided ways of defining the national community in terms of suffering and outrage.

To the extent that the nation was imagined as a community set in an inviolate space, actual or feared invasion readily seemed akin to rape and violation. Britain's muted invasion fear in the autumn of 1914 was expressed vicariously through the plight of Belgium and imagined through the violation of British homes. Tales of raped women in Belgium and France merged into the rape of Belgium itself and suggested the threat to Britain. William Le Queux's lurid account in *German Atrocities: A Record of Shameless Deeds*, for example, turned rape and mutilation into a premeditated feature of German policy towards Belgium: 'The wild orgies of blood and debauchery, the atrocious outrages, murders, and mutilations, the ruthless violation and killing of defenceless women, girls, and children of tender age, have been, it is now admitted by the Germans themselves, carried out with their full knowledge, and even as part of the actual plan of campaign of their War-Lords.'[27] A recruiting pamphlet used in the Irish and British campaigns in 1914, which showed a brutish German soldier standing on the body of a dead woman with a doll nearby, his bayonet erect and dripping with blood, encapsulated the fate of Belgium in an image of rape and family violation which implied that the Germans would do the same if they invaded Britain.[28]

In France, where a vulnerable population disproportionately composed of women and children had been abandoned to the invader, rape and mutilation were no less symbolic to the nation. In addition to the general polarization of male and female spheres in the nineteenth century, a political tradition reaching back to the French Revolution placed women and children in a tutelary relationship to the nation through the male citizen and soldier, responsible for their protection.[29] Invasion, which was deeply etched in historical memory (1792–4, 1870), violated family ideology in both Republican and Catholic variants. The lines of Rouget de Lisle's

Marseillaise made the link explicit: '[The enemy] comes right into our homes, to slit the throats of our sons, of our [women] companions', runs one line, immediately followed by an appeal to male citizens to rise up *en masse* and repel the foe ('Aux armes, citoyens!' etc.). These words spoke directly to the experience of 1914, as suggested by a wartime set of engravings illustrating the Marseillaise by the French artist, Auguste Roubille (illustrations 30 and 31). Significantly, Rouget de Lisle's ashes were transferred to the Hôtel des Invalides on 14 July 1915.[30] Expressing the nation's plight through images of violated women and children carried the message that only the male warrior could redeem the victims' fate.

Ruth Harris and Stéphane Audoin-Rouzeau have shown how the link between real women's bodies and the body politic provided an especially troubling expression of the national trauma of invasion, in the form of an intense debate in 1915 over the 'child of the barbarian', the offspring of French women raped by German soldiers.[31] In early January, the journalist Jean d'Orsay published an apocryphal tale in *Le Matin* concerning a Belgian priest who had counselled women pregnant through rape by German soldiers to abort their four- or five-month-old foetuses. Although discredited, the story triggered a stormy debate.[32] Maurice Barrès, the nationalist writer, suggested a month later, in *L'Echo de Paris*, that local feeling among women in his native Lorraine strongly favoured the destruction of the 'virus' left by the invader, and he tacitly endorsed the implied solution of abortion or infanticide ('What jury would condemn them?').[33] In the months that followed, elite circles divided over whether temporary suspension of the anti-abortion laws should indeed be permitted for women in this situation, or whether the 'child of the enemy' should be kept and if so, whether he (and he was usually imagined with his father's gender) could ever become a good Frenchman.[34]

The debate revolved around the role of biology and culture in the constitution of the national community, and the nature of maternal sentiment. Fears of demographic vulnerability, belief in the universal values of Republicanism, and conservative Catholic family values had combined to make the French less receptive to eugenics than pre-war Britain or Germany. Consequently, a strong, heterogeneous coalition (including Republicans and even socialists, Catholics, and feminists) opposed a suspension of the ban on abortion, however limited. Whether French mothers should raise the little enemy in their midst, converting him by maternal love and Republican patriotism or Catholic values into a Frenchman, or

[margin handwritten note: abortion, children of German invaders conceived through rape]

marked similarities to Revolutionary iconography

30   The Marseillaise and 'German atrocities'

whether they should place the unwanted reminder of personal and national humiliation in state care, was a further division within the maternalist camp. Either way, belief in the power of education to redeem the child of the enemy and turn him into a true Frenchman was an important component of the debate.

The maternalist coalition was certainly more influential than the opposite viewpoint which favoured the physical elimination of the enemy's seed. Yet, as Stéphane Audoin-Rouzeau has pointed out, the degree of support for the latter position shows just how much the war fostered biological assumptions about the national community. The position was starkly stated by Paul Rabier, a doctor who considered that abortion was simply an extension of

31   The Marseillaise and the national response: the *levée en masse*

the struggle for survival on the battlefield: 'The enemy is the enemy and wherever he inserts himself and digs in, we have to dislodge and kill him, that is war! [...] Suppressing an embryo of a few weeks does not seem to me to be murder [...] any more than killing a German with a bullet or a bayonet.'[35] Others drew on current medical and biological theories to present the child of the enemy as a malignant medical condition, or even as a threat to national bloodlines. This fear connected with current concerns over the heritability of madness, syphilis, criminality, and alcoholism − all easily projected onto the image of the invader. 'The child of the Boche', wrote one commentator, 'can only be a brute, an idiot or a criminal degenerate.'[36] This was the 'enemy within' with a vengeance.

Popular sympathy for this position was dramatically demonstrated by the trial of Joséphine Barthélemy in early 1917. Accused of killing her infant at birth the previous summer, Barthélemy, who had been repatriated from the occupied Meurthe-et-Moselle, claimed to be the victim of rape by two Germans. Her defence lawyer not only underlined her harrowing life under the German occupation but also generalized the case by claiming that Joséphine Barthélemy was only one of many such victims, and he summoned up the spectre of these 'sons of Germany who will later mingle in France anonymously and with impunity'. He argued that thwarted maternal instinct had inspired a legitimate hatred for the child of the enemy whom she was forced to carry. By placing the suffering of raped women on an equal footing with that of the soldiers fighting to liberate the fatherland, he expressed the gendered compact on which national defence rested. As Barrès and others had predicted, no jury would convict and Barthélemy was duly acquitted.[37]

It has been shown in chapter 5 that it is almost impossible to determine how many women became pregnant through rape by German soldiers. The government took the matter seriously enough to formulate and publicize its policy, which maintained the ban on abortion but helped women place the offspring of German rapes in total secrecy with the Public Assistance.[38] The official commission on German war crimes clearly expected to find evidence of significant violation of French women by German soldiers when it entered the territory abandoned by the German army in its retreat to the Siegfried Line, in spring 1917. In reality the incidence was very low, the problem being rather that of French women who had cohabited more or less willingly with enemy soldiers.[39]

The debate on the children of German rape is important ultimately because it expressed in its most extreme form a gendered vision of the national community. The drama of the enemy foetus was a stark reflection of the military impotence of French males, and many of the fantasies associated with the issue concerned the difficulty of accepting that the enemy had permanently violated what French soldiers had failed to defend. The 'child of the barbarian' codified as an 'atrocity' narrative the fantasies of rape and mutilation which had been male responses to the invasion itself.

National victimhood was represented by the violation of place as well as body. Louvain, Rheims cathedral, and to a lesser extent the medieval Cloth Hall at Ypres (whose destruction by artillery fire occurred as mobile warfare came to an end) are the clearest examples. As Pierre Loti, the

French novelist, put it with characteristic hyperbole: 'The tortured, the hanged, the women and children shot or mutilated will soon have perished in their poor anonymous graves, and then the world will no longer remember them. But these ruins [lying] on the ground, these innumerable ruins of museums or churches, how many devastating pieces of evidence for the prosecution, and [ones] which will last!'[40] The destruction of the historic university library of Louvain far outweighed the killing of 248 civilians in the Allied case against Germany. At Rheims, no civilians were executed at all; what counted was the supposedly wilful destruction of a pre-eminent French place of national memory.[41] These cases, however, were exceptional only in their national and international resonance, not in their essence. Time and again, 'German atrocities' were portrayed as the destruction of a locality replete with historical and cultural significance.

Much had contributed to the sense of place in early twentieth-century Europe. A long peace interrupted by fewer wars than preceding epochs, a deepening historical awareness, and the transport revolution helped create a sense of the architectural patrimony of cities, towns, and even villages as something which defined local identity and connected it to the nation. Tourism, with its monuments, beauty-spots, and potted local histories, contributed to a heightened sense of place. The invasion of 1914 fell like an axe across this idealization of locality. Significantly, a form of tourism (or pilgrimage) occurred while the invasion was still in progress, as fascinated civilians sought a glimpse of the smoking ruins left by the barbaric invader. *Bruxellois* streamed northward to see the site of heavy fighting after the counter-attacks by the Belgian army from Antwerp.[42] Parisians likewise visited the devastation left by the German retreat from the Marne.[43] The press took readers on vicarious tours of the destruction in the Meurthe-et-Moselle.

For the British, the sites of 'atrocities' (unless internationally famous, like Rheims and Louvain) were devoid of precise significance. But in Belgium and especially France, where the people of the liberated zone became free to talk about the experience, the Germans were accused of violating the history and identity of localities by the deliberate targeting of buildings in reprisal for supposed civilian resistance. Local narratives contrasted the peaceable landscape, pre-war prosperity, and centuries of historical evolution with the brutal incursion of the invaders.

In a typical example, Loup Bertroz, a local newspaper editor, published an account of the devastation of Senlis by the Germans, which opened with a guide-book description of the town.[44] The locality was firmly linked to the destiny of the nation ('The origin of the city is very ancient; its name has been associated across the centuries with the different phases of our [national] history'), while its tourist qualities were also evoked. 'Pretty Senlis is not only renowned for its monuments and its history but equally appeals to tourists for the marvellous sites in its environs which offer visitors the occasion for delightful walks.' Bertroz then recounted the partial destruction wrought by the Germans from 1 to 5 September and the martyrdom of the mayor, Eugène Odent. Accompanying photographs showed the town's shattered streets and blackened public buildings.

Such commemorative accounts amounted to a veritable genre during the war. A series of books was published in 1915–16 on the devastated villages of Lorraine. A local doctor, Viriot, wrote the volume on Noményy, typically evoking the village's historic and geographic identity: '[Noménny's] archaeological and historical memorials attracted scholars; economists, agronomists, merchants, even industrialists found all they needed for the creation of various businesses. Life was easy, everything smiled on this exquisite little place.'[45] The subsequent account of the events of 1914 which terminated with a description of the ruins served as an ordering narrative which restored the trauma to historical time and began to make it explicable. The same function was performed at Gerbéviller by the Nancy artist, Victor Prouvé, who was invited to record the village's devastation in the autumn of 1914.[46] A special issue of the art journal *L'Art et les Artistes* was devoted in 1915 to the portrayal of historically and culturally defined localities as the victims of enemy violation, focusing on the destruction by the 'modern vandals' of village churches and local historical monuments throughout the entire invasion zone.[47] Tourist guides for 'pilgrims' to the sites of deliberate devastation were also published in 1915–16 in order, as one put it, to sustain the memory of 'the victims of these outrages perpetrated on the land of France', and to nourish 'a relentless hatred' of the enemy.[48]

Remembrance provided a third expression of national victimhood. The death and devastation occasioned by German atrocities generated a powerful local need to grieve and also to order the memory of the trauma through memorialization. This was difficult in Belgium under the German occupation. Commemorative masses were held in the late autumn of 1914 as the civilian dead were disinterred from collective and hastily dug graves and properly buried. But the occupying authorities frequently forbade memorials or censored inscriptions which implied German guilt. The same difficulties applied in occupied France. But in the zone liberated by the victory of the Marne, local suffering and commemoration were openly symbolized as national victimhood.

The cultural model most readily available for this purpose was martyrdom. In its religious form, martyrdom requires no personal qualification other than the violent sacrifice of the innocent for the cause; as such, it traditionally provided the surest route to sainthood within the Catholic church. By the First World War, the concept had long been secularized, with patriotic and other varieties of martyrdom embodying the values of different political creeds.[49] The events of the invasion supplied a number of exemplary cases, both religious and secular, in which individual martyrdom linked local memory with national outrage.

French and Belgian priests who had been particularly maltreated by German soldiers served as exemplary martyrs for both faith and country. The aged priest of Varreddes in the Seine-et-Marne, for example, who had been unjustly accused of signalling to the French army from his church tower, badly beaten, and killed, soon achieved martyr status. One publication portrayed him as incarnating the proud resistance of 'the violated Marne [. . . as] the shield of civilization'.[50] In similar fashion, the death of a parish priest of Saint-Dié (Vosges), during its brief occupation, the brutal treatment and death of the curé of Sompuis (Marne) during his deportation, or the killing of various Belgian priests, all provided deaths which exemplified Catholic suffering at the hands of the invader.[51]

Martyrdom also served to describe the collective fate of the church. This was particularly important in France where, unlike in Belgium, official and popular secularism meant that Catholicism had no axiomatic claim to speak for the nation. On the contrary, anticlerical suspicion of the Vatican's temporizing over the issues at stake in the war, and the susceptibility of Catholics to the charge of split allegiance – to the international church as well as to the nation – placed French Catholics on the defensive.[52] Willette summed up the difficulties in a cartoon which portrayed the 'truth' about the invasion of Belgium in the form of a priest and a baby with severed hands beating at the doors of the Vatican in front of an impassive Swiss guard (illustration 32).[53] The killing of some 22 French priests by the invading German troops therefore represented a powerful claim of collective martyrdom for the church, which adapted the memory of persecution at the hands of the French Revolution to the events of 1914. Bishop Turinaz of Nancy echoed Bishop Heylen in Namur. After naming the 11 priests of

32 At the doors of the Vatican: 'Open, open, it is unfortunate Belgium' (Adolphe Willette, 1915)

his diocese shot by the Germans (some allegedly after torture), Turinaz denied the existence of francs-tireurs, attributing any shooting to drunken, pillaging German soldiers, or occasionally to rear-guard resistance by French soldiers. In a Lenten address in 1915, he accused the German troops of conducting a religious war which deliberately targeted churches and sacred objects (such as the despoiled tabernacle at Gerbéviller) and sought to destroy Catholicism in the name of *Kultur*.[54] Here, martyrdom supplied a familiar language which expressed the suffering of Lorraine and northern France, and the symbolic victimhood of the nation, in Catholic terms.

But martyrdom easily encompassed all victims of the invasion. The German practice of making hostages out of local dignitaries ensured that there was no shortage of secular martyrs, often suffering their fate with stoic or heroic patriotism. The mayor of Badonviller, awarded the Légion d'honneur in August 1914, the executed mayor of Senlis, or Tielemans, the burgomaster of Aarschot, were only some of the victims who particularized the collective fate of the invaded zone. Secular martyrdom was as easily mythified as religious martyrdom, especially given a tradition of juvenile patriotism dating back (in the French case) to Barra, the Republican boy hero of the French Revolution. The legend (distilled from a real event) of the young Émile Desprès, from the Nord, recalled this tradition. Desprès was supposed to have been offered his life by a German officer who was about to execute a group of French hostages, including a wounded sergeant accused of shooting a German soldier who had tried to rape a Frenchwoman. But to secure his freedom, the youth had to kill the French sergeant himself. Desprès pretended to agree to the diabolical compact, only to turn his firearm on the German officer at the last moment, following which he was himself brutally executed. Youthful patriotism redeemed the humiliation of the invasion – positively inverting the symbolic victimhood of the children with severed hands.[55] The British acquired their own martyr in the person of Edith Cavell, executed in Brussels by the Germans in October 1915 for helping trapped Allied soldiers to escape. The explanation for the outpouring of British emotion on her death, apart from the fact that as a nurse she embodied wartime female selflessness, lies in the way her tale particularized the surrogate relationship of British opinion with the invasion of Belgium by providing a direct victim.[56]

Martyrdom was perhaps most important as an attribute of the localities which had suffered from the German atrocities. By late 1914, the term 'martyr' was being applied to the worst-affected villages of the Meurthe-et-

Moselle. The French Commission used it for No- mény, whose utter desolation it described in the following terms: 'Apart from a few houses still standing near the station [...], all that remains of this little town is a succession of broken and blackened walls, in the midst of piles of rubble in which can be seen, here and there, partly calcinated animal bones and the carbonized remnants of human corpses.'[57] The commission included photos of these scenes in its first report. A parliamentary commission on social assistance proposed that the ruins of Nom ény should be preserved as a monument, 'attesting forever to our suffering and the ignominy of our enemies'. Gerbéviller likewise became a site of pilgrimage from September 1914, culminating in a visit in late November by the government and the President of the Republic, Poincaré, during which the latter awarded the Republican Légion d'honneur to Sister Julie, the heroic nun who had kept a first-aid station going throughout the battle. The same debate took place over whether to preserve the ruins as a monument to German atrocities. This anticipated by 30 years the discussion which was to occur over Oradour-sur-Glane, the village destroyed with its inhabitants by the SS in 1944, which eventually was commemorated in this fashion.[58]

Naturally, the situation in Belgium and occupied France was different. Yet if a war culture could not exist in the same way under enemy domination, the memory of enemy atrocities committed during the invasion remained a vital touchstone.[59]

Accounts circulated inside occupied Belgium conveying the sense of shock left by the events of the invasion. As some semblance of normal life returned, civilians sought to comprehend what had occurred. Some in a privileged position conducted their own inquiries. The retired academic, Jean Chot, toured Namur province in the winter of 1914–15 interviewing survivors and witnesses of German atrocities for a manuscript that was not published until 1919.[60] Canon Jean Schmitz in Namur and Norbert Nieuwland of the Abbey of Maredsous, near Dinant, tried to establish accurate death lists and gather witness statements, though they too only published the fruits of their work after the war.[61] Nieuwland, however, printed an anonymous 'Dinant Necrology' as early as the end of August 1914.[62] This was one of a host of publications that tried to commemorate the victims while exonerating them from German accusations of treacherous warfare.[63] In effect, this clandestine literature was the Belgians' rejoinder to the German military inquiries and the campaign of German self-justification culminating in the White Book.

Some of the civilian inquiries were published abroad. Jean Massart, the biologist who organized the Belgian response to the German 'Appeal to the World of Culture!', wrote an account of life under the occupation which he published on his escape to France in 1915. In this, he not only refuted the German version of the invasion of 1914, but independently came to a similar conclusion to that of van Langenhove on the mythic sources of the franc-tireur fear in the German army.[64] Gustave Somville, who conducted his own investigation into events around Liège, likewise managed to escape to Britain where he wrote his account.[65] Maurice Tschoffen's report on Dinant was published from Holland in 1917. Tschoffen conducted an inquiry both among his fellow deportees while imprisoned at Kassel, and in Dinant on his return in 1915. Like Nieuwland's anonymous necrology, his report was an attempt to list all the civilian victims. It also expressed the outrage of Belgian victims, dismissing the White Book's charge of Belgian civilian resistance as myth.[66]

Establishing the facts was one thing; discrediting the perpetrators' account, both abroad and within Belgium, where German censorship held sway, was another. As we have seen, the Belgian bishops undertook this role on behalf of the occupied population. But they were not alone. Other attempts by Belgian civilians to reject the German interpretation of 1914, as well as to oppose an increasingly harsh occupation policy, produced a culture of patriotic resistance. One of the most remarkable expressions of this resistance was the clandestine press, and especially the mercurial *La Libre Belgique* which, starting publication in February 1915, goaded the occupying authorities for the remainder of the war.

The first issue of *La Libre Belgique* declared that 'there is something stronger than the Germans, [and it] is the truth.' The paper's declared function was thus to contest the German version of events, and 'German atrocities' were central to this enterprise. An early editorial on the Belgian government's attempt to create a conscript army (by calling all men of 18 to 25 to escape to France) linked the 'new Belgium' being forged on the battlefield to the redemption of the victims of the invasion. 'Those who fell in the trenches of Liège and on the plains of Haelen; those who lie under the ruins of Louvain and Termonde, the mothers who have been assassinated and the children who have been massacred await their righteous avengers.'[67] In Belgium as in France and Britain, the violation of women and the family was used to endorse the military mobilization of men.

La Libre Belgique also sought to establish what had occurred during the invasion. It publicized clandestine literature (such as a series of brochures on 'Martyred Belgium'), including eye-witness accounts.[68] It disparaged the flood of German publications in Belgium which maintained the German accusations of a vicious Belgian population.[69] It scrutinized German military inquiries among Belgian civilians, and accused the army in April 1915 of suppressing civilian testimony on Louvain.[70] When the White Book appeared, *La Libre Belgique* expressed scorn at the German justification of harsh repression by the claim that they were 'forced into it by francs-tireurs of both sexes and all ages, from three weeks to 90 years old'.[71]

In short, *La Libre Belgique* analysed the 'German atrocities' in similar vein to the Allied governments. An early article commented that '[German] "Kultur" has nothing in common with French, Belgian, English, Spanish, Italian or American culture. It is not civilization; the way the German invaders have behaved in our country and in northern France since last August demonstrates this beyond all doubt [...].'[72] The Hague Conventions were invoked to show that the German army had comprehensively violated international law.[73] The paper moved on to other concerns after 1915, but the invasion remained a reference point. In denouncing Flemish collaborators in 1917, for example, the paper measured their betrayal against Liège, Louvain, Termonde, Dinant, Dixmuide and the 'thousands of corpses of their brothers'.[74] The call for resistance to the German occupation with its requisitioning, deportations, and attempt to divide the country between Flanders and Wallonia drew on the language of German 'crimes' established in 1914.[75]

Belgian experience of the German occupation cannot be reduced to the stance of *La Libre Belgique* or that of other clandestine publications. The use the Germans were able to make of Flemish separatism points to one internal division, and by 1917–18 a desperately hungry population was concerned mainly with survival. Yet the trauma of the invasion and atrocities of 1914 could not be resolved while the Germans remained, enforcing their own version of events.[76] Although the culture of patriotic resistance was expressed in middle-class and mainly (but not exclusively) French-language publications, it had broader support, as indicated by the enormous popularity of Cardinal Mercier. It continually recharged the atrocities of 1914 with emotive meaning, using the same basic language as the war cultures of Belgium's allies. All the major works, including the Bryce Report, the Belgian official reports, and the brochures of the French

Comité d'Études et de Documents (among them Bédier's two pamphlets) circulated secretly, and were even reprinted underground. Raemaekers' cartoons were likewise distributed in a banned review, *La Cravache*.[77] In this way, the original subjects of the 'German atrocities' were reinforced in their sense of national victimhood by representations of those same events fed back from Britain, France, and their own exiled government.

The patriotic culture of wartime Germany was no less developed than that of the Allies.[78] But it was more difficult for the events of 1914 to shape the image of the enemy for the same reasons that the German government found it hard to mount a coherent international propaganda effort on the issue. The ferocious franc-tireur preying on hapless German soldiers, rightfully punished by the army, gradually faded, including from the illustrated periodicals where he had figured in the first nine months of the war.[79] The public could not be presented with individualized victims and perpetrators or with detailed narrative accounts such as those which gave the 'German atrocities' their substance in the Allied countries. Rather, the German treatment of the issue at home reflected the essentially defensive position adopted internationally. A vein of satirical comment developed on the Allied 'atrocity' accusations, especially the obviously mythic elements. Already in September 1914, a cartoon in *Simplicissimus* portrayed a group of Parisians clustered around the Venus de Milo in the Louvre, gathering yet more evidence of German barbaric war tactics to be sent to the neutral powers (illustration 33).[80] Photographs published in reviews in 1915 showed German soldiers feeding Belgian civilians, with the ironic title: 'German Barbarians'. In early 1917, a German official film, made to counter the highly successful British film of the *Battle of the Somme*, was full of defensive and mocking references to the Allied 'atrocity' accusations of 1914–15. One caption, for example, under the stark ruins of shattered buildings, asked 'Who are the Barbarians?', while another underlined the Allied artillery's destruction of the church in Péronne by referring to the silence of the Entente press which had condemned the Germans over Rheims cathedral.[81] But such irony underlined the difficulty of directly using the Belgian and French 'atrocities' of 1914, as opposed to Allied hypocrisy, in depicting the enemy for home audiences.

As with Germany's foreign propaganda, other issues were employed to demonize the enemy. The alleged mistreatment of German prisoners and above all the use of colonial troops were obvious candidates.[82] In 1918, a propaganda campaign accompanied the German spring offensive which

> This propaganda is needed, as the correspondence that we have received in recent days suffices to show. Hundreds of primary school teachers from the most diverse regions of France are urging us to act, are crying 'Help!', and affirm to us that the inhabitants of their communes are extraordinarily ignorant of the truth and consider those who talk of German crimes to be weak in the head. Such ignorance [...], were it to continue, would constitute a grave peril for the *patrie*; it would make people ready to entertain the worst suggestions.[87]

This last phrase could only mean a negotiated peace, so that Malvy linked continued belief in German 'atrociousness' to the popular will to endure until total victory had been achieved.

In February 1916, another body with a similar title, the Ligue Souvenez-Vous (Remember! League) had been founded nationally (the Ligue du Souvenir remained rooted in Lorraine).[88] Souvenez-Vous enjoyed the support of the political, intellectual, and artistic elites of the capital under the presidency of Jean Richepin (poet, essayist, and member of the Académie Française), and by the end of 1916 it had a presence in almost half the unoccupied French départements.[89] Its task, too, was to challenge the *endormeurs* ('putters to sleep'), or those who diminished the memory of the crimes of 1914 and other 'atrocities', whether by flagging patriotism or outright 'internationalism'.[90] It aimed to sustain what Richepin called the 'sacred hatred' of the barbarian enemy who sought to extinguish the 'civilization of justice, charity, law, liberty, and light' for which the French were fighting.

The Ligue Souvenez-Vous held meetings and distributed brochures and posters. In late 1916, it saturated France with a poster showing a German commercial traveller calling at a house in post-war France with his wartime incarnation behind him, flaming torch in one hand and a knife dripping blood in the other, and the stark reminder that they were one and the same person ('ne l'oubliez jamais!' – 'never forget it!').[91] The league also issued a résumé of the major Allied reports of 1914–15 with lurid illustrations.[92] In October 1917, it organized an exhibition in Paris on 'German crimes' (advertised by three different posters evoking the 'atrocities' of 1914), which subsequently toured the provinces (illustration 34).[93]

Britain and France, like other combatant nations, experienced growing war weariness in 1916–17. The world of the front was one from which civilians were largely excluded. Expressions of moral horror were reserved for

34 Recalling atrocities: poster for an exhibition, Paris, October 1917

the war itself as much as for the enemy who, on occasion at least, could be seen as a fellow-victim. The terminology of 'carnage', 'butchery', and above all 'sacrifice' became increasingly commonplace and found an echo in the flagging mobilization of civilian energies for the apparently endless struggle. In both Britain and France, civilian adhesion to the war effort became a matter of acute concern to the state in 1917.[94]

Both countries, in consequence, experienced a concerted remobilization of political and cultural energies behind the war effort largely from above. Ostensibly autonomous bodies, the Union des Grandes Associations contre la Propagande Ennemie (UGACPE) in France, and the National War Aims Committee in Britain (NWAC), enjoyed state backing as they sought to reanimate the war culture of the early years and stiffen national resolve.[95] These campaigns focused on the total defeat of Germany, the superior strength of the western Allies, and a variety of plans for the post-war international order. In both cases, this involved re-emphasizing the intrinsic evil of the enemy, and hence the 'German atrocities' of 1914.

The Ligue Souvenez-Vous operated under the UGACPE, but the latter also produced its own atrocity propaganda, extending the atrocity accusations of 1914 to the German occupation of France, the execution of Edith Cavell, and the scorched earth policy practised by the German army as it withdrew to the Siegfried Line in February 1917.[96] In Britain, the NWAC invoked German war crimes in France and Belgium or at sea, including the 'German Crimes Calendar' for 1918, with a different 'atrocity' for each month.[97] It produced a 'national film', which imagined England in the grips of a German occupation and drew on the outrage provoked by the forced German enrolment of women for work in occupied France. The film was shot in Chester, with a number of the local women resisting the barbarism of hordes of German soldiers who dragged them to lorries for deportation.[98] The Ministry of Information produced a brief film clip also touching on the 'atrocities' theme. With the title, *The Leopard's Spots*, the film took the same theme as the Souvenez-Vous poster, that of the barbarous German soldier reappearing as an innocent commercial traveller after the war.[99] German brutality to innocent Belgians, especially women and children, figured in hundreds of sermons by British Protestant clergymen in the last year of the conflict as a means of opposing pacifists and conscientious objectors.[100]

Although unable to reproduce the self-mobilization of the earlier part of the war, the campaigns of the UGACPE and NWAC probably contributed, along with other factors, to the improvement of civilian and military morale in 1918.[101] The campaigns were helped by events. As both countries withstood the final German offensive, the language of 1914 was reactivated by renewed fear of invasion, refugees, bombardment of Paris and London (by long-range artillery of the former and by aircraft of both), and the determination to resist defeat, although there was no German brutality towards civilians on the earlier pattern. Moreover, as the Allied armies gradually reversed the German offensive and moved by early autumn into areas occupied by the Germans throughout the war, accounts emerged of the events of four years before, as well of the subsequent occupation. By the time of the Armistice, the French Commission was conducting investigations in the regions that it had previously been unable to visit, and three deputies had addressed parliament on the trauma of the occupation of Lille and the deportation of women and girls for forced labour.[102] The end of the war evoked its beginning, and this resulted in a hardening mood of retribution.

In the case of the USA, something like the war culture of the beginning of the conflict was created in the last 18 months of the war. Partly because much American opinion remained indifferent to the war, if not outright resistant, and partly because the mechanisms of commercial and political mobilization were more highly developed than virtually anywhere else, a formidable combination of voluntarist self-mobilization and state-directed propaganda defined and propagated the national cause. This centred on a demonized view of 'German atrocities', by land and sea, which was rooted in the prototypal events of August–October 1914.

As with Britain and France in autumn 1914, public emotion generated spy mania, fear of invasion, and the persecution of scapegoats. The 'war preparedness' movement, associated with politicians such as Theodore Roosevelt, converted the conviction of many Americans that the Germans were guilty of 'atrocities' in 1914–15 into an embryonic vision of the enemy. The successful film, *Battle Cry of Peace*, for example, made in 1915 with Roosevelt's backing as a call for a nation in arms, portrayed the brutal occupation of New York by an unidentified enemy acting for all the world like the American cartoonists' version of the Germans in Belgium. Yet the representation of German 'atrociousness' in the cinema during the neutrality period was also censored, while films condemning the war (such as D. W. Griffith's *Intolerance* and Thomas Ince's *Civilization*, both in 1916) provided an alternative vision.[103] Woodrow Wilson, after all, was re-elected in November 1916 on a promise to keep America out of the war.

Once the conflict was joined, however, these constraints were removed. The official Committee on Public Information (CPI), which publicized the nation's case for going to war, harnessed many of America's leading academics to the task of providing the necessary documentation for a populist campaign. The CPI's director, George Creel, a progressive Democrat, skilfully blended Wilsonian idealism with persuasive techniques, though he avoided the intolerant fervour of the independent pro-war patriotic bodies.[104]

The CPI reworked 'German atrocities' from an American angle. The *War Cyclopedia*, edited by Frederic L. Paxson of the University of Wisconsin, stated: 'The first months of the war witnessed the inauguration by Germany of a policy of terror in the invaded districts of Belgium and France designed to facilitate the control of conquered territory. Villages and towns were burned, wounded soldiers massacred, non-combatants shot or maimed, women outraged, and children tortured by the soldiery.'[105] Dana Munro, professor of medieval history at Princeton, edited the most sustained case made by the CPI against *German War Practices*. This drew on State Department papers and German testimony (including the war diary extracts published by Bédier) in order to show that 'German atrocities' in 1914 were systematic and rooted in the political philosophy of the *Kaiserreich*. In deference to German-American sensibilities, however, dissident German voices were given prominence, including soldiers who had written to the American ambassador in Berlin protesting against the brutality of the army to civilians and enemy soldiers.[106] The CPI also publicized the Hague Convention on Land Warfare, with distinguished academic lawyers contrasting its observance by the Allied forces with its supposedly systematic flouting by the German army.[107]

Relatively sober in tone and content, these publications provided 'atrocity' material for the CPI campaign. One of the 'illustrative' speeches circulated to the 75,000 'four-minute men' (who delivered short patriotic speeches) explicitly referred to Munro's *German War Practices* for evidence of Prussian 'frightfulness' in Belgium, the exposure of which to ordinary Americans was to culminate in the question: 'Now, then, do you want to take the *slightest* chance of meeting Prussianism here in America?'[108] The evidence of a Brooklyn clergyman and associate of Theodore Roosevelt, Newell Dwight Hillis, suggests that 'German atrocities' were used in American war loan campaigns. Initially sceptical, Hillis had been persuaded by reading Bryce of the reality of German war crimes. During

35   'Remember Belgium': American war loan poster

the first war loan campaign, in the spring of 1917, he claimed that he had
been constantly asked: '"What about the German atrocities? Do they not
represent falsehoods invented by the enemy states?"' Sponsored by a group
of New York bankers, Hillis was sent to France on a fact-finding mission in
order to be able to address subsequent war loan meetings with greater
authority on the issue, and in rather more lurid language than that of the
CPI publications.[109] American war loan and recruitment posters confirm
that the 'German atrocities' of 1914 were vital in painting the dehumanized visage of the enemy (illustration 35).[110]

Part IV
The impossible consensus: German atrocities and memories of war from 1919

1   Versailles

From the outset, the Allied governments had considered German atrocities as violations of international law and potentially subject to future judicial process. Under French and Belgian law, enemy soldiers could be tried by courts-martial for war crimes, even in their absence, and the French military justice service prepared charges throughout the conflict. Prosecution of war crimes by national criminal courts was likewise possible, though the absence of extradition agreements was a major drawback. The idea of a supranational tribunal to try war crimes proved contentious. The question of whether responsibility for war crimes extended to those in command, including the Kaiser, also produced differences between the Allies.

However, the form that war crimes prosecutions might take only began to emerge piecemeal during the war. In 1915–16, the British government threatened to pursue those responsible for a string of 'atrocities', including U-boat warfare and the executions of Edith Cavell and Captain Charles Fryatt, a steamer captain accused of trying to ram a U-boat.[1] In France, the deportation by the Germans of women and girls from Lille and the deliberate devastation of territory in the withdrawal to the Siegfried Line resulted in new calls for legal retribution.[2] In the difficult mid-period of the war, government leaders were reluctant to encourage expectations of early victory by threatening war crimes trials.[3] Nonetheless, the French Ministry of Justice drafted plans in 1917 to prosecute German war criminals before an inter-Allied criminal court.[4]

Although the German government requested an armistice on the basis of President Wilson's Fourteen Points, the mood of retribution in France and Britain kept punishment for enemy atrocities and especially prosecution of the Kaiser on the agenda. On 4 October 1918, the French government promised that criminals who had breached 'international law and the fundamental principles of all human civilization' would be held 'morally, judicially, and financially responsible'.[5] The bulk of the French press and public opinion agreed, and political leaders from the left to the right urged the trial of the Kaiser by an international tribunal.[6] Clemenceau, visiting London in early December, accused the Kaiser and his 'accomplices' of committing 'the greatest crime in history', and agreed with Lloyd George to seek Wilhelm II's extradition from his Dutch exile.[7] Clemenceau also set up a Consultative Juridical Committee under Frédéric Larnaude, dean of the Paris Law Faculty, which published a report on the Kaiser's guilt in war crimes for the peace conference.[8]

Since Britain had not been invaded, and in consequence could seek less by way of financial reparation, a moral and legal judgment against Germany was even more urgent there.[9] On 1 November, the Attorney-General, Sir Frederick Edwin Smith, established a Committee of Inquiry into Breaches of the Laws of War which recommended the prosecution of the Kaiser before an Allied tribunal both for war crimes and (with a dissenting minority) for having provoked the war.[10] Lloyd George referred to the prosecution of the Kaiser and of war criminals during the general election, issuing a 'Final Manifesto of Six Points' on 11 December 1918, the first two of which were 'Trial of the Kaiser' and 'Punishment of those responsible for atrocities'.[11] But he did not whip up a campaign in favour of prosecuting war criminals; as in France, this was a popular cause which had no need of being invented by politicians.[12]

It was, then, with Franco-British agreement that war crimes were placed top of the agenda for the peace conference when it opened in Paris in mid-January 1919.[13] A Commission on the Responsibilities of the Authors of the War and the Enforcement of Penalties was set up under the American Secretary of State, Robert Lansing, to report on both German culpability for the outbreak of war and German military conduct. It consisted of 15 members, two each from the British Empire, France, Italy, Japan, and the USA, and one each from five other Allied countries, including Belgium.[14] It was soon bitterly divided between the Franco-British and the American delegates.

Although American entry into the war had been accompanied by a popular campaign to vilify Germany, Wilson remained sceptical of atrocity accusations by both sides, and both he and Lansing refused to admit that international law as it stood placed any restrictions on whether, or how, sovereign states might wage war. The lack of precedent for an international tribunal and the difficulty of trying cases on the basis of retrospective law also troubled the American administration. These views were voiced on the commission by the eminent American lawyer, James B. Scott, who had been a delegate to the 1907 Hague conference.[15] They were sharply at odds with the British Committee of Inquiry, represented on the Paris commission by Sir Ernest Pollock, the English Solicitor-General. The Americans also crossed swords with the French delegation, which presented a new version of the 1917 Ministry of Justice proposal for an international criminal court, under the auspices of the League of Nations, an idea backed by Pollock and Lloyd George.[16]

The conflict deepened as the commission's work moved into subcommittee stage. One subcommittee looked at specific criminal acts and concluded that the Central Powers had indeed waged war 'by barbarous or illegitimate methods'. It devised 32 categories of war crime, headed by civilian massacres and the execution of hostages, appended a list of alleged incidents, many from 1914, and recommended the creation of a permanent body to undertake fuller investigation.[17] In another subcommittee, dealing with the legal consequences of war crimes, there was open confrontation when the British, French, and Belgians forced through the proposal for an international tribunal against Lansing's opposition. The subcommittees also dealt with the question of the responsibility of the head of state (Article 227), concluding that the Kaiser had deliberately caused the war and could be held legally responsible. This was distinct from the subsequently notorious Article 231, which proclaimed Germany's and her allies' responsibility for the war as the legal basis for German financial liability. Article 231 emerged in fact from the Commission on Reparations.[18]

The European majority in the Commission on Responsibilities proposed the establishment of an international court composed of Allied judges to try all those, including heads of state, who were accused of ordering or failing to prevent war crimes, and national military tribunals to deal with minor cases. Deadlock was broken only by Wilson's suggestion that the Americans produce a dissenting minority report. This argued that there was no basis in law for enforcing moral precepts of humanity, no precedent for establishing an international court or trying a head of state, and that failing to prevent a crime was invalid as a legal principle unless there were clear lines of command.[19]

The division was renewed when Clemenceau, Lloyd George, and Wilson discussed the issues in April. Despite a more conciliatory policy towards Germany on territorial issues, Lloyd George still asserted Germany's moral responsibility for the origin and conduct of the war. He and Clemenceau rejected Wilson's contention that German military conduct differed little from that during the Franco-Prussian War. Clemenceau retorted: 'They were brutal in 1870; but we did not have to reproach them with crimes [committed] by order, and there was not, during [that] war or immediately after it, the same hatred of the German soldier that you will find today among the belligerent [powers].' Lloyd George added that the Germans had practised a policy of brutality, particularly evident in submarine warfare, and that 'there would be no point in making peace if all these crimes remained unpunished.'[20] On 8 April, the two sides were locked in disagreement over the trial of war criminals, including the Kaiser.

The conflict was resolved when Wilson and Lansing partially gave way, and presented the draft of what were to become Articles 227 to 230 of the treaty.[21] Article 227 arraigned Wilhelm II on ethical, rather than strictly legal, grounds, for a 'supreme offence against international morality and the sanctity of treaties', and sought his extradition from Holland for trial before an Allied tribunal. Articles 228–30 obliged the German government to hand over those of its nationals accused of violating 'the laws and customs of war' for trial before the military tribunals of the Allied countries, with composite military tribunals where more than one Ally was concerned (see appendix 3 below). The essential principle of German legal culpability for war crimes, and the trial of the Kaiser for starting the war were thus secured by the French and British governments, but without entrenching war crimes in international law or achieving a permanent international court for prosecuting war criminals.

When the German delegation was presented with the peace terms on 7 May, the clauses on responsibilities became the focal point of the German strategy to reject the treaty. The repudiation of the Allied charge of sole German war guilt by the German Foreign Minister, Brockdorff-Rantzau, must be seen in the context of the conflict within the German government. The SPD, which dominated the early Weimar governments, chose to have little influence on Germany's peace strategy, and foreign policy was left in the hands of the unreformed Foreign Ministry.[22]

From the end of hostilities, the Foreign Ministry conducted a campaign of 'obfuscation' on 'war guilt' and German military conduct, distorting the evidence and hampering the publication of unwelcome documents.[23] It attempted continually to provoke confrontation with the Allies and, against the intentions of the cabinet, invested the 'war guilt' complex with special meaning.[24] On war crimes, it envisaged the resumption of the propaganda battle on the lines drawn up by the German White Book of 1915.

Some members of the cabinet (Erzberger of the Centre Party, David of the SPD, and even President Ebert) initially wanted a different policy. On the question of responsibility for the war, they envisaged publication of the collection of diplomatic documents on the outbreak of war, compiled by the leading Marxist theoretician, Karl Kautsky, which was highly damaging to the Imperial government. This amounted to a policy of discontinuity, by which the old regime was denounced and the Allies shown that Germany had turned a new leaf, possibly obtaining better peace terms. But the conservative Foreign Ministry saw this policy as betrayal by 'radical elements'. The government agreed, and in early April 1919 it was decided to delay publication of Kautsky's documents until after the peace treaty.

The same choice applied in relation to German wartime military conduct. Here, conservative civil servants took the offensive by publishing material accusing the Allies of war crimes.[25] Both issues were the remit of a new section in the Foreign Ministry, established in late 1918 to defend Germany against the expected charge of sole war guilt and the demand for the surrender of war criminals. At first simply called the Special Bureau v. Bülow, after its founder, it was renamed the Kriegsschuldreferat (War Guilt Section) or Schuldreferat in 1920. For the next 15 years, it emitted a stream of 'innocentist' propaganda defending Germany against Allied charges over the cause and conduct of the war.[26]

The Schuldreferat was attached to the Office for Peace Negotiations, which co-ordinated the production of memoranda for the guidance of the German peace delegation on a range of subjects including war crimes.[27] The historical division of the General Staff, for example, supplied a report which denied Allied charges that the German army had violated international law in its conduct of warfare and recalled uncomfortable incidents in the not so distant past of its accusers, notably the South African War and Sherman's 'march to the sea' in the American Civil War.[28] It was these memoranda of the Office for Peace Negotiations, with their continuity of wartime arguments, that informed the German peace strategy, not the views of the revolutionary government.

When Brockdorff-Rantzau received the draft treaty in Versailles on 7 May 1919, he exceeded cabinet instructions by denouncing it for the charge of sole German war guilt (an expression it did not contain).[29] Although Rantzau promised that Germany would not 'trivialize the responsibility of the men who conducted the political and military war and deny outrages against international law', he suggested that every European nation had its war criminals, and demanded an impartial, neutral investigation of guilt for the outbreak and conduct of the war.[30] Against the express decision of the cabinet, Rantzau sent the Allies a memorandum signed by four eminent, internationally respected experts who had been summoned to

Versailles by the German delegation, professors Hans Delbrück, Albrecht Mendelssohn Bartholdy, and Max Weber, and Count Montgelas. The professors' memorandum of 28 May, largely ghost-written by the German delegation, rejected the thesis of sole German responsibility.[31] In its counterproposals of 29 May, the German delegation claimed the treaty was impossible to execute, rejecting in particular Articles 227 and 228, and demanded negotiations. The supporting press campaign also quoted these articles rather than Article 231 to sustain rejection of the treaty.[32]

The German case was not unreasonable in theory. On war guilt they stated that 'no one single fact had caused the war', and unilateral incrimination of Germany was therefore unjustified. On atrocities, Brockdorff-Rantzau argued (like Wilson and Lansing) that the extradition of alleged war criminals could not be reconciled with principles of international or German law, for the courts would be composed of the victors who were themselves parties. Instead, the Germans called for an international court, which would decide only which acts committed in the war were to be considered violations of international law and to which any party could refer for a ruling. The prosecution of such crimes would remain within national jurisdictions. All other misdeeds, as with previous peace treaties, would be amnestied.[33]

In practice, the counterproposals were entirely unrealistic, since they amounted to a demand for Germany to be treated as an equal in the investigation and prosecution of war crimes, which was bound to be regarded as a provocation. Yet this was their real purpose, as part of Brockdorff-Rantzau's strategy to prepare Germany for the rejection of the treaty and the resumption of hostilities. This strategy was based on the gamble that the peoples of the enemy nations would not support their governments, and a revolutionary crisis would force the victors to undertake a radical revision of the treaty.[34] The German Foreign Ministry was thus prepared to pursue a policy of catastrophe in which the ruin of Germany (by invasion or revolution, or both) might also ruin her enemies.[35]

The Allied reply of 16 June restated the views underlying Articles 227 to 231 and gave Germany an ultimatum to accept the treaty or face renewed war. It asserted that after 1871 Germany, 'true to the Prussian tradition', had systematically worked towards war in order to dominate Europe, and was 'responsible for the savage and inhuman manner in which it was conducted'. Not content with violating the neutrality of Belgium, '[the Germans] deliberately carried out a series of promiscuous shootings and burnings with the sole object of terrifying the inhabitants into submission by the very frightfulness of their action.' The note listed several other 'barbarities', and concluded that the conduct of Germany was 'almost unexampled in human history'.[36] This (unlike the treaty) was an explicitly moral condemnation, and may have been designed to prepare the victor nations for the resumption of war.[37] Signed by Clemenceau but drafted by Lloyd George's adviser, Philip Kerr, the ultimatum testified to the solidity of the Franco-British agreement on German responsibility for the outbreak and conduct of the war. The German delegation left Paris, and recommended to the cabinet the rejection of the treaty.

In the short term, the German 'catastrophist' strategy (*Katastrophenpolitik*) worked. As is well known, the cabinet and the Reich President rejected the treaty as 'intolerable' and 'unfulfillable'. In the session of the National Assembly on 12 May, moral outrage was intensified by successively more radical speeches from deputies of all parties except the left-wing Independent Social Democrats (USPD), and climaxed in Minister-President Scheidemann's rhetorical question: 'Which hand would not wither that places us in such chains?' The effect on the German public was electric: there was a massive mobilization of opinion against the treaty, with hundreds of rallies and demonstrations, many including protests specifically against the extradition of the Kaiser and Germans accused of war crimes.[38] The Foreign Ministry thus succeeded in stirring up a popular movement which constricted the government's freedom of decision.

In the medium term, the strategy failed. The government was unable to force a radical revision of the treaty. It is even dubious whether it impressed most Germans. As the head of the Schuldreferat, Freytag, wrote in July 1919, 'broad sections of the population were convinced of German war guilt.'[39] The chief of the British Military Mission, General Neill Malcolm, noted that while feeling against the extradition of the Kaiser, Hindenburg, and leading officers was very strong in the army and in the parties of the right and centre, it was 'not at all strong among the Majority Socialists or the Independents'. There was 'little feeling anywhere against handing over for trial subordinates actually accused of outrages [...] there might even be a balance of feeling in our favour.'[40] The Allied ultimatum was the moment of truth for the German army. Although the disarmament clauses threatened the livelihood of many officers, it was extradition proceedings, and their affront to the collective honour of the army, that aroused the strongest outrage. This concern lay behind a meeting on 19 June 1919 of some 30

General Staff officers and generals with Defence Minister Noske to discuss whether to sign the treaty. Noske, who had rejected the very possibility of German atrocities when confronted by his Belgian Socialist colleagues in 1914, was urged by the officers to establish a military dictatorship. Although Noske, supported by General Groener, acting as spokesman for the OHL, managed to convince them the treaty had to be signed, their support was conditional on rejection of the 'Schmachparagraphen' (or 'shame paragraphs', as the 'responsibilities' clauses were dubbed).[41] General von Lüttwitz, who was commander of Brussels in August 1914 and now controlled the Berlin area, told Noske that if the peace were accepted 'the mass of the good troops [...] would take up a position against the government'.[42]

The Bauer government's proposal to sign the treaty without accepting Articles 227 to 231 made no impression on the victors, and the Allied reply on 22 June, which insisted on immediate and unconditional signing of the treaty, caused a grave crisis. It created the 'urgent danger', according to Lüttwitz, that the officer corps would mutiny. Noske, now losing his nerve, told the SPD parliamentary group that invasion by the enemy armies was to be preferred, for acceptance would bring chaos and the destruction of the army and the Reich. He announced his resignation, but the SPD begged him to stay on. The Centre Party voted to reject the treaty and resign from the government, creating a potential majority against ratification.[43]

This crisis was overcome through the intervention of the President, acting in concert with Erzberger. Ebert asked the OHL for its opinion on unconditional acceptance. General Groener stated that military resistance was futile, and that Noske would have to issue a public appeal to the army, warning the men and officers to 'do their damned duty [...] and not let down the Fatherland in its hour of danger'.[44] Ebert called the party leaders to a meeting on 23 June, and Erzberger bluntly asked each of those opposed to ratification: were they willing to form a government which would face up to the resumption of hostilities? The liberal DDP and DVP replied with a clear 'no', and the conservative DNVP with an evasive 'no'.[45]

This had the necessary effect. Noske withdrew his resignation, as did the Centre Party, and the treaty was finally signed on 28 June. While the Reichswehr temporarily gave up hope of an armed rising, the demand not to surrender alleged war criminals to the Allies was the one constant in its politics, and a deep gulf opened up between the Republic and the army.[46]

For the time being, the army kept its peace. But in the long term the catastrophist peace strategy had a devastating effect on the legitimacy of the Republic, for the government proved unwilling to call the bluff of the Foreign Ministry and the right-wing parties by confronting them with the army's confession of impotence. Although nationalist outrage at the treaty was not spontaneous popular fury, but 'public' anger induced by the propaganda apparatus co-ordinated by the Foreign Ministry, successive democratic governments acquiesced in the resulting patriotic self-deception and nationalist mythology.[47]

Germany was not merely divided between those who wanted to reject the Allied accusations and realists who knew that Germany could not put up military resistance. The revolution allowed critical voices to emerge, some of which were genuinely troubled by Allied war crimes charges. The executive of the Soldiers' Council, for example, equated German military brutality in Belgium during the war with counter-revolutionary violence at home, and it called on the government to prosecute 'those persons who have been guilty of major crimes in Belgium before pressure is exerted by the Allies'.[48] At the same time, in November 1918, some prominent figures from the political centre (ranging from conservative liberals like Hans Delbrück and Friedrich Naumann to moderate Social Democrats and trade union leaders like Carl Legien) urged the government to form an 'impartial commission' to investigate charges of German cruelty in warfare which had been raised 'not only by enemies, but by many soldiers'.[49] Reluctantly, the government established such a body under the Centre Party leader, Erzberger, but its work was disrupted by revolutionary unrest in early 1919, its composition was changed, and it failed to make a thorough inquiry.[50]

The closest Germany came to critically investigating German war crimes was the establishment by the National Assembly of a special commission of inquiry (*Untersuchungsausschuß*) into the origins of the war, wartime peace initiatives, and the causes of the defeat. Its origins went back to early March 1919, when Otto Landsberg, the Social Democratic Minister of Justice, proposed a bill, later modified by the liberal Interior Minister Hugo Preuß, to establish a tribunal, with punitive powers, to investigate the degree of German co-responsibility for the outbreak of war and whether enemy charges of German war crimes were justified. But the bill was not given its first reading by the National Assembly until 28 July, after the signature of the peace, and the proposal was implemented in the form of a parliamentary commission of inquiry. This was constituted on 21 August

1919 and it worked throughout the Weimar Republic.[51] The third of its four subcommittees was charged with investigating whether the German army and government had violated the laws of war. A special tribunal (or *Staatsgerichtshof*) was to hear cases submitted by any of the four subcommittees.

In principle, the Third Subcommittee offered the centre-left, which dominated the National Assembly until the elections of June 1920, the opportunity for a serious investigation of German war crimes. But the commission as a whole turned out to be a boomerang which could equally be used by the right to accuse the left of betrayal and to draw it into deeper complicity on Germany's war record. The Third Subcommittee ended up as a general inquiry into all war crimes, Allied and German, which took eight years to publish a report whitewashing the German military.[52] More dramatically symptomatic of the difficulties faced by an independent inquiry was the appearance of Hindenburg as a star witness before a packed session in November 1919 of the Second Subcommittee, which investigated the possibility of a negotiated peace during the war. Hindenburg had been invited by a centre-right deputy, and in full dress-uniform he used the occasion to formulate the 'stab in the back' theory of Germany's defeat, blaming the 'November criminals' and exonerating the military leadership and the old regime.[53]

The SPD was the party best placed by its strength and role in government in the early Weimar Republic to enforce an independent inquiry. However, the SPD, in the light of its complex relationship with the army and the war, decided against repudiating Germany's war record, in part because this would have broken the crucial alliance with the army which the SPD government members (and especially Noske) saw as their defence against the revolutionary left. Repudiation would also have exposed the SPD to public scrutiny of its own wartime role, not only in supporting the war from beginning to end, but also in defending the conduct of the military. Even if it was critical of the Imperial government, the SPD remained convinced that Germany had been encircled and faced invasion in 1914, and it refused to swallow the Allied thesis embodied in the peace treaty.[54]

From this perspective, the 'responsibilities clauses' looked like a manifestation of unabated wartime enmity. Relativizing German war guilt and alleged war crimes was a logical answer both to the party's dependence on the army and to its rejection of the Allied version of the new international order. The Allies' exclusion of the Germans from the peace negotiations and their insistence that the 'responsibilities' clauses were non-negotiable facilitated the attempt by Brockdorff-Rantzau and the German peace delegation to paint a picture of national humiliation, thus underwriting the SPD's Faustian pact with the Foreign Ministry and the army.

Although only one element of a complex peace settlement which came to be dominated by reparations, the question of war crimes and extradition was no less emotive and symbolically charged after the signature of the Versailles Treaty than before, attracting more press attention in Germany than German 'guilt' for the outbreak of war.[55] This was due to its role both as a signifier of the war's meaning for the former belligerents and as a touchstone for the tense relationship between the German army and its new political masters.

Throughout summer and autumn 1919, the Allies sought to implement clauses 227–30 in the face of stubborn German defiance. Although it quickly became apparent that the Dutch would not yield up the exiled Kaiser, Allied demands for the extradition of German army and navy officers, together with some of the most senior political figures of the old regime, pushed the German military into a frenzy of activity. The Foreign and Reichswehr Ministries set up a special office to prepare the defence of officers arraigned on war crimes charges. General Groener simply advised those with a 'bad conscience' to 'disappear', and soon there was a secret organization to help them do just that. Connected with extreme right-wing groups and officers' associations, it prepared 6,000–8,000 hiding-places in Germany and neutral countries in summer and autumn 1919, and Freikorps stormtroopers stood by to prevent the arrest of suspects and spirit them away.[56]

Threatened extradition of German officers for war crimes trials also contributed to the right-wing violence which culminated in the Kapp Putsch on 13 March 1920. The attempt on Erzberger's life on 26 January was partly due to his warning in a speech on 25 July 1919 that he might be forced to publish the wartime record of the government's right-wing enemies. This was interpreted as a personal threat to extradite them to the Allies.[57] Although the Kapp Putsch was in the event occasioned by the implementation of the disarmament clauses of the treaty, the Freikorps, the Reichswehr, and the right-wing organizers were equally agitated by extradition. In February 1920 the Chief of the Troop Office (the de facto General Staff), General von Seeckt, argued for defying extradition by force, and considered a new scheme for a military dictatorship under Noske.[58] The fiasco of the Kapp Putsch one month later, and the depth of popular support for the Republic it revealed, showed the hollowness of the government's claim that its security would be imperilled by taking measures that upset the military.

Yet throughout the second half of 1919, the German government invoked the danger of a military putsch in order to resist pressure from the Allies for the delivery of alleged German war criminals. The threat worked to the extent that by August both Lloyd George and Clemenceau agreed to a smaller, symbolic number of accused, though the French reserved the right to demand the full complement eventually.[59] But in mid-October, the German government moved from seeking a delay to complete abandonment of the policy of extraditions. This important change was occasioned by the re-entry into the cabinet of the German Democratic Party (DDP), which saw the issue as a chance to prove how 'national' liberals could be. A DDP leader, Eugen Schiffer, who became Minister for Justice, welcomed the 'possibility of catastrophe', and renewed the threats that revolutionary upheaval would be the inescapable consequence of extradition.[60] On 5 November, Baron Kurt von Lersner, the German representative responsible for negotiating the implementation of the peace treaty, called on the Allies to drop extradition, proposing that German courts should be allowed to prosecute accused German war criminals.[61]

The Allies flatly rejected this suggestion.[62] The Commission on the Organization of Mixed Tribunals, which was responsible for carrying out Articles 228–30, had begun amalgamating the national extradition lists, coming up with 1,590 names of alleged German war criminals wanted for trial. At a Franco-British meeting in London in mid-December, Lloyd George proposed its reduction to 50 or 60. Clemenceau remained privately sympathetic to the 'symbolic' approach. But the demands by French and Belgian officials for the ultimate trial of the full list could not be opposed in public.[63] It was eventually agreed to seek some further reduction of numbers.

The British representatives succeeded in having the list pared to 862 suspects.[64] These consisted of 334 each from the lists of Belgium and France (making up three-quarters of the final list), 97 from the British list (including nine Turkish citizens accused in connection with the Armenian genocide), 51 from the Polish, 41 from the Romanian, 29 from the Italian, and four from the Serb-Croat-Slovene lists. The total was 890 persons or groups because certain names were included from more than one national list. Prominent figures in military and public life were named, including field marshals Hindenburg, Bülow, and Mackensen, generals Ludendorff, Hausen, Kluck, Stenger, d'Elsa, Deimling, and Marwitz, and Crown Prince Wilhelm and Crown Prince Rupprecht of Bavaria, along with the former Chancellor Bethmann Hollweg. The British list included Admiral Tirpitz, other leading admirals, and twenty U-boat commanders.

The individuals sought for extradition were charged with various types of crime committed in all theatres throughout the war. From the extradition lists it is possible to calculate the number of charges under a particular category of crime, in order to ascertain the relative importance attributed by the Allies to the different types of offence. The resulting total of 1,059 is higher than that of the 890 names listed for extradition because many were accused of crimes under more than one category (appendix 4). The 'German atrocities' of 1914 constituted 405 of the 1,059 charges, the bulk of them (396, or 37 per cent of the overall total) relating to the invasion of Belgium and France, the remaining 9 (1 per cent) to Poland. Of the Belgian and French charges (over three-quarters of the total), the invasion of 1914 accounted for 48 per cent and 50 per cent respectively. Figure 3 shows that at 188 (18 per cent), the killing of civilians during the invasion of Belgium and France was the largest category of war crime.[65] This compared with deportation to Germany (16 per cent), crimes in POW camps (14 per cent), and naval war crimes (3 per cent). Cruelty to civilians and destruction of property during the invasion also figured prominently at 6 per cent and 9 per cent respectively. Despite the inevitably approximate nature of the numbers derived from the extradition lists, they demonstrate that the memory of 1914 decisively influenced Allied policy on legal retribution against the former enemy.

The total remained too high for the British. Lloyd George repeated that only a few notorious offenders should be tried, though on these he meant business: 'If even 20 were shot it would be an example.'[66] But the Allied governments failed to agree a further reduction, and on 20 January they decided to publish a list of 853 Germans.[67] Meanwhile the German campaign against extradition reached a climax, with street violence and mass meetings denouncing the affront to national honour and any hint of government compliance. Noske, with characteristic modesty, told the British that if the Allies insisted on extradition, he would resign and abandon Germany to the resulting chaos.[68] The French came under similar pressure.[69]

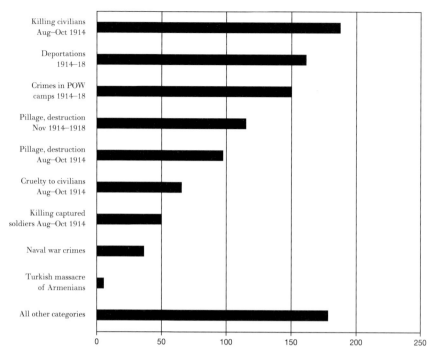

Figure 3 Individuals sought by category of war crime for extradition, January 1920 (see appendix 4)

At the end of January Lloyd George finally accepted that Lersner's proposal of trials in Germany provided the way out of the crisis, and he privately put the compromise to Millerand, who had succeeded Clemenceau as Prime Minister shortly before. Like his predecessor, Millerand had some sympathy with Lloyd George's attempt to find an accommodation with the former enemy. But he was tied by his own government's commitment to strict fulfilment of the treaty, and he insisted on handing the full extradition list to the German delegation on 3 February. Driven by French public opinion, neither Clemenceau nor Millerand could afford to yield on extradition, given the continued importance of 'German atrocities'.[70]

Lersner, however, refused to transmit the list to the German government. He returned the original to Millerand, resigned, and left next day for Berlin. In his letter of protest he said he had repeatedly told the Allies that it would be impossible to find German officials who would collaborate in extraditing their fellow-countrymen.[71] In fact, Lersner was acting against of 1914. These were the execution of captured French soldiers in Lorraine in August 1914 on the order of Major-General Stenger, the shooting of civilians at Jarny, and the destruction of Nomény with the loss of 55 inhabitants.[88]

Despite their limitations, the Leipzig proceedings presented the first opportunity to confront from both sides the events that lay behind some of the bitterest Allied accusations. The German state prosecutor, using Allied evidence and witnesses, would charge named individuals for particular acts which were deemed by the Allies to be war crimes. The accused would have the full backing of state-supplied evidence and German defence witnesses to justify their actions and reject the Allied legal definition of war crimes. Yet if a slim chance existed that wartime Allied atrocity allegations might be converted into a sustainable judicial process, the gulf separating the two sides was too wide and the legitimacy accorded the proceedings in Germany too tenuous for it to succeed.

Even bringing the cases to trial encountered deep German reservations. The German government came under pressure from German innocentist campaigners to oppose the entire process and publish a list of German counter-accusations of Allied war crimes. The government delayed initiating proceedings for as long as it could, despite growing Allied pressure. Matters came to a head in early May 1921, when the Allies threatened to occupy the Ruhr over German obstruction of reparations, disarmament, and war crimes trials. The centre-right Fehrenbach government resigned and its centre-left successor, under Centre Party leader Josef Wirth, began the trials speedily. The new policy was one of damage limitation, doing the minimum necessary to fulfil the peace terms and avoid sanctions (hence its refusal to publish the countercharges of Allied war crimes) while minimizing nationalist hostility.[89]

This is not to say that the proceedings which opened on 23 May 1921 before the Criminal Senate of the Reichsgericht in Leipzig were a charade. The German judicial system enjoyed real independence from government, as centre-left politicians in Weimar learned. The court president, Dr Karl Schmidt, conducted the trials with punctilious fairness and courtesy towards both Allied witnesses and the top-level delegations from Britain, France, and Belgium which attended the prosecution of 'their' cases.[90] More obvious bias came in the declared reluctance of the Reich Prosecutor, Dr Ludwig Ebermayer, who brought the Allied cases, to proceed against career officers and servicemen whom he considered to be the embodiment of patriotic duty. The Germans also enjoyed an important political discretion in deciding the legal admissibility of the cases and the order in which they would be brought. Finally, the atmosphere of the trials was unavoidably partisan. Apart from the Allied delegations and representatives of the world press, the courtroom was packed with a largely hostile German public. Opportunities were rife for demagogic speeches by the defence and expressions of hatred towards Allied witnesses and observers.[91]

The four British cases (three of the seven having been abandoned owing to the absence of the accused) were the first to be heard. This primacy was almost certainly political. Ebermayer acted in a dilatory fashion in relation to the Belgian and French material (ignoring the cases relating to 1914), while he was quite keen to proceed in the British cases, especially those to do with naval warfare.[92] This probably stemmed from the German view that the British set the greatest store by the Leipzig proceedings, that they would be the easiest to satisfy, and that once satisfied, the impetus for the trials would abate. The British cases, unlike the massacres, incendiarism, and deportations of 1914, were also relatively simple to settle without major discredit to the army.

Light sentences were given to three junior officers in a wartime prison camp for brutality towards British prisoners. However, a U-boat commander who had torpedoed a hospital ship, the *Dover Castle*, was found innocent on the grounds that he had merely obeyed German naval orders to sink hospital ships in designated zones in reprisal for the supposed Allied use of such vessels to transport war materials. The court did not query the orders as such. As if to compensate the British, the Reichsgericht subsequently initiated a case on its own account concerning the sinking of another hospital ship, the *Llandovery Castle*, by a different U-boat. Although the U-boat commander was safely in exile, the court found two subordinates guilty – not for attacking the ship, though it was far outside the zones designated for this type of action, but for failing to act against their commander when he fired on the survivors in their lifeboats. None of the judgments in the British cases called the principles of German war conduct into question. They merely found individuals guilty of gratuitously offending against basic humanity.

Although German opinion was divided, with liberals welcoming the independence of the court and nationalists condemning the ten-year sentences given to the naval officers, British opinion was by and large satisfied. The English Solicitor-General, Sir Ernest Pollock, reported to that the order 'not to take prisoners' was questioned by his sergeant but the response was 'Brigadebefehl' (brigade order). The sergeant banned his men from carrying it out, but while advancing across the parade ground, Ernst heard Major Müller give the order to shoot Frenchmen lying in a hollow. Even more importantly, one-year volunteer Schmerber heard Major Müller say to four officers and Crusius: 'Brigade order: all wounded soldiers and other individual [French] soldiers are not to be taken captive, but shot.' The officers were disquieted by this, but Müller told them: 'It was a necessary measure for Major-General Stenger had found that French troops fired treacherously at the Germans. Also no manpower was available for the transport of the prisoners.' Egged on by Müller and Crusius with the words 'Don't you know the brigade order yet?', soldiers then killed about 20 wounded Frenchmen.

Together with evidence from captured German war diaries, which the witnesses were unable to disown, there was sufficient evidence to show that some form of verbal order was issued by Stenger on 21 August.[98] The French, moreover, could prove that a written order was issued on 26 August at the battle of Thiaville, notably from an inquiry conducted in 1915 among 16 prisoners of IR 112 and 142, as well as from the deposition already referred to by an Alsatian medical officer in IR 112. The recently published diary of the Alsatian recruit, Dominik Richert, confirms the second Stenger order. In fact Richert intervened in one instance to prevent the killing of captured Frenchmen.[99]

Nonetheless, the court declared there was no case against General Stenger. Instead, it found his subordinate, Crusius, guilty of manslaughter and sentenced him to two and a half years' imprisonment. Stenger emerged from the court carrying flowers from his admirers. He received so many letters 'congratulating him on his order to give no quarter' that he placed an advertisement in the press to express his gratitude.[100] After his own trial, he was active in the campaign to support the accused in further war crimes trials, sending out circulars to collect money.[101] As late as April 1922 he anticipated a renewed call by the Entente for extradition, which he fully expected the German government would refuse. In this, he wrote, it needed the support of the entire people:

The question of the alleged war criminals is *not a party question*, for the 890 persons on the extradition list come from *all* classes of our people. It also offends the sense of justice of *everyone* that only Germany has to conduct such trials, while the notorious war criminals of the Entente, about whom we have abundant prosecution evidence, escape scot-free. Our *people in arms* in the years 1914–18 is owed a self-evident debt of gratitude, by ensuring that its glorious deeds are kept clear of the dirt of slander.[102]

Stenger's acquittal outraged the French. On 8 July their delegation was recalled from Leipzig, never to return, leaving the cases of Jarny and No, meny unheard.[103] The Avocat Général, Matter, who led the official team, noted that inadequate French preparation (especially in relation to fool-proof witness statements) had combined with German bias and obstruction to defeat the case against Stenger.[104] In his report to the government, he underlined the hostility displayed towards the Alsatian witnesses, who were constantly interrupted and questioned on their family origins and wartime conduct, and whose evidence counted for nothing against a Prussian general. Overall, Matter came to the opposite conclusion to his English counterpart, Sir Ernest Pollock. He told the government that the Germans had not fulfilled the undertaking made to the Allies in 1920 that when holding war crimes trials on German soil, they would 'rise above [their] own feelings [and] dominate [their] national prejudices', and he advised against further participation.[105] The French reproached the British for accepting the Leipzig verdicts, and the Prime Minister, Briand, denounced the 'parody' of the trials to parliament.[106]

The Leipzig proceedings failed both as a war crimes tribunal and as a means of resolving opposed national views of the events of 1914. If Leipzig was victors' justice, it was on the terms of the vanquished, satisfying no one except the British government, which had decided to move beyond the whole business. Briand, meanwhile, had begun to seek a more conciliatory approach towards Germany, and he recommended to an inter-Allied meeting in August 1921 that the issue of the trials should be referred to a body of 'high legal authorities' so that 'time would [...] be gained and public opinion would have a chance to die down'.[107] This struck a chord with the British government, which readily agreed, and with the Wirth govern- ment in Germany. But French public and press opinion did not die down. In response to the Leipzig trials, Briand was lobbied in the summer and autumn 1921 by outraged French veterans' and ex-prisoner-of-war associa- tions demanding renewed action against German war criminals; in December he received a similar petition from the Ligue Souvenez-Vous.[108]

He summoned a meeting of the legal experts of the Inter-Allied Commission on Leipzig on 6–7 January 1922.

The outcome of this meeting destroyed any idea that the war crimes issue would simply fade away. The Inter-Allied Commission condemned the Leipzig trials as 'highly unsatisfactory' and recommended that the Allies should resume the demand for extradition.[109] This idea was bluntly rejected by the Wirth government, supported by general press hostility and nationalist demonstrations.[110] In March 1922, President Ebert visited the centenary memorial to the 1813 Battle of Leipzig and publicly defended the work of the Supreme Court against 'official foreign criticism'.[111] At the same time, a new French government took office under the wartime president of the Republic, Raymond Poincaré, who was intent on pursuing a tougher policy towards Germany on the fulfilment of the peace treaty. Poincaré's immediate goal was tightening sanctions in order to ensure the delivery of reparations. German refusal to comply with Articles 228–30 provided him with additional leverage on the former Allies for action against Germany. Like Briand, Poincaré was also subject to strong public resentment at German behaviour. He, too, received a petition from the Ligue Souvenez-Vous. Moreover, as a Lorrainer who had personally and officially shared the outrage at 'German atrocities' during the invasion, he felt strongly on the issue. For these reasons, he urged the British to act on the recommendations of the Inter-Allied Commission on the Leipzig Trials and renew the demand for extradition.[112]

The British rejected the proposal outright when the French tabled it at a conference of ambassadors on 26 July 1922. In a compromise solution which barely disguised the fact that co-operation between the former Allies on the war crimes issue had broken down, a note was issued to the German government stating that the Allied governments condemned the Leipzig trials and reserved the right to pursue the full implementation of Articles 228–30. An additional note reserved the right of prosecution in absentia.[113] In reality, the lack of political will to pursue extradition, especially on the part of the British, meant that the long German campaign to frustrate the prosecution of war criminals had succeeded.

Yet the issue did not quite end there. Following Leipzig, the French proceeded with trials of German war criminals by court-martial in absentia. The aborted hearing of the case of Nomény, for example, was followed by the court-martial trial of the accused in Nancy, a decision announced by the Minister of Justice at Nomény as he awarded the Croix de guerre to the town in September 1921.[114] Poincaré expanded the process in April 1922 to include all 2,000 Germans on the original French list. This now became the principal judicial means of dealing with wartime German atrocities, and by December 1924 more than 1,200 Germans had been found guilty. The centre-left government which came to office in June 1924, under Edouard Herriot, did not stop the trials, but Herriot ordered the Ministries of Justice and War to exercise the 'greatest discretion [...] vis-à-vis the press', suggesting that the public mood had begun to change.[115] The Belgians likewise conducted a substantial number of prosecutions by courts-martial not only of cases on the extradition list but of other German soldiers.[116]

The Reichsgericht, for its part, worked its way through all 853 accused whose names had been made public in February 1920.[117] Its purpose was to exonerate the officers and men who were being condemned in their absence by the French and Belgians. Neither the French nor the Belgian authorities informed the German government of their courts-martial judgments, so the German embassies in Paris and Brussels relied on the daily newspapers in order to report the names of those found guilty to the Foreign and Defence Ministries. The Reich Prosecutor then instituted proceedings against them, and if, as was usually the case, these ended with a non-prosecution or an acquittal, the decision was publicized in the German, and if possible, international press. Those condemned by a foreign court who wished to make a statement in the newspapers were given official help to do so.[118] The issue remained one of military honour, with all that this implied for the political rehabilitation of the German army.

The conflicting judgments of the Allied courts-martial and the Reichsgericht sprang from continuing differences in interpretation of the laws of war combined with the German belief in a People's War conducted by francs-tireurs. Three examples illustrate the distinction. In October 1924, a court-martial of the French 20th Army Corps in Nancy tried a number of senior Bavarian officers in absentia for the mass execution at Gerbéviller, imposing death sentences on them. The official German story, published in the Reichsarchiv history in 1925, was that the 31st Infantry Division had been involved in bitter fighting in which it faced a well-prepared franc-tireur attack. The Reichsgericht found that the German soldiers, encountering 'treacherous' franc-tireur resistance, behaved lawfully.[119]

The swathe of destruction cut by the Third Army through Namur province and north-eastern France was likewise the subject of opposed judgments. The Belgian and French governments accused seven generals of responsibility for the destruction of Dinant, Rethel, and elsewhere. Furthermore, on 9 May 1925 a Belgian court-martial at Dinant sentenced a number of German officers in their absence for the killings in August 1914.[120] The Leipzig court dismissed all these charges in November–December 1925. One of the seven generals was Johannes Meister, who (as colonel) commanded Grenadier Regiment 101 in August 1914, and who had been charged by the Belgians on 19 June 1922 with the 'systematically inhumane conduct of his troops from 19 to 27 August', and in particular with ordering the execution of a number of civilians at Les Rivages (Dinant) on 23 August. The Reichsgericht noted that this event was the subject of one German internal investigation in 1915 (the inquiry for the White Book) and another in 1920. The court repeated that the troops were fired on by civilians, even women and children. Although some witnesses confirmed that civilians, including women and children, were killed as hostages, the court found 'no evidence to show the execution was unlawful. Nor could it be proved that the defendant issued an order to shoot the civilians.'[121] The court likewise found in relation to the six other generals that no acts 'punishable in German law' had been committed.[122]

In January 1925 the court-martial of Liège and Luxembourg provinces condemned Colonel von Hedemann and General Thessmar to death in absentia for the collective execution at Arlon, on 26 August 1914. Even Berthold Widmann, the Foreign Ministry's consultant lawyer, admitted that in this instance the Reichsgericht investigation had not been able to find any justification of these executions, or evidence of franc-tireur acts in Rossignol. Yet the court decreed that it was 'not improbable' that the executed Belgians might have been 'partly' guilty of treacherous or illegal acts against German troops, and it placed the accused 'outside prosecution'.[123]

The trial by French and Belgian courts-martial of alleged war criminals and the parallel hearings of the Reichsgericht show just how irreconcilable the two sides remained over the events of 1914. The issue poisoned relations between the former belligerent powers into the mid-1920s, not least because Germans condemned by the French and Belgian tribunals were liable to arrest if they set foot in those countries, and thus found their ability to travel humiliatingly curtailed. Only in the second half of the 1920s were these sanctions dropped by the French and Belgian authorities and the courts-martial abandoned.[124] In Germany, the issue continued to rankle. Out of 907 cases heard on the basis of the Allied extradition list, nine ended with judgments – five acquittals and four convictions of subaltern soldiers. For most of the remainder, the Reichsgericht had decided by 1925 – on the basis of preliminary proceedings at which the accused did not have to appear – that there was no case to answer.[125] The court even reversed the guilty verdicts in the *Llandovery Castle* case.[126] The activities of the Reichsgericht relating to war crimes continued until the Nazis, on coming to power, ended them.

3   War cultures after the war

In many ways, the Treaty of Versailles amounted to a continuation of the wartime cultural mobilization. Peacemaking raised the meaning of the war and the reasons for which so many died. Of course, many individuals were indifferent to the claims and rhetoric of wartime in their desire to re-establish personal normality.[127] Others repudiated them. But the continuing controversy over war crimes indicates that the process of cultural demobilization was a difficult one.

In the British case, the vengeful Germanophobia which accompanied the general election in December 1918 had cooled by 1921. There were no pressure groups urging the punishment of German war crimes, as in France. The press by and large endorsed the government's qualified acceptance of the Reichsgericht verdicts. The French ambassador in London wrote in May 1922 that British opinion was 'quite indifferent' to the question of punishing German war criminals and would be roused to hostility not by German avoidance of war crimes trials but by renewed French attempts to carry these out.[128] Lloyd George's desire to normalize relations with Germany, even to the point of accepting a moratorium on reparations payments, was in tune not only with perceived British interests in re-establishing a European balance of power but also with a public desire to return to peacetime normality. Significantly, when a statue of Edith Cavell was unveiled in St Martin's Place, London, on 17 March 1920, the tone of the ceremony was remarkably free of recrimination and the memorial bore Cavell's own words: 'Patriotism is not enough. I must have no hatred or bitterness for anyone.'[129] This was the shift in mood captured by John Maynard Keynes's immensely successful polemic, *The Economic Consequences of the Peace*, whose real target was the continued wartime

Poincaré tried to force the German government to gather evidence for use in the French courts-martial and even to extradite the Crown Prince as a war criminal.[144] With regard to war crimes, as in other respects, the Ruhr occupation saw the last efflorescence of the French war culture.

The invasion of 1914, symbolic for the nation, had only been experienced by a minority in France, whereas it proved central to Belgian memory following the war. When the government re-established itself in Brussels in early 1919, it instituted a second commission to investigate German war crimes during the invasion, along with various aspects of the occupation. The commission was reorganized under the Justice Ministry in July 1919, with a smaller membership composed of leading academics, lawyers, and civil servants, including Henri Pirenne, now rector of the University of Ghent. Over the following three years, the commission re-examined the events of 1914 as systematically as it could in disturbed post-war conditions, interviewing witnesses anew and eliminating all uncorroborated incidents. It endorsed the essential conclusions of the wartime commission. It denied the existence of Belgian francs-tireurs, a point on which every burgomaster of places cited in the German White Book was interrogated. It confirmed the essentially irrational and spontaneous nature of the franc-tireur myth-complex. But it also found that the 'legend of the francs-tireurs was, in the last analysis, created or at least suggested in order to justify and explain the "reprisals" by which [the Germans] pretended to make the war shorter and more humane.' It was, in short, the product of German military doctrine.[145]

The official inquiry was only the most important in a deluge of publications. Jean Schmitz, secretary of the diocese of Namur, and Norbert Nieuwland of the abbey of Maredsous, could publish the multivolume history of German war crimes during the invasion of Namur province and Belgian Luxembourg, for which they had separately gathered clandestine witness statements during the war.[146] This amounted to over 2,000 pages essentially on the central two weeks of the franc-tireur myth-complex, from 18 to 31 August 1914. As Bishop Heylen commented, it was simultaneously a record of German cruelty and a memorial to the endurance of the civilian population and the heroism of the soldiers.[147] Other clandestine wartime accounts appeared. Jean Chot issued the report of his trip gathering evidence on German atrocities in the winter of 1914–15.[148] The unfinished history of the invasion undertaken by Godefroid Kurth, the retired professor of history at the University of Liège who had died in January 1916, appeared with a chapter exposing the 'legend of the francs-tireurs' and an appendix on the massacres of Aarschot, based on Kurth's personal investigation. Kurth, according to Cardinal Mercier's preface, wrote as an admirer of Germany who was devastated by 'the invasion, its original iniquity, its atrocities and its lies'.[149]

Much of the post-war literature recorded outrage at particular atrocities. The massacre of 383 civilians at Tamines on 21 August 1914 had been ignored by the German White Book, and thus figured less prominently in the wartime battle of words. In 1919, a Jesuit local historian published his own inquiry among survivors in order to provide a 'true' account, to give the victims a voice, and edify the 'pilgrims' who would come to pay patriotic homage to the 'martyrs' of the town. The book rejected the suggestion of an Austrian resident of Tamines that there had been franc-tireur activity, maintaining that 'neither the intellectual part of the population nor the working class dreamed of opposing the Germans' progress with force.' The real cause lay in the widespread German fantasy that they faced partisan resistance, so that 'at the first shot they cried out that there were francs-tireurs.'[150] Lemaire's account was relatively restrained. Others, such as a series entitled 'The Martyrs' Cry', called frankly for vengeance: 'All Belgians, all the peoples of the universe, must know how much worse are the atrocities carried out by the armies of the German Empire than even the official reports relate. The sorrowful multitude of our martyrs calls with a great cry for avenging justice.'[151]

Dinant was a particularly acute case. In a public ceremony at the beginning of December 1918, a local lawyer, Édouard Gérard, read out an oath on behalf of the municipal council to a large gathering of townspeople. He defiantly rejected the 'calumny' of the franc-tireur legend and called on the Allied governments to prosecute the German soldiers responsible for the massacre. The ceremony of the 'oath of Dinant' was repeated for the benefit of the British and American troops who had liberated the town.[152] A 'calvary' of the principal execution sites was rapidly established and eventually marked with monuments. In the summer of 1921 a local paper stated a common Dinant feeling when it attacked Lloyd George for supposedly expressing himself satisfied at the outcome of the Leipzig trials, and angrily asked whether 'we ought to be satisfied that these bandits who were guilty [...] of horrors, some of which we still cannot recount, should still be at liberty'.[153] Many Belgian localities had comparable memories. It is thus not surprising that the Leipzig proceedings should have encountered scepticism or that German war crimes should have remained a live issue.

1919, dedicated to the proposition of a 'new nationalism' on the basis of honesty about German conduct in the war. Like Schwertfeger, he believed in the reality of the franc-tireur war and considered it justified by the precedent of the German War of Liberation in 1813 and the 1907 Hague Convention. Unlike Schwertfeger, he condemned the response of collective reprisals, whose origins he traced to European colonial warfare.[177] Another dissident, Walter Oehme, who had been present at the destruction of Kalisz in Poland in 1914 and who was angered by the lack of official admission of responsibility for it, published a book in 1920 with the provocative title, 'A Confession of German Guilt: Contributions on German War Conduct'. This dealt with the 'atrocities' committed against Belgian civilians.[178] Oehme, too, assumed there had been a justifiable Belgian '*Volkskrieg*', in combating which the German army had committed excesses.[179]

In 1921, the philosopher and peace campaigner Friedrich Wilhelm Foerster published a brochure condemning German war conduct and occupation policy, especially the deportation of girls and women from Lille. Generally, German pacifists were unwilling to accept specifically German guilt for either the outbreak or conduct of the war.[180] Foerster was an exception, readily blaming both on German militarism, by which he meant not just the Supreme Command but also the elite of teachers, professors, war theologians, journalists, and industrialists.[181] Such an analysis echoed wartime condemnations by the Allies but did not contain a precise investigation of the events of 1914. The most remarkable German attempt to deal with the latter as German war crimes was undoubtedly the book published in 1924 by Lilly Jannasch. The daughter of a German bank director and a French mother, Jannasch also assumed that Belgian franc-tireur resistance was real but justified. She used the Allied wartime publications, however, including the French official reports and Bédier's pamphlets, to document the German response and to argue that it epitomized the spirit of militarism and expansionism that lived on in the new Germany. Jannasch stated that reconciliation between the former belligerent powers could only occur once Germany had come to terms with its war crimes, but she also showed why the climate of opinion in early Weimar Germany made this unlikely: 'The courageous proclamation of the truth is taxed with treason, and the person who obstinately sticks to this task is immediately singled out for the bullets and clubs of the Pangermanists.'[182]

By the tenth anniversary of the outbreak of the war, the issue of 'German atrocities' during the invasion of France and Belgium was no closer to being settled than when it first arose. The Peace Treaty, infused with the war cultures of both sides, had made 'German atrocities' one of the prime irritants that kept hatred alive. Significantly, even the few dissidents in Germany who called for some form of moral reparations for the conduct of the army did not understand the role of the franc-tireur myth-complex. The climate of antagonism between the former belligerent nations militated against any neutral and impartial investigation of what had happened during the invasion. The Allied attempt to have alleged war criminals extradited was perceived by many Germans to be victors' justice, which indeed it was. The unwilling German judicial process against the accused was conducted in a spirit of partisan self-defence. Failure to resolve the conflict resulted from the weak Allied hold on post-war Germany, growing divergence of French and British policy, and indirectly from the withdrawal of American support for the new European order. It also stemmed from the manipulation of the war crimes issue by the conservative elites and the nationalist right in Germany, for whom restoring the prestige of the old army was vital, and from a wider German rejection of the peace settlement as a whole.

10   German atrocities and the politics of memory

After the occupation of the Ruhr, diplomatic détente and the return of domestic political calm permitted the demobilization of wartime cultures, especially in the former Allied countries. Memory of the war did not fade, but its human cost now predominated as individuals and whole societies slowly came to terms with the legacy of industrialized mass death. In Germany, the process was complicated by the verdict of 1918: the nationalist right never culturally demobilized but continued to seek ways of overturning the humiliation of Versailles. Still, in this changed climate one would expect interest in the 'German atrocities' of 1914 to have rapidly diminished.

The reverse proved to be the case. True, the end of war crimes proceedings removed the international controversy of the early 1920s. But the issue did not disappear. Between the mid-1920s and the Nazi arrival in power in 1933, the atrocities continued to provoke dissension. There was, moreover, a major reordering of their meaning whose effects have lasted to the present.

1   The pacifist turn: German atrocities as Allied propaganda

After the Great War, a minority current of opinion in Britain and France challenged the notion of unilateral German guilt for the outbreak and conduct of the war. This stance was rooted in the conviction that the real atrocity was war itself. It claimed that all belligerent countries had their share of responsibility for the catastrophe and should ensure that it never happened again. This viewpoint had emerged during the war in groups which resisted the process of cultural mobilization with its demonization of the enemy, such as the Société d'Études Documentaires et Critiques sur la Guerre in France and the Union of Democratic Control (UDC) in Britain.[1] Once the war was over, individuals from these and other groups attacked the 'responsibilities clauses' of the Treaty of Versailles and urged the dismantling of the wartime frame of mind as the prerequisite for a lasting peace.

This pacifist critique entailed a relativization of the 'German atrocities' question at several levels. First was the moral condemnation of the slaughter of 9 million men, by comparison with which the alleged atrocities during the invasion of Belgium and France, or German naval warfare, paled into insignificance. A second claim was that the war crimes of which the Germans stood accused were no worse than atrocities committed by Allied soldiers. Atrocities were part of the inherent awfulness of war. But most important of all was the argument that German atrocities were really the product not of German brutality but of Allied propaganda.

This last thesis was argued most influentially by two books, one French and one British, which appeared in the course of the 1920s. Georges Demartial, a French civil servant and militant pacifist who had taken a leading part in the Société d'Études Documentaires et Critiques, published a study of the mobilization of wartime 'consciousness' in 1922, much of which was devoted to 'German atrocities'. In common with many of the pacifists of the 1920s, Demartial presented his work as an attempt to re-establish the intellectual 'community of truth' which had been fractured during the war. He rejected the war culture and the moral 'excommunication' of Germany which went with it.[2] He used a scattering of examples in order to equate Allied and German atrocities, such as the *Baralong* affair and evidence from the UDC on Allied soldiers shooting prisoners. He also cited Shaw's 'Common Sense about the War' to deny that the bombarding of Rheims cathedral was an atrocity at all, and he concluded that: 'It is abominable moral cowardice to attribute the atrocity of this war to Germany, since the atrocity is inherent in war itself.'[3]

Demartial went further, however. A central article of the pacifist critique held that, left to themselves, 'the people' would not have embarked on war. 'Lies' about the war and the enemy had to be manufactured in order to enrol them in the modern equivalent of a war of religion, and central among these was the imputation of 'all the atrocities imaginable' to the German army.[4] Demartial's denunciation of atrocity propaganda, and ultimately of the entire Allied war culture, pointed to the revision of Articles 227–31 of the Treaty of Versailles.

Demartial argued that the Allies had used biased accusations against the Germans at Leipzig because all the crimes of which the latter were accused had in reality been committed by Allied forces as well. He cited Stülpnagel's 'The Truth about German War Crimes' in support of this point. Much of the argument concerned the massacre of prisoners for which there was no shortage of anecdotal evidence incriminating Allied soldiers. But Demartial made little attempt to dissect the events of 1914. He did not analyse the Allied cases which were left unheard at Leipzig, such as Jarny, Nomény, or Andenne. He dismissed the evidence of the war diaries discussed by Bédier. He also used German accounts of the Russian invasion of East Prussia as a moral counterweight to the German invasion in the west. Demartial certainly highlighted a weakness of the Allied case when he called for an impartial investigation of all atrocity charges by the League of Nations. But from the belief that each side's accusations would cancel the other it was a short step to declaring that Leipzig represented nothing more than the cynical prolongation of wartime hatred by the Allied governments; Demartial concluded that the task of pacifism was to inoculate public opinion against all propaganda.[5]

In Britain, Arthur Ponsonby's *Falsehood in Wartime* paralleled Demartial's argument. Ponsonby was a former diplomat and radical Liberal who became a prominent Labour MP after the war. During the conflict he had been an active member of the UDC, which had done more than any other organization to denounce atrocity propaganda.[6] In the second half of the 1920s he developed a 'humanitarian pacifism', based on what, to him, was the obvious pointlessness of war, and became the most prominent peace crusader in Britain.[7] In 1925, Ponsonby launched his campaign with a manifesto, *Now is the Time*, which he dedicated to 'the millions who have fallen in war', and which identified the 'great conspiracy' by which governments manipulate public opinion into accepting, and even glorifying, war. The real battle was to establish democratic control over diplomacy so as to unmask the 'conspiracy' and oppose the 'war mentality'.[8] It was a logical extension to publish *Falsehood in Wartime* in 1928 as an exposure of wartime propaganda.[9]

Ponsonby's subject was the cynical deception of credulous public opinion. Although he looked at lies about the causes of war and war aims, and acknowledged the role of rumour and hysteria, the book was principally concerned with 'the exaggeration and invention of atrocities [... as] the main staple of propaganda', especially by government and the press.[10] In reality, much of what Ponsonby evoked was the Allied mythologization of 'German atrocities' whose roots lay in the hysteria of French and Belgian civilians and Allied soldiers. His book had chapters on the 'mutilated nurse', the 'Belgian baby without hands', and the myth of the crucified Canadian soldier, this last being picked up in the Ypres salient and reported in *The Times* in May 1915.[11] He underscored the sheer unlikelihood of such tales, as well as the failure of journalism to check them. He also emphasized cases of deliberate fabrication. Most famous of these was the German 'corpse factory', a report of 1917 that the Germans were rendering the bodies of their dead soldiers for use in various kinds of war production. Related in *The Times* and elsewhere, it was not denied (though also not promoted) by official British propaganda agencies, and was only finally exposed and laid to rest in 1925. The notoriety it achieved in that year helped discredit British wartime propaganda, especially in the USA.[12]

Ponsonby did not, however, see the relationship between Allied myths and the complex events of the invasion itself. He ignored the franc-tireur mythology, and thus also the ensuing German 'reprisals'. Moreover, he constantly hinted that atrocity legends were deliberately circulated by the press in order to stoke up wartime passions, rather than allowing that they might be a symptom of those passions. The result was a discussion of atrocity tales divorced from the issues and wartime mentalities which had given them meaning. But it served to make the case of government manipulation and pointed to the conclusion that 'international war is a monster born of hypocrisy, fed on falsehood, fattened on humbug, kept alive by superstition, directed to the death and torture of millions [...].'[13]

In both Britain and France, the charge that 'German atrocities' were simply Allied propaganda was part of a campaign to revise the 'responsibilities' clauses of the Treaty of Versailles and dismantle bellicose mentalities. This was especially clear in France, where hatred of the wartime enemy remained stronger down to the occupation of the Ruhr than in Britain.[14] Overlapping networks of individuals from the Société d'Études Documentaires, the review *Clarté*, the left wing of the Socialist Party, and the French Communist Party portrayed atrocities as characteristic of war as a whole and denounced the attempted French prosecution of German war criminals. German claims of supposed rapes by black troops from the occupation army in the Rhineland were endorsed as proof of equivalent Allied atrocities.[15] The attack on 'Poincaré-la-Guerre', while mainly concerned with French responsibility for the war, dismissed Allied atrocity charges against Germany; Demartial's book was part of this assault.[16] The call for revision of the treaty became the focus for radical (or 'integral') pacifism in the later 1920s, notably with Victor Margueritte's campaign for Franco-German reconciliation.

Margueritte was an anti-establishment novelist who in 1925 fronted a public appeal signed by a group of pacifist intellectuals which urged 'moral disarmament' (the term Hitler had rejected) as the real basis for peace. In effect, this meant dismantling wartime mentalities which blocked the way to a genuine Franco-German rapprochement. France would therefore have to abandon not simply Article 231 of the Treaty of Versailles, as the basis of unjust reparations claims, but Articles 227–30 which 'sustain hatred with [their quest for] reprisals'.[17] Margueritte pursued the themes of the appeal in *L'Évolution*, the review he founded the following year. *L'Évolution* saw war, not capitalism, as the great evil, and favoured gradual but ineluctable 'progress' which would lead to 'reconciliation between the enemies of yester-year'. As part of its exposure of the war mentalities, the review published extracts from the works of Ponsonby and Demartial on atrocity propaganda.[18]

Margueritte's and Ponsonby's campaigns were a new departure within pacifism in France and Britain. Not only was their moral repudiation of war absolute but it came from the specific experience of 1914–18. 'Atrocity' tales were seen as central to the mental mobilization which had allowed cynical governments to unleash unprecedented carnage. 'Moral disarmament' therefore denied the reality of German atrocities in 1914 and repudiated the use of atrocity propaganda to saddle Germany with guilt for the real atrocity, war itself. This was not the view taken by mainstream pacifism, which placed its faith in rational schemes for mediating international conflict, embodied by the League of Nations. Such 'old-style' pacifism could readily justify the war effort in 1914–18 as necessitated by the unprovoked aggression of imperial Germany, and thus defend the peace settlement, while hoping that a new approach to international relations would make such wars a thing of the past.[19]

Nevertheless, radical and old-style pacifists agreed on the need for détente. Their case was reinforced by a broader revision of the popular memory of the war in France and Britain at several levels. First, the brutality of military behaviour towards civilians in the entire cycle of armed conflict from 1914 to the early 1920s relativized Allied accusations against Germany. In the demonology of French and British conservatism, Bolshevik 'terror' began to rival 'German atrocities'. Although attempts were made to link them (*Boche* sounded like *Bolchévique*), it was just as logical to rehabilitate Germany as a bulwark against Bolshevism or, like Lloyd George, to play down atrocities in both in the interest of reconciling them to the post-war order.[20] Elsewhere, British colonial repression provided troubling echoes of the charges against Germany, which the Germans themselves were not slow to exploit.[21] India and Ireland supplied particular hostages to fortune. True, the government and the House of Commons censured General Dyer for the Amritsar massacre of 1919, indicating that 'Prussianism' (the criticism levelled at him in India and by the left wing in Britain) was not the systematic policy of British rule.[22] But the government implicitly condoned collective reprisals against civilians in the Irish War of Independence in 1919–21 in the face of Opposition outrage. The Labour Party set up its own commission to investigate British 'atrocities', while *The Nation*, which was the voice of the Liberal conscience that had embraced the war in 1914, now portrayed Britain as a world pariah owing to behaviour which, it argued, paralleled that of the Germans in Belgium.[23] When the German White Book of 1915 finally appeared in a British edition in 1921, it was presented by its translator, an Oxford academic, former MP, and wartime staff officer, as an answer to the Bryce Report and as an ironic comment on British action in Ireland.[24]

Secondly, the perceived failure of a hardline policy against Germany brought a revulsion against the crude formulations of the war culture, and desire for an alternative framework of diplomatic relations. British opinion had broadly reached this stage by 1921 and hence showed little interest in the Leipzig trials. In France, the reaction came later. The 1925 Treaty of Locarno, which guaranteed the post-war frontiers of France, Belgium, and Germany and established a framework of arbitration for future disputes, seemed to indicate, along with German entry into the League of Nations the following year, that the war was finally over and an era of diplomacy between equals had begun. Reparations were not relinquished. Even the French Socialists continued to justify them by virtue of Germany's responsibility for the outbreak of war.[25] Nor were conventional concerns with military security and the balance of power abandoned. Briand, the principal architect of the new French policy, was no more a pacifist than Poincaré had earlier been a militarist.[26] But the public language of diplomacy changed to one of peace and reconciliation.

When Briand greeted the German delegation on its admission to the League of Nations in September 1926, he declared: 'The war is over [...]

mobilization for war in 1917–18 and helped justify disengagement from European affairs by a substantial, isolationist, portion of American opinion. Allied propaganda, and especially atrocity propaganda, was criticized for having played a key role in bringing America into the war (hence the reaction to the 'corpse conversion' fabrication when it broke in 1925). This reaction affected historians, journalists, and broader public debate.[38] The American historical profession was riven both by internal criticisms of the role played by academics in wartime and by a major public conflict over responsibility for the outbreak of war. This pitted those who maintained the wartime orthodoxy against revisionists who exonerated Germany, epitomized by the flamboyant historian and publicist, Harry Elmer Barnes.[39] It is not accidental if the most important work on propaganda, which for the first time became the object of serious academic inquiry, was both American and preoccupied by atrocity stories. As a doctoral student in political science at the University of Chicago in the 1920s, Harold Lasswell took the war as a case-study for developing a 'socio-psychological' approach to the nature of propaganda. His chapter on 'satanism' — that is, the demonization of the enemy — centred on atrocity myths.[40] The fullest historical treatment of the German atrocities anywhere was written at the end of the inter-war period, in an isolationist vein, by an American historian, James Morgan Read, who saw the phenomenon essentially as propaganda.[41]

By an irony of history, the 'revisionists' at the German Foreign Ministry and German nationalists saw 'German atrocities' and 'war guilt' in similar terms to pacifists and left-liberals in former Allied countries. There was agreement that 'German atrocities' were essentially an Allied invention and both sides called for revision of the responsibilities clauses of the peace treaty. Of course, the broader political visions at stake were totally different. But Hitler in *Mein Kampf* (1925–6) portrayed atrocity propaganda as a brilliant Allied (and essentially British) victory against Germany in terms which oddly foreshadowed Ponsonby's analysis.[42] Indeed, *Falsehood in Wartime* was well received in Germany, where the Foreign Ministry regarded it as the 'best and most effective book [...] against war atrocity lies' and assisted its publication in French and German. It was reissued during the Nazi period.[43] So much did Allied pacifist and German revisionist views parallel each other that German revisionists were able to make good use of the work of Allied pacifists. The campaign waged by the Schuldreferat to prove Germany's innocence in both the cause and the conduct of the war involved considerable subsidies to favourable foreign publications, including Margueritte's review *Évolution*. Individual authors, among them Margueritte and Demartial in France and Fay and Barnes in the USA, were aided in the production, translation and circulation of their works, in Margueritte's case to the tune of 500,000 Reichsmark.[44] The view that 'German atrocities' were little more than Allied propaganda made for strange bedfellows.

2   Locarno and the politics of memory

As far as the former Allied governments were concerned, the Treaty of Locarno in 1925 meant a new approach to international relations based on the rehabilitation of Germany, but not revision of Versailles. By contrast, to German diplomacy Locarno meant the opportunity to revise Versailles, including the responsibilities clauses.[45] With the waning of Allied interest in war crimes, it might have been logical for the German revisionist campaign to concentrate on Article 231, reparations, and the withdrawal of Allied troops from the Rhineland. These were indeed central issues for the Germans from 1925 until the end of the Allied occupation in 1930 and the end of reparations in 1932. They provided a solid reason for not jeopardizing German–Belgian relations by raising the 'atrocities' question when most Belgians had welcomed the Locarno accords.[46]

Yet so long as war crimes remained part of the moral foundation of the peace settlement, they retained a significance far beyond Belgian–German relations. If the Foreign Ministry wavered over pursuing the revision of Articles 227–30, its own Schuldreferat and the Reichswehr Ministry showed no such reticence since they wished to strengthen the legitimacy of the army within Weimar and defend the honour of millions of veterans by restating the official German version of events in 1914. For the Schuldreferat it was axiomatic that the two questions of guilt for the war and guilt for the conduct of the war were one entity; it was necessary to fight against both accusations and 'defend the honour of the old army (especially [on] "Belgian atrocities", [and the] franc-tireur question)'.[47] This, however, meant reviving the acrimony between the two countries.

Early in 1926 Reichswehr Minister Geßler approached the Foreign Ministry suggesting that it should campaign against Articles 227–30.[48] Geßler felt it was obvious that 'the spreading of lies about our conduct of war, in short about the alleged German barbarities, is far more injurious to our inquiry into the franc-tireur war on 30 August while Vandervelde was at the League of Nations in Geneva, where Briand and Austen Chamberlain (the British Foreign Secretary) told him of their disapproval. Vandervelde had begun to doubt the wisdom of his own initiative, unsuccessfully asking Chamberlain to 'help him out of the hole into which he has got'.[85] On 2 September, Vandervelde had to agree in cabinet to drop the proposal, over which Belgian and German diplomacy then drew a veil.[86] The abortive inquiry thus revealed the dangers of reopening the franc-tireur controversy. Yet it also showed that failing to do so kept the memory of 1914 charged with the potential for conflict.

The truth of both lessons was demonstrated over the subsequent six years before the Nazis came to power. The former Allied countries showed a strong desire to downgrade the events of 1914 which was frustrated by the unqualified reassertion of the wartime German position. When in late July 1927, Poincaré (as Prime Minister) inaugurated the reconstructed town hall at Orchies, burned down by the Germans in September 1914, he deplored the Reichstag report and the campaign of the German nationalist press in favour of the franc-tireur thesis. But he affirmed that 'as soon as [the Germans] stop misleading the world, as soon as they no longer contest the responsibility of the Central Empires for the explosion of the war and the excesses committed during [military] operations, we shall gladly speak of these tragic episodes as far distant events, classified in the archives of History.'[87] The London *Times* likewise observed that British opinion wished for nothing better than to forget the 'atrocities' but was prevented from doing so by German behaviour.[88] The Belgian government favoured a degree of amnesia over the atrocities question in the interest of co-operation with Germany. The Prime Minister, Jaspar, felt that an inquiry would only make Belgian–German relations more tense and 'maintain the mood of war instead of creating a mood of peace'.[89] The German Foreign Ministry, preoccupied with securing lower reparations and an early end to the Allied occupation of the Rhineland, also sought to restrain the most trenchant German denunciations of a Belgian People's War in 1914.[90]

But disruptive elements on both sides refused to realign their memory of 1914 with the requirements of Locarno diplomacy. In Germany, the Foreign Ministry's tactics of rapprochement, which meant downplaying the memory of 1914, conflicted with the goal of contesting and removing the 'responsibility clauses', pursued by its own Schuldreferat. Nationalist veterans' organizations and politicians and civil servants defending the 'honour' of the army had a particular interest in sustaining the thesis of the wartime White Book. In Belgium and France, the resigned stance of political leaders faced with an unmodified official German thesis on wartime atrocities contrasted with hardening local memories of victimhood at German hands. The result was a series of conflicts over the irreconcilable memory of the 'atrocities', especially between Germany and Belgium.

Memorials played a central role. Monuments were erected across the invasion zone of Belgium and France throughout the 1920s and inaugurated in ceremonies which recalled both the events and the language of wartime enmity. In France, Badonviller, Nomény, and Gerbéviller all acquired the status of *villes-martyres*. When Albert Lebrun, Vice-President of the Senate, unveiled the Nomény monument on 30 September 1928, he still found it hard to believe that 'a great people which prided itself on its civilization [...] could knowingly and deliberately [...] carry out acts whose horror defied the most warped imagination'.[91] At the inauguration of the Badonviller monument a year later, the mayor spoke of 'the barbaric method of the enemy [with] robbery, pillage and arson carried out scientifically', while Painlevé, Minister of War, referred to 'horrors whose traces have not been entirely effaced'.[92] Yet the status of 'martyred town' was at best a regional one confined to French Lorraine, and compared to the original events the inaugural ceremonies enjoyed little national coverage.

The typical form of the monuments suggests why. As has already been noted, the civilian victims were usually incorporated into a monument to the fallen soldiers of the locality, similar to those erected throughout France. Nomény was an exception, with a separate monument to civil victims, and in the Nord there were also monuments to civilians killed during the occupation, as opposed to the invasion.[93] But even in Nomény, the civil and military monuments stood next to each other and were inaugurated on the same occasion.[94] 'Martyr' status was thus conferred by reference to the victorious *poilu*, and it was the sacrifice of the soldiers (not the civilians) which subsequently determined the political meaning of the war, including the shift to rapprochement with Germany after Locarno. Gerbéviller demonstrates how limited was the autonomous impact of the memory of the invasion. In 1924, the unveiling of the monument was marred when the local branch of the right-wing Ligue des Patriotes accused the centre-left government, which had replaced Poincaré after the occupation of the Ruhr, of being 'shirkers and defeatists' who would betray the 'blood of those who gave France victory'.[95] So offensive was this that

Gerbéviller had humiliatingly to solicit the status of 'martyr' already granted to Badonviller and Nomény, and when this was grudgingly given in 1930, it came with little publicity in a ceremony held safely in the nearby administrative centre of Lunéville.[96] Thus a nationalist attempt to use local suffering in 1914 in order to reject Franco-German détente only succeeded in further marginalizing the memory of the invasion.

In Belgium, commemorating the victims of German atrocities recalled the direct experience of a much larger proportion of the population. Many sites of what have been defined in this study as 'major incidents' were marked by monuments dedicated solely or essentially to the civilian dead — such as Battice and other localities around Liège, Aarschot, and Tamines, where an inconsolable female figure threw up her arms over a massive plinth inscribed: 'To the martyrs of the 22 August 1914' (illustration 36). The civilians from Rossignol executed at Arlon on 26 August 1914 were disinterred in 1920 and, in the presence of King Albert, Bishop Heylen of Namur, and a host of Belgian and foreign dignitaries, seen off in a cortège which wound through villages decked with garlands and arches until it arrived in Rossignol, where the bodies were interred in a mausoleum. A monument, whose frieze (carved by the nationally known sculptor, Frans Huygelen) depicted a victim of the 'German atrocities' at rest under the national flag, with the victorious Allied armies on one side and the grief-stricken people of Rossignol on the other, was unveiled at the mausoleum by Queen Elisabeth in 1925. The Queen was given a bouquet of flowers by a girl who had lost several of her family in the execution.[97]

Local memory of German atrocities thus held wider sway than in France, but two Belgian sites had a national and even international signif-icance by virtue of the attention they had attracted during the war — Dinant and Louvain. It was here that the real battle of memory was joined with German nationalist politicians and veterans. Initially, the different massacre sites in Dinant were each commemorated separately. But in the mid-1920s, the commemorative effort was co-ordinated by the municipal-ity, with sculptural plaques and inscriptions of a unified design marking the individual sites and a monument erected outside the town hall. This ensemble was commissioned from Frans Huygelen and inaugurated on 23 August 1927. While the town hall monument was inoffensive, several of the plaques at execution sites graphically portrayed the events they commem-orated (e.g. the Bourdon wall, see illustration 37). Moreover, the inscrip-tions translated the hatred still palpable in the town by recording the

36 Monument to civilian 'martyrs', Tamines (inter-war postcard)

'martyrdom' of the 674 'innocent victims of German barbarism' (at the town hall monument), or the 'Teutonic fury' (at the Tschoffen wall).[98]

The town hall memorial was unveiled in the presence of Crown Prince Leopold, Defence Minister de Broqueville, and the French Minister for Pensions, Louis Marin. The ceremony was followed a few days later by the inauguration of a monument to the French soldiers killed defending the town, at which the guest of honour, Marshal Pétain, defined Belgium as the 'advance guard of Latindom'.[99] The response in Germany was one of outrage – doubtless exacerbated by the fact that Vandervelde's offer of an international inquiry still lay on the table. The German ambassador in Brussels protested against the Dinant monument complex. Vandervelde expressed some sympathy with German feelings, and claimed that he also found the reliefs 'deplorable', though Prime Minister Jaspar and other ministers upheld the historical judgements conveyed by the monuments.[100] The German right-wing and Catholic press condemned the Belgians for reviving 'atrocity legends'. Nationalist veterans' associations, especially from Saxony (home of the XIIth Army Corps), demanded a government protest against the defamation of German military honour.[101] Only with difficulty did the Foreign Ministry manage to dissuade the German

37   The Bourdon wall monument, commemorating the massacre
at Les Rivages, Dinant (inter-war postcard)

Officers' League (Deutscher Offizier-Bund) from pursuing this course
because of 'the overwhelming evidence against us in the case of Dinant'.[102]

The response of Germany's nationalist veterans to the summer's controversy over the Belgian 'People's War' was summed up by no less a person
than Field Marshal Hindenburg, now President of the Republic, when he
inaugurated the grandiose monument to the 1914 victory against the
Russians at Tannenberg, on 18 September 1927, which he portrayed as a
supreme act of self-defence. He not only denied the Allied thesis of German
responsibility for the outbreak of war but affirmed that 'the German army

waged the war with clean hands', and he offered once again to submit the issue to international adjudication. Stresemann endorsed this stance in an interview published by *Le Matin* in Paris, when he suggested that Hindenburg's views on German motivation and military behaviour in 1914 were 'a common conviction among all Germans'. In a bid to reopen the memory of 1914, Stresemann called for 'moral questions of extreme human importance' arising from the war to be submitted to the arbitration provisions of Locarno.[103]

Even more revealing of the tensions caused by the memory of 1914 was the uproar provoked the following summer, in 1928, by the inauguration of the rebuilt university library in Louvain. As in Dinant, the renewal of municipal life in the early post-war years had been marked by bitter memories of 1914 and overt hostility to Germany. At the reopening of the university in 1919, the rector, Mgr Ladeuze, who had witnessed the sack of the town in 1914 and reported on it to the Vatican, condemned the obstinate German belief in the 'legend of the francs-tireurs'. Arguing that nothing could excuse the destruction of the library, he declared: 'At Louvain, Germany disqualified itself as a nation of thinkers.'[104] The events of 1914 were literally engraved in the municipal memory of Louvain when the 'martyrs' monument' was erected in the station square. It carried panels (by Marcel Wolfers) which portrayed terrified refugees and civilians facing execution (illustration 38). The monument stood over a mausoleum containing 138 of the victims and was unveiled in 1925 by Marshal Foch who, in front of Queen Elisabeth and Cardinal Mercier, invoked the 'martyrdom of Louvain [whose] tragic horror has been recorded by history forever'.[105]

In view of such local consensus, it is not surprising that the reconstruction of the university library (whose precious works Germany was obliged to replace by Article 247 of the Versailles Treaty) should also have been seen as a memorial to the events of 1914. The project was a remarkable expression of the American sympathy for Belgium which had been so manifest in the Hoover Commission for Relief in Belgium which helped feed the country from 1915 to 1917. The president of Columbia University, Nicholas Murray Butler, a prominent educationalist and liberal Republican, played a leading role in raising American funds, while Whitney Warren, a francophile New York architect who was personally connected to Butler, designed the new building in neo-Renaissance style.[106] In fact, Warren was the driving force. He was strongly committed both to European architecture and to the Allied

38   The 'martyrs' monument', Louvain: The executed (inter-war postcard)

cause from the outset, reporting to the US Embassy in Paris in 1914 on the destruction of Rheims cathedral by the Germans.[107] Reconstructing Louvain library was a personal crusade. Warren's feelings about his own and his country's role were shared by Cardinal Mercier, who suggested to him in 1921 that an inscription should figure on the building stating: 'Furore teutonico diruta, dono americano restituta' (Destroyed by the German fury, restored by American gift).[108] As Warren's drawings make clear, he endorsed the sentiment enthusiastically (illustration 39) and incorporated the Latin motto into an ornamental balustrade on the exterior of the building. 'Furor teutonicus', or the 'German fury', was a term dating back to the Roman poet Lucan, which had been used by the Kaiser before the war, and by both German and Allied propaganda in 1914–15.[109] It provoked a different kind of furore in the changed climate of Locarno politics.

By 1927, as the library neared completion, the balustrade with its defiant inscription began to alienate the academic community at Louvain. The need to resume international academic life and renew the scientific 'community of truth' conflicted with national antagonisms derived from the war. The death of Cardinal Mercier in 1926 undoubtedly helped this process. Only Simon Deploige (like the rector, Ladeuze, a participant in the

DESIGN FOR THE LIBRARY
AT LOUVAIN
DESTROYED BY THE GERMANS ·1914
RESTORED BY AMERICA ·1922
WARREN AND WETMORE ARCHITECTS

39   The new Louvain university library: architects' sketch (1922)

events of 1914) continued to support Warren's inscription. In December 1927, Ladeuze wrote to Warren summarily dropping the inscription from the plans. The letter, which was widely published in the press, explained that the decision implied no acceptance of the German version of events, but simply recognized that the inscription would make it impossible for German academics to come to Louvain for scientific collaboration. Functional reconciliation required a degree of official amnesia.[110]

Warren insisted on maintaining the inscription, not least because he felt it to be a legacy from Cardinal Mercier to the Belgian people. This placed him on a collision course with the academic community in Louvain and also with shifting opinion in the USA. Not merely isolationists, but liberal public figures who wished America to play a role in building European harmony based on Locarno and the League of Nations, opposed prolonging wartime hatreds. Foremost among these was Nicholas Murray Butler, who by 1927 was president of the Carnegie Endowment for International Peace and an enthusiastic supporter of Locarno diplomacy. One indication of the changed climate of American opinion was the difficulty in raising funds to complete the library, with the Carnegie Endowment and the Hoover Commission for Relief in Belgium stepping in to bridge the deficit. This resulted in direct American pressure to drop the inscription. As the *New York Times* put it: 'there are many persons who feel as the [Carnegie] Foundation does, namely, that if the people are to go on indefinitely fighting the war, lasting peace will be an empty phrase and the struggle will be resumed at some future date.'[111]

Warren, however, was equally strongly backed in Belgium by numerous veterans' organizations, Franco-Belgian friendship societies, and sizeable elements of the press and the political establishment. In June 1928, Whitney Warren brought the by now notorious inscription to Louvain for installation, only to have it confiscated by the university. After a fierce polemic between Warren and Ladeuze, the inauguration of the library in early July took place with the balcony empty of inscription and under siege conditions. The government sought to reduce the official and diplomatic presence to a minimum and a large police force kept demonstrators well away from the ceremony. The French ambassador nonetheless attended and reported to Briand that although the proceedings promised to be anticlimactic, they were redeemed by an aircraft which curved overhead depositing thousands of leaflets on the assembled dignitaries – bearing the inscription 'Furore teutonico diruta, dono americano restituta.'[112]

Immediately following the opening, the empty balustrade was smashed by one of the Belgian foremen working on the library, Félix Morren, who declared on his arrest that: 'We aren't all *Boches* in Louvain yet.' It transpired that Morren had been wounded as a 15-year-old by the Germans in 1914 and later deported under harsh conditions. When he tried to destroy the balustrade again in 1933, he stated at his trial that he was acting less against the university than against the 'policy of forgetting' the events of 1914 practised by Belgian governments since the Armistice.[113] The affair ended with Warren failing in his legal action against the university to have the inscription installed, and he gave the ornament to a close Belgian associate, Pierre de Soete, a sculptor and occasional journalist with nationalist leanings.[114] As de Soete pointed out in an article published in *Le Soir* in January 1928 entitled 'Louvain et Locarno', the root of the discord lay in the amnesia required by the politics of rapprochement with Germany, and the conflict this provoked with Belgian memory of the war.[115]

Other incidents expressed the continued tension between hardline Belgian and German memories of 1914. In 1930, a large painting entitled 'The Mutilation of Belgium' which hung in the Musée Royal de l'Armée in Brussels (in the 'Trophy Hall' commemorating the victory of 1918) was removed after protest by the German ambassador. Its dominant image, needless to say, was the mythic child with severed hands (illustration 40). The incident prompted the Liberal daily *L'Indépendance belge* to publish a list of all the children who, according to the official commissions of inquiry, had been the real victims of German violence during the war.[116] The resumption of tourism also occasioned clashes. Not only were German visitors sometimes set upon in Belgium, but the municipal councils of Aarschot and Dinant took the Baedeker company to court in 1932–3 over the new edition of its Belgian guide, which summarized the official German view of events in the two towns in August 1914 as franc-tireur ambushes which caused the German army to carry out mass executions. Baedeker, after consulting the German Foreign and Reichswehr Ministries, agreed to republish the book with a statement admitting that the events of 1914 were still the subject of disagreement between Belgium and Germany. But despite pressure from the Belgian government, the two towns rejected this compromise and the sale of the German and English editions of the book was banned in Belgium until Baedeker produced a satisfactory revision. The German Foreign and Reichswehr Ministries reimbursed its not inconsiderable legal costs.[117]

This battle of memories deepened the divisions opened inside Germany by the 1927 Reichstag report on 'The Belgian People's War'. The Social Democrats now cautiously endorsed the Belgian view of events in Dinant and Louvain. *Vorwärts* concluded: 'If it is true that old people, women, and children were shot as hostages – and it is difficult to doubt it in view of the detailed descriptions – then the events of Dinant remain as a stain in the history of German warfare.'[118] When Fernand Mayence, professor of classical archaeology at Louvain, published a brochure in January 1928 refuting the allegations of the 1927 Reichstag report, he explained the 'legend of the francs-tireurs of Louvain' as a 'mass psychosis' with panic shooting by German soldiers. This view was accepted by *Vorwärts*, which talked of a 'terrible misunderstanding, a general hallucination'.[119] Mayence's brochure made a deep impact in Germany where 15,000 copies were distributed, 7,000 to professors and secondary school teachers.[120] A similar repudiation was written for the municipality of Dinant by Maurice

40 'The Mutilation of Belgium' hanging in the Royal Army Museum, Brussels (removed in 1930)

Tschoffen and Norbert Nieuwland. Distributed in even greater numbers in Germany (200,000 by June 1930), its explanation of the events as a 'collective hallucination' by the German soldiers was again endorsed by *Vorwärts*, along with other Social Democratic and pacifist newspapers.[121]

Such a stance was not easy for the SPD. In August 1928, the party accepted the Belgian case on the franc-tireur war at the congress of the Labour and Socialist International, held in Brussels. Paul Löbe, SPD President of the Reichstag, stated: 'The question of the alleged atrocities is very difficult for us [...] The SPD is convinced that some of the serious accusations cannot be denied. I am therefore of the opinion that Germany owes Belgium moral satisfaction.'[122] The *Kölnische Zeitung* called Löbe's speech 'most unfortunate', reminding its readers that during an invasion such as that of 1914, 'necessity knows no law.'[123] Moreover, the SPD ministers in the Great Coalition government, from 1928 to 1930, could not follow this change in the party's attitude. On the contrary, they resisted calls for a fresh inquiry, and Carl Severing, SPD Minister of the Interior, commissioned the Reich Archive to produce a book with the opposite goal, of proving the 'Belgian popular war'.[124]

German pacifist circles were even clearer in their condemnation of German militarism for the atrocities of 1914. Like Social Democrats they welcomed the Louvain and Dinant brochures. When the Reich Ministry of Posts banned Nieuwland and Tschoffen's account of Dinant in March 1929, German pacifist organizations ordered the book in bulk, with the Berlin branch of the German Peace Society alone distributing several thousand copies.[125] Catholic pacifists triggered a reaction within German Catholicism. Most Catholic newspapers and the Centre Party supported the centre-right consensus on German military innocence in 1914. But certain Catholic pacifist journals, and notably the Munich-based *Allgemeine Rundschau*, which devoted four issues to German–Belgian reconciliation in 1929–30, embraced the Belgian version of events. The editor, Georg Moenius, travelled to Belgium with Friedrich Wilhelm Foerster, the leading secular pacifist, in order to investigate the German war crimes in Louvain, Dinant, and Tamines, and consulted Mayence and Nieuwland in the process. In the *Allgemeine Rundschau* of 14 September 1929, Moenius attempted to explain the 'franc-tireur psychosis' of the German soldiers as a pathological delusion. In this and other articles, Moenius, Foerster, Mayence, and Nieuwland stressed the need for the 'moral liquidation' of the war by seeking the historical truth, and all of them condemned the German army for major war crimes.[126] Articles by Wendel in *Vorwärts* and *Tagebuch*, and by Foerster in his new *Die Zeit*, also argued that Germany owed Belgium 'moral reparation'.[127] Such statements angered the Centre Party and the influential *Kölnische Volkszeitung* which, as in 1914–15, sought to restore good relations between Belgian and German Catholics while refusing to accept that German soldiers had committed atrocities.[128] It was the Cologne paper that now argued for amnesia as it resentfully accused Moenius and Foerster of disturbing peace and reconciliation with unnecessary memories.[129]

German Communism, like its French counterpart, was less consistently interested in the question of German war crimes owing to its rejection of all capitalist wars, of which atrocities were taken to be a common feature. Nonetheless, individual testimony surfaced to condemn the wartime actions of the German army. The most interesting was that of the Saxon nobleman Arnold von Golßenau, who as a Communist author used the pseudonym Ludwig Renn. He provided a detailed account of the fighting around Dinant, which he experienced at first hand, in his semi-autobiographical novel *Krieg* ('War'), published in 1929. Written from the perspective of an ordinary soldier, Renn's account is evasive on the question of Belgian civilian resistance. Unexpectedly coming under fire, the protagonist attributes it to 'these damned Belgians'. But a fellow soldier tells him that it was only the echo of firing elsewhere. A series of houses are stormed in a small settlement in most of which there are only terrified civilians. But in the last, a farm, the German soldiers open a trap-door from which 'rose a civilian smiling evilly. He roused a horrible feeling in me.' Though describing the 'rage' evoked by francs-tireurs, the protagonist saves the Belgian's life by sending him off on stretcher duty. Next day, however, he notices that the farm has been burned down, only to be told that two German soldiers had been shot by the occupants who were themselves executed and the farm destroyed. But doubts remained: '[That] it should turn out so exactly to be true seemed too simple to me. I did not quite believe [...] that it had been our particular farm.'[130]

Thus, in an anti-war novel written in the same realistic vein as Remarque's *All Quiet on the Western Front*, the belief in the franc-tireur thesis was restated. But Renn revised his opinion the same year, publishing an article in *Linkskurve*, the organ of the League of Proletarian Revolutionary Writers of Germany, in which he explained how the senses were deceived in Dinant. He admitted that he had believed he was under fire from the houses in Dinant though the shooting came in reality from French soldiers on the other side of the river: 'But we believed we were being shot at by the inhabitants, and executed civilians *en masse*.'[131]

On the other side, Germany's official history of the war, written by a team of archivists and former General Staff officers at the Reich Archive and published from 1925, unquestioningly repeated the accusations of a Belgian People's War. At numerous points it charged civilians with firing at the invading troops. For example, it referred to the 'fanatical resistance of the population' at Dinant, but made no mention of 'reprisals' or the execution of 674 civilians.[132] Although fierce fighting at Tamines was recorded, no mention was made of the 383 civilians executed there. Significantly, the Reich Archive history ignored the fighting against the Belgian army on the northern flank from 20 August. No mention was made of the Belgian attack from Malines on 24–26 August and the fighting near Louvain in which it resulted. This omission can only be explained as an attempt to hide the real chain of causation of the destruction of Louvain in favour of the franc-tireur explanation.

Likewise, regimental histories replicated in miniature the arguments of the White Book and the innocentist campaign.[133] IR 125 from Württemberg, which was involved in the chaotic battle in fog on 22 August at Baranzy in Belgian Luxembourg and killed many civilians, recalled that the Belgian civilian population, despite the 'warning' of the war of 1870–1, participated in the fighting and had to pay for it.[134] The publication by IR 165 depicted its passage from Liège to Louvain as if it had to run a virtual gauntlet of attacks by treacherous civilians, and remarked that 'it goes without saying that civilians who engaged in fighting were not treated very gently.'[135] Articles bearing the same message appeared in the nationalist war veterans' press, such as the *Stahlhelm* and *Deutsche Treue* ('German Loyalty', organ of the National Association of German Officers).[136] Overall, the regimental memory enshrined in these official histories and veterans' accounts was the German counterpart of the local Belgian monuments to the civilian victims.

The German Foreign Ministry, for its part, wished even more than the Belgian government to let war crimes fade away. In 1928, Bernhard W. von Bülow, director of the European Department (II), argued that pursuing the issue could only be 'extremely disadvantageous' for Germany. He asked the Schuldreferat to use its influence to stop all meetings and publications on 'the war atrocities in Belgium', and he stressed that the regular departments, not the Schuldreferat, must keep control of the issue because it had become a liability.[137] By itself, the Schuldreferat might have found it hard to go against the senior officials. But it had a powerful ally in the Reichswehr Ministry which felt that the counter-offensive for which it had been calling since 1926 was now imperative. In a memorandum of December 1928, it proposed taking action against the 'hate-filled Belgian war propaganda' which was 'the most serious injury to German honour', and recommended preparing an 'official historical study' based on unused records in the Reich Archive, the Reichsgericht war crimes trials, and the files of the former Military Investigation Department for Violations of the Laws of War.[138]

The Reichswehr had more on its agenda than irritation at local Belgian commemoration of the 'German atrocities' of 1914. Restoring the 'honour' of the old army was seen as vital for the 'maintenance of the good reputation of the present Reich army which emerged from it'. Moreover, it would serve to unify German society, which 'was divided into two camps', those who could not understand why the government patiently tolerated the enemy attacks against German honour, and those who concluded from the government's silence that the Belgian standpoint was correct.[139] The proposed counter-offensive was thus intended to reject cultural demobilization and to attempt to remobilize wartime mentalities.

The principal result of the Reichswehr Ministry's initiative was a book commissioned (as noted) by the Interior Minister, Severing, vetted and approved by the Schuldreferat, and reluctantly sanctioned (and funded) by the senior functionaries in the Foreign Ministry.[140] The book was prepared by an archivist at the Reich Archive in Potsdam, Robert Oszwald, and published in July 1931 with the title *Der Streit um den belgischen Franktireurkrieg* ('The Dispute about the Belgian Franc-Tireur War').[141] As anticipated, it was based on an impressive amount of material, including 4,500 files covering 900 German army units. But it was a far from dispassionate inquiry. Oszwald enjoyed close links with nationalist veterans and was a member of the DNVP.[142] In 1928–9, he had published a series of articles foreshadowing the book in the right-wing journal *Deutscher Offizier-Bund* ('German Officers' League').[143]

Essentially, Oszwald pursued the strategy mapped out by Schwertfeger in 1920. He blamed Belgium for illegal resistance of the German invasion by civilians in general and the non-active Garde Civique in particular.[144] As we have argued, there was little if any basis for such a view.[145] Oszwald's intention was to force the Belgians to agree to an inquiry using archive material in both countries. This, as he explained to the German Chancellor, Brüning, would exonerate the German people from the accusation of 'barbaric warfare'. His hope, no doubt, was to marshal evidence of an illegal Belgian 'popular war' which would justify the conduct of the German troops, even if a partial admission of guilt were made. This would suffice to call Articles 227 to 230 of the Treaty of Versailles into question, and destroy the legitimacy of reparations.[146] By and large, the book was greeted enthusiastically by the German press. Schwertfeger praised it in the *Kölnische Zeitung*, the *Hannoverscher Kurier*, and the *Deutscher Offizier-Bund*. Not only the nationalist but also the Catholic and democratic newspapers gave it lengthy coverage, while the conservative historian Hans Herzfeld wrote that Oszwald had succeeded in 'refuting the Belgian arguments using Belgian and French material'.[147]

Senior staff in the Foreign Ministry, however, found Oszwald an embarrassment. They refused to have his book translated into foreign languages, deeming it 'not suitable for extensive utilization for propaganda'. The Director of the Reich Archive Historical Department, von Haeften, found some of Oszwald's material contradictory, including two documents which 'seriously incriminate the German troops' concerning the 'punishment of Andenne' and the shooting of Belgian priests. It was not, he concluded, 'in the interest of Germany to direct the attention of the world to the events of August and September 1914 in Belgium'.[148]

Oszwald's team maintained the momentum of its campaign. Retired Lieutenant-Colonel Alfons Fonck, as has already been noted, sought to prove that 128 officers and soldiers had been injured or killed by shotgun fire in 1914.[149] But his book was coolly received in the moderate and left-wing press in Germany, for all its endorsement by the Nazis and the right.[150] *Vorwärts*, in a devastating critique, pointed out that if the injuries in question really came from Belgian shotguns, this would disprove the thesis of a premeditated *Volkskrieg*, since only a government of 'incurable idiots would equip its freeshooters with shotguns'.[151] Even Oszwald accepted this verdict.[152]

The Schuldreferat went so far as to persuade Albert Einstein, known internationally not only as Germany's most renowned scientist but also as a pacifist, to broker a meeting between Norbert Nieuwland, the Belgian historian of the invasion, and Professor Walther Schücking, the German legal historian and moderate pacifist, with a view to resolving the Belgian–German quarrel over the 'German atrocities'. The pair met twice in 1929–30. Although Einstein intended a free exchange of views, Nieuwland and Schücking spoke in an official capacity, the latter having been instructed by Oszwald and Widmann, consultant to the Schuldreferat, only to discuss incidents up to 15 August 1914. This eliminated Dinant, Aarschot, Tamines, and Louvain from consideration and focused on the German thesis of the fanatical franc-tireur war. Nieuwland conceded that 'in some localities' there might have been francs-tireurs, though this had not been proved. But he wanted a public declaration by 'respected German private persons' that the major massacres breached international law.[153] For the Schuldreferat, this was unthinkable.

In similar fashion, the suggestion made by Oszwald in his own book that an international commission of inquiry should settle the franc-tireur issue was taken up by Fernand Mayence of Louvain. But, as before, the Schuldreferat wanted it to concentrate exclusively on the first half of August 1914, so that the mass executions which took place during the main invasion, and which Widmann internally admitted were unjustified, could be excused by prior Belgian 'guilt'. Inevitably, this attempt at an understanding got no further than mutual recriminations.[154] One further initiative might have reconciled the opposed sides. In March 1932 Vandervelde, now in opposition, proposed that a joint commission of Belgian and

German historians, none of whom had any prior connection with the question, should investigate the 'franc-tireur' war under the chairmanship of Henri Pirenne, and produce an independent report. The German Foreign Ministry expressed interest in the proposal, despite the reservations of the Reichswehr Ministry, but no further steps had been taken when the Nazis came to power, and the Belgian government dropped the idea.[155] By the nature of the events of 1914, consensus on the invasion required such compromises in the German position that these would endanger the revisionist campaign. Consequently, the Schuldreferat could not afford to allow truly independent discussions, the German Foreign Ministry preferred silence, and the tension between the Foreign and Reichswehr Ministries remained unresolved.

The last salvo of the inter-war battle of memory came from Belgium. As early as 1928 the idea had emerged of one further monument in Dinant to the suffering of all Belgian civilians during the war. The fate of the town would thus symbolize the martyrdom of the nation. The initial proponent was Édouard Gérard, author of the 'oath' of December 1918, who imagined the monument as a library documenting the facts of the events.[156] This and other ideas fell by the way, but in July 1932 new life was breathed into the project by a meeting between Sasserath, the burgomaster of Dinant, and none other than Pierre de Soete. De Soete offered to design a monument which would honour the intention of Gérard's original project by 'responding to the outrage of the infamous German calumnies' while incorporating Whitney Warren's defiant inscription from Louvain, of which de Soete still had custody.[157] De Soete's plan included an obelisk 150 metres high, and in 1933 the municipality designated the Place d'Armes, near the Tschoffen wall, as the site.

From the start, the monument stirred bitter opposition, locally, nationally, and from Germany. Catholic opinion (Walloon and Flemish) rejected the incorporation of the Louvain inscription as an anticlerical manoeuvre designed to attack moves towards reconciliation with German Catholics. The provocative nature and history of the inscription also fuelled recriminations from local and national opinion, which felt that it needlessly exposed Belgium's international vulnerability, especially after the Nazis came to power. There was outrage in Saxony, where the local *Dresdner Anzeiger* maintained that the Saxon veterans who had suppressed the Dinant rising were 'patriots who acted not out of blind hatred but patriotic self-sacrifice'. In 1933, under strong German pressure, King Albert and the

41 'Furore teutonico': the Dinant national monument to the victims of German atrocities. Inaugurated 1936, destroyed by the Germans, 1940

Prime Minister, de Broqueville, tried to persuade Sasserath and the Dinant council to drop the inscription. Influential local luminaries such as Gérard and Tschoffen also opposed the project on the grounds of national security.[158] The controversy affected fund-raising so that the monument had to assume more modest dimensions. When completed in 1936, it consisted of a centre-piece some 9 metres high, composed of a giant hand raised in the solemn 'oath of Dinant' to uphold the truth of the events of 1914, and flanked by two walls surmounted by the first portion of the Louvain inscription, 'Furore teutonico'. Below were engraved the names of the 674 victims at Dinant, while columns at either end bore the place names of the principal German atrocities in Belgium (illustration 41).[159]

The inauguration on 24 August 1936 was boycotted by church and state. Indeed, Paul-Henri Spaak, Foreign Minister in the government which had just re-established Belgian neutrality in a desperate bid to stay out of the looming European war, appealed in vain to Sasserath to drop the inscription shortly before the ceremony.[160] So far had the climate of opinion changed since the unveiling of the municipal monument nine years earlier that on this occasion the two patrons of the French support committee, Marshals Pétain and Franchet d'Esperey, stayed away. Although a large crowd heard Sasserath describe the monument as Dinant's final answer to the 'calumnies' that had been reawakened with the 1927 Reichstag report, it was purely local and the monument had fierce detractors in the town itself.[161] With the Rhineland reoccupied by German troops, civil war in Spain, and public opinion in Belgium (as in France and Britain) split between anti-fascism and appeasement, the tensions of 1936 completed the marginalization of the memory of 1914 – even on the site of the atrocities.

3   The Second World War and after

The arrival of the Nazis in power polarized the battle of memory in its most extreme positions. In a referendum held in December 1929, only 14 per cent of the German electorate had voted for a 'Law against the Enslavement of the German People', formulated by the extreme right-wing parties in order to reject the 'war guilt' articles of the Versailles Treaty, along with the Young Plan on reparations.[162] In effect, majority opinion supported the Locarno diplomacy of Stresemann, with its aim of revising Versailles by persuasion and its ambivalence over whether the Allied case on 'German atrocities' was best contested or allowed to die. Once in power, Hitler revised the post-war settlement unilaterally, so that when in 1937 he told the Reichstag that he was 'revoking' Germany's signature to the Versailles Treaty, the campaign conducted by the Schuldreferat became redundant.[163]

Bodies such as the Reich Archive or the army's military history section maintained an interest. Occasional new documents supporting the Allied case required repudiation. In 1934, for example, the Polish doctor, Jacobson, who had been a medical orderly with IR 49 in August 1914, published his memoirs, once more exposing the franc-tireur illusion and the savage German response.[164] But in Germany the issue was no longer contentious. It was axiomatic for the regime that there had been a Belgian 'People's War', that it had been illegitimate, and that the Allies had twisted German reprisals into atrocity propaganda. This had defamed the army and helped underpin an unjust peace – which the Führer was busy tearing up. In the former Allied countries, the threat now posed by Germany was a reason for repressing, not recalling, the memory of 1914. The quantity of Belgian publications on the issue tailed off in the later 1930s, while in France a maverick far-right journalist from Lille, Antoine Redier, was an isolated voice in pointing to the German atrocities of 1914 as a warning against Hitler.[165]

As the Nazis remobilized the language of war, they moved beyond the way it had been deployed in 1914–18, while also making knowing reference to the earlier usage. Unlike nationalist Germany of the Great War, the Nazis affirmed, even rejoiced in, 'barbarism' as a hallmark of the new German culture. Hitler referred to Nazi Germany as young, barbarian, and vital, and 'hardness' and unsentimentality became key attributes of idealized Nazi manhood. The leading sociologist, Werner Sombart, who in his 1915 pamphlet, 'Merchants and Heroes', had portrayed the war as a clash between hollow English commercialism and German 'Kultur', now openly assumed the mantle of barbarism in *Deutscher Sozialismus*, the work with which he greeted the Nazi regime in 1934. 'We are called barbarians', he declared. 'Good – we accept the insult and turn it into a word of honour. We are barbarians and proud of being so, and we will remain so.'[166] This semantic shift foreshadowed a radicalization of violence in the construction of a new order.

Ominously, the Nazi regime made wide use of 'atrocity' propaganda. It displayed outraged innocence at claims of German atrocities by its political enemies, and from 1933 denounced 'world Jewry' for conducting 'atrocity propaganda' against Germany.[167] In 1937, the catalogue to the 'degenerate art' exhibition condemned those anti-war painters who, like Otto Dix and George Grosz, had incited sedition by depicting German soldiers as drunkards and brutes possessed by lust, and who had given 'sustenance to the Allied allegations of German war atrocities'.[168] Conversely, the Foreign Ministry invented 'atrocity' charges, especially against the Poles, in order to justify expansionist ambitions in the late 1930s. These were circulated in reports similar in tone and format to those of the First World War – logically, since the hope of achieving expansion without intervention by the major western powers, including the USA, meant paying lip-service to the notion of an international public sphere, on which the propaganda campaigns of 1914–18 had been premised.[169] The reflex persisted as parody. The Foreign Ministry condemned 'Bolshevik atrocities' in 1942 when any idea of a common public sphere (along with international law) had perished with German occupation policy in Poland and with racial war against the USSR.[170]

The invasion of the Low Countries and France reawakened memories of the atrocities of 1914 on both sides. Acutely conscious of what they considered to be the brilliant Allied propaganda victory in the previous war, the Nazi leadership took care to avoid any repetition in 1940. In early mid-May,

Goebbels noted repeatedly in his diary that his ministry was repudiating all enemy atrocity stories, 'so that no legend can be created'. He later added: 'The psychological situation at present is most favourable for us. All neutral countries are full of admiration. What a transformation since 1914!'[171] But countering enemy accusations was only half of it. Avoiding incidents which gave rise to them was crucial. At the Nuremberg trial of major war criminals in 1945–6, the German defence lawyer Stahmer, in denying the charge of conspiracy to commit war crimes, stated that 'at the beginning of the war every endeavour was made to wage war with decency and chivalry', as proved by 'the orders of the High Command regulating the behaviour of the soldiers in Norway, Belgium, Holland'.[172]

The evidence certainly suggests that the German army tried to avoid a repeat of 1914. Incidents reminiscent of the franc-tireur scare sometimes occurred, as at Vinkt, in Belgium, where a number of villagers were executed following alleged civilian resistance.[173] An exception to the rule of relative respect for civilian life and property in western Europe was aerial warfare, with the machine-gunning of columns of fleeing civilians and the bombing of civilian targets, notably in Rotterdam on 14 May, with the death of 980 inhabitants. The reluctance of Allied propaganda to take this up, or of the Dutch to indict German leaders at Nuremberg for the destruction of Rotterdam, is explained by the subsequent bombing of German cities by the British.[174] Yet there was nothing like the German execution of over 6,000 civilians in a similar period during the earlier invasion.

German units were under strict orders to behave impeccably. Although the possibility of civilian resistance had been foreseen, francs-tireurs were to be tried by court-martial and genuine militiamen and organized volunteers were to be treated as prisoners of war.[175] Hitler personally issued an order to the Wehrmacht on 7 July 1940 enjoining all troops 'to exercise restraint in their dealings with the population of the occupied enemy territory, as befits a German soldier'. He warned that soldiers who committed 'punishable acts – also against the population' would face 'ruthless prosecution', in serious cases even the death penalty.[176] This order, which flies in the face of common assumptions about Europe under Nazi domination, is partly explained by Nazi racial distinctions between western and eastern Europe, but it also reflected the need to ensure that Germany's enemies had no grounds for atrocity propaganda reminiscent of 1914–15.

The response of French and Belgian civilians to the invasion was equally shaped by the memory of 1914. The marginalization of the 'German atrocities' in inter-war opinion was swiftly reversed with the shock of the Nazi *Blitzkrieg*. This is not to say that memories of the earlier invasion were the only cause of the massive exodus of over 8 million French and up to 2 million Belgians (about one-fifth of the population in each case). Reasonable fears of aerial bombing and more recent myths, such as those of the 'fifth column' or of ferocious German parachutists, played their part. But the memory of real atrocities in 1914 and of the subsequent occupation helped generate a panic which this time assumed national proportions.[177] The prefect of the Oise, for example, considered that 'the memories of the Great War and the harshness of life at that period had a great deal to do' with the flight of the population of Beauvais.[178] The inhabitants of Orchies left at the first sign of bombardment on 10 May 1940 by a reflex 'probably connected to the events of 1914'.[179] The myths as well as the memories of 1914 played a role. Simone de Beauvoir encountered terrified refugees in the west of France who spoke of children with severed hands, while interviews with inhabitants of Caen in Normandy, who were young girls in 1940–4, underline the extent to which their mothers experienced the *exode* through the imagery of the previous invasion, especially rapes and mutilated children.[180]

All the more surprising, therefore, was the contrast between anticipation and experience, at least initially. Time and again, Belgian and French civilians were surprised by the overall restraint of the German soldiers. The prefect of the Ardennes, despite the material ravages caused by the invasion, spoke of the invaders' 'cordiality' and 'correctness', while his colleague in Belfort remarked on their 'courteous behaviour'. A deputy of the Seine-Inférieure and the prefects of the Oise and the Seine-et-Oise all used similar terms.[181] The American journalist William Shirer noted on entering Paris that the inhabitants who had remained behind were 'all the more amazed at the very correct behaviour of the troops – so far'.[182] As one youngster of 1940 recalled after a friendly encounter with a German soldier: 'I had read so many of the little pink books that lay in the school library, which endlessly described the brutal behaviour of the soldiers of William II in 14–18. Could the [soldier] whom I'd just seen, and who had said [...] that the weather was hot, belong to the same race?'[183]

The degree to which German conduct during the invasion and occupation was influenced by the memory of Allied accusations of 'German atrocities' in 1914 is further indicated by the extraordinary efforts of the army and regime to set the record straight from their point of view. Whereas the military war memorials of the Great War were left intact, the most defiant monuments to the civilian victims of the 'German atrocities' were destroyed. One of the first acts of the German invaders as they arrived in Dinant was to demolish the 'Furore teutonico' monument. Offending inscriptions were chiselled off other monuments in the town, including Huygelen's group outside the town hall and other plaques.[184] At Louvain one half of the plaque at the city hall, listing the names of the civilian 'heroic martyrs', was ripped out, while the other half, commemorating the deeds of the Belgian army, was left intact.[185] During the three-day battle for the city, the university library with its reassembled collections paid for by German reparations was once again burned down. Whether this was a deliberate act of German revenge, as the Belgian War Crimes Commission maintained, or a by-product of battle, is uncertain. German propaganda blamed the British troops who had defended Louvain, in order to reverse the propaganda verdict of 1914.[186] A one-sided battle of the texts also continued as the Germans censored Belgian school-books which taught an unacceptable version of the history of the Great War or mentioned German atrocities.[187]

Reversing the victors' verdict of 1919 meant a trip to the archives. In what must have been the biggest historical research project carried out during the war, the Director of the German Army Archives, von Rabenau, appointed deputies to Brussels and Paris as soon as the cities had been captured in order to seize material on a range of historical subjects, including the events of 1914, and dispatch it to Germany. The Supreme Command of the Wehrmacht, directly presided over by Hitler, informed the commander of the German invasion forces in Belgium and northern France on 6 July 1940: 'We have the greatest interest in the archives of the Belgian General Staff [...] From them exact proof can perhaps be provided to show that the "German atrocities in Belgium", which were used at the time to whip up hatred against us in the whole world, had their origin in the Belgian General Staff which incited the Belgian civil population to resist the German invasion and which even put its soldiers in civilian clothing and had them shoot at our troops.'[188] Unsurprisingly, satisfactory material was not forthcoming, and Major von Harbou, chief of staff of the military commander in Belgium and northern France, wrote to Rabenau on 18 August 1940, explaining why the mission was unlikely to succeed:

Dear General,

I should like to make a personal comment on the instructions you sent to your commissioner here concerning 'German atrocities' and 'sentences against Germans accused of war crimes'. I was involved in the very first days in Belgium in 1914 and from the start I had the impression that the *malheur* was the result purely of the unfortunate institution of the Garde Civique. These people were armed and wearing civilian clothing and were out and about when our unexpected invasion took place. Some of them fired, most did not, but all were treated as armed civilians by us. After a few hours every civilian was treated as an enemy. Whoever shot from a house was regarded as a franc-tireur, even if he was a Belgian soldier. Enormous nervousness on our side; and then Germans shot at Germans.

I do not think anything good will come out of this matter. It will hardly be possible to find anything to implicate Belgium. Apart from that, I would advise not to do anything, at least for the time being.[189]

Notwithstanding Harbou's scepticism, the hunt for material on the 'franc-tireur war' in Belgium and France continued throughout the occupation. As late as 7 August 1944, the day before the archive commission in Paris disbanded, files concerning the court-martialling of German war criminals in absentia during the 1920s were being sent to the German army archives in Potsdam.[190]

German concern with the 'atrocities' of 1914 during the Second World War displayed the characteristic duality which lay at heart of the original phenomenon. A belief that Germany had been the victim of Allied atrocity propaganda led to obsessive efforts to establish the 'truth' about 1914. Yet the equally strong conviction that a real franc-tireur war had been put down by legitimate harshness evoked parallels in the new conflict. As noted, the German armies expected that they might meet franc-tireur resistance when they invaded France and the Low Countries. They simply wished to avoid the kind of panicky response that would feed propaganda victories to the Allies. Should there be real combat with civilians, nothing had happened since the First World War to change the German army's basic intolerance of the phenomenon or its doctrine of harsh reprisals, especially since the principles of the Hague Convention had made such little headway in German official thinking. Indeed, the terms of the Armistice with France, signed on 22 June, stated that any Frenchmen who continued to fight would be punished as francs-tireurs.[191] Inevitably, German military belief about what had really happened in 1914 served as a reference point for new situations.

This was clearly the case in the east. The invasion of Poland was initially governed by the same rules of combat that had obtained in the German army in 1914.[192] On 3 September 1939, Himmler ordered the SS and police units which followed the regular Wehrmacht troops to shoot on the spot Polish insurgents caught resisting or with weapons in their hands. The army was susceptible to the same kind of 'franc-tireur' paranoia as in 1914, provoked by the nervousness of raw troops, the inevitable 'friendly fire' incidents, 'senseless firing at non-existent freeshooters [*Freischärler*]', but also real rear-guard actions conducted by Polish soldiers and militiamen. Civilians were massacred in Bromberg and Czestochowa in early September after such incidents.[193] While SS Einsatzgruppen and police units, not the army, were primarily responsible for converting such arbitrary repression of civilians into a war of racial annihilation, they appropriated the language and concepts of the army in doing so. On 21 September 1939, Heydrich informed the Einsatzgruppen that the reason for the collection of all Polish Jews in a few large cities, preparatory to the secret final goal of deportation to a Jewish reservation in eastern Poland, was that 'Jews [were] prevalent in franc-tireur attacks and in pillaging.'[194] Using the image of the franc-tireur, and thus of a treacherous, dangerous enemy, a seamless continuum could be constructed in which the army, too, would lose its remaining inhibitions against killing civilians.

Well before the invasion of the Soviet Union, Hitler declared in the notorious 'Commissar Order' of March 1941, that the Hague Conventions (which the USSR had not signed) would not apply. A string of orders spelt out the implications, and while Nazi racial ideology, loathing of Communism, and fear of Bolshevik 'atrocities' all contributed to the anticipated ruthlessness towards enemy civilians, this also drew on the army's memory of the franc-tireur war of 1914. On 13 May 1941, Marshal Keitel ordered that francs-tireurs should be 'liquidated without pity by the combat unit from which they flee', while an Army High Command order of 4 June 1941 decreed that 'agitators, Bolsheviks, francs-tireurs, saboteurs, and Jews' should be exterminated.[195] On 11 June, General Staff officers and court-martial judges were told that their '*sense of justice has to take second place behind the necessity of war*', and that they must 'return to the old custom of warfare; our present law of war was only laid down after the World War. One of the two enemies must perish; bearers of the enemy view are not to be conserved, but liquidated. The term "freeshooter" [*Freischärler*] encompasses also the civilian who calls for obstruction (e.g. propagandists, leaflet distributors, those who destroy German orders, arsonists [...] etc.).'[196]

Hitler himself looked back to the crucial precedent of 1914. Thinking about partisans shortly after the invasion of Russia, he recalled that:

> The old Reich knew already how to act with firmness in the occupied areas. That's how attempts at sabotage to the railways in Belgium were punished by Count von der Goltz. He had all the villages burnt within a radius of several kilometres, after having had all the mayors shot, the men imprisoned, and the women and children evacuated. There were three or four acts of violence in all, then nothing more happened.[197]

In fact the memory was exaggerated. After one incident of railway line sabotage on 25 September 1914, Goltz took hostages and threatened ruthless reprisals in case of repetition.[198] However, what matters is the use Hitler made of the memory of the franc-tireur war to justify escalating brutality against civilians in 1941.[199]

In the USSR, partisan resistance was negligible in the first six months of the German invasion, although by mid-1942 it had attracted upwards of 150,000 combatants. It was therefore not the cause of German brutality towards civilians, though it doubtless reinforced it.[200] In other areas of German-occupied Europe, the emergence of resistance movements was met with collective reprisals which also drew on the precedent of 1914. Admittedly, the legal justification of civilian resistance did not extend to occupation, as opposed to invasion, the revisions of the Hague and Geneva conventions between the wars having failed to resolve this issue. But whatever the status of armed opposition to enemy occupation, it remained illegal under Article 50 of the Hague Convention on Land Warfare for the occupier to impose collective punishment for the acts of guilty individuals (see appendix 2). Yet this is precisely how the German occupation forces responded, as in 1914.

In France, initial 'correctness' by German troops quickly changed in the face of the growing Resistance which was met with hostage-taking and reprisals. The military governor of France in 1940–2, responsible for initiating executions of hostages, was none other than Otto von Stülpnagel, the prominent 1920s innocentist campaigner against Allied war crimes charges. During his term of office, 375 hostages were condemned to death and 221 executed.[201] In fact, there was a clash of views on how widespread hostage shooting should be. Stülpnagel felt that limited executions plus large-scale deportation of Communists and Jews to the east would be a more effective deterrent, and he eventually resigned over the issue. With the first attacks on Wehrmacht personnel in August 1941, Keitel (Chief of Staff), acting on behalf of Hitler, insisted that Communist prisoners be shot in increasing numbers in reprisal, a policy continued by Stülpnagel's successor, his cousin Heinrich von Stülpnagel. But the disagreement was only one of degree since no one denied the principle of collective culpability.[202]

From June 1942, the policy of hostage executions was gradually abandoned in favour of a military campaign against the Resistance. This in turn displayed distinct similarities with 1914. In February 1944, the commander-in-chief in the west ordered troops facing attack to: '(a) Return fire immediately! If innocent people are hit, it is regrettable, but only the terrorists are to blame; (b) Immediately seal off the area around the scene of the crime and arrest all civilians in the vicinity regardless of their estate and identity; (c) Immediately burn down houses from which shots were fired.'[203] In March 1944, Keitel ordered that partisans were to be killed in fighting and only brought before a court-martial if they escaped death and were subsequently arrested. They were not to be treated as prisoners of war. Perhaps sobered by the thought of the post-war consequences of his actions, Heinrich von Stülpnagel, in one of his last orders as governor in July 1944, reminded the occupation forces: 'No German soldier should assault the defenceless, the helpless, women, and children! However difficult the conditions of partisan warfare make it to distinguish between friend and foe, it is the first duty of the German soldier to spare the innocent.'[204] But it was too late to prevent notorious atrocities such as those at Nîmes, in March 1944, Ascq (near Lille) in April, Tulle on 9 June, and Oradour-sur-Glane on 10 June 1944, where 642 inhabitants, including women and children, were killed by a Waffen-SS division in 'reprisal' for a Resistance ambush, and the village destroyed. As the Germans withdrew from France, they engaged in atrocities against the civilian population on a scale which was only being established 50 years later.[205] Comparable reactions to resistance occurred in other countries. In Italy, German soldiers massacred civilians in various incidents as punishment for partisan activity.[206] Mark Mazower has argued that the legacy of 1870 and 1914, along with Nazi racial views, helped determine the brutality of Wehrmacht actions against villages in Greece.[207]

German military behaviour towards civilians in the Second World War, for all its distinctiveness, was thus connected to the mythic franc-tireur war of 1914 by historical memory, individual experience, and military doctrine. Myth, however, at least in the form of the extraordinary collective delusion of 1914, was precisely one of the differences. Brutality against civilians in the opening phase of the First World War came from above and below. Panic-driven violence emerged from below due to the circumstances of combat, as well as to longer-term mentalities and cultural stereotypes, and was endorsed and generalized by express orders and military doctrine. Anti-partisan measures in the Second World War, by contrast, were carefully planned by Hitler and the army to ensure that violence and terror were used in a controlled fashion to subjugate civilian populations and eliminate resistance. As such, they were a structural part of the motivation and maintenance of discipline of the new German army.[208]

By the same token, the ubiquitous feeling of the invaded populations in 1914 that they had been unjustly held responsible for a resistance which, even if legal, was virtually non-existent had no parallel in the Second World War. Rather, the problem was the relationship between real resistance movements and the populations in whose name they claimed to act, but who often bore the brunt of reprisals. In the French case, however, those who resisted certainly owed something of their sense of legitimacy to the image of the franc-tireur of 1870, and through that to the 'People's War', the *levée en masse*. This was the myth at the heart of the political culture of Republicanism which expressed the state's right to call on the citizen to defend the nation, and which justified the patriot in taking up arms even in the absence of the Republic. The ideological impulse which had contributed in 1914 to the Allied, and especially the French, defence of the right to a spontaneous *levée en masse* was a strong element in the French Resistance of 1940–4.[209]

Indeed, two major Resistance groups were called after the francs-tireurs, the Communist organization Francs-Tireurs et Partisans, and the moderate Republican organization, Franc-Tireur. Among the members of the latter was none other than Marc Bloch. Frequent reference was made to the *levée en masse* and to the victorious battle of Valmy in 1792 against the Prussian army – an historical moment which fused the figure of the volunteer with Republican defence against the German enemy. As one poster on the walls of Paris in 1943 summed it up: '*La Patrie en Danger. 1792–1943. To Save France like our Great Ancestors the Volunteers of the Levée en Masse*'.[210] So ingrained was the reflex that a 'national insurrection' coinciding with the

Allied invasion of France became the guiding vision of many, especially the Communists.[211] De Gaulle likewise considered from 1942 that a 'national insurrection' was inseparable from 'national liberation'. Although the French military, the British and American governments, and more conservative elements of the Resistance, were sceptical, 'national insurrection' was duly declared to coincide with D-Day. In the face of furious German reprisals against the population, this was converted into a more limited military operation.[212] But what matters here is the reflex; many could not imagine the liberation of France without a *levée en masse* of the kind the Germans had mistakenly imagined they faced in 1914.

In Britain, which knew neither occupation nor resistance, the memory of the 'German atrocities' in 1914 related differently to the experience of the Second World War, though in ways that also reflected the duality of the original phenomenon as myth and event. The legacy of the pacifist turn resulted in widespread scepticism towards new reports of enemy atrocities. George Orwell commented in 1944 that the reaction against the 'German atrocities' of 1914 had made it more difficult to arouse opinion against 'fascist aggression' after 1933. '"Atrocities" had come to be looked on as synonymous with "lies"', he argued. 'The stories about the German concentration camps were atrocity stories: therefore they were lies — so reasoned the average man.'[213] Poignant support for Orwell's observation comes from Victor Gollancz, the left-wing Jewish publisher, who in 1942 issued a pamphlet to inform the public about the Nazi mass murder of the Jews. Before embarking on this vital task, Gollancz summarized at length the standard pacifist dismissal of atrocities as lies, stating that 'nothing is baser than "atrocity mongering" for its own sake, or, worse, for the sake of stirring up hatred against the enemy.' And he concluded that 'war is [...] one vast atrocity' and that punishing the enemy simply prepared for future wars.[214] Only after this elaborate disclaimer could Gollancz tell the news of the genocide which seemed to make both the war and punishment indispensable.

Orwell's argument applied not only to public opinion, but also to government. In 1942 the British and American governments received many reports confirming that the Nazis were engaged in mass extermination of civilians in eastern Europe, but they reacted with scepticism. The reluctance to believe the reports, and when they finally believed them, to publicize them, owed much to the conviction that German atrocities during the Great War had been grossly exaggerated by Allied propaganda and hence subsequently discredited.[215]

Yet as evidence piled up that the enemy was guilty not only of the new crime of 'genocide' but also of widespread war crimes under the Hague and Geneva conventions, the Allies began to prepare post-war criminal proceedings. This revived the language and precedent of the First World War. The Hague Convention on Land Warfare was invoked by the governments in exile in London in January 1942, when they collectively denounced the Nazis for 'terror characterized amongst other things by imprisonments, mass expulsions, the execution of hostages and massacres'.[216] Within a year, Roosevelt, Churchill, and Molotov signalled their intent to try German atrocities and war crimes by special tribunal. Although there was no agreement until summer 1945 on the form of what became the Nuremberg International Military Tribunal, the lesson of the Leipzig 'fiasco' of 1921 permeated the preparatory work.[217] The Allied leaders who established the United Nations Commission for the Investigation of War Crimes in October 1943 held that failure to convict German war criminals after 1919 'had undoubtedly sowed the seeds for ruthless disregard by the Nazis, two decades later, of accepted principles of international law governing the conduct of war'.[218] When the Nuremberg and other war crimes trials were finally held, the objections raised in 1919–21 against the status of international law, holding subordinates responsible, or the inequity of singling out enemy war crimes were dismissed. Justice was this time made firmly on the victors' terms.

Inevitably after 1945, in a world coming to terms with unprecedented war crimes, genocide, mass bombing of civilians, and nuclear weapons, the German atrocities of 1914 paled into relative insignificance. Yet their public memory did not completely die. Rather, it reflected the special relationship each country had with the First World War.

In Britain, the pacifist turn regained its predominance. If most Britons saw the Second World War as just and necessary, they subscribed to a more ambivalent view of the First World War as a testament to the tragedy of modern warfare, which propaganda had helped make possible.[219] The French were still conscious of having fought for survival in the First World War, symbolized by its veterans, but they now had a more recent and complex memory of invasion and suffering to come to terms with. It supplied its own imagery of martyrdom (e.g. Oradour) as well as redemption through the mythified history of the Resistance and de Gaulle.[220] The invasion of 1914 was once again reduced to at best a regional memory.[221]

Not suprisingly, the events of 1914 remained most controversial in Belgium and Germany. In Belgium, the more recent experience reinforced the earlier without supplanting it. In Germany, however, distancing the new Federal Republic from the 'exceptionality' of the Nazi period meant reasserting the respectability of the Second Reich. This gave the innocentist case on Germany's war aims and war conduct in 1914 continued political as well as historical relevance. None of this should be exaggerated. The actors were principally professional historians rather than diplomats and politicians. But the German atrocities of 1914 remained a potentially troubling issue in Belgian–German relations, despite partnership in NATO and economic co-operation.

Conscious of this, a meeting of Belgian and German historians in 1954 produced a set of recommendations for reconciling the opposed interpretations. German military conduct was explained by the unexpected resistance of the Belgian army and the 'psychosis of the franc-tireur war'; the German charge of organized, illegal civilian resistance was declared to be 'absolutely false'. This marked an important advance but still had its limitations as an accurate portrayal of events. The German franc-tireur thesis was equated with the false Belgian 'propaganda theses of particular German cruelties, such as the severed children's hands'. But the latter had never been defended by the Belgian authorities, whereas the German government had long propounded the franc-tireur argument against its own better knowledge. Moreover, German war crimes in 1914 were described as 'isolated excesses', thus ignoring their true extent.[222]

The impetus for a fresh examination came from Fernand Mayence. In 1955 he reported on the issue to the Belgian Royal Academy, referring to his personal experience of the sack of Louvain and his 1928 pamphlet. Mayence felt it important that Belgium's professional modern historians should condemn the 'historical fraud' of the German case before the amnesia, or at least silence, of the post-war decade consigned the matter to oblivion. To this end, he revived his 1931 proposal for a joint commission of Belgian and German historians, and approached Professor Franz Petri, cultural historian at the University of Münster, whom he had known since the early 1930s.[223] Petri had begun to work on the issue as a young historian in 1930–1, but after coming to the conclusion that the Belgian version of events in Andenne was probably correct, he declined to pursue it further for fear of jeopardizing his career. During the Second World War he was part of the German administration in Belgium responsible for the

'Germanization' of the universities. After 1945, he distanced himself from the ideology and practice of National Socialism, but found it hard to deal critically with his own role in the Nazi occupation.[224]

This makes his collaboration with Mayence all the more remarkable. For in 1956, the two men established a joint committee with three historians from each side. Mayence chose de Sturler and van der Essen (who had served on the Belgian War Crimes Commission during the Second World War, and testified at Nuremberg). Petri selected Rothfels and Conze.[225] Mayence had hoped that a joint declaration might resolve the matter quickly. Petri responded that a thorough scholarly study was necessary to enable his German colleagues to come to a reasoned judgement. He told Mayence and Conze that he had long been convinced that there had been no organized Belgian franc-tireur war, that no German publication (including the White Book and the 1927 Reichstag report) had provided evidence of this, and that German scholarship was honour-bound to renounce this thesis. Petri's standpoint differed from that of his Belgian colleague only in nuances. He interpreted the franc-tireur war as a 'tragic mistake of the German army' and not a deliberate lie, and he was not prepared to rule out the possibility of individual civilian resistance. Mayence reluctantly agreed to wait for the results of the planned study.[226]

Petri's research strategy was ingeniously simple, namely to investigate the reliability of the German White Book. He asked his young assistant, Peter Schöller, to undertake a study of Louvain. Possibly ill-health prevented Petri taking up the case of Andenne again, as he originally intended. Another researcher proved unable to carry out his work on Dinant. But the German half of the committee decided that Louvain by itself would suffice for the Belgian–German agreement.[227]

The entire initiative thus turned on Peter Schöller's study, *Der Fall Löwen* ('The Case of Louvain'), which was published simultaneously in German, Flemish, and French in 1958.[228] The key to Schöller's deconstruction of the White Book was the Ministry of War's internal draft on Louvain of January 1915, provided by Conze who inherited it from his father-in-law, who had worked for the Army Command in Hanover.[229] This allowed Schöller to expose the selection and suppression of evidence that made the White Book a cover-up for the real explanation – the franc-tireur myth and German military panic. Although he also showed that belief in an uprising was genuine, Schöller concluded that the violence of the German reaction would have been unjustified even if the attacks had been real. In effect, he overturned the official case defended since 1914 and achieved the German self-criticism that some in Germany had called for in the 1920s.

The reception of the book demonstrated the changed climate since the inter-war period. It was endorsed by all three German members of the joint committee. Conze, it is true, cavilled at the use of 'crime' (*Verbrechen*) to describe the reaction of German soldiers who genuinely believed themselves to have been ambushed, lest this should justify the war crimes Articles of the Versailles Treaty.[230] Rothfels's signature was especially important, however, not only because he was chairman of the newly founded Institute for Contemporary History, Munich, and of the powerful Association of German Historians from 1958 to 1962, but also because he had been a volunteer in 1914 and was one of several nationalist historians prominent in the anti-Versailles campaign in the 1920s.[231] Petri, in his introductory essay, wrote that 'the previous German version of the events of August [1914] in Belgium should no longer be disseminated', and he concluded with an apology to Louvain and its inhabitants.[232] No less significantly, the three Belgian committee members found the study 'so complete' they had nothing to add or change.[233] Schöller's study thus represented a consensus by professional historians on the sack of Louvain. Broadly favourable scholarly reception of the book, in Germany and abroad, underlined the point.[234]

Schöller's work gained wider public recognition and provided the occasion for political reconciliation. It was generally welcomed by the German as well as the Belgian press, and received benevolent radio commentary in Frankfurt and Bavaria.[235] Mindful, no doubt, that the stain of 'cultural atrocity' was unhelpful to German foreign policy, the leading political figures of the Federal Republic embraced the book. Chancellor Adenauer (who, with Robert Schuman, had been awarded an honorary degree in Louvain early in 1958) informed Petri and Schöller that he had read it with interest, and found it proof that 'historical scholarship in the service of the truth is able to contribute to understanding between peoples.' The Foreign Minister, Heinrich von Brentano, and Federal President Heuß sent similar letters.[236] On 6 May 1958, the German members of the joint committee, together with Schöller, were guests of honour at a reception in Louvain. Thielemans, the burgomaster and deputy for Louvain, welcomed the committee's work as 'moral reparation' for the franc-tireur calumny.[237] Petri and Schöller were presented with plaques by the university the following day, and Mayence subsequently wrote to Schöller that: 'You have given me, in the evening of my life, the incomparable satisfaction of seeing that my efforts of more than 40 years have not been in vain, and that the total truth has at last been acknowledged. For this I thank you warmly.'[238]

Yet it would be wrong to suggest that Schöller's book exorcized the ghost of the German atrocities in 1914. Most obviously, the scope of the study restricted its import. There was no attempt to gauge the real dimensions of the franc-tireur myth and the German response. And while Schöller was sensitive to the mythic and cultural, as well as circumstantial, causes of the German delusion, he did not discuss army orders and the chain of responsibilities.[239] Petri pointed to a paradox whereby the mere allegation of civilian resistance was felt to be a lying insult in 1914 but was openly espoused as a principle by the Belgian Resistance in 1940–5.[240] Two basic questions, the legitimacy of resistance, and of the repression practised in 1914, remained unresolved. The Belgian–German committee achieved consensus via the lowest common denominator – that of condemnation of an illusion based on panic which fuelled an undisciplined overreaction.

This makes it surprising that in the more abrasive atmosphere of the 1960s, with its probing questions about the German past, the German atrocities of 1914 did not resurface. The conservative historian Gerhard Ritter, who had fought in the First World War, dismissed the issue with a footnote in his massive work on German militarism.[241] Fritz Fischer, the Hamburg historian who controversially reopened the question of German war guilt in 1914, and with it the deeper connections between the *Kaiserreich* and National Socialism, deliberately avoided the related issue of German military conduct towards civilians which he judged to be still deeply divisive.[242] Despite more recent studies on specific aspects of the question, the consensus of the German innocentist campaign of the 1920s has not been reversed in the reference literature in Germany.[243] In the 1970s, West German schoolbooks still spoke of the executions of the citizens of Louvain as 'Belgian war propaganda'.[244] The most authoritative German encyclopaedia, *Brockhaus*, maintained in its 1996 edition that *Franktireurs* were irregular fighters against the Germans in France in 1870–1 and again in Belgium and France in 1914; yet its references to the destruction of Louvain and Dinant contained no mention of mass executions. Thomas Nipperdey's acclaimed history of the Wilhelmine Empire depicts the invasion of Belgium in 1914 in a way that recalls the discredited White Book of 1915: Belgian francs-tireurs were the cause of 'nervousness' among the German troops, who reacted 'sometimes with unplanned severity'; 'Small incidents [...] and war damage to cultural monuments' were inflated by Allied propaganda into 'Hun barbarities' and 'German atrocities'.[245]

If Schöller's conclusions have not revised broader German historical understanding of the 1914 invasion of France and Belgium, they were too radical for many veterans. In fact, Schöller received hostile and approving letters from former soldiers in equal measure. But the critics were a vocal lobby and the language was often vituperative.[246] One expressed his regret that the historian had not been on the receiving end of the ambush in Louvain ('You might well have got a pot of boiling water poured over your faker's brain or a shotgun blast in your faker's breast'), and informed him that in his own squadron, an officer and 12 men had been found in a barn with their throats cut. He concluded by dismissing Schöller as 'the shabbiest professor I have ever encountered [...] Only professors in today's democracy could be so degenerate.'[247] Kiel, home of the former IXth Reserve Corps which had been involved in Louvain, was a centre of criticism by veterans.[248] Likewise, a former NCO in IR 162, which came from Lübeck and had been stationed in Louvain, wrote a bitter review which cited soldiers' letters published in the Lübeck press in 1914, all of them affirming that there had been a civilian ambush.[249]

Other hostile comment came from the *Deutsche Soldatenzeitung*, a military paper which, without having seen Schöller's book, claimed the author had 'rehabilitated the Belgian francs-tireurs and defamed the German soldiers of 1914'. Why, it asked, was there any need to reopen the question which had been clarified adequately by the White Book and the Reichstag investigation of 1927? Schöller's most persistent critic was Johann Kühl, from Kiel, who denounced Schöller as a 'notorious liar' and later issued a brochure disputing his arguments.[250] Overall, the hostile veterans' reaction is best understood as the last collective breath of the original franc-tireur delusion, and as an expression of loyalty to the 'honour' of the old army.

Conversely, the restrictive focus of the committee of Belgian and German historians left intact much of the local Belgian memory of the German atrocities in 1914. The ceremony of reconciliation at Louvain in May 1958 remained unique. Elsewhere, the original feelings of victimhood at German hands and outrage at the German refusal to acknowledge wrongdoing have persisted, in attenuated form, to the present. In Aarschot, for example, a chapel was built in 1964 alongside an earlier monument at the site of the collective execution in which the burgomaster, Tielemans, and his brother and son died. It bears the inscription in Flemish: 'We have pardoned the guilty: the victims we do not forget.' The memory of the executions is preserved by statues, school projects, and an annual commemorative mass. Much of this collective memory has been sustained by the efforts of a Catholic priest, Father Jozef De Vroey, who was an infant when his father was executed in August 1914, and who published a history to coincide with the inauguration of the new chapel on the fiftieth anniversary of the events.[251]

Likewise in Dinant, the events of 1914 continue to be marked with a mass every 23 August. The celebrants have been closely connected with the destruction of the town, including notably Mgr Himmer, Bishop of Tournai and grandson of the manager of the cloth factory in Leffe who was shot in 1914, and Canon Albert Herbecq, who with his brother Eugène (also a priest), witnessed the events as children and saw their father narrowly escape execution. The homilies delivered in the 1980s and 1990s on this occasion carried the same message: the perpetrators of the crimes of August 1914 are forgiven, but witness must continually be borne to the events so long as the innocence of the victims goes unacknowledged.[252] This, too, is a distant expression of the trauma and outrage of the civilian victims in 1914.

Memories of 1914 have proved as fiercely contested as the events themselves. Bolstered by the official denial represented by the White Book and the inter-war campaign against the Versailles war crimes Articles, the franc-tireur complex constituted the official German record of the events, which had important consequences for the German treatment of civilians in the Second World War. The intervention by professional historians after 1945 to discredit the official thesis in the case of Louvain, significant though it was, did not result in a reassessment of the history of the German atrocities in 1914, nor could it dislodge the continued belief by some veterans in the original franc-tireur myth. In fact, the historical debate on the connections between the Second and Third Reichs starting in the early 1960s carefully avoided the issue of German military doctrine and conduct towards civilians.

Condemnation of the 'German atrocities' in the Allied countries during the Great War gave way to scepticism and denial in the inter-war period owing to changes in the retrospective meaning attributed to the war as a whole. The imaginary and mythic dimension which had always been there on the Allied side became the principal explanation once the 'German atrocities' were reinterpreted by many as largely Allied propaganda. This belief was only partially and temporarily reversed during the Second World War when the planning of war crimes proceedings raised the precedent of the earlier conflict. Even in Belgium, the experience of the German atrocities became an essentially local memory. The memories of the German atrocities have remained, for the lifetime of those involved, unreconciled.

Conclusion and perspectives

This study has focused on the events which occurred during the German invasion of France and Belgium in 1914 and which rapidly acquired the label of 'German atrocities' on one side, although the Germans thought of them as an illegitimate 'People's War' which justified a harsh response. For the first time, the evidence from both sides has been examined, and we have confirmed the wartime official estimates that some 6,500 civilians were killed in Belgium and France from August to October 1914. There were other incidents during the First World War which may be classified as atrocities or which were felt to be so at the time, but the nature of the atrocities of 1914 and the controversy they aroused make them a distinct historical phenomenon.

The conflict between the two incompatible atrocity accusations and their mutual denial by each side has been resolved. The Great Fear which swept through the invading German armies took the form of a collective delusion that enemy civilians were engaged in massive resistance in a franc-tireur war. The combination of the trauma of combat with ideological and cultural predispositions – the expectation of a *levée en masse* on the pattern of 1870 and the paranoid world-view of a great part of the officer corps – generated this myth-complex. The delusion developed such force that it persuaded one million men of the reality of a chimera.

We can state categorically that there was neither collective civilian resistance nor military action by franc-tireur units as in 1870–1. There were a few isolated cases of individual civilians firing on Germans, but none of these incidents provoked mass executions such as those of Dinant, Louvain, or Liège in Belgium, and Nomény, Longuyon, and Haybes in France. The subsequent explanation offered by German innocentist literature in the 1920s that the Belgian Garde Civique was at the root of the perceived

[handwritten marginal note:] Do they prove their case conclusively?

right / wrong
legal / illegal

franc-tireur incidents concerns only a minority of cases. In itself, this did nothing to exonerate the German army, for the participation of such a civilian militia, to the extent that it occurred, was self-evidently legal, no surprise to the German army leadership, and should not have occasioned reprisals on non-combatants. In fact, most German atrocities took place where no Garde Civique was involved, and the Germans did not even claim that it existed in France.

The German response to imagined enemy atrocities in 1914 cannot be explained exclusively by reference to circumstance, myth, and cultural predisposition. While violence against civilians before 18 August came largely from the autonomous action of troops in the field, the main invasion was characterized by orders given by the OHL and army commanders to expect civilian resistance and impose collective penalties in which the 'innocent' would suffer with the 'guilty'. Many German soldiers admitted, at least in their private letters and diaries, that atrocities were being ordered. Undoubtedly the calculation of the German supreme command and government was analogous to those on war finance: just as the costs of the war would be extracted from Germany's defeated and occupied enemies, the principle 'might is right' would expunge war crimes from the historical record. The full expression of doubts that surfaced inside Germany during the war among soldiers, Catholics, Socialists, intellectuals, and extending even to the Chancellor and his closest advisers, therefore had to be resisted in order to maintain a united front in response to the Allied propaganda campaign. The results of Peter Schöller's pioneering work on Louvain can be confirmed: the White Book of 1915 was a product of Foreign Ministry manipulation, not only on Louvain, but in its entirety, containing distorted witness evidence and omitting all statements by German soldiers or Belgian civilians that endangered the official German construction of the 'franc-tireur war'.

Of course, modern war and the violence of invasion were traumatic to both sides, and French and Belgian civilians and retreating Allied soldiers displayed mythologizing tendencies of their own. Rumours spread by soldiers and civilians and the hysterical reaction of refugees from the war zone produced an atrocity fear which caused the mass flight of hundreds of thousands in 1914. Although Allied governments were quick to use the opportunities presented by the enemy's way of warfare to mobilize opinion at home and in neutral countries, it was mainly unofficial and informal sources, not officialdom, which disseminated lurid and sensationalist propaganda. Much of this had its origin in the mythic accounts of trauma-tized witnesses. But Allied myths and propaganda responded to the reality of the brutal German repression of an imagined People's War. This created the basic difference in the way the 'atrocities' issue gave meaning to the war and helped shape its memories on the two sides.

For all the distinctiveness of the German atrocities of 1914, a set of perspectives has been opened up in the course of this study which relates the phenomenon to broader questions. Those questions in turn help define the full meaning and significance of the events of 1914. The first such perspective is provided by the relationship between armies and enemy civilians.

Fear of civilians and brutality towards them were not confined to the German army. The unexpected chaos of war as vast armies criss-crossed frontiers in eastern and western Europe resulted in violence against civil-ians in various places in 1914–15. However, the comparison with other invasions, though limited by the inadequacy of current research, has revealed that the violence was greater in Belgium and France than else-where (excluding the very different cases of Turkish Armenia and the Russian retreat of 1915), partly because the fantasy of civilian resistance was so intense and widespread, and partly because German army policy soon transformed spontaneous local responses into something that was more than indiscipline.

The source of this particular attitude and doctrine is to be found in the long-term hostility of the Prusso-German armies to the involvement of irregular civilian levies in warfare. No army likes to be preyed on by guer-rillas. But the German response went beyond the experience and memory of the Franco-Prussian war.[1] The reaction was rooted in a deep ideological aversion to the politicized citizen who viewed warfare as an extension of politics, or worse, of revolution. This was especially so for the German elites, which, after the wars of unification, saw an army rooted by short-term conscription in the nation, and officered by upper-class professionals, as a curb on democracy and a guarantee against revolution. Partisan warfare in this perspective was subversion. Hence it was not accidental, or merely circumstantial, that the German military should have created a collective fantasy in 1914 of one of its own worst fears.[2]

This attitude remained firm during the inter-war period. This is shown by the Reichswehr's defence of the German response in 1914 as a matter of honour, despite the fact that the senior military hierarchy was simultaneously giving consideration to a radical plan during Weimar for a doomsday defence of Germany from invasion by all-out civilian resistance. After conventional rearmament this idea only re-emerged in the dying days of the Second World War, with the creation of the *Volkssturm*, which explicitly referred to the precedent of 1813.[3] Prior to that, the army, and above all Hitler, still preferred to think of resolving Germany's problems on foreign soil through invasion by a sophisticated conscript army firmly under professional control. Not surprisingly, the fear of civilian resistance resurfaced, with similar responses. This time there was no franc-tireur fantasy. Indeed, still convinced that the Allies had brilliantly twisted legitimate German reactions in 1914 into anti-German propaganda, the Nazi and military leaderships took considerable care during the invasion of the Low Countries and France in 1940 not to offer such hostages to fortune again. But once irregular resistance emerged to occupation in western and southern Europe, the response was recognizably related to that of 1870 and 1914. Anti-partisan warfare on the eastern front, however, while beginning within traditional, 1914-style categories, was soon radicalized and transformed into a part of the Nazi war of racial conquest.

None of this means that the German army is the only one to have treated civilians as the enemy or to have wreaked vengeance on a vulnerable population considered to be the source of military resistance. The Germans themselves, when seeking historical parallels for their actions in 1914 to use against the Allies, turned to the American Civil War and the South African War, 1899–1902.[4] In both cases, civilian irregulars were used by the side operating on home territory. In both, the invading army engaged in collective reprisals against innocent civilians. Confederate guerrillas in Missouri were met with brutal semi-official retaliation by Union forces.[5] In response to the illegality of the rebellion as a whole, Sherman in late 1864 to early 1865 pursued a scorched earth policy through Georgia and especially South Carolina, though property rather than civilian lives was the target. Sheridan likewise laid waste the Shenandoah Valley.[6] In South Africa, the British used terror against Boer guerrilla resistance in 1900–2, with the systematic burning of farmhouses, though not the execution of civilians, and the deportation of women and children to camps. Deaths in the latter were due to mismanagement rather than policy, however, and resulted in an outcry in Britain.[7]

In effect, civil and colonial wars in the nineteenth and twentieth centuries are two arenas which have been prolific in brutality between *inevitably, huh?*

soldiers and civilians. Civil wars, by their very nature, break down the distinction between combatant and non-combatant, leading to the targeting of the civilian population, although precisely this tendency led to the first code of military conduct, the Lieber Code of 1863 drawn up by the Union in the American Civil War. The more ideological civil wars become, the more easily the distinction between soldier and civilian vanishes, so that the Russian Civil War of 1918–20 and the Spanish Civil War both witnessed massacres of civilians on a considerable scale – though possibly not with the intensity of what occurred within a fortnight in Belgium and France in the second half of August 1914.[8] The Irish War of Independence, which for the British was a cross between a civil rebellion and a colonial war, likewise resulted in licensed terror by police and army against the civilian population.

Even more devastating for civilians than civil wars were the European colonial wars, especially those against indigenous peoples. Echoes of this reality invested the events of 1914 in various ways, with the Belgians discovering as a symbol of their own victimization the 'severed hands' which they stood accused of using as punishment in the Congo, the Germans condemning the British and French for using 'savage' colonial troops, and Belgian or French civilians occasionally comparing their treatment by the invaders with German colonial warfare. All European powers in the nineteenth and early twentieth centuries practised ferocious repression of colonized peoples through one-sided warfare and by massacring civilians. The Germans took the palm, with their genocidal war against the Herero and Nama of German South-West Africa in 1904–7. But the British also waged war in a brutal manner in the Sudan and in Nigeria.[9] Military and paramilitary forces in the United States and Australia massacred indigenous populations on a substantial scale.[10]

Yet the point for contemporaries was that 1914 was not a civil or colonial war, but a conflict between European states, indeed between those 'great world-dominating nations of white race', as Freud called them, which prided themselves on constituting civilization and which had been expected to find 'another way of settling misunderstandings and conflicts of interest'.[11] Here, the distinction between combatant and non-combatant was meant to be at its clearest and the assumption that warfare was in some measure rule-bound and subject to codes of morality most developed. Paradoxically, the fundamental conflict of interpretation in 1914 stemmed from this shared assumption. For by the German military's understanding

(margin note: how defensible is the German position?)

of the 'laws and customs of war', uncontrolled civilian participation in fighting was the height of barbarity, recalling as it did both the savagery of the colonial sphere or backward regions of Europe and also the advanced tendency to the politicization of warfare. Conversely, in Allied eyes, the German reluctance to recognize the right of a population to a *levée en masse* and the harsh imposition of collective reprisals equally represented barbarity and the breach of international law.

How absolute was this difference of view is impossible to say. No counterfactual analysis allows us to assert, as some have implied, that the British or French armies would have responded in the same manner as the Germans in 1914 faced with the same provocation.[12] The fact that the provocation was illusory itself suggests the power of particular mentalities and predispositions on the part of the German military hierarchy which combined a fear of Clausewitz's own observation on the increased involvement of the people in warfare with a Clausewitzian commitment to using the most ruthless means needed to win victory.[13] It is entirely possible that in the supercharged atmosphere of August 1914 a French invasion of Germany such as that envisaged in Plan XVII, encountering civilian harassment, would have resulted in violent responses. But would French commanders have used human shields in combat? Would General Joffre have declared it policy that villages should be burned in collective reprisal for resistance and that local irregulars bearing arms should be shot, as did General von Bülow within five days of the war beginning? More significantly, would French political leaders have endorsed such actions? Would President Poincaré have condemned the enemy government in front of the world for fomenting a *levée en masse*, as did the Kaiser? The differences in past experience and mentality suggest not, since the demonology of the 'People's War' (in the European theatre at least) did not have the same potency for these armies and states. But we cannot be sure.

(margin note: what if the roles were reversed?)

This reverse case, however, did not occur, whereas German military harshness did, and it constituted a powerful negative example for the Allies. The distinctions that we are making should in no way be understood as essentialist. They were conditioned by particular historical developments, such as the role and influence of the military within the conservative political culture of Imperial Germany and the significance of European land warfare for German politics between 1870 and 1945. Later, in the 1950s, the French army demonstrated that it was capable of sustained brutality against civilians in the face of irregular warfare in Algeria. For the French, this conflict was a mixture of civil insurrection, colonial war, and Communist plot, somewhat like the Irish War of Independence for Britain, though on a vaster scale. Here, too, there was domestic dissent.[14]

All this suggests a second perspective on the German atrocities of 1914 which is that of the legal norms of war between sovereign states. It would be easy to dismiss these as a nineteenth-century illusion faced with the harsh realities of twentieth-century warfare. But the 1907 Hague Convention on Land Warfare was clearly an article of faith for much of educated opinion in the Allied countries, and it deeply troubled the defence conducted by the German establishment in the later 1920s. The Geneva Convention of 1906 on the treatment of enemy soldiers was broadly accepted by all parties. Despite the Stenger case, there is no evidence of a German military policy of shooting captured enemy soldiers, though the practice came to be quite widespread on both sides. Yet over the treatment of civilians in the event of irregular or guerrilla resistance, there was a sharp clash of views.

However much the German approach may have been based on an old-fashioned dislike of citizens involving themselves in combat (other than as docile conscripts), its effect was to reduce the distinction between combat-ant and non-combatant without which the laws of war lose much of their point. Of course, adequate 'rules of engagement' (as the American army dubbed them in Vietnam) may present real difficulties when conventional armies face partisans embedded in a local population.[15] But German mili-tary doctrine in 1914 refused to recognize the problem whereas the Hague Convention on Land Warfare at least gave a partial answer. The Allies never ceased pointing out that even if the German illusion of a franc-tireur war had been a reality, the response would still have been unjustified and largely illegal. Whatever else Articles 228–30 of the Treaty of Versailles and the fiasco of Leipzig achieved, they embodied that argument. The hyper-sensitivity of the German military to the accusation of wrongdoing in 1914 reaffirmed its doctrine of the illegality of enemy irregular warfare during Weimar. This provided one strand of its descent into lawlessness and barbarity during the Third Reich.

Conversely, the preservation of the notion of international law in war was an important concern of the Allies in 1939–45, in spite of all the problems presented by waging total war against a totalitarian foe. This was reflected not only in the Nuremberg tribunal and the construction of the new legal category of genocide, but also by war crimes trials for German (and

Japanese) brutality towards enemy servicemen and civilians on grounds comparable to those of 1914. Like proceedings after the First World War, these represented victors' justice inasmuch as potential cases of Allied crimes (such as British area bombing) were not entertained. They were similarly curtailed by a changing international conjuncture – in this case, the onset of the Cold War.[16] Nonetheless, the impulse to regulate the tumultuous experience of the previous decade led to the rewriting of the international law of war in 1949, with four new Geneva conventions, and in no area more controversially so than that of military conduct towards civilian resisters and non-combatants. If military establishments in the victor powers (notably Britain) were wary of tipping the balance too much in favour of guerrilla warfare, former occupied countries with resistance movements succeeded in getting the Hague definition of acceptable civilian participation in combat extended from invasions to occupations. The Convention on the Protection of Civilian Persons in Time of War so defined the rights of inhabitants of invaded and occupied territory as to outlaw explicitly almost all the acts which the German armies committed in 1914, including pillage and hostage-taking.[17]

How this legal redefinition of relations between soldiers and civilians worked out in the subsequent 50 years, so often characterized by implacable guerrilla warfare and ferocious responses by conventional forces (as in Algeria and Vietnam), is beyond our scope. It marks precisely the point at which colonial and post-colonial conflicts were brought into the purview of international law.[18] But the point is that after the climactic confrontation of national armies in the mid-twentieth century, international law was deemed more, not less, relevant to regulating war. Events in the former Yugoslavia and Rwanda in the 1990s, including the establishment of international tribunals to try crimes against humanity, whether genocide, 'ethnic cleansing', or military massacres of civilians, lent fresh relevance to international law on war. Conflict over the German atrocities of 1914, in this perspective, was part of an enduring attempt to submit war to legal and moral norms.

A very different, third, perspective on those same events is provided by the complex of irrational responses – fear, hatred, myth, hysteria – which played a central role on both sides. Faith in rationality may not have been so characteristic a feature of bourgeois culture before 1914 as is sometimes supposed. Fascination with violence and irrationality was increasingly insistent in art, thought, and politics.[19] The war itself, which was organized

[margin handwriting: issue less about proper conduct, more about immorality of war]

according to the norms of modern bureaucratic rationality, conjured up collective passions and irrationality on a devastating scale. The fixation with atrocities by both sides was part of this development. From one angle, the parallel myth-complexes of the *Franktireurkrieg* and 'severed hands' can be interpreted as discrete examples of the kind of false rumour, hysteria, and panic which occur in a variety of settings, from wars to stock markets, and which have been studied by social psychologists and sociologists.[20] The exaggeration of German and Allied witness evidence in 1914–15 may also be understood in terms of the phenomenon of invented or symbolic memory, which has been highlighted by current concern with childhood trauma. But while both viewpoints help in understanding how myth-complexes operate, they tell us little about their historical origins or significance.

Here, the work of early modern historians, who necessarily grapple with mentalities which are very different from their own, has shown the way in exploring the insights that Marc Bloch drew from his experience in the Great War on the relationship between 'false rumours', myths, and underlying cultural patterns, or mentalities. As we have suggested in chapter 3, Georges Lefebvre's book on the Great Fear of 1789 was a pioneering study. The history of religious belief (especially of the seventeenth-century witch craze), and of early modern popular culture more generally, has important lessons to offer. For it suggests among other things that there is no hard and fast line between 'popular' and 'elite' responses (both may share and even jointly generate hysteria and myth), that the printed word (books, pamphlets, newspapers) may well play a crucial role in amplifying and disseminating myths, which cannot therefore be seen as belonging in a purely oral domain, and that legal or quasi-legal proceedings help fix myths as official narratives – or do just the opposite. All these points apply equally to the contemporary period.

More important still, it is clear that underlying mentalities and the collective energies linked to these provide a vital medium in which myths and other kinds of collective self-suggestion become substantive historical phenomena, with a capacity to shape actions and events. It is because ephemeral myths draw on more enduring reservoirs of symbolism that they are capable of momentarily condensing meaning. What is true of the largely religious cultures of the early modern period is no less true of the largely secularized cultures of the twentieth century, though since this is our world it may be harder for us to see it. The national and ideological beliefs which drove the two world wars in Europe, and which made them 'total' conflicts at the level of the collective imaginings of the societies concerned, generated the categories of antagonism from which atrocity myths were fashioned.[21] In this process, collective hysteria, rumour, and mythic fantasy were not the opposite of the organizational rationality of the military or the state, nor merely the raw material of calculating propagandists who rationally manipulated the passions of the masses. They were part of the bureaucratic process and integral to the propaganda.

Nothing illustrates this better than the role of the German military command structure in generating the collective fantasy of the francs-tireurs of 1914 and in organizing a response which provided a paradoxical justification for the sweeping Allied categorization of German 'frightfulness'. But the German atrocities of 1914 were also part of a wider phenomenon – namely, the tendency for atrocities to be committed against those who have been predefined as atrocious. The victims, in other words, have first to be imagined as actual or potential perpetrators. The demonization of the enemy by a variety of secular myths and fantasies, and the baneful consequences of this when translated not simply into spontaneous irrationality but into the orchestrated actions of immensely powerful organizational structures, bedevilled twentieth-century Europe. In this sense, the capacity for atrocity is deeply inscribed in modern society and the German atrocities of 1914 are merely a fragment of a much larger picture.[22]

This tendency of course has its antidote in a clearer understanding of how atrocities are imaginatively constructed, as well as committed. Romain Rolland was groping for precisely this when, without dismissing the reality of the brutalities that were occurring (in the manner of George Bernard Shaw), he appealed for an end to the self-mobilization of intellectuals behind the war and a return to a critical, and self-critical, stance. The inter-war tendency to dismiss the 'German atrocities' question as manipulative Allied propaganda was not helpful in this regard. The unravelling of the processes by which 'atrocities', real or invented, are used to designate an enemy and manipulated in conscious and half-conscious ways is by no means a developed reflex among journalists and commentators even now, as coverage of the wars in former Yugoslavia has demonstrated.[23]

A fourth perspective on the events of 1914 is provided by the subsequent memories of them. There was no monolithic collective memory in the case of either Germany or the former Allied countries. Memories differed with particular groups and evolved over time. The major shift was undoubtedly what we have called the 'pacifist turn', in which the retrospective reaction in the victor societies against the overwhelming human cost of the war favoured the reinterpretation of German atrocities as Allied propaganda. Liberals and socialists in particular, whose vision of a pacific and open diplomacy was premised on rational and democratic peoples, found the propaganda thesis a useful scapegoat for the manifestly violent and impassioned conduct of those same peoples during the war. As well as producing an unholy alliance of views with German nationalists, this had the effect of reducing the events of 1914 to a regional memory.

If the memories were multiple, so too was the nature of the war. The meaning which contemporary home front opinion gave the war was substantially determined by its opening phase. While the conflict lasted, the circumstances of its outbreak and the initial experience of actual or potential violation – personal, local, and national – provided much of the justification for fighting and shaped attitudes to the eventual peace. For the western powers in particular, invasion stood at the heart of the war experience, directly for Belgium and France, vicariously for Britain and later America. 'German atrocities' acquired much of their emotive and mythic force because they distilled this larger preoccupation. The shadow of invasion also haunted the German soldier through his fear of the franc-tireur and inhered in the myths and memories of the brief Russian incursion of August 1914 into East Prussia.

Retrospectively, however, the 'fictive communities' of mourning which proliferated in all the former combatant societies sought to come to terms not with this opening phase but with the overwhelming military experience of industrialized trench warfare.[24] Allied opinion was freed by victory to confront the question of whether the outcome was worth this price. Inevitably the German atrocities, as a signifier of the trauma of 1914 which pointed to the absolute necessity of the subsequent four and a half years' slaughter, were obscured by this dominant memory except in the regions concerned. It was as if two frameworks of remembrance existed, which could not be reconciled easily or even at all. This was most painfully obvious in Belgium, where regional memory increasingly clashed with the logic of national self-preservation through an accommodation with Germany. In France, and even more in Britain or America, the German atrocities of 1914 faded with the significance of the invasions they incarnated. In Germany, paradoxically, invasion came with the peace, with the occupation of the Rhineland. This revived the view that the atrocities question was an Allied fabrication and a double injustice, by reference to post-war events as well as to 1914. The memory of the German atrocities thus acquired its full resonance from the shifting experience of invasion on the two sides. In this sense, it was related to a central aspect of European war in the twentieth century, but one which was far more widely characteristic, and symbolic, of the Second World War than the First.

One final perspective requires comment. Central to this study has been the view that 'atrocities' are a culturally constructed and historically determined category.[25] This is clearly shown by the opposed ideas which Germans and Allies had about the same set of events in August–October 1914. The discord sprang partly from different views of what had happened, but even more from divergent views on what both sides agreed had happened – namely, collective reprisals carried out by the German army. These were undoubtedly war crimes by reference to the prevailing legal yardstick, the 1907 Hague Convention on Land Warfare, which Germany had signed, and which was the direct ancestor of the current legal norm enshrined in the 1977 Additional Protocols to the Geneva Conventions of 1949. However, by its own institutional memory and conventions the German army considered the real atrocity to be mass civilian resistance. Hence, there is nothing absolute or immutable about a term such as 'atrocities' or even 'war crimes'.

More significant than the issue of relative meaning, however, is that of proportionality. Why should we be concerned with what, after all, were only 6,500 civilian deaths and the destruction of 20,000 buildings in the light of all that has happened since? In what sense by our moral measure at the turn of the twentieth century were these 'atrocities', or even significant war crimes, at all?

The answer to these questions lies in the importance of the moral measure itself.[26] It would be unfair to dismiss those who condemned German atrocities in 1914 as merely naïve, deluded, or guilty of more than the normal quota of human inconsistency. By the standards of the time, the events were deeply shocking to broad sections of opinion in Allied countries, as indeed the same events, misunderstood by opinion in Germany, were considered shocking there for different reasons. The sense of shock in both cases reflected the encounter of pre-war sensibilities with the violence and destructiveness unleashed by the German invasion. The shock looked both forward and back. It involved revulsion at events (real and presumed) which was rooted in pre-war standards of 'civilized' behaviour and in the attempt to apply these standards as legal norms. Yet it also sought a new language to describe the conflict, whose violence and exaggeration on both sides (ferocious francs-tireurs, barbarous German soldiers) was itself part of the 'brutalization' of political life and everyday experience brought about by the war.[27] Ultimately, the conflict between Germany and the Allies over the events of 1914 was about the boundaries between soldier and civilian, and about the norms and purpose of military force in a rapidly changing world — in short, about the moral yardstick of atrocity itself. If we look back with a different scale of atrociousness, we should recognize that this scale has its own history to which, for the reasons explained in this book, the German atrocities of 1914 belong.

Appendices

Appendix 1 German atrocities in 1914: incidents with ten or more civilians killed. For abbreviations, see Note, pp. 440–1

Key date	Place	Province/ department	Civilians killed	Buildings destroyed	Combat related	Panic	Human shield	Deportations	German units
5 Aug.	Berneau	Liège (B)	10	80	no	yes	no	no	IR25, IR89, IR90. Possibly Cav. Div. 2 or 4
5 Aug.	Micheroux	Liège (B)	11	24	yes	yes	no	no	IR27, IR165
5 Aug.	Poulseur	Liège (B)	13	25	yes	yes	yes	no	IR82, IR83; IR73 & 74 (possibly Kür. 6)
5 Aug.	Soumagne	Liège (B)	118	101	yes	no	yes	no	IR27 (IR165 not confirmed)
6 Aug.	Battice	Liège (B)	33	147	yes	yes	no	no	IR16, IR165
6 Aug.	Blégny-Trembleur	Liège (B)	19	46	yes	no	no	no	IR16
6 Aug.	Esneux	Liège (B)	20	25	no	yes	no	no	IR73, IR74. Perhaps also IR82 & IR83
6 Aug.	Hermée	Liège (B)	11	149	yes	no	no	no	IR89, IR90. Jäg. Batl. 7 & 9
6 Aug.	Sprimont	Liège (B)	40	60	yes	no	no	no	IR73, IR74. Possibly D19
6 Aug.	Magnée	Liège (B)	17	14	yes	no	no	no	IR20, IR35. Field Art. 39
6 Aug.	Olne-St Hadelin	Liège (B)	64	46	yes	yes	yes	no	IR20, IR35. Field Art. 39
6 Aug.	Retinne	Liège (B)	40	18	yes	yes	yes	no	IR27, IR165. Perhaps also IR16, IR153
6 Aug.	Romsée	Liège (B)	27	40	yes	yes	yes	no	IR35, IR20
6 Aug.	Warsage	Liège (B)	14	25	no	yes	no	no	IR89, IR90
7 Aug.	Herstal	Liège (B)	27	10	yes	no	no	no	IR89, IR90
7 Aug.	Lixhe	Liège (B)	11	9	no	no	no	no	IR90. Probably IR89
7 Aug.	Louveigné	Liège (B)	28	77	no	no	no	no	IR73. Perhaps IR82 & IR83 but not confirmed
8 Aug.	Baelen	Liège (B)	16	8	no	yes	no	no	Perhaps IR35 & IR20; IR13 & IR158 are unlikely, but possible
8 Aug.	Francorchamps	Liège (B)	14	25	yes	yes	no	no	IR74. Possibly also IR39 & IR56
8 Aug.	Herve	Liège (B)	38	300	no	no	no	no	Possibly IR39, IR165, or Hus 10
8 Aug.	Melen	Liège (B)	108	60	yes	no	no	no	IR56, IR165 when 11 were killed on 6 August; possibly present on 8 August

Key date	Place	Province/ department	Civilians killed	Buildings destroyed	Combat related	Panic	Human shield	Deportations	German units
9 Aug.	St Truiden	Limburg (B)	21	?	no	no	no	no	Leib-Hus.-Brig.
10 Aug.	Linsmeau	Brabant (B)	18	7	yes	no	no	no	Units of IInd Cav. Corps
10 Aug.	Jarny	Meurthe-et-Moselle (F)	15	?	no	no	no	no	Unknown
11 Aug.	Bazailles	Meurthe-et-Moselle (F)	25	45	yes	no	no	no	D25
12 Aug.	Badonviller	Meurthe-et-Moselle (F)	10	85	yes	no	no	no	BIR1, BIR 2, BIR 16, BILWR
14 Aug.	Barchon	Liège (B)	32	110	no	yes	no	no	IR85 probably; IR165 is unlikely
15 Aug.	Wandre	Liège (B)	31	15	no	no	no	no	IR16, IR53, Field Art. 26
16 Aug.	Visé	Liège (B)	23	600	no	yes	no	yes	IR52, IR75, P(Königsberg), Cav.
18 Aug.	Haccourt	Liège (B)	16	80	no	yes	no	no	U9, IR73
18 Aug.	Heure-le-Romain	Liège (B)	28	83	no	yes	no	no	IR73
18 Aug.	Schaffen	Brabant (B)	23	175	yes	no	no	no	IR49, IR149
18 Aug.	Tongeren	Limburg (B)	12	12	no	yes	no	yes	RIR72
19 Aug.	Aarschot	Brabant (B)	156	366	no	yes	yes	yes	IR49, IR140. D 12; Field Art. 17; some units of 3rd Inf. Div.
19 Aug.	Attenrode	Brabant (B)	10	19	yes	no	no	no	Cav., probably PHus3
19 Aug.	Linden	Brabant (B)	19	96	yes	no	no	no	Unknown
19 Aug.	Lubbeek	Brabant (B)	18	45	no	no	no	no	Unknown
19 Aug.	Herselt	Antwerp (B)	23	5	yes	no	no	no	Probably 6th Inf. Brig. (IR34, IR42)
20 Aug.	Liège	Liège (B)	67	42	no	yes	no	yes	IR15, IR39, IR57, IR165, Jäg 7
20 Aug.	Erezée-Briscol	Luxembourg (B)	11	16	no	yes	no	no	RIR106, RJäg. 13
20 Aug.	Andenne/Seilles	Namur (B)	262	210	yes	yes	no	no	IR83, GRR1, GRR2, P28
20 Aug.	Franc-Waret	Namur (B)	22	10	yes	no	no	no	3rd Guards Inf. Div., regt unknown
20 Aug.	Somme-Leuze	Namur (B)	11	21	no	no	no	yes	Field Art. 11
20 Aug.	Molenstede	Brabant (B)	11	30	yes	no	no	no	Unknown
20 Aug.	Wespelaar	Brabant (B)	18	48	yes	no	no	no	Unknown
20 Aug.	Nomény	Meurthe-et-Moselle (F)	55	200	yes	no	yes	no	BIR2, BIR4, BIR8. Possibly Res.HusR 2
21 Aug.	Arsimont	Namur (B)	13	126	yes	no	yes	no	GGrenR1
21 Aug.	Auvelais	Namur (B)	44	127	yes	no	yes	no	On 22 Aug: GGrenR 2 & 4

21 Aug.	Audun-le-Roman	Meurthe-et-Moselle (F)	13	388	yes	no	no	no	Possibly units of 34th Div., or of 6th Cav. Div.
21 Aug.	Mont-Saint-Martin	Meurthe-et-Moselle (F)	16	76	yes	no	no	no	IR121, IR122
22 Aug.	Anloy	Luxembourg (B)	49	32	yes	no	yes	no	IR115, IR116
22 Aug.	Mussy-la-Ville	Luxembourg (B)	13	55	yes	no	yes	no	Probably IR123, 124, 120, and 127
22 Aug.	Neufchâteau	Luxembourg (B)	20	21	yes	no	no	no	21st R Div.
22 Aug.	Tintigny	Luexmbourg (B)	63	183	yes	no	yes	no	IR38, IR51, IR157, IR10, IR11
22 Aug.	Tamines	Namur (B)	383	240	yes	no	yes	no	IR77
22 Aug.	Bouffioulx	Hainaut (B)	10	32	yes	no	no	no	Probably 37th Brig.
22 Aug.	Charleroi	Hainaut (B)	32	156	yes	no	yes	no	RIR78
22 Aug.	Couillet	Hainaut (B)	18	406	yes	no	yes	yes	19th R Div.
22 Aug.	Farciennes	Hainaut (B)	20	146	no	no	yes	no	Unknown
22 Aug.	Monceau	Hainaut (B)	63	248	yes	no	yes	no	D1, RUR2
22 Aug.	Montignies-sur-Sambre	Hainaut (B)	35	103	yes	no	yes	no	19th R Div.
22 Aug.	Baranzy	Luxembourg (B)	27	86	yes	no	no	yes	IR119, IR121, IR122, IR125, IR127
22 Aug.	Maixe	Meurthe-et-Moselle (F)	10	36	yes	no	no	no	Bav. Light Cav. 3 (possibly BIR 23, Bav. Field Art. 12)
22 Aug.	Chénières	Meurthe-et-Moselle (F)	22	95	?	no	no	no	IR22
22 Aug.	Fillières	Meurthe-et-Moselle (F)	10	33	yes	no	no	yes	9th R Div.
22 Aug.	Landres	Meurthe-et-Moselle (F)	10	67	?	no	no	no	33rd Div., 3rd Cav. Div.
22 Aug.	Mercy-le-Haut	Meurthe-et-Moselle (F)	10	0	yes	no	no	no	86th Brig.
22 Aug.	Saint-Pancré	Meurthe-et-Moselle (F)	10	27	?	no	no	no	Unknown
23 Aug.	Ethe	Luxembourg (B)	218	256	yes	no	no	no	IR46, IR47, IR50, IR6
23 Aug.	Bièvre	Namur (B)	17	72	yes	no	no	no	IR28, IR29, IR68, IR69. Kür.8
23 Aug.	Bouge	Namur (B)	17	48	yes	no	no	no	IR71, IR95
23 Aug.	Bouvignes	Namur (B)	31	20	yes	no	no	no	IR178
23 Aug.	Dinant	Namur (B)	674	1,100	yes	yes	yes	yes	IR100, IR101, IR103, IR108, IR178, IR182. Field Art. 12, Field Art. 48
23 Aug.	Hastière-par-delà	Namur (B)	19	98	yes	no	no	no	IR103, IR104, IR133
23 Aug.	Spontin	Namur (B)	44	131	no	yes	no	no	IR103, RIR101
23 Aug.	Waulsort	Namur (B)	14	11	yes	no	yes	no	IR181
23 Aug.	Flénu	Hainaut (B)	12	12	yes	no	yes	yes	Unknown
23 Aug.	Jemappes	Hainaut (B)	11	?	yes	no	no	no	6th Division

Key date	Place	Province/department	Civilians killed	Buildings destroyed	Combat related	Panic	Human shield	Deportations	German units
23 Aug.	Nimy	Hainaut (B)	13	30	yes	no	yes	no	Unknown
23 Aug.	Quarégnon	Hainaut (B)	66	137	yes	no	no	no	IR24, Field Art. 18
23 Aug.	Ville-Pommeroeul	Hainaut (B)	14	0	yes	no	no	no	7th Division; IR165
23 Aug.	Fresnois-la-Montagne	Meurthe-et-Moselle (F)	51	99	yes	no	no	no	IR62, IR125
23 Aug.	Saint-Léger	Luxembourg (B)	11	6	no	yes	no	no	Unknown
24 Aug.	Bertrix	Luxembourg (B)	11	4	no	yes	no	no	IR115, 116, 117, 118
24 Aug.	Houdemont	Luxembourg (B)	11	68	no	yes	no	no	IR23
24 Aug.	Izel	Luxembourg (B)	20	161	no	no	no	no	Unknown
24 Aug.	Latour	Luxembourg (B)	71	0	yes	no	no	no	IR50, IR6
24 Aug.	Offagne	Luxembourg (B)	13	22	no	no	no	no	IR118
24 Aug.	Hermeton-sur-Meuse	Namur (B)	10	78	yes	no	no	no	IR106
24 Aug.	Namur	Namur (B)	30	110	no	yes	yes	no	IR71, GGrenR5, Foot Art. 18
24 Aug.	Pommeroeul	Hainaut (B)	15	23	yes	no	yes	no	Perhaps IR165
24 Aug.	Gerbéviller	Meurthe-et-Moselle (F)	60	455	yes	no	no	yes	IR60, IR166, Bläg2
24 Aug.	Longuyon	Meurthe-et-Moselle (F)	60	213	yes	yes	no	no	IR122, IR125, IR156
24 Aug.	Haybes	Ardennes (F)	61	596	yes	no	yes	no	IR133, IR179, Hus19
24 Aug.	Rouvres	Meuse (F)	47	150	yes	no	no	no	Bav. 33 Res. Div.
25 Aug.	Anthée	Namur (B)	13	71	?	no	no	no	IR104, IR106, RHusR18
25 Aug.	Romedenne	Namur (B)	11	122	yes	no	no	no	IR104, IR106
25 Aug.	Surice	Namur (B)	56	132	yes	no	no	no	IR104, IR106, IR107, H19, FA77
25 Aug.	Hofstade	Brabant (B)	10	?	yes	no	yes	no	IR48
25 Aug.	Louvain	Brabant (B)	248	2,000	yes	yes	no	yes	LW35, LW53, RHusR6, IR162, Units of: LW53, LW55, IR163, LSBatl. Neuss, RIR94, RIR31, et al.
25 Aug.	Zempst	Brabant (B)	14	40	yes	no	no	yes	RIR12
25 Aug.	Veltem	Brabant (B)	18	40	yes	no	no	no	Unknown

Date	Location	Region							Units
25 Aug.	Lunéville	Meurthe-et-Moselle (F)	19	70	no	yes	no	no	IR14, Bav. Cav. Div., Bav. Jäg., 5th Bav. Res. Div., U7
25 Aug.	Jarny	Meurthe-et-Moselle (F)	13	22	no	yes	no	no	BIR4, BIR66, BIR68
25 Aug.	Margny	Ardennes (F)	42	71	no	no	no	no	IR38, IR10
25 Aug.	Quérénaing	Nord (F)	21	?	yes	?	?	?	Unknown
25 Aug.	Vicoigne	Nord (F)	15	?	yes	?	?	?	Unknown
25 Aug.	Sedan	Ardennes (F)	23	many	yes	no	yes	no	IR25, IR28
26 Aug.	Arlon	Luxembourg (B)	133	100	no	no	no	no	LS (Gotha)
26 Aug.	Korbeek-Lo	Brabant (B)	16	132	no	no	no	yes	Unknown
26 Aug.	Rotselaar	Brabant (B)	19	67	yes	no	no	yes	Unknown
26 Aug.	Frasnes-lez-Couvin	Namur (B)	10	145	no	no	no	no	IR101, IR104, IR100, RIR103
26 Aug.	Maubert-Fontaine	Ardennes (F)	11	?	yes	no	no	no	H18
28 Aug.	Werchter	Brabant (B)	20	270	no	no	no	no	Unknown
30 Aug.	Saulces-Monclin	Ardennes (F)	14	88	yes	no	no	no	IR102
31 Aug.	Rethel	Ardennes (F)	15	many	no	no	no	no	IR178 (+ other rgts of 32 Inf. Div.?)
2 Sep.	Senlis	Oise (F)	21	105	yes	no	yes	no	Unknown
4 Sep.	Lebbeke	East Flanders (B)	29	0	no	no	yes	yes	18th RDiv
6 Sep.	Bignicourt-sur-Saulx	Marne (F)	12	30	?	no	no	yes	Unknown
16 Sep.	Frasnes-lez-Couvin	Namur (B)	34	0	no	no	no	yes	Unknown
27 Sep.	Aalst	East Flanders (B)	20	some	yes	yes	no	no	LW27, LIR73
19 Oct.	Beerst	West Flanders (B)	14	?	no	no	no	no	Unknown
19 Oct.	Ledegem	West Flanders (B)	18	34	no	no	no	no	RIR242
19 Oct.	Roeselare	West Flanders (B)	51	252	yes	yes	no	no	RIR235, RIR236
19 Oct.	Staden	West Flanders (B)	18	no	yes	yes	no	no	RIR214, RIR213
19 Oct.	Vladslo	West Flanders (B)	10	no	yes	yes	no	no	Probably 45rd RDiv.
20 Oct.	Zarren	West Flanders (B)	11	118	yes	no	no	no	RIR201, RIR202, RIR203, RIR204
20 Oct.	Handzame	West Flanders (B)	12	?	yes	yes	no	no	P209
21 Oct.	Esen	West Flanders (B)	47	many	yes	no	no	yes	RIR202, RIR203, RIR204

Note to appendix 1

Appendix 1 presents a database consisting of incidents during the invasion of Belgium and France in August–October 1914 in which German soldiers deliberately killed ten or more civilians. The table is analysed in chapter 2. The following methodology has been applied to assemble the database.

Any cut-off point for the number of victims is arbitrary. The justification for the choice of incidents in which ten or more civilians were killed is a practical one. It yields a manageable number of cases for quantitative analysis – a total of 129 – and there is no *a priori* reason for supposing that including incidents with fewer than ten civilian deaths would produce different conclusions.

The 'incident', which is used as the unit of investigation, requires definition. An incident is a related set of events which had an internal logic and unity, even if it lasted for a number of days. This has meant critically reconstructing the available official data for civilian deaths, which are often recorded in the form of all the deliberate killings in a given place for the duration of the invasion, irrespective of the number of separate incidents involved. Sometimes more than one incident occurred in a particular place, but the only data used are those relating to the particular incident in which ten or more civilians died. In two locations where two such incidents occurred, Jarny and Frasnes-lez-Couvin, they are listed separately.

On occasions, some victims were killed not at the core site of the incident but in another locality. Whether this was part of the original incident or constituted a new one has been evaluated on the facts of each case. In Arlon, in Luxembourg province (Belgium), for example, 108 of the 133 civilians executed were being deported from Rossignol, a village over 25 kilometres away where other inhabitants had been killed on the spot. But the role already established for Arlon as a centre of courts-martial for supposed civilian resisters and as a place of killings makes it reasonable to treat the execution of the 108 from Rossignol as part of the incident of Arlon. Admittedly, this logic derives from the perpetrators' perspective. Rossignol, rather than Arlon, was where the incident was seared into local memory and commemorated. On other occasions, killings which took place in separate administrative jurisdictions were really part of the one incident, and have been classified accordingly. The case of Dinant in Belgium, for example, includes the killing of civilians on the same day (23 August) in the suburbs of Leffe, Neffe, and Anseremme. Nearby Bouvignes, however, has been counted as a distinct incident, though closely related to the assault on Dinant by the German Third Army.

For each case, ten variables have been established: key date (the pivotal date in the escalation of the incident into one in which ten or more civilians died, rather than its starting date, though the two may coincide); place; province or département, with country identification (B for Belgium, F for France); number of civilians deliberately killed (incidental victims of warfare being excluded); number of buildings deliberately destroyed (collateral destruction likewise being ignored); whether the incident was directly related to combat between German and Allied troops; whether there was a 'panic' by the Germans, meaning a manifestation of collective hysteria akin to a riot which the local command had trouble controlling; whether the German troops used civilians as a 'human shield' against Allied soldiers; whether civilians were deported either a significant distance in occupied territory or to Germany itself (in contrast to localized expulsion from the incident site); and the German units involved. One other potential variable, that of rape, has not been included for the reasons discussed in chapter 2.

In the case of the German units responsible, the following initials for the different types of army unit have been employed together. The standard unit was the regiment; where the usual unit was a battalion, this has been stated; where the unit could not be established, the next largest (brigade or division) has been named. IR has been used for infantry regiment, including fusilier and grenadier regiments; Cav. Div. (cavalry division), Cav. Corps (cavalry corps); G (guards); GRR (guards reserve regiment); GGrenR (guards grenadier regiment); Kür. (cuirassiers); Jäg. (Jäger – light infantry – battalion); D (dragoons); Field Art. (field artillery); Foot Art. (foot artillery, i.e. heavy artillery); Hus (hussars); LS (Landsturm, the senior category of reserve unit by age); LW (Landwehr, the intermediary category of reserve unit by age); P (pioneer battalion); and UR (Uhlan regiment – lancer). The prefix B or Bav. to any of the above indicates that the regiment belonged to the Bavarian Army, which had its own numbering system (thus BIR2 is the Second Bavarian Infantry Regiment). The prefix R to any of the above indicates a reserve regiment (thus RIR103 is the 103rd Reserve Infantry Regiment). In some cases civilian witnesses were unable to identify the regiment involved. German sources have been used to state which units were in the place on the day in question.

Each of the 129 incidents has been examined in as much detail as possible from archival and published sources in Germany and the Allied countries. Since the Allies were the accusers, they made the most systematic collection of evidence, particularly regarding civilian casualties and the destruction of property. The returning Belgian government in 1919 restructured its inquiry, effectively making it a second official commission, in order to use the evidence of those who had remained in the country during the occupation in re-examining the war crimes of 1914. The first commission had depended heavily on refugee witnesses.

These three official inquiries provide the essential source material for establishing the incidents with ten or more civilian deaths during the invasion of Belgium and France.[1] However, it is important to note some limits to the coverage of the French Commission. Hampered like the first Belgian Commission by lack of direct access to incident sites that remained under enemy occupation throughout the war, it completed its task in the winter of 1918–19. In doing so, however, it was interested as much in German occupation policy as in events that had occurred during the invasion. Unlike in the Belgian case, there was no systematic attempt to reinvestigate the events of August–October 1914 in the former occupied regions, and one département which bore the full brunt of the German invasion in late August 1914, the Ardennes, was never investigated by the French Commission at all. The departmental archives of the Ardennes, Meurthe-et-Moselle, Nord, and Pas-de-Calais have therefore been used to supplement the published reports of the official French Commission.[2] But the picture remains incomplete for France. Details are sketchy for some of the incidents in which ten or more civilians lost their lives and a small number of such incidents may have escaped detection entirely.

Several other Allied sources of documentation have been used in establishing the database. First, the investigation carried out by Schmitz and Nieuwland for Namur and Luxembourg, based on detailed interviews with civilian survivors and witnesses, represents an invaluable additional source on these two Belgian provinces, since it goes into considerably more detail than even the second official commission, which it can be used to cross-check.[3] Working independently during the war, Schmitz and Nieuwland combined forces after the war to produce a multivolume history of the invasion of the two provinces that extensively cites witness evidence.[4]

Secondly, the archives of the Belgian and French official commissions provide further qualitative evidence, in the form of unpublished witness statements.[5] These rarely throw additional light on the numbers killed and the scale of destruction, since these calculations were included in the published evidence. But they clarify the evolution of some incidents, and thus help to establish other variables. Finally, the voluminous contemporary published sources from Allied and neutral countries have also been used to reconstruct each incident and to clarify the variables, notably the connection between the incident and combat, the presence or absence of panic by German soldiers, the use of human shields, and deportations. The evidence from the official reports for the numerically recorded variables (civilian deaths and buildings destroyed) has normally been preferred to occasionally conflicting evidence from other sources on these variables for the sake of consistency. This practice has only been departed from where the detailed case analysis suggested the alternative estimate to be more accurate.

German documentation available for constructing the database is of two types. The German response to the official Allied reports, the White Book of May 1915, published by the German Foreign Ministry, was derived from a number of inquiries by the German military authorities into the events of the invasion which resulted in prior reports printed by the Prussian Ministry of War purely for internal circulation in the winter of 1914–15. These reports were heavily edited by the Foreign Ministry in order to make its case, the German counter-accusation of illicit civilian resistance.[6]

Given the difference of perspective, the information is radically opposed to that contained in the Allied official reports. In a total of 70 appendices containing witness evidence (66 devoted to the 'eastern frontier' of Belgium, and four respectively to the major incidents of Aarschot, Andenne, Dinant, and Louvain), there is little detail on what, by the argument of the report, were justifiable German 'reprisals', and nothing on the number of civilian deaths resulting from them. By the same token, however, the

White Book did not deny the civilian deaths and destruction of buildings detailed in the Belgian and French official reports, so that the latter remain uncontested as sources for these variables in the database. More surprisingly perhaps, little attempt was made in the White Book to estimate the number of German soldiers killed by the alleged civilian attacks, making it impossible to incorporate this information into the database. This, along with the fact that a good deal of the evidence initially cited by the Ministry of War reports was sufficiently doubtful to be dropped from the White Book, indicates that the Germans lacked the kind of evidence for their hypothesis of a franc-tireur war that the Allies possessed in abundance for German atrocities. The White Book was also much more limited in its scope. No French cases were considered at all, and with just over 30 incidents referred to in which ten or more civilians died, its coverage of these incidents was about a quarter that of our database.

The White Book apart, however, a mass of German documentation, both archival and in various published forms, provides crucial evidence on the incidents with ten or more civilians killed, as well as on the different perceptions of these by the two sides involved. The same is true for the depositions, however selectively used, on which the White Book itself was based. Accordingly, this German material has been used together with Allied sources in order to establish many of the variables of the database. It has been particularly important in identifying the units of the German army involved. This was one of the most unreliable aspects of the Allied official investigations. Quite apart from the fact that in some cases German units hid their bright badges in fear of franc-tireur attacks, terrified civilian witnesses often failed to identify the units responsible or misidentified them. German sources, and especially the Reichsarchiv's official history of the war, have therefore been used in order to complement and correct Allied sources in establishing the German units involved.[7]

Finally, the military history of the invasion which constitutes the context for the 129 incidents helps to determine several variables, notably the relationship of each case to combat and the incidence of panic and use of human shields. It has been reconstructed using the official military histories from both sides, as well as other contemporary and secondary published works.[8]

Appendix 2 Hague Convention (IV) Respecting the Laws and Customs of War on Land (1907)

Section I – On Belligerents

Article 1

The laws, rights, and duties of war apply not only to armies, but also to militia and volunteer corps fulfilling the following conditions:

1. To be commanded by a person responsible for his subordinates;
2. To have a fixed distinctive emblem recognizable at a distance;
3. To carry arms openly; and
4. To conduct their operations in accordance with the laws and customs of war.

In countries where militia or volunteer corps constitute the army, or form part of it, they are included under the denomination 'army.'

Article 2

The inhabitants of a territory which has not been occupied, who, on the approach of the enemy, spontaneously take up arms to resist the invading troops without having had time to organize themselves in accordance with article 1, shall be regarded as belligerents if they carry arms openly and if they respect the laws and customs of war [...]

Section II – Hostilities

Article 25

The attack or bombardment, by whatever means, of towns, villages, dwellings, or buildings which are undefended is prohibited [...]

Article 27

In sieges and bombardments all necessary steps must be taken to spare, as far as possible, buildings dedicated to religion, art, science, or charitable purposes, historic monuments, hospitals, and places where the sick and wounded are collected, provided they are not being used at the time for military purposes.

It is the duty of the besieged to indicate the presence of such buildings or places by distinctive and visible signs, which shall be notified to the enemy beforehand.

Article 28

The pillage of a town or place, even when taken by assault, is prohibited. [...]

Section III – Military Authority over the Territory of the Hostile State

Article 46

Family honor and rights, the lives of persons, and private property, as well as religious convictions and practice, must be respected.

Private property can not be confiscated.

Article 47

Pillage is formally forbidden. [...]

Article 50

No general penalty, pecuniary or otherwise, shall be inflicted upon the population on account of the acts of individuals for which they can not be regarded as jointly and severally responsible [...]

Article 56

The property of municipalities, that of institutions dedicated to religion, charity and education, the arts and sciences, even when state property, shall be treated as private property.

All seizure of, destruction or willful damage done to institutions of this character, historic monuments, works of art and science, is forbidden, and should be made the subject of legal proceedings.

Source: James Brown Scott (ed.), *Texts of the Peace Conferences at the Hague, 1899 and 1907* (Boston and London, 1908), pp. 209–29.

Appendix 3 The Treaty of Versailles, Articles 227–230

Part VII – Penalties

Article 227

The Allied and Associated Powers publicly arraign William II of Hohenzollern, formerly German Emperor, for a supreme offence against international morality and the sanctity of treaties [...]

Article 228

The German Government recognises the right of the Allied and Associated Powers to bring before military tribunals persons accused of having committed acts in violation of the laws and customs of war. Such persons shall, if found guilty, be sentenced to punishments laid down by law. This provision will apply notwithstanding any proceedings or prosecution before a tribunal in Germany or in the territory of her allies.

The German Government shall hand over to the Allied and Associated Powers, or to such one of them as shall so request, all persons accused of having committed an act in violation of the laws and customs of war, who are specified either by name or by the rank, office or employment which they held under the German authorities.

Article 229

Persons guilty of criminal acts against the nationals of one of the Allied and Associated Powers will be brought before the military tribunals of that Power.

Persons guilty of criminal acts against the nationals of more than one of the Allied and Associated Powers will be brought before military tribunals composed of members of the military tribunals of the Powers concerned.

In every case the accused will be entitled to name his own counsel.

Article 230

The German Government undertakes to furnish all documents and information of every kind, the production of which may be considered necessary to ensure the full knowledge of the incriminating acts, the discovery of offenders and the just appreciation of responsibility.

Source: Harold W. V. Temperley (ed.), *A History of the Peace Conference of Paris* (6 vols, London, 1920–4), vol. 3, *Chronology, Notes and Documents* (1920), pp. 212–13.

Appendix 4 Allied demands for the extradition of enemy war criminals, 1920

Category of crime	Number of individuals sought on war crimes charges by prosecuting country							
	Belgium	France	Britain	Italy	Poland	Romania	Serb-Croat-Slovene Kingdom	Total
Killing civilians, Aug.–Oct. 1914	99	89			4			192
Cruelty to civilians, Aug.–Oct., 1914	66							66
Killing captured soldiers, Aug.–Oct. 1914		50						50
Pillage, arson, destruction, theft, Aug.–Oct. 1914	3	89			5			97
Subtotal	**168**	**228**			**9**			**405**
Killing civilians, Nov. 1914–Nov. 1918	2	4			15	17	1	39
Cruelty to civilians, Nov. 1914–Nov. 1918	21				6	10		37
Killing captured soldiers, Nov. 1914–Nov. 1918		2						2
Pillage, arson, destruction, theft, Nov. 1914–Nov. 1918	6	57		3	40	9	3	118
Subtotal	**29**	**63**		**3**	**61**	**36**	**4**	**196**
Turkish massacre of Armenians			7					7
Military responsibility for criminal orders	3	4	7			1		15
Political responsibility for criminal orders		2	2					4
Bombardment of open cities and aerial warfare on civilians			5					5
Cultural atrocities		16			2			18
Destructions during retreat, 1917 and 1918		34						34
Rape	1	8						9

Category of crime	Number of individuals sought on war crimes charges by prosecuting country							
	Belgium	France	Britain	Italy	Poland	Romania	Serb-Croat-Slovene Kingdom	Total
Crimes in POW camps (including deaths)	5	67	58	16		5		151
Deportations, 1914–18	139	26						165
Forced labour, including prostitution	3	12						15
Criminal acts of naval warfare			24	11				35
Subtotal	151	169	103	27	2	6		458
Total	348	460	103	30	72	42	4	1,059

Note to appendix 4

The table shows the relative importance of different categories of war crime calculated by the number of individuals charged under them according to the lists of alleged war criminals wanted for extradition from Germany by former Allied states and newly independent states in eastern Europe (Bundesarchiv, Berlin, R 3003 Generalia/56: Liste des personnes désignées par les puissances pour être livrées par l'Allemagne [...]).The total of individuals charged from the seven national lists (Belgium, France, Britain, Italy, Poland, Romania, and the Serb-Croat-Slovene Kingdom) is 1,059. As far as possible, double-counting of the same individual for a given charge has been elimi-nated. The figure is still higher than that of the simple aggregate of individuals sought for extradition according to the same lists (890) because a number of individuals were charged with crimes in more than one category. General von Bülow, for example, was wanted on the French list for crimes in five categories.

We have devised the categories of crime in the table from the charges on the lists in order to achieve systematic classification of the charges. Four categories of crime (killing civilians; cruelty to civilians; killing captured soldiers; pillage, arson, destruc-tion, theft) classify charges relating to the invasions of August–October 1914 and, calculated as a subtotal of the table, indicate the weight of the invasions of 1914 in the war crimes charges as a whole. The same four categories have been applied to war crimes alleged to have occurred between November 1914 and November 1918. These have been calculated as a second subtotal for comparative purposes. A further 11 cate-gories of crime (Turkish massacre of Armenians to naval war crimes) have been used to classify the remaining war crimes. Crimes in some of these categories (e.g. cultural atrocities, deportations) may have occurred during the invasions of 1914, but in the absence of dates they have not been included in the crimes (and subtotal) relating to 1914.

Presenting the material statistically is difficult owing to the lack of uniform criteria in all national lists. In the Belgian list, only 44 separate incidents were listed under 'killing of civilians, August–October 1914'. Naturally, for such cases as Dinant, Louvain, etc., several named officers were held responsible. On the French list, 89 names were associated with 81 incidents in this category. The Belgian list also contains 66 unnamed commanders of identified units charged with 'systematically inhumane conduct of their troops' (see category cruelty to civilians, August–October 1914). In the corresponding French category, neither the individuals nor the incidents are sufficiently well defined to be included. The British list includes nine Turks sought for extradition if found in Germany. Two were accused of political responsibility for the Turkish 'massacres' of Armenians (the term 'genocide' was not coined until 1944), and have been so listed, while seven were accused of direct involvement in the massacres.

Notes

Bibliographical abbreviations

AD	Archives Départementales
ADAP	*Akten zur Deutschen Auswärtigen Politik*
AGR	Archives Générales du Royaume (Brussels)
AN	Archives Nationales (Paris)
BA	Bundesarchiv
BA-MA	Bundesarchiv-Militärarchiv (Freiburg)
BDIC	Bibliothèque de Documentation Internationale Contemporaine (Paris)
BfZ	Bibliothek für Zeitgeschichte (Stuttgart)
CE	Commission d'enquête
CPHDC	Centre for the Preservation of Historical Documentary Collections (Moscow)
DBFP	*Documents on British Foreign Policy*
GLA	Badisches Generallandesarchiv (Karlsruhe)
HStA	Sächsisches Hauptstaatsarchiv (Dresden)
HStA-MA	Württembergisches Haupstaatsarchiv-Militärarchiv (Stuttgart)
KA	Bayerisches Hauptstaatsarchiv-Kriegsarchiv (Munich)
MAE	Ministère des Affaires Étrangères (Paris)
MHC	Musée d'Histoire Contemporaine (Paris)
MRA	Musée Royal de l'Armée (Brussels)
PAAA	Politisches Archiv des Auswärtigen Amts (Bonn; now Berlin)
PRO	Public Record Office (London)
RBLDAG	*Revue Belge des Livres, Documents et Archives de la Guerre 1914–18*
SHA	Service Historique d l'Armée de Terre (Vincennes)
TCD	Trinity College, Dublin
UGACPE	Union des Grandes Associations contre la Propagande Ennemie

Introduction

1   Fernand van Langenhove, *Comment naît un cycle de légendes. Francs-tireurs et atroc-ités en Belgique* (Lausanne and Paris, 1916); English translation, *The Growth of a Legend: A Study Based upon the German Accounts of Francs-Tireurs and 'Atrocities' in Belgium* (London, 1916); German translation, *Wie Legenden entstehen! Franktireurkrieg und Greueltaten in Belgien* (Zürich, 1917).

2   Marc Bloch, 'Réflexions d'un historien sur les fausses nouvelles de la guerre', in Bloch, *Écrits de guerre, 1914–1918*, ed. Étienne Bloch, introd. Stéphane Audoin-Rouzeau (Paris, 1997), pp. 169–84, originally published in the *Revue de synthèse*, 1921.

3   E.g. James M. Read, *Atrocity Propaganda 1914–1919* (New Haven, 1941); and Harold D. Lasswell, *Propaganda Technique in World War I* (1927; new edn, Cambridge, Mass., 1971), esp. ch. 4, 'Satanism', devoted to 'atrocity' fabrications.

4   For the best discussion from this last angle, see Trevor Wilson, 'Lord Bryce's Investigation into Alleged German Atrocities in Belgium, 1914–15', *Journal of Contemporary History*, 14/3 (1979), pp. 369–83, also Wilson, *The Myriad Faces of War: Britain and the Great War, 1914–1918* (Cambridge, 1986), pp. 182–91.

5   Peter Schöller, *Der Fall Löwen und das Weißbuch. Eine kritische Untersuchung der deutschen Dokumentation über die Vorgänge in Löwen vom 25. bis 28. August 1914* (Cologne and Graz, 1958); translated into French as *Le Cas de Louvain et le Livre Blanc allemand* (Louvain and Paris, 1958), and also into Flemish.

6   Lothar Wieland, *Belgien 1914. Die Frage des belgischen 'Franktireurkrieges' und die deutsche öffentliche Meinung von 1914 bis 1936* (Frankfurt, Berne, New York, 1984).

7   Michael Jeismann, *Das Vaterland der Feinde. Studien zum nationalen Feindbegriff und Selbstverständnis in Deutschland und Frankreich, 1792–1918* (Stuttgart, 1992).

8   Ruth Harris, 'The "Child of the Barbarian": Rape, Race and Nationalism in France during the First World War', *Past and Present*, 141 (1993), pp. 170–206; Stéphane Audoin-Rouzeau, *L'Enfant de l'ennemi (1914–1918). Viol, avortement, infanticide pendant la grande guerre* (Paris, 1995).

9   John Horne and Alan Kramer, 'German "Atrocities" and Franco-German Opinion, 1914: The Evidence of German Soldiers' Diaries', *Journal of Modern History*, 66/1 (1994), pp. 1–33; John Horne, 'Les Mains coupées. "Atrocités allemandes" et opinion française en 1914', in Jean-Jacques Becker, Jay Winter, Gerd Krumeich, Annette Becker and Stéphane Audoin-Rouzeau (eds), *Guerre et cultures, 1914–1918* (Paris, 1994), pp. 133–46; Alan Kramer, 'Les "Atrocités allemandes": mythologie populaire, propagande et manipulations dans l'armée allemande', in Becker et al., *Guerre et cultures*, pp. 147–64; Alan Kramer, '"Greueltaten". Zum Problem der deutschen Kriegsverbrechen in Belgien und Frankreich 1914', in Gerhard Hirschfeld and Gerd Krumeich, with Irina Renz (eds), *Keiner fühlt sich hier mehr als Mensch ... Erlebnis und Wirkung des Ersten Weltkriegs* (Essen, 1993), pp. 85–114; John Horne and Alan Kramer, 'War between Soldiers and Enemy Civilians, 1914–1915', in Roger Chickering and Stig Förster (eds), *Great War, Total War: Combat and Mobilization on the Western Front, 1914–1918* (Cambridge, 2000), pp. 153–68; John Horne, 'Corps, lieux et nation. La France et l'invasion de 1914', *Annales: Histoire, Sciences Sociales*, 1 (2000), pp. 73–109; Alan Kramer, 'Der Umgang mit der Schuld. Die "Schuld im Kriege" und die Republik von Weimar', in Dietrich Papenfuß and Wolfgang Schieder (eds), *Deutsche Umbrüche im 20. Jahrhundert* (Cologne and Weimar, 2000), pp. 75–94; John Horne, 'Defining the Enemy: War, Law and the Levée en Masse in Europe, 1870–1945', in Daniel Moran and Arthur Waldron (eds), *The People in Arms: Military Myth and Political Legitimacy since the French Revolution* (Cambridge, forthcoming).

10   The papers of the two Belgian Commissions (one established during the war, the other after it) are in Archives Générales du Royaume (AGR), Brussels, Commission d'Enquête (CE), III 374 B1; the French Commission's papers are in Archives Nationales (AN), Paris, AJ4. The principal German archives containing testimony by

soldiers are Bundesarchiv-Militärarchiv (BA-MA), Freiburg; Württembergisches Hauptstaats-archiv-Militärarchiv (HStA-MA), Stuttgart; Sächsisches Hauptstaats-archiv (HStA), Dresden; Bayerisches Hauptstaatsarchiv, Kriegsarchiv (KA), Munich.

11 Jean Schmitz and Norbert Nieuwland, *Documents pour servir à l'histoire de l'invasion allemande dans les provinces de Namur et de Luxembourg* (7 vols, Brussels and Paris, 1919–24).

1 German invasion, part 1

1 Reichswehrministerium, *Sanitätsbericht über das deutsche Heer [...] im Weltkrieg, 1914–1918* (3 vols, Berlin, 1934–8), vol. 3 (1934), appendix, p. 5 (for the size of the German invasion force); Gerhard Ritter, *The Schlieffen Plan: Critique of a Myth* (1956; English translation, New York, 1958); John Keegan, *Opening Moves: August 1914* (New York, 1971), pp. 8–55; Holger Herwig, *The First World War: Germany and Austria-Hungary 1914–1918* (London, 1997), pp. 43–74. Estimates of the size of the German forces on the western front, including the defensive lines on the Rhine, range between 1.3 and 1.6 million men: Reichsarchiv, *Der Weltkrieg 1914 bis 1918. Die militärischen Operationen zu Lande* (14 vols, Berlin, 1925–44), vol. 1, *Die Grenzschlachten im Westen* (1925), pp. 69, 646.

2 For the military history of the events discussed in this and the following chapter, see the German official history, Reichsarchiv, *Weltkrieg*, vol. 1; ibid., vol. 3, *Der Marne-Feldzug von der Sambre zur Marne* (1926); the French official history, Ministère de la Guerre, *Les Armées françaises dans la grande guerre* (103 vols, Paris, 1922–37), vol. 1, *La Bataille des frontières jusqu'au 23 août 1914* (1936); anon., *La Belgique et la guerre* (4 vols, Brussels, 1921–8), vol. 2, Jacques Cuvelier, *L'invasion allemande* (1921), and vol. 3, Maurice Tasnier and R. van Overstraeten, *Les Opérations militaires* (1926); *The Times History of the War* (21 vols, London, 1914–20), vol. 1 (1914) and vol. 2 (1915); *La Guerre de 1914. L'Action de l'armée belge pour la défense du pays et le respect de sa neutralité. Rapport du commandement de l'armée. Période du 31 juillet au 31 décembre 1914* (Paris, 1915), also translated into English; J. M. Kennedy, *The Campaign round Liège* (London, 1914); Léon van der Essen, *The Invasion and the War in Belgium from Liège to the Yser* (London, 1917); L. Koeltz, *La Guerre de 1914–1918. Les Opérations militaires* (Paris, 1966), pp. 64–155; Keegan, *Opening Moves*; Herwig, *The First World War*, pp. 75–125.

3 The conventional total is 25,000 infantry: Reichsarchiv, *Weltkrieg*, vol. 1, pp. 108–9; Generalstab des Heeres, *Der Handstreich gegen Lüttich vom 3. bis 7. August 1914* (Berlin, 1939), p. 71. This appears to be an underestimate. The force consisted of six infantry brigades, composed of two regiments each, plus an additional regiment, making a total of 13 infantry regiments, plus five Jäger (light infantry) battalions. However, it appears that the regiments were instructed not to mobilize their full complement: IR 165, for example, was ordered to limit its companies to 175 men instead of the normal complement of 250 (Otto Fließ and Kurt Dittmar, *5. Hannoversches Infanterie-Regiment Nr. 165 im Weltkriege* (Oldenburg and Berlin, 1927), pp. 5, 14). Thus there were about 30,000 infantrymen, to which should be added three cavalry divisions (8,000 cavalrymen), pioneers, and artillery, which the *Handstreich* ignores. The initial assault force must thus have had about 39,000 soldiers.

4 *Handstreich gegen Lüttich*, p. 56; Tasnier and van Overstraeten, *Opérations militaires*, p. 36.

5 Jean Stengers, 'L'Entrée en guerre de la Belgique', *Guerres Mondiales et Conflits Contemporains*, 179 (1995), pp. 13–33 (here 21–2). Laurence van Ypersele, *Le Roi Albert. Histoire d'un mythe* (Ottignies, 1995), pp. 138–42.

6 Luc de Vos, *Het effectief van de Belgische Krijgsmacht en de Militiewetgeving, 1830–1940* (Brussels, 1985), pp. 315, 326–35.

7 Georges Hautecler (ed.), *Le Rapport du général Leman sur la défense de Liège en août 1914* (Brussels, 1960), pp. 103–4; Reichsarchiv, *Weltkrieg*, vol. 1, pp. 113, 114–16; Carl Ernst, *Der Große Krieg in Belgien. Beobachtungen, seinen ehemaligen hannoverschen Landsleuten gewidmet* (Gembloux, 1930), pp. 16–19, on the German losses and retreat.

8 Nine infantry brigades and two additional regiments, plus cavalry and heavy artillery (calculated from Reichsarchiv, *Weltkrieg*, vol. 1, pp. 117–20); Tasnier and van Overstraeten, *Opérations militaires*, p. 55.

9 Reichsarchiv, *Weltkrieg*, pp. 119–20; *Handstreich gegen Lüttich*, p. 62; Tasnier and van Overstraeten, *Opérations militaires*, pp. 54–63.

10 Keegan, *Opening Moves*, pp. 82–92; Ritter, *The Schlieffen Plan*, p. 175. For German losses, see *Handstreich gegen Lüttich*, pp. 78–9, which gives 3,458 infantry soldiers killed, wounded, or missing just in the three days 4–6 August. The estimate of 5,300 casualties is by Heutter, an engineer from Zürich who conducted inquiries travelling through Belgium in early 1915; Heutter wrote 5,300 killed, which is almost certainly too high. AGR, Brussels, Commission d'enquête sur la violation du droit des gens (hereafter CE), III 374 B1, 12. Report by Heutter, submitted via the Belgian legation, Berne, to the Belgian government's Commission of Inquiry (hereafter Heutter report), p. 9.

11 Henri Davignon, *German Posters in Belgium: Their Value as Evidence* (London, 1918), pp. 2–3.

12 Commission d'enquête sur la violation des règles du droit des gens, des lois et des coutumes de la guerre, *Rapports sur la violation du droit des gens en Belgique* (Paris and Nancy, 1915–16, 2 vols, hereafter referred to as Belgian First Commission), 17th report, vol. 2, pp. 56–7; Gustave Somville, *Vers Liège. Le chemin du crime. Août 1914* (Paris, 1915, based on an inquiry carried out in the Liège district in late 1914–early 1915, and also translated into English), pp. 155–7; *Le Soir*, 6 August 1914, for Belgian soldiers using the houses in their fighting.

13 Belgian First Commission, 17th report, vol. 2, pp. 55–6 (which gave nine deaths); Commission d'enquête sur les violations des règles du droit des gens, des lois et des coutumes de la guerre (4 vols, Brussels, 1921–3, hereafter referred to as Belgian Second Commission), vol. 1 (2 parts), *Rapports sur les attentats commis par les troupes allemandes pendant l'invasion et l'occupation de la Belgique* (Brussels, 1922), vol. 1, part 1, p. 15, gives ten deaths; Somville, *Vers Liège*, pp. 165–9; the Dutch paper, *De Tijd*, 8 August 1914, cited in *Le XXe Siècle*, 10 August 1914. On the nocturnal panic, see the two army reports in Bundesarchiv (BA) Koblenz, NL 15/97: M/S Foerster: Stellungnahme zu der Ausarbeitung des Oberstlts [...] Fonck, fol. 9–10: 2nd Battalion, Field Artillery Regiment 60, and Fusilier Regiment 90.

14 Belgian First Commission, 17th report, vol. 2, p. 52; Somville, *Vers Liège*, p. 65 (for quotation); AGR, Brussels, CE, III 374 B1, 81b, testimony Julien Christiane, 23 September 1914. In Battice, three villagers were executed on the grounds of suspicious behaviour on 4 August (Belgian Second Commission, vol. 1, part 1, p. 50; Somville, *Vers Liège*, p. 56).

15 See appendix 1 below. We have calculated the number of inhabitants killed in incidents with ten or more civilian dead ('major incidents') as 679. Since 168 were killed

in 51 incidents in which fewer than ten died, the total is 847. There is no estimate available for the number of civilians wounded by German soldiers. The number of buildings deliberately destroyed refers only to those in places where 'major incidents' occurred. Again, the true total is higher.

16 Belgian First Commission. An English translation was published, but all page references are to the French language original. The aim of the commission was to establish the violations of the 'rights of people and the duty of humanity' committed by the Germans (Belgian First Commission, vol. 1, p. 41). The second commission was established in 1919 to study all aspects of the invasion and occupation. The reports were not translated into foreign languages. For the history of the first commission, see chapter 6, and of the second commission, see chapter 9. For Belgian sources on Liège, see also Essen, *The Invasion and the War in Belgium*, pp. 49–99; Somville, *Vers Liège, passim*; and anon., *La Belgique martyre. Les atrocités allemandes dans les environs de Verviers* (Verviers, n.d., but post-war).

17 Centre for the Preservation of Historical Documentary Collections (CPHDC), Moscow, 1256-5-47, fol. 10, war diary 34th Infantry Brigade, report Gen. v. Kraewel, at 09.15 (German time) on 6 August 1914, for the order to retreat; Tasnier and van Overstraeten, *Opérations militaires*, p. 53.

18 Somville, *Vers Liège*, pp. 225–33. Belgian First Commission, 17th report, vol. 1, p. 68, puts the beginning of the reprisals at 4 am on 6 August, rather than 4 pm. Cf. Belgian Second Commission, vol. 1, part 1, pp. 36–7.

19 The executions were on 6 and 7 August (Belgian First Commission, 16th report, vol. 2, pp. 31–48). This report was based on the testimony of Ferdinand Fléchet, the burgomaster of Warsage, who escaped across the Dutch border to Maastricht, where he made a lengthy statement which was reproduced by the Dutch *Nieuwe Rotterdamsche Courant* and from there by the international press (e.g. *Le Temps*, 14 August 1914).

20 There is no reliable narrative of the fighting at Herstal on 7 August. This account has been constructed by deduction from *Handstreich gegen Lüttich*, pp. 27–30, and Somville, *Vers Liège*, pp. 215–17.

21 Belgian Second Commission, vol. 1, part 1, p. 302.

22 *Handstreich gegen Lüttich*, p. 33; Tasnier and van Overstraeten, *Opérations militaires*, p. 41 (who underestimate the size of the German force by calling it a battalion); Belgian Second Commission, vol. 1, part 1, p. 302; Somville, *Vers Liège*, pp. 192–3.

23 Belgian First Commission, 17th report, vol. 2, pp. 54–5. The Belgian Second Commission wrongly dates this execution to 6 August (vol. 1, part 1, p. 26). Witness statements taken in 1919 and reproduced in the Second Commission (vol. 1, part 1, pp. 343–4) confirm both the anger of the Germans and the absence of any charge of civilian resistance, let alone any form of interrogation. Two of the witnesses even claimed to have seen an officer fire with his pistol in the air in order to trigger the men's belief in resistance. The account is confirmed in all essentials by Somville, *Vers Liège*, pp. 131–46, and *La Belgique martyre*, p. 44. Witness statements cited by the Belgian consul, Maastricht, at the session of the CE on 7 May 1915 are at AGR, Brussels, CE, III 374 B1, 81a.

24 Belgian First Commission, 17th report, vol. 2, pp. 54–5; Somville, *Vers Liège*, pp. 133–6.

25 Somville, *Vers Liège*, p. 129. The First and Second Commission reports wrongly date this incident to the night of 4–5 August. Cf. correct dating in *Handstreich gegen Lüttich*, pp. 16–17, and Cuvelier, *L'invasion allemande*, p. 95.

26 Somville, *Vers Liège*, pp. 122–5; Belgian Second Commission, vol. 1, part 1, pp. 27–8.

27 Somville, *Vers Liège*, pp. 86–7, corroborated by Belgian First Commission, 17th report, vol. 2, p. 53, although the latter incorrectly gives the date as 5 August.

28 Somville, *Vers Liège*, p. 57; Belgian First Commission, 17th report, vol. 2, p. 52 (giving 35 victims).

29 Testimony in Belgian Second Commission, vol. 1, part 1, pp. 24–6, 342. The Germans held an inquiry into the massacre of Melen-La Bouxhe on 16 February 1915 at the Kommandantur of Liège, with 17 civilian witnesses called (Somville, *Vers Liège*, p. 90). This was not referred to by the official German report, *Die völkerrechtswidrige Führung des belgischen Volkskriegs* (Berlin, 1915).

30 The Belgian Second Commission gives a generalized account (vol. 1, part 1, pp. 52–3); Belgian First Commission, 17th report (vol. 2, pp. 52–3) and Somville (*Vers Liège*, pp. 64–84) are more precise and corroborate each other in essentials. Both attribute responsibility to IR 39. *Handstreich gegen Lüttich* (p. 62) confirms that IR 39 arrived that day from Germany. But the Swiss engineer Heutter, in his report to the Belgian government, suggested that a cavalry squadron engaged in the attack on Fléron was responsible (AGR, Brussels, CE, III 374, B1, 12). Somville noted that the enraged commander of a newly arrived cavalry unit shouted: 'The whole town must be burned. The inhabitants keep firing even when their houses are in flames' (*Vers Liège*, p. 71). This may have been the 10th Hussar Regiment, attached to the 14th Brigade.

31 *Handstreich gegen Lüttich*, pp. 36–9; Somville, *Vers Liège*, pp. 96–196; Belgian Second Commission, vol. 1, part 1, pp. 372–4 (testimony of burgomaster of Olne). The Belgian accounts are corroborated by *La Belgique martyre*, pp. 6–15 (testimony of widow and daughter of teacher of Saint-Hadelin). Belgian and German accounts confirm that IR 20 and Fusilier Regiment 35 were responsible.

32 Somville, *Vers Liège*, pp. 110, 114–15.

33 Ibid., pp. 116, 121, corroborated by the Belgian Second Commission, vol. 1, part 1, p. 31.

34 *Handstreich gegen Lüttich*, pp. 42–51.

35 Belgian Second Commission, vol. 1, part 1, pp. 72–4; Somville, *Vers Liège*, p. 49.

36 Somville, *Vers Liège*, pp. 24–36; Belgian Second Commission, vol. 1, part 1, pp. 86–7.

37 *La Belgique martyre*, pp. 105–18 (esp. 116–17). Belgian witnesses categorically denied shooting. The main details are confirmed by AGR, Brussels, CE, III 374 B1, 81a; Belgian First Commission, 17th report, pp. 59–61; Belgian Second Commission, vol. 1, part 1, p. 78; Somville, *Vers Liège*, pp. 19–23. Emil Waxweiler, *Hat Belgien sein Schicksal verschuldet?* (Zürich, 1915, pp. 243–4), explained that the three shots that prompted the German actions in Francorchamps were fired by a small Belgian cavalry patrol that ambushed a German column; since the Germans had thus far not encountered Belgian army units in the area, they assumed the shots had been fired by civilians.

38 See chapter 3 for a fuller discussion of this point.

39 Bundesarchiv-Militärarchiv (BA-MA), Freiburg, N 324–36, Karl von Einem gen. v. Rothmaler, letters to his wife.

40 BA-MA, Freiburg, N 324-26, war diary von Einem, 9 August 1914; Belgian First Commission, 6th report, vol. 1, pp. 78–9, for the text of Bülow's proclamation.

41 Politisches Archiv des Auswärtigen Amts (PAAA) Bonn, R 20880. fol. 8–9: commentary by the Kaiser on a message from the Belgian government informing the German government of the uniforms worn by the Garde Civique (9 August 1914, i.e. date of

receipt).

42 Instruction of 4 August 1914, signed by Paul Berryer, Minister of the Interior; original draft in AGR, Brussels, CE, III 374 B1, 49; reproduced in Henri Davignon (ed.), *Belgium and Germany: Texts and Documents* (London, 1915), p. 27.

43 Instruction of 5 August, in *Le Soir*, 8 August 1914. Leman's appeal was posted on 4 August, the Minister's instruction of 4 August on 5 August (Davignon, *Belgium and Germany*, p. 24).

44 Belgian Second Commission, vol. 1, part 1, pp. 247–8. According to the deputy mayor of Arlon, Reuter, French patrols had been sighted in the area between 2 and 12 August (ibid., p. 562). For the execution of deputy commissioner Lempereur: ibid., pp. 571–2. Cf. *L'Avenir de Luxembourg*, 8 August 1914, translation of extract in KA Kriegsarchiv (hereafter KA), Munich, HS 2259. *Le XX Siècle*, 10 August, reported that the woman was shot dead by the dragoons. For the myth of the young girl as combatant: BA, Potsdam, Sachthematische Sammlung 267, Lt Glückmann, war diary, 1914–15, diary entry 14 August. Cf. also Schmitz and Nieuwland, *L'invasion allemande*, vol. 7, pp. 265–6; Reichsarchiv, *Der Weltkrieg*, vol. 1, p. 132.

45 Archives Départementales (hereafter AD) Meurthe-et-Moselle, 86J5, Commission pour une histoire de la guerre franco-allemande, report of the primary school teacher of Audun-le-Roman, E. Véron. This commission was set up in 1914 to gather materials (including eye-witness accounts) for a history of the war, its papers only being rediscovered in 1996. In addition to the Departmental Archives of the Meurthe-et-Moselle, the principal sources are the official French commission set up to investigate German war crimes, whose 12 reports were published between January 1915 and 1919 under the title *Commission instituée en vue de constater les actes commis par l'ennemi en violation du droit des gens (décret du 23 septembre 1914). Rapports et procès-verbaux d'enquête* (hereafter French Commission), and the extensive archives of this commission, to be found in the AN, Paris, series AJ4.

46 *L'Est républicain* and *Le Temps*, 12 August 1914; French Commission, reports 10–12, pp. 23, 106.

47 AD Meurthe-et-Moselle, 86J4 2, report of C. Humbert, director of the school at Jarny, 14 December 1914. The French Commission, 5th report, pp. 25–9, relates a second incident which occurred in Jarny on 25 August, when at least 13 inhabitants were killed. The execution of the 15 Italian workers was added to this total by a number of witnesses. However, the testimony of the director of the school (who was also secretary to the mayor) is quite precise on 10 August as the date of the execution of the 15 Italians, the more so since the director left Jarny on 14 August. His report was written for the departmental commission on the history of the war. Ordering dogs to be shot was almost certainly part of the detailed instructions drawn up by the French government (including evacuations) to reduce the vulnerability of frontier regions during the mobilization.

48 French Commission, reports 10–12, pp. 24, 108–9.

49 *Le Temps*, 18 and 20 August 1914 ('Les Atrocités allemandes en Meurthe-et-Moselle'); French Commission, 3rd report, pp. 29–30, 145–9. The official history of the Bavarian army insisted that francs-tireurs had been present in Blâmont: Karl Deuringer, *Die Schlacht in Lothringen und in den Vogesen 1914. Die Feuertaufe der Bayerischen Armee* (2 vols, Munich, 1929), vol. 1, p. 52.

50 *L'Est républicain*, 20 August 1914; *Le Temps*, 20 August 1914; French Commission, 5th report, pp. 24–6, 121–30. A report by the school teacher of Badonviller, drawn up

for the departmental commission on the history of the war, confirms the accounts of witnesses cited by the official commission (AD Meurthe-et-Moselle, 86J 7, report of 13 September 1915, signature illegible). As with Blâmont, the Bavarian army's official history maintained the franc-tireur accusation (Deuringer, *Schlacht in Lothringen*, vol. 1, pp. 65–70). An officer of the third battalion, Bavarian IR 2, described the summary execution of civilians 'responsible' for resistance as francs-tireurs: KA, Munich, HS 2301, Eugen von Frauenholz, 'Erinnerungen an meine Soldatenzeit 1901–1918' (manuscript), p. 208.

51 E.g., in Parux on 10 August, the village was burned and six villagers were shot after a Landwehr company met resistance in taking it. The inhabitants denied any participation. Deuringer, *Schlacht in Lothringen*, vol. 1, p. 52; KA, Munich, HS 2762, Josef Clement, 10 August 1914, for the testimony of a soldier; AN AJ4 26, deposition of a nun, Marie Macron, 16 October 1914, whose nephew was among the six executed.

52 AN, Paris, AJ4 7, deposition Schoff, 11 October 1914.

53 Badisches Generallandesarchiv (GLA), Karlsruhe, 456 F1/205, commander XIVth Army Corps to Seventh Army, 13 August 1914; ibid., report of 28 August 1914.

54 Report in *Le Matin*, 18 August 1914, and *Le Temps*, 20 August 1914.

55 KA, Munich, BIR 1, official war diary, 11 August 1914.

56 PAAA, Bonn, R20880, fol. 12–13, Chief of the General Staff to the Foreign Ministry, 12 August 1914; *Norddeutsche Allgemeine Zeitung*, 14 August 1914.

57 National Archives, Washington, D.C., State Department, series M 367 (World War I and its Termination), 763.72116/ 1–79 (Illegal and Inhumane Warfare), telegram sent to State Department via German Embassy in Stockholm, 18 August 1914.

58 *La Guerre de 1914. L'action de l'armée belge*, pp. 49–93; Essen, *The Invasion and the War in Belgium*, pp. 177–84, 209–33.

59 F. Vliegen, *La Tragédie de Visé et la captivité des civils en Allemagne* (Liège, n.d., but 1919), pp. 3–4. Vliegen was a witness of the events and a deportee.

60 Belgian Second Commission, vol. 1, part 1, p. 19. Somville confirms that the new troops were from Königsberg (*Vers Liège*, p. 210), as did the Dutch journalist, L. Mokveld ('rough fellows from East Prussia'), in *De Overweldiging van België* (Rotterdam, 1916), translated into English as *The German Fury in Belgium* (London, 1917), p. 72.

61 The published depositions in the Belgian Second Commission report all concur that late in the evening of 15 August there was a fierce fusillade (lasting perhaps 15 minutes) and that in the morning it was announced that civilians had fired and that the town would be razed (pp. 316–39). An unpublished witness account maintains that a German patrol fired on German army telephonists on the left bank of the Meuse, in the night of 15–16 August, and that in order to cover up this 'friendly fire' incident, the destruction of Visé was decreed. (Statement made by Cerfont in Maastricht, 19 August, AGR, Brussels, CE, III 374 B1, 81b.)

62 Mokveld, *The German Fury*, pp. 72–3.

63 Belgian Second Commission, vol. 1, part 1, p. 18.

64 Letter, 18 August 1914, in Erich von Tschischwitz (ed.), *General von der Marwitz. Weltkriegsbriefe* (Berlin, 1940), p. 22.

65 BA, Koblenz, NL 15/97, Stellungnahme Foerster, fol. 11. Fifty-two members according to Belgian sources. They remained in Germany for five months (Cuvelier, *L'invasion allemande*, pp. 180–1).

66 Belgian First Commission, 17th report, vol. 2, pp. 71–2; Belgian Second Commission, vol. 1, part 1, pp. 272–3. A letter of apology for the pillaging and burning of Tongeren

was sent from the First Army headquarters at Louvain, on 21 August 1914, signed by Colonel von Bergmann. It may well have been prompted by a report from Lieutenant Heuke (probably of IR 42) who according to the Belgian report was in command of Tongeren, and who was critical of the passing troops and of the orders for 'reprisal' given by their unidentified commander (ibid., p. 272).

67 Mokveld, *The German Fury*, p. 47.

68 See in particular the evidence of the Liège police officer Neujean, given in August 1919 (Belgian Second Commission, vol. 1, part 1, pp. 374–83). Belgian sources identified the troops incorrectly as active, not reserve regiments.

69 Somville, *Vers Liège*, pp. 247–8. The tone of this account suggests that Somville witnessed the events himself.

70 Belgian Second Commission, vol. 1, part 1, p. 379: testimony by Neujean. Neujean also indicated that in an interview with a German lieutenant in 1917, the latter admitted that the story of the Russian students was a legend in which no one in Germany believed any longer, though he still held inhabitants responsible for firing on the Germans (cf. also Somville, *Vers Liège*, pp. 249–50).

71 Somville, *Vers Liège*, p. 212; Vliegen, *La Tragédie de Visé*, p. 14.

72 PAAA, Bonn, R 20882, fol. 65: report by Justizrat Dr Bodenheimer on a statement made to him and Prof. O. Warburg by the Persian subject Josef Soltanitzki, 7 September 1914. Soltanitzki witnessed the events in Liège on 21–22 August, and was told by German officers that soldiers had been shot at from the library of the Jewish students. Soltanitzki knew the library was closed, and obtained confirmation from Daltour, a major in the Garde Civique, that the students had not fired.

73 Belgian Second Commission, vol. 1, part 2, pp. 9–10 and 16.

74 Belgian First Commission, 15th report, p. 26; Belgian Second Commission, vol. 1, part 2, pp. 10, 351–5 (evidence of R. P. De Beucker, priest at Schaffen); corroboration from the unpublished testimony of Joseph Rymen, AGR, Brussels, CE, III 374 B1, 81b. IR 49 was in the IInd Army Corps and in the area of Diest-Schaffen on 18 August (Reichsarchiv, *Weltkrieg*, vol. 1, p. 215; Tasnier and van Overstraeten, *Opérations militaires*, p. 88).

75 Quoted by Joseph Bédier, *Les Crimes allemands d'après des témoignages allemands* (Paris, 1915), pp. 10–11. For a discussion of the German soldiers' *Kriegstagebücher*, or war diaries, as a significant source for German mentalities during the invasion, see chapter 3 below.

76 AGR Brussels, III 374 B1, CE, 32, typescript of inquiry for Cardinal Mercier into maltreatment of the priest. This is confirmed by the report of the German Military Governor in Belgium, Bissing, to Quartermaster-General West, 28 February 1915, CPHDC Moscow, 1415-1-55. For German evidence of the Belgian army in Diest-Schaffen on 18 August, see CPHDC Moscow, 1275–5–62, fol. 8, translation of diary of Belgian lieutenant Ghobert, 7th Line Regiment, Antwerp, entry for 18 August 1914.

77 Tasnier and van Overstraeten, *Opérations militaires*, pp. 94–5; Belgian First Commission, 1st, 3rd, 4th, 5th, 10th, and 21st reports; Belgian Second Commission, vol. 1, part 2, pp. 31–51, 364–84; *Die völkerrechtswidrige Führung*, pp. 89–103; the Belgian response, Ministère des Affaires Etrangères and Ministère de la Justice (eds), *Réponse au Livre blanc allemand du 10 mai 1915* (Paris, 1916), pp. 150–78; E. Alexander Powell, *Fighting in Flanders* (London, 1914), pp. 86–92; L.-H. Grondijs, *Les Allemands en Belgique. (Louvain et Aerschot) Notes d'un témoin hollandais* (Paris and Nancy, 1915; English translation, New York, 1916), pp. 16–28; Godefroid Kurth,

Le Guet-apens prussien en Belgique (Paris and Brussels, 1919), pp. 207–26; and Jozef De Vroey, *Aarschot op Woensdag 19 Augustus 1914* (Aarschot, n.d., but 1964). The 8th Brigade also comprised the 12th Dragoons Regiment, 17th Field Artillery Regiment, the 2nd Military Police Troop, and supply and medical columns (BA-MA, Freiburg, PHD 6/145, Ministry of War, Military Investigation Department for Violations of the Laws of War: memorandum on the events in Aarschot, 19 and 20 August 1914, sent to the Chancellor, 7 January 1915, *passim*).

78 Belgian First Commission, 5th report, vol. 1, p. 65, based on the statement by a Belgian soldier who escaped by remaining in the river pretending to be dead. For corroboration by one of the monks of the Sacred Heart Order in Aarschot, see Belgian Second Commission, vol. 1, part 2, pp. 368–9.

79 Belgian First Commission, 1st report, p. 44, and Second Commission, vol. 1, part 2, pp. 37–9. The original statement by an Aarschot primary school teacher, Julian van Praets, whose second, post-war deposition was used by the Second Commission, confirms that six civilians were shot in the morning of 19 August, although they were simply standing in the corridor of a house. Praets was categoric that no civilian fired on the Germans. (AGR, Brussels, CE, III 374 B1, 81b.) A contradictory account, suggesting that the six executed civilians had resisted, comes in the unused and second-hand account of Baron de Trannay, living some ten miles from Aarschot at Tongerlo. The primary school head teacher, Reusel, had told him that in spite of the mayor's instructions, the six had offered resistance. On what basis he said this, and whether he was merely relaying the German accusation, is not clear. A shadow of ambiguity remains over this incident.

80 Belgian First Commission, 5th report, pp. 65–6.

81 BA-MA, Freiburg, PHD 6/145, Ministry of War, memorandum on Aarschot, deposition Folz, pp. 16–17; Belgian Second Commission, vol. 1, part 2, pp. 51 and 383–4. The Germans conducted a ballistic test in 1915 which confirmed that the shots had indeed come from outside, at street level, on the far side of the square (Belgian Second Commission, vol. 1, part 2, p. 41).

82 BA-MA, Freiburg, PHD 6/145, memorandum on Aarschot, deposition Folz, pp. 16–17.

83 AGR, Brussels, CE, III 374 B1, 26, dossier on preparation of the Belgian response to the German White Book, especially a long memorandum by its president, Cooremans, pointing out that at Aarschot, as elsewhere, while the possibility of individual acts, though unproved, existed, concerted resistance was out of the question. Father Jozef De Vroey, whose father was among those executed on 19–20 August and who has made the atrocity at Aarschot the subject of intensive study, rules out the possibility of civilian resistance. However, he records that four Aarschot families told him they had seen 'francs-tireurs' firing (interview with John Horne, Aarschot, 1 May 1996). The authors would like to express their gratitude to Father De Vroey for sharing with them his knowledge of the events at Aarschot and their place in the memory of the townspeople.

84 BA-MA, Freiburg, PHD 6/145, memorandum on Aarschot, deposition Jenrich, pp. 10–11.

85 BA-MA, Freiburg, PHD 6/145, memorandum on Aarschot, deposition Karge, p. 13.

86 'Fosse Mommens', Belgian Second Commission, vol. 1, part 2, pp. 42–3, 375–6; BA-MA, Freiburg, PHD 6/145, memorandum on Aarschot, deposition Karge, p. 14.

87 Belgian Second Commission, vol. 1, part 2, p. 377; BA-MA, Freiburg, PHD 6/145, memorandum on Aarschot, deposition Jenrich, p. 11. Remarkably, this statement was

reproduced in *Die völkerrechtswidrige Führung* (p. 97), which maintained that 88 'free-shooters' had been executed at Aarschot (ibid., p. 91).

88 Belgian First Commission, 4th report, vol. 1, pp. 58–63, also Belgian Second Commission, vol. 1, part 2, pp. 31–6 (inquiry carried out by S. Orts, the secretary of the First Commission, in early September, when the Belgian army briefly regained the town).

89 Belgian Second Commission, vol. 1, part 2, p. 45; Grondijs, *Les Allemands en Belgique*, pp. 23–4.

90 Belgian Second Commission, vol. 1, part 2, p. 47.

91 AGR, Brussels, CE, III 374 B1, 81b (deposition Julian van Praets). This provides a much more detailed description than his 1919–20 deposition to the Second Commission report, though the essentials are the same. For the Sacred Heart fathers, see Belgian Second Commission, vol. 1, part 2, pp. 364–8 (depositions of Jean van Kerckhoven and Eugène de Busschère).

92 Belgian Second Commission, vol. 1, part 2, p. 382 (deposition of Joseph Meehus, priest).

93 According to Jozef De Vroey, 169 were killed, most of them 'family men', leaving 234 orphans. Also, 416 houses, rather than the 316 recorded by the Belgian commision, were destroyed. Interview with J. Horne, Aarschot, 1 May 1996. The additional 13 victims are accounted for by the killings of Aarschot citizens elsewhere, including nearby villages, and at Louvain. (De Vroey, *Aarschot, passim.*)

94 BA, Berlin, R 3003 ORA/RG bJ 594/20, vol. 1, fol. 5–8 and 10–13: report Bronsart von Schellendorf to Reichswehr Ministry, 5 June 1920; cf. ibid., fol. 41, report Captain Wabnitz, 15 March 1920; Reichsarchiv, *Weltkrieg*, vol. 1, pp. 217–18, 408–10; Tasnier and van Overstraeten, *Opérations militaires*, p. 102; Belgian First Commission, 11th and 21st reports ; Belgian Second Commission, vol. 1, part 1, pp. 97–110 and 424–66; Jean Schmitz and Norbert Nieuwland, *Documents pour servir à l'histoire de l'invasion allemande dans les provinces de Namur et de Luxembourg* (7 vols, Brussels and Paris, 1919–24), vol. 2, pp. 25–93; *1914. Enquêtes à Dinant, Andenne, Tamines et Luxembourg belge* (n.pl., n.d.); *Pages du livre de douleurs de la Belgique* (n.pl., n.d., a clandestine wartime Belgian publication), pp. 17–23.

95 BA, Berlin, R 3003 ORA/RG bJ 594/20, vol. 1, fol. 5–8 and 10–13: reports Bronsart von Schellendorf and Wabnitz; Belgian Second Commission, vol. 1, part 1, pp. 98–100.

96 Schmitz and Nieuwland, *L'invasion allemande*, vol. 2, p. 83 (priest's quotation); Belgian Second Commission, vol. 1, part 1, p. 102; *Enquêtes à Dinant*, pp. 14–15.

97 Report of the court-martial of the 1st Guards Reserve Division (Second Army) to the commander of the Namur siege troops, General von Gallwitz, 21 August 1914, cited in Robert Paul Oszwald, *Der Streit um den belgischen Franktireurkrieg. Eine kritische Untersuchung der Ereignisse in den Augusttagen 1914 und der darüber bis 1930 erschienenen Literatur unter Benutzung bisher nicht veröffentlichten Materials*, (Cologne, 1931), pp. 147–8. According to one official war diary, total losses were six men and two officers killed, and 60 injured (BA, Berlin, R 3003 ORA/RG bJ 594/20, vol. 1, fol. 108: extract from war diary, 1st Company, Pioneer Battalion 28, 20 August 1914). The assertion of a concerted attack was made by Bronsart von Schellendorf (ibid., fol. 5–8 and 10–13), and by Major Scheunemann (ibid., fol. 19–22); cf. *Die völkerrechtswidrige Führung*, p. 109.

98 Bibliothek für Zeitgeschichte (BfZ), Stuttgart, NL Klitzing, Reserve Lieutenant Betke von Klitzing, First Guards Reserve Regiment, to his wife, 21 August 1914.

99   BA, Berlin, R 3003 ORA/RG bJ 594/20, vol. 1, fol. 108: extract from war diary, 1st
     Company, Pioneer Battalion 28, 20 August 1914; fol. 41: report Wabnitz, 15 March
     1920.

100 BA, Berlin, R 3003 ORA/RG bJ 594/20, vol. 1, fol. 108: extract from war diary, 1st
     Company, Pioneer Battalion 28, 20 August 1914.

101 Belgian First Commission, 21st report, vol. 2, p. 124.

102 Belgian Second Commission, vol. 1, part 1, p. 104.

103 Belgian Second Commission, vol. 1, part 1, pp. 103, 435–41.

104 BA, Berlin, R 3003 ORA/RG bJ 594/20, vol. 1, fol. 10–13, report Bronsart von
     Schellendorf, 5 June 1920; ibid., fol. 19–22, report Scheunemann, 12 September 1920;
     ibid., vol. 1, fol. 79, statement Wabnitz, 3 August 1920.

105 BA, Berlin, R 3003 ORA/RG bJ 594/20, vol. 1, fol. 79, statement Wabnitz, 3 August
     1920; vol. 1, fol. 163–6, deposition Woite; fol. 128, statement Franz Worms, 3rd
     Company, Guards Reserve Rifle Battalion. For the execution figures, see report of the
     court-martial of the 1st Guards Reserve Division to General von Gallwitz, 21 August
     1914, cited in Oszwald, *Der Streit*, pp. 147–8.

106 AGR, Brussels, CE, III 374 B1,12, Heutter report, pp. 13–15. The figure of 800 civil-
     ians rounded up in the central square given by Belgian sources is confirmed by the
     German court-martial report.

107 Several witnesses quoted by Schmitz and Nieuwland and by the Second Commission
     report, notably Eva Comes, confirmed the role of Junge. The Second Commission was
     not certain that Bronsart ordered the executions (Belgian Second Commission, vol. 1,
     part 1, p. 109). Two clandestine Belgian accounts had a Major Scheunemann, or
     Schoeneman, intervening towards the end of the events in the square (*Pages du livre
     de douleurs*, p. 17; *1914. Enquêtes à Dinant*, pp. 15–16). In his testimony to Schmitz and
     Nieuwland, the lawyer Maurice Monjoie also identified Scheunemann (*L'invasion
     allemande*, vol. 2, p. 68). Belgian witnesses thus named more or less correctly most of
     the German officers involved.

108 Belgian Second Commission, vol. 1, part 1, pp. 106 and 450; Schmitz and Nieuwland,
     L'invasion allemande, vol. 2, p. 50.

109 Belgian Second Commission, vol. 1, part 1, pp. 102–3, 455.

110 According to the evidence of one of the group of three, Félix Heurter, who was injured
     but survived by feigning death, there was no semblance of a court-martial or even
     interrogation (Schmitz and Nieuwland, *L'invasion allemande* vol. 2, pp. 51–2). Both
     the Second Commission report and Schmitz and Nieuwland agree on the heightened
     tension caused by the arrival of the German NCO's corpse.

111 The group from the rue d'Horseilles was taken more or less straight to the execution
     ground (Belgian Second Commission, vol. 1, part 1, p. 457, evidence of Edouard Noël).
     It is not clear whether the other 'suspects', classified before their arrival, were added
     to this cortège or executed separately, as was certainly the case with some, in
     surrounding streets. The latter is the impression conveyed by *1914. Enquêtes à Dinant*,
     p. 16, and some of the witnesses quoted in the Second Commission report.

112 AGR, Brussels, CE, III 374 B1, 12, Heutter report, pp. 13–15.

113 Schmitz and Nieuwland, *L'invasion allemande*, vol. 2, pp. 55 and plate 21; *Pages du
     livre de douleurs*, p. 18; Davignon, *German Posters in Belgium*, p. 28.

114 Franz Petri and Peter Schöller, 'Zur Bereinigung des Franktireurproblems vom
     August 1914', *Vierteljahrshefte für Zeitgeschichte*, 9 (1961), p. 244.

115 BA, Berlin, R 3003 ORA/RG bJ 594/20, vol. 1, fol. 41: report Wabnitz, 15 March 1920;

Schmitz and Nieuwland, *L'invasion allemande*, vol. 2, p. 68 (Monjoie's evidence).

116 Davignon, *German Posters in Belgium*, pp. 44 and 48 (for the two posters); Schmitz and Nieuwland, *L'invasion allemande*, vol. 2, p. 64.

117 Schmitz and Nieuwland, *L'invasion allemande*, vol. 2, p. 61; vol. 1, part 1, p. 443.

118 Keegan, *Opening Moves*, p. 104; Tasnier and van Overstraeten, *Opérations militaires*, pp. 96–121; van der Essen, *The Invasion and the War in Belgium*, pp. 141–55.

119 Schmitz and Nieuwland, *L'invasion allemande*, vol. 2, p. 263.

120 Belgian First Commission, 11th report, pp. 130–3; Belgian Second Commission, vol. 1, part 1, pp. 122–8, 473–7; Schmitz and Nieuwland, *L'invasion allemande*, vol. 2, pp. 261–332 (312 for quotation); Davignon, *German Posters in Belgium*, p. 45.

121 Davignon, *German Posters in Belgium*, pp. 11, 15.

122 Brand Whitlock, *Belgium under the German Occupation: A Personal Narrative* (2 vols, London, 1919), vol. 1, pp. 74–6, 81 (quotation); H. Marchant, *Historique des troupes territoriales en Belgique en 1914. Groupement Clooten: Gardes Civiques, Gendarmerie, Corps de Volontaires* (Ixelles, 1938), pp. 14–15.

123 See appendix 1 below.

124 The destruction of the archives of the Prussian army at Potsdam during the Second World War severely reduces the primary sources relating to the First and Second Armies during the invasion. For military events on the Sambre, see Ministère de la Guerre, *Les Armées françaises dans la grande guerre*, vol. 1, part 2, *Annexes* (1922), pp. 564, 660; Reichsarchiv, *Weltkrieg*, vol. 1, pp. 358–9; and *Le Combat d'Arsimont. Les 21 et 22 août 1914 à la 19e Division* (Nancy, Paris, Strasbourg, 1926). For the massacre at Tamines, see Belgian First Commission, 11th and 21st reports; Belgian Second Commission, vol. 1, part 1, pp. 143–6, 477–9; Schmitz and Nieuwland, *L'invasion allemande*, vol. 3, pp. 75–154 ; and A. Lemaire, *La Tragédie de Tamines (21, 22 et 23 août 1914)* (Tamines, 1919).

125 Belgian Second Commission, vol. 1, part 1, pp. 147–8; Schmitz and Nieuwland, *L'invasion allemande*, vol. 3, pp. 41–59, 63–6.

126 Belgian First Commission, 11th report, p. 134 (for the Garde Civique and the civilian audience); Schmitz and Nieuwland, *L'invasion allemande*, vol. 3, pp. 79–80. The captain of the Garde Civique made it clear how much of a hindrance civilians were in this first phase of the battle (Lemaire, *La Tragédie de Tamines*, pp. 187–9).

127 Reichsarchiv, *Weltkrieg*, vol. 1, pp. 358–9.

128 AGR, Brussels, CE, III 374 B1, 20, deposition Jules Bruyère on the human shield.

129 Lemaire, *La Tragédie de Tamines*, p. 145; Schmitz and Nieuwland, *L'invasion allemande*, vol. 3, pp. 104–5. Reichsarchiv, *Weltkrieg*, vol. 1, pp. 358–9, confirms that IR 77 was present.

130 Belgian Second Commission, vol. 1, part 1, pp. 143–4; cf. Lemaire, *La Tragédie de Tamines*, p. 163.

131 Lemaire, *La Tragédie de Tamines*, pp. 125–90 (extensive survivor witness statements); AN, Paris, AJ4 20, deposition Laurent Ferdinant on rifle butts; Schmitz and Nieuwland, *L'invasion allemande*, vol. 3, fig. 89, post-war commemorative photograph showing the high number of survivors.

132 See discussion of the German White Book in chapter 6.

133 Sources on Louvain are: Belgian First Commission, 2nd, 3rd, 5th, and 21st reports; Belgian Second Commission, vol. 1, part 2, pp. 63–102, 393–525; three eye-witness accounts, René Chambry, *La Vérité sur Louvain* (Paris, 1915), English translation, *The Truth about Louvain* (London, 1915); Grondijs, *Les Allemands en Belgique*; A.

Fuglister, *A Neutral Description of the Sack of Louvain* (Concord, N.H., 1929); *Pages du livre de douleurs*, pp. 57–75. The principal secondary work, which contains a critical analysis of the German White Book, is Peter Schöller, *Der Fall Löwen und das Weißbuch. Eine kritische Untersuchung der deutschen Dokumentation über die Vorgänge in Löwen vom 25. bis 28. August 1914* (Cologne, Graz, Louvain, 1958), also in French and Flemish. Cf. Lothar Wieland, *Belgien 1914. Die Frage des belgischen 'Franktireurkrieges' und die deutsche öffentliche Meinung von 1914 bis 1936* (Frankfurt, Berne, New York, 1984), pp. 32–9; and Wolfgang Schivelbusch, *Die Bibliothek von Löwen. Eine Episode aus der Zeit der Weltkriege* (Munich and Vienna, 1988), pp. 13–50.

134 Wieland, *Belgien 1914*, p. 34. See also PAAA, Bonn, R 20882, fol. 75–87: report by Dillen, Prior of the Dominican Order at Louvain, 4 September 1914.

135 PAAA, Bonn, R 20882, fol. 75–87: report by Dillen; Chambry, *The Truth about Louvain*, pp. 11–15; Wieland, *Belgien 1914*, p. 35 (for the poster).

136 Schöller, *Der Fall Löwen*, pp. 34–5, for basis of calculation of troop numbers. For intimidation, see Belgian Second Commission report, vol. 1, part 2, e.g. pp. 416–17 (deposition of Émile Schmit); Grondijs, *Les Allemands en Belgique*, pp. 39–41; and Wieland, *Belgien 1914*, pp. 35–6.

137 Reichsarchiv, *Weltkrieg*, vol. 1, pp. 217 and 365.

138 AGR, Brussels, CE, III 374 B1, 81a, testimony of G. Bruylants, professor at Louvain and president of the Académie Royale de Médecine, who witnessed the events of the night of 25 August and investigated them the following day; Belgian Second Commission, vol. 1, part 2, pp. 419 (testimony of Émile Schmit) and 431 (testimony of Baron Orban de Xivry), on David-Fischbach's murder; ibid., numerous witnesses on the events of the night, including Alfred Nérincx, professor of international law at the university who took over as burgomaster on 29 August (pp. 394–6); Grondijs, *Les Allemands en Belgique*, pp. 48–67; *Pages du livre de douleurs*, pp. 57–72; Chambry, *The Truth about Louvain*, pp. 21–32.

139 Vatican Archive, Affari Ecclesiatici Straordinari, Belgio, 1907–1914, pos. 199, fasc. 101, undated report by Ladeuze, almost certainly early 1915, fol. 68. Cf. testimony of Ladeuze to the Belgian Second Commission, vol. 1, part 2, pp. 466–70.

140 Grondijs, *Les Allemands en Belgique*, p. 54; Fuglister, *A Neutral Description*, pp. 16–17.

141 Grondijs, *Les Allemands en Belgique*, p. 52.

142 Belgian First Commission, 5th report, pp. 68–74; Vatican Archive, Ladeuze report, fol. 61; Chambry, *The Truth about Louvain*, pp. 40–58; Schöller, *Der Fall Löwen*, pp. 63–6 (for shooting on 28 August).

143 Grondijs, *Les Allemands en Belgique*, p. 64 (civic guard), and Belgian Second Commission, vol. 1, part 2, p. 518 (testimony Professor Luis Maldague).

144 Papers of Peter Schöller, in possession of Frau Dr H. Ditt, Münster, Heinrich Richard (German veteran), to Petri, 23 July 1958; Schöller, *Der Fall Löwen*, pp. 41–4; PAAA, Bonn, R 20882, fol. 75–87: report by Dillen, 4 September 1914, fol. 78–9.

145 Vatican Archive, Affari Ecclesiatici Straordinari, Belgio, 1907–1914, pos. 199, fasc. 101, Ladeuze report, fol. 59–61, and ibid., Segretaria di Stato, 244 D7 (Belgio), f. 108, Simon Deploige, 'Le Point de vue des catholiques belges', appendix 4, 'Explication des excès commis par les troupes allemandes en Belgique', pp. 1–2.

146 Grondijs, *Les Allemands en Belgique*, p. 37; Vatican Archive, Ladeuze report, fol. 69.

147 Vatican Archive, Ladeuze report, fol. 71.

148 Belgian Second Commission, vol. 1, part 2, pp. 472–3 (testimony of Monsignor Jules De Becker, professor at Louvain and rector of the American College). Dupierreux referred to the destruction of the library of Alexandria by the Arabs in the seventh century.

149 Belgian Second Commission, vol. 1, part 2, pp. 468–70 (testimony of Ladeuze); Grondijs, *Les Allemands en Belgique*, pp. 81–2 (insults to clerics), 89–107 (Tervueren and Lüttwitz); Whitlock, *Belgium under the German Occupation*, vol. 1, pp. 114–16.

150 Mokveld, *The German Fury in Belgium*, pp. 121–2, 129; *Die völkerrechtswidrige Führung*, appendix D, summary memorandum, p. 236.

151 Reichsarchiv, *Weltkrieg*, vol. 1, p. 506 (position of the First Army on 25 August); ibid., vol. 3, p. 328, on the strategic position.

152 Essen, *The Invasion of Belgium*, pp. 185–98. In the zone of the fighting, Hofstade was burned on 25 August, with ten civilian dead and over 100 (including women and children) used as a human shield. In nearby Zempst, 14 civilians were killed and 34 deported to Germany. At Veltem, on the afternoon of 25 August, civilians were accused of firing and 18 were executed (Belgian Second Commission, vol. 1, part 2, pp. 109, 138–40, 552–8). Among the villages near Louvain that suffered was Korbeek-Lo, which was pillaged and razed on 26 August, with 16 inhabitants killed and many of the rest expelled or deported to Liège. See appendix 1 below.

153 *Les Armées françaises dans la grande guerre*, vol. 1, part 2, *Annexes*, p. 726; Keegan, *Opening Moves*, pp. 98–109.

154 The essential Belgian sources for Dinant are three inquiries. The first is that of the state prosecutor, Maurice Tschoffen, an eye-witness who, on return from deportation to Germany in November 1914, conducted a scrupulous inquiry under the nose of the Germans. This was published in the Belgian First Commission, 20th report, vol. 2, pp. 85–98. A second inquiry was carried out by the post-war commission which corroborated Tschoffen's account in every major particular, though it revised the total killed upward to 665 (Belgian Second Commission, vol. 1, part 1, pp. 151–68). A third inquiry was that of Schmitz and Nieuwland, conducted separately by the two men during the war and amalgamated after the war as *L'invasion allemande*, vol. 4 (2 parts) being devoted to the events at Dinant. For Schmitz and Nieuwland's work, see chapter 9. The German inquiry was published in *Die völkerrechtswidrige Führung*, appendix C, pp. 116–229. For the production of this account, see chapter 7. The Belgian official rebuttal came in *Réponse au Livre blanc allemand*, pp. 199–289. Tschoffen also responded with a volume published in Holland, *Le Sac de Dinant et les légendes du Livre blanc allemand du 10 mai 1915* (Leiden, 1917). Nieuwland and Tschoffen produced a definitive total of 674 civilian deaths in *La Légende des francs-tireurs de Dinant. Réponse au mémoire de M. le professeur Meurer de l'université de Wurzbourg* (Gembloux, 1928), p. 86.

155 Friedrich Max Kircheisen (ed.), *Des Generalobersten Frhrn. v. Hausen Erinnerungen an den Marnefeldzug 1914. Mit einer einleitenden kritischen Studie* (Leipzig, 1920; 2nd edn, 1922), p. 108.

156 Schmitz and Nieuwland, *L'invasion allemande*, vol. 1, pp. 132–51 (Somme-Leuze, in Namur province), and vol. 1, pp. 116–32 for Erezée, in northern Luxembourg province; HStA, Dresden, 40870, 96th Foot Artillery Battalion, diary entry 20 August 1914, and ibid., 40949, munition column 260, 96th Foot Artillery Battalion, diary entry 20, 21, and 22 August 1914 (for Champlon and Hargimont, in northern Luxembourg).

157 HStA, Dresden, 36404, war diary 1st Battalion, Foot Artillery Regiment 19, diary entries 20 and 21 August 1914.

158 From the Second Battalion, Fusilier Regiment 108, and 1st Company, Pioneer Battalion 12.

159 The Reichsarchiv official history made no mention of the raid. The account in *Die völkerrechtswidrige Führung* called it a 'reconnaissance in force' and emphasized civilian ambush (Appendix C, pp. 117 and 128–32). Evidence of panic (see below) was likewise suppressed. For the reaction of the inhabitants, see Belgian First Commission, 20th report, vol. 2, p. 87, and 21st report, vol. 2, p. 125, testimony of Mme D. For corroboration of drunkenness, *De Telegraaf* (Amsterdam), 8 December 1914, evening edition, in CPHDC Moscow, 1467-1-12, fol. 128–30 (report by Staller). For casualties see Schmitz and Nieuwland, *L'invasion allemande*, vol. 4, part 2, p. 282.

160 BA, Berlin, R 3003/ORA/RG bJ 198/20, vol. 2, fol. 43–9, battalion report. The brigade commander was Major-General von Watzdorf.

161 HStA, Dresden, Zeitgeschichtliche Sammlung 75, No. 1: Kurt Rasch (2nd Battalion, IR 108) to his parents, 22 August 1914. The battalion report mentioned similar figures for losses.

162 BA, Berlin, R 3003/ORA/RG bJ 198/20, vol. 2, fol. 43–9 (battalion report).

163 M. Larcher, *Le 1er Corps à Dinant, Charleroi, Guise (août 1914)* (Paris, 1932), p. 28; Belgian First Commission, 20th report, vol. 2, p. 87 (testimony of Tschoffen) for French patrols on the east bank; BA, Berlin, R 3003/ORA/RG bJ 198/20, vol. 2, fol. 29 and reverse, extract from report by 2nd Battalion IR 108.

164 Evidence of the burgomaster of Bouvignes, Ludovic Amand, in Schmitz and Nieuwland, *L'invasion allemande*, vol. 4, part 2, p. 96.

165 Service Historique de l'Armée de Terre (hereafter SHA), Vincennes, 26N 735, journal des marches, 273e RI; *Historique de 273e régiment d'infanterie pendant la guerre 1914–1918* (Nancy, Paris, Strasbourg, n.d.), pp. 4–5.

166 SHA, Vincennes, 26N 735. The regimental diary of French IR 273 puts the time of retreat at 3 pm. But the burgomaster of Bouvignes' testimony is that the French were fleeing as the Germans arrived, around 6.30 pm. This is corroborated by the fact that the civilians who had hidden in the basement of the cloth factory at Leffe gave themselves up around 5 pm, when the Germans were still firing from the factory windows. The factory was only slightly upstream from Bouvignes, which it overlooked on the opposite bank (Schmitz and Nieuwland, *L'invasion allemande*, vol. 4, part 2, pp. 93, 236). The discrepancy may well be accounted for by a small French rear-guard. The bulk of French IR 273 disengaged mid-afternoon.

167 CPHDC Moscow, 1467-1-12, fol. 117, deposition NCO Zschocke, 9th company, IR 103, 13 December 1914.

168 CPHDC Moscow, 1467-1-11, fol. 99, transcript of an undated, unsigned statement by Sergeant Franz Stieping [*sic*]. The saw-mill was probably in reality a disused paper factory.

169 CPHDC Moscow, 1467-1-11, fol. 18, deposition Stiebing, Ersatzbataillon IR 178, 5 February 1915.

170 Schmitz and Nieuwland, *L'invasion allemande*, vol. 4, part 2, pp. 80–91, evidence of Adrien Borrelly, prior of the abbey.

171 Testimony of Isabelle Himmer, adult daughter of the manager, in Schmitz and Nieuwland, *L'invasion allemande*, vol. 4, part 2, pp. 94–5.

172 Schmitz and Nieuwland, *L'invasion allemande*, vol. 4, part 2, pp. 99–123.

173   Belgian First Commission, 20th report, vol. 2, p. 91 (Tschoffen report).
174   HStA, Dresden, Zeitgeschichtliche Sammlung 73, diary Wilhelm Clemens, IR 182, entry for 23 August.
175   Additional evidence to that in Schmitz and Nieuwland from Jean Chot, *La Furie allemande dans l'entre Sambre-et-Meuse (journées des 23, 24, 25 et 26 août 1914)* (Charleroi, 1919), p. 76, whose informants in the winter of 1914–15 confirmed that the Germans had systematically set fire to houses.
176   Nieuwland and Tschoffen, *La Légende des francs-tireurs de Dinant*, p. 42.
177   Schmitz and Nieuwland, *L'invasion allemande*, vol. 4, part 2, pp. 123–84.
178   Belgian First Commission, 20th report, vol. 2, pp. 88, 92–3 (Tschoffen report).
179   Ibid., pp. 88–9.
180   CPHDC Moscow, 1467-1-12, fol. 35–6, deposition Major Walter von Loeben, commander of a battalion in Grenadier Regiment 100, 15 February 1915. He was a captain in command of the third company at the time of the execution. Count Kielmannsegg's deposition, cited in the White Book, confirmed that he had given the order for the execution of 'about 100 guilty inhabitants'; he reiterated the presumption of civilian resistance (*Die völkerrechtswidrige Führung*, p. 134). That the victims of the execution were selected arbitrarily on the order of the battalion commander was confirmed by Lieutenant von Haugk, battalion adjutant in Grenadier Regiment 100, in a deposition of 16 February 1915: BA, Berlin, R 3003/ORA/RG bJ 304/20, appendix 17.
181   Belgian Second Commission, vol. 1, part 1, pp. 485–7 (testimony of Nestor Trembloy and Prosper Massart). Schmitz and Nieuwland provide further corroboration (*L'invasion allemande*, vol. 4, part 2, pp. 158–64).
182   Belgian First Commission, 20th report, vol. 2, p. 88 (Tschoffen report).
183   Ibid., p. 89.
184   Earlier the French had fired from the village of Neffe, and may well still have had soldiers there at this point. But French IR 273 was also retreating from the Dinant bridge up the Philippeville road to Onhaye, from which it could fire at the Germans at Les Rivages.
185   For a discussion of these opposed accounts, see Schmitz and Nieuwland, *L'invasion allemande*, vol. 4, part 2, pp. 184–8; *Die völkerrechtswidrige Führung*, appendices 39–48 (pp. 55–64).
186   Schmitz and Nieuwland, *L'invasion allemande*, vol. 4, part 2, pp. 188–200. See, in particular, the account of Félix Bourdon, ibid., pp. 192–6. Cf. Chambre des Représentants, *Séance du 13 juillet 1927. Rapport présenté aux Chambres Législatives par M. le Ministre des Affaires Étrangères* [i.e. Vandervelde] *sur certaines affirmations de la Commission d'Enquête du Reichstag au sujet d'une prétendue guerre de francs-tireurs en Belgique*, p. 12, which gives the lower figure of 77, rather than the 90 victims mentioned in Schmitz and Nieuwland.
187   Schmitz and Nieuwland, *L'invasion allemande*, vol. 4, part 2, pp. 206–28.
188   BA, Berlin, R 3003/ORA/RG bJ 307/20, vol. 1, fol. 6–7, statement General Meister, 30 November 1920; ibid., fol. 102: statement by Meister's batman, Ernst Stürzkober, 27 December 1921. Naturally, it is possible that Stürzkober was seeking to protect his former master out of continuing loyalty. But the evidence connecting Meister with the execution order is thin, whereas there is a confession as well as corroboration in regard to Major Schlick.
189   BA, Berlin, R 3003/ORA/RG bJ 307/20, vol. 1, fol. 104–5, statement P. Fritz, 27

December 1921, lance-corporal in 9th company, IR 101. On the impossibility of the group of civilians having fired, ibid., fol. 130, statement Walter Hoßfeld, 7 February 1922, and fol. 136–7, statement Paul Stier, 14 February 1922. On the culpability of Schlick, see also ibid., vol. 1, fol. 93–4: statement Lieutenant Schuster.

190 BA, Berlin, R 3003/ORA/RG bJ 307/20, vol. 1, fol. 107, statement Schlick, 28 December 1921.

191 BA, Berlin, R 3003/ORA/RG bJ 304/20, report NCO Bieligk, 8 April 1920.

192 AGR, Brussels, CE, III 374 B1, 21, deposition Lieutenant Loustalot, Bordeaux, 16 June 1915.

193 Belgian First Commission, 20th report (Tschoffen report), vol. 2, pp. 91–2.

194 Schmitz and Nieuwland, *L'invasion allemande*, vol. 4, part 2, pp. 125, 201, 269–77.

195 Belgian Second Commission report, vol. 1, part 1, pp. 190–1, 520–1; Schmitz and Nieuwland, *L'invasion allemande*, vol. 4, part 1, pp. 54–64. Unfortunately, lack of German archival evidence makes full study of these incidents impossible.

196 Belgian Second Commission report, vol. 1, part 1, pp. 182–6, 501–11; Schmitz and Nieuwland, *L'invasion allemande*, vol. 5, pp. 194–216.

197 HStA, Dresden, Zeitgeschichtliche Sammlung 75, No. 8: letter Captain F. Heinzmann, Reserve IR 101, to his wife, 23 August 1914.

198 Belgian Second Commission, vol. 1, part 1, pp. 117–19, 470–533; Schmitz and Nieuwland, *L'invasion allemande*, vol. 4, part 1, pp. 96–125. The German units involved were IR 103 and probably also Reserve IR 101. For the treatment of Spontin by the official German inquiry in 1915, see chapter 6.

2 German invasion, part 2

1 Reichsarchiv, *Der Weltkrieg 1914 bis 1918. Die militärischen Operationen zu Lande* (14 vols, Berlin, 1925–44), vol. 1, *Die Grenzschlachten im Westen* (1925), pp. 303–45, 537–67; Ministère de la Guerre, *Les Armées françaises dans la grande guerre* (103 vols, Paris, 1922–37), vol. 1, *La Bataille des frontières jusqu'au 23 août 1914* (1936), pp. 210–11; Jean Schmitz and Norbert Nieuwland, *Documents pour servir à l'histoire de l'invasion allemande dans les provinces de Namur et de Luxembourg* (7 vols, Brussels and Paris, 1919–24), vol. 6, *La Bataille de Neufchâteau et de Maissin* (1924), pp. 5–22, and vol. 7, *La Bataille de la Semois et de Virton* (1924), pp. 5–20; L. Koeltz, *La Guerre de 1914–1918. Les opérations militaires* (Paris, 1966), pp. 62, 75–7; John Keegan, *Opening Moves: August 1914* (New York, 1971), pp. 73–81.

2 See appendix 1 below. To the major incidents in Belgian Luxembourg totalling 660 deaths (excluding Erezée-Briscol which was the responsibility of the Third Army) must be added those that took place in the northern Meurthe-et-Moselle at Audun-le-Roman (13), Mont-Saint-Martin (16), Chénières (22), Fillières (10), Landres (10), Mercy-le-Haut (10), Saint-Pancré (10), Fresnois-la-Montagne (51), Longuyon (60), and in the Ardennes at Margny (42) and Sedan (23). All were the responsibility of the Fourth and Fifth Armies. This total of 927 deaths must be supplemented by the incidents with fewer than ten dead, making an approximate death toll of 1,000.

3 The post-war Belgian commission wrongly stated that there was no battle at Anloy, though it reported the violence against civilians (Belgian Second Commission, vol. 1, part 1, pp. 217–18, 549–51); cf. the much more detailed account in Schmitz and Nieuwland, *L'invasion allemande*, vol. 6, pp. 137–52 (p. 143 for the primary school teacher's evidence).

4 Schmitz and Nieuwland, *L'invasion allemande*, vol. 6, pp. 69–71 (p. 71 for quotation, from a notice in French posted in the town on the evening of 22 August).

5 Belgian Second Commission, vol. 1, part 1, pp. 260–1, 582–6; Schmitz and Nieuwland, *L'invasion allemande*, vol. 7, pp. 91–101. The Second Commission wrongly gives a total of 30 dead, contradicted by its own evidence of 40 killed in the collective shooting (from Albert Lamotte, brother of the burgomaster, in Belgian Second Commission, vol. 1, part 1, pp. 582–3). The corrected figure of 63 is derived from both sources. Cf. the apologetic accounts in Reichsarchiv, *Weltkrieg*, vol. 1, pp. 314–15, and Kurt Ernst Gottfried von Bülow, *Preußischer Militarismus zur Zeit Wilhelms II. Aus meiner Dienstzeit im Heer* (Schweidnitz, 1930), pp. 135 and 140. According to one German army report the ambush on the Germans near Tintigny was carried out by foresters wearing uniform; the Belgian government had given the German government official notice of their status as combatants: BA, Koblenz, NL 15/97, Stellungnahme Foerster … fol. 12.

6 Belgian Second Commission, vol. 1, part 1, pp. 248–9; Bayerisches Hauptstaatsarchiv-Kriegsarchiv (KA), Munich, HS 2259, statement by von Hedemann, Landsturm-Infanterie-Bataillon Gotha, attached to Hurt's report to the Imperial German Court, Arlon, 16 March 1915.

7 On Arlon and Rossignol, see Belgian Second Commission, vol. 1, part 1, pp. 247–50 and 562–72 ; Schmitz and Nieuwland, *L'invasion allemande* vol. 8, pp. 44–71.

8 Reichsarchiv, *Weltkrieg*, vol. 1, pp. 312–15 and 332; Schmitz and Nieuwland, *L'invasion allemande*, vol. 7, pp. 61–70; Joseph Hubert and Joseph Neujean, *Rossignol. Les Drames de l'invasion allemande dans le Luxembourg belge* (1922; new edn, Tamines, 1938), pp. 89–132. The Belgian sources particularly identified IR 62 and 157, but implicated also IR 23 and 63.

9 Schmitz and Nieuwland, *L'invasion allemande*, vol. 7, pp. 61–70, 203.

10 Ibid., pp. 201–3.

11 Ibid., p. 201. The story was published in *L'Indépendance luxembourgeoise*, 24 August 1919, and confirmed on 4 July 1923 in a report by Koenig, Criminal Police Inspector of Luxemburg (Schmitz and Nieuwland, *L'invasion allemande*, vol. 7, p. 201, n. 3).

12 Ibid. pp. 201–4, who give the figure as 122, which can be taken as the more accurate since Schmitz and Nieuwland provide a list of names; Belgian Second Commission, vol. 1, part 1, pp. 247–50, which gives the figure as 121; Hubert and Neujean, *Rossignol*, pp. 126–32. Of the total, 108 were from Rossignol, seven from Breuvanne, five from Saint-Vincent, and two from Tellancourt (France).

13 KA, Munich, HS 2259, report Landsturm-Infanterie-Bataillon Gotha, 16 March 1915.

14 HStA-MA, Stuttgart, M660, Pezold diary, 18 October 1914, pp. 67–8 (comment of Schenkelberger, a factory-owner).

15 Schmitz and Nieuwland, *L'invasion allemande*, vol. 7, pp. 265–6 (Ethe) and 313 (Goméry).

16 Reichsarchiv, *Weltkrieg*, vol. 1, pp. 252, 303–8, 318–19; Belgian sources for Ethe are the Second Commission, vol. 1, part 1, pp. 251–3, and Schmitz and Nieuwland, *L'invasion allemande*, vol. 7, pp. 263–310 (p. 270 for events at Belmont, suggesting that IR 46 was responsible).

17 Accounts of Baulard, the burgomaster (who survived the collective execution), and of Louis Authelet-Claisse, in Schmitz and Nieuwland, *L'invasion allemande*, vol. 7, pp. 283–4, and 285–7.

18 Ibid., pp. 310–33; French Commission, report 3, pp. 11–16, 73–80; and two French

eye-witness accounts, A. Grasset, *Vingt jours de guerre aux temps héroïques. Carnet de route d'un commandant de compagnie. (Août 1914)* (Paris and Nancy, 1918), esp. pp. 238–79, and J. Simonin, *De Verdun à Mannheim. Ethe et Goméry (22, 23, 24 août 1914)* (Paris, 1917).

19   KA, Munich, HS 2259, report by 20th Infantry Brigade, unsigned, but probably by its commander Major-General von der Horst, 1 September 1914, attached to Hurt's report to Imperial German Court, Brussels, 31 March 1915. Von der Horst incorrectly dated the incident as occurring on 27 August; this was altered by General Hurt to 22 August; from the context it is clearly 23 August.

20   Schmitz and Nieuwland, *L'invasion allemande*, vol. 7, pp. 292–5 (evidence of four survivors).

21   Ibid., pp. 295–7.

22   KA, Munich, HS 2259, report by 20th Infantry Brigade, 1 September 1914; ibid., report by IR 50, 5 December 1915; Schmitz and Nieuwland, *L'invasion allemande*, vol. 8, pp. 306–10. The other units involved were Grenadier Regiment 6 and the First Mounted Jäger Regiment. For civilian losses, see also *La Belgique et la guerre* (4 vols, Brussels, 1921–8), vol. 2, Jacques Cuvelier, *L'invasion allemande* (1921), pp. 163–4.

23   Schmitz and Nieuwland, *L'invasion allemande*, vol. 7, pp. 366–73, 378–82. Belgian Second Commission, vol. 1, part 1, p. 256, gives the figures of 24 killed in Baranzy, but ignores three villagers asphyxiated in their burning houses and the 80 houses destroyed. It also fails to include Baranzy in its overall listing of incidents. In this case, the figures of Schmitz and Nieuwland are preferred for the statistical analysis in appendix 1 below. On the 'friendly fire' incidents, see HStA-MA, Stuttgart, M660, NL Ebbinghaus, book 5: war diary kept by Lt Alfred Roth, entry for 22 August, pp. 8–10. On the executions from the German perspective: HStA-MA, Stuttgart M660, NL Dr Max Flammer, diary entry 23 August, p. 9.

24   HStA-MA, Stuttgart, M660, NL Ebbinghaus, book 4, Ebbinghaus diary, entry for 22 August, fol. 9.

25   French Commission, 12th Report, pp. 25–6, 111–13.

26   Ibid., pp. 28–9, 124–7.

27   AD Meurthe-et-Moselle, 86J5, Commission pour une histoire de la guerre franco-allemande, testimony of E. Véron, the primary school teacher; French Commission, 5th report, pp. 26–7, 131–9.

28   French Commission, reports 10–12, pp. 24–5, 109–11 (Fillières); ibid., pp. 26, 114–18 (Chénières); ibid., pp. 27, 119–20 (Landres); ibid., pp. 28, 122–4 (Mercy-le-Haut); ibid., pp. 27, 120–2 (St Pancré).

29   French Commission, reports 10–12, pp. 30–1, 147–56.

30   HStA-MA, Stuttgart, M1/7, 20, Heeresabwicklungsamt Württemberg to Heeresabwicklungsamt Preußen, Abtl. für Völkerrechtsverletzungen U.5., [?] March 1920. At least one detachment of IR 123 was also present.

31   HStA-MA, Stuttgart, M660 NL Ebbinghaus, book 8, report by Captain Fauser, 23 August 1914, p. 21. An unclear pencil addition to the typescript may read '(20 Mann)' – i.e. that 20 civilians were killed.

32   Reichsarchiv, *Weltkrieg*, vol. 1, p. 342; French Commission, 12th report, pp. 29, 144. The French Commission also places Bavarian IR 22 in Longuyon, but this appears to be on the basis of one witness and is certainly a mistaken identification, probably for IR 122. Bavarian regiments were in the Sixth Army, which was not present in this sector.

33   AD Meurthe-et-Moselle, 8R 200, sub-prefect to the prefect, 7 December 1914; French

Commission, reports 10–12, pp. 29–30, 127–46.

34 Statement of Beck, 10 January 1919 (French Commission, reports 10–12, pp. 127–9).

35 Marie Mandrier, a refugee, 25 February 1915 (French Commission, reports 10–12, p. 131).

36 HStA-MA, Stuttgart, M660, NL Ebbinghaus, book 4, Ebbinghaus diary, entry 23 August, fol. 17.

37 HStA-MA, Stuttgart, M660, NL Ebbinghaus, book 5, diary Lt Roth, 25–27 August, pp. 13–16.

…he Bayerisches Kriegsarchiv), *Die Schlacht in Lothringen und in … Feuertaufe der Bayerischen Armee* (2 vols, Munich, 1929), vol. …2; Reichsarchiv, *Weltkrieg*, vol. 1, p. 208; *Les Armées françaises,* …–331; Koeltz, *La Guerre de 1914–1918*, pp. 71–2; Keegan, *Opening …s*, vol. 1, part 1, p. 308.

…1st report, p. 113, testimony of the farmer, Charles Gourier; A. …*s à Nomény (août 1914)* (Nancy, 1916), p. 38.

…1st report, pp. 109–24 (esp. evidence of Virginie Maire, p. 117). …s of civilian evidence on Nomény are the published report, vol. 1, …*es Allemands à Nancy*, who used the manuscript evidence of the …ditionally, interviewed as eye-witness M. Muller, professor of …MAE, Paris, P 1463, vol. 1098, deposition G. Munier, 27 August, …. J. Pilloy, fol. 208–9.

…ng are SHA, Vincennes, 26N 736, regimental diary of French IR …*llemands à Nomény*; *Historique du 277e régiment d'infanterie* …8; *Historique du 325e régiment d'infanterie* (Paris, n.d.), pp. 6–9; … de Nomény (20 août 1914)', *Le Pays lorrain*, August 1933, pp. …barricade (p. 353); Deuringer, *Schlacht in Lothringen*, vol. 1, pp.

…*régiment d'infanterie*, pp. 7–8. This wrongly states that the …from Nomény having set fire to it that night. As the official …ed, the Germans were still in possession next day. …1st report, p. 117 (evidence of Virginie Maire). …me Kieffer, the wife of the other dead father, confirms Maire's …7–18).

…*s à Nomény*, pp. 81–6. Two more were killed in the artillery …ne disappeared. Viriot claimed that a further 20 died from …ock. None of these have been counted in the death-toll of the …ma…

…Deuringer, *Schlacht in Lothringen*, vol. 1, pp. 185–6.

50 Antoine Redier, *Les Allemands dans nos maisons* (1938; 2nd edn, Paris, 1945), p. 73.

51 Deuringer, *Schlacht in Lothringen*, p. 188.

52 SHA, Vincennes, 16N 1603, vol. A III: Q.G.A., 27 February 1915, translated extract of war diary Fischer, Bavarian IR 8; Joseph Bédier, *Comment l'Allemagne essaye de justifier ses crimes* (Paris, 1915), pp. 22–3, reproduces the extract in facsimile and provides a transcription and translation. The two translations differ slightly, but neither distorts the meaning of the original.

53 Evidence of Dieudonné, the justice of the peace who fled on 8 August (Viriot, *Les Allemands à Nomény*, p. 33). The only mention of a civilian caught engaging in resistance relates to Rouvres, in the département of the Meuse (Deuringer, *Schlacht in Lothringen*, p. 187).

54 French Commission, 1st report, pp. 27–9, 138–48; E. Badel et al., *Gerbéviller-la-martyre. Documentaire, histoire anecdotique* (Nancy, n.d., but 1915); Robert Creusat, *La Victoire oubliée. Gerbéviller-Rozelieures, août-septembre 1914* (Lunéville, 1986). Creusat was a local doctor whose childhood had been dominated by the collective memory of the events of 1914.

55 Creusat, *La Victoire oubliée*, pp. 201, 211.

56 French Commission, 1st report, p. 28. Mirman, the prefect of the Meurthe-et-Moselle, describes entering Gerbéviller and finding the corpses at La Prêle – a meadow just outside the town (ibid., p. 142). Details are scarce, and there is no German corroboration.

57 Marianne Freiemuth, 76 years, in ibid., p. 145.

58 Creusat, *La Victoire oubliée*, p. 201. The French Commission established during its visit in November 1914 that 36 corpses had been found at that point, with possibly 100 people missing.

59 Testimony of Auguste Kislique, lieutenant in the Fire Service, who saw a 'Bavarian' shot down by the French Chasseurs-à-pied and heard the Germans blame civilians (French Commission, 1st report, p. 139).

60 KA, Munich, HS 2309, war diary Rudolf Ritter von Xylander, diary entry 24 August 1914. This was, we assume, Major Ritter von Xylander, member of the General Staff of the Sixth Army, not General Ritter von Xylander, commander of the 1st Bavarian Army Corps, who was probably in the area of Baccarat on 24–25 August.

61 Letter to John Horne from M. and Mme André Pierson, Gerbéviller, 6 June 1996.

62 Badel, *Gerbéviller-la-martyre*, p. 40. This is longer than (and taken on a different occasion from) Sister Julie's published evidence in the official Commission report. Cf. the corroborating testimony of Céline Mercier (AN, Paris, AJ4 16 [Montpellier], 12 October 1914).

63 Peck's testimony is in AN, Paris, BB18 2568 2 (Ministère de la Justice), preparation for Leipzig trials, Lunéville dossier, and also MAE, Paris, Série internationale, Y, Violations du droit des gens en France, 95 (March 1919–December 1922), M. Sornay, French Consulate in Düsseldorf, to Foreign Ministry, 7 October 1921.

64 French Commission, 1st report, pp. 23–6, 122–35; E. Badel, *Lunéville (août–septembre 1914)* (Nancy, 1915).

65 Deuringer, *Schlacht in Lothringen*, vol. 1, p. 303; *Les Armées françaises dans la grande guerre*, vol. 1, part 1, *La Bataille des frontières*, p. 331.

66 The pillage referred to in the French reports is confirmed by various German witnesses: KA, Munich, HS 2234, war diary Bertold Schenk von Stauffenberg (2nd Infantry Munitions column), entry for 24 August 1914; and KA, Munich, HS 2309, war diary Rudolf Ritter von Xylander, entry for 24 August 1914, who deplored the depredations of the 'Prussians' in Lunéville, i.e. of the XXIst Army Corps.

67 Deuringer, *Schlacht in Lothringen*, vol. 2, pp. 378, 402–4, 413–48, esp. 435.

68 On 3 September, the Germans displayed a poster in the town cataloguing their accusations against the inhabitants on 25 August: firing on Red Cross teams, ambushing supply columns, and shooting at the hospital full of German wounded, for which the town was to be fined 650,000 francs (French Commission, 1st report, p. 26).

69 KA, Munich, HS 2234, Bertold Schenk von Stauffenberg, war diary, 25 August 1914, pp. 11–12.
70 French Commission, 1st report, pp. 26–7.
71 Deuringer, *Schlacht in Lothringen*, vol. 2, p. 459.
72 KA, Munich, HS 2740, Albert Ritter von Beckh, diary entry 25 August, pp. 51–2.
73 French Commission, 1st report, pp. 26–7.
74 KA, Munich, HS 2696 Kriegserinnerungen des Oberst Joseph von Tannstein gen. Fleischmann, entry 25 August 1914, p. 16.
75 Georges Gromaire, *L'Occupation allemande en France (1914–1918)* (Paris, 1925), pp. 30–1. This incident was not investigated by the official commission nor is it mentioned in the memoir of Félix Trépont, Prefect of the Nord, in AN, Paris, 96 AP 1.
76 Reichsarchiv, *Weltkrieg*, vol. 1, pp. 551–2; French Commission, reports 10–12, pp. 163–84 (p. 180 for the civilian casualties). The soldiers were from the 33rd Bavarian Reserve Division.
77 AD Ardennes, 12J 1, Émile Marlier, 'Les Ardennes envahies', part 1, 'La Guerre de 1914–18 dans les Ardennes'; part 2, 'L'Arrivée des allemands' (manuscript, 1937 and 1933 respectively). Part 1 is a 913-page document on the military events. Part 2 (169 pages) provides a place-by-place account of the impact of the invasion and of German war crimes. Marlier's modest goal was to collect primary source materials (written and oral) for future historians of the Ardennes in 1914 (part 1, pp. ii–iii).
78 The captured war diary of a lieutenant in IR 178 (XIIth Army Corps) revealed that Gué d'Hossus was burned and some villagers thrown into the flames on 26 August after a shot was fired, though the diarist thought that this had been accidentally discharged by a German soldier, cited in Joseph Bédier, *Les Crimes allemands d'après des témoignages allemands* (Paris, 1915), p. 11; Jacques de Dampierre, *Carnets de route de combattants allemands* (Paris and Nancy, 1916), pp. 1–71 (whole text); Marlier, 'L'Arrivée des allemands', pp. 20–2.
79 On Haybes, see Marlier, 'L'Arrivée des allemands', pp. 7–18; Jean Chot, *La Furie allemande dans l'entre-Sambre-et-Meuse (journées des 23, 24, 25 et 26 août 1914)* (Charleroi, 1919), pp. 145–88; Marie-Louise Dromart, *Sur le chemin du calvaire* (Paris, 1920); Louis de la Hamaide, *Histoire de Haybes sur Meuse*, pp. 71–6 (account of the priest of Haybes, Abbé Hubert); R. Szymanski, *Les Ardennes, terre de France oubliée en 1914–1918* (n. pl., 1984), pp. 49–53. For the suggestion of the foresters, see Chot, *La furie allemande*, pp. 150–1. The authors would like to thank Monsieur Marc Servant, of Charleville-Mézières, for having put them in touch with local historians of Haybes and providing them with documentation on the events of August 1914.
80 Marlier, 'L'Arrivée des allemands', p. 9.
81 Bédier, *Les Crimes allemands*, p. 22 (war diary of soldier Schiller, IR 133).
82 Marlier, 'L'Arrivée des allemands', p. 9.
83 HStA Dresden, Zeitgeschichtliche Sammlung 75, No. 38, combat report by Major (retd) Rothlaufs, 8 September 1915.
84 Marlier, 'L'Arrivée des allemands', pp. 10–11.
85 Chot, *La Furie allemande*, pp. 172–7.
86 Marlier, 'L'Arrivée des allemands', pp. 19–20, 28–31, 43–5, 55–72 and 72–7.
87 Ibid., pp. 130–6 and 107–13; French Commission, 5th report, pp. 9, 41–8 (Sedan).
88 AN, Paris, F7 12938, report of general commanding the Sixth Region to Prefect of the Meuse, 27 August 1914 on obstruction by refugees; for overall figures see chapter 5.

89 Jules Maurin, *Armée, guerre, société. Soldats languedociens (1889–1919)* (Paris, 1982), p. 345.

90 Marlier, 'L'Arrivée des allemands', pp. 22–6.

91 Ibid., pp. 43–5 (a fourteenth civilian was killed on 1 September); Reichsarchiv, *Weltkrieg*, vol. 3, *Der Marne-Feldzug. Von der Sambre zur Marne* (1926), p. 62.

92 Marlier, 'L'Arrivée des allemands', pp. 55–72; Dampierre, *Carnets de route de combattants allemands*, pp. 43–4 (anonymous diarist of IR 178). Regiments identified by the French sources were IR 182, 101, 103, 178, and 18th Hussars; Reichsarchiv, *Weltkrieg*, vol. 3, pp. 62, 111.

93 Koeltz, *La Guerre de 1914–1918*, pp. 79–143; Keegan, *Opening Moves*, pp. 114–59; Holger Herwig, *The First World War: Germany and Austria-Hungary 1914–1918* (London, 1997), pp. 100–5.

94 André de Maricourt, *Le Drame de Senlis. Journal d'un témoin. Avant, pendant, après août–septembre 1914* (Paris, 1916), pp. 88–9; French Commission, 1st report, pp. 37–8, 185–92; Loup Bertroz, *Senlis pendant l'invasion allemande, 1914, d'après le carnet de notes d'un senlisien* (Senlis, n.d., but 1915). In the absence of the Prussian army archives the only evidence of the German units involved comes from official histories: Reichsarchiv, *Weltkrieg*, vol. 3, p. 210.

95 Bertroz, *Senlis*, p. 27.

96 French Commission, 1st report, pp. 15, 79–80; ibid., 5th report, pp. 13, 63–4.

97 AN, Paris, AJ4 19, deposition of Hippolyte Bouvry, deputy mayor of Marfaux.

98 French Commission, 5th report, pp. 30–2, 37–8, 150–7, 170–9; L. Colin, *Les Barbares à la trouée des Vosges. Récits des témoins* (Paris, 1915), pp. 67–162 (Saint-Dié). Reichsarchiv, *Weltkrieg*, vol. 3, pp. 276–9, 284–5.

99 Charles Berlet, *Réméréville. Un village lorrain pendant les mois d'août et septembre 1914* (Paris, 1918), pp. 49–55; French Commission, 1st report, pp. 34, 174–5.

100 See chapters 5 and 8 below.

101 French Commission, 1st report, p. 37 (Néry).

102 French Commission, 3rd report, p. 37 (Corporal Gaston Lenoir, French IR 317, near Albert in the Somme). For further evidence of human shields, see French Commission, 3rd report, pp. 7–9.

103 French Commission, 5th report, pp. 36, 171–2 (evidence of Georges Visser, one of the survivors); Colin, *Les Barbares à la trouée des Vosges*, p. 103; Bédier, *Les Crimes allemands*, pp. 19–20; Bédier, *Comment l'Allemagne essaye de justifier ses crimes*, p. 27. The account was by a Lieutenant Eberlein, published in the *Münchner Neueste Nachrichten*, 7 October 1914. Cf. Eberlein's post-war justification, published under a pseudonym: KA, Munich, MKr 13390, report Dr Ritter, 14 October 1919. Eberlein was probably in the 30th Reserve Division.

104 Schmitz and Nieuwland, *L'invasion allemande*, vol. 5, pp. 108–12. See also Szymanski, *Les Ardennes*, p. 62.

105 French Commission, 2nd report, *passim* (p. 75 for list of camps); Fernand Passelecq, *Déportation et travail forcé des ouvriers et de la population civile de la Belgique occupée (1916–1918)* (Paris and New Haven, 1928), p. 5. See also Annette Becker, *Oubliés de la grande guerre. Humanitaire et culture de guerre, 1914–1918. Populations occupées, déportés civils, prisonniers de guerre* (Paris, 1998), pp. 53–6.

106 *La Belgique et la guerre*, vol. 3, Maurice Tasnier and R. van Overstraeten, *Opérations militaires* (Brussels, 1926), pp. 185–218; Leon van der Essen, *The Invasion and the War in Belgium from Liegè to the Yser* (London, 1917), pp. 209–33, 275–350; Koeltz, *La*

Guerre de 1914–1918, pp. 143–55; Herwig, *The First World War*, pp. 114–17.

107 Belgian Second Commission, vol. 1, part 2, pp. 239–41, 596–605. On Aalst, ibid., pp. 250–3, 620–8.

108 See Belgian Second Commission, vol. 1, part 2, pp. 320–5, 633–7 (Roeselare); ibid., pp. 332–5, 640–3 (Staden); AN, Paris, AJ4 3, testimony of Alphonse Roulers (Roeselare) and Louis Huyghe (Staden), refugees in the Gers, south-western France.

109 Belgian Second Commission, vol. 1, part 2, pp. 328, 639–41 (Ledegem), 344–8, 658–65 (Esen).

110 The massacre of French deportees at Frasnes-lez-Couvin in Belgium has been counted as a French incident.

111 Calculated from: Belgian Second Commission, vol. 1, part 1, pp. 605–23; ibid., vol. 1, part 2, pp. 679–704. The number respectively of 'minor' incidents and resultant deaths in each province is: Antwerp, 19 and 44; Brabant, 75 and 195; East Flanders, 16 and 28; West Flanders, 27 and 74; Hainaut, 54 and 206; Liège, 51 and 168; Limburg, 23 and 52; Luxembourg, 38 and 104; Namur, 80 and 229.

112 The incidents in Brabant and Hainaut, plus Tongeren in Limburg, and Andenne, Namur, and Tamines in Namur province.

113 Namur province plus Erezée-Briscol in northern Luxembourg.

114 Belgian First Commission, 10th and 15th reports; French Commission, 1st report, p. 9.

115 John Horne and Alan Kramer, 'War between Soldiers and Enemy Civilians, 1914–15', in Roger Chickering and Stig Förster (eds), *Great War, Total War: Combat and Mobilization on the Western Front, 1914–1918* (Cambridge and New York, 2000), pp. 153–68. For the military background, Norman Stone, *The Eastern Front 1914–1917* (London, 1975).

116 Imanuel Geiss, 'Die Kosaken kommen! Ostpreußen im August 1914', in Geiss, *Das deutsche Reich und der Erste Weltkrieg* (1978; 2nd edn; Munich, 1985), pp. 62–3; Denis Showalter, *Tannenberg: Clash of Empires* (Hamden, Conn., 1991), p. 159.

117 Auswärtiges Amt, *Greueltaten russischer Truppen gegen deutsche Zivilpersonen und deutsche Kriegsgefangene* (Berlin, 1915); English language summary, *Memorial on Atrocities Committed by Russian Troops upon German Inhabitants and Prisoners of War* (Berlin, 1915).

118 *Greueltaten russischer Truppen*, appendices 22 and 28.

119 CPHDC Moscow, 1275-5-63, fol. 36–7 (Pillkallen). For Neidenberg, and the Russian conviction of coming under civilian attack, see Alfred Knox, *With the Russian Army 1914–1917* (2 vols, London, 1921), vol. 1, pp. 57, 62; Showalter, *Tannenberg*, pp. 219–21.

120 CPHDC Moscow, 1275-5-63, fol. 38, Ermittlungskommission der privaten Feuerversicherungsgesellschaften, Kreis Pillkallen, Regierungsbezirk Gumbinnen. According to this collection of reports, the total number of German civilians killed in the Russian invasion was only 44 (or 34), over a period of four months (ibid., fol. 6–7).

121 The Bavarian emissary to Berlin, Count Lerchenfeld to Bavarian Minister-President Hertling, 14 September 1914, cited in Geiss, 'Die Kosaken kommen!', pp. 62–3. The commission was also 'unable to find a single case of mutilation such as chopped-off hands, etc.', ibid.

122 Erich Ludendorff, *Meine Kriegserinnerungen 1914–1918* (Berlin, 1919), pp. 24–5, 53.

123 Dennis Showalter refers to 'the myth of East Prussia's harrowing at the hands of the Cossack hordes – a myth kept alive during and long after the war for political, ethnic and ideological reasons' (*Tannenberg*, p. 159). Cf. Holger Herwig, who subscribes to the myth of the 'Russian terror in East Prussia' (*The First World War*, p. 128).

in Jean-Pierre Rioux and Jean-François Sirinelli (eds), *Pour une histoire culturelle* (Paris, 1997), pp. 183–92. For conspiracy theories in phenomena of collective delusion, see Raoul Girardet, *Mythes et mythologies politiques* (Paris, 1986), pp. 25–62 ('La conspiration').

11 Georges Lefebvre, *The Great Fear of 1789: Rural Panic in Revolutionary France* (1932; English translation, introd. George Rudé, London, 1973).

12 Ibid., pp. 210–11.

13 Ibid., pp. 50 (quotation) and 53–6 (examples). For the 'Irish night', see George H. Jones, 'The Irish Fright of 1688: Real Violence and Imagined Massacre', *Bulletin of the Institute of Historical Research*, 55 (1982), pp. 148–53.

14 Lefebvre, *The Great Fear*, p. 50.

15 Ibid.

16 Ibid., pp. 123 (quotation), 148–55.

17 Ibid., pp. 202–11.

18 Quoted in Gustave Somville, *Vers Liège. Le chemin du crime. Août 1914* (Paris, 1915), pp. 167–8.

19 French Commission, 12th report, pp. 24–5.

20 BA-MA, Freiburg, N266/69 Aug. v. Cramon. Meine Erlebnisse im Weltkriege – Frankreich 1914. The village was unnamed, but was probably in Belgium between Bastogne and the Luxemburg border (Cf. Reichsarchiv, *Der Weltkrieg, 1914 bis 1918. Die militärischen Operationen zu Lande* (14 vols, Berlin, 1925–44), vol. 1, *Die Grenzschlachten im Westen* (1925), pp. 105–6, 132 and map 1, 'Die Aufmärsche'). The men killed must have been from the 7th Hussars, in the 16th Infantry Division.

21 Lothar Wieland, *Belgien 1914. Die Frage des belgischen 'Franktireurkrieges' und die deutsche öffentliche Meinung von 1914 bis 1936* (Frankfurt, Berne, New York, 1984), pp. 19–20.

22 PAAA, Bonn, R 20880, fol. 12–13, Chief of the General Staff to the Foreign Ministry, 12 August 1914; *Norddeutsche Allgemeine Zeitung*, 14 August 1914. Moltke's 'Warning' was a reply to the Belgian diplomatic note of 8 August, informing the German government of the mobilization and uniforms of the Garde Civique.

23 Langenhove, *Cycle de légendes*, pp. 214–15; see also chapter 8 below.

24 Pierre Mille, 'Lettre de Belgique', *Le Temps*, 22 August 1914.

25 Wilhelm Nau, *Beiträge zur Geschichte des Regiments Hamburg* (5 vols, Hamburg, 1924–6), vol. 1, *Der Marsch auf Paris* (1924), p. 12.

26 *Kriegsfahrten deutscher Maler. Selbsterlebtes im Weltkrieg 1914–1915* (Bielefeld and Leipzig, n.d., but 1916), pp. 92–5.

27 MAE, Paris, film P1463, vol. 1098, fol. 101–9.

28 *Parole. Deutsche Krieger-Zeitung. Amtliche Zeitung des Deutschen Kriegerbundes*, 23 August 1914, in Bundesarchiv (BA), Potsdam, Reichskanzlei 2401/2. The report was taken from the *Magdeburger Zeitung*.

29 *Die völkerrechtswidrige Führung des belgischen Volkskriegs* (Berlin, 1915), p. 107, appendix B, Summary Report.

30 See chapter 2 above. For further examples, see *Die völkerrechtswidrige Führung*, p. 4.

31 L. Mokveld, *The German Fury in Belgium* (London, 1917), pp. 121–2. Manteuffel's published evidence to the official German inquiry did not refer to the story (*Die völkerrechtswidrige Führung*, appendix D3, pp. 247–9). When Manteuffel was investigated by a German court-martial judge in January 1921 because the Belgians wished him to be prosecuted for war crimes, he made a more oblique claim about disguised

soldiers in relation to the shooting on 28 August: 'I did not witness inhabitants of Louvain taking part in fighting against German troops, nor can I provide any evidence of such participation by the population. I later heard that Belgian soldiers in civilian clothing were said to have shot at the German troops' (Peter Schöller, *Der Fall Löwen und das Weißbuch. Eine kritische Untersuchung der deutschen Dokumentation über die Vorgänge in Löwen vom 25. bis 28. August 1914* (Cologne and Graz, 1958), p. 70).

32 *Die völkerrechtswidrige Führung*, pp. 239–43, appendix D1.

33 BA-MA, Freiburg, PHD 6/145, appendix 3, p. 12 (deposition Karge, 15 November 1914). The official German inquiry into Andenne held that the townsfolk admitted that two Flemish soldiers of Belgian IR 8 stayed behind in Andenne, put on civilian clothes, and fired on the Germans (*Die völkerrechtswidrige Führung*, pp. 112–13, appendix B 4, report of Lieutenant Goetze, 8 January 1915).

34 Loup Bertroz, *Senlis pendant l'invasion allemande, 1914, d'après le carnet de notes d'un senlisien* (Senlis, n.d., but 1915), p. 28.

35 French Commission, 5th report, pp. 29, 146; KA, Munich, HS 2301, Eugen von Frauenholz, 'Erinnerungen an meine Soldatenzeit 1901–1918', p. 209.

36 Captain Meyer, Landwehr Squadron of the Salzwedel Uhlans (HStA-MA, Stuttgart, M660 NL Pezold, diary entry 29 October 1914, p. 81).

37 *Le Temps*, 21 August 1914, report by the police commissioner of Conflans-Jarny. Corroboration comes from the doctor of Jarny, Henri Bastien, who attended the dying Collignon and heard the story from him (French Commission, 5th report, pp. 142–3).

38 *Die völkerrechtswidrige Führung*, p. 109, appendix B1, report of Freiherr von Langermann.

39 BA-MA, Freiburg, PHD 6/145, Ministry of War, Military Investigation Department for Violations of the Laws of War: memorandum on the events in Aarschot, 19 and 20 August 1914, sent to the Chancellor, 7 January 1915, deposition Karge, p. 12. On Karge's role, see chapter 1 above.

40 E.g. Joppécourt, French Commission, 12th report; Andenne: Jean Schmitz and Norbert Nieuwland, *Documents pour servir à l'histoire de l'invasion allemande dans les provinces de Namur et de Luxembourg* (7 vols, Brussels and Paris, 1919–24), vol. 2, p. 50.

41 See chapter 1 for Aarschot and Andenne. For Badonviller, see *L'Est Républicain*, 20 August 1914, for the citation of Légion d'honneur; AD Meurthe-et-Moselle, 86J 1 (Commission pour une histoire de la guerre franco-allemande), report of the director of the school at Badonviller, 13 September 1915; French Commission, 5th report, pp. 24–6, 121–30.

42 See chapter 7, 'Catholics'.

43 Nau, *Beiträge zur Geschichte des Regiments Hamburg*, vol. 1, p. 16, diary entry for 13 August 1914.

44 *Lettres des evêques de Namur et de Liège concernant les atrocités allemandes dans leurs diocèses* (Rome, 1916), pp. 111–12. See also Belgian First Commission, vol. 2, 17th report, p. 57 (Visé); *Les Atrocités allemandes dans les environs de Verviers* (Verviers, n.d.), p. 8 (Olne); Somville, *Vers Liège*, p. 116 (Forêt); F. Vliegen, *La Tragédie de Visé et la captivité des civils en Allemagne* (Liège, n.d., but 1919), pp. 3–4.

45 BA-MA, Freiburg, N30/52, Beseler, letter to his wife, 16 August 1914.

46 For Schaffen, see chapter 1 above. For Aarschot, see the deposition of the priest, Joseph Meeus, in Belgian Second Commission, vol. 1, part 2, p. 382.

47 Wojciech Jacobson, *Z Armja Klucka na Paryz. Pammielnik lekarza – Polaka* (Torun, 1934); French translation, *En Marche sur Paris avec l'armée prussienne du Général von*

Kluck (Brussels, 1937), pp. 38–9. Jacobson was a Polish medical officer with IR 49 and a sceptical witness of the events. See also Belgian Second Commission, vol. 1, part 2, pp. 52–3, 384 for Gelrode. The priest of Gelrode was executed in Aarschot. On 28 August 1914, 97 inhabitants (both sexes and all ages) were deported to Munster camp.

48 AGR, Brussels, CE, III, 374 B1, 34, deposition by Wladyslaus Ossowski entitled 'Die deutschen Barbaren in Belgien – ich selbst der Augenzeuge'.

49 L.-H. Grondijs, *Les Allemands en Belgique. (Louvain et Aerschot) Notes d'un témoin hollandais* (Paris, 1915), p.18; Louise Mack, *A Woman's Experiences in the Great War* (London, 1915), p. 43.

50 Ernst Rump, private papers, Hamburg, Kriegsbriefe: letter to his wife, 27 August 1914.

51 Ernst Rump, private papers, Hamburg, Kriegsbriefe: letter to his parents, 5 September 1914. For the battle for Dendermonde, see Belgian Second Commission, vol. 1, part 2, pp. 239–41, 596–605; *La Belgique et la guerre* (4 vols, Brussels, 1921–8), vol. 3, M. Tasnier and R. van Overstraeten, *Les Opérations militaires* (1926), p. 133.

52 Schmitz and Nieuwland, *L'invasion allemande*, vol. 4, part 2, pp. 80–91 (evidence of Adrien Borrelly, prior of the Abbey).

53 *Kölnische Zeitung*, 16 September 1914; Belgian Second Commission report, vol. 1, part 1, pp. 117–19, 470–3; Schmitz and Nieuwland, *L'invasion allemande*, vol. 4, part 1, pp. 96–125.

54 Belgian Second Commission, vol. 1, part 1, pp. 190–2, 520–1, 524–5; Schmitz and Nieuwland, *L'invasion allemande*, vol. 4, part 1, pp. 54–68.

55 See chapter 2 above for Haybes. For Villers-en-Fagne, see Jacques de Dampierre, *Carnets de route de combattants allemands* (Paris, 1916), pp. 28–9 (diary of officer of IR 178). Curiously, the Second Belgian Commission makes no mention of the priest's death or the presence of IR 178 (vol. 1, part 1, pp. 196–7). What matters here is the mythology of the resistant priests, of which the anonymous officer's diary provides clear proof. For Marlemont-la-Ginguette and Sault-lès-Rethel, see AD Ardennes, 12J 1, Émile Marlier, 'Les Ardennes envahies', part 2, 'L'Arrivée des allemands', pp. 36–9 and 67 respectively.

56 BA-MA, Freiburg, N 266/69 Aug. v. Cramon. Meine Erlebnisse im Weltkriege – Frankreich, 1914, fol. 8, undated diary entry between 17 and 21 August.

57 Schmitz and Nieuwland, *L'invasion allemande*, vol. 6, pp. 134–7 (Bertrix), 143 (Anloy); Belgian Second Commission, vol. 1, part 1, p. 220.

58 Schöller, *Der Fall Löwen*, pp. 61–6.

59 BA, Berlin, 07.01, 2465/3, fol. 45: von Wandel, War Ministry, to Reich Chancellor, Reich Department of the Interior, Chief of General Staff, etc., 11 December 1914. Cf. ibid., fol. 23: von Wandel, War Ministry, to Chancellor, Chief of General Staff, etc., 30 September 1914. Jacques Fontana, *Les Catholiques français pendant la grande guerre* (Paris, 1990), p. 311, gives a figure of 17 priests arrested.

60 *Les Alsaciens-Lorrains en France pendant la guerre* (Paris, 1915), pp. 34–41.

61 KA, Munich, HS 2696, Kriegserinnerungen des Oberst Joseph von Tannstein gen. Fleischmann, entry for 5 August 1914.

62 French Commission, 5th report, pp. 29, 141–2; Eugène Griselle, *Le Martyre du clergé français* (Paris, 1915), pp. 48–9.

63 Franciscus, *'Gott mit uns!' Dieu avec nous!* (Paris, 1916), pp. 264–6.

64 French Commission, 1st report, pp. 10, 54–5.

65 French Commission, 5th report, pp. 8–9, 41–8; Griselle, *Le Martyre du clergé français*, pp. 51–61. The identity of the German regiment responsible is not known.

66 Langenhove, *Cycle de légendes*, pp. 54–67.

67 CPHDC, Moscow, 1467-1-12, fol. 112–15, deposition Oberleutnant Reichel, IR 177, 12 December 1914.

68 *Berliner Lokal-Anzeiger*, 31 August 1914, cited in Langenhove, *Cycle de légendes*, pp. 71–2.

69 Belgian Second Commission, vol. 1, part 2, pp. 364–8 (depositions of Jean van Kerckhoven and Eugène de Busschère).

70 Ibid., p. 446 (deposition of Pierre-François Claes).

71 Vatican Archive, Segretaria di Stato, 244 D7 (Belgio), f. 105, report by Tacci, nuncio, to Gasparri (Secretary of State, Vatican), 23 December 1914, on the action of Sarzana who deputized for Tacci.

72 Grondijs, *Les Allemands en Belgique*, p. 19.

73 See chapter 1 above.

74 *De Telegraaf*, 7 August 1914, evening edition; untitled report 'from a special correspondent in Maastricht'.

75 'Un furieux assaut contre Herstal. Résistance héroïque de la population', *Le XXe Siècle* (Brussels), 12 August 1914; *Le Soir* (Brussels), 13 August 1914; 'Women against Uhlans. Germans Repulsed by Boiling Water. Defence of Herstal', *The Times*, 12 August 1914 (a report from Reuters in Paris, which had 2,000 Germans 'disabled by wounds and scalds'). For the disclaimer, see *Le XXe Siècle*, 14 August 1914.

76 The argument of the German press was summarized by an anonymous brochure, *Der Franktireurkrieg in Belgien. Geständnisse der belgischen Presse* (Stuttgart and Berlin, 1915), pp. 10–11, which used a Belgian press report on Herstal (among others) as an admission of the reality of the franc-tireur war.

77 CPHDC, Moscow, 1256-5-47, fol. 2, report by two men of Jäger Battalion 7, Maastricht, to General Command VIIth Army Corps, Münster.

78 BA, Koblenz, NL 15/402, lecture by Schwertfeger in the Foreign Ministry, 12 March 1920, p. 7. Schwertfeger was naturally less candid in his book, *Die Grundlagen des belgischen Frantireurkrieges 1914* (Berlin, n.d., but 1920), pp. 84–6. On Schwertfeger's role in the 'innocentist' campaign generally, see chapter 9 below.

79 *Germania*, 18 August 1914. Liège was a centre of the Marxist left of the Parti Ouvrier Belge. There were also revolutionary syndicalist currents in the principal industrial centres of Wallonia.

80 *Hamburgischer Correspondent*, 20 August 1914.

81 Paul Oskar Höcker, *An der Spitze meiner Kompagnie. Drei Monate Kriegserlebnisse* (Berlin, 1914), pp. 28–30; see also the discussion of Höcker in van Langenhove, *Cycle de légendes*, pp. 150–8.

82 Belgian First Commission, vol. 2, 17th report, p. 53; Somville, *Vers Liège*, p. 90. Belgian Second Commission, vol. 1, part 1, p. 24, gives 108 victims of whom seven were women and 13 were children under 16 years.

83 *Die völkerrechtswidrige Führung*, p. 76, appendix 56 (evidence of Paul Blankenburg, IR 165).

84 *Hamburgischer Correspondent*, 20 August 1914.

85 BA, Potsdam, 92: Sachthematische Sammlung 267, Glückmann, KTB 1914–1915, diary entry 14 August.

86 Schmitz and Nieuwland, *L'invasion allemande*, vol. 7, p. 308.

87 In reality, one married woman (Marie Hurieaux-Goffinet) was killed with her husband. See chapter 2 above.

88 AGR, Brussels, CE, III 374 B1, 21, summary by Lieutenant Loustalot, 16 June 1915. *Die völkerrechtswidrige Führung*, pp. 181–201, appendix C (Dinant), C43, 44, 47, 56, 60, 61, for women and children in combat.

89 *Die völkerrechtswidrige Führung*, appendix D25, p. 280–1 (hearsay evidence of August Zander, 3rd Ersatz Co., IR 165, on hot tar); Joachim Delbrück (ed.), *Der deutsche Krieg in Feldpostbriefen* (10 vols, Munich, 1915–17), vol. 1, *Lüttich/Namur/Antwerpen* (1915), p. 154.

90 Belgian Second Commission, vol. 1, part 2, pp. 328, 639–41; see also chapter 2 above.

91 Godefroid Kurth, *Le Guet-Apens prussien en Belgique* (Paris and Brussels, 1919), p. 208. Tilly, commander of the Catholic League during the Thirty Years' War, besieged Protestant-held Magdeburg in 1631; when it fell, the population was slaughtered by undisciplined troops and the town was unintentionally burned down. In Protestant mythology, Tilly became the 'butcher of Magdeburg'.

92 AD Ardennes, 12J 1, Émile Marlier, 'Les Ardennes envahies', part 2, 'L'Arrivée des allemands', p. 14, drawing on the evidence of Marie-Louise Dramard, 'Rapport sans commentaires sur les atrocités commises par les allemands à Haybes du 24 au 27 août 1914', *Journal des Régions dévastées*, 21 December 1919. For Surice, see Schmitz and Nieuwland, *L'invasion allemande* vol. 5, pp. 194–210 (205 for myth).

93 Bloch, 'Les fausses nouvelles de la guerre', p. 178.

94 See chapter 1 above.

95 Mokveld, *The German Fury*, p. 90.

96 AD Meurthe-et-Moselle, 86J 7: C. Antoine and S. Lhuillier, 'Notes sur l'invasion allemande, août 1914'. The German officer was Baron von Beust-Koenigssee.

97 French Commission, 1st report, p. 116 (evidence of Barbe Conrad on Nomény); AN, Paris, AJ4 11, testimony of Mme Armentin, a refugee at Annecy, on Gerbéviller; and Charles Berlet, *Réméréville. Un village lorrain pendant les mois d'août et septembre 1914* (Paris, 1918), p. 27.

98 *Die völkerrechtswidrige Führung*, appendix D 35 and 37, pp. 293, 297–300 (Louvain); appendix C 73 and 78, pp. 214, 219 (Dinant); appendix 66, p. 87, for evidence of Captain Troeger, RIR 204, about the victims from RIR 203 between Ghent and Torhout. See chapter 2 above for Esen and Zarren.

99 AD Nord, 9R 17, reports of the prefect to the Minister of the Interior, 23 , 25, and 28 September 1914; 9R 21, reports of police commissioner, Lille, to Prefect, 23 September 1914 (information culled from refugees), and 25 September 1914 (news of burning of Orchies and reported comment of a German officer to the effect that the inhabitants had stripped the corpses and cut off their ears); Auswärtiges Amt, *Über die Verletzung der Genfer Konvention vom 6. Juli 1906 durch französische Truppen und Freischärler* (Berlin, 1914), appendix 5 (report of medical majors Neumann and Grünfelder, Valenciennes, 26 September 1914); E. Draux, *Nouvelle Histoire d'Orchies* (Lille, 1980), pp. 122–36. Orchies was never investigated by the French official commission.

100 Auswärtiges Amt, *Verletzung der Genfer Konvention*, appendix 5.

101 AD Nord, 9R 22, report from Tourcoing (unsigned) on the poster; Draux, *Nouvelle histoire d'Orchies*, p. 135, for the text.

102 The conventional idea that public opinion responded to the outbreak of war with unbridled chauvinism has been challenged, even deconstructed. See Jean-Jacques Becker, *1914. Comment les français sont entrés dans la guerre* (Paris, 1977); Jean Stengers, 'L'Entrée en guerre de la Belgique', *Guerres Mondiales et Conflits Contemporains*, 179 (1995), pp. 13–33; Gerd Krumeich, 'L' Entrée en guerre en Allemagne', in Jean-Jacques

Becker and Stéphane Audoin-Rouzeau (eds), *Les Sociétés européennes et la guerre de 1914–1918* (Paris, 1990), pp. 65–74; Wolfgang Kruse, *Krieg und nationale Integration. Eine Neuinterpretation des sozialdemokratischen Burgfriedensschlusses 1914–15* (Essen, 1993); Benjamin Ziemann, *Front und Heimat. Ländliche Kriegserfahrungen im südlichen Bayern 1914–1923* (Essen, 1997), pp. 39–54; and Jeffrey T. Verhey, *The Spirit of 1914: Militarism, Myth, and Mobilization in Germany* (Cambridge, 2000). There is no detailed study of public opinion and British entry into the war.

103 Auswärtiges Amt (Germany), *Denkschrift über die Behandlung der deutschen Konsuln in Rußland und die Zerstörung der deutschen Botschaft in Petersburg* (Berlin, 1915); K.U.K. Ministerium des Äußern (Austria-Hungary), *Sammlung von Nachweisen für die Verletzungen des Völkerrechtes durch die mit Österreich-Ungarn kriegführenden Staaten*, 31 January 1915 (Vienna, 1915), pp. 3–116. For the German accusations regarding Belgium see Ilse Meseberg-Haubold, *Der Widerstand Kardinal Merciers gegen die deutsche Besetzung Belgiens 1914–1918. Ein Beitrag zur politischen Rolle des Katholizismus im ersten Weltkrieg* (Frankfurt and Berne, 1982), p. 47. For the Belgian refutation of the German charges in relation to Antwerp, see the report of the state prosecutor in Antwerp (25 August 1914), a copy of which was sent to the Holy See (Vatican Archive, Seg. di Stato, 244 D7 (Belgio), f. 107). For German confirmation, see Meseberg-Haubold, *Der Widerstand* (citing Delbrück, Interior Minister, to Jagow, Foreign Minister, 4 September 1914). The events in question took place on 4–5 August, and according to the state prosecutor's inquiry, were limited to attacks on property.

104 Becker, *1914*, pp. 505–10; David French, 'Spy Fever in Britain, 1900–1915', *Historical Journal*, 21/2 (1978), pp. 364–70.

105 Becker, *1914*, pp. 498–510. The Paris attacks came mainly on 2–3 August. In Lille, German businesses were attacked on the night of 4 August, resulting in 20 arrests (AN, Paris, F7 12938, prefect's report, 5 August 1914; P. Trochon, *Lille avant et pendant l'occupation allemande* (Tourcoing, 1922), p. 6). In the Pas-de-Calais, the prefect warned the government that 'very serious incidents' would occur if the German emigrant workers in the region were not quickly evacuated (AN, Paris, F7 12938, prefect's report, 4 August 1914).

106 *Le Soir* (Brussels), 6 August 1914 and, for the quotation, 8 August 1914 (editorial, 'Cela doit cesser'); *Le Temps* (Paris), 7 August 1914; Brand Whitlock, *Belgium under the German Occupation: A Personal Narrative* (2 vols, London, 1919), vol. 1, pp. 52–6.

107 *The Times*, 12 August 1914; Panikos Panayi, *The Enemy in our Midst: Germans in Britain during the First World War* (New York and Oxford, 1991), pp. 223–9.

108 KA, Munich, HS 3393 Hans Ritter von Seißer: war diary 4th (Bavarian) Infantry Division, diary entries 2–5 August 1914; Fritz Fischer, *War of Illusions: German Policies from 1911 to 1914* (1969; English translation, London, 1975), pp. 508–9; Verhey, *The Spirit of 1914*, pp. 75–6.

109 Michael MacDonagh, *In London during the Great War: The Diary of a Journalist* (London, 1935), p.15. For the suspicion of poisoned bread, see also *The Times*, 12 August 1914 ('Germans in London').

110 AN, Paris, F7 12938, Lot, prefect's reports of 15 and 16 August 1914; ibid., Lot-et-Garonne, prefect's report 9 August; ibid., Lozère.

111 See chapter 2 above.

112 Colmar Freiherr von der Goltz, *Das Volk in Waffen. Ein Buch über Heerwesen und Kriegführung unserer Zeit* (1883; 6th edn, revised 'on the basis of the experiences of the World War', Berlin, 1925), p. 1; Arden Bucholz, *Moltke, Schlieffen, and Prussian*

War Planning (Providence and Oxford, 1991), pp. 156–7. Schlieffen's conclusions on his historical studies were published in the *Vierteljahrshefte für Truppenführung und Heereskunde*, 1909–13, in Großer Generalstab (ed.), *Alfred von Schlieffen: Gesammelte Schriften* (2 vols, Berlin, 1913), vol.1, and in a separate volume, *Cannae* (Berlin, 1913).

113   Four weeks, according to Lerchenfeld, the Bavarian ambassador to Berlin, on 31 July 1914 (Fischer, *War of Illusions*, p. 503); three weeks according to the OHL representative at the Austrian Army Command, General von Freytag-Loringhoven, writing to Admiral von Müller, the Chief of the German Naval Cabinet (Georg Alexander von Müller, *Regierte der Kaiser? Kriegstagebücher, Aufzeichnungen und Briefe des Chefs des Marine-Kabinetts Admiral Georg Alexander von Müller 1914–1918* (Göttingen, Berlin, Frankfurt, 1959), pp. 73–4 (diary entry 2 December 1914). It seems that Moltke extended the timescale to six weeks in his conversation with Conrad von Hötzendorf at Karlsbad in May 1914 (Franz Conrad von Hötzendorf, *Aus meiner Dienstzeit 1906–1918* (5 vols, Vienna, 1921–5), vol. 3, p. 673).

114   Gerhard Ritter, *The Schlieffen Plan: Critique of a Myth* (1956; English translation, New York, 1958), pp. 66–7.

115   Bucholz, *Moltke*, p. 319.

116   Reichsarchiv, *Weltkrieg*, vol. 1, pp. 108–20, *passim*.

117   BA-MA, Freiburg, N 324/26, General Karl von Einem, commander of the VIIth Army Corps, letter to his wife, 8 August 1914. Cf. ibid., war diary, entry 9 August 1914.

118   Generalstab des Heeres (ed.), *Der Handstreich gegen Lüttich vom 3. bis 7. August 1914* (Berlin, 1939), p. 12.

119   Erich von Tschischwitz (ed.), *General von der Marwitz. Weltkriegsbriefe* (Berlin, 1940), pp. 21–2 (letters 13 and 18 August 1914). For Tongeren, see chapter 1 above.

120   Schöller papers, von Trotta genannt Treyden, Karlsruhe, to Petri, 11 June 1958.

121   AGR, Brussels, CE, III 374 B1, 21: summary of inquiry among captured troops of the XIIth Army Corps by Lieutenant Loustalot (hereafter Loustalot report), 16 June 1915, p. 19; BA Berlin, R 3003/ORA/RG, bJ 307/20 vol. 1, fol. 102, statement Ernst Stürzkober, Dresden, 27 December 1921.

122   BA-MA, Freiburg, N 30/52. Beseler did not witness at first hand any of the fighting during the invasion.

123   BA-MA, Freiburg, N 324/26 von Einem: Bericht an das Reichsarchiv Potsdam über die Marneschlacht 1914. Transcript from personal war diary, entry of 12 August.

124   Belgian Second Commission, vol. 1, part 2, pp. 173–5.

125   Ivan Bloch, *The Future of War in its Technical, Economic, and Political Relations* (1898; English translation, London, 1900); John Ellis, *The Social History of the Machine Gun* (1976; new edn, London, 1993), chs 3 and 5; Tim Travers, *The Killing Ground: The British Army, the Western Front and the Emergence of Modern Warfare, 1900–1918* (London, 1987), pp. 62–82; Dieter Storz, *Kriegsbild und Rüstung vor 1914. Europäische Landstreitkräfte vor dem Ersten Weltkrieg* (Herford, Berlin, Bonn, 1992).

126   BA, Berlin, 1501/12276, fol. 157–69: Dr Bruno Borchardt, 'Merkwürdigkeiten beim Schießen', in Julian Borchardt (ed.), *Lichtstrahlen. Bildungsorgan für denkende Arbeiter*, 3/7 (2 April 1916), pp. 159–63.

127   Jacobson, *En marche sur Paris*, p. 30.

128   BA-MA, Freiburg, N 324/26, war diary, entry for 4 September, fol. 24. Major-General Schwarte was commander of the 79th Infantry Brigade (IR 56 and 57).

129   E.g. Geoffrey Best, 'Restraints on War by Land before 1945', in Michael Howard (ed.), *Restraints on War: Studies in the Limitation of Armed Conflict* (Oxford, 1979), pp.

17–37 (here p. 25). For contemporary American witness views on the apparent efficiency of the German army in 1914, see E. Alexander Powell, *Fighting in Flanders* (London, 1914), p. 131 ('a mighty and highly efficient machine which is directed by a cold and calculating intelligence in far-away Berlin'); Whitlock, *Belgium under German Occupation*, vol. 1, pp. 81–2 ('modern science yoked to the chariot of autocracy').

130 *Der Handstreich gegen Lüttich*, pp. 44–7.

131 HStA-MA, Stuttgart, M660, NL Flammer, diary, 25 August 1914, p. 10 reverse. The typed transcript has 'Ligneulx', a misreading for 'Signeulx', a village three kilometres west of Baranzy.

132 KA, Munich, HS 3372 war diary, Leonhard Eisenbeiß, pp. 8–9. There thus appear to have been no civilian casualties. There were other serious friendly fire incidents on 24 August between Markirch and the Col de St Marie in Alsace, with at least seven killed and 30 wounded: KA, Munich, HS 2694 (Georg Rosentreter), diary entry, 24 August 1914, pp. 10–11. Another instance in Alsace in BA-MA, Freiburg, MSg2/3112, Aufzeichnungen Karl Gruber, c.10 August 1914.

133 CPHDC, Moscow, 1415-1-54, fol. 270 and 273, circular found in home of Antwerp schoolteacher van Ruy, in Malines. Almost identical copy in Carl Ernst, *Der Große Krieg in Belgien. Beobachtungen, seinen ehemaligen hannoverschen Landsleuten gewidmet* (Gembloux, 1930), pp. 33–4. Schmitz and Nieuwland, *L'invasion allemande*, vol. 2, pp. 61–2, for the contemporary French translation. CPHDC, Moscow, 1415-1-54, fol. 269: Kaiserl. Dt. Gericht des General-Gouvernement in Belgien to Abt. IIb, 21 June 1915, confirmed the existence of the proclamation and indicated that von Bassewitz was in the Second Army and town commandant at Huy.

134 Cf. AGR, Brussels, CE, III 374 B1, 81a: e.g. session 30 September 1914: letter by chief medical officer Fritz Scheel, reserve medical company, 17th Res. Div, 9th AC, to Emma Trotsch, Halberstadt, 6 September 1914; session 20 October 1914, extract from war diary Gustave (*sic*) Klein, Landsturm.

135 Jacobson, *En marche sur Paris*, p. 31.

136 Cited in Joseph Bédier, *Comment l'Allemagne essaye de justifier ses crimes* (Paris, 1915), pp. 11–12.

137 KA, Munich, HS 2677 Otto Freiherr von Berchem, manuscript of memoirs 'Aus meinem Leben', entry for 10 August, p. 110. Cf. also HStA, Dresden, Zeitgeschichtliche Sammlung 75, No. 6, letter Fritz Schreiber, 29 August 1914.

138 AD Meurthe-et-Moselle, 86J 12, evidence of A. Wibrotte, 30 September 1915.

139 HStA-MA, Stuttgart, M660 NL Gleich, diary entry 10 August, book 153, pp. 37–8.

140 Ibid., diary entry 11 August 1914, pp. 39–40.

141 KA, Munich, HS 2358, Joseph Müller, war diary, vol. 1, diary entries 12–14 August 1914, pp. 29–30.

142 KA, Munich, HS 2301, Eugen von Frauenholz, 'Erinnerungen an meine Soldatenzeit 1901–1918', typescript, p. 209.

143 See chapters 1 (Liège) and 2 (Lorraine) above. For the impact of the collapse of the XVth Army Corps on French opinion, see Becker, *1914*, pp. 546–9.

144 *Schwäbischer Merkur*, 10 August 1914, morning edition. No court-martial records survive.

145 Deuringer, *Die Schlacht in Lothringen*, vol. 1, p. 64.

146 *Kriegsfahrten deutscher Maler*, p. 96. No date was given for the incident, and the text has 'Evelebbe', a mistake for Evelette. The Belgian source gives the date and the name

of the hanged man, Henry Jules, clog-maker (Belgian Second Commission, vol. 1, part 1, p. 111).

147 CPHDC, Moscow, 1467-1-12, fol. 114, deposition Sergeant Langenhan, 13 December 1914. The place given is Le Bniey, which is almost certainly a mistaken transcription of a name that has not been identified.

148 Belgian Second Commission , vol. 1, part 1, p. 256. For Baranzy, see chapter 2 above.

149 KA, Munich, HS 2259, report on the interrogation of the francs-tireurs held prisoner at Magdeburg, 16 September 1914.

150 Alfons Fonck, *Schrotschüsse in Belgien* (Berlin, 1931).

151 KA, Munich, HS 2259: 'Aufstellung der deutschen Verluste durch belgische Freischärler in 5 belgischen Provinzen', Foreign Ministry, 6 June 1916. The survey covered the provinces of Liège, Luxembourg, Namur, Brabant, and Hainaut.

152 The principal sources for the Garde Civique are two works justifying German military conduct in 1914 published between the wars, and a number of Belgian publications: Schwertfeger, *Grundlagen*; Robert Paul Oszwald, *Der Streit um den belgischen Franktireurkrieg. Eine kritische Untersuchung der Ereignisse in den Augusttagen 1914 und der darüber bis 1930 erschienenen Literatur unter Benutzung bisher nicht veröffentlichten Materials* (Cologne, 1931); Lucien Laudy, 'La Garde Civique non active en 1914', *Carnet de la Fourragère*, 1/3 (1925), pp. 73–7; H. Marchant, *Historique des troupes territoriales en Belgique en 1914. Groupement Clooten: Gardes Civiques, Gendarmerie, Corps de Volontaires* (Ixelles, 1938); E.-A. Jacobs, 'La Garde Civique de la province de Liège en 1914', in *Fédération des Cercles d'Archéologie et d'Histoire de Belgique, XLIVe Session. Congrès de Huy* (2 vols, 1976), vol. 2, pp. 526–8; Jacobs, 'Les Oubliés. Le rôle de la Garde civique en août 1914' in *Le Roi Albert et ses soldats* (Brussels, 1973), pp. 9–15. For the numbers, see Oszwald, *Der Streit*, pp. 9–10.

153 Cf. Schwertfeger, *Grundlagen*, pp. 92–3.

154 Oszwald, *Der Streit*, p. 73.

155 *L'Indépendance belge*, cited in ibid., p. 52; cf. also *Le Petit Bleu*, 5 August 1914; and *Anvers-Bourse*, 5 August 1914 (ibid., pp. 53–4).

156 *Le Soir*, 4 August 1914, cited in Oszwald, *Der Streit*, p. 52.

157 Cited in Oszwald, *Der Streit*, p. 52.

158 Jacobs, 'La Garde Civique', p. 527. See also various Belgian newspaper accounts, 6–11 August, cited in Oszwald, *Der Streit*, pp. 35–6.

159 Tasnier and Overstraeten, *Les Opérations militaires*, p. 82; Oszwald, *Der Streit*, pp. 12–13; Jacobs, 'La Garde Civique de la province de Liège en 1914'.

160 Musée Royal de l'Armée (hereafter MRA), Brussels, 'Rapport sur les événements [...] depuis le 31 juillet 1914 jusqu'au 10 août 1914', typescript of report by Joseph Knapen, Garde Civique commander; Belgian Second Commission, vol. 1, part 1, pp. 279–80. Four more inhabitants were killed in a further incident on 11 August. The Belgian Second Commission mentioned neither the role nor deportation of the Garde Civique.

161 *Le XXe Siècle*, 7 August 1914; emphasis in the original.

162 Cited in Oszwald, *Der Streit*, p. 70.

163 Schwertfeger, *Grundlagen*, pp. 81–2.

164 *Le XXe Siècle*, 16 and 20 August 1914.

165 Schwertfeger, *Grundlagen*, p. 95; circular of the provincial government of Namur to the heads of the local administrations, 15 August 1914, in ibid., appendix 27, p. 193.

166 Schwertfeger, *Grundlagen*, p. 96; also circular of provincial government of Namur 15 August 1914, in ibid., appendix 27, p. 193; circular of provincial government of

Brabant, 18 August, in ibid., appendix 30, p. 197; circular of provincial government of Namur, 19 August, in ibid., appendix 33, p. 203. On the disbanding of the Garde Civique in Namur province between 17 and 21 August, Ernst, *Der Große Krieg in Belgien*, p. 54, and Marchant, *Groupement Clooten*, p. 16.

167　AN, Paris, F7 12840 and 12841, on the *gardes civils*. On nationalist sentiment and pre-war invasion scares in the Meurthe-et-Moselle, see Jean-François Eck, 'Louis Marin et la Lorraine, 1905–1914. Le pouvoir local d'un parlementaire sous la IIIe République' (Doctorat de Troisième Cycle, Institut d'Études Politiques, Paris, 1980), pp. 377–86.

168　For the phenomenon more generally, see Bloch, 'Les fausses nouvelles de la guerre', and two contemporary collections, Albert Dauzat, *Légendes, prophéties et superstitions de la guerre* (Paris, n.d.), and Lucien Graux, *Les Fausses Nouvelles de la grande guerre* (7 vols, Paris, 1918–20).

169　PAAA, Bonn, R 19881, fol. 44, telegram Grand Headquarters, Koblenz, to Ministry of the Interior, Berlin, 6 August 1914.

170　BA-MA, Freiburg, N 266/69 Aug. v. Cramon. Meine Erlebnisse im Weltkriege – Frankreich 1914, diary entry 7 August 1914.

171　Ibid., diary entry dated between 8 and 10 August.

172　Dampierre, *Carnets de route allemands. Traduction intégrale*, pp. 3–71 (here, pp. 5, 19–20, 28, 30–1, 43–4).

173　KA, Munich, HS 3372, war diary, Leonhard Eisenbeiß, p. 4.

174　KA, Munich, HS 2740, Albert Ritter von Beckh, pp. 39–40 (diary entry 20 August 1914).

175　Mokveld, *The German Fury*, p. 89.

176　Alan Kramer, '"Greueltaten". Zum Problem der deutschen Kriegsverbrechen in Belgien und Frankreich 1914', in Gerhard Hirschfeld, Gerd Krumeich, and Irina Renz (eds), *Keiner fühlt sich hier mehr als Mensch … Erlebnis und Wirkung des Ersten Weltkriegs* (Essen, 1993), pp. 85–114; Kramer, 'Les "Atrocités allemandes": mythologie populaire, propagande et manipulations dans l'armée allemande', in Jean-Jacques Becker et al. (eds), *Guerre et cultures, 1914–1918* (Paris, 1994), pp. 147–64.

177　Powell, *Fighting in Flanders*, pp. 125–8.

178　AGR, Brussels, CE, III 374 B1, 21: Loustalot report, pp. 12–13 (quotation, p. 12).

179　Ibid., pp. 14–15.

180　Ibid., p. 12.

181　Ibid., pp. 14–15. The soldier was from the 12th Jäger Battalion.

182　Ibid., pp. 15–16. The men on whose evidence Loustalot based his story were Delling, IR 103, and Bieler, 12th Jäger Battalion.

183　*Kölnische Volkszeitung*, 16 September 1914, cited in Langenhove, *Cycle de légendes*, p. 176.

184　*Kölnische Volkszeitung*, 10 August 1914, cited in ibid., pp. 125–7.

185　*Kölnische Volkszeitung*, 12 August 1914, cited in ibid., p. 130.

186　*Kölnische Zeitung*, 9 August 1914, 1st morning edition.

187　Ibid., 11 August 1914, 1st morning edition; Kurt Koszyk, *Deutsche Pressepolitik im Ersten Weltkrieg* (Düsseldorf, 1968), p. 23. Cf. *Schwäbischer Merkur*, 12 August 1914, afternoon edition: collection of Belgian 'atrocities' committed by civilians, cited from the *Kölnische Zeitung*.

188　The first on 9 August was based on the reports of refugees returning to Berlin from Belgium, and the second on 12 August, reflecting to a limited extent the change of tone throughout the German press, was entitled 'The shameful deeds in Belgium' (*Norddeutsche Allgemeine Zeitung*, 9 August, 1st edition; 12 August, 2nd edition).

189 E.g. *Vorwärts*, 9 August 1914; *Kölnische Zeitung*, 9 August (2nd morning edition); *Kölnische Volkszeitung*, 10 August (morning edition), *Norddeutsche Allgemeine Zeitung*, 9 August 1914, 2nd edition.

190 E.g. Delbrück (ed.), *Der deutsche Krieg in Feldpostbriefen*, vol. 1; Hans Leitzen (ed.), *Der große Krieg 1914–15 in Feldpostbriefen. Neue Folge* (Wolfenbüttel, 1915); and Hermann Sparr (ed.), *Feldpostbriefe 1914. Berichte und Stimmungsbilder von Mitkämpfern und Miterlebern* (Leipzig, 1915); Langenhove, *Cycle de légendes*, pp. 194–5.

191 *Leipziger Neueste Nachrichten*, 20 October 1914, cited in Langenhove, *Cycle de légendes*, pp. 62–3.

192 *Deutsche Tageszeitung*, 19 August 1914, morning edition.

193 Here we differ from Lothar Wieland who correctly notes that atrocity stories in the press had the opportunity to influence the troops waiting to be transported to Belgium, but uses this to explain why large-scale mass executions took place only after 18 August (*Belgien 1914*, pp. 19–23). This exaggerates the role of the press and fails to recognize that both the franc-tireur belief and the first mass executions at Liège predated any press accounts of civilian resistance.

194 *Kölnische Volkszeitung*, 15 September 1914; van Langenhove, *Cycle de légendes*, p. 214.

195 Paul R. Krause, 'Franktireure', *Die Gartenlaube. Illustriertes Familienblatt*, 36 (1914), pp. 764–6.

196 Arnulf Volkmar, 'Ein Edelmann. Novelle aus dem Deutsch-Französischen Kriege 1870/71', *Illustrirte Zeitung*, 27 August 1914.

197 KA, Munich, HS 2643, General Konrad Krafft von Dellmensingen, diary II, pp. 6–7 (20 September 1914).

4 Memories, mentalities, and the German response to the 'franc-tireur war'

1 The *Dictionnaire Littré* of 1878 defines francs-tireurs as 'soldiers of certain mobile corps created during the wars of the revolution'. The current *Dictionnaire Robert* confirms the Revolutionary origin of the term (1792).

2 Jean-Paul Bertaud, *The Army of the French Revolution: From Citizen-Soldiers to Instruments of Power* (Princeton, 1988); Alan Forrest, *Soldiers of the French Revolution* (Durham, N.C., 1990); Peter Paret, 'Conscription and the End of the Ancien Regime in France and Prussia', in Paret, *Understanding War: Essays on Clausewitz and the History of Military Power* (Princeton, 1992), pp. 53–74.

3 Charles de Freycinet, *La Guerre en province pendant le siège de Paris, 1870–71* (Paris, 1871), p. 10.

4 'Volontaires et Francs-Tireurs!', engraving, 1870, Bibliothèque Sainte-Geneviève, Paris; François Roth, *La Guerre de 70* (Paris, 1990), pp. 224–6; Robert Molis, *Les Francs-Tireurs et les Garibaldi. Soldats de la République. 1870–1871 en Bourgogne* (Paris, 1995).

5 Stéphane Audoin-Rouzeau, *1870. La France dans la guerre* (Paris, 1989), p. 205.

6 Michael Howard, *The Franco-Prussian War: The German Invasion of France, 1870–1871* (1961; new edn, New York, 1990), pp. 249–56; Markus Hauser, *Der Kampf*

Irregulärer im Kriegsrecht (Artikel 1 und 2 der Landkriegsordnung 1907) (Bad Ragaz, 1937), p. 9; Audoin-Rouzeau, *1870*, pp. 198, 210–19.

7 Helmuth von Moltke, *Moltkes Militärische Korrespondenz. Aus den Dienstschriften des Krieges 1870/71*, ed. Großer Generalstab (Berlin, 1897), part 3, telegram of 1 October 1870, p. 318.

8 Telegram from HQ (Versailles) to Second Army Command, 7 November 1870, ibid. p. 368. Cf. the warning to all army commands and military governors to be on guard against surprise attacks by armed civilians, to take hostages as a precaution, and carry out the 'harshest punishments', telegram 5 December 1870, ibid., pp. 422–3. Cf. telegram 7 January 1871 to General von Werder, on need for 'ruthless punishment of individuals and entire villages' in case of insurgency in Lorraine, ibid., p. 510.

9 Mark Stoneman, 'The Bavarian Army and French Civilians in the War of 1870–71', Master's dissertation, University of Augsburg, 1994, chs 4 and 7, for this example and an illuminating discussion. We would like to thank the author for showing us his work.

10 Amédée Brenet, *La France et l'Allemagne devant le droit international pendant les opérations militaires de la guerre de 1870–71* (Paris, 1902), pp. 12–15; Moltke, *Moltkes Militärische Korrespondenz*, pp. 531–2.

11 Walter Laqueur, *Guerrilla: A Historical Study* (London, 1977), p. 85.

12 For this new image of warfare, see Stoneman, 'The Bavarian Army', pp. 93–7.

13 Helmuth von Moltke, *Moltke in seinen Briefen. Mit einem Lebens- und Charakterbild des Verewigten* (Berlin, 1902), pp. 225–6.

14 Otto Pflanze, *Bismarck: der Reichsgründer* (Munich, 1997), p. 486.

15 Julius von Hartmann, *Kritische Versuche, Nr. 2: Militärische Notwendigkeit und Humanität* (1878), cited in Hauser, *Der Kampf Irregulärer*, p. 10.

16 *Des Generalobersten Frhrn. v. Hausen Erinnerungen an den Marnefeldzug 1914. Mit einer einleitenden kritischen Studie*, ed. Fr. Max Kircheisen (1920; 2nd edn, Leipzig, 1922), *passim*.

17 Generalfeldmarschall Colmar Freiherr von der Goltz, *Denkwürdigkeiten*, ed. Friedrich Freiherr von der Goltz and Wolfgang Foerster (Berlin, 1929), p. 48 and *passim*.

18 Cf. Generaloberst von Einem, *Erinnerungen eines Soldaten 1853–1933* (Leipzig, 1933), esp. p. 12; and Junius Alter (ed.), *Ein Armeeführer erlebt den Weltkrieg. Persönliche Aufzeichnungen des Generalobersten v. Einem* (Leipzig, 1938), esp. p. 14.

19 *Kölnische Zeitung*, 9 August 1914, 1st morning edition.

20 This is a major topic for research in its own right. Unfortunately, neither of two recently published books on the education of Prussian officers discusses the military-historical content of their education. Cf. Steven E. Clemente, *For King and Kaiser! The Making of the Prussian Army Officer, 1860–1914* (New York, Westport, London, 1992); John Moncure, *Forging the King's Sword: Military Education between Tradition and Modernization: The Case of the Royal Prussian Cadet Corps, 1871–1918* (New York and Frankfurt, 1993). An excellent bibliography of published memoirs, diaries, and contemporary military-political writings is in Thomas Rohkrämer, *Der Militarismus der 'kleinen Leute'. Die Kriegervereine im Deutschen Kaiserreich 1871–1914* (Munich, 1990).

21 Helmuth von Moltke, *Geschichte des deutsch-französischen Krieges von 1870–71* (Berlin, 1891), pp. 165–70.

22 Ibid., pp. 233–4.

23 Hans von Kretschman, *Kriegsbriefe aus den Jahren 1870/71*, ed. Lily Braun (12th edn, Berlin, 1911), p. 138 (letter 29 September 1870).

24 Ibid., p. 92.

25 Goltz, *Denkwürdigkeiten*, p. 62 (letter of 26 November 1870) and p. 65 (letter of 24 December 1870).

26 Colmar von der Goltz, *Léon Gambetta und seine Armeen* (Berlin, 1877), translated as *Gambetta et ses armées* (Paris, 1877), esp. pp. 3–6, and 431–65; E. Carrias, *La Pensée militaire allemande* (Paris, 1948), p. 297.

27 Colmar von der Goltz, *Das Volk in Waffen. Ein Buch über Heerwesen und Kriegführung unserer Zeit* (1883; 6th edn, revised 'on the basis of the experiences of the World War' by Friedrich Freiherr von der Goltz, Berlin, 1925), p. v. Translated into English as *The Nation in Arms: A Treatise on Modern Military Systems and the Conduct of War* (London, 1906).

28 August Keim, *Erlebtes und Erstrebtes. Lebenserinnerungen von Generalleutnant Keim* (Hanover, 1925), p. 196.

29 Geoffrey Best, 'Restraints on War by Land before 1945', in Michael Howard (ed.), *Restraints on War: Studies in the Limitation of Armed Conflict* (Oxford, 1979), pp. 17–37; Geoffrey Best, *Humanity in Warfare: The Modern History of the International Law of Armed Conflicts* (London, 1980; new edn, 1983), pp. 128–215. For the Brussels conference, see James Lorimer, *The Institutes of the Law of Nations* (2 vols, Edinburgh, 1883–4), vol. 2, pp. 337–402. On the Hague conferences, see Christian Meurer, *Die Haager Friedenskonferenz* (2 vols, Munich, 1907), esp. vol. 2, *Das Kriegsrecht der Haager Konferenz*; and James B. Scott, (ed.), *Texts of the Peace Conferences at the Hague, 1899 and 1907* (Boston and London, 1908).

30 John Horne, 'Defining the Enemy: War, Law and the *Levée en masse* in Europe, 1870–1945', in Daniel J. Moran and Arthur Waldron (eds.), *The People in Arms: Military Myth and Political Legitimacy since the French Revolution* (Cambridge, forthcoming).

31 Cited in Lorimer, *Law of Nations*, vol. 2, p. 356. This was Article 10 of the Brussels accord, which became Article 2 of the Hague conventions in 1899, in which the definition of the status of the belligerent was more logically placed at the head of the accords (James B. Scott (ed.), *The Proceedings of the Hague Peace Conferences: Translation of the Official Texts* (5 vols, New York, 1920–1), vol. 1, pp. 53–4, 253–4).

32 Cited in Meurer, *Kriegsrecht*, vol. 2, p. 87.

33 Scott, *Hague Peace Conferences*, vol. 1, pp. 552–4.

34 Ibid.

35 Michael Howard, *War in European History* (Oxford, 1976), pp. 86–7; Paret, 'Conscription and the End of the Ancien Regime'; Peter Paret, *Clausewitz and the State: The Man, his Theories, and his Times* (1976; new edn, Princeton, 1985), p. 214.

36 Meurer, *Kriegsrecht*, vol. 2, pp. 58–69.

37 Jan Philipp Reemtsma, 'Die Idee des Vernichtungskrieges. Clausewitz – Ludendorff – Hitler', in Hannes Heer and Klaus Naumann (eds), *Vernichtungskrieg. Verbrechen der Wehrmacht 1941–1944* (1995; new edn, Frankfurt, 1997), pp. 380–4; Paret, *Clausewitz*, p. 236.

38 Paret, *Clausewitz*, p. 77; Gordon A. Craig, *The Politics of the Prussian Army 1640–1945* (1955; new edn, Oxford, 1964), chs 2–4, passim.

39 By Article 1 of the main agreement, which covered procedure. The substantive articles came as an appendix.

40 *Kriegsbrauch im Landkriege* (Berlin, 1902), translated into English as *The German War Book: Being 'The Usages of War on Land' issued by the Great General Staff of the German Army*, with a critical introduction by J. H. Morgan (London, 1915).

41 Ibid., pp. 52–4, quotation p. 54.

42 Ibid., p. 55.

43 Ibid., pp. 60–1.

44 See chapters 9 and 10 below.

45 Meurer, *Die Haager Friedenskonferenz*, vol. 2, p. 17. Meurer cited the *Kriegsbrauch* frequently throughout his book.

46 *Felddienstordnung* (Berlin, 1908).

47 *Felddienstordnung*, p. 104.

48 Ibid., appendix II: Anlage zum Abkommen betreffend die Gesetze und Gebräuche des Landkriegs vom 18.10.07, December 1911.

49 On the War Academy, Arden Bucholz, *Moltke, Schlieffen, and Prussian War Planning* (Providence and Oxford, 1991), pp. 185–91.

50 BA, Berlin, R 3003/ORA/RG, bJ 307/20, vol. 2, fol. 125, statement to the Reich prosecutor in war crime investigations by Major (retired) Georg von Mücke, Dresden, 12 January 1923. Cf. the experience of Lothar Engelbert Schücking ('War der Franktireurkrieg verboten?', *Die Weltbühne*, 13 September 1927, pp. 396–7), who recalled a court-martial judge in Belgium who was about to convict members of the Garde Civique as francs-tireurs. When Schücking pointed out the right of civilians to resist, the officer confessed he knew nothing of the Hague Convention.

51 August von Janson, *Der junge Infanterieoffizier und seine taktische Ausbildung* (Berlin, 1900).

52 Otto von Moser, *Die Führung des Armeekorps im Feldkriege* (Berlin, 1910). Similar assumptions in Friedrich Immanuel, *Taktische Aufgaben für Übungen und Kriegsspiel in Verbänden aller Art bis zum Armeekorps einschließlich* (4th edn, Berlin, 1914) (preface dated July 1913), tasks 79 and 80.

53 Moser, *Die Führung des Armeekorps*, pp. 19, 27.

54 Ibid., pp. 61, 67.

55 Friedrich von Bernhardi, *Reiterdienst. Kritische Betrachtungen über Kriegstätigkeit, Taktik, Ausbildung und Organisation unserer Kavallerie* (Berlin, 1910), p. 9. *Deutschland und der nächste Krieg* (Stuttgart and Berlin, 1912), translated into English as *Germany and the Next War* (London, 1912). By 1914, there had been nine German and 16 English impressions.

56 Bernhardi, *Reiterdienst*, pp. 53, 56, 59, 70, 137, 152, 258.

57 Friedrich Immanuel, *Handbuch der Taktik* (2 vols, Berlin, 1910), part 2, pp. 159–60, 255–8.

58 Konrad Lehmann and [Eggert] von Estorff, *Dienstunterricht des Offiziers. Anleitung zur Erteilung des Mannschaftsunterrichts in Beispielen* (Berlin, 1908), pp. 154–7.

59 Louis von Scharfenort, *L'interprète militaire. Zum Gebrauch in Feindesland, sowie behufs Vorbereitung für die Dolmetscherprüfung mit den Lösungen der schwierigeren Texte aus '225 deutsche Aufgaben'* (Berlin, 1906), pp. 43 and 51.

60 AGR, Brussels, CE III 374 B1, 21: Summary by Loustalot, 16 June 1915, p. 17.

61 Karl Krafft, *Handbuch für die Vorbereitung zur Kriegsakademie. Zugleich ein Ratgeber für die wissenschaftliche Beschäftigung jüngerer Offiziere* (Berlin, 1903), pp. 228–9.

62 Goltz, *Denkwürdigkeiten*, pp. 284–5, letter to Mudra, 24 August 1907.

63 Notes by Major W. von Hahnke on Schlieffen's memorandum of 28 December 1912,

cited in Gerhard Ritter, *The Schlieffen Plan: Critique of a Myth* (1956, English translation: London, 1958), p. 181.

64 Oberst von Zimmermann, 'Milizheere (Schluß). Die Heere der französischen
Republik im Kriege 1870/71', *Vierteljahrshefte für Truppenführung und Heereskunde*
10/4 (1913), pp. 694–731 (here pp. 708–9).

65 Ibid., p. 730.

66 A. Pingaud, 'Impressions de guerre allemandes en 1870', *Revue des Deux Mondes*, 15
September 1915, pp. 371–95; Stoneman, 'The Bavarian Army and French Civilians',
chs 4 and 7.

67 Friedrich Gerstäcker, *Die Franctireurs. Erzählung aus dem deutsch-französischen
Kriege* (Jena, n.d., but *c*.1871).

68 Friedrich Gerstäcker, *Kriegsbilder eines Nachzüglers aus dem deutsch-französischen
Kriege* (Jena, n.d., but *c*.1871), pp. 18–19.

69 Walter Bloem, *Volk wider Volk* (Leipzig, 1912), pp. 326–7.

70 Seestern (pseudonym for Ferdinand Grautoff), *1906. Der Zusammenbruch der alten
Welt* (Leipzig, n.d., 2nd edn [1907]). It apparently sold no fewer than 150,000 copies
(Fernand van Langenhove, *Comment naît un cycle de légendes. Francs-tireurs et atroc-
ités en Belgique* (Lausanne and Paris, 1916), p. 115).

71 Nicholas Stargardt, *The German Idea of Militarism: Radical and Socialist Critics
1866–1914* (Cambridge, 1994), esp. pp. 19–48.

72 David Schoenbaum, *Zabern 1913: Consensus Politics in Imperial Germany* (London,
1982); Hans-Ulrich Wehler, 'Symbol des halbabsolutistischen Herrschaftssystems.
Der Fall Zabern von 1913/14 als Verfassungskrise des Wilhelminischen Kaiserreichs',
in Wehler (ed.), *Krisenherde des Kaiserreichs 1871–1918. Studien zur deutschen Sozial-
und Verfassungsgeschichte* (Göttingen, 1970), pp. 65–84.

73 Richard J. Evans, *Kneipengespräche im Kaiserreich. Stimmungsberichte der
Hamburger Politischen Polizei 1892–1914* (Reinbek bei Hamburg, 1989), pp. 341–6,
384–7.

74 For the historiography of 'mentalities' as principally defined by the *Annales* school in
France, see Peter Burke, *The French Historical Revolution: The Annales School
1929–89* (Cambridge, 1990), pp. 67–74.

75 Geoff Eley, *Reshaping the German Right: Radical Nationalism and Political Change
after Bismarck* (New Haven and London, 1980), pp. 160–205; Wolfgang J. Mommsen,
'The Prussian Conception of the State and the German Idea of Empire: Prussia and
the German Empire in Recent German History', in Mommsen, *Imperial Germany
1867–1918: Politics, Culture, and Society in an Authoritarian Empire* (1990; English
translation, London, 1995), pp. 43–4.

76 Richard J. Evans, 'In Search of German Social Darwinism: The History and
Historiography of a Concept', in Manfred Berg and Geoffrey Cocks (eds), *Medicine
and Modernity: Public Health and Medical Care in Nineteenth- and Twentieth-
Century Germany* (Washington, D.C., and Cambridge, 1997), pp. 55–80.

77 Roger Chickering, 'Die Alldeutschen erwarten den Krieg', in Jost Dülffer und Karl
Holl (eds), *Bereit zum Krieg. Kriegsmentalität im wilhelminischen Deutschland
1890–1914. Beiträge zur historischen Friedensforschung* (Göttingen, 1986), pp. 21–3;
Roger Chickering, *We Men Who Feel Most German: A Cultural Study of the Pan-
German League, 1886–1914* (Boston, London, Sydney, 1984).

78 The authors are grateful to Dr. med. Birgitta Rüth-Behr, Hamburg, for discussion of
this point.

79 For example, the future chief of the OHL, Falkenhayn; see Holger Afflerbach, *Falkenhayn. Politisches Denken und Handeln im Kaiserreich* (Munich, 1994), p. 102.

80 Bernhardi, *Der nächste Krieg*, pp. 82 and 16–25. For the reaction to Bernhardi see Fritz Fischer, *War of Illusions: German Policies from 1911 to 1914* (1969; English translation, London, 1975), pp. 242–4; Wolfgang J. Mommsen, *Großmachtstellung und Weltpolitik 1870–1914. Die Außenpolitik des Deutschen Reiches* (Frankfurt and Berlin, 1993), pp. 228 and 241.

81 Daniel Frymann (i.e. Heinrich Claß), *Wenn ich der Kaiser wär. Politische Wahrheiten und Notwendigkeiten* (Leipzig, 1912). Cf. BA, Berlin, NL Gebsattel, 90 Ge 4/1, fol. 6, Gebsattel to 'Daniel Frymann', 28 May 1913.

82 BA, Berlin, NL Gebsattel, 90 Ge 4/1, fol. 61, Claß to Gebsattel.

83 Chickering, *We Men Who Feel Most German*, pp. 115, 107–13.

84 Marilyn Shevin Coetzee, *The German Army League: Popular Nationalism in Wilhelmine Germany* (New York and Oxford, 1990), pp. 86–7.

85 Fischer, *War of Illusions*, pp. 105–9, 282–6, 452.

86 Goltz, *Denkwürdigkeiten*, pp. 335–8.

87 On Social Darwinism in the world-view of the ex-servicemen, see Rohrkrämer, *Militarismus der 'kleinen Leute'*, pp. 252–62.

88 Belgian Second Commission, vol. 1, part 1, pp. 14–15.

89 BA-MA, Freiburg, N 30/52, Beseler to his wife from Thildonck, 23 August 1914.

90 Ibid., Beseler to his wife from Dieghem (near Brussels), 25 and 28 August 1914.

91 BA, Berlin, NL Gebsattel, 90 Ge 4/1, fol. 196–7, Gebsattel to Claß, 16 August 1914.

92 BA-MA, Freiburg, MSg2/3112, notes by Karl Gruber, *c.* 26 August 1914, p. 22.

93 *Rheinisch-Westfälische Zeitung*, 1 January and 12 February 1914, cited in Kurt Koszyk, *Deutsche Pressepolitik im Ersten Weltkrieg* (Düsseldorf, 1968), pp. 88–9.

94 Gerd Krumeich, 'The Myth of Gambetta and the "People's War" in Germany and France, 1871–1914', in Stig Förster and Jörg Nagler (eds), *On the Road to Total War: The American Civil War and the German Wars of Unification, 1861–1871* (Cambridge, 1997), p. 645.

95 Bucholz, *Moltke*, p. 268.

96 Wolfgang J. Mommsen, 'Culture and Politics in the German Empire', in Mommsen, *Imperial Germany*, p. 122; Paul Weindling, *Health, Race and German Politics between National Unification and Nazism, 1870–1945* (1st edn 1989; Cambridge, 1993), p. 56.

97 Thomas Nipperdey, *Deutsche Geschichte 1866–1918*, vol. 1, *Arbeitswelt und Bürgergeist* (1st edn 1990; 3rd rev. edn, Munich, 1993), p. 478. Margaret Lavinia Anderson, 'Windhorsts Erben. Konfessionalität und Interkonfessionalismus im politischen Katholizismus 1890–1918', in Winfried Becker and Rudolf Morsey (eds), *Christliche Demokratie in Europa: Grundlagen und Entwicklungen seit dem 19. Jahrhundert* (Cologne and Vienna, 1988), pp. 69–90, here pp. 86–7.

98 *Germania*, 18 August 1914. Cf. also Lothar Wieland, *Belgien 1914. Die Frage des belgischen 'Franktireurkrieges' und die deutsche öffentliche Meinung von 1914 bis 1936* (Frankfurt, Berne, New York, 1984), pp. 70–1, citing *Kölnische Volkszeitung*, 16 and 18 August.

99 Georg Alexander von Müller, *Regierte der Kaiser? Kriegstagebücher, Aufzeichnungen und Briefe des Chefs des Marine-Kabinetts Admiral Georg Alexander von Müller 1914–1918*, ed. Walter Görlitz (Göttingen, 1959), p. 57.

100 Wenninger diary, 6 September 1914, in Bernd F. Schulte, *Europäische Krise und Erster Weltkrieg. Beiträge zur Militärpolitik des Kaiserreichs, 1871–1914* (Frankfurt,

1983), p. 259. For the Kaiser's anti-Catholicism see also Fritz Fischer, 'Exzesse der Autokratie. Das Hale-Interview Wilhelms II. vom 19. Juli 1908', in Fischer (ed.), *Hitler war kein Betriebsunfall. Aufsätze* (Munich, 1992), pp. 104–35, here pp. 114–15.

101   On the military's fear of proletarian insurrection, see Bernd F. Schulte, *Die deutsche Armee 1900–1914. Zwischen Beharren und Verändern* (Düsseldorf, 1977), who incorrectly depicts it as the army's dominating concern.

102   Schulte, *Die deutsche Armee*, p. 545; Stig Förster, *Der doppelte Militarismus. Die deutsche Heeresrüstungspolitik zwischen Status-Quo-Sicherung und Aggression 1890–1913* (Stuttgart, 1985), pp. 191–2. The order was issued by General von Bissing, who in November 1914 became military governor of Belgium.

103   Bundesarchiv-Militärarchiv (BA-MA), Potsdam, PH2/466: Ministry of War, Berlin, to Chief of General Staff, 8 February 1912. Cf. also Förster, *Der doppelte Militarismus*, p. 193.

104   BA, Berlin, Reichskanzlei 2463, fol. 17–19: Moltke to Bethmann Hollweg, 23 August 1914. This document is published also in Helmut Otto and Karl Schmiedel (eds), *Der erste Weltkrieg. Dokumente* (1st edn 1977; Berlin (DDR), 1983), pp. 77–9.

105   Belgian Second Commission, vol. 2, *Rapports sur les déportations des ouvriers belges et sur les traitements infligés aux prisonniers de guerre et aux prisonniers civils belges* (Brussels and Liège, 1923); Annette Becker, *Oubliés de la Grande Guerre. Humanitaire et culture de guerre 1914–1918. Populations occupées, deportés civils, prisonniers de guerre* (Paris, 1998), pp. 57–77.

106   KA, Munich, HS 2259, minutes of conference of military governors, Brussels, 10 November 1914.

107   Jean-Marie Mayeur, *Autonomie et politique en Alsace. La constitution de 1911* (Paris, 1970), pp. 185–92; P. Dollinger (ed.), *L'Alsace de 1900 à nos jours* (Toulouse, 1979), chs 1 and 2.

108   Alan Kramer, '*Wackes* at War: Alsace-Lorraine and the Failure of German National Mobilization, 1914–1918', in John Horne (ed.), *State, Society and Mobilization in Europe during the First World War* (Cambridge, 1997), pp. 105–21. For a more pessimistic evaluation of the attempted integration of the two provinces, see Hans-Ulrich Wehler, 'Unfähig zur Verfassungsreform. Das "Reichsland" Elsaß-Lothringen von 1870 bis 1918', in Wehler, *Krisenherde des Kaiserreichs*, pp. 30–51.

109   Over 17,000 and 8,000 respectively (Kramer, '*Wackes* at War', pp. 108, 111).

110   On this process, see ibid., pp. 106–12, and on German Lorraine, François Roth, 'Lorraine annexée et Lorraine occupée, 1914–1918', in Jean-Jacques Becker and Stéphane Audoin-Rouzeau (eds), *Les Sociétés européennes et la guerre de 1914–1918* (Paris, 1990), pp. 289–309 (here pp. 290–2).

111   HStA-MA, Stuttgart, M660 Res. Lt. Dr. Adolf Spemann. Diary entry, 14 August 1914, p. 3, at Benfeld.

112   HStA-MA, Stuttgart, M660, NL Oberstleutnant Gerold von Gleich, 'Meine Erlebnisse im Feldzug 1914. I. Teil: Der Feldzug in Lothringen im August 1914. Niederschrift im April 1915 begonnen.' Book 153, diary entries 4–5 August 1914, pp. 10–13.

113   KA, Munich, HS 2358, war diary Joseph Müller, 8 August 1914.

114   KA, Munich, HS 3411/1 war diary Clauß, 12 August 1914.

115   J. Rossé et al. (eds.) on behalf of the friends of Abbé Dr Haegy, *Das Elsaß von 1870–1932* (4 vols, Colmar, n.d., but 1936), vol. 1, *Politische Geschichte*, pp. 237–8.

116   Roth, 'Lorraine annexée', p. 291.

117   KA, Munich, HS 2373, Die Schlacht bei Weiler am 18.8.1914: 'Die Augusttage von

1914 in Weiler im Elsaß' – from the diary of Fräulein Emilie Dietz, diary entries 3 and 17–19 August 1914. Cf. Reichsarchiv, *Der Weltkrieg 1914 bis 1918. Die militärischen Operationen zu Lande* (14 vols, Berlin, 1925–44), vol. 1, *Die Grenzschlachten im Westen* (1925), map 4. The troops were probably the 1st Battalion, Bavarian Reserve IR 11.

118 KA, Munich, HS 2373, deposition by Catholic priest Alfons Kappler, 14 October 1914, before military tribunal of XVth Army Corps, Strasbourg.

119 KA, Munich, HS 2373, report by court-martial counsellor Hauck to deputy command, XVth Army Corps, 16 November 1914. This did not prevent the Bavarian official history from repeating the claim that the villagers helped to conceal the French; this was sufficient reason to burn down the village (*Die Schlacht in Lothringen*, vol. 1, p. 139).

120 E.g. in the case of St Moritz, or that of Burzweiler, quoted in chapter 1 above, where a tribunal found that German 'friendly fire', not civilian resistance, was to blame (*Das Elsaß*, vol. 1, p. 238).

121 *Kaiserliche Verordnung über die Strafrechtspflege bei dem Heere in Kriegszeiten und Kaiserliche Verordnung über das außerordentliche kriegsrechtliche Verfahren gegen Ausländer und die Ausübung der Strafgerichtsbarkeit gegen Kriegsgefangene. Vom 28. Dezember 1899* (Berlin, 1911), in BA-MA, Freiburg, PHD 3/217. BA, Berlin, R 3003 Generalia, 59, envelope 1c, containing Armee-Verordnungsblatt, 2 August 1914.

122 HStA, Dresden, 40164, order issued by von Laffert, commander of XIXth Army Corps, 14 August 1914.

123 BA, Berlin, R 3003/ORA/RG, bJ 307/20, vol. 2 fol. 96, order of the day, XIIth Army Corps, Corps Headquarters Burg Reuland, 15 August 1914.

124 Hausen, *Erinnerungen an den Marnefeldzug*, pp. 104–5, 107–9. See chapter 1 above.

125 HStA, Dresden, 26882, IR 134: divisional order, 15 August 1914.

126 HStA, Dresden, 40164, Foot Artillery Battalion 58, Battalion order, 14 August 1914; ibid., Battalion order, 17 August 1914.

127 Jean Chot, *La Furie allemande dans l'entre-Sambre-et-Meuse (journées des 23, 24, 25 et 26 août 1914)* (Charleroi, 1919), p. 67.

128 HStA, Dresden, Zeitgeschichtliche Sammlung 75, No. 1: Kurt Rasch to his parents, 22 August 1914.

129 BA, Berlin, R 3003/ORA/RG, bJ 198/20, vol. 2, fol. 30, extract from war diary Rifle Regiment 108.

130 AGR, Brussels, CE III 374 B1, 21, statement by Otto Kuchler (*sic*: Küchler?), drummer in IR 103, 7th co., from Bautzen, 30 April 1915 (translated from French).

131 AGR, Brussels, CE III 374 B1, 21, Loustalot inquiry, statement by Rudolph Grimmer, IR 108, 1st company, 15 March 1915.

132 AGR, Brussels, CE III 374 B1, 21, Loustalot inquiry, statements by Ewald Breitschneider, 5th company, IR 108, and Johannes Peisker, NCO in 7th company, IR 108, 15 March 1915.

133 AGR, Brussels, CE III 374 B1, 21, Loustalot inquiry, statement by Paul Pfeiffer, 4 May 1915.

134 General von Wenninger, cited in Schulte, *Europäische Krise*, p. 224.

135 HStA-MA, Stuttgart, M79/11b, Falkenhayn to War Minister at Grand Headquarters (transcript).

136 CPHDC, Moscow, 1415-1-51. Undated wall poster; attached note states: 'Aus: 6. Res.Div. Aushänge 10.8. – 21.8.14'. The poster cannot have been used before 17 August, when the IIIrd Reserve Corps entered Belgian territory. Cf. Reichsarchiv,

Weltkrieg, vol. 1, p. 130. The wording suggests this poster was used by all advancing divisions. It was signed 'supreme commander of the army', but it is not clear if this was Moltke, as commander-in-chief of all the armies, or the commander of the army containing the 6th Reserve Division.

137   Henri Davignon, *German Posters in Belgium: Their Value as Evidence* (London, 1918). Bülow stated that 110 had been executed; the true figure was 262 for Andenne and Seilles, with 110 in one single execution.

138   CPHDC, Moscow, 1415-1-54, fol. 84: undated, unsigned note, probably by staff of Governor-General, Brussels, January 1915.

139   Otto and Schmiedel (eds), *Der erste Weltkrieg*, document 19, pp. 80–4.

140   KA, Munich, HS 2643, Konrad Krafft von Dellmensingen, Tagebuch II, p. 3, entry 19 September, and p. 18, 23 September, noting a conversation with his army commander, Prince Rupprecht of Bavaria.

141   Whether there was conscious emulation of the British policy during the South African War of detaining Boer and African civilians, including women and children, in concentration camps cannot be investigated here.

142   KA, Munich, HS 2643, Konrad Krafft von Dellmensingen, Tagebuch II, p. 71, 9 October 1914. Indeed, the Schlieffen Plan made no mention of combating civilian insurgency, either by deportation or military repression.

143   *Die Kämpfe der deutschen Truppen in Südwestafrika*, ed. Kriegsgeschichtliche Abteilung I des Großen Generalstabes, vol. 1 (Berlin, 1906), p. 207, cited in Ernst Otto, *Schlieffen und der Generalstab. Der preußisch-deutsche Generalstab unter Leitung des Generals von Schlieffen 1891–1905* (Berlin [DDR], 1966), p. 214. Schlieffen wrote of 80,000 people killed.

144   Robert von Friedeburg, 'Konservatismus und Reichskolonialrecht. Konservatives Weltbild und kolonialer Gedanke in England und Deutschland vom späten 19. Jahrhundert bis zum Ersten Weltkrieg', *Historische Zeitschrift*, 263 (1996), pp. 345–93, here p. 382.

145   Cf. ibid., p. 385.

146   Bucholz, *Moltke*, p. 315.

147   Carl von Clausewitz, *On War*, ed. and trans. Michael Howard and Peter Paret (1832; Princeton, 1984), pp. 75–8.

148   Hew Strachan, 'Clausewitz and the Rise of Prussian Hegemony', in Strachan, *European Armies and the Conduct of War* (London, 1983), pp. 90–107, here pp. 103–4.

149   Goltz, *Das Volk in Waffen*, section 6.

150   Theodor Wolff, *Tagebücher 1914–1919. Der Erste Weltkrieg und die Entstehung der Weimarer Republik in Tagebüchern, Leitartikeln und Briefen des Chefredakteurs am 'Berliner Tageblatt' und Mitbegründers der 'Deutschen Demokratischen Partei'*, ed. Bernd Sösemann (Boppard, 1984), part 1, p. 168, diary entry 17 February 1915.

151   HStA, Dresden, 26882, divisional order of the day, staff headquarters, Hargnies, 26 August 1914; emphasis added.

152   HStA-MA, Stuttgart, M660 NL Pezold, diary entry, 15 August 1914, p. 2.

153   PAAA, Bonn, R 22382, Graf von Pfeil, 27th Division, to Generalkommando, 14 August 1914, transcript in Grand Headquarters to Reichskanzler, 29 August 1914.

154   HStA-MA, Stuttgart, M660 NL Pezold, diary entry 14 September 1914, p. 25. Crown Prince Wilhelm was commander of the Fifth Army.

155   HStA-MA, Stuttgart, M660, NL Pezold, p. 70, 21 October 1914.

156   Ibid., 12 November 1914 (comments of Lieutenant Veiel).

157 *Hamburger Volkszeitung*, 25 August 1927. The article was reprinted in *Rote Fahne*, 11 September 1927, an extract appeared in the pacifist journal *Das Andere Deutschland*, 10 September 1927, and the entire article there on 6 April 1929 (Wieland, *Belgien 1914*, pp. 242–3, 471, n. 441).

158 BA, Berlin, R 3003/ORA/RG bJ 307/20 vol. 1, fol. 209, deposition Major Alfred Stübel, Dresden, 15 April 1922. Stübel was commander of 6th company, Grenadier Regiment 101.

159 Hans-Ulrich Wehler, *Deutsche Gesellschaftsgeschichte* (3 vols, Munich, 1987–95), vol. 3, *Von der 'Deutschen Doppelrevolution' bis zum Beginn des Ersten Weltkrieges 1849–1914* (1995), pp. 1248–9.

5 Allied opinion and 'German atrocities', August–October 1914

1 *Le Temps*, 7 August 1914.

2 'L'Empire des barbares. Nouvelles atrocités', *Le Matin*, 11 August; *Le Temps*, 12 August (both reporting a French government communiqué).

3 'L'Assassinat de Warsage', *Le Temps*, 14 August 1914; 'Leurs atrocités', *Le Matin*, 15 August 1914. This second story underplayed the total of 18 civilians who in fact perished (Belgian Second Commission, vol. 1, part 2, pp. 150 and 562–3).

4 'Crimes allemands dans la Haute-Alsace', *Le Matin*, 16 August 1914; *Le Temps*, 17 August 1914.

5 'L'État d'esprit des soldats allemands', *Le Temps*, 17 August 1914.

6 'Bandits. Ils avouent leurs vols, leurs pillages, leurs incendies' and 'Les Atrocités allemandes', *Le Matin*, 18 August 1914; 'Les Atrocités allemandes. En Meurthe-et-Moselle', *Le Temps*, 20 August 1914.

7 National Archives, Washington, D.C., State Department, M367, 763.72116/ 80–170, for the series of French protest notes; the first three notes were reproduced in *Le Temps*, starting with that of 16 August, under the headline 'Les Atrocités allemandes', *Le Temps*, 22 August 1914.

8 AD Nord, 9R 15; AD Pas-de-Calais, R 857; also in *Le Temps*, 22 August 1914. The list was to be based on impartial testimony and updated twice monthly.

9 Belgian First Commission, vol. 1, p. 41; *Le Soir* (Brussels), 9 August 1914.

10 'Nouvelles inexactes', *Le Soir*, 8 August 1914; *The Times*, 10 August 1914. For the false rumour, J. M. Kennedy, *The Campaign round Liège* (London, 1914), pp. 35–6.

11 'Les Barbares', *Le Soir*, 11 August 1914. The report was compiled principally from the Dutch Catholic paper, *De Tijd*, with additional material from the *Nieuwe Rotterdamsche Courant*. *Le Soir* first carried news of the Berneau and Warsage incidents, both from Dutch papers, on 10 August.

12 From 16 August, there was a string of press releases on 'German atrocities'.

13 'Les Atrocités allemandes en Belgique. Un réquisitoire', *Le Matin*, 25 August 1914; AGR, Brussels, Broqueville papers, 442 (Commission d'enquête), typescript of the original; English version published (*inter alia*) in *Daily Mail*, 26 August 1914.

14 W. Breton, *Un Régiment belge en campagne (1er août–1er janvier 1915). Quelques fastes du 2e chasseurs à pied* (Paris and Nancy, 1916), p. 26.

15 F.-H. Grimauty, *Six mois de guerre en Belgique par un soldat belge. Août 1914–février 1915* (Paris, 1915), p. 47. No date or place is indicated, but the author subsequently fell back in defence of Brussels, so he was on the line of the Gette in the week before 18 August.

16 Roland de Marès, *La Belgique envahie* (Paris, 1915), p. 62. The eminent Belgian histo-
    rian and eye-witness of the invasion, Henri Pirenne, confirmed in his post-war study
    that news of German behaviour at Liège and Namur was scarce and hardly credited,
    whereas events at Aarschot and Louvain provoked a 'collective panic' which contin-
    ued until October (*La Belgique et la guerre mondiale* (Paris, 1928), pp. 64–5).

17 AD Meurthe-et-Moselle, 8R 172, dossier on the alert of 27 November 1912; cf. Jean-
    François Eck, 'Louis Marin et la Lorraine 1905–1914. Le pouvoir local d'un parlemen-
    taire sous la IIIe République', troisième cycle thesis, Institut d'Études Politiques,
    Paris, 1980), pp. 377–80.

18 AN, Paris, F7 12938, Meuse, prefect's report, 12 August 1914. The latter is almost
    certainly a reference to the incident at Affléville on 9 August. AN, Paris, F7 12938,
    Meurthe-et-Moselle, prefect's report, 18 August 1914.

19 Ibid., prefect's report, 27 August 1914.

20 'A Nomény', *L'Est républicain*, 22 August 1914.

21 AN, Paris, F7 12938, Meurthe-et-Moselle, prefect's report, 27 August 1914; appeal by
    General Durand, 'Habitants de Nancy', *L'Est républicain*, 23 August 1914.

22 AN, Paris, F7 12938, Meuse, prefect's report of 25 August 1914.

23 AD Nord, 9R 20, report of the special police commissioner attached to the First Army
    Region, 21 August 1914, for the fall of Brussels; ibid., report of the sub-prefect of
    Avesnes, 24 August 1914; ibid., report of the sub-prefect of Dunkerque, 23 August
    1914. See also P. Trochon, *Lille avant et pendant l'occupation allemande* (Tourcoing,
    1922), p. 13, for an appeal for calm by the mayor of Lille on 24 August.

24 AN, Paris, 96 AP 1, 'Mémoire de Félix Trépont, préfet de Lille sous l'occupation alle-
    mande' (a retrospective account), pp. 80–1, for the mood in Lille; AD Nord 9R11,
    circular to mayors and police commissioners, 29 August 1914.

25 AN, Paris, F7 12938, Pas-de-Calais, prefect's report, 25 August 1914.

26 AN, Paris, F7 12939, Vosges, prefect's reports of 19 and 27 August 1914; see also L.
    Colin, *Les Barbares à la trouée des Vosges. Récits des témoins* (Paris, 1915), p. 73.

27 AN, Paris, F7 12939, Seine-et-Marne, prefect's report, 1 September 1914; AN, Paris,
    F7 12937, Aube, prefect's report, 8 September 1914.

28 AN, Paris, F7 12939, Seine-Inférieure, prefect's report, 31 August 1914.

29 Ibid., Haute-Saône, prefect's report, 30 August 1914. This was despite the 'emotion'
    caused on 26 August by news of the French withdrawal from nearby southern Alsace.

30 Ibid., Ain, prefect's report, 22 August 1914; ibid., Tarn-et-Garonne, prefect's report, 26
    August 1914. The prefect of the Oise considered that the wounded in the hospital
    trains which passed through his département spread 'quite unbelievable tales' of
    battle to local inhabitants (AN, Paris, F7 12938, Oise, prefect's report, 26 August 1914).

31 AN, Paris, F7 12937, Calvados, prefect's report, 25 August 1914.

32 AN, Paris, F7 12939, Deux-Sèvres, prefect's report, 2 September 1914; ibid., Var,
    prefect's report, 1 September 1914. In the case of the Var, the prefect described the
    Belgian refugees as 'victims of spoliation and barbary'. The poster in the Deux-Sèvres,
    issued by the prefect as he prepared to receive 5,000 French and Belgian refugees,
    called on the inhabitants of the département to 'welcome into your homes these
    country folk from Flanders, Picardy, Belgium or Lorraine, who [...] have had the pain
    of witnessing the pillage and the burning of their family assets, and who, in many
    cases after being forced to submit to hateful violence, are even now wandering the
    roads of France'.

33 Jean-Jacques Becker, *1914. Comment les français sont entrés dans la guerre* (Paris,

1977), pp. 523–58.

34 As early as 4 September, the general commanding the Tenth Army region (Brittany) asked the press to refrain from all propaganda concerning 'German atrocities'. For this and Millerand's instruction, see AD Ille-et-Vilaine, 4M censure (uncatalogued).

35 Pirenne, *La Belgique et la guerre mondiale*, pp. 275–82. Pirenne puts the refugees temporarily flooding into Holland at a million, but gives no evidence or source for this figure. The American ambassador to Holland reckoned that by October, there were more than 400,000 refugees in that country, 'all of them in a state of extreme poverty and distress' (National Archives, Washington, D.C., State Department, M 367, 763.72/ 1076–1196, 14 October 1914). The lower figure is used here, but it remains a guess. In France, there were 445,000 assisted French refugees by January 1915 and 154,000 assisted Belgians, most of whom must have entered France by October 1914. The assisted were reckoned as 70 per cent of the total, giving over 500,000 French and 200,000 Belgian refugees. A proportion of the French refugees may have been displaced by trench warfare rather than the invasion. Four hundred thousand thus seems a safer calculation for the number of refugees directly resulting from the invasion. (Michel Huber, *La Population de la France pendant la guerre* (Paris, 1931), pp. 172–87.)

36 Private diaries and memoirs, published and unpublished, have been used irrespective of the region from which their author came. Additionally, one area on the south coast of England (West Sussex) has been examined at archival level.

37 Arnold Bennett, *The Journals of Arnold Bennett*, vol. 2, *1911–1921* (London, 1932), pp. 98, 101.

38 Diary of Miss M. B. Peterkin, Imperial War Museum (manuscripts).

39 John H. Morgan, *German Atrocities: An Official Investigation* (London, 1916).

40 The *Times* journalist, Michael MacDonagh, saw the first wounded soldiers from the BEF at Waterloo Station on 30 August, and noted that 'they all looked dazed' (*In London during the Great War: The Diary of a Journalist* (London, 1935), p. 19).

41 Andrew Clark, *Echoes of the Great War: The Diary of the Reverend Andrew Clark, 1914–1919* (Oxford, 1985), pp. 33, 37 (entries for 20–21 November and 7–11 December 1914).

42 *Observer and West Sussex Recorder*, 23 September 1914 (Ivan Malcom, MP). See also ibid., 9 and 16 September.

43 AN, Paris, AJ4 10. The total number of depositions is slightly less than the total of 284 incidents since some described more than one incident.

44 Jean Schmitz and Norbert Nieuwland, *Documents pour servir à l'histoire de l'invasion allemande dans les provinces de Namur et de Luxembourg* (7 vols, Brussels and Paris, 1919–24), vol. 4, part 2, p. 194.

45 Belgian First Commission, 3rd report, vol. 1, p. 56.

46 AN, Paris, AJ4 19, dossier on Épernay, deposition by Mme Rainguet.

47 AN, Paris, AJ4 5, deposition of 6 January 1915.

48 Ibid., deposition of 6 November 1914.

49 AN, Paris, AJ4 16, deposition of 29 April 1915. One bourgeois, the composer Albéric Magnard, was so resolved to protect his property that he shot the first two German soldiers who tried to enter his house, killing one and wounding the other, before taking his own life. The Germans burned the house down and pillaged the village (French Commission, 1st report, pp. 39, 197–8).

50 AN, Paris, AJ4 16, deposition of Mme Comte, from Veley (20 April 1915).

51 Hélène Pittard (under pseudonym N. Roger), *Le Passage des évacués à travers la Suisse* (2 vols, Paris and Neuchatel, n.d., but 1915 or 1916), vol. 1, *Les Evacués à Genève*, p. 27.

52 Testimony of Louis Donnet, the deputy priest of the church of Les Alloux in Tamines, in Schmitz and Nieuwland, *L'invasion allemande*, vol. 3, p. 105.

53 AGR, Brussels, CE, III, 374 B1, 54.

54 AN, Paris, AJ4 30, deposition of Brigadier Gervaise to the Director-General of the Customs Service, 25 June 1915.

55 Belgian First Commission, 17th report, vol. 2, p. 54.

56 AN, Paris, AJ4 19, deposition (1 November 1914) of an old labourer who witnessed the incident which he claimed took place on 6 September 1914.

57 See chapter 1 above.

58 Deposition of Mme Jacques, whose husband and son both perished (Schmitz and Nieuwland, *L'invasion allemande*, vol. 5, p. 205).

59 AD Meurthe-et-Moselle, 8R 172, letter to Mirman, 12 September 1914.

60 AGR, Brussels, CE, III, 374 B1, 81b, manuscript letter, 22 August 1914.

61 AN, Paris, AJ4 5, deposition of Claude Millenin, landlord.

62 Schmitz and Nieuwland, *L'invasion allemande*, vol. 2, p. 312.

63 For the notices, see anon., *Les Affiches de guerre à Roubaix, à Tourcoing, à Lille, en Belgique. Avis, appels, proclamations, sentences, et documents divers des autorités françaises et allemandes. Août à fin décembre 1914* (Roubaix, 1915), and Henri Davignon, *German Posters in Belgium: Their Value as Evidence* (London, 1918).

64 Testimony of Abbé Moreaux, in Schmitz and Nieuwland, *L'invasion allemande*, vol. 5, p. 105.

65 French Commission, 1st report, pp. 91–2.

66 Ibid., pp. 156–7.

67 AN, Paris, AJ4 5, deposition of François Betancourt, the assistant mayor, 11 December 1914.

68 AN, Paris, AJ4 17 (Nîmes), deposition of Claudius Gravier, French IR 61.

69 First Belgian Commission, 2nd report, vol. 1, pp. 49–50.

70 French Commission, 3rd and 4th reports, pp. 10–23 (p. 14 for the quotation).

71 AN, Paris, AJ4 23 (Riom), deposition of Gaston Le Quemer, soldier in French IR 94 (20 October 1914); AJ4 22 (Quimperlé), deposition of Léon Boinville, French IR 350 (26 November 1914).

72 Morgan, *German Atrocities*, pp. 123–57.

73 French Commission, 3rd and 4th reports, p. 19.

74 AN, Paris, AJ4 9, (Bourges). His report receives corroboration from a fellow-soldier in IR 146, who was convalescing far away in Pau, but who at Morhange on the same date had seen at 40 yards distance 'a dragoon stretched out on the ground, wounded, whom two German infantry soldiers finished off with their rifle butts' (AN, Paris, AJ4 20, Pau, deposition of Paul Rouer, 30 October 1914).

75 AN, Paris, AJ4 14, Limoges, in one of a number of depositions concerning such incidents in the German advance to the Marne and subsequent retreat.

76 French Commission, 3rd and 4th reports, pp. 66–73; AN, Paris, BB 18 2568 4, report of the French Embassy, Berne, 22 September 1914, for Zimmerman's evidence. For the post-war trial of Stenger, see chapter 9 below.

77 See chapter 2 above.

78 French Commission, 3rd and 4th reports, pp. 9–10; Belgian First Commission, 7th report, vol. 1, pp. 89–92. The Bryce Report did not raise the issue of dumdum bullets.

79 Exploding bullets were banned by the St Petersburg Declaration of 1868 and soft-nosed bullets by the Hague Convention of 1907. For the interrogation of the German prisoner, see SHA, Vincennes, 22N 297, Deuxième bureau, 6th Army Corps, 1914–15; for the order issued by the German High Command, on 24 September 1914, see AN, Paris, AJ4 44, report on dumdums by the 2e Bureau, Eighth Army, 14 December 1914.

80 AN, Paris, AJ4 16, note of 16 November 1914 from Dr Paul Caillol, military hospital number 5, Narbonne; ibid., report of 14 October by Dr Jean Arrons, director of the military hospital at Prades; AN, Paris, AJ4 22, note on 'balles explosives' by the professor of surgery at the Maritime Hospital, Brest.

81 French Commission, 1st report, p. 8. The Belgian report shared the judgement, considering in the case of Luxembourg province, for example, that it was 'beyond doubt that rapes have been very frequent' (Belgian First Commission, 8th report, vol. 1, p. 109). See also *Report of the Committee on Alleged German Outrages Appointed by His Britannic Majesty's Government and Presided over by the Right Hon. Viscount Bryce, O.M.*, Cd 7894 (London, 1915), pp. 47–53.

82 AD Pas-de-Calais, R 587, letter of the mayor of Sailly-sur-la-Lys to the prefect of the Pas-de-Calais, 10 June 1916; AD Meurthe-et-Moselle, 8R 200, interview of Gabrielle T., aged 39, on 13 February 1915 concerning her rape on 6 September 1914 by two German soldiers while her ten-year-old daughter was in the next room; Belgian First Commission, 8th report, vol. 1, p. 109.

83 Stéphane Audoin-Rouzeau, *L'Enfant de l'ennemi (1914–1918). Viol, avortement, infanticide pendant la grande guerre* (Paris, 1995), ch. 2.

84 Here, the invasion of 1914 differs from the official condoning of rape by the Red Army in eastern Germany in 1945 and the deliberate use by Bosnian Serb soldiers of rape as an instrument of 'ethnic cleansing' in 1992–3. On the former, see Atina Grossmann, 'A Question of Silence: The Rape of German Women by Occupation Soldiers', *October 72* (Spring 1995), p. 43–63, and Norman Naimark, *The Russians in Germany: A History of the Soviet Zone of Occupation, 1945–1949* (Cambridge, Mass. and London, 1995), pp. 69–140.

85 French Commission, 1st report, pp. 16–17, 43, 87–8, 216; AN, Paris, AJ4 5 (Amiens), deposition of Emma P., plus corroborating statement by her mother.

86 AN, Paris, AJ4 19 (Paris), deposition of Louise F., including details omitted from the account in French Commission, 1st report, pp. 16, 85. The published account mistakenly gives the daughter's age as 13, instead of three.

87 AN, Paris, AJ4 4 (Aix), deposition of 28 October 1914.

88 Belgian First Commission , 4th report, p. 61.

89 AGR, Brussels, CE, III, 374 B1, 81a, deposition of Private Verbiest, Belgian IR 2, corroborated by that of Private Vervynckt, Belgian IR 7, both made on 8 October 1914.

90 French Commission, 1st report, pp. 21–3, 29; AN, Paris, AJ4 15 (Lyon), deposition of Gérard de Langlade, brigadier in Artillery Regiment 20, on Nomény; AJ4 17 (Nîmes), deposition of Pierre Guyon concerning Gerbéviller.

91 The theme of male rape is not entirely absent, but seems to have existed more as a form of speculation or fantasy on the part of male witnesses, and thus as an additional symbolic register for expressing the trauma and impotence of being invaded. In the case of Gerbéviller, two witnesses agreed that four of the male corpses left by the Germans had had the trousers removed and the ankles bound, and that one or two of them had had their sexual organs mutilated. One of the two witnesses thought it

possible that one of the male victims had 'suffered a special kind of outrage', though the official commentary considered it impossible to say (French Commission, 1st report, pp. 29, 140–1).

92 French Commission, 1st report, p. 172.

93 Ibid., pp. 41, 208.

94 Ruth Harris, 'The "Child of the Barbarian": Rape, Race and Nationalism in France during the First World War', *Past and Present*, 141 (1993), pp. 170–206, esp. p. 186.

95 French Commission, 1st report, pp. 20, 104–5.

96 AN, Paris, AJ4 44, deposition of Georges Cuvellier, French IR 148.

97 In order of citation, AN, Paris, AJ4 20 (Pau), deposition of Fernand Douillard (French IR 62), 27 October 1914; ibid., deposition of François Héno (French IR 116, also 27 October 1914, suggesting, given their different units, that one was inspired by the other); AN, Paris, AJ4 22 (Rennes), deposition of Arthur Potiron (French IR 69); AN, Paris, AJ4 21 (Poitiers), deposition of Edmond Grizaud (French IR 93), 31 October 1914; AN, Paris, AJ4 (Rennes), deposition of Alexis Mulot (French IR 64), 16 November 1914, who placed the incident on 23 August. The testimony of both Mulot and Potiron was forwarded by the Procureur Général of Rennes to the Belgian authorities (AGR, Brussels, CE, III, 374 B1, 20).

98 Audoin-Rouzeau, *L'Enfant de l'ennemi*, pp. 90–8. Audoin-Rouzeau makes the point about the home front representation of the issue. But the unpublished deposition witnesses demonstrate that the myth expressing the trauma came from the narratives of soldier witnesses, real or imaginary. For the wider home front treatment of this theme, see chapter 8 below.

99 AN, Paris, AJ4 9 (Bourges), deposition of Hippolyte Coutant. He was told by a local girl that the woman had been raped the evening before. See also AN, Paris, AJ10 (Caen), statements by Jean Vandebrugge and Léopold Guillemin, both Belgian soldiers; AN, Paris, AJ4 25 (Toulouse), deposition Paul Morel, French IR 1 (1 December 1914), recounting the stories of Belgian civilians in Namur province about women whose breasts had been cut off; ibid., deposition of Georges Hequet, French IR 284 (1 December 1914), who swore that he had seen the body of a pregnant woman in Belgium whose breasts had been mutilated (suggesting that such stories were circulating in the military hospitals of Toulouse); AGR, Brussels, CE, III, 374 B1, 20, report by the police of Trouville (France) on the account given by a Belgian refugee, exceptionally a woman, who recounted that in Liège and Herstal the Germans had cut off women's breasts to stop them suckling children; ibid., deposition of Winaud Médard, Belgian soldier, sent on by the judicial authorities in the Tarn, where he was a refugee. In an example which portrays perfectly the evidential ambiguity of the story, a French soldier in Colonial IR 22 claimed that the inhabitants of a village in Belgium, some 60 miles from the Meuse, showed him and his comrades the body of a woman whose breasts had been cut off, but 'I couldn't verify if she had been mutilated as was said because she was clothed' (AN, Paris, AJ4 16 (Montpellier), deposition of Jean-François Joseph).

100 E.g. AN, Paris, AJ4 18 (Orléans), deposition of Urbain Bourieux, 3rd Zouaves; AN, Paris, AJ4 20 (Pau), deposition of Joseph Defossez, 3rd Belgian Regiment of Heavy Cavalry, in hospital in Pau; ibid., deposition of François-Bertrand Bazet, a priest working in the hospital of Pau; ibid., deposition of Louis Decrook, a Belgian miner and refugee; AN, Paris, AJ4 21 (Poitiers), deposition of Arthur Rippe, soldier in French IR 123; AN, Paris, AJ4 22 (Rennes), deposition of Eugène Gaudin, French IR

25, concerning the supposed mutilation of the breast of a mother suckling her baby; AN, Paris, AJ4 23 (Riom), deposition of Alphonse Verbrugge, 2nd Belgian Grenadiers; and AN, Paris, AJ4 25 (Toulouse), Joseph Jouva, a miner from Liège province.

101 AGR, Brussels, CE, III 374, B1, 81a, testimony of soldier Verbiest.

102 Klaus Epstein, *Matthias Erzberger and the Dilemma of German Democracy* (1959; new edn, New York, 1971), p. 122; Vatican Archive, Affari Ecclesiastici Straordinari, folder 116, text of an interview by Cardinal Gasparri, Secretary of State, 18 March 1916. Cardinal Mercier, the Primate of Belgium, and Heylen, Bishop of Namur, had also been asked about the matter when they visited Rome, according to Gasparri. The former cited only three cases of nuns raped by German soldiers, while the latter considered that isolated cases apart, the story had no foundation. A copy of this interview was sent to the Bavarian ambassador at the Vatican, assuring him that 'it corresponds to the truth' (ibid., Gasparri to Baron Ritter von Grünstein, 8 April 1916).

103 On the constructed nature of narrative and the malleable role of memory in relation to this, see Donald P. Spence, *Narrative Truth and Historical Truth: Meaning and Interpretation in Psychoanalysis* (New York, 1982), esp. pp. 166–72.

104 AN, Paris, BB18 2568 2 (Ministry of Justice), Procureur Général of Amiens, 9 November 1917, reporting on the difficulties in getting details of German soldiers responsible for rape and murder in Hazebrouck, October 1914, in inquiries carried out shortly after the events.

105 E.g. the French prefects' evidence, cited above, on the role played by the tales in provoking the civilian exodus of late August–early September.

106 John Horne, 'Les Mains coupées. "Atrocités allemandes" et opinion française en 1914', in Jean-Jacques Becker et al. (eds), *Guerre et Cultures, 1914–1918* (Paris, 1994), pp. 133–46.

107 AN, Paris, AJ4 3 (Agen).

108 AN, Paris, AJ4 18 (Orléans).

109 AN, Paris, AJ4 10 (Caen). A separate deposition under her married name to the judicial authorities in Caen stated that the Germans had killed children with poisoned sweets at Tourcoing, in the Nord.

110 AGR, Brussels, CE, III, 374 B1, 20, material sent by the president of the French Commission to the Belgian Commission, 28 December 1914.

111 AN, Paris, AJ4 3 (Agen).

112 AN, Paris, AJ4 27, deposition of Charles Leroux.

113 AN, Paris, AJ4 30 (from the Ministry of Finance), deposition of Brigadier Gervaise.

114 AN, Paris, AJ4 6 (Angers), depositions of sergeants Henri Turpin and Édouard Deleval. French IR 43 was part of the Ist Army Corps (Fourth Army) and the encounter took place at Gérin on 22 August. See chapter 1 above for the raid.

115 AN, Paris, AJ4 23 (Riom).

116 AN, Paris, AJ4 3 (Agen).

117 AN, Paris, AJ4 21 (Poitiers).

118 See chapter 6 below. The French authorities investigated a claim by a Madame d'Héricaut, president of the Ligue des Femmes Françaises (the leading middle-class women's organization) in the Artois region, that she was taking care of a child with 'severed hands' in the Pas-de-Calais. This resulted in a confession by Mme d'Héricault that she was only repeating a rumour and not referring to her own experience (AD Pas-de-Calais, R 857, statement by Mme d'Héricault, n.d., and accompanying letter

from the president of the Cour des Comptes to the prefect of the Pas-de-Calais, 21 April 1916). The Vatican enquired into a rumour from Switzerland, in mid-1916, about a little Belgian girl recovering in hospital after the Germans had amputated her hand. The tale was without foundation (Vatican Archive, Affari Ecclesiastici Straordinari, Belgio, 217).

119 Stéphane Audoin-Rouzeau, *La Guerre des enfants 1914–1918: essai d'histoire culturelle* (Paris, 1993), ch. 3.

120 *L'Illustration*, 24 October 1914, report on the massacres of No025y and Gerbéviller by Gabriel Louis-Jaray, who accompanied the nationalist writer and journalist, Maurice Barrès, to his native Lorraine in October. *Le Matin*, 25 October, ran a story on 'Ce qui reste de Revigny' (near Bar-le-Duc) which arose from the visit of the French official commission. A visit by Mirman to the devastated villages of Lorraine generated a report in *Le Temps* ('Gerbéviller', 28 November 1914) and the cover story of *L'Excelsior*, 29 November 1914, the latter including two pages of photos.

121 'A travers les villes mortes', *Le Matin*, 11 September, 'Les Barbares ont passé par là', 14 September, 'Les Étapes de l'ignominie', 16 September, and 'Qu'on pense à nous', an appeal by the parliamentary deputy of the Oise, 19 September 1915; 'De Paris à la ligne de feu', *Le Temps*, 24 September, and 'Autour de la bataille', 6 October 1915; *L'Excelsior*, 9 October 1914, on Compiègne; 'L'Oeuvre des vandales', 11 October, on Orchies; 'Après le passage des allemands', 18 September 1914, on Senlis, with two pages of photos; and 21 September 1914, on hostage-taking.

122 'En Belgique', *Le Temps*, 14 September 1914. The only indication of the number of deaths was the supposed execution of a 'hundred notables'. The 11th Belgian report (15 January 1915) was the first to detail events in Namur province.

123 'La Belgique ensanglantée', *L'Illustration*, 12 September 1914. The Belgian Commission's identical conclusion was given in a press release by the Ministry of Foreign Affairs and widely reproduced in the Allied press on 30 August.

124 'Le Journal de marche d'un officier saxon', *Le Temps*, 26 October 1914; *The Times*, 19 October 1914.

125 'Le Fléau allemand à Nancy', *Le Temps*, 24 August 1914; 'L'Héroïque sacrifice d'un vaillant pays', *Le Matin*, 27 August 1914, and 'Journal de Charleroi. Récit d'un témoin', 14 October.

126 E.g. 'La Sauvagerie allemande', *L'Est républicain*, 19 August 1914, which unselfconsciously describes how witness accounts were uncritically transcribed in the newspaper editing room.

127 'La Belgique envahie', *Le Temps*, 2 September 1914.

128 Michael Jeismann, *Das Vaterland der Feinde. Studien zum nationalen Feindbegriff und Selbstverständnis in Deutschland und Frankreich 1792–1918* (Stuttgart, 1992), pp. 346–7.

129 *Le Matin*, 21 September 1914; *La Guerre sociale*, 8 October 1914.

130 *Excelsior*, 26 August 1914. Cf. the photo-journal, *Le Miroir*, 30 August ('Allies and enemies are treated the same') and 27 September 1914.

131 C. Noiht, *Les Barbares modernes. Les atrocités et cruautés exercées par les allemands en Belgique, en Alsace-Lorraine et en France pendant la guerre de 1914* (2 vols, Paris, 1914), vol. 1, p. 79. The story was published in identical form in several papers, including the *Bulletin des Armées de la République*, 18 August 1914, p. 2, and *Le Matin*, 18 August 1914 ('Sauvages. Ils ont fusillé un enfant de sept ans. Ils méritent tous les représailles'), but not *Le Temps*.

132 The poem, 'The Child with the Wooden Gun', was published in the *Bulletin des Armées de la République* on 23 August 1914; it held the Kaiser accountable for the death of the innocent child. A verse of the poem was cited on the postcard shown in illustration 10.

133 'Une Main coupée', *Le Matin*, 29 August 1914.

134 Louis-Lucien Klotz, *De la guerre à la paix. Souvenirs et documents* (Paris, 1924), pp. 33–5.

135 A fine collection of 'atrocity' postcards (numbering at least 100) is in the Musée d'Histoire Contemporaine, Paris.

136 Cf. the military service law of 1905 which made explicit reference to 1793. John Horne, 'Defining the Enemy: War, Law and the Levée en Masse in Europe, 1870–1945', in Daniel Moran and Arthur Waldron (eds), *The People in Arms: Military Myth and Political Legitimacy since the French Revolution* (Cambridge, forthcoming); Gerd Krumeich, 'The Myth of Gambetta and the "People's War" in Germany and France, 1871–1914', in Stig Förster and Jörg Nagler (eds), *On the Road to Total War: The American Civil War and the German Wars of Unification, 1861–1871*, (Washington, D.C., and Cambridge, 1997), pp. 641–55.

137 Jean Norton Cru, *Témoins. Essai d'analyse et de critique des souvenirs de combattants édités en français de 1915 à 1928* (Paris, 1929), pp. 38–59.

138 For the distinction between French 'civilization' and German 'culture', see Pierre Bénéton, *Histoire des mots. Culture et civilisation* (Paris, 1975). On the Franco-Prussian War as a cultural conflict, see Oriel Reshef, *Guerres, mythes et caricature. Au berceau d'une mentalité française* (Paris, 1984); Stéphane Audoin-Rouzeau, *1870. La France dans la guerre* (Paris, 1989), pp. 268–72, 321; and Annette Becker, 'L'Étranger au temps de la guerre de 1870–1871', in Jean-Pierre Jessenne (ed.), *L'Image de l'autre dans l'Europe du nord-ouest à travers l'histoire* (Lille, 1996), pp. 123–32. For the role of the negative enemy stereotype in the construction of national identity between 1870 and 1914, see Claude Digeon, *La Crise allemande de la pensée française (1870–1914)* (Paris, 1959) and Jeismann, *Vaterland der Feinde*.

139 Paul M. Kennedy, *The Rise of the Anglo-German Antagonism, 1860–1914* (London, 1980), pp. 251–88, 306–20; Samuel Hynes, *The Edwardian Turn of Mind* (Princeton, 1968), pp. 15–53; Ignatius F. Clarke, *Voices Prophesying War: Future Wars, 1763–3749* (1966; 2nd edn, Oxford, 1992), ch. 4; Jonathan Steinberg, 'The Copenhagen Complex', *Journal of Contemporary History*, 3 (1966), pp. 23–46.

140 *Annales parlementaires de Belgique, Chambre des Représentants. Session Extraordinaire de mardi 4 août 1914*, for the speech of Albert I; Pirenne, *La Belgique et la guerre mondiale*, chs 1 and 2; M. R. Thielemans and E. Vandewoude (eds), *Le Roi Albert à travers ses lettres inédites, 1882–1916* (Brussels, 1982); Laurence van Ypersele, *Le Roi Albert. Histoire d'un mythe* (Ottignies, 1995), pp. 137–53.

141 *Report of the International Commission to Inquire into the Causes and Conduct of the Balkan Wars* (London, 22 February 1914). The liberal *Frankfurter Zeitung* carried items (based on reports in *The Times* and the *Daily Telegraph*) on 'atrocities' committed in the Balkan War on 3 December, 11 December, 17 December, and 23 December 1913 ('Butchery on both sides'). Not only liberal opinion was outraged by the atrocities. The anonymous author of a report on the capture of Janinu by the Greeks in the journal of the Prussian General Staff condemned the 'atrocities' committed by Greek soldiers against Turkish civilians. (Anon, 'Die Einnahme von Janinu durch die Griechen', *Vierteljahrshefte für Truppenführung und Heereskunde* 10/4 [1913], pp. 783–90, here p. 789.)

142 E.g. R. Jacomet, *Les Lois de la guerre continentale* (Paris, 1913), with preface by Louis
     Renault (pp. 6–16).

143 See chapter 1 above.

144 AD Nord 9R 12, 'dossiers documentaires [...] sur les lois de la guerre, convention de
     Genève, convention de la Haye etc.'; AN, Paris, F7 12840, report by Ministry of the
     Interior summarizing the debate on the *gardes civils*.

145 'La Situation en Belgique', *Le Temps*, 1 September 1914.

146 *Le Temps*, 27 October 1914.

147 AN, Paris, AJ4 19 (Paris), Coulommiers district, for reference to 'bandits'. Both civilians
     and soldiers used the term 'barbarians', e.g., ibid., Madame Louvet in Épernay canton
     who saw her husband beaten up and killed by 'these barbarians'; AN, Paris, AJ 44, the
     French soldier, Georges Cuvellier, whose patrol in Belgium met the woman bruised and
     raped by German soldiers, and who later claimed to have seen a house containing
     wounded French soldiers set on fire, who concluded that the Germans were 'barbarians'.

148 Ministère de l'Instruction et des Beaux-Arts, *Documents officiels. Les Allemands
     destructeurs de cathédrales et de trésors du passé. Mémoire relatif aux bombardements
     de Reims, Arras, Senlis, Louvain, Soissons, etc. accompagné de photographies et de pièces
     justificatives* (Paris, 1915), pp. 5–24 (illustration facing p. 12 for German poster);
     anon., *Germany's Violations of the Laws of War 1914–15: Compiled under the Auspices
     of the French Ministry of Foreign Affairs* (London, 1915), pp. 298–307 (statements by
     cathedral officials and local French commander). The official German press commu-
     niqué (WTB report in *Kölnische Zeitung*, 23 September 1914, 1st morning edition)
     denied that the cathedral was targeted.

149 National Archives, Washington, D.C., State Department papers, M367.763 72116/
     1–79, text of the French government's communiqué on Rheims; *Le Temps*, 30 August
     1914 (for Louvain). See also 'Vandalisme germanique', *Le Temps*, 21 September 1914,
     and 'Rançon et symbole', *Le Temps*, 22 September 1914, on the destruction of Louvain
     and Rheims.

150 Schmitz and Nieuwland, *L'invasion allemande*, vol. 2, p. 68.

151 See chapter 6 below.

152 Jean Stengers, *Congo. Mythes et réalités* (Louvain-la-Neuve, 1989), pp. 141–4.
     According to Stengers, the hands were amputated mainly from corpses whereas the
     myth portrayed the living being mutilated. Cf. Thomas Pakenham, *The Scramble for
     Africa* (London, 1991), pp. 585–601.

153 *Le Charivari*, 24 January 1915.

154 Richard Holt, *Sport and Society in Modern France* (London, 1981), pp. 126–31;
     Richard J. Evans, *Rituals of Retribution: Capital Punishment in Germany, 1600–1987*
     (London, 1996), pp. 207–445, *passim*.

155 Peter Gay, *The Bourgeois Experience: Victoria to Freud* (5 vols, London and New York,
     1984–98), vol. 3, *The Cultivation of Hatred* (1993), pp. 514–27.

156 Frédéric Chauvaud, *De Pierre Rivière à Landru. La violence apprivoisée au XIXe siècle*
     (Brussels, 1991), ch. 9; Corbin, *Le Village des cannibales*, ch. 4; Alain Corbin, 'Le Sang
     de Paris. Réflexions sur la généalogie dans l'image de la capitale', in Corbin, *Le Temps,
     le désir, l'horreur* (Paris, 1991), pp. 215–25; Karen Halttunen, 'Humanitarianism and
     the Pornography of Pain in Anglo-American Culture', *American Historical Review*
     100/2 (1995), pp. 303–34.

157 The literature on Jack the Ripper is voluminous. On his French equivalents, see A.
     Lacassagne, *Vacher, l'éventreur et les crimes sadiques* (Lyon, 1899), esp. pp. 250–3.

6 The battle of official reports and the tribunal of world opinion

1 See the case of the supposed abduction of children from Paris in 1750 and the 'rumour' of young girls spirited away to the white slave trade in Orléans in 1969 (Arlette Farge and Jacques Revel, *The Rules of Rebellion: Child Abductions in Paris in 1750* (1988; English translation, Cambridge, 1990); Edgar Morin, *Rumour in Orleans* (1969; English translation, London, 1971), pp. 17–43).

2 The French note of 18 August 1914, while denying any civilian participation in combat, argued that if any Frenchmen 'impelled by the wish to defend their hearths [...] spontaneously took up arms', this would conform to the second Article of the Hague Convention on Land Warfare.

3 AGR, Brussels, Broqueville papers, 442 (Commission d'enquête); Henri Davignon, *Belgium and Germany: Texts and Documents* (London, 1915), p. 35; Michel Dumoulin (ed.), *Jules Destrée. Souvenirs des temps de guerre* (Louvain, 1980), introduction, p. 20.

4 Belgian First Commission, vol. 1, pp. 52–3.

5 The eighth report dealt with Luxembourg (December 1914) and the 11th with Dinant (January 1915). The 16th and 17th reports dealt with Liège, the 22nd with Hainaut. One further report was published, but the focus switched to German actions during the occupation (Belgian First Commission, 23rd report (Le Havre, 1917)).

6 'Le Nombre total des victimes civiles faites en Belgique par les armées allemandes d'invasion', in Bureau Documentaire Belge, *Cahiers documentaires. Recueil méthodique de documents sur la guerre européenne rassemblés et publiés avec le concours du Bureau Documentaire Belge* (Le Havre, 1914–18), 26 November 1915, p. 7. Cf. the total of 5,521 established by our calculations. See chapter 1 above, p. 74.

7 *Le Temps*, 14 October 1914, for Briand's circular.

8 In late December 1914, the Prime Minister, Viviani, reassured a deputy, Henri Galli, that publication was imminent of a report that would condemn the 'collective murder and pillage that the Germans call war' (*Le Temps*, 7 January 1915).

9 *The Diary of Lord Bertie of Thame: 1914–1918* (2 vols, London, 1924), vol. 1, p. 67; James M. Read, *Atrocity Propaganda 1914–1919* (New Haven, 1941), ch. 6.

10 *Le Livre rouge allemand. Un document écrasant. Les atrocités allemandes. Texte complet du rapport officiel de la commission instituée en vue de constater les actes commis par l'ennemi en violation du droit des gens* (Paris, 1915), sold in a cheap edition at 50 centimes. Illustrated versions were G. d'Ostoya, *Le Livre des atrocités allemandes d'après les rapports officiels. Estampes de G. d'Ostoya* (Paris, n.d.), and *Les Atrocités allemandes en France. Reproduction intégrale des rapports officiels des 17 décembre 1914 et 8 mars 1915. Illustrations de Maurice Leroy* (Paris, n.d.).

11 'Le Pillori', *Le Temps*, 9 January 1915, (editorial).

12 For the Foreign Office response to the various 'atrocity' reports, see the file PRO, London, FO 372/495, which includes reports from the Belgian, Swiss, and French governments. Further reports are in FO 372/496.

13 *Lord Riddell's War Diary, 1914–1918* (London, 1933), p. 52 (entry for 16 January 1915).

14 *The Black Book of the War: German Atrocities in France and Belgium* (London, 1915), which was the French report plus the first eight Belgian reports; *German Atrocities in France* (London, n.d., but 1915). The official translation was *German Atrocities in France: Report Presented by the Commission Instituted with a View to Investigating*

Acts Committed by the Enemy in Violation of International Law (London, 1916). For the question of translation of the French first report in English, see Read, *Atrocity Propaganda*, pp. 154–5.

15 Herbert Asquith, *The War, its Causes and its Message: Speeches delivered by the Prime Minister August–October 1914* (London, 1914), p. 14. Cf. PRO, London, FO 372/495/53825: Sir Charles Mathews, Director of Public Prosecutions, to Davidson, Foreign Office, 24 September 1914, on the Attorney-General's request to collect evidence on German atrocities in Belgium.

16 *Report of the Committee on Alleged German Outrages appointed by His Britannic Majesty's Government and presided over by the Right Hon. Viscount Bryce, O.M.* Cd. 7894 (London, 1915), p. 3; Asquith to George V, 16 September 1914, MSS Asquith (Bodleian Library, Oxford), vol. 7, fol. 240–2.

17 PRO, London, FO 372/495/53825, Sir Charles Mathews, Director of Public Prosecutions, to Davidson, Foreign Office, 24 September 1914, requesting an introduction to the Belgian Legation. The Home Office also supplied the president of the Belgian inquiry in London in the person of Sir Mackenzie Chalmers, a former Under-Secretary of State at the Home Office. See Belgian First Commission, 10th and 21st reports, and Henri Davignon, *Souvenirs d'un écrivain belge, 1879–1945* (Paris, 1954), pp. 235–44. Davignon was sent by Cooremans, president of the Belgian Commission, then in Antwerp, to conduct the London operation, where he remained as the key figure behind Belgian wartime propaganda in Britain. He was the son of Julien Davignon, Foreign Minister in the Belgian government-in-exile in 1914–15.

18 PRO, London, HO 45/11061/266 503, no. 7, Morgan to the Home Office. A summary was published in *The Nineteenth Century and After* (June 1915), and subsequently distributed in translation abroad; Morgan presented his full report as *German Atrocities: An Official Investigation* (London, 1916).

19 See Asquith's reply to a parliamentary question by Ronald McNeill on 15 September 1914 concerning the need to obtain 'unimpeachable' evidence of the 'gross violations of civilized warfare committed by German officers and men' which were reported by wounded soldiers (Bodleian Library, Oxford, MSS Asquith, vol. 87, fol. 152).

20 *Report of the Committee on Alleged German Outrages*, p. 3; Bodleian Library, Oxford, MSS Bryce, vol. 147, Sir John Simon to Bryce, 4 December 1914, asking him to chair the committee.

21 This was a concern of Foreign Office official, Eustace Percy, who wrote to the future chairman of the committee of inquiry, Lord Bryce, setting out his fears that the Allied case in the USA would be damaged by such exaggerated press coverage (Percy to Bryce, 26 October 1914, Bodleian Library, Oxford, MSS Bryce, vol. 239, fol. 73–81). Even inveterate anti-German officials at the Foreign Office, such as Eyre Crowe, firmly rejected attempts to use tales of mutilation to sway American opinion (Peter Cahalan, *Belgian Refugee Relief in England during the Great War* (New York, 1932), p. 115). The private emphasis throughout of the senior politicians involved in setting up the committee was on gathering 'trustworthy' information on German atrocities (Asquith to the King, 10 December 1914, in Bodleian Library, Oxford, MSS Asquith, vol. 7, fol. 240–2).

22 H. A. L. Fisher, *James Bryce* (2 vols, London, 1927); *Dictionary of National Biography, 1922–1930* (London, 1937), pp. 127–35; Keith Robbins, 'History and Politics: The Career of James Bryce', in Robbins (ed.), *Politicians, Diplomacy and War in Modern British History* (London, 1994), pp. 189–214.

23 Trevor Wilson, 'Lord Bryce's Investigation into Alleged German Atrocities in Belgium, 1914–15', *Journal of Contemporary History* 14/3 (1979), pp. 369–83, and also Wilson, *The Myriad Faces of War: Britain and the Great War, 1914–1918* (Cambridge, 1986), ch. 17, for a fine study of the Bryce Committee, from the standpoint of British attitudes towards the war. Brief, dismissive discussions are contained in Michael L. Sanders and Philip M. Taylor, *British Propaganda during the First World War* (London, 1982), pp. 143–4, and Gary S. Messinger, *British Propaganda and the State in the First World War* (Manchester, 1992), pp. 70–84.

24 James D. Squires, *British Propaganda at Home and in the United States from 1914 to 1917* (Cambridge, 1935), p. 31.

25 *Report of the Committee on Alleged German Outrages* and *Appendix: Evidence and Documents laid before the Committee on Alleged German Outrages*, Cd. 7895 (London, 1915).

26 Report of the Committee on Alleged German Outrages., pp. 7–8. Some material was included concerning French civilians or 'outrages' against British troops on French soil, mainly as a result of the witness evidence gathered by J. H. Morgan in France.

27 Attempts to locate this material in the papers of Lord Bryce in the Bodleian Library, Oxford, and in the PRO in Chancery Lane and Kew (Home Office papers) have drawn a blank. Trevor Wilson rightly discounts the notion that Bryce himself had the material destroyed, and points out that the ruling by the Home Secretary, Sir John Simon, that the witness evidence should not be communicable during the war for fear of reprisals in occupied Belgium, but retained for subsequent verification, was perfectly reasonable (*Myriad Faces of War*, p. 189). Apparently the Bryce Committee materials were destroyed by the Home Office between 1922 and 1939, as stated by an undated, unsigned note from the Home Office to the Public Record Office: PRO, London, HO 45/11061/266503. The reason remains a mystery. Cf. Read, *Atrocity Propaganda*, p. 206, and PRO, London, FO 370/587/L1185, which indicates that exhaustive searches in the Home Office and the Foreign Office were made but failed to find the Bryce Committee papers.

28 Cf. Stéphane Audoin-Rouzeau, *L'Enfant de l'ennemi (1914–1918). Viol, avortement, infanticide pendant la grande guerre* (Paris, 1995), pp. 40–1.

29 *Report of the Committee on Alleged German Outrages*, pp. 25–6; cf. Belgian First Commission, 2nd report, vol. 1, pp. 48–9.

30 The Bryce witness recorded the bodies of six dead labourers along the road (*Report of the Committee on Alleged German Outrages*, p. 26). The Belgian Second Commission gave the total dead as five from the village, including one woman, who was shot but may also have been bayoneted. Six inhabitants from Zempst were shot at Eppeghem (Belgian Second Commission, vol. 1, part 2, pp. 141, 681, and 686).

31 *Report of the Committee on Alleged German Outrages*, p. 26; Belgian Second Commission, vol. 1, part 2, pp. 136–7, 681.

32 *Report of the Committee on Alleged German Outrages*, p. 26; Belgian Second Commission, vol. 1, part 2, pp. 138, 683 (Hofstade); pp. 137, 687 (Weerde).

33 *Report of the Committee on Alleged German Outrages*, p. 50.

34 Ibid., pp. 41–2; Belgian First Commission, 12th report (January 1915), which drew some general conclusions.

35 French Commission, 1st report, p. 8.

36 Morgan, *German Atrocities*, pp. 52–3; Fisher, *James Bryce*, vol. 2, p. 135.

37 Simon to Bryce, 4 December 1914, quoted in Wilson, *Myriad Faces of War*, p. 185.

38   Irene Cooper Willis, *England's Holy War: A Study of English Liberal Idealism during the Great War* (New York, 1928), pp. 86–134, esp. 128–32.

39   M. Brock and E. Brock (eds), *H. H. Asquith: Letters to Venetia Stanley* (Oxford, 1985), letters of 29 August and 31 August 1914 (pp. 204 and 209 respectively).

40   Ibid., letter of 1 October 1914, p. 258; J. H. Whitehouse, *Belgium at War: A Record of Personal Experiences* (Cambridge, 1915), with an introduction by Lloyd George (esp. p. 17).

41   *Report of the Committee on Alleged German Outrages*, p. 61. Cf. Bryce, *The Attitude of Great Britain in the Present War* (London, 1916), in which Bryce claimed that 'England stands for a pacific as opposed to a military type of civilisation' (p. 17).

42   Wilson, *Myriad Faces of War*, ch. 17, for the fullest statement of this argument and a detailed examination of Cox's objections.

43   Ibid., p. 185.

44   Simon to Bryce, 8 December 1914, in Bodleian Library, Oxford, MSS Bryce, vol. 247, fol. 11–13, clarifying the terms of reference and operation of the committee.

45   *Report of the Committee on Alleged German Outrages*, p. 43.

46   Henri Davignon, *La Conduite des armées allemandes en Belgique et en France d'après l'enquête anglaise* (Paris, 1915), esp. pp. 28–9. This was a sequel to Davignon's account of the findings of the Belgian Commission's inquiry in Britain, *Les Procédés de guerre des allemands en Belgique* (Paris, 1915). In retrospect, Davignon considered that the Bryce Report 'reached the same conclusions as our more modest commission [...] We carefully remained quite independent of each other, [and were] happy at such an opportune mutual confirmation' (*Souvenirs d'un écrivain belge*, p. 244).

47   Robert P. Oszwald, *Der Streit um den belgischen Franktireurkrieg. Eine kritische Untersuchung der Ereignisse in den Augusttagen 1914 und der darüber bis 1930 erschienenen Literatur, unter Benutzung bisher nicht veröffentlichten Materials* (Cologne, 1931), p. 123.

48   CPHDC, Moscow, 1467-1-12, fol. 153, von Wandel, War Ministry, 9 September 1914. The instruction had reached down to regimental level by 22 September 1914 (HStA, Dresden, 40434, Detachment Sachsse, order of 22 September 1914). This is a slightly different version which requested evidence of the *Volkskrieg*.

49   PAAA, Bonn, R 22383, 'Völkerrechtswidrige Führung des belgischen Volkskrieges' (no foliation), Zimmermann, Foreign Ministry Berlin to Foreign Ministry GHQ, 16 September 1914. The General Staff and War Ministry having moved to Grand Headquarters at the front, the bodies left in Berlin were known as the Deputy General Staff and Deputy War Ministry.

50   PAAA, Bonn, R 22383, Zimmermann, Foreign Ministry Berlin, to Jagow, Foreign Ministry GHQ, 24 September 1914.

51   CPHDC, Moscow, 1467-1-12, fol. 106, War Ministry Investigation Department to XIIth Army Corps, 16 November 1914; emphasis in original. This same formulation was repeated in many other requests for evidence. Statements recorded in this file and 1467-1-11 date from late November 1914 to February 1915, with one statement by NCO Max Schubert from as early as 29 September 1914 (1467-1-11, fol. 24).

52   'De verwoesting van Dinant. Een tweede Leuven' ('The Devastation of Dinant. A Second Louvain'), in CPHDC, Moscow, 1467-1-12, fol. 128–9. The original report appeared in *De Telegraaf*, Amsterdam, 8 December 1914, and was widely republished abroad (PAAA, Bonn, R 20890, fol. 98–107).

53   CPHDC, Moscow, 1467-1-12, fol. 133, Deputy General Staff, department III b to

General-Gouvernement, Brussels, 7 January 1915; CPHDC, Moscow, 1467-1-12, fol. 125, Foreign Ministry to War Ministry, Military Investigation Department, 9 January 1915, requesting material to counter 'the very unfavourable impression which has been created in the neutral countries by Staller's report'.

54 CPHDC, Moscow, 1467-1-12, fol. 10, corps order of the day, 12 February 1915.

55 PAAA, Bonn, R 22383, Scheüch, War Minister at GHQ to Secretary of State in the Foreign Ministry at GHQ, 25 September 1914.

56 PAAA, Bonn, R 22383, Under-Secretary of State Zimmermann, Berlin, to Secretary of State, 13 October 1914.

57 PAAA, Bonn, R 22386, Wedding (legal department, Foreign Ministry) to von Grünau, 10 April 1915.

58 *Die völkerrechtswidrige Führung des belgischen Volkskriegs* (Berlin, 1915). An abbreviated version appeared in English translation as *The Belgian People's War, a Violation of International Law. Translations from the Official German White Book, Published by the Imperial Foreign Office* (New York, 1915), and an even shorter abridgement was published in French, *La Conduite contraire au droit des gens de la population belge dans sa lutte contre les troupes allemandes* (Berlin, 1915). Translations into other languages included Swedish and Spanish. The full text appeared in English only after the war (Ernest N. Bennett, *The German Army in Belgium: The White Book of May 1915. With a Foreword on Military Reprisals in Belgium and Ireland* (London, 1921)). On Bennett's translation and introduction, see chapter 10 below.

59 *Die völkerrechtswidrige Führung*, p. 1.

60 Several copies of the original report by the War Ministry Investigation Department (in fact dated 12 January 1915) are extant, e.g. BA-MA, Freiburg, PHD 6/145.

61 Peter Schöller, *Der Fall Löwen und das Weißbuch. Eine kritische Untersuchung der deutschen Dokumentation über die Vorgänge in Löwen vom 25. bis 28. August 1914* (Cologne and Graz, 1958), pp. 23–6. For the circumstances that led Schöller to produce his work, see chapter 10.

62 Schöller, *Der Fall Löwen*, pp. 37–8, 41–4.

63 The original materials collected by the War Ministry Military Investigation Department, consisting of some 600 pages of depositions mainly by German officers and soldiers, and a few Belgian depositions, are extant in the CPHDC, Moscow: 1467-1-12 (book 1), and 1467-1-11 (book 2).

64 CPHDC, Moscow, 1467-1-12, fol. 35–6, deposition of Major Walter von Loeben, commander of a company of the 100th Grenadier Regiment, 15 February 1915.

65 Haugk testified that Kielmannsegg gave the order to shoot a number of 'suspicious' men who had been taken captive simply because the firing from the houses and the river-bank did not stop. BA, Berlin, R 3003/ORA/RG bJ 304/20, vol. 2, no foliation, transcript of 'appendix 17', Neufchatel, 16 February 1915, Lieutenant von Haugk, battalion adjutant in IR 100. This 'appendix' was not in the White Book, and was thus part of the original War Ministry report.

66 *Die völkerrechtswidrige Führung*, p. 134.

67 CPHDC, Moscow, 1467-1-11, fol. 99, transcript of an undated, unsigned statement by Stieping [*sic*].

68 *Die völkerrechtswidrige Führung*, appendix C31, p. 169.

69 CPHDC, Moscow, 1467-1-11, fol. 18, deposition Stiebing, 5 February 1915. See also chapter 1 above, p. 47.

70 BA, Berlin, R 3003/ORA/RG bJ 307/20, vol. 1, fol. 89–90. Hauth was killed in action

11 days later. Ibid., R 3003/ORA/RG bJ 307/20, vol. 2, fol. 27 rev., list of officers of IR 101.

71 PAAA, Bonn, R 22386, telegram Zimmermann to von Stumm, 19 April 1915.

72 *Die völkerrechtswidrige Führung*, pp. 140, 154, 168.

73 CPHDC, Moscow, 1467-1-12, fol. 291, Bauer and Wagner, undated draft, probably to the General Staff, February 1915. Bauer and Wagner had repeated their request to d'Elsa on 28 January for a report on the events in Dinant – CPHDC, Moscow, 1467-1-11, fol. 64.

74 CPHDC, Moscow, 1467-1-12, fol. 37–61: approximately 44 pages of handwritten notes by Schweinitz, apparently extracts from depositions by both German and Belgian witnesses, but lacking details of dates, places or names. The evidence of Nicolas Tock, one of the survivors of the mass execution at Les Rivages, who testified to the arbitrary and groundless killing of unarmed villagers and steadfastly maintained that civilians had not fired, was likewise suppressed by the editors (BA, Berlin, R 3003/ORA/RG, bJ 307/20, vol. 1, fol. 87–8. Nicolas Tock, 24, servant, Dinant. Transcript from the files of the War Ministry, vol. 15, Beiheft zu Heft 2, fol. 13–14).

75 CPHDC, Moscow, 1467-1-12, fol. 25, court-martial official Schweinitz, XIIth Army Corps, to all units. Madame Poucelet made her signed deposition in Dinant on 11 January 1915.

76 First Belgian Commission, 20th report, vol. 2, p. 96; Jean Schmitz and Norbert Nieuwland, *Documents pour servir à l'histoire de l'invasion allemande dans les provinces de Namur et de Luxembourg* (7 vols, Brussels and Paris, 1919–24), vol. 4, part 2, *Le Combat de Dinant. Le sac de la ville* (1922), pp. 265–6.

77 Combat report of 100th Grenadier Regiment, *Die völkerrechtswidrige Führung*, appendix C6, p. 133; Acting Sergeant-Major Bartusch, ibid., appendix C10, p. 137. Lieutenant-Colonel Count Kielmannsegg referred to 'about a hundred guilty inhabitants of the male sex [who] were shot by my direction and in accordance with an order given by higher authority', ibid., C7, p. 134.

78 *Die völkerrechtswidrige Führung*, appendix C26, p. 158, evidence of Captain Wilke, sixth company, IR 178.

79 Ibid., p. 117.

80 Ibid., pp. 33–42.

81 Schmitz and Nieuwland, *L'invasion allemande*, vol. 7, pp. 306–8. Corroboration of a German investigation of the killings at Arlon, Ethe, and neighbouring villages is in KA, Munich, HS 2259, papers of Friedrich Hurt, Military Governor of Luxembourg Province, 1914–15, Hurt to Imperial German Court of the General-Gouvernement in Belgium, Brussels, 31 March 1915.

82 Gustave Somville, *Vers Liège. Le chemin du crime. Août 1914* (Paris, 1915), pp. 90–1, 188, 212–13 and 233.

83 Oszwald claimed that the omission of civilian evidence in the White Book was intentional. One reason was to protect Belgian witnesses from prosecution by the Belgian state; another was that those 'guilty' of franc-tireur activity were unlikely to incriminate themselves (*Der Streit*, p. 150). That the German military should have been so solicitous of Belgian civilians whom it considered collectively guilty of a *Volkskrieg* is unlikely.

84 *Die völkerrechtswidrige Führung*, p. 235, and criticisms in the official Belgian reply: Ministère des Affaires Étrangères et Ministère de la Justice, *Réponse au Livre blanc allemand du 10 mai 1915* (Paris, 1916), pp. 63–73.

85 The White Book stated that 'even members of the clergy' had participated in the fighting (p. 2), a claim supported in the appendices (appendix 43 and 47). The report on Dinant repeated the general claim (p. 122), with one supporting deposition (C 18). The full weight of the charge rested on the clergy of Louvain (p. 236). General Boehn, in the first deposition, claimed there was firing from an abbey; he included the bizarre claim of a hussar that he had been fired on by 12 clergymen (D 1, p. 242). Cf. also D 2, 34, 37, 38, 42, 48.

86 Fernand Mayence (ed.), *La Correspondance de S. E. le Cardinal Mercier avec le gouvernement général allemand pendant l'occupation 1914–1918* (Brussels and Paris, 1919), pp. 25–6, for the initial letter of von Bissing to Cardinal von Hartmann immediately after the former's appointment, asking for his help in mediating with the Belgian hierarchy; Vatican Archives, Segretaria di Stato, 244 D7 (Belgio), f. 107, letter of Frühwirth, Papal nuncio in Munich, to the Vatican, reporting on the correspondence between Hartmann and Bissing, 4 January 1915. This includes a copy of a letter by Bissing to Hartmann, 28 December 1914, which spelt out the policy of 'pacification' and expressed gratitude to Hartmann for his mediation.

87 BA-MA, Freiburg, PHD 6/145, War Ministry, 'Anschuldigungen gegen die Deutschen wegen der Behandlung der belgischen Geistlichen', 22 January 1915; PAAA, Bonn, R 20891, fol. 84: the original letter signed by Wandel to the Chancellor, 22 January 1915, bears pencilled deletions, suggesting that the letter was to be sent as a telegram to the German diplomatic representatives. The memorandum was reported in the *Nieuwe Rotterdamsche Courant*, 23 March 1915.

88 *Die völkerrechtswidrige Führung*, appendix A.

89 Walter Görlitz (ed.), *Regierte der Kaiser? Kriegstagebücher, Aufzeichnungen und Briefe des Chefs des Marine-Kabinetts Admiral Georg Alexander von Müller 1914–1918* (Göttingen, Berlin, Frankfurt 1959), pp. 62–3, 30 September 1914.

90 PAAA, Bonn, R 22383, Scheüch, War Minister at GHQ to Secretary of State, Foreign Ministry, at GHQ, 2 October 1914.

91 Belgian Second Commission, vol. 1, part 2, pp. 407–8: evidence of Professor Alfred Nerinckx, temporary burgomaster from 29 August 1914.

92 Theodor Wolff, *Tagebücher 1914–1919. Der Erste Weltkrieg und die Entstehung der Weimarer Republik in Tagebüchern, Leitartikeln und Briefen des Chefredakteurs am 'Berliner Tageblatt' und Mitbegründers der 'Deutschen Demokratischen Partei'*, ed. Bernd Sösemann (Boppard, 1984), part 1, pp. 154–5, 9 February 1915.

93 PRO, London, HO45/11061/266 503, H. A. L. Fisher, the University, Sheffield, to Sir C. Schuster, Home Office, 26 July 1915.

94 PRO, London, HO 45/11061/266 503, Schuster to Aitken, Home Office, 29 July 1915.

95 *Réponse au Livre blanc allemand du 10 mai 1915*. Published in English as *Reply to the German White Book of the 10th May 1915* (London, 1918). For the process of composition of the *Réponse au Livre blanc*, and direct proof that it did not suppress contradictory evidence, see AGR, Brussels, CE, III, 374, B1, 20.

96 Fernand Passelecq, *La Réponse du gouvernement belge au Livre blanc allemand du 10 mai 1915. Étude analytique de la publication officielle du gouvernement belge* (Paris, 1916), published in English as *Truth and Travesty: An Analytical Study of the Reply of the Belgian Government to the German White Book* (London, 1916).

97 BA, Koblenz, NL 15/402, lecture by Schwertfeger to the staff of the Auswärtiges Amt on Belgian affairs, 12 March 1920, pp. 17–18. It is not known why the White Book did not include estimates of German losses caused by Belgian francs-tireurs. For

the internal calculations of these by the German army, see chapter 3 above.

98 Somville, *Vers Liège*, p. 282.

99 Fernand Passelecq, *Francs-tireurs et atrocités belges. Un cycle de légendes allemandes* (Le Havre, n.d., but early 1916), pp. 25–8.

100 Ibid. This originally appeared as a long article in *Le Correspondant*, 25 December 1915. The appendix of van Langenhove's book was devoted to a tabular critique of the White Book's testimony (*Cycle de légendes*, pp. 246–51).

101 Passelecq, *Francs-tireurs*, pp. 12–13.

102 AGR, Brussels, Broqueville papers, 443, 'Mission aux États-Unis'.

103 On the concept of the 'public sphere', see in particular Jürgen Habermas, *The Structural Transformation of the Public Sphere* (1962; English translation, Cambridge, Mass., 1989). On two crucial paradigms of the liberal construction of an international opinion, see Geoffrey Best, *Humanity in Warfare: The Modern History of the International Law of Armed Conflicts* (London, 1980; new edn, 1983) and Sandi E. Cooper, *Patriotic Pacifism: Waging War on War in Europe 1815–1914* (New York and Oxford, 1991).

104 For the founding of the Bureau Documentaire Belge, see AGR, Brussels, Archives de la guerre, T 179. The organization of the missions is documented in the papers of the prime minister of the government in exile, AGR, Brussels, Broqueville papers, 478–84. See also Suzanne Tassier, *La Belgique et l'entrée en guerre des États-Unis (1914–1917)* (Brussels, 1951), ch. 3; Dumoulin, *Jules Destrée*, esp. pp. 20–54; Michel Dumoulin, 'La Propagande belge dans les pays neutres au début de la première guerre mondiale (août 1914–février 1915)', *Revue Belge d'Histoire Militaire*, 22 (1977), pp. 246–59.

105 Lucy Masterman, *C. F. G. Masterman* (London, 1939), pp. 272–86, for an account by Masterman's widow; and among the works which deal with Wellington House, Squires, *British Propaganda*, pp. 25–34; Sanders and Taylor, *British Propaganda*, pp. 38–43; and Messinger, *British Propaganda*, pp. 24–69.

106 Ministère des Affaires Étrangères, *Les Violations des lois de la guerre par l'Allemagne* (Paris, 1915), translated into English as *Germany's Violations of the Laws of War, 1914–1915: Compiled under the Auspices of the French Ministry of Foreign Affairs* (London, 1915), and also into Italian. There is no comprehensive published work on French war propaganda, but see Jean-Claude Montant, 'La Propagande extérieure de la France pendant la première guerre mondiale. L'exemple de quelques neutres européens', 9 vols, thèse de doctorat, Université de Paris I, 1988.

107 Kurt Koszyk, *Deutsche Pressepolitik im Ersten Weltkrieg* (Düsseldorf, 1968), pp. 26 and 239ff. Cf. Jürgen von Ungern-Sternberg and Wolfgang von Ungern-Sternberg, *Der Aufruf 'An die Kulturwelt!' Das Manifest der 93 und die Anfänge der Kriegspropaganda im Ersten Weltkrieg* (Stuttgart, 1996), pp. 126–35. This last account is full of detail but fails to use the records of the Foreign Ministry.

108 Emmet Crozier, *American Reporters on the Western Front 1914–1918* (New York, 1959), pp. 26–54.

109 Powell, *Fighting in Flanders*, pp. 86–98.

110 *New York Tribune*, 31 August 1914; Richard Harding Davis, *With the Allies* (London, 1915), pp. 80–95.

111 *Saturday Evening Post* (Philadelphia), 14 November 1914; Irvin S. Cobb, *The Red Glutton: With the German Army at the Front* (London, 1915), pp. 32–120.

112 PAAA, Bonn, R 20880, fol. 71–2, memorandum Hammann, Foreign Ministry, on a

conversation with von Gwinner, director of the Deutsche Bank, who had been present at the meeting, 24 August 1914. Gwinner stressed that Gerard, the American ambassador, was especially supportive of the idea. No trace of this appears in the memoirs published by the ambassador in 1917, after American entry into the war on the Allied side (James W. Gerard, *My Four Years in Germany* (New York, 1917)).

113 Cited in Ilse Meseberg-Haubold, *Der Widerstand Kardinal Merciers gegen die deutsche Besetzung Belgiens 1914–1918. Ein Beitrag zur politischen Rolle des Katholizismus im ersten Weltkrieg* (Frankfurt, 1982), p. 47. In effect, Bethmann Hollweg related to the journalists the content of the telegram he sent to Woodrow Wilson, along with that from the Kaiser (see chapter 3). The message was drafted on 2 September, given to the American ambassador on 4 September, and published in the *Norddeutsche Allgemeine Zeitung* on 7 September (PAAA, Bonn, R 20881, fol. 74, telegram Chancellor to Foreign Ministry, 2 September 1914; *Norddeutsche Allgemeine Zeitung*, 7 September 1914; Gerard, *My Four Years in Germany*, p. 210).

114 Davis, *With the Allies*, pp. 80–95.

115 National Archives (Washington, D.C.), State Department, M 367; 763.72116/1–79 (Illegal and Inhumane Warfare), ambassador in Berlin to State Department, 14 September 1914, for the text of the journalists' declaration; PAAA, Bonn, R 20888, fol. 162, for the tour organized by the German Foreign Ministry; Crozier, *American Reporters on the Western Front*, pp. 40–2. Davis, Will Irwin (*Collier's Magazine*), and Gerald Morgan (*Metropolitan Magazine*) did not sign.

116 PAAA, Bonn, R 20886, fol. 115, transcript of the Deputy General Staff, Brose, to Foreign Ministry, 8 October 1914. The typewritten drafts of the articles, written on 5 October, are in this file, fol. 117–23. For Cobb's denial of any pro-German bias, see *The Red Glutton*, pp. 80–1.

117 Squires, *British Propaganda*, pp. 43–4.

118 Jörg Nagler, 'From Culture to *Kultur*: American Perceptions of Imperial Germany, 1871–1914', unpublished paper presented to the conference, Images and Multiple Implications: American Views of Germany and German Views of America from the 18th to the 20th Centuries, Kalamazoo College, April 1993. The authors would like to thank Professor Nagler for allowing them to consult this paper.

119 Frederick C. Luebke, *Bonds of Loyalty: German Americans and World War I* (De Kalb, Ill., 1974), pp. 83–113.

120 George S. Viereck, *Spreading Germs of Hate* (London, 1931), pp. 48–59; Luebke, *Bonds of Loyalty*, pp. 91–3.

121 *The Fatherland*, 30 September 1914, 'Who Maims the Dead?' (on Powell) and 'German Atrocities a Myth' (on the Aachen declaration); 6 September 1914, '"German Brutality"', on Louvain.

122 Viereck, *Spreading Germs of Hate*, pp. 55–6. Viereck participated in the propaganda outfit run by Privy Councillor Bernhard Dernburg on Broadway; Reinhard R. Doerries, 'Promoting *Kaiser* and *Reich*: Imperial German Propaganda in the United States during World War I', in Hans-Jürgen Schröder (ed.), *Confrontation and Cooperation: Germany and the United States in the Era of World War I, 1900–1924* (Providence and Oxford, 1993), pp. 135–65.

123 State Department, M 367, 763.72116, telegram Brand Whitlock to Jennings Bryan, 29 September 1914. See also Brand Whitlock, *Belgium under the German Occupation: A Personal Narrative* (2 vols, London, 1919), vol. 1, pp. 99–154, for a balanced and acute account of the action of the German army. Corroboration comes in the published

account by the secretary of the American Embassy in Brussels, Hugh Gibson, *A Diplomatic Diary* (London, 1917), *passim*.

124 Arthur S. Link (ed.), *The Papers of Woodrow Wilson*, vol. 32, *January 1–April 16 1915* (Princeton, 1980), pp. 42–3 (note from William Jennings Bryan to Wilson on making a statement about the absence of any American obligation), and pp. 60–1 (Wilson's reply that such a statement would lack moral force, so that it was preferable to make no statement).

125 See, in particular, the influential study by Squires, *British Propaganda*, which drew on some of the post-war revelations by those (such as Sir Gilbert Parker) most active in the campaign.

126 Bodleian Library, Oxford, MSS Simon, vol. 50, fol. 100–1, Bryce to Sir Courtney Ilbert, 9 September 1914. For Masterman's opposition to the proposed tour, see Lucy Masterman, *C. F. G. Masterman*, p. 276.

127 Wilson, *Myriad Faces of War*, p. 190.

128 Michel Dumoulin, 'La Propagande belge en Italie au début de la première guerre mondiale (août-décembre 1914)', *Bulletin de l'Institut Historique Belge de Rome*, 46–47 (1976–7), pp. 335–67; L. Claeys-Boovaert and J. van Humbeeck, 'Les Discours de la propagande belge en Italie. 1914–1918', *Risorgimento*, 21 (1979), pp. 23–46, esp. p. 42.

129 Jules Destrée, *En Italie avant la guerre, 1914–1915* (Brussels and Paris, 1915), esp. pp. 20–54; Dumoulin, *Jules Destrée*; Claeys-Boovaert and van Humbeeck, 'Les Discours de la propagande belge', pp. 23–46. The Rome committee produced six brochures in Italian on its own account in 1915, five of which concerned in whole or in part the atrocities issue. It also distributed brochures produced by other agencies on the same theme (Dumoulin, *Jules Destrée*, pp. 46–7); AGR, Brussels, CE, III, 374, B1, 30, reports of Mélot to the Foreign Ministry on the Belgian propaganda mission to Italy; Auguste Mélot, *L'Invasione tedesca nel Belgio. Discorso pronunciato da M. Mélot, deputato di Namur al Gabinetto Cattolico di Milano il 23 novembre del 1914* (Milan, n.d., but 1914). Mélot also published a longer booklet on atrocities through the Belgian Catholic propaganda campaign in Rome (*L'Invasione di Belgio. Una guerra ingiusta e barbara* (Rome, 1915)).

130 Destrée, *En Italie avant la guerre*, p. 91; Destrée, *Le Atrocità tedesche. Documenti ufficiali pubblicati da Giulio Destrée, Deputato di Charleroy* (Milan, 1914); Dumoulin, 'La Propagande belge en Italie', p. 346.

131 *New York Times*, 22 September 1914, p. 10 (editorial). National Archives (Washington, D.C.), State Department, 367.763 72116, memorandum on the 'Destruction of Historical Monuments in Europe 1914–15', 31 March 1915, listing the principal protests received.

132 PAAA, Bonn, R 20883, fol. 5, German Embassy Rome to Reich Chancellor, 6 September 1914.

133 Wolff, *Tagebücher 1914–1919*, p. 135 (11 December 1914).

134 PAAA, Bonn, R 20886, fol. 148, [signature illegible] to Geheimer Rat Dr. Wilhelm von Bode, 6 October 1914. Leading German cultural experts, too, realized that Louvain and Rheims had 'done more damage abroad [...] than two lost battles': Winfried Speitkamp, '"Ein dauerndes und ehrenvolles Denkmal deutscher Kulturtätigkeit". Denkmalpflege im Kaiserreich 1871–1918', *Die Alte Stadt. Vierteljahreszeitschrift für Stadtgeschichte, Stadtsoziologie und Denkmalpflege*, 18/2 (1991), p. 195.

135 Alberto Monticone, *La Germania e la neutralità italiana* (Bologna, 1971), esp. chs 2 and 7, provides a detailed political and organizational account of this battle, but

neither relates it to the events of the war nor investigates in detail its themes. No cultural history of the battle of the belligerents for Italian opinion in 1914–15 seems to have been written.

136 Karl Lange, *Marneschlacht und deutsche Öffentlichkeit 1914–1939. Eine verdrängte Niederlage und ihre Folgen* (Düsseldorf, 1974), p. 76, citing Friedrich Max Kircheisen, a German author who lived in Geneva.

137 PAAA, Bonn, R 20881, fol. 28, telegram envoy Berne, 31 August 1914; *Neue Zürcher Zeitung*, 29 August 1914.

138 PAAA, Bonn, R 20886, fol. 38, telegram envoy Berne to Foreign Ministry, 3 October 1914.

139 Dumoulin, *Jules Destrée*, pp. 19–20. AGR, Brussels, CE, III, 374, B1, 30, report of Waxweiler on Belgian mission to Switzerland, 4 March 1915.

140 PAAA, Bonn, R 20883, fol. 135–6, Handelsvertragsverein – Verband zur Förderung des deutschen Außenhandels to Foreign Ministry, 15 September 1914.

141 E.g. PAAA, Bonn, R 20888, fol. 42, German Embassy Lisbon to Reich Chancellor Bethmann Hollweg, 28 September 1914. On Portuguese opinion and the 'atrocities' issue, see Filipe Ribeiro de Meneses, 'The Failure of the Portuguese First Republic: An Analysis of Wartime Political Mobilization', Ph.D. thesis, Trinity College Dublin, 1996, pp. 95–8.

142 PAAA, Bonn R 20885, fol. 2, telegram envoy Kristiania to Foreign Ministry, 24 September 1914.

143 Wolff, *Tagebücher 1914–1919*, part 1, pp. 104–5.

144 PAAA, Bonn, R 20883, fol. 103.

145 PAAA, Bonn, R 20891, fol. 98–103.

146 Émile Waxweiler, *La Guerre de 1914. La Belgique neutre et loyale* (Paris and Lausanne, 1915), but first published in Geneva in December 1914, and translated into German as *Der europäische Krieg. Hat Belgien sein Schicksal verschuldet?* (Zürich, 1915). It was also translated into English, Italian, Russian, and Spanish. Section 5 dealt with the franc-tireur war. The German response was Richard Graßhoff, *Belgiens Schuld. Zugleich eine Antwort an Prof. Waxweiler* (Berlin, 1915), translated into English as *The Tragedy of Belgium: An Answer to Professor Waxweiler* (New York, 1915).

147 See in particular Graßhoff, *Belgiens Schuld*, pp. 44–64 ('The People's War'); also Lothar Wieland, *Belgien 1914. Die Frage des belgischen 'Franktireurkrieges' und die deutsche öffentliche Meinung von 1914 bis 1936* (Frankfurt, Berne, New York, 1984), pp. 87–92. Cf. Oszwald, *Der Streit*, p. 139.

148 BA-MA, Freiburg, PH2/35: Militäruntersuchungsstelle für Verletzungen des Kriegsrechts, *Widerlegung der von der französischen Regierung erhobenen Anschuldigungen*, published by the Foreign Ministry via the WTB agency on 11 January 1915.

149 For Lunéville, see chapter 2 above.

150 *Über die Verletzung der Genfer Konvention vom 6. Juli 1906 durch französische Truppen und Freischärler* (Berlin, 1914), also translated into French and English.

151 *Völkerrechtswidrige Verwendung farbiger Truppen auf dem europäischen Kriegsschauplatz durch England und Frankreich* (Berlin, 1915), translated into English, French, and Dutch. For German protests in 1870 see Amédée Brenet, *La France et l'Allemagne devant le droit international pendant les opérations militaires de la guerre de 1870–71* (Paris, 1902), pp. 47–9.

152 Cf. Audoin-Rouzeau, *L'Enfant de l'ennemi*, pp. 35–6.

153 Auswärtiges Amt, *Der Baralong-Fall* (Berlin, 1916); Alan Coles, *Slaughter at Sea: The Truth behind a Naval War Crime* (London, 1986), citing *The Times*, 19 and 20 January 1916; *Verhandlungen des Deutschen Reichstages. Stenographische Berichte*, vol. 306, cols 669–675 (15 January 1916), for the Reichstag debate.

154 PAAA, Bonn, R 22386, Wedding (legal department, Foreign Ministry) to von Grünau, Berlin, 10 April 1915.

155 Fritz Fischer, *Germany's Aims in the First World War* (1961; English translation, London, 1967), pp. 95–120; Stig Förster, 'Der deutsche Generalstab und die Illusion des kurzen Krieges 1871–1914. Metakritik eines Mythos', *Militärgeschichtliche Mitteilungen*, 54 (1995), pp. 61–95; Holger Herwig, *The First World War: Germany and Austria-Hungary, 1914–1918* (London, 1997), pp. 6–62.

7 Communities of truth and the 'atrocities' question

1 E.g. 'Zarismus oder Kultur? Die Greuel des Krieges', *Hamburger Echo*, 11 August 1914.

2 *Hamburger Echo*, 15 August 1914.

3 *Vorwärts*, 22 October 1914.

4 Kurt Koszyk, *Deutsche Pressepolitik im Ersten Weltkrieg* (Düsseldorf, 1968), pp. 147–8. This was no doubt a reference to the article 'Gegen die Barbarei', *Vorwärts*, 24 August 1914.

5 'A Propos d'atrocités', *L'Humanité*, 7 September 1914. *Le Matin* was the target.

6 *La Guerre sociale*, 24 and 26 August 1914 respectively.

7 Pierre Renaudel, 'A Propos des atrocités', *L'Humanité*, 5 October 1914.

8 *Vorwärts*, 10 September 1914; Wolfgang Kruse, *Krieg und nationale Integration. Eine Neuinterpretation des sozialdemokratischen Burgfriedensschlusses 1914–15* (Essen, 1993), pp. 93, 126–7.

9 Adolph Koester and Gustav Noske, *Kriegsfahrten durch Belgien und Nordfrankreich 1914* (Berlin, n.d., but 1915), pp. 4–5. The reports also appeared in *Vorwärts*.

10 Ibid., pp. 13, 20, 25–6.

11 Auguste Dewinne, editor of the Brussels Socialist paper, *Le Peuple*, as quoted in an account by P. Nordrenge, 'Lettre du Havre', in *L'Indépendance belge*, 6 November 1914. The French Socialist Party received an account of the visit from the Parti Ouvrier Belge ('Socialistes belges et allemands', series of three articles in *L'Humanité*, 16–18 December 1914). For other accounts by Belgian socialists, see Émile Vandervelde, *La Belgique envahie et le socialisme international* (Paris, 1917), pp. 204–7, and Émile Royer, *German Socialists and Belgium* (London, n.d., but 1915), pp. 33–4.

12 Nordrenge, 'Lettre du Havre', *L'Indépendance belge*, 6 November 1914; 'Karl Liebknecht a fait une enquête en Belgique', *L'Humanité*, 21 December 1914 (for the details of the reported incident of the 'francs-tireurs'). Karl Meyer, *Karl Liebknecht: Man without a Country* (Washington, D.C., 1957), p. 57. Liebknecht did not refer to 'German atrocities' in his famous declaration of 2 December 1914 when he refused to vote for war credits in the Reichstag.

13 Erich Matthias and Susanne Miller (eds), *Das Kriegstagebuch des Reichstagsabgeordneten Eduard David 1914 bis 1918* (Düsseldorf, 1966), p. 41, diary entry 25 September 1914.

14 Kruse, *Krieg und nationale Integration*, p. 210; Theodor Wolff, *Tagebücher 1914–1919. Der Erste Weltkrieg und die Entstehung der Weimarer Republik in Tagebüchern, Leitartikeln und Briefen des Chefredakteurs am 'Berliner Tageblatt' und Mitbegründers der 'Deutschen Demokratischen Partei'*, ed. Bernd Sösemann (Boppard, 1984), part 1, p. 187.

15 Eisner to Heine, 11 February 1915, cited in Kruse, *Krieg und nationale Integration*, p. 211.

16 Vandervelde, *La Belgique envahie*, pp. 155–231, for this exchange (quotation, p. 168). See also Jules Destrée, *Les Socialistes et la guerre européenne 1914–1915* (Paris, 1916), pp. 13–21.

17 *Le Parti Socialiste belge et la guerre* (July 1917).

18 Canon van Ballaer, *Benoit XV et la Belgique pendant les premiers mois de son pontificat* (Louvain, 1922); F. Peemans, 'Tensions dans les relations belgo-vaticanes en 1914–1918', *Risorgimento*, 21 (1979), pp. 173–94; Ilse Meseberg-Haubold, *Der Widerstand Kardinal Merciers gegen die deutsche Besetzung Belgiens 1914–1918. Ein Beitrag zur politischen Rolle des Katholizismus im Ersten Weltkrieg* (Frankfurt, 1982); Jacques Fontana, *Les Catholiques français pendant la grande guerre* (Paris, 1990), pp. 169–92; Francis Latour, *La Papauté et les problèmes de la paix pendant la grande guerre* (Paris, 1996).

19 *The Voice of Belgium: Being the Wartime Utterances of Cardinal Mercier* (London, 1917), pp. 1–2.

20 Vatican Archive, Segretaria di Stato, 244 D7 (Belgio), f. 105.

21 Ibid., copy of letter from Sarzana to Goltz, 14 September 1914.

22 Ibid., reports by Sarzana dated 5 October 1914, 29 October 1914, and 22 November 1914; report by Tacci to Gasparri of 23 December 1914.

23 Vatican Archive, Segretaria di Stato, 244 A1b (Imparzialità della S. Sede), 2063, f. 64, report of Tacci, 'Sopra lo stato di guerra in Belgio', 6 December 1914, reproduced in van Ballaer, *Benoît XV*, pp. 18–19.

24 Vatican Archive, 244 D7 (Belgio), f. 107, protest sent via the Papal nuncio in Antwerp, 20 September 1914. The same message was conveyed by the Belgian Ambassador to the Vatican, Baron d'Erp (Julien Davignon, Belgian Minister of Foreign Affairs, to Baron d'Erp, 17 September 1914, and D'Erp's covering letter to Cardinal Ferrata of 20 September 1914, Vatican Archive, Segretaria di Stato, 244 D7 (Belgio), f. 107). For corroboration of the Vatican's attitude, see the account by the rector of the Institut Catholique de Paris, Alfred Baudrillart, of his visit to Rome in autumn 1914 (*Les Carnets du Cardinal Alfred Baudrillart. 1er août 1914 – 31 décembre 1918* ed. Paul Christophe (Paris, 1994), pp. 107 and 117).

25 *L'Osservatore romano*, 8 October 1914.

26 *Les Carnets du Cardinal Alfred Baudrillart*, p. 86 (entry for 13 October 1914).

27 Vatican Archive, Segretaria di Stato, 244 D7 (Belgio), f. 105.

28 Ibid., Mélot to Benedict XV.

29 Ibid., note in Gasparri's hand of meeting with Mélot, November 1914 (no day given).

30 Vatican Archive, Segretaria di Stato, 244 D7 (Belgio), f. 107, Hartmann to Gasparri, 13 August 1914. Hartmann referred to the 'warring parties', but in the context of his letter he could only have meant the Belgians.

31 Vatican Archive, Segretaria di Stato, 244 D7 (Belgio), f. 105, Mercier to Benedict XV, 25 November 1914.

32 Ibid.; reproduced in Ballaer, *Benoît XV*, pp. 15–16 (Ballaer was unaware that

Benedict's letter had been solicited by Mercier).

33 Vatican Archive, Segretaria di Stato, 244 A1b (Imparzialità della S. Sede), f. 64, Gasparri to Tacci, 16 December 1914.

34 Meseberg-Haubold, *Der Widerstand*, p. 55. The letter was passed to Mercier by Cardinal Hartmann of Cologne.

35 Meeting of 16 December 1914: *La Correspondance de S.E. le Cardinal Mercier avec le Gouvernement Général allemand pendant l'occupation 1914–1918* (Brussels and Paris, 1919), ed. Fernand Mayence, p. 13. Mercier reiterated the point in a letter of 28 December 1914 (ibid., p. 29).

36 Mercier to Hartmann, 28 December 1914, in *La Correspondance du Cardinal Mercier*, pp. 11–12.

37 *The Voice of Belgium*, pp. 8–12. The letter was published by the archdiocesan printer, and widely disseminated in the Allied press. For the original French text, see *Patriotisme et Endurance. Lettre pastorale de Son Éminence le Cardinal Mercier, Archévêque de Malines, noël 1914* (Paris, 1915).

38 Vatican Archive, Affari Ecclesiastici Straordinari, Belgio, 1915, 200–02, fasc. 102, Tacci to Gasparri, 3 January 1915, describing German reactions; ibid., uncatalogued papers of Brussels nunciature 'Durante la guerra', box 93, undated letter of Tacci on the same subject; *La Correspondance du Cardinal Mercier*, pp. 26–46.

39 Meseberg-Haubold, *Der Widerstand*, pp. 66–7.

40 PAAA, Bonn, R 20891, fol. 122, Prussian Embassy, Rome, to Foreign Ministry, Berlin, 24 January 1915; cf. Meseberg-Haubold, *Der Widerstand*, p. 218, n. 99.

41 Ballaer, *Benoît XV*, pp. 25–6; Meseberg-Haubold, *Der Widerstand*, p. 68.

42 Vatican Archive, papers of the Brussels nunciature 'Durante la Guerra', box 93, Benedict XV to Mercier, 23 January 1915.

43 Vatican Archive, Affari Ecclesiastici Straordinari, Belgio, 200–02, fasc. 102, printed text of the Lenten address, *Mandement de carême de l'an de grâce 1915* (n.pl., n.d.), and Tacci to Gasparri, 28 February 1915, detailing the battle between Heylen and the Military Governor of Namur and indicating the passages changed under German duress, including one which stated that it was not possible to establish whether individual civilians had committed crimes (*Mandement de carême*, p. 7).

44 Vatican Archive, Segretaria di Stato, 244 D7 (Belgio) f.107, 'Réponse pour le diocèse de Namur [...] à la note du 22-1-1915 [...] au Chancelier von Bethmann-Hollweg et publiée [...] dans le *Nieuwe Rotterdamsche Courant* de mardi, 23 mars 1915', 10 April 1915, pp. 2–3. Tacci sent a copy to the Vatican at Heylen's request with a covering note (16 April 1915) making it clear that the response had been delivered to the occupation government in Brussels.

45 Vatican Archive, Segretaria di Stato, 244 D7 (Belgio) f. 107, 'Réponse pour le diocèse de Namur', pp. 5–6.

46 Jean Schmitz and Norbert Nieuwland, *Documents pour servir à l'histoire de l'invasion allemande dans les provinces de Namur et de Luxembourg* (7 vols, Brussels and Paris, 1919–24), vol. 1, pp. vii–xii; Michel Majoros, 'Collection de documents relatifs à la guerre de 1914–1918 rassemblés par le chanoine Jean Schmitz. Inventaire' (Namur, 1991), pp. i–iii (typescript in the Archives de l'État).

47 *Lettres des évêques de Namur et de Liège concernant les atrocités allemandes dans leur diocèse* (Rome, 1916), p. 23.

48 Vatican Archive, Segretaria di Stato, 244 D7 (Belgio) f. 107, copies of the report sent by Heylen and the letter sent by Archbishop Rutter of Liège to von Bissing (with

copies to the Vatican and the international diplomatic corps), dated 31 October and 25 October 1915 respectively. The texts circulated without German permission in Belgium and were published in Rome in 1916 (*Lettres des evêques de Namur et de Liège*).

49 Vatican Archive, Segretaria di Stato, 244 D7 (Belgio) f. 107, Tacci to Gasparri, 10 November 1915, reporting on a meeting with Baron von der Lancken, head of the political affairs department of the German military government, on 9 November.

50 *Les Évêques de Belgique aux évêques d'Allemagne et d'Autriche-Hongrie.* It was issued on 24 November 1915 and signed by Mercier, Heylen, Rutten, and Crooy, Bishop-Elect of Tournai. Cardinal Hartmann later told Gasparri that the German hierarchy had already privately been contacted by Mercier on the subject and rejected the idea, so that the published initiative was a means of continuing opposition to the German government and the Vatican rather than a real hope that such a commission might prove possible (Vatican Archive, Affari Straordinari, Belgio, 211, fasc. 114, Hartmann to Gasparri, 16 January 1916).

51 Comité Catholique de Propagande Française à l'Étranger, *La Guerre allemande et le catholicisme* (Paris, 1915); *Les Carnets du Cardinal Alfred Baudrillart*, pp. 170–1; Fontana, *Les Catholiques français*, pp. 329–38.

52 *La Guerre allemande*, pp. 81–140 ('La Guerre aux églises et aux prêtres').

53 Lothar Wieland, *Belgien 1914. Die Frage des belgischen 'Franktireurkrieges' und die deutsche öffentliche Meinung von 1914 bis 1936* (Frankfurt, Berne, New York, 1984), p. 76.

54 Klaus Epstein, *Matthias Erzberger and the Dilemma of German Democracy* (1959; new edn, New York, 1971), p. 101.

55 A. J. Rosenberg, *Der deutsche Krieg und der Katholizismus* (Paderborn, 1915), translated into English as *The German War and Catholicism: German Defense against French Attacks* (St Paul, Minn., 1916), esp. ch. 3.

56 Vatican Archive, Affari Ecclesiastici Straordinari, 211, fasc. 114, Tacci to Gasparri, 13 January 1916.

57 KA, Munich, HS 1592, pp. 7–9: 'Tätigkeits-Bericht der Politischen Abteilung bei dem General-Gouverneur in Belgien von Anfang November 1915 bis Ende Januar 1916.' See also Meseberg-Haubold, *Der Widerstand*, pp. 91–3.

58 Vatican Archive, Segretaria di Stato, 244 D7 (Belgio), f. 108, typescript on 'Le Point de vue des catholiques belges dans la guerre de 1914'; see also A. Druart, 'Mgr Simon Deploige au Vatican', in 'La Belgique, l'Italie et le Saint-Siège', *Risorgimento*, 21 (1979), pp. 155–71. Deploige was sent to the Vatican from December 1914 to July 1915 by the Belgian government. For Ladeuze, see Vatican Archive, Affari Ecclesiastici Straordinari, Belgio, 199, fasc. 101, a secret, handwritten 20-page report by Ladeuze 'establishing the innocence of the civil population and highlighting the wrong committed against the Catholic university' (p. 1).

59 The idea came from the Belgian government-in-exile in April 1915, but was eagerly taken up by the Vatican (Vatican Archive, Affari Straordinari, Belgio, 204 – reconstitution of Louvain Library). Benedict XV himself endorsed it, but a communication from Tacci on 6 October 1915 made it clear that the scheme was mistaken and would only worsen the Belgian population's attitude to the Vatican (Vatican Archive, papers of the Brussels nuncio, 1914–18 (uncatalogued), box 93).

60 Meseberg-Haubold, *Der Widerstand*, pp. 91–3.

61 *Les Évêques de Belgique*, p. 8; *La Correspondance du Cardinal Mercier*, pp. 47–53, for

Mercier's suggestion of a joint Belgian–German tribunal to investigate the killing of priests in his own diocese.

62 *Les Évêques de Belgique*, p. 17.

63 Vatican Archive, Affari Ecclesiastici Straordinari, Belgio, 211, fasc. 114, Gasparri to Frühwirth, nuncio in Munich, 14 and 22 January 1916.

64 Vatican Archive, Affari Ecclesiastici Straordinari, Belgio, 211, fasc. 114, printed reply 'Eure Eminenz! Hochwürdigste Herren Bischöfe!'; also Meseberg-Haubold, *Der Widerstand*, pp. 97–109.

65 Meseberg-Haubold, *Der Widerstand*, p. 103.

66 Ibid., p. 287, n. 75.

67 Faulhaber to Knöpfler, 22 October 1915, cited in ibid., p. 288, n. 79.

68 CPHDC, Moscow, 1415-1-55, untitled report, Governor-General Baron Bissing to Generalquartiermeister West, 28 February 1915. Transcript made in the Reichsarchiv, 30 June 1928. Meseberg-Haubold (*Der Widerstand*, p. 83, and pp. 243–4, nn. 29 and 35) knew only an abbreviated version which omits the essential paragraph in which Bissing confirmed the execution of 47 Belgian priests.

69 Bissing visited the priest on 25 January 1915. See the testimony of the priest, J. H. Segers, gathered by Cardinal Mercier's inquiry (AGR, CE, III 374 B1, 32), and the published deposition by Segers in the second, post-war commission's report (Belgian Second Commission, vol. 1, part 2, pp. 353–4).

70 Hermann-Josef Scheidgen, *Deutsche Bischöfe im Ersten Weltkrieg. Die Mitglieder der Fuldaer Bischofskonferenz und ihre Ordinariate 1914–1918* (Cologne, Weimar, Vienna, 1991), p. 296, quoting Bertram to Hartmann, 27 September 1917 (*sic*), in fact 1914).

71 PAAA, Bonn, R 20888, fol. 32, transcript Brose, Deputy General Staff of the Army, Berlin, to all Deputy General Commands, 17 September 1914; ibid., fol. 35–6.

72 Bernhard Duhr, S.J., *Der Lügengeist im Völkerkrieg. Kriegs-Märchen* (Munich and Regensburg, 1915).

73 Wieland, *Belgien 1914*, p. 75; Fernand van Langenhove, *Comment naît un cycle de légendes. Franc-tireurs et atrocités en Belgique* (Lausanne and Paris, 1916), p. 13.

74 *Pax-Informationen*, 24 February 1915, cited by Robert Paul Oszwald, *Der Streit um den belgischen Franktireurkrieg. Eine kritische Untersuchung der Ereignisse in den Augusttagen 1914 und der darüber bis 1930 erschienenen Literatur unter Benutzung bisher nicht veröffentlichten Materials* (Cologne, 1931), p. 138.

75 For intellectuals and the war, and especially for the reaction to 1914, see Roland Stromberg, *Redemption by War: The Intellectuals and 1914* (Lawrence, Kans., 1982); Robert Wohl, *The Generation of 1914* (Cambridge, Mass., 1979); Modris Eksteins, *Rites of Spring: The Great War and the Birth of the Modern Age* (London, 1989); Christophe Prochasson and Anne Rasmussen, *Au nom de la patrie. Les intellectuels et la première guerre mondiale* (Paris, 1996); Martha Hanna, *The Mobilization of Intellect: French Scholars and Writers during the Great War* (Cambridge, Mass., 1996); Fritz Ringer, *The Decline of the Mandarins: The German Academic Community, 1890–1933* (1969; new edn, Hanover and London, 1990); Reinhard Rürup, 'Der "Geist von 1914" in Deutschland. Kriegsbegeisterung und Ideologisierung des Krieges im Ersten Weltkrieg', in Bernd Hüppauf (ed.), *Ansichten vom Krieg. Vergleichende Studien zum Ersten Weltkrieg in Literatur und Gesellschaft* (Königstein/Ts, 1984), pp. 1–30; Wolfgang J. Mommsen (ed.), *Kultur und Krieg: Die Rolle der Intellektuellen, Künstler und Schriftsteller im Ersten Weltkrieg* (Munich, 1996); Wolfgang J. Mommsen, 'German Artists, Writers, and Intellectuals and the Meaning of War,

1914–18', in John Horne (ed.), *State, Society and Mobilization in Europe during the First World War* (Cambridge, 1997), pp. 21–38 ; Stuart Wallace, *War and the Image of Germany: British Academics, 1914–1918* (Edinburgh, 1988), esp. chs 1 to 3; Samuel Hynes, *A War Imagined: The First World War and English Culture* (London, 1990), chs 1 to 3.

76 Jean-Jacques Becker, *1914. Comment les français sont entrés dans la guerre* (Paris, 1977); Hanna, *The Mobilization of Intellect*, pp. 78–105.

77 Trevor Wilson, *The Myriad Faces of War: Britain and the Great War* (Cambridge, 1986), pp. 24–6.

78 Werner Sombart, *Händler und Helden: Patriotische Besinnungen* (Leipzig and Munich, 1915).

79 Ringer, *Decline of the Mandarins*, pp. 180–99; Rürup, 'Der "Geist von 1914"'; Mommsen, 'German Artists, Writers, and Intellectuals and the Meaning of War', pp. 28–31; Eksteins, *Rites of Spring*, pp. 76–80.

80 *Vossische Zeitung*, 20 August 1914, reported in *The Times*, 25 August ('England's "Indelible" Shame'). For a contemporary translation into English, P. van Houtte, *The Pan-Germanic Crime: Impressions and Investigations in Belgium during the German Occupation* (London, 1915), pp. 155–6.

81 *The Times*, 18 September 1914. The list of signatories was organized by the Liberal minister, Charles Masterman, who at the beginning of September had established a discreet anti-German propaganda agency at the behest of the government. See Lucy Masterman, *C. F. G. Masterman* (London, 1939), pp. 272–7; Gary S. Messinger, *British Propaganda and the State in the First World War* (Manchester, 1992), p. 36.

82 *Why We Are at War: Great Britain's Case* (Oxford, 1914). For the theologians' manifestos, see *The Times*, 30 September 1914, and W. B. Selbie, *The War and Theology* (1915). See also Wallace, *War and the Image of Germany*, chs 1 and 2; Arlie J. Hoover, *God, Germany and Britain in the Great War: A Study in Clerical Nationalism* (New York, Westport, London, 1989); Hartmut Pogge von Strandmann, 'The Role of British and German Historians in Mobilizing Public Opinion in 1914', in Benedikt Stuchtey and Peter Wende (eds), *British and German Historiography 1750–1950. Traditions, Perceptions, and Transfers* (Oxford, 2000), pp. 337–47.

83 'La Défense du goût français', *Le Temps*, 19 September 1914, citing the Société des Artistes Français. The list of boycotting bodies included the Société Française d'Archéologie (*Le Temps*, 7 October 1914), the Société d'Auteurs et de Compositeurs Dramatiques (ibid., 17 October), the Académie des Inscriptions et des Belles Lettres (ibid., 25 October), the Académie des Sciences (ibid., 5 November), and the Société de l'École des Chartes (ibid., 8 November).

84 'L'Italie intellectuelle proteste contre l'incendie de Louvain', *Le Temps*, 2 September 1914. At the end of September, several German professors of history and art in Rome protested against accusations in the Italian press about alleged German responsibility for the destruction of Rheims cathedral, though the German embassy in Rome considered the gesture to be in vain (PAAA, Bonn, R 20886, fol. 48, German embassy Rome to Foreign Ministry, 29 September 1914). For the USA, see the *New York Times*, 22 and 23 September 1914 (letters among others from Charles W. Eliot, former president of Harvard, and David Jordan, former president of Stanford).

85 Bernhard vom Brocke, '"Wissenschaft und Militarismus." Der Aufruf der 93 "An die Kulturwelt!" und der Zusammenbruch der internationalen Gelehrtenrepublik im Ersten Weltkrieg', in William M. Calder III, Helmut Flashar and Theodor Lindken

(eds), *Wilamowitz nach 50 Jahren* (Darmstadt, 1985), pp. 649–719. For the fullest study of the Appeal, see Jürgen von Ungern-Sternberg and Wolfgang von Ungern-Sternberg, *Der Aufruf 'An die Kulturwelt!' Das Manifest der 93 und die Anfänge der Kriegspropaganda im Ersten Weltkrieg* (Stuttgart, 1996). For contemporary transla-tions of the text of the Appeal into English, see van Houtte, *Pan-Germanic Crime*, pp. 155–61, and into French, *Le Temps*, 13 October 1914, and Louis Dimier, *L'Appel des intellectuels allemands* (Paris, 1915), pp. 46–63.

86 Ungern-Sternberg and Ungern-Sturnberg, *Der Aufruf*, pp. 18–20. That no victims of blinding were found in German hospitals is indicated by the omission of this accusa-tion from the first draft in the final version. Cf. ibid., p. 50.

87 For the ambiguous remarks of the naval intelligence chief, Captain Löhlein, see Ungern-Sternberg and Ungern-Sternberg, *Der Aufruf*, p. 22.

88 Wolff, *Tagebücher 1914–1919*, p. 106, nn. 6–10.

89 On this division, see Ringer, *The Decline of the Mandarins*, pp. 189–99, and Fritz Fischer, *Germany's Aims in the First World War* (1961; English translation, London, 1967), pp. 155–73.

90 Ulrich von Wilamowitz-Moellendorf, *My Recollections, 1848–1914* (1929; English translation, London, 1930), pp. 382–3; *Revue Belge des Livres, Documents et Archives de la Guerre 1914–18 (RBDLAG)* 11 (1935–6), pp. 480–1; Ungern-Sternberg and Ungern-Sternberg, *Der Aufruf*, p. 23.

91 For the text, see Klaus Böhme (ed.), *Aufrufe und Reden deutscher Professoren im Ersten Weltkrieg* (Stuttgart, 1975), pp. 49–50, and Brocke, '"Wissenschaft und Militarismus"', p. 717. For the context see Ringer, *The Decline of the Mandarins*, pp. 182–3, and Ungern-Sternberg and Ungern-Sternberg, *Der Aufruf*, p. 129.

92 Cited in Ungern-Sternberg and Ungern-Sternberg, *Der Aufruf*, p. 61.

93 Ibid., p. 63.

94 In 1919, a German pacifist, Dr Hans Wehberg, carried out an inquiry among the signatories as to their motive in signing the Appeal and their current view of their 1914 reasoning. Out of 58 surviving signatories who answered Wehberg, 16 refused to retract anything (probably the true figure was 20, but no more) while at least 47 now no longer wished to support the Declaration on all its contentions (Ungern-Sternberg and Ungern-Sternberg, *Der Aufruf*, pp. 74–5). Wehberg's inquiry was published in the *Berliner Tageblatt*, 28 October 1919, and as a brochure, *Wider den Aufruf der 93! Das Ergebnis einer Rundfrage an die 93 Intellektuellen über die Kriegsschuld* (1920). Cf. *RBDLAG*, 11 (1935–6), pp. 480–1.

95 Cited in Ungern-Sternberg and Ungern-Sternberg, *Der Aufruf*, pp. 208–9. Cf. James Sheehan, *The Career of Ludwig Brentano* (Chicago, 1966), pp. 186–9.

96 Wolff, *Tagebücher, 1914–1919*, pp. 104–5.

97 Ibid., pp. 112, 119, 122; cf. Ungern-Sternberg and Ungern-Sternberg, *Der Aufruf*, pp. 65–6.

98 The 'Appeal' appeared in the German press on 4 October 1914. But it had been published in the Swiss press and received by individual intellectuals abroad on 1–2 October (Ungern-Sternberg and Ungern-Sternberg, *Der Aufruf*, pp. 25–6). *The Times* provided a brief summary on 8 October. *Le Temps* published the full text in Paris on 13 October, having been sent it from a correspondent in Geneva who had received his own copy. The declaration of the 4,000 university professors was published on 16 October in the German press and as a brochure on 23 October.

99 *Le Temps*, 17 and 25 October 1914.

100 Session of 31 October, reported in *Le Temps*, 31 October 1914.

101 *Le Temps*, 5 November 1914.

102 *Le Temps*, 8 November 1914.

103 H. A. L. Fisher, *James Bryce* (2 vols, London, 1927), vol. 2, p. 277; Wallace, *War and the Image of Germany*, pp. 40–1, 192.

104 *The Times*, 21 October 1914. For the text, see also van Houtte, *Pan-Germanic Crime*, pp. 161–8.

105 Romain Rolland, *Journal des années de guerre 1914–1919* (Paris, 1952), p. 127; Ungern-Sternberg and Ungern-Sternberg, *Der Aufruf*, p. 68 (letter by Sudermann to his wife).

106 Carol S. Gruber, *Mars and Minerva: World War I and the Uses of the Higher Learning in America* (Baton Rouge, La., 1975), pp. 46–80; Peter Novick, *That Noble Dream: The 'Objectivity Question' and the American Historical Profession* (New York, 1988), pp. 112–16.

107 Hugo Münsterberg, *The War and America* (New York, 1914), pp. 19–20 and 177–9.

108 *The Fatherland*, 30 September 1914 (for Münsterberg) and 11 November 1914 (for the Appeal).

109 S. H. Church, *The American Verdict on the War* (Baltimore, 1915), p. 42.

110 Novick, *That Noble Dream*, pp. 114–15.

111 Eric Thiers, 'Intellectuels et culture de guerre 1914–1918. L'exemple du Comité d'Études et de Documents sur la Guerre', DEA dissertation, École des Hautes Études en Sciences Sociales, Paris, 1996, p. 62. The details that follow on the composition and operation of the committee come mainly from this study.

112 *Le Temps*, 5 November 1914. For the memory of 1870–1, see Ernest Lavisse, *L'Invasion dans le département de l'Aisne* (Laon, 1872), cited in Annette Becker, 'L'Étranger au temps de la guerre de 1870–1871', in Jean-Pierre Jessenne (ed.), *L'Image de l'autre dans l'Europe du nord-ouest à travers l'histoire* (Lille, 1996), pp. 123–32. On Lavisse, see Pierre Nora, 'Lavisse, instituteur national', in Nora (ed.), *Les Lieux de mémoire. La République, la Nation, les France* (3 vols, Paris, 1997), vol. 1, pp. 239–75, and Gerd Krumeich, 'Ernest Lavisse und die Kritik an der deutschen "Kultur", 1914–1918', in Mommsen, *Kultur und Krieg*, pp. 143–54.

113 Émile Durkheim, *L'Allemagne au dessus de tout* (Paris, 1915), esp. pp. 4, 14. For Durkheim's role on the committee, see Stephen Lukes, *Émile Durkheim: His Life and Work* (London, 1973), pp. 547–59.

114 Charles Andler and Ernest Lavisse, *Pratique et doctrine allemandes de la guerre* (Paris, 1915); Ernest Lavisse (ed.), *L'Allemagne et la guerre de 1914–15* (Paris, 1915). Section 3 of the latter summarized Andler and Lavisse's brochure on the German conduct of the war.

115 Joseph Bédier, *Les Crimes allemands d'après des témoignages allemands* (Paris, 1915), translated into English as *German Atrocities from German Evidence* (Paris, 1915), and *Comment l'Allemagne essaye de justifier ses crimes* (Paris, 1915), appearing in English as *How Germany Seeks to Justify Her Atrocities* (Paris, 1915). See John Horne and Alan Kramer, 'German "Atrocities" and Franco-German Opinion, 1914: The Evidence of German Soldiers' Diaries', *Journal of Modern History*, 66/1 (1994), pp. 1–33.

116 Both Hubert Grimme, professor at the University of Münster, and Max Kuttner, professor at the Royal Augusta School in Berlin, had known Bédier when he studied 'scientific' philology in Germany in the late 1880s, Kuttner as one of his teachers. Both

men produced stinging rejections of Bédier's interpretations. See Hubert Grimme, *Ein böswilliger Sprachstümper über 'deutsche Kriegsgreuel'. Entgegnung auf 'Les Crimes Allemands par Joseph Bédier'* (Münster, 1915), and Max Kuttner, *Deutsche Verbrechen? Wider Joseph Bédier, 'Les Crimes allemands'. Zugleich eine Antwort aus französischen Dokumenten* (Bielefeld and Leipzig, 1915).

117 André Gide, *Journal d'André Gide 1889–1939* (Paris, 1951), pp. 500–1 (entry for 15 November 1914).

118 George Bernard Shaw, *Bernard Shaw: Collected Letters*, vol. 3, *1911–1925*, ed. Dan H. Laurence (London, 1985), letters respectively to Robert Loraine, 13 December 1914 (p. 279) and George Cornwallis-West, 2 October 1914 (p. 253).

119 George Bernard Shaw, 'Common Sense about the War', in *The Works of Bernard Shaw*, vol. 21, *What I Really Wrote About the War* (London, 1930), pp. 23–115, here p. 114.

120 Michael Holroyd, *Bernard Shaw* (5 vols, London, 1988–92), vol. 2, *1898–1918: The Pursuit of Power* (London, 1989), p. 346.

121 Romain Rolland, *Au-dessus de la mêlée* (Paris, 1915), first published in the *Journal de Genève*, 15 September 1914, and translated into English as *Above the Battlefield* (Cambridge, 1914).

122 'Lettre ouverte à Gerhart Hauptmann', originally published in the *Journal de Genève*, 29 August 1914, reproduced in Rolland, *Au dessus de la mêlée*, pp. 5–8, and with Hauptmann's reply, 'Louvain … Reims', *Éditions des Cahiers Vaudois* (Lausanne, 1914), pp. 123–9. Hauptmann's reply was published in the *Vossische Zeitung*, 10 September 1914. A Rubens painting had been destroyed in the bombardment of Malines cathedral.

123 Rolland published his rejoinder to the Appeal in the *Journal de Genève*, on 10 October 1914, under the title 'De deux maux, le moindre: pangermanisme ou panslavisme?' (reproduced in *Au-dessus de la mêlée*, pp. 39–56). For the campaign of protest, see 'Louvain … Reims', *Éditions des Cahiers Vaudois*. The respondents included noted neutral and Russian intellectuals and artists, including Stravinsky, Miguel de Unamuno, and the Italian historian Guglielmo Ferrero, as well as French and British signatories.

124 'Inter arma caritas', in Rolland, *Au-dessus de la mêlée*, pp. 57–71 (originally published in the *Journal de Genève*, 30 October 1914); Rolland, *Journal des années de guerre*, p. 76.

125 Rolland, *Au-dessus de la mêlée*, p. 28.

126 'Lettre à ceux qui m'accusent' (17 November 1914), in ibid., p. 81.

127 Rolland, *Journal des années de guerre*, pp. 90–1 (October 1914), 127–8 and 133–5 (November 1914); *Romain Rolland, Stefan Zweig, Briefwechsel, 1910–40* (2 vols), vol. 1, *1910–1923* (Berlin, 1987), Zweig to Rolland, 19 October and 3 November 1914, pp. 78–82 and 89–90 respectively; Stefan Zweig, *The World of Yesterday* (London, 1943), pp. 184–95. The publication of Thomas Mann's *Gedanken im Kriege* ('Thoughts in Time of War'), which defended German *Kultur* against the pretensions of western 'civilization', signalled the impossibility of the venture for Zweig, although Rolland resolved to continue his 'task of Cassandra'.

128 Pirenne had initially refused to believe the accounts of 'German atrocities' and felt sure that his German colleagues would 'be infuriated at the statesmen and rulers of Europe who had ended a century of peace'. See Bryce Lyon, *Henri Pirenne: A Biographical and Intellectual Study* (Ghent, 1974), pp. 215–19. Ungern-Sternberg and Ungern-Sternberg point out that Pirenne's rupture with Lamprecht may have

prompted the latter to distance himself from the Appeal (*Der Aufruf*, p. 69).

129 Jean Massart, *Les Intellectuels allemands et la recherche de la vérité* (Paris, 1918), first published in the *Revue de Paris*, 1 October 1918.

130 For the case of Freemasonry, see C. Magnette, *Correspondance du grand maître de la maçonnerie belge, le frère Charles Magnette, avec les grands loges de la maçonnerie allemande* (Paris, 1915).

8 Wartime culture and enemy atrocities

1 For the concept of a 'war culture', see the pioneering work of Stéphane Audoin-Rouzeau, especially *La Guerre des enfants, 1914–1918* (Paris, 1993), p. 65, and Annette Becker, *War and Faith: The Religious Imagination in France 1914–1930* (1994; English translation, Oxford, 1998); Jean-Jacques Becker et al. (eds), *Guerre et cultures 1914–1918* (Paris, 1994), esp. 'Avant-propos', pp. 7–10; Stéphane Audoin-Rouzeau and Annette Becker, 'Violence et consentement. La "culture de guerre" du premier conflit mondial', in Jean-Pierre Rioux and Jean-François Sirinelli (eds), *Pour une histoire culturelle* (Paris, 1997), pp. 251–71; and Stéphane Audoin-Rouzeau and Annette Becker, *14–18. Retrouver la guerre* (Paris, 2000).

2 For 'self-mobilization', see John Horne, 'Mobilizing for "Total War", 1914–1918', in Horne (ed.), *State, Society and Mobilization in Europe during the First World War* (Cambridge, 1997), pp. 1–17. For the concept as applied to pre-war Wilhelmine Germany, see Richard J. Evans, 'Introduction', in Evans (ed.), *Society and Politics in Wilhelmine Germany* (London, 1978), p. 28.

3 Marc Augé, *Le Sens des autres. Actualité de l'anthropologie* (Paris, 1994); John Horne, 'L'Étranger, la guerre et l'image de "l'autre", 1914–1918', in Jean-Pierre Jessenne (ed.), *L'Image de l'autre dans l'Europe du Nord-Ouest à travers l'histoire* (Lille, 1996), pp. 133–44.

4 R. Douglas, 'Voluntary Enlistment in the First World War and the PRC', *Journal of Modern History*, 42 (1970), pp. 564–85; Peter Simkins, *Kitchener's Army: The Raising of the New Armies, 1914–1916* (Manchester, 1988), pp. 61–3, 125; Nicholas Hiley, 'The News Media and British Propaganda 1914–18', in Jean-Jacques Becker and Stéphane Audoin-Rouzeau (eds), *Les Sociétés européennes et la guerre de 1914–1918* (Paris, 1990), pp. 175–81. Among the official literature issued by the Parliamentary Recruiting Committee in Britain, see no. 18, 'Germany's Barbaric Treatment of the Belgian People', and *The Truth about German Atrocities: Founded on the Report of the Committee on Alleged German Outrages* (London, 1915).

5 Paul Bew, *John Redmond* (Dublin, 1996), pp. 37–9.

6 Mark Tierney, Paul Bowen, and David Fitzpatrick, 'Recruiting Posters', in David Fitzpatrick (ed.), *Ireland and the First World War* (Dublin, 1986), pp. 47–58. The percentage estimate is based on figures from the above essay using the large collection of recruiting posters in the Trinity College Dublin (TCD) Library (Papyrus 16, 1–12, and Papyrus 53, 54 and 55). See also David Fitzpatrick, 'The Logic of Collective Sacrifice: Ireland and the British Army, 1914–1918', *Historical Journal*, 38/4 (1995), pp. 1017–30.

7 TCD Library, Papyrus 55d, poster 109.

8 TCD Library, Papyrus 55a, poster 24; Papyrus 55c, poster 93; Pauline Codd, 'Recruiting and Responses to the War in Wexford', in Fitzpatrick (ed.), *Ireland and the First World War*, pp. 15–26, here pp. 23–4.

9   TCD Library, Papyrus 55a, poster 9.

10 TCD Library, Papyrus 55c, poster 89, and Papyrus 55a, poster 12, respectively.

11 *Le Temps*, 30 November 1914; Karin Wolf, *Sir Roger Casement und die deutsch-irischen Beziehungen* (Berlin, 1972), pp. 27–8; Brian Inglis, *Roger Casement* (1973; new edn, Belfast, 1993), pp. 293–4.

12 M. J. Champcommunal, *Les Lois de la guerre (guerre sur terre). Leur violation systématique par l'Allemagne. Réparations et sanctions. Conférence donnée le samedi 27 novembre 1915 dans la grande salle de l'Hôtel-de-Ville de Limoges* (Paris, 1915).

13 J. Valéry, *Les Crimes de la population belge. Réplique à un plaidoyer pour le gouvernement allemand* (Paris, 1916); J. H. Morgan, *German Atrocities: An Official Investigation* (London, 1916). Cf. A. Mailler, *De la distinction entre les combattants et les non-combattants comme base du droit de guerre* (Paris, 1916), a Paris law thesis that drew directly on the events of 1914, and George W. Scott (professor of international law at Columbia University) and James W. Garner (professor of political science at the University of Illinois), *The German War Code Contrasted with the War Manuals of the United States, Great Britain and France*, Committee on Public Information Series, no. 11 (Washington, D.C., February 1918).

14 Jean Santo, *Les Crimes allemands et leur châtiment* (Paris, n.d., but 1916), also reproduced as postcards.

15 Theodore Cook, *Kaiser, Krupp and Kultur* (London, 1915) and *Kultur and Catastrophe* (London, 1915). *The Field* also produced its own synopsis of the official reports of the Allied countries, *The Crimes of Germany* (London, 1917).

16 James F. Willis, *Prologue to Nuremberg: The Politics and Diplomacy of Punishing War Criminals of the First World War* (Westport, Conn., and London, 1982), pp. 16–22, 30–2. The French Commission, 7th report, also dealt with naval war crimes (pp. 9–14, 35–92).

17 French Commission, reports 10–12; Belgian First Commission, 23rd report; Annette Becker, *Oubliés de la grande guerre. Humanitaire et culture de guerre 1914–1918. Populations occupées, déportés civils, prisonniers de guerre* (Paris, 1998), pp. 68–77.

18 The Armenian genocide was a distinct, but minority, current in the literature on enemy 'atrocities', e.g. Arnold Toynbee, *Armenian Atrocities: The Murder of a Nation* (London, 1915). For Bryce and the Armenians, see Keith Robbins, 'Lord Bryce and the First World War', in Robbins (ed.), *Politicians, Diplomacy and War in Modern British History* (London and Rio Grande, Ohio, 1994), pp. 189–214, here pp. 198–202.

19 Among the best-known publications by neutral witnesses condemning 'German atrocities' were that of the Dutch former professor at the Dordrecht Technical Institute, L. H. Grondijs, *Les Allemands en Belgique (Louvain et Aerschot). Notes d'un témoin hollandais* (Paris, 1915), translated into English as *The Germans in Belgium* (New York, 1916); the book written by the journalist L. Mokveld, who covered the invasion for a leading Dutch Catholic paper, *De Overweldiging van België* (Rotterdam, 1916), translated into English as The *German Fury in Belgium* (London, 1917); and the work of a francophile Greek international lawyer, Léon Maccas, *Les Cruautés allemandes. Réquisitoire d'un neutre* (Paris, 1915), translated into English as *German Barbarism: A Neutral's Indictment* (London, 1916).

20 *The Times*, 18 November 1915 ('The Cartoonist of the War: A Dutchman's Genius: Biting Satires'); Ariane de Ranitz, *'Met een Pen en een Potlood als Wapen!' Louis Raemaekers (1869–1956). Schets van een Politiek Tekenaar* (n.pl., 1989).

21 *The 'Land and Water' Edition of Raemaekers' Cartoons* (London, 1916), unpaginated, but p. 7.

22 *Le Temps*, 8, 9, and 14 February 1916. Raemaekers had been published in *Le Journal* and awarded the Légion d'honneur the previous year. But it was only with this visit that he was able to receive the honour in person. He was acclaimed by fellow cartoonists, and the weekly satirical pictorial journal, *La Baïonnette*, ran a special issue in homage to him (10 February 1916). Raemaekers' exhibition, at the Galerie Georges-Petit, made a considerable impact. *Le Temps* (14 February) makes it clear that it was the same exhibition as that already presented in London. Like *The Times*, the paper emphasized the witness quality of the drawings – 'leur invraisemblable accent de vie' (their incredible likeness to life).

23 Ranitz, 'Met een Pen', p. 337; Louis Raemaekers, *The Great War: A Neutral's Indictment. One Hundred Cartoons by Louis Raemaekers* (London, 1916) – 1,050 copies of the de luxe edition were produced, but the images were disseminated in all manner of editions and formats for the remainder of the war.

24 Texts extracted from official reports or eye-witness accounts were added in the book versions. Many of the cartoons of 'German atrocities' in Belgium had been executed before Raemaekers had seen the reports of the official commissions (J. Murray Allison (ed.), *Raemaekers' Cartoon History of the War* (London, 1919), pp. xiv–xv).

25 See chapter 2 above and appendix 1.

26 C. Vuille, *L'Affaire Raemaekers. Compte-rendu d'un procès intenté à Me Charles Vuille devant la Haute Cour Pénale Fédérale* (Neuchâtel, n.d., but 1918). The German government also pressured the Spanish government into temporarily forbidding a Raemaekers exhibition in Madrid in November 1916 (*The Times*, 15, 29, and 30 November 1916).

27 William Le Queux, *German Atrocities: A Record of Shameless Deeds* (London, 1914), p. 5. Le Queux, the *Daily Mail* journalist, had written a string of pre-war invasion novels.

28 The illustration was used in a British recruiting pamphlet and adapted to the Irish campaign with the words: 'Irishmen! Remember Belgium.'

29 Dorinda Outram, *The Body and the French Revolution: Sex, Class and Political Culture* (New Haven, London, 1989), pp. 153–64; Lynn Hunt, *The Family Romance of the French Revolution* (London, 1994), pp. 68–9.

30 Auguste Roubille, *La Marseillaise* (n.pl., n.d., *c*.1915); Maurice Agulhon, 'Marianne en 14–18', in Becker et al., *Guerre et cultures*, pp. 373–84; Michel Vovelle, 'La Marseillaise. War or Peace', in Pierre Nora (ed.), *Realms of Memory: Rethinking the French Past* (7 vols, 1984–92; English translation, 3 vols, New York, 1996–8), vol. 3, *Symbols* (1998), pp. 29–74.

31 Ruth Harris, 'The "Child of the Barbarian": Rape, Race and Nationalism in France during the First World War', *Past and Present*, 141 (1993), pp. 170–206; Stéphane Audoin-Rouzeau, *L'Enfant de l'ennemi (1914–1918). Viol, avortement, infanticide pendant la grande guerre* (Paris, 1995), ch. 3; also Nicoletta Gullace, 'Sexual Violence and Family Honor: British Propaganda and International Law during the First World War', *American Historical Review*, 102/3 (1997), pp. 714–47.

32 Jean d'Orsay, 'Pour la race!', *Le Matin*, 7 January 1915. For the discrediting of the story, see 'L'Attentat et l'enfant', *Le Matin*, 26 January 1915; Harris, '"Child of the Barbarian"', p. 191; and Audoin-Rouzeau, *L'Enfant de l'ennemi*, p. 100.

33 *L'Écho de Paris*, 10 February 1915.

34 G. Docquois, *La Chair innocente. L'enfant du viol boche* (Paris, n.d., but 1917).

35 P. Rabier, *La Loi du mâle. A propos de l'enfant du barbare* (Paris, 1915), pp. 17, 60.

36 Jehan Rictus, in Docquois, *La Chaire innocente*, p. 90; Harris, '"Child of the Barbarian"', pp. 193–4.

37 Docquois, *La Chaire innocente*, pp. 153–225; Audoin-Rouzau, *L'Enfant de l'ennemi*, pp. 13–31, for an exemplary analysis.

38 Ministère de l'Intérieur, *Mesures d'assistance à l'égard des femmes qui ont été victimes des violences de l'ennemi. Circulaires du Ministère de l'Intérieur en date du 24 mars 1915* (Paris, 1915); Judith Wishnia, 'Natalisme et nationalisme pendant la première guerre mondiale', *Vingtième siècle*, 45 (1995), pp. 30–9.

39 French Commission, 9th report, pp. 22–32. The original documentation, in AN, Paris, AJ4 27, makes it clear that the question of rapes by the occupier was systematically asked but that few accounts were forthcoming.

40 Pierre Loti, *La Grande Barbarie (fragments)* (Paris, 1915), p. 9.

41 Jacques Le Goff, 'Reims, City of Coronation', in Nora (ed.), *Realms of Memory*, vol. 3, *Symbols*, pp. 193–251.

42 *Pages du livre de douleurs de Belgique* (n.pl., n.d.), p. 49.

43 André de Maricourt, *Le Drame de Senlis. Journal d'un témoin. Avant, pendant, après août–septembre 1914* (Paris, 1916), p. 146; *Le Cri de Paris*, 29 November 1914 ('Faits divers').

44 Loup Bertroz, *Senlis pendant l'invasion allemande, 1914, d'après le carnet de notes d'un senlisien* (Senlis, n.d., but 1915), pp. 7–14.

45 André Viriot, *Les Allemands à Nomény (août 1914)* (Nancy, 1916). Other volumes in the series included Émile Badel, *Lunéville (août–septembre 1914)* (Nancy, 1915), and Émile Badel et al., *Gerbéviller-la-martyre. Documentaire, historique, anecdotique* (Nancy, n.d., but 1915). The series had official support; the prefaces were written by Mirman, prefect of the Meurthe-et-Moselle, and in the case of Viriot's volume on Gerbéviller, the Ministry of Foreign Affairs provided a subsidy.

46 Badel et al., *Gerbéviller-la-martyre*, pp. 42–3. Prouvé, whose invitation came from the mayor of Nancy, drew on the tales of victims for his drawings which were published in Gustave Geffroy (ed.), *La Grande Guerre par les artistes* (Paris, n.d., but 1915).

47 'Les Vandales en France', *L'Art et les Artistes* (1915).

48 Alexandre Arsène and Paul Ginisty, *Le Livre du souvenir. Guide du voyageur dans la France envahie en 1914* (Paris, 1916), p. 1. See also Octave Beauchamp, *Les Cités meurtries. Les champs de bataille 1914–1915* (Paris, n.d., but 1915 or 1916). This large-format illustrated guide was published by a tourism magazine, *Le Tour de France. Guide du touriste*, as a guide for 'pilgrimage to the sacred ruins of the murdered cities'; all the towns and villages included (Rheims, Arras, Gerbéviller, Senlis, etc.) were chosen as the victims not of combat but of deliberate destruction.

49 P. Delooz, 'Towards a Sociological Study of Canonized Sainthood in the Catholic Church', in Stephen Wilson (ed.), *Saints and their Cults: Studies in Religious Sociology, Folklore and History* (Cambridge, 1983), pp. 189–216, esp. 205–7; A. Soboul, 'Religious Feeling and Popular Cults during the French Revolution: "Patriot Saints" and Martyrs for Liberty', in ibid., pp. 217–32.

50 F. Martin-Ginouvrier, *Le Martyre du curé de Varreddes* (Barcelona and Paris, 1918), p. 5 (for the quotation). See also F. Lebert, *Varreddes. Le martyre des otages* (2nd edn, Paris, 1917), and chapter 3 above.

51 For France, see Bishop Turinaz, 'En Lorraine', *La Croix*, 12 October 1914; Franciscus,

'*Gott mit uns!' Dieu avec nous!* (Paris, 1916); Abbé Eugène Griselle, *Le Martyre du clergé français* (Paris, 1915); and Gabriel Langlois, *Le Clergé, les catholiques et la guerre* (Paris, 1915), pp. 26–63 ('Héroïsme du clergé civil'). For Belgium, see Auguste Mélot, *Le Martyre du clergé belge* (Paris, 1915).

52 Fontana, *Les Catholiques français pendant la grande guerre*, pp. 123–67; James McMillan, 'French Catholics: *Rumeurs Infâmes* and the *Union Sacrée*, 1914–1918', in Frans Coetzee and Marilyn Shevin-Coetzee (eds), *Authority, Identity and the Social History of the Great War* (Oxford and Providence, 1995), pp. 113–32.

53 *Le Rire rouge*, 27 February 1915 ('Ouvrez! … ouvrez! … C'est l'infortunée Belgique!', by A. Willette).

54 Franciscus, *'Gott mit uns!' Dieu avec nous!*, pp. 264–5 and 311–24, for both documents.

55 Stéphane Audoin-Rouzeau, 'L'Enfant héroïque en 1914–1918', in Becker et al. (eds), *Guerre et cultures*, pp. 173–82. For one of the many accounts of Émile Desprès, see *La Guerre européenne de 1914–1915. L'invasion allemande en France et en Belgique. La fin des barbares. Les atrocités commises par les allemands* (Paris, n.d., but 1915), 3 issues, part 2.

56 Charles Sarolea, *The Murder of Nurse Cavell* (London, 1915), p. 51; Trevor Wilson, *The Myriad Faces of War: Britain and the Great War, 1914–1918* (Cambridge, 1986), pp. 744–5.

57 French Commission, 1st report, pp. 21–2, 23.

58 Viriot, *Les Allemands à Nomény*, p. 13; Badel et al., *Gerbéviller-la-martyre*, pp. 47–53; Sarah Farmer, *Martyred Village: Commemorating the 1944 Massacre at Oradour-sur-Glane* (London, 1999), pp. 59–98.

59 Sophie De Schaepdrijver, 'Occupation, Propaganda, and the Idea of Belgium', in Aviel Roshwald and Richard Stites (eds), *European Culture and the Great War: The Arts, Entertainment, and Propaganda, 1914–1918* (Cambridge, 1999), pp. 267–94.

60 Jean Chot, *La Furie allemande dans l'entre-Sambre-et-Meuse (journées des 23, 24, 25 et 26 août 1914)* (Charleroi, 1919).

61 Jean Schmitz and Norbert Nieuwland, *Documents pour servir à l'histoire de l'invasion allemande dans les provinces de Namur et de Luxembourg* (7 vols, Brussels and Paris, 1919–24).

62 Anon., *Nécrologie dinantais. La vérité sur les massacres de Dinant* (Dinant, n.d., but 1914). For the genesis of the *Nécrologie*, see Jean Massart, *La Presse clandestine dans la Belgique occupée* (Paris, 1917), p. 20, translated into English as *The Secret Press in Belgium* (London, 1918), and Schmitz and Nieuwland, *L'invasion allemande*, vol. 4, part 2, p. 18.

63 Other examples include *Pages du livre de douleurs* which covered Leffe, Sorinne, Andenne, Charleroi; *Louvain; 1914. Enquêtes à Dinant, Andenne, Tamines et Luxembourg belge* (n.pl., n.d.); *Au long de la voie sanglante. Les étapes douloureuses* (Dinant, n.d.); *Les Boches à Surice. Les Huns en Belgique* (n.pl., n.d.).

64 Jean Massart, *Comment les belges résistent à la domination allemande: contribution au livre des douleurs de la Belgique* (Paris and Lausanne, 1916), translated into English as *Belgians under the German Eagle* (London, 1916), pp. 66–73 (English version).

65 Gustave Somville, *Vers Liège. Le Chemin du crime. Août 1914* (Paris, 1915), translated into English as *The Road to Liège: The Path of Crime, August 1914* (London, 1916).

66 Maurice Tschoffen, *Le Sac de Dinant et les légendes du Livre blanc allemand du 10 mai 1915* (Leiden, 1917), pp. 236–7.

67 *La Libre Belgique*, 4 (February 1915).

68 'La Belgique martyre', *La Libre Belgique*, 6 (March 1915); Massart, *La Presse clandestine*, pp. 6–8.

69 Massart, *Belgians under the German Eagle*, pp. 98–108.

70 *La Libre Belgique*, 17 (April 1915). Issue no. 25, May 1915, reported that the German military were using menaces to extract suitable evidence from Belgian civilian witnesses on the Tamines massacre.

71 *La Libre Belgique*, 31 (June 1915).

72 'La Kultur', *La Libre Belgique*, 5 (March 1915).

73 E.g., 'Les Lois de la guerre d'après les nations civilisées et les lois allemandes de la guerre', *La Libre Belgique*, 12 and 13 (1915); and a report of Louis Renault's address to the Sorbonne on the laws of war in *La Libre Belgique*, 29 (June 1915).

74 *La Libre Belgique*, 115 (March 1917).

75 E.g. the last issue of the paper, 171, November 1918.

76 Henri Pirenne, *La Belgique et la guerre mondiale* (Paris, 1928), which accords considerable importance to the 'atrocities' question (esp. pp. 54–6); De Schaepdrijver, 'Occupation, Propaganda and the Idea of Belgium'.

77 Massart, *The Secret Press in Belgium*, pp. 5–10. A semi-regular clandestine fly-sheet, entitled *Le Belge*, published a summary of Joseph Bédier's pamphlet, *Les Crimes allemands*, in its November 1915 issue, under the heading 'Leurs atrocités avouées'. The original also circulated in Belgium, but was, according to *Le Belge*, difficult to procure (copy in the BfZ, Stuttgart).

78 In addition to Wolfgang J. Mommsen, 'German Artists, Writers and Intellectuals and the Meaning of War', in Horne, *State, Society and Mobilization*, see Hans Weigel et al., *Jeder Schuss ein Russ. Jeder Stoss ein Franzos. Literarische und graphische Kriegspropaganda in Deutschland und Österreich 1914–1918* (Vienna, 1983); Michael Jeismann, *Das Vaterland der Feinde. Studien zum nationalen Feindbegriff und Selbstverständnis in Deutschland und Frankreich 1792–1918* (Stuttgart, 1992), pp. 299–338; Wolfgang Kruse, *Krieg und nationale Integration. Eine Neuinterpretation des sozialdemokratischen Burgfriedensschlusses 1914–15* (Essen, 1993); Wolfgang J. Mommsen, *Bürgerliche Kultur und künstlerische Avantgarde 1870 bis 1918. Kultur und Politik im deutschen Kaiserreich* (Frankfurt and Berlin, 1994), pp. 117–67; Wolfgang J. Mommsen (ed.), *Kultur und Krieg. Die Rolle der Intellektuellen, Künstler und Schriftsteller im Ersten Weltkrieg* (Munich, 1996); and Matthew Stibbe, *German Anglophobia and the Great War, 1914–1918* (Cambridge, 2001), pp. 49–79.

79 The authors would like to thank Dr Beth Irwin Lewis, Wooster College, Ohio, for her work in establishing this point. It is confirmed by the popular illustrated journal *Die Gartenlaube*, in which the theme of atrocities and francs-tireurs featured repeatedly in August–November 1914, but disappeared thereafter.

80 Ragnvald Blix, 'In der Lügenfabrik' ('In the Lie Factory'), *Simplicissimus*, 26 (22 September 1914).

81 *Bei unseren Helden an der Somme*, BUFA, 1917 (copy in Bundesarchiv-Filmarchiv Potsdam); Susanne Brandt, 'Bilder von der Zerstörung an der Westfront und die doppelte Verdrängung der Niederlage', in Gerhard Hirschfeld et al. (eds), *Kriegserfahrungen. Studien zur Sozial- und Mentalitätsgeschichte des Ersten Weltkriegs* (Essen, 1997) pp. 439–54, here p. 444.

82 Eberhard Demm, 'Propaganda and Caricature in the First World War', *Journal of Contemporary History*, 28 (1993), pp. 163–92, here 176; Stibbe, *German Anglophobia*, pp. 38–43.

83 *Kölnische Zeitung*, 28 March 1918 ('Der Krieg gegen die Zivilbevölkerung').

84 Léon Mirman, *Sur la tombe des martyrs. Sur la tombe des héros* (Nancy, n.d., but 1916), p. 11.

85 Mirman, *Sur la tombe des martyrs*, p. 5.

86 L. Mirman, G. Simon, and G. Keller, *Leurs Crimes* (Nancy, 1916), pp. 62–3. The book was translated into English as *Their Crimes* (London, 1917), and into German in 1919.

87 AD Loire, 29M 9 (Ligue du Souvenir).

88 *Souvenez-vous! Ligue pour perpétuer le souvenir des crimes allemands. Statuts* (Paris, 1916), copy in BDIC, Paris.

89 *Bulletin de la Ligue Souvenez-Vous*, 1 (January 1917), pp. 4–5. It listed 36 départements, excluding the Seine (Paris), as having corresponding members or committees.

90 L'Union des Grandes Associations contre la Propagande Ennemie (UGACPE), published minutes, 28 May 1918, report of the Ligue Souvenez-Vous, pp. 23–30. The term *endormeurs* was coined by Maurice Donnay, of the Académie Française, in *Bulletin de la Ligue Souvenez-Vous*, January 1917, pp. 5–6.

91 *Bulletin de la Ligue Souvenez-Vous*, January 1917, p. 9 (reproduction of the poster).

92 UGACPE, published minutes, 28 May 1918, pp. 28; J. Escudier and J. Richepin, *Le Livre rouge des atrocités allemandes d'après les rapports officiels des gouvernements français, anglais et belges par l'image [...] 40 estampes hors texte [...] par J.-G. Domergue* (Paris, n.d.).

93 UGACPE, published minutes, 28 May 1918, pp. 27–8. The posters for the exhibition were executed by Lucien Jonas, Charles Jouas, and Barrère. Illustration 34 shows that by Jouas. The exhibition ran for a month in Paris and contained a variety of illustrations and exhibits, including clubs supposedly used by the Austro-Hungarian army for dispatching wounded enemy soldiers, which had been helpfully lent by the Italian government. It was visited by Poincaré, President of the Republic.

94 Wilson, *Myriad Faces of War*, pp. 507–40; John M. Bourne, *Britain and the Great War, 1914–1918* (London, 1989), pp. 199–224; Pierre Renouvin, 'L'Opinion publique et la guerre en 1917', *Revue d'histoire moderne et contemporaine*, 15/1 (1968), pp. 4–23; Jean-Jacques Becker, *The Great War and the French People* (1980; English translation, Leamington Spa, 1985), pp. 217–35.

95 John Horne, 'Remobilizing for "Total War": France and Britain, 1917–1918', in Horne, *State, Society and Mobilization*, pp. 195–211.

96 Géo London, *Ils ont détruit sans nécessité militaire* (Paris, n.d., but late 1918); L. Guillet, *Souvenez-vous! La barbarie allemande* (Paris, n.d., but 1917).

97 PRO, London, T102/20, 'Publications issued by the Department of Publicity (NWAC)'. These included 'Murder Most Foul', by the American publicist, Newell Dwight Hillis, 'Devils of the Deep', by the American consul at Queenstown, Ireland, and 'If the Kaiser Governed Britain', by William Stephen Sanders.

98 Nicholas Reeves, *Official British Film Propaganda during the First World War* (London, 1986), pp. 125–32.

99 Ibid., pp. 203–5.

100 Arlie J. Hoover, *God, Germany, and Britain in the Great War: A Study in Clerical Nationalism* (New York, Westport, London, 1989), pp. 110–11.

101 See Horne, 'Remobilizing for "Total War"'.

102 French Commission, 10th, 11th and 12th reports; *Les Atrocités allemandes à Lille. Trois témoignages de députés socialistes* (Paris: UGACPE, 1919).

103 Kevin Brownlow, *The War, the West and the Wilderness* (London, 1979), pp. 30–8, 69–77; Craig W. Campbell, *Reel America and World War I: A Comprehensive Filmography and History of Motion Pictures in the United States, 1914–1920* (Jefferson, N.C., and London, 1985), pp. 25–47.

104 George Creel, *How We Advertised America* (New York, 1920); James R. Mock and Cedric Larson, *Words that Won the War: The Story of the Committee on Public Information 1917–1919* (Princeton, 1939), based on the archives of the CPI; David Kennedy, *Over Here: The First World War and American Society* (New York, 1980), pp. 59–63; J. Michael Sproule, *Propaganda and Democracy: The American Experience of Media and Mass Persuasion* (Cambridge, 1997), pp. 6–16.

105 Frederic L. Paxson et al., *War Cyclopedia: A Handbook for Ready Reference on the Great War* (Washington, D.C., 1918), p. 22.

106 Dana Munro (ed.), *German War Practices* (Washington D.C.: CPI, January 1918), pp. 18–19; Frederic L. Paxson, *Pre-War Years, 1913–1917* (Boston, 1936), pp. 168–9 (praising the relatively sober tone of Munro's publication). See also Carol S. Gruber, *Mars and Minerva: World War I and the Uses of the Higher Learning in America* (Baton Rouge, LA, 1975), pp. 118–61.

107 Scott and Garner, *The German War Code*.

108 Mock and Larson, *Words that Won the War*, p. 123.

109 Newell D. Hillis, *German Atrocities: Their Nature and Philosophy* (New York, 1918), esp. pp. 7–9.

110 'Remember Belgium', poster by Young Ellsworth for the fourth war loan campaign, in *Quand les affiches s'en vont en guerre. 1917–1918. Deux années d'affiches de guerre américaines* (Brussels, 1986), pp. 71 and 219.

111 Brownlow, *The War, the West and the Wilderness*, pp. 131–4; Campbell, *Reel America and World War I*, pp. 59–60; Leslie Midkiff DeBauche, 'Mary Pickford's Public on the Home Front', in Karel Dibbets and Bert Hogenkamp (eds), *Film and the First World War* (Amsterdam, 1995), pp. 149–59.

112 Campbell, *Reel America and World War I*, p. 60.

113 James W. Gerard, *My Four Years in Germany* (New York, 1917); Brownlow, *The War, the West and the Wilderness*, pp. 135–9; Campbell, *Reel America and World War I*, pp. 97–9.

9 The moral reckoning: Versailles and the war crimes trials

1 James F. Willis, *Prologue to Nuremberg: The Politics and Diplomacy of Punishing War Criminals of the First World War* (Westport, Conn., and London, 1982), pp. 23–36, and especially Asquith's speech to the House of Commons on 31 July 1916 (cited p. 31); Annie Deperchin-Gouillard, 'Responsabilité et violation du droit des gens pendant la première guerre mondiale. Volonté politique et impuissance juridique', in Annette Wieviorka (ed.), *Les Procès de Nuremberg et de Tokyo* (Brussels, 1996), pp. 25–49.

2 Jacques Dumas, *Les Sanctions pénales des crimes allemands* (Paris, 1916); *Revue des Deux Mondes*, 15 August 1916, p. 958; Willis, *Prologue to Nuremberg*, pp. 33–4.

3 Lothar Wieland, *Belgien 1914. Die Frage des belgischen 'Franktireurkrieges' und die deutsche öffentliche Meinung von 1914 bis 1936* (Frankfurt, Berne, New York, 1984), pp. 33–5. Briand as Prime Minister in late 1916 was forced to endorse Asquith's call of 31 July for criminal proceedings against the authors of the deportations, but warned against diverting attention from the military struggle.

4 AN, Paris, BB 18 2568 2 (Ministère de la Justice), 'Projet de convention pour assurer le châtiment des crimes ennemis', 24 April 1917, and evidence of inquiries conducted in 1917–18.

5 *Le Temps*, 7 October 1918; Willis, *Prologue to Nuremberg*, pp. 50–1.

6 Pierre Miquel, *La Paix de Versailles et l'opinion publique française* (Paris, 1972), pp. 237–9. See in particular the inquiry opened by *Le Matin* on the question in January 1919.

7 General Jean-Jules Mordacq, *Le Ministère Clemenceau. Journal d'un témoin* (4 vols, Paris, 1930–1), vol. 3, *Novembre 1918–juin 1919* (1931), p. 27; David Stevenson, *French War Aims against Germany 1914–1919* (Oxford, 1982), p. 158.

8 Miquel, *La Paix de Versailles*, p. 238, n. 2; Frédéric Larnaude and Albert de Lapradelle, *Examen de la responsabilité pénale de l'Empereur Guillaume II* (Paris, 1918).

9 As noted by Clemenceau's personal adviser, General Mordacq, when visiting London with Clemenceau in December 1918 (*Le Ministère Clemenceau*, vol. 3, p. 27).

10 PRO, London, FO 608/245 (Memorandum submitted to the British Delegates to the Commission on the Responsibilities for the War), fol. 172A–173; ibid., fol. 511–83, for the committee's 'Interim Reports'. Cf. Willis, *Prologue to Nuremberg*, pp. 54–9.

11 Cited in John Maynard Keynes, *The Economic Consequences of the Peace* (London, 1919), p. 131.

12 Caroline Playne, *Britain Holds On, 1917–18* (London, 1933), pp. 390–2; Willis, *Prologue to Nuremberg*, pp. 49–64. For a balanced appraisal of the 1918 election which repudiates Keynes's view that Lloyd George made jingoistic use of the war crimes theme (*Economic Consequences*, pp. 127–33), see Kenneth O. Morgan, *Consensus and Disunity; The Lloyd George Coalition Government, 1918–1922* (Oxford, 1979), pp. 38–41.

13 *The Times*, 27 January 1919, p. 10; Willis, *Prologue to Nuremberg*, pp. 65–6.

14 James Brown Scott, 'The Trial of the Kaiser', in Edward M. House and Charles Seymour (eds), *What Really Happened at Paris* (New York, 1921), pp. 231–58, at p. 233.

15 Scott, 'The Trial of the Kaiser', *passim*.

16 Willis, *Prologue to Nuremberg*, pp. 70–1.

17 *Le Temps*, 17 March 1919, for the categories; Albert de Lapradelle (ed.), *La Paix de Versailles* (14 vols, Paris, 1929–39), vol. 3, *Responsabilités des auteurs de la guerre et sanctions* (1930), pp. 235–60 (first subcommittee); ibid., pp. 295–324 (third subcommittee, on consequences of war crimes); Willis, *Prologue to Nuremberg*, pp. 72–3; Walter Schwengler, *Völkerrecht, Versailler Vertrag und Auslieferungsfrage. Die Strafverfolgung wegen Kriegsverbrechen als Problem des Friedensschlusses 1919/20* (Stuttgart, 1982), pp. 71–124.

18 See appendix 3 below; for the genesis of Article 231, Philip M. Burnett, *Reparations at the Paris Peace Conference: From the Standpoint of the American Delegation* (2 vols, New York, 1940), vol. 1, pp. 66–70.

19 Willis, *Prologue to Nuremberg*, pp. 75–7 (evidence of Lansing's desk diary for Wilson's suggestion); *Violations of the Laws and Customs of War: Report of the Majority and Dissenting Reports of the American and Japanese Members of the Commission on Responsibilities at the Conference of Paris, 1919*, Pamphlet 32 (Oxford, 1919); also in Lapradelle, *Responsabilités des auteurs de la guerre*, pp. 461–556.

20 Mordacq, *Le Ministère Clemenceau*, vol. 3, pp. 187–8; Paul Mantoux (ed.), *Les*

Délibérations du Conseil des quatre (24 mars–28 juin 1919) (2 vols, Paris, 1955), vol. 1, pp. 123–4 (session of 2 April); Maurice Hankey, *The Supreme Control: At the Paris Peace Conference 1919* (London, 1963), p. 114.

21 Mantoux, *Les Délibérations du Conseil des quatre*, pp. 184–96; Willis, *Prologue to Nuremberg*, pp. 77–86.

22 Ulrich Heinemann, *Die verdrängte Niederlage. Politische Öffentlichkeit und Kriegsschuldfrage in der Weimarer Republik* (Göttingen, 1983), p. 35.

23 Holger H. Herwig, 'Clio Deceived: Patriotic Self-Censorship in Germany after the Great War', in Keith Wilson (ed.), *Forging the Collective Memory: Government and International Historians through Two World Wars* (Providence and Oxford, 1996), pp. 87–127.

24 Schwengler, *Völkerrecht*, p.138. A Commission on Violations of International Law and the Customs of War by Members of the Entente Armies was set up in the Foreign Ministry under Major Otto von Stülpnagel to collect incriminating material as well as material to be used in defence of Germans accused of crimes (ibid., pp. 138–9, n. 74).

25 *ADAP*, series A, vol. 1, document 160: Dieckhoff to Bülow, 5 March 1919, pp. 270–1. Dieckhoff was reporting on the views of Foreign Minister Brockdorff-Rantzau and the head of the Office for Peace Negotiations, Count von Bernstorff. On the Kautsky documents, see Eric J. C. Hahn, 'The German Foreign Ministry and the Question of War Guilt in 1918–1919', in Carole Fink, Isabel V. Hull, and MacGregor Knox (eds), *German Nationalism and the European Response, 1890–1945* (London, 1985), pp. 53–5, and Heinemann, *Die verdrängte Niederlage*, pp. 74–8. The decision to campaign on the issue of military conduct was supported by the General Staff in a memorandum to the Foreign Ministry of 20 April 1919 with a countercharge accusing the French of war crimes and hypocrisy (Schwengler, *Völkerrecht*, p. 162, n. 175).

26 Herwig, 'Clio Deceived', pp. 91–9; Wolfgang Jäger, *Historische Forschung und politische Kultur in Deutschland. Die Debatte 1914–1980 über den Ausbruch des Ersten Weltkrieges* (Göttingen, 1984), pp. 46–7; Wieland, *Belgien 1914*, pp. 115–20.

27 Heinemann, *Die verdrängte Niederlage*, pp. 38–9.

28 Alma Luckau, *The German Delegation at the Paris Peace Conference* (New York, 1941), p. 37.

29 Hahn, 'German Foreign Ministry', pp. 59–60, 66–7. Rantzau chose the most provocative of several drafts at his disposal (Schwengler, *Völkerrecht*, pp. 177–8; Michael Dreyer and Oliver Lembcke, *Die deutsche Diskussion um die Kriegsschuldfrage 1918/19* (Berlin, 1993), pp. 131–2). That the Allies never officially advanced a thesis of 'sole German war guilt' was admitted by the head of the Zentralstelle für Erforschung der Kriegsursachen (Central Office for Research on the Causes of the War), the 'scholarly' front organization of the Foreign Ministry, Alfred von Wegerer, in internal reports. Article 231 spoke only of Germany and its allies as the cause of all losses and damages (Heinemann, *Die verdrängte Niederlage*, p. 230).

30 Schwengler, *Völkerrecht*, p. 179.

31 *Papers Relating to the Foreign Relations of the United States: The Paris Peace Conference 1919*, vol. 6 (Washington D.C., 1946), pp. 781–94, for the memorandum; Schwengler, *Völkerrecht*, pp. 185–6; Heinemann, *Die verdrängte Niederlage*, pp. 40 and 45; Dreyer and Lembcke, *Die deutsche Diskussion*, pp. 131–2, 146–7.

32 Luckau, *The German Delegation*, document 57, pp. 369–71; Dreyer and Lembcke, *Die deutsche Diskussion*, pp. 181–2.

33 Schwengler, *Völkerrecht*, pp. 190–1; cf. also Jäger, *Historische Forschung*, p. 32.

34 Schwengler, *Völkerrecht*, p. 191.

35 Cf. Hahn, 'German Foreign Ministry', pp. 43–70. For the distinction between the policies of catastrophe and fulfilment (*Katastrophenpolitik* and *Erfüllungspolitik*), see Detlev Peukert, *The Weimar Republic: The Crisis of Classical Modernity* (1987; English translation, London, 1991), pp. 55–7.

36 Luckau, *The German Delegation*, pp. 411–12.

37 Cf. Schwengler, *Völkerrecht*, pp. 194–5.

38 Ibid., pp. 197–201.

39 Memorandum Freytag, 24 July 1919, cited in Heinemann, *Die verdrängte Niederlage*, p. 56.

40 *Documents on British Foreign Policy 1919–1939* (hereafter *DBFP*), First Series, vol. 6 (London, 1956), document 84, General Malcolm (Berlin) to Director of Military Intelligence at the British Peace Delegation in Paris, 6 August 1919, p. 124.

41 Schwengler, *Völkerrecht*, pp. 217–19. Cf. Johannes Erger, *Der Kapp-Lüttwitz-Putsch. Ein Beitrag zur deutschen Innenpolitik 1919/20* (Düsseldorf, 1967), document 1, p. 303: Groener at meeting of OHL officers, 12 July 1919, reporting on meeting of 19 June 1919. For wider military protests against the treaty, especially the extradition clauses, see Schwengler, *Völkerrecht*, pp. 204–5.

42 Cited in Schwengler, *Völkerrecht*, p. 227, n. 472.

43 Ibid., pp. 227–8.

44 Ibid., pp. 228–9.

45 Klaus Epstein, *Matthias Erzberger and the Dilemma of German Democracy* (1959; new edn, New York, 1971), p. 322.

46 Erger, *Der Kapp-Lüttwitz-Putsch*, pp. 26–31; Schwengler, *Völkerrecht*, pp. 226–7, 233–5.

47 Cf. Herwig, 'Clio Deceived'.

48 *Vorwärts*, 29 November 1918, 'Ein Staatsgerichtshof für Vergehen in Belgien verlangt'. Cf. Schwengler, *Völkerrecht*, pp. 143–6.

49 'Die Grausamkeiten der Kriegführung' (The cruelties of warfare): *Norddeutsche Allgemeine Zeitung*, 20 November 1918; Schwengler, *Völkerrecht*, p. 164; Willis, *Prologue to Nuremberg*, p. 82. Cf. Gregor Huch, 'Kommission Schücking', in *Der Deutsche*, 15 September 1919, pp. 7–8.

50 Huch, 'Kommission Schücking', pp. 9–12.

51 Schwengler, *Völkerrecht*, pp. 157–60; Heinemann, *Die verdrängte Niederlage*, pp. 23–4; Herwig, 'Clio Deceived', p. 108.

52 See chapter 10 below.

53 Erich Eyck, *A History of the Weimar Republic* (1954–6; English translation, 2 vols, Cambridge, Mass., 1962–7), vol. 1, pp. 134–9; Herwig, 'Clio Deceived', p. 109.

54 Abraham Berlau, *The German Social Democratic Party 1914–1921* (1949; new edn, New York, 1975), pp. 285–318.

55 Dreyer and Lembcke, *Die deutsche Diskussion*, pp. 181–2.

56 Schwengler, *Völkerrecht*, pp. 246–50.

57 Epstein, *Matthias Erzberger*, pp. 329–30.

58 Willis, *Prologue to Nuremberg*, pp. 121–2; Schwengler, *Völkerrecht*, pp. 314–16.

59 *DBFP*, First Series, vol. 6, document 104, Balfour to Earl Curzon, 11 August 1919, p. 144; ibid., document 106, Earl Curzon to Balfour (Paris), 13 August 1919, p. 146; ibid., document 126, transcription of telephone message from Lloyd George to Balfour, 20 August 1919, pp. 174–5; cf. *DBFP*, First Series, vol. 1, document 32, appendix C,

Dupont, mission militaire française, Berlin, to Marshal Foch, 4 August 1919, pp. 397–8; David Watson, *Georges Clemenceau: A Political Biography* (London, 1974), p. 359.

60 Schwengler, *Völkerrecht*, pp. 258–64, citing a memorandum by Schiffer, 22 October, in the Schiffer papers (ibid., p. 262).

61 *DBFP*, First Series, vol. 6, document 256, Sir E. Crowe (Paris) to Earl Curzon, 6 November 1919, with enclosed communication from Simson, German Foreign Ministry, to the Peace Conference, 4 November 1919, pp. 332–4. Cf. Schwengler, *Völkerrecht*, pp. 265–6.

62 Schwengler, *Völkerrecht*, p. 271 (Allied note of 1 December 1919).

63 For Clemenceau's public attitude, see his speech of 11 October 1919 to the French Senate, during which he produced a large file from the Under-Secretary of Military Justice in which 'are related the abominable crimes of the entire German soldiery, with the names of the criminals and supporting evidence [...] We cannot provide an amnesty for things like that, it's impossible [...]' (Georges Clemenceau, *Discours de paix* (Paris, 1938), pp. 233–81, at p. 265). Clemenceau adopted the same position in the debate on the issue by the Chamber of Deputies on 7 November (Mordacq, *Le Ministère Clemenceau*, vol. 4, *Juillet 1919–janvier 1920* (1931), pp. 167–8. Cf. Willis, *Prologue to Nuremberg*, pp. 117–18; Schwengler, *Völkerrecht*, pp. 325–7).

64 *DBFP*, First Series, vol. 9, document 559, Meeting of the Commission on the Organization of Mixed Tribunals, Paris, 13 January 1920, pp. 602–11; *DBFP*, First Series, vol. 2, document 78, Meeting of Allied Representatives, 20 January 1920, pp. 927–8.

65 See also appendix 4.

66 *DBFP*, First Series, vol. 2, document 73, Meeting of the heads of delegations [...] at Paris, 15 January 1920, pp. 886–7; Schwengler, *Völkerrecht*, p. 332.

67 The total was reduced to 853 after elimination of double-counting of individuals within and between the different lists.

68 *DBFP*, First Series, vol. 9, document 567, Kilmarnock to Curzon, 26 January 1920, p. 618.

69 *ADAP*, series A, vol. 3, document 14, pp. 33–4: Foreign Minister Hermann Müller (SPD) to embassy Vienna, 20 January 1920.

70 Schwengler, *Völkerrecht*, p. 332; Marjorie Farrar, *Principled Pragmatist: The Political Career of Alexandre Millerand* (New York and Oxford, 1991), pp. 234–6.

71 *ADAP*, series A, vol. 3, document 26, Lersner to Foreign Ministry, 4 February 1920, attaching Lersner to President Millerand, 3 February 1920, pp. 50–2; Willis, *Prologue to Nuremberg*, pp. 120–1.

72 Schwengler, *Völkerrecht*, p. 304.

73 Wieland, *Belgien 1914*, p. 100; Willis, *Prologue to Nuremberg*, p. 123.

74 *DBFP*, First Series, vol. 9, document 595, Kilmarnock to Curzon, 5 February 1920, p. 650; ibid., document 597, Kilmarnock to Curzon, 5 February 1920, p. 651.

75 *Berliner Tageblatt*, 5 February 1920, cited in Schwengler, *Völkerrecht*, p. 305.

76 BA, Berlin, R 3003 Generalia/51, fol. 25, Stülpnagel (head of the Central Office for Violations of International Law) to Reich Prosecutor Leipzig, 12 September 1920.

77 Eduard Meyer (ed.), *Für Ehre, Wahrheit und Recht. Erklärung deutscher Hochschullehrer zur Auslieferungsfrage* (Berlin, 1919); Schwengler, *Völkerrecht*, p. 283.

78 *DBFP*, First Series, vol. 9, document 38, Kilmarnock to Curzon, 10 February 1920, p. 57. A correspondent of the *Berliner Tageblatt*, Captain Persius, made similar remarks

to another British correspondent. Ibid., n. 4.

79 E.g. the view of a British military intelligence officer, Colonel Roddie, and the new chargé d'affaires in Berlin, Lord Kilmarnock, who transmitted the catastrophe thesis (ably fed them by Noske) to London in January 1920, contributing to the abandonment of the extradition policy (Willis, *Prologue to Nuremberg*, p. 121).

80 Morgan, *Consensus and Disunity*, p. 140.

81 At a conference in London on 12 February 1920 (*DBFP*, First Series, vol. 7, documents 1–4, pp. 1–29, *passim*).

82 *ADAP*, series A, vol. 3, document 63, Sthaner, chargé d'affaires, London, to Foreign Ministry, 10 March 1920, p. 114. Cf. Willis, *Prologue to Nuremberg*, pp. 123–4.

83 *Verhandlungen der Deutschen Nationalversammlung. Stenographische Berichte*, vol. 332 (16 January–30 March 1920), 4 March 1920, cols 4668–9.

84 *Freiheit. Berliner Organ der Unabhängigen Sozialdemokratie Deutschlands*, 9 February 1920, evening edition; 11 February 1920, morning edition; 11 February 1920, evening edition; 13 February 1920, morning edition, with extracts from evidence on the Stenger case and the killing of civilians in Mulhouse, Reiningen, and Burzweiler; it called for punishment for such 'atrocities'.

85 *DBFP*, First Series, vol. 9, document 584, Kilmarnock to Curzon, 3 February 1920, p. 638.

86 At least in Bavaria: Benjamin Ziemann, *Front und Heimat. Ländliche Kriegser- fahrungen im südlichen Bayern 1914–1923* (Essen, 1997), pp. 379–80. Richard Bessel (*Germany after the First World War* (Oxford, 1993), pp. 262–3) is undoubtedly correct in stating that pacifism failed to make a significant impact on the political culture of Weimar Germany. But popular opinion, as opposed to extreme right-wing organizations, did not necesarily accept the myths of nationalist propaganda. Cf. *DBFP*, First Series, vol. 9, document 609, Kilmarnock to Curzon, 7 February 1920, p. 674. Schwengler's opinion (*Völkerrecht*, p. 291) that the majority of the Germans opposed extradition cannot be proved or disproved. More important here is the extent of popular mobilization on the issue, which on the basis of attendance at rallies and demonstrations is rather unimpressive.

87 *DBFP*, First Series, vol. 8, pp. 234–52.

88 BA, Berlin, R 3003 Generalia/56: Première liste des personnes designées par les puissances alliées pour être jugées par la cour suprème de Leipzig; AN, Paris, BB 18 2568 2, for the preparatory dossiers on the cases of the Stenger order, Jarny, and Gerbéviller.

89 Peukert, *The Weimar Republic*, p. 58.

90 This was the judgement of the official French mission, otherwise deeply critical of the Leipzig proceedings (MAE, Paris, Série Z, Europe, Allemagne 1918–29, 589, 'Sanctions aux violations du droit des gens: punition des coupables: mission de l'avocat général Matter au procès de Leipzig'). It was also that of the British observer, Claud Mullins (*The Leipzig Trials* (London, 1921), p. 43).

91 For the proceedings, see House of Commons, *Parliamentary Papers*, 1921, vol. 12, *German War Trials*, Cmd 1450. For a summary of the trials and a description of the atmosphere, see Mullins, *The Leipzig Trials*. For historical accounts, see Willis, *Prologue to Nuremberg*, pp. 126–47, and Jean-Jacques Becker, 'Le Procès de Leipzig', in Wieviorka (ed.), *Les Procès de Nuremberg et de Tokyo*, pp. 51–60.

92 See BA, Berlin, R 3003 Generalia/52. The French and Belgian cases attracted very little correspondence, mainly related to maltreatment of prisoners and individual crimes against property and individuals in the years 1916–18.

93 *Parliamentary Debates*, Commons, 5th series, vol. 146 (1921), pp. 1534–6; *ADAP*, series A, vol. 5, p. 139.

94 Mullins, *The Leipzig Trials*, pp. 136–51; Willis, *Prologue to Nuremberg*, pp. 134–5.

95 Joanna Bourke, *An Intimate History of Killing: Face-to-Face Killing in Twentieth-Century Warfare* (London, 1999), ch. 6, 'Atrocity'.

96 *Le Temps*, for the quotation; AN, Paris, BB 18 25684 (Ministry of Justice), for the summarized testimony in the case. On suspicion of Alsatian soldiers in the German army, see Alan Kramer, '*Wackes* at War: Alsace-Lorraine and the Failure of German National Mobilization, 1914–1918', in John Horne (ed.), *State, Society and Mobilization in Europe during the First World War* (Cambridge, 1997), pp. 105–21.

97 All the summarized testimony is from the record of the judgment in the Reichsgericht case, 6 July 1921: AN, Paris, BB 18 25684 (Ministry of Justice).

98 French Commission, 3rd report (1 May 1915), p. 71, evidence of diarist Rothacker, IR 142.

99 Dominik Richert, *Beste Gelegenheit zum Sterben. Meine Erlebnisse im Kriege 1914–1918*, ed. Angelika Tramitz and Bernd Ulrich (Munich, 1989), pp. 36–9.

100 The United Nations War Crimes Commission, *History of the United Nations War Crimes Commission and the Development of the Laws of War* (London, 1948), pp. 50–1.

101 HStA-MA, Stuttgart, M660 NL Ebbinghaus, book 2: letters and appeals on the 'war accused', circular from Stenger, April 1922, Bad Oeynhausen.

102 Ibid., emphasis in the original.

103 Willis, *Prologue to Nuremberg*, pp. 135–7.

104 MAE, Paris, Série Z, Europe, Allemagne 1918–29, 589, 'Sanctions aux violations du droit des gens [. . .]: mission [. . .] Matter', notes of Matter on the trials.

105 Ibid., report of Matter and his colleagues to the government, 12 July 1921.

106 *Journal Officiel, Chambre des Députés, Débats Parlementaires*, 1921, p. 988; Édouard Clunet, 'Les Criminels de guerre devant le Reichsgericht à Leipzig', *Journal du Droit International*, 48 (1921), pp. 440–7; Willis, *Prologue to Nuremberg*, pp. 136–7.

107 MAE, Paris, Série Z, Europe, Allemagne 1918–29, 575: 'Notes du secrétaire français prises au cours de la réunion tenue le vendredi 10 août 1921 [. . .] Quai d'Orsay' (esp. for the outrage of the Belgian Prime Minister, Jaspar, at the German conduct of the Leipzig trials); *DBFP*, First Series, vol. 15, appendix 2, document 103 (British Secretary's notes of Allied Conference [. . .] August 13 1921); Willis, *Prologue to Nuremberg*, p. 140.

108 MAE, Paris, Série Z, Europe, Allemagne 1918–29, 576, reply by Briand to president of Association des Camarades de Combat, 16 August 1921; reply to Anciens Prisonniers de Guerre des Associations Normandes, Bretonnes, Perchoises, Sarthoises, et Mayennaises, 17 September 1921; petition of Ligue Souvenez-Vous, 9 December 1921.

109 MAE, Paris, Série Z, Europe, Allemagne 1918–29, 577, dossier on the 'Commission des Coupables', 7 January 1922; Willis, *Prologue to Nuremberg*, p. 140.

110 Willis, *Prologue to Nuremberg*, p. 141. The French embassy in Berlin considered that 'for once' German press opinion was united in rejecting renewed extradition, with even *Vorwärts* considering it a 'political aberration' (MAE, Paris, Série Z, Europe, Allemagne 1918–29, 577, French embassy to Paris, 15 January 1922).

111 MAE, Paris, Série Z, Europe, Allemagne 1919–29, 577, telegram from consul, Leipzig, to French embassy, Berlin, 9 March 1922.

112 MAE, Paris, Série Z, Europe, Allemagne 1918–29, 579, petition of Ligue Souvenez-

Vous, demanding the implementation of the Inter-Allied Commission's resolution by the ambassadors' conference, 11 July 1922; *Bulletin de la Ligue Souvenez-Vous*, January 1923, p. 2.

113 *DBFP*, First Series, vol. 20, document 26, p. 530 (Sir P. Cheetham, Paris, to Balfour, 2 August 1922), on Conference of Ambassadors on 2 August, which agreed to the British compromise counterproposals; PAAA, Bonn, R 26578, memorandum Wendschuch, 23 August 1925, p. 7, for the note informing the German government of the new Allied policy. See also Willis, *Prologue to Nuremberg*, pp. 141–2, and Schwengler, *Völkerrecht*, pp. 351–2.

114 MAE, Série Z, Europe, Allemagne 1918–29, 576, circular 'Jugement des coupables de guerre', 13 September 1921; Clunet, 'Les Criminels de guerre devant le Reichsgericht', p. 446.

115 Willis, *Prologue to Nuremberg*, pp. 141–4.

116 PAAA, Bonn, R 26578, memorandum Wendschuch, 3 August 1925, pp. 8–12. A list of 35 of those accused by the Belgian courts-martial, with sentences passed on some, can be found at CPHDC, Moscow, 1256-1-13, fol. 59–89.

117 BA, Berlin, R 3003/ORA/RG, Reich Prosecutor's files.

118 PAAA, Bonn, R 26578, memorandum Wendschuch, 3 August 1925, pp. 8–12.

119 The officers concerned were Lieutenant-General Albert von Berrer (commander of the 31st Infantry Division), Brigadier-General Clauß (commander of the 6th Bavarian Infantry Brigade), Colonel Hucker (commander of IR 166), and several other officers of IR 137, 160, and 166 (HStA-MA, Stuttgart, M660, NL Berrer, book 46: cutting from an unnamed, undated newspaper). Berrer had in fact been killed in combat in 1917. The Reichsgericht examination is not properly documented in this file.

120 BA, Berlin, R 3003/ORA/RG bJ 307/20, vol. 2, fol. 155, transcript of note from German embassy, Brussels, 9 May 1925.

121 HStA, Dresden, Zeitgeschichtliche Sammlung 78, war diary Meister, including decision of the Reichsgericht, 11 December 1925. The files of the Reich Prosecutor's office show that Meister was placed outside prosecution on 27 November 1925 (BA, Berlin R 3003/ORA/RG, bJ 307/20, vol. 2, fol. 159).

122 Major-General Waldemar Richter, commander of Field Artillery Regiment 28; Major-General Erich Wagner, commander of Field Artillery Regiment 64; Lieutenant-General Gustav von der Decken, commander of IR 100; Lieutenant-General Mathias Hoch, commander of IR 103; Lieutenant-General Count Vitzthum von Eckstädt, commander of IR 108; and Lieutenant-General Friedrich von der Decken, commander of IR 134.

123 Joseph Hubert and Joseph Neujean, *Rossignol. Les drames de l'invasion allemande dans le Luxembourg belge* (1922; new edn Tamines, 1938), pp. 131–2; PAAA, Bonn, R 26279, Widmann to König, Schuldreferat, Foreign Ministry, 17 April 1931, with undated memorandum by Widmann.

124 Willis, *Prologue to Nuremberg*, p.145.

125 PAAA, Bonn, R 26578, memorandum Wendschuch, 3 August 1925, p. 8. Cf. Schwengler, *Völkerrecht*, p. 359. Willis, *Prologue to Nuremberg*, p. 146, has a slightly different formulation, viz that 861 of 901 cases were declared *nolle prosequi*.

126 Willis, *Prologue to Nuremberg*, p. 146. This decision was not made public.

127 Most forcefully argued for the case of Germany, by Bessel, *Germany after the First World War*, pp. 254–84.

128   MAE, Paris, Série Z, Europe, Allemagne 1918–29, 578, French ambassador, London, to Minister of Foreign Affairs, Paris, 'Au sujet des coupables de guerre', 16 May 1922. The ambassador's view was informed by his dealings with the senior Foreign Office official, Sir Eyre Crowe.

129   British law officers had determined by February 1920 that, though dealt with harshly, Cavell had been legally executed by the Germans, and she was eliminated from the British list of German war crimes (Willis, *Prologue to Nuremberg*, p. 128). The bust in St Martin's Place, London, testified to the continuing cult of Edith Cavell as the embodiment of heroic British womanhood. Yet the inscriptions on the statue ('Humanity', 'Devotion', 'Fortitude', and 'Sacrifice'), and the tone of the inaugural ceremony, were free of overt hatred and antagonism towards Germany (*The Times*, 17 October 1920, p. 10, for the statue; ibid., 18 March, p. 13, for the ceremony, and p. 17, editorial).

130   Keynes, *Economic Consequences*, pp. 250–1; Robert Skidelsky, *John Maynard Keynes: Hopes Betrayed 1883–1920* (London, 1983; new edn, 1992), pp. 393–4.

131   Jean-Jacques Becker and Serge Berstein, *Victoire et frustration, 1914–1929* (Paris, 1990), p. 155.

132   French Commission, reports 10–12 (Paris, 1919).

133   E.g. *Les Atrocités allemandes pendant la guerre 1914–1918. Rapports officiels. Die deutschen Greueltaten während des Weltkrieges 1914–1918. Nach den amtlichen Berichten* (Paris, n.d., but 1919); anon., *Culture. Les crimes allemands. Kultur. Die deutschen Verbrechen* (Paris, Nancy, Strasbourg, 1919).

134   *Bulletin de la Ligue Souvenez-Vous* (BDIC, Paris), especially running front page extract from Clemenceau's verdict on Leipzig (for quotation), and 'Faut-il haïr l'Allemagne?' ('Is it Necessary to Hate Germany?'), in *Bulletin*, July 1924, p. 7. The participating organizations included the right-wing Ligue des Patriotes and Ligue des Chefs de Section, but also the mainstream Republican Ligue de l'Enseignement.

135   Alexandre Mérignhac and E. Lémonon, *Le Droit des gens et la guerre de 1914–1918* (2 vols, Paris, 1921). The conclusion stated the case against Germany and described the process to prosecute war criminals from the end of the war to the eve of the Leipzig trials (pp. 539–673). The same broad line was taken by the leading French periodical on international law, the *Journal du Droit International*.

136   E.g. Georges d'Ostoya, *Le Livre des atrocités allemandes d'après les rapports officiels* (Paris, 1920), which was a new edition of a wartime illustrated work drawn very loosely from the official reports; or the equally bloodcurdling drawings by Maurice Neumont, also well known for his wartime drawings of 'German atrocities', in Henri d'Orcines, *Leurs exploits* (Étampes, n.d., but 1919).

137   E.g. Lucien Normand, *Le Châtiment des crimes allemands* (Paris, 1919) (Ligue des Patriotes), which argued that severe reparations were the price of Germany's collective responsibility for the wartime crimes.

138   Jacques Bainville, *Les Conséquences politiques de la paix* (Paris, 1920).

139   Antoine Prost, *Les Anciens Combattants et la société française, 1914–1939* (3 vols, Paris, 1977), vol. 3, *Mentalités et idéologies*, p. 78; Annette Becker, *Les Monuments aux morts. Mémoire de la grande guerre* (Paris, 1988).

140   Annette Becker finds little evidence of direct representation of civilian victims but plenty of evidence of the redemptive *poilu* for the Nord ('D'une guerre à l'autre. Mémoire de l'occupation et de la résistance: 1914–1945', *Revue du Nord*, 306, 1994, pp. 453–65). She confirms the complementarity of civilian suffering and military

triumph more generally in *Les Monuments aux morts*, pp. 77–9. For the evidence on the Ardennes, where German atrocities were represented on monuments, see Jean-Pierre Marby, 'Les Monuments aux morts ardennais de la grande guerre', *Revue historique ardennaise*, 22 (1987), pp. 137–53. For the Meurthe-et-Moselle, see AD Meurthe-et-Moselle, 1M1670, Hommages publics, inaugurations (Badonviller), with an account from *L'Indépendant de Lunéville*, 3 October 1929, and chapter 10 below.

141 Jacques Néré, *The Foreign Policy of France from 1914 to 1945* (1974; English translation, London, 1975), p. 56, and John Keiger, *Raymond Poincaré* (Cambridge, 1997), pp. 240–73.

142 Henry Salomon, *Les Allemands peints par eux-mêmes* (Dunkirk, 1921), pp. vii–xi (p. xi for the quotation).

143 Édouard Bonnefous, *Histoire politique de la troisième république*, vol. 3, *L'après-guerre (1919–1924)* (Paris, 1968), pp. 326–8. The resolution of the Communist deputy, Paul Vaillant-Couturier, was defeated by 487 votes to 65. The Chamber of Deputies voted that Viviani's speech be posted in every commune in France, a distinction reserved for speeches concerning the 'state of the nation'.

144 Willis, *Prologue to Nuremberg*, p. 143. The British refused to participate in the attempt to extradite the Crown Prince.

145 Commission d'enquête sur les violations des règles du droit des gens, des lois et des coutumes de la guerre, *Rapports sur les attentats commis par les troupes allemandes pendant l'invasion et l'occupation de la Belgique*, vol. 1, part 1 (Brussels and Liège, 1922), pp. xiv–xxv (p. xxiv for the quotation). Volume 1 consisted of two parts which covered in more detail the same incidents as the 22 reports of the wartime commission. The second volume covered the mistreatment of civilian and military prisoners (1923), the third the economic exploitation of Belgium (1921), and the fourth was on the legal measures imposed by the German occupation (1923). A pamphlet sumarized the findings of the Second Commission, Baron Albéric Rolin, *Les Allemands en Belgique 1914–1918. Conclusions de l'enquête officielle belge* (Liège, 1925), esp. pp. 18–20 (on German military doctrine).

146 Jean Schmitz and Norbert Nieuwland, *Documents pour servir à l'histoire de l'invasion allemande dans les provinces de Namur et de Luxembourg* (7 vols, Brussels, 1919–24).

147 Ibid., Vol. 1, p. v.

148 Jean Chot, *La Furie allemande dans l'entre Sambre-et-Meuse (journées des 23, 24, 25 et 26 août 1914)* (Charleroi, 1919). See chapter 8 above.

149 Godefroid Kurth, *Le Guet-apens prussien en Belgique* (Paris and Brussels, 1919), p. xii.

150 A. Lemaire, *La Tragédie de Tamines (21, 22 et 23 août 1914)* (Tamines, 1919), pp. 110, 115. Lemaire was responding to the use made by Richard Graßhoff's wartime brochure for the German War Ministry of the statement by Graf, an Austrian inhabitant of Tamines.

151 *Collection 'le cri des martyrs'. Enquêtes officieuses sur les brigandages allemands en Belgique, lors de l'invasion d'août 1914. Publication hebdomadaire* (Dinant, n.d., but 1919–20); *Le Martyre de Dinant* (5th edn, Dinant, 1920), pp. 7–8.

152 For the commemoration of the events of Dinant, see the remarkable study by Axel Tixhon, 'Le Souvenir des massacres du 23 août 1914 à Dinant. Étude des commémorations organisées durant l'entre-deux-guerres', Licence dissertation, Université Catholique de Louvain-la-Neuve, 1995. The authors would like to thank Axel Tixhon for his generosity in giving them a copy of his work. See also Édouard Gérard, *La Mort de Dinant. Histoire d'un crime (21, 23, 24 et 25 août 1914)* (Dinant, 1919), trans-

lated into English as *The War in Belgium, 1914–1918: The Atrocities at Dinant* (Brussels, 1919).

153 *Le Petit Moniteur de la Région de Dinant*, 23 August 1921.

154 Peukert, *Weimar Republic*, pp. 66–77.

155 Alexander von Kluck, *Der Marsch auf Paris und die Marneschlacht 1914* (Berlin, 1920), pp. 23–4; Fr. Max Kircheisen (ed.), *Des Generalobersten Frhrn. v. Hausen Erinnerungen an den Marnefeldzug 1914. Mit einer einleitenden kritischen Studie* (Leipzig, 1920; 2nd edn, 1922), pp. 129, 138–9. On Ludendorff, see chapter 2 above.

156 Kriegsministerium und Oberste Heeresleitung, *Die deutsche Kriegführung und das Völkerrecht. Beiträge zur Schuldfrage* (Berlin, 1919), translated into French as *Le Commandement en chef allemand pendant la guerre et le droit des gens. Étude sur la question des culpabilités* (Berlin, 1919).

157 Otto von Stülpnagel, *Die Wahrheit über die deutschen Kriegsverbrechen. Die Anklagen der Verbandsmächte in Gegenüberstellung zu ihren eigenen Taten* (Berlin, 1920; 4th edn, 1921).

158 BA, Berlin, R 3003 Generalia/51, fol. 25, Stülpnagel to Reich Prosecutor Leipzig, 12 September 1920.

159 Cited in Wieland, *Belgien 1914*, pp. 109–12.

160 Bernhard Schwertfeger, *Belgische Landesverteidigung und Bürgerwacht (garde civique) 1914. Im amtlichen Auftrag bearbeitet* (Berlin, 1920), republished as *Die Grundlagen des belgischen Franktireurkrieges 1914. Das deutsche amtliche Material* (Berlin, n.d., but 1920); PAAA, Bonn, R 26432, Schwertfeger to Ministerialdirektor (Schwendemann, head of the Schuldreferat), 30 January 1930. Schwertfeger received a stipend of 500 marks a month on condition that he wrote five articles. This was no trivial amount, being almost three times the average industrial worker's annual wage that year of 2,131 marks.

161 Wieland, *Belgien 1914*, pp. 106–7.

162 BA, Koblenz, NL 15/180, Schwertfeger to Direktor Schmidt, Verlag Reimar Hobbing, Berlin, 14 February 1920.

163 Wieland, *Belgien 1914*, pp. 107–9. One positive review was in the *Deutsche (Norddeutsche) Allgemeine Zeitung*, 8 April 1920.

164 BA, Koblenz, NL 15/402 (Schwertfeger papers). For the lecture series, see *ADAP*, series A, vol. 2, document 193, pp. 350–1: Haniel von Haimhausen, Under-Secretary, 13 October 1919. The lectures were given as part of a series on 'war guilt' and war crimes.

165 BA, Koblenz, NL 15/402, lecture by Schwertfeger to staff of the Foreign Ministry, 11 March 1920, pp. 7–8.

166 Ibid., 11 March 1920, pp. 17–18.

167 BA, Koblenz, NL 15/402, lecture by Schwertfeger to staff of the Foreign Ministry, 12 March 1920, pp. 19–21.

168 On the countercharges, see Schwengler, *Völkerrecht*, pp. 302–3. Stülpnagel was the author of the list (BA, Berlin, R 3003 Generalia/51, fol. 25, Stülpnagel to Reich Prosecutor Leipzig, 12 September 1921). On the front organization, the Arbeitsausschuß Deutscher Verbände, see Heinemann, *Die verdrängte Niederlage*, pp. 16, 120–54.

169 *Tägliche Rundschau*, 6 March 1920. Cf. *Kreuzzeitung*, 6 April 1921, evening edition.

170 August Gallinger, *Gegenrechnung. Verbrechen an kriegsgefangenen Deutschen* (Leipzig and Munich, 1921); translated into English as *The Countercharge: The*

Matter of War Criminals from the German Side (Munich, 1922), and into Swedish, Spanish, and Japanese. See also Willis, *Prologue to Nuremberg*, p. 131.

171 Gallinger, *Gegenrechnung*, pp. 143, 146.

172 Keith Nelson, 'The "Black Horror on the Rhine": Race as a Factor in Post-World War I Diplomacy', *Journal of Modern History*, 42/4 (1970), pp. 606–27; Berlau, *The German Social Democratic Party*, pp. 305–7. The French government avoided using colonial troops in the occupation of the Ruhr in 1923 so as not to give more propaganda hostages to the German government.

173 Werner Maser, *Hitler's Letters and Notes* (1973; English translation, London, 1976), pp. 270–1. The phrase was 'moralische Entwaffnung'. Hitler's notes read: 'And moral disarmament./ destruction of the "national sense"/ of national pride/ Extradition (War Criminals)'.

174 Bessel, *Germany after the First World War*, pp. 258–9.

175 *Vorwärts*, 7 February 1920, cited in Schwengler, *Völkerrecht*, p. 309; Remmele to Chancellor, 7 February 1920, cited in ibid., p. 310.

176 Karl Kautsky, *Wie der Weltkrieg entstand. Dargestellt nach dem Aktenmaterial des Deutschen Auswärtigen Amts* (Berlin, 1919), p. 159. Significant sections of the brochure were published in *The Times*, 29 November 1919, and *Nieuwe Rotterdamsche Courant*, 29 November. Kautsky's work was highly damaging to the record of the Imperial government, and the Foreign Ministry managed to delay its publication from March to November 1919, until the peace conference was safely concluded (Hahn, 'The German Foreign Ministry', pp. 53–5; Heinemann, *Die verdrängte Niederlage*, pp. 74–8).

177 Gregor Huch, 'Die belgische Schande. Ein Briefwechsel aus Kriegszeit und ein Nachwort', *Der Deutsche*, 15 September 1919, pp. 13–72.

178 Walter Oehme (ed.), *Ein Bekenntnis deutscher Schuld. Beiträge zur deutschen Kriegsführung* (Berlin, 1920), see esp. pp. 63–7.

179 Oehme, *Bekenntnis*, p. 65.

180 Karl Holl and Wolfram Wette (eds), *Pazifismus in der Weimarer Republik. Beiträge zur historischen Friedensforschung* (Paderborn, 1981), pp. 47–50.

181 Friedrich Wilhelm Foerster, *Zur Beurteilung der deutschen Kriegsführung* (Berlin, 1921).

182 Lilli Jannasch, *Untaten des preußisch-deutschen Militarismus* (Wiesbaden, 1924), translated into English as *German Militarism at Work: A Collection of Documents* (London, 1926), and into French as *Les Atrocités allemandes de la grande guerre d'après des documents authentiques* (Paris, 1925). The police in Frankfurt suspected Jannasch of espionage. She was co-signatory of an appeal of the Franco-German League for the Rights of Man, and in October 1925 published 'Thoughts on Prussian Militarism' in the pacifist journal *Die Menschheit*, prompting the police to search the editor's house (PAAA, Bonn, R 26578, Police President, department 1A to Stieve, Foreign Ministry, 1 April 1926).

10 German atrocities and the politics of memory

1 For the Société d'Études, see Christophe Prochasson, *Les Intellectuels, le socialisme et la guerre 1900–1938* (Paris, 1993), pp. 162–7, 212–13 ; Emmanuel Naquet, 'La Société d'études documentaires et critiques sur la guerre. Ou la naissance d'une minorité pacifiste au sein de la Ligue des Droits de l'Homme', in 'S'engager pour la paix dans la

France de l'entre-deux-guerres', *Matériaux pour l'histoire de notre temps* (Paris), 30 (1993), pp. 6–10. For the UDC, see Marvin Swartz, *The Union of Democratic Control in British Politics during the First World War* (Oxford, 1971).

2 Georges Demartial, *La Mobilisation des consciences. La guerre de 1914* (Paris, 1922; enlarged edn, 1927), pp. 7–11, 15–29.

3 Ibid., pp. 28–9.

4 Ibid., pp. 133–4.

5 Ibid., pp. 252–79.

6 See, for example, the *Journal of the Union of Democratic Control* for a series of articles in 1916 exposing Allied atrocity tales.

7 Martin Ceadel, *Pacifism in Britain 1914–1945: The Defining of a Faith* (Oxford, 1980), pp. 80–3.

8 Arthur Ponsonby, *Now is the Time: An Appeal for Peace* (London, 1925), p. 30.

9 Arthur Ponsonby, *Falsehood in Wartime: Containing an Assortment of Lies Circulated Throughout the Nations During the Great War* (London, 1928).

10 Ibid., pp. 128–34.

11 *The Times*, 10 May 1915 (original report) and 15 May 1915 (letters to the editor).

12 Ponsonby, *Falsehood in Wartime*, pp. 102–13. See also 'Kadaver', *The Nation*, 31 October 1925, pp. 171–2, for a history of the legend; cf. Michael L. Sanders and Philip M. Taylor, *British Propaganda during the First World War, 1914–18* (London, 1982), pp. 146–8

13 Ponsonby, *Falsehood in Wartime*, p. 142.

14 The call for a 'cultural demobilization' was implicit, rather than explicit, in Arthur Ponsonby's 'Peace Letter', a campaign refusing 'to support any government which resorts to arms', which garnered 128,770 signatures in 1927 (*The Times*, 9 December 1927; Ceadel, *Pacifism in Britain*, p. 80).

15 The Communist paper *L'Humanité* and the Socialist *Le Populaire* both condemned the Allied attempt to prosecute alleged German war criminals at Leipzig and else- where, and the Communists, in particular, alleged that a French general (Martin de Bouillon) had, like Stenger, given an order to shoot German prisoners (Sixte Quenin, 'A Leipzig et à Paris. Chacun défend ses assassins', *Le Populaire*, 14 July 1921).

16 John Keiger, *Raymond Poincaré* (Cambridge, 1997), pp. 198–9; Édouard Bonnefous, *Histoire politique de la troisième république* (8 vols, Paris, 1965–86), vol. 3, *L'Après- guerre (1919–1924)* (1968), pp. 326–8.

17 *Appel aux consciences. Vers la paix. Avec un avant-propos de Victor Margueritte* (Paris, 1925), p. 30.

18 Patrick de Villepin, 'La Revue *Évolution* et le pacifisme révisionniste (1926–1933)', *Matériaux pour l'histoire de notre temps*, 30 (1993), pp. 11–13; 'La conscience universelle', manifesto in the first issue of *L'Évolution*, 15 January 1926, pp. 1–6. The French appeal inspired a similar British appeal, signed by leading pacifists including J. M. Keynes, H. N. Brailsford, Bertrand Russell, and V. Woolf (*L'Évolution*, 15 January 1926, pp. 33–6).

19 Norman Ingram, *The Politics of Dissent: Pacifism in France 1919–1939* (Oxford, 1991), pp. 14–15, for the term 'old-style pacifism' and the distinction in France. For the British distinction in terms of absolute 'pacifism' (a neologism of the author's) and a more qualified 'pacifism', see Ceadel, *Pacifism in Britain*, pp. 9–17.

20 Jean-Jacques Becker and Serge Berstein, *Histoire de l'anti-communisme en France* (2 vols, Paris, 1987), vol. 1, *1917–1940*, pp. 40–1; Philip Knightley, *The First Casualty:*

The War Correspondent as Hero, Propagandist and Myth Maker (London, 1982), pp. 140–1. On Lloyd George's attitude to Russia, see Kenneth O. Morgan, *Consensus and Disunity: The Lloyd George Coalition Government 1918–1922* (Oxford, 1979), pp. 109–18.

21 E.g. August Gallinger, *The Countercharge: The Matter of War Criminals from the German Side* (Munich, 1922), pp. 7–8. The theme of brutality in the colonies had been used by both sides in the 'war of words' during the war. For British examples, see *German Atrocities and the Breaches of the Rules of War in Africa*, Cd 8306 (London, 1916) and *Reports on Treatment by the Germans of British Prisoners and Natives in German East Africa 1917–18*, Cd 8689 (London, 1918).

22 Derek Sayer, 'British Reaction to the Amritsar Massacre, 1919–1920', *Past and Present*, 131 (1991), pp. 130–64.

23 'The Character of the Irish Terror', *The Nation*, 1 January 1921. In 1921, the *Nation* devoted far more space to British military misconduct in Ireland than to the Leipzig trials. See also the Labour Party, *Report of the Labour Commission to Ireland* (London, 1921). The left-wing weekly, the *New Statesman*, compared British repression in Ireland with the Germans in Belgium ('The Spokesman of Civilization', *New Statesman*, 16 October 1920, pp. 36–7). See also David Fitzpatrick, *The Two Irelands, 1912–1939* (Oxford, 1998), pp. 89–93, and Charles Townshend, *The British Campaign in Ireland, 1919–1921: The Development of Political and Military Policies* (Oxford, 1978), pp. 159–60.

24 Ernest N. Bennett (ed. and trans.), *The German Army in Belgium: The White Book of May 1915. With a Foreword on Military Reprisals in Belgium and Ireland* (London, 1921), pp. xi–xii (introduction); Demartial, *La Mobilisation des consciences*, p. 274 (details on Bennett).

25 Richard Gombin, *Les Socialistes et la guerre. La S.F.I.O. et la politique étrangère française entre les deux guerres mondiales* (Paris and The Hague, 1970), pp. 22–84.

26 Jacques Néré, *The Foreign Policy of France from 1914 to 1945* (1974; English translation, London, 1975), pp. 91–2.

27 Georges Bonnefous, *Histoire politique de la troisième république*, vol. 4, *Cartel des gauches et union nationale (1924–1929)* (1973), pp. 186–7.

28 The evolution of the press bore this out. Of the four mass-circulation national papers, all of which supported Poincaré's foreign policy in the early 1920s, three backed Briand in the later 1920s, with only *Le Journal* favouring the strict application of Versailles (Claude Bellanger et al., *Histoire générale de la presse française* (5 vols), vol. 3, *De 1871 à 1940* (Paris, 1972), pp. 512–27).

29 Antoine Prost (ed.), *Les Anciens Combattants 1914–1940* (Paris, 1977), p. 65.

30 Antoine Prost, *Les Anciens Combattants et la société française 1914–1939* (3 vols, Paris, 1977), vol. 3, *Mentalités et idéologies*, pp. 77–119.

31 Adrian Gregory, *The Silence of Memory: Armistice Day 1914–1946* (Oxford and Providence, 1994), pp. 118–48.

32 Paul Fussell, *The Great War and Modern Memory* (New York and London, 1975), pp. 3–35; Samuel Hynes, *A War Imagined: The First World War and English Culture* (London, 1990), pp. 423–63.

33 Robert Graves, *Goodbye to All That* (1929; new edn, Oxford and Providence, 1995), pp. 69, 167–8). On Graves, see Fussell, *The Great War and Modern Memory*, pp. 216–17.

34 C. E. Montague, *Disenchantment* (1922; new edn, 1940), p. 119. Montague had been a

journalist with the *Manchester Guardian*. On the discrediting of the press in Britain, see also Fussell, *The Great War and Modern Memory*, p. 316. For the same point in relation to France, see Thomas Ferenczi, 'Les Transformations du journalisme', in Sylvie Caucanas and Rémy Cazals (eds), *Traces de 14–18* (Carcassonne, 1997), pp. 59–66, at pp. 59–60.

35 Jean Galtier-Boissière, *Histoire de la guerre*, part 1, *Le Crapouillot*, August 1932, pp. 91–3. Galtier-Boissière drew heavily on Ponsonby's evidence.

36 Philip Gibbs, *Realities of War* (London, 1929), pp. 329–30. Gibbs, it seems, wanted to have it both ways: he also conceded (p. 327) that not all the stories of atrocities had been faked by propaganda. For the wartime account, see Philip Gibbs, *The Soul of the War* (London, 1915), pp. 129–56.

37 Robert Graves and Alan Hodge, *The Long Week-End: A Social History of Great Britain 1918–1939* (London, 1940), pp. 14–17.

38 Ulrich Heinemann, *Die verdrängte Niederlage. Politische Öffentlichkeit und Kriegsschuldfrage in der Weimarer Republik* (Göttingen, 1983), pp. 231–3. J. Michael Sproule, *Propaganda and Democracy: The American Experience of Media and Mass Persuasion* (Cambridge, 1997), pp. 37–52.

39 Peter Novick, *That Noble Dream: The 'Objectivity Question' and the American Historical Profession* (New York, 1988), pp. 207–24; Ellen L. Evans and Joseph O. Baylen, 'History as Propaganda: The German Foreign Ministry and the "Enlightenment" of American Historians on the War-Guilt Question, 1930–1933', in Keith Wilson (ed.), *Forging the Collective Memory: Government and International Historians through Two World Wars* (Oxford and Providence, 1996), pp. 151–77.

40 Harold Lasswell, *Propaganda Technique in World War I* (new edn, Cambridge, Mass., 1971), pp. 77–101; Sproule, *Propaganda and Democracy*, pp. 68–9.

41 James M. Read, *Atrocity Propaganda 1914–1918* (New Haven, 1941).

42 Adolf Hitler, *Mein Kampf* (1925–6; English translation, London, 1969), pp. 161–9.

43 *Akten zur deutschen auswärtigen Politik* (*ADAP*), series B, vol. 16, document 209, memorandum Schwendemann (Schuldreferat), 9 February 1931. A very favourable review of the book had appeared in the innocentist journal *Der Weg zur Freiheit*, 1 July 1928, pp. 201–4. Ponsonby's book was published as *Lügen in Kriegszeiten* (Berlin, 1930), and reissued in 1931. A German translation of the eighth British edition (1940) was published as *Lügen im Kriege. Eine Auswahl von Lügen, die während des Weltkrieges bei den Völkern in Umlauf waren* (Berlin, 1941).

44 Villepin, 'La Revue *Évolution*', p. 12; Holger H. Herwig, 'Clio Deceived: Patriotic Self-Censorship in Germany after the Great War', in Wilson, *Forging the Collective Memory*, pp. 87–127, at pp. 100–4. Margueritte was connected with the official German innocentist organization, the Zentralstelle für Erforschung der Kriegsursachen (Heinemann, *Die verdrängte Niederlage*, p. 330, n. 83, and pp. 95–7). Initially, Margueritte took the semi-official German revisionist periodical, *Kriegsschuldfrage*, edited by Alfred von Wegerer, as a model for *Évolution*. The German Schuldreferat considered that the review had been founded with their money (*ADAP*, series B, vol. 16, document 26, memorandum de Haas, 28 October 1930: 'Financial commitments of the Schuldreferat', p. 60). Overall, the Schuldreferat contributed a massive 2.8 million francs to *Évolution* (Villepin, 'La Revue *Évolution*', pp. 11, 13; Heinemann, *Die verdrängte Niederlage*, pp. 113–15).

45 Jon Jacobson, *Locarno Diplomacy: Germany and the West 1925–1929* (Princeton, 1972).

46 For Belgium and Locarno, see Jane K. Miller, *Belgian Foreign Policy between Two Wars, 1919–1940* (New York, 1951), pp. 190–2. Hermann Pünder, State Secretary in the Reich Chancellery, told a meeting of ministers on 20 September 1926 that 'no country in the world is at the present moment a better friend of Germany than Belgium' (*Akten der Reichskanzlei. Weimarer Republik. Die Kabinette Marx III und IV. 17. Mai 1926 bis 29. Januar 1927. 29. Januar 1927 bis 29. Juni 1928*, vol. 1, ed. Günter Abramowski (Boppard 1988), document 83, p. 215).

47 *ADAP*, series B, vol. 16, document 209, memorandum Schwendemann, 9 February 1931, p. 525.

48 PAAA, Bonn, R 26578, Reichswehr Minister to Foreign Ministry, 22 February 1926.

49 PAAA, Bonn, R 26578, Reichswehr Ministry, Central Office for Violations of International Law in the Truppenamt (Zentralstelle für Völkerrechtsverletzungen) to Foreign Ministry, Press Department, and ibid., Reichswehr Ministry, Truppenamt, to Foreign Ministry, both 4 January 1926; emphasis in the original. The General Staff having been dissolved under the terms of the Treaty of Versailles, the Truppenamt was its *de facto* successor.

50 PAAA, Bonn, R 26578, Reichswehr Ministry, Central Office for Violations of International Law in the Truppenamt, to Stieve, Schuldreferat, Foreign Ministry, 21 April 1926; *Die Legende von den abgehackten Kinderhänden* (1926).

51 See chapter 9 above.

52 *Das Werk des Untersuchungsausschusses der Verfassunggebenden Deutschen Nationalversammlung und des Deutschen Reichstags 1919–1928*, ed. Johannes Bell, Walter Schücking, and B. Widmann, third series, *Völkerrecht im Weltkrieg*, 4 vols in 5 parts; vol. 2, *Der belgische Volkskrieg* (Berlin, 1927), p. 33.

53 See chapter 4 above.

54 *ADAP*, series A, vol. 5, document 202: memorandum Weber (representative of the Foreign Ministry in the Third Subcommittee) 28 November 1921, pp. 413–15. Cf. *ADAP*, series A, vol. 6, document 7, Foreign Minister Rathenau to Reichstag Deputy Fleischer, 10 March 1922, pp. 14–16, with identical passages; emphasis added. See also Heinemann, *Die verdrängte Niederlage*, p. 193. This report was published in May 1929 as part of the first series on the prehistory of the war. Cf. BA Berlin, R 1501/25810.

55 According to a leading member of the subcommittee, and secretary of the overall Reichstag Commission, Eugen Fischer-Baling, 'Der Untersuchungsausschuß für die Schuldfragen des ersten Weltkrieges', in Alfred Herrmann (ed.), *Aus Geschichte und Politik. Festschrift zum 70. Geburtstag von Ludwig Bergstraesser* (Düsseldorf, 1954), p. 137.

56 *Der belgische Volkskrieg*, pp. 135–9.

57 Papers of Peter Schöller, in possession of Frau Dr H. Ditt, Münster, Fischer-Baling to Schöller, 4 September 1957. On the conversion of the parliamentary inquiry into a test of German foreign policy, see Heinemann, *Die verdrängte Niederlage*, p. 197.

58 For the Reichstag debate of 18 May 1927 on the third report on international law in the war, see Heinemann, *Die verdrängte Niederlage*, pp. 202–3; MAE, Paris, Série Y, Affaires internationales, 1918–40', 93 (Violations du droit des gens), French ambassador, Berlin, to Briand, 18 and 19 May 1927, with account of Bell's presentation of the report to the Reichstag; National Archives (Washington, D.C.), State Department, 367 763.72116/611–80, report by the US ambassador, Schurman, to the State Department on Bell's speech and its reception, 19 May 1927; Hubert Frank, 'Kriegsreichstag 1927',

Die Menschheit, 27 May 1927.

59   Lothar Wieland, *Belgien 1914. Die Frage des belgischen 'Franktireurkrieges' und die deutsche öffentliche Meinung von 1914 bis 1936* (Frankfurt, Berne, New York, 1984), pp. 130–1; Heinemann, *Die verdrängte Niederlage*, pp. 197–8.

60   *Anklage und Widerlegung. Taschenbuch zur Kriegsschuldfrage* ('Accusations and Refutations: Pocket-book on the War Guilt Question'). Heinemann, *Die verdrängte Niederlage*, p. 203.

61   Heinemann, *Die verdrängte Niederlage*, pp. 202–3.

62   *Vorwärts*, 19 May 1927.

63   Frank, 'Kriegsreichstag 1927'.

64   F. von der Marwitz, 'Die preußischen Kriegsverbrechen', *Die Menschheit*, 3 June 1927.

65   *Rapport présenté aux Chambres Législatives par M. le Ministre des Affaires Étrangères sur certaines affirmations de la Commission d'Enquête du Reichstag au sujet d'une prétendue guerre de francs-tireurs en Belgique* (Brussels, Chambre des Représentants, no. 321, séance du 13 juillet 1927). It was one of three reports, the other two concerning the violation of Belgian neutrality and the deportation of Belgian labour.

66   *Rapport présenté aux Chambres Législatives*, pp. 2–4.

67   Ibid., p. 5; cf. Belgian First Commission, 3rd report, p. 57.

68   *Rapport présenté aux Chambres Législatives*, p. 5.

69   Ibid., p. 9.

70   Quoted in the report of the American ambassador to the State Department, 19 May 1927, in National Archives (Washington, D.C.), State Department, 367 763.72116/611–680.

71   *Rapport présenté aux Chambres Législatives*, p. 16.

72   MAE, Paris, Série Y, Affaires internationales, 1918–40, 100, report of Herbette, French ambassador in Brussels, 24 July 1927; Paul Hymans, *Mémoires*, (2 vols, Brussels, 1958), vol. 2, p. 591.

73   *Rapport présenté aux Chambres Législatives*, p. 15.

74   MAE, Paris, Série Y, Affaires internationales, 1918–40, 100, Herbette, French ambassador in Brussels, 'Enquête sur les francs-tireurs belges', 25 August 1927, on Belgian press reaction. *Le Peuple*, the Socialist daily, was the most enthusiastic supporter of Vandervelde's initiative. *Le Soir* was cautious, urging such an inquiry only under the aegis of the League of Nations.

75   Jules Destrée, 'Tribune libre', *Le Soir*, 24 September 1927.

76   MAE, Paris, Série Y, Affaires Internationales, 1918–40, 100, 'Enquête sur les francs-tireurs belges', for negative comment by the bulk of the Belgian press.

77   *ADAP*, series B, vol. 6, document 79, pp. 166–7 (note from Schubert to Belgian envoy in Berlin, 1 August 1927). Keller, the German ambassador, saw Vandervelde three weeks later, on 20 August, to express the German government's interest in his suggestion of an 'impartial commission of inquiry' (*Le Soir*, 21 August 1927).

78   *Deutsche Allgemeine Zeitung*, 20 August 1927. Cf. Wieland, *Belgien 1914*, pp. 146–8.

79   PAAA, Bonn, R 29138, fol. 22–4, unsigned memorandum for Secretary of State von Schubert, 22 July 1927.

80   *Le Soir*, 21 August 1927; Wieland, *Belgien 1914*, pp. 148–53.

81   MAE, Paris, Série Y, Affaires internationales, 1918–40, 100, report of Herbette, French ambassador in Brussels, to Paris, 25 July 1927. According to this, Jaspar, the Prime Minister, Brocqueville, who had been Prime Minister throughout the war and was now Minister of Defence, and Hymans, a member of the wartime government

who was now Minister for Justice, all opposed the idea of an international commission. For confirmation, see Hymans, *Mémoires*, vol. 2, pp. 585–94.

82 MAE, Paris, Série Y, Affaires internationales, 1918–40, 100, French ambassador to Paris, 30 August 1927, 'L'Enquête sur les francs-tireurs. Opinion du Nonce Apostolique'.

83 MAE, Paris, Série Y, Affaires internationales, 1918–40, 100, Berthelot, head of the French Ministry of Foreign Affairs, to French ambassador, Brussels, 27 August 1927 (asking him to convey this view to Vandervelde), and to French embassies in Prague, Rome and Warsaw, 5 September 1927, 'Commission d'enquête franco-belge'.

84 MAE, Paris, Série Y, Affaires internationales, 1918–40, 100, Victor Basch to Briand, 14 September 1927; Briand to Basch, 30 September 1927.

85 *DBFP*, series 1A, vol. 3, document 297: Lindsay to Chamberlain, 11 August 1927, pp. 517–18, extract from undated minute by Chamberlain.

86 Wieland, *Belgien 1914*, pp. 162–5.

87 *Le Temps*, 25 July 1927; AD Nord, M 145a, Orchies, 24 juillet 1927. Venue de M. Raymond Poincaré. For the events at Orchies in 1914, see chapter 3.

88 'Futile Propaganda', editorial in *The Times*, 2 August 1927, which endorsed Poincaré's speech at Orchies.

89 Hymans, *Mémoires*, vol. 2, p. 589.

90 Jacobson, *Locarno Diplomacy*, pp. 143–83, for German foreign policy priorities.

91 *L'Est républicain*, 1 October 1928.

92 AD Meurthe-et-Moselle, 1M 1670, Hommages publics, inaugurations (Badonviller), with an account from *L'Indépendant de Lunéville*, 3 October 1929. See also AD Meurthe-et-Moselle, 2R 147bis, Monuments aux morts, for lists of the monuments commemorating the invasion.

93 See chapter 9 above.

94 AD Meurthe-et-Moselle, 1M 670, Hommages publics, inaugurations: Nomény.

95 AD Meurthe-et-Moselle, WO/1683, Monuments aux morts; Gerbéviller, report of the Sub-Prefect of Lunéville to the Prefect, 21 October 1924.

96 AD Meurthe-et-Moselle, WO/1683, Monuments aux morts: Gerbéviller.

97 Joseph Hubert and Joseph Neujean, *Rossignol. Les Drames de l'invasion allemande dans le Luxembourg belge* (1922; new edn, Tamines, 1938), pp. 167–92; 'A la Mémoire des habitants de Rossignol', brochure produced for the inauguration of the monument, 1925 (BfZ, Stuttgart). The girl was Hortense Thiry.

98 Axel Tixhon, 'Le Souvenir des massacres du 23 août 1914 à Dinant. Étude des commémorations organisées durant l'entre-deux-guerres', Licence dissertation, Université Catholique de Louvain-la-Neuve, 1995, pp. 123–30, and Wieland, *Belgien 1914*, p. 153.

99 Tixhon, 'Le Souvenir des massacres du 23 août 1914', pp. 48–9.

100 *ADAP*, series B, vol. 6, pp. 248–50 (document 119); *Der Weg zur Freiheit*, 7/19 (1 October 1927), pp. 289, 292, 300.

101 Wieland, *Belgien 1914*, pp. 153–60. The right-wing *Hamburger Nachrichten* (25 August 1927) referred to 'a monument to slander' ('Der Verleumdung ein Denkmal'), saying that it represented a continuation of 13 years of Belgian atrocity propaganda.

102 *ADAP*, series B, vol. 6, document 170, p. 389, n. 3; Köpke to the German ambassador in Brussels, 10 September 1927, cited in Wieland, *Belgien 1914*, pp. 160–1.

103 *Der Weg zur Freiheit*, 7/19, 1 October 1927, for Hindenburg's speech; Gustav Stresemann, *Gustav Stresemann: His Diaries, Letters and Papers* (3 vols, 1933; English translation, London, 1940), vol. 3, pp. 212–15, for Hindenburg's speech and

Stresemann's response. Stresemann's views were published in *Le Matin*, 25 September 1927. See George Mosse, *Fallen Soldiers: Reshaping the Memory of the World Wars* (New York, 1990), pp. 96–7, for the Tannenberg monument.

104 P. Ladeuze, *Le Crime allemand contre l'université de Louvain. Les leçons de la guerre. (Discours prononcé au Grand Auditoire du Collège du Pape Adrien VI, à Louvain, le 21 janvier 1919, pour l'ouverture solennelle des cours de l'université de Louvain, après la grande guerre)* (Louvain, 1919), cited in *RBLDAG*, 3 (1926–7), pp. 167–8. For Ladeuze and the Vatican during the war, see chapter 7 above.

105 *RBLDAG*, 3 (1926–7), p. 225.

106 For secondary works on the Louvain controversy, see Wieland, *Belgien 1914*, pp. 187–213, and Wolfgang Schivelbusch, *Die Bibliothek von Löwen. Eine Episode aus der Zeit der Weltkriege* (Munich and Vienna, 1988). The following account also utilizes the papers of Nicholas Murray Butler in the Butler Library, Columbia University, reports by the French ambassador to Belgium in MAE, Paris, Série Y, Affaires internationales, 1918–40, 100, and contemporary Belgian publications. Butler headed the fund-raising committee, which used the Columbia alumni network, but Warren played the key organizational role (Butler papers, Warren to Butler, 10 January, and reply 12 January, 1922).

107 National Archives, Washington, D.C., State Department, M367, 763.72116, Whitney Warren to Herrick (US ambassador in Paris), 28 September 1914; Thomas B. Mott, *Myron T. Herrick, Friend of France: An Autobiographical Biography* (New York, 1929), pp. 190–1. Warren had been appointed a foreign associate of the Académie des Beaux-Arts in Paris in 1909 (Butler papers, correspondence, Butler to Warren, 3 November 1909).

108 For Mercier's role, see Pierre de Soete, *Furore teutonico, 1914–1929* (Brussels, n.d., but 1929 or 1930), p. 20.

109 Lucan, *Belli Civilis*, ed. A. E. Housman (Oxford, 1926), Book 1, lines 255–6 (p. 11). The authors are indebted to Dr Judith Mossman, Trinity College, Dublin, for tracing the origin of the term. In November 1913, the Belgian King Albert was told by the Kaiser and Moltke that war with France was inevitable; Moltke told him a German victory was absolutely certain, because on hearing the cry 'War against France' the German people would unleash a 'colossal' wave and the 'Furor Teutonicus' would smash everything in its path (Fritz Fischer, *War of Illusions: German Policies from 1911 to 1914* (1969; English translation, London, 1975), pp. 226–7).

110 MAE, Paris, Série Y, Affaires Internationales, 1918–40, 100, Herbette to Briand, 16 April 1928 (copy of letter); de Soete, *Furore teutonico*, p. 31; Butler papers, correspondence, Ladeuze to Nicholas Murray Butler, 7 December 1927, for similar sentiments.

111 *New York Times*, 8 October 1928. Butler hinted as early as 1925, in a letter to Simon Deploige who headed the Louvain end of the financial operation, that funding was getting harder (Butler papers, correspondence, Butler to Deploige, 2 December 1925). Cf. *RBLDAG*, 3 (1926–7), pp. 103–4.

112 MAE, Paris, Série Y, Affaires internationales, 1918–40, 100, series of reports by Herbette to Briand, summer 1928, esp. 4 July 1928.

113 MAE, Paris, Série Y, Affaires internationales, 1918–40, 100, Herbette to Briand, 17 July 1928; *RBLDAG*, 12 (1936–7), pp. 158–9.

114 MAE, Paris, Série Y, Affaires internationales, 1918–40, 100, Herbette to Briand, 17 October 1928 and 18 December 1930; French chargé d'affaires to Herriot, 25 August 1932. Warren won the initial case against Ladeuze in Louvain, but the court of appeal

in Brussels found in favour of the university in 1930, a verdict upheld by the supreme appeal court (Cour de Cassation) in 1932.

115 *Le Soir*, 10 January 1928; de Soete, *Furore teutonico*, p. 28.

116 *L'Indépendance belge*, 26 September 1930, cited in *RBLDAG*, 7 (1931), p. 15. The artist, Brignoli, was from Bergamo. He wrote an open letter to *L'Indépendance belge* on 8 August 1930 in which he explained how much he admired Belgium in 1914 and how 'The mutilation of the innocent child symbolized the pride and uprightness of Belgium in its awareness that resistance to the enemy was impossible.' The painting had been hanging in the museum since 1920 (MAE, Paris, Série Y, Affaires internationales, 1918–40, 100, Herbette to Briand, 2 October 1930).

117 *RBLDAG*, 8 (1932), pp. 181–2; ibid., 9 (1933–4), pp. 7–9; MAE, Paris, Série Y, Affaires internationales, 1918–40, 100, ambassador to Quai d'Orsay, 17 December 1931, 20 December 1931, and 11 May 1933; Wieland, *Belgien 1914*, pp. 371–83.

118 'Die Greuel von Dinant', *Vorwärts*, 9 September 1927, cited in Wieland, *Belgien 1914*, p. 171.

119 Fernand Mayence, *La Légende des francs-tireurs de Louvain. Réponse au mémoire de M. le Professeur Meurer de l'Université de Würzburg* (Louvain, 1928), translated into German as *Die Legende der Franktireurs von Löwen. Antwort auf das Gutachten des H. Professors Meurer von der Universität Würzburg* (Louvain, 1928), and also distributed in English, Flemish, Spanish, and Italian; *Vorwärts*, 9 February 1928, cited in *RBLDAG*, 4 (1927–8), p. 443.

120 'Louvain et la légende des francs-tireurs', in *RBLDAG*, 6 (1929–30), pp. 125–33; Wieland, *Belgien 1914* p. 199; *Vorwärts*, 9 February 1928, cited in Wieland, *Belgien 1914*, pp. 189–90. The clash between Meurer and Mayence was widely commented on in the international press. Each author published further articles in the original languages and in English in the American review, *Current History*, July 1928: 'The Blame for the Sack of Louvain' (title of issue); Christian Meurer, 'The Case for the Germans', pp. 556–66; Fernand Mayence, 'The Belgian Rejoinder', pp. 566–71.

121 Norbert Nieuwland and Maurice Tschoffen, *La Légende des francs-tireurs de Dinant. Réponse au mémoire de M. le professeur Meurer de l'Université de Wurzbourg* (Gembloux, 1928), translated into German as *Das Märchen von den Franktireurs von Dinant. Antwort auf das Gutachten von Professor Meurer von der Universität Würzburg* (Gembloux, 1928), and also issued in English, Flemish, Italian, and Spanish versions; *Vorwärts*, 18 January 1929.

122 *Kölnische Zeitung*, 11 August 1928; *RBLDAG*, 5 (1928–9), pp. 133–4.

123 *Kölnische Zeitung*, 11 August 1928.

124 Wieland, *Belgien 1914*, p. 315.

125 Ibid., pp. 234–40, 245.

126 'L'"Allgemeine Rundschau" poursuit sa campagne pro-belge', in *RBLDAG*, 6 (1929–30), pp. 122–37; Wieland, *Belgien 1914*, pp. 280–3.

127 Schwendemann, the director of the Schuldreferat, considered these articles (without any evidence) to be a prelude to new financial demands from Belgium. He was, naturally, strictly against any concessions to the Belgians (*ADAP*, series B, vol. 16, document 174, memorandum Schwendemann, 24 March 1930, pp. 408–11).

128 See chapter 7 above.

129 *RBLDAG*, 6 (1929–30), p. 126.

130 Ludwig Renn, *War* (1929; English translation, London, 1929; 1984 edn), pp. 29–40.

131 'Dinant – L'auteur de "Guerre", M. Ludwig Renn, avoue qu'il s'est trompé',

RBLDAG, 6 (1929–30), pp. 289–90. Renn's recantation was publicized in the Belgian press, notably *Le Soir*, 21 November 1929.

132 On Dinant, Reichsarchiv, *Der Weltkrieg 1914 bis 1918* (14 vols, Berlin, 1925–44), vol. 1, *Die Grenzschlachten im Westen* (1925), pp. 376–80. The manuscripts of the Reich Archive war history were examined before publication by the Schuldreferat to ensure nothing incriminating appeared (*ADAP*, series B, vol. 16, document 209, memorandum Schwendemann, 9 February 1931, p. 528).

133 For a Belgian critique, see F. Vandaele, 'Une Offensive de mensonges. Les historiques des régiments allemands', *Revue Générale* (Brussels), 15 July 1932, pp. 31–50, cited in *RBLDAG*, 8 (1932–3), pp. 453–4.

134 General Reinhold Stühmke, *Das Infanterie-Regiment 'Kaiser Friedrich, König von Preußen' (7. Württ.) Nr. 125 im Weltkrieg 1914–1918* (Stuttgart, 1923), pp. 9–12. It mentions franc-tireur attacks in Baranzy, Musson, and St Pancré.

135 Otto Fließ and Kurt Dittmar, *5. Hannoversches Infanterie-Regiment Nr. 165 im Weltkriege* (Oldenburg and Berlin, 1927), pp. 7–10, 20. See also the history of the 3rd Grenadier Guards Regiment, which claimed to have been attacked by francs-tireurs in Belgium and France: *Das Königin Elisabeth Garde-Grenadier-Regiment Nr. 3, 1914–1918* (Oldenburg and Berlin, 1921), pp. 11–13.

136 Wieland, *Belgien 1914*, pp. 207–11.

137 Memorandum von Bülow, 18 September 1928, in *ADAP*, series B, vol. 10, document 32, pp. 95–6.

138 PAAA, Bonn, R 29140, fol. 18–19, Reichswehr Minister to Foreign Minister, [19] December 1928; ibid., fol. 20–6, 'Denkschrift über die gegen die belgische Propaganda zu ergreifenden Maßnahmen', and fol. 29, appendix 2 to this memorandum.

139 PAAA, Bonn, R 29140, fol. 18–19, Reichswehr Minister to Foreign Minister, [19] December 1928, fol. 24–6, 'Denkschrift'.

140 Wieland, *Belgien 1914*, p. 346, citing Schwendemann to Joos, 2 August 1930; PAAA, Bonn, R 26279, König, Schuldreferat, to Oszwald, 2 May 1931.

141 Robert Paul Oszwald, *Der Streit um den belgischen Franktireurkrieg. Eine kritische Untersuchung der Ereignisse in den Augusttagen 1914 und der darüber bis 1930 erschienenen Literatur unter Benutzung bisher nicht veröffentlichten Materials*, (Cologne, 1931). So discreet was the Foreign Ministry's involvement that no mention was made of it in the book, although it subsidized the work (via the Schuldreferat) to the tune of at least 30,000 Reichsmark, or roughly 350,000 euros in prices of 2001 (PAAA, Bonn, R 26279: Reich Ministry of Finance to Foreign Ministry, 24 March 1931).

142 Oszwald was born in 1883, married a Fleming, was assistant lecturer in history, University of Leipzig, 1908–9, and worked for the Saxon Historical Commission 1912–15. In 1915–16 he worked in the Political Department of the Governor-General in Belgium at Antwerp, in 1916–17 in Ghent, and in 1917–18 in the Political Department, Brussels. In 1920 he became an archivist at the Reichsarchiv. He published widely on Flemish–Walloon relations. (Wieland, *Belgien 1914*, p. 479, n. 602.)

143 In fact, the publisher of the *Kölnische Volkszeitung* (Ibid., pp. 207–11, 345–6).

144 Oszwald, *Der Streit*, p. 76.

145 Cf. chapter 3.

146 Wieland, *Belgien 1914*, pp. 349–52.

147 Ibid., pp. 353–60; *Historische Zeitschrift*, 146, 1932, pp. 189–90. Hans Herzfeld was decorated as an officer in the war, and was opposed to the Weimar Republic and western democracy (Rüdiger vom Bruch and Rainer A. Müller, *Historikerlexikon. Von der Antike bis zum 20. Jahrhundert* (Munich, 1991), p. 135).

148 PAAA, Bonn, R 26279, von Haeften for von Friedberg, 7 August 1931.

149 Alfons Fonck, *Schrotschüsse in Belgien* (Berlin, 1931).

150 The German Association wrote to the Foreign Ministry expressing its disappointment that many well-known personalities in Germany had declined to review Fonck's work (PAAA, Bonn, R 26279, Draeger, Arbeitsausschuß Deutscher Verbände, to König, Foreign Ministry, 28 April 1931).

151 Hermann Wendel, 'Schrotschüsse in Belgien', *Vorwärts*, 11 May 1931. Wendel was a leading Social Democratic pacifist.

152 Cited in Wieland, *Belgien 1914*, pp. 336–7. Wieland casts doubt on the authenticity of Fonck's research. After all, the War Ministry Investigation Department could have published the results of its own research in 1915, but failed to do so (ibid., pp. 327–8). A fair assessment would be that the research was 'authentic', but the interpretations skewed and the conclusions absurd.

153 PAAA, Bonn, R 26279, Widmann to König, Foreign Ministry, 11 April 1931, 'Unterlage für eine Aufzeichnung'; BA Berlin, R 1501/25810, fol. 102: President of the Reichsarchiv to Reich Minister of the Interior, 30 May 1929. On Einstein, Fritz Stern, *Dreams and Delusions: The Drama of German History* (London, 1988), pp. 39–41; Siegfried Grundmann, *Einsteins Akte* (Heidelberg, 1997). *RBLDAG*, 6 (1929–30), pp. 288–9; cf. Wieland, *Belgien 1914*, pp. 213–14, 217–20.

154 Fernand Mayence, 'Lettre ouverte à Oszwald, à propos de son livre récent sur les francs-tireurs en Belgique', *Le Soir*, 6 August 1931, cited in *RBLDAG*, 7 (1931), p. 357. Among the other Belgians who polemicized with Oszwald was A. Lemaire (the Jesuit historian of the Tamines massacre), *La Controverse des 'francs-tireurs'. Lettre ouverte à M. le Dr. R. P. Oszwald, conseiller supérieur d'archives et membre des archives du Reich* (Brussels, 1932). Cf. Wieland, *Belgien 1914*, pp. 361–5.

155 *Le Peuple*, 20 March 1932; BA Berlin, R1501, 25811, fol. 206–7, German embassy, Brussels, to Foreign Ministry, Berlin, 21 March 1932; *ADAP*, series B, vol. 20, document 50, memorandum Köpke, 14 April 1932, pp. 116–18; Wieland, *Belgien 1914*, pp. 365–8.

156 T. Heyse, 'Furore teutonico', in *RBLDAG*, 12 (1936–7), pp. 158–60, 304–14; Wieland, *Belgien 1914*, pp. 383–91; and Tixhon, 'Le Souvenir des massacres', pp. 142–60.

157 Quotation by the association supporting the museum project announcing de Soete's offer, cited in Tixhon, 'Le Souvenir des massacres', p. 143. See also MAE, Paris, Série Y, Affaires internationales 1918–40, 100, chargé d'affaires to Herriot, 25 August 1932.

158 MAE, Paris, Série Y, Affaires internationales, 1918–40, 100, chargé d'affaires in Brussels to Paul-Boncour, 7 September 1933; A. Boissier (consul-general, Dresden) to Paul-Boncour, 30 September 1933; Tixhon, 'Le Souvenir des massacres', p. 148 (Gérard) and 156 (Tschoffen). The chargé d'affaires in Brussels considered that the Nazi threat and the desire to conciliate Ladeuze and the Catholic hierarchy explained the government's attitude.

159 Tixhon, 'Le Souvenir des massacres', p. 155.

160 Ibid., p. 159.

161 Heyse, 'Furore teutonico', *RBLDAG*, 12 (1936–7), pp. 309–12.

162 Jacobson, *Locarno Diplomacy*, pp. 353–4.

163   Herweg, 'Clio Deceived', pp. 284–5.

164   Wojcieck Jacobson, *Z Armja Klucka na Paryz; Pammielnik lekarza – Polaka* (Torun, 1934); translated into French as *En marche sur Paris avec l'armée prussienne du Général von Kluck* (Brussels, 1937), esp. ch. 2.

165   For Belgium, see the evidence of the *RBLDAG*; Antoine Redier, *Les Allemands dans nos maisons* (Paris, 1938; 2nd edn, 1945).

166   Werner Sombart, *Deutscher Sozialismus* (Berlin, 1934), p. 160; for Sombart's wartime work, see ch. 7 above.

167   Victor Klemperer, *LTI. Notizbuch eines Philologen* (1957; 16th edn, Leipzig, 1996), diary entry 27 March 1933, p. 44.

168   *Entartete 'Kunst'. Ausstellungsführer* (Berlin, n.d., but 1937), pp. 12–14, facsimile in Stephanie Barron (ed.), *'Entartete Kunst'. Das Schicksal der Avantgarde im Nazi-Deutschland* (1991; new edn, Munich, 1992), pp. 370–2.

169   Auswärtiges Amt, *Documents Relative to Polish Atrocities* (1940; English translation, Berlin, 1940); and *The Polish Atrocities against the German Minority in Poland* (1940; English translation, Berlin, 1940).

170   Auswärtiges Amt, *Bolschewistische Verbrechen gegen Kriegsrecht und Menschlichkeit: Dokumente zusammengestellt vom Auswärtigen Amt* (Berlin, 1942).

171   Elke Fröhlich (ed.), *Die Tagebücher von Joseph Goebbels. Sämtliche Fragmente*, part 1, *Aufzeichnungen 1924–1941*, vol. 4, *1.1.1940–8.7.1941* (Munich, New York, London, Paris, 1987), p. 154 (diary entry for 11 May 1940); pp. 155–9 (diary entries 12 and 15 May).

172   *Trial of the Major War Criminals before the International Military Tribunal. Nuremberg 14 November 1945–1 October 1946*, vol. 27 (Nuremberg, 1948), p. 516.

173   Commission des Crimes de Guerre, *Les Crimes de guerre commis lors de l'invasion du territoire national, mai 1940. Les massacres de Vinkt* (Liège, 1948); P. Taghon, *Mai 40. La campagne de dix-huit jours* (Paris and Louvain-la-Neuve, 1989), p. 185. Of 12 reports by the Belgian War Crimes Commission, 1945–9, only two concerned 1940 (Vinkt and Louvain). The remainder concerned the German retreat in 1944–5 and the camp at Breendonck.

174   Gerhard L. Weinberg, *A World at Arms: A Global History of World War II* (Cambridge, 1994), pp. 125–6. For civilian deaths, see Peter Calvocoressi and Guy Wint, *Total War: Causes and Course of the Second World War* (1972; new edn, 2 vols, London, 1979), vol. 1, p. 132. For British reluctance to target civilians in 1940, see Max Hastings, *Bomber Command* (London, 1979), pp. 85–105.

175   Hans Umbreit, 'Les Projets allemands et les premières semaines d'occupation', in Maurice Vaïsse (ed.), *Ardennes 1940* (Paris, 1991), pp. 235–46; Hans-Adolf Jacobsen (ed.), *Dokumente zur Vorgeschichte des Westfeldzugs 1939–1940* (Göttingen, 1956), document 49 (untitled, undated fragment), p. 172.

176   BA Berlin, R 43 II/676 microfiche 1, fol. 59: the Führer and supreme commander of the Wehrmacht, 7 July 1940. This was circulated also to the SS, police, and the various civilian authorities which might have sent non-army personnel to France. Ibid., fol. 61: the chief of the Reich chancellery, Lammers, 24 July 1940. Lammers added that this Führer decree applied to all occupied enemy areas, including Poland, Norway, the Netherlands, Belgium, Luxembourg. It clearly did not apply in Eastern Europe.

177   Jean Vidalenc, *L'Exode de mai–juin 1940* (Paris, 1957), pp. 68, 415; Gérard Giuliano, 'L'Exode des populations ardennaises en mai–juin 1940', in Vaïsse, *Ardennes 1940*, p. 206; J. Gérard-Libois and José Gotovitch, *L'An 40. La Belgique occupée* (Brussels,

1971), pp. 234–5.

178 AN, Paris, F1C III 1176 (Oise), report of prefect, 30 June 1940.

179 G. Lhomme, *Notes sur les événements de mai 1940 à Orchies*, cited in Vidalenc, *L'Exode*, p. 68.

180 Simone de Beauvoir, *La Force de l'âge* (Paris, 1960), p. 508; Jill Sturdee, 'War and Memory of Childhood: The Children of Caen and the Nazi Occupation', unpublished paper presented at the conference on War and Memory in the Twentieth Century, University of Portsmouth, 25–27 March 1994. The authors would like to thank Dr Sturdee for permission to cite her paper.

181 AN, Paris, F1C III 1138 (Ardennes); 1142 (Territoire de Belfort); 1176 (Oise); 1188 (Seine-Inférieure); 1190 (Seine-et-Oise).

182 William L. Shirer, *Berlin Diary: The Journal of a Foreign Correspondent 1934–1941* (London, 1941), pp. 321–3, 17 June 1940 (cf. also p. 286, entry for 20 May 1940).

183 Cited in Gérard Giuliano, Jacques Lambert, and Valérie Rostowsky, *Les Ardennais dans la tourmente. De la mobilisation à l'évacuation* (Charleville-Mézières, 1990), p. 439.

184 Tixhon, 'Le Souvenir des massacres', pp. 161–2.

185 Shirer, *Berlin Diary*, p. 282 (20 May 1940).

186 Ibid., p. 280 (20 May 1940) and pp. 338–9 (26 June 1940); *Trial of the Major War Criminals*, vol. 6 (1947), pp. 534–5 (testimony of L. Van der Essen); Schivelbusch, *Die Bibliothek von Löwen*, pp. 173–8. Van der Essen was a Louvain historian, adviser to the government in exile during the First World War, and member of the Belgian War Crimes Commission during and after the Second. In this capacity he investigated the second destruction of the library, concluding that its destruction was a deliberate act of the Wehrmacht (*War Crimes committed during the Invasion of the National Territory May 1940 – The Destruction of the Library of the University of Louvain* (Liège, 1946)).

187 *Trial of the Major War Criminals*, vol. 6, p. 535 (testimony of Van der Essen).

188 CPHDC, Moscow, 1256-1-13, fol. 52: quartermaster-general V, Supreme Army Command, to military commander in Belgium and Northern France, 6 July 1940; transcript in the files of the Director of Military Archives, Potsdam (Chef HA).

189 CPHDC, Moscow, 1256-1-13, fol. 56: Harbou to Rabenau, 18 August 1940. Major Christian von Harbou was indeed a participant in the invasion of Belgium in August 1914: cf. PAAA, Bonn, R 20880, fol. 8–9: commentary by the Kaiser on a message from the Belgian government, received 9 August 1914. After 20 July 1944 Harbou was executed for participating in the conspiracy against Hitler (Walter Görlitz (ed.), *Regierte der Kaiser? Kriegstagebücher, Aufzeichnungen und Briefe des Chefs des Marine-Kabinetts Admiral Georg Alexander von Müller 1914–1918* (Göttingen, 1959), p. 407).

190 CPHDC, Moscow, 1256-1-58, fol. 19–23 (dissolution of the commission); Bundesarchiv-Militärarchiv (BA-MA), Potsdam, microfilm WF-10/20966, Knorr to Chef der HAe Potsdam, 7 August 1944 (court-martial material).

191 William L. Shirer, *The Collapse of the Third Republic. An Inquiry into the Fall of France in 1940* (1969; new edn, London, 1972), p. 1014.

192 Weinberg, *A World at Arms*, pp. 58–9; Michael Wildt, draft chapter, 'Polen 1939', esp. p. 12. The authors are grateful to Dr Wildt for making available to them his draft manuscript.

193 Ibid., pp. 19–20 and 39 (citing an order of the 17th Division, 4 September 1939).

194 Ibid., p. 27.

195 Michael Veuthey, 'Guerrilla Warfare and Humanitarian Law', *International Review of the Red Cross*, 234 (1983), pp. 115–37, cited in H. A. Wilson, *International Law and the Use of Force by National Liberation Movements* (Oxford, 1988), pp. 34–52. Cf. Geoffrey Best, *Humanity in Warfare: The Modern History of the International Law of Armed Conflicts* (1980; new edn, London, 1983), pp. 238–9, and Omer Bartov, *Hitler's Army: Soldiers, Nazis and War in the Third Reich* (New York, 1992), pp. 179–86.

196 BA-MA, Potsdam, WF-03/32772, no. 8522 194–5. Tätigkeitsbericht Nr. 2, Panzer-Gruppe 3, Abt. Ic, 1 January 1941–11 August 1941, speech by Lieutenant-General Müller on 11 June 1941 (emphasis in the original).

197 *Hitler's Table Talk 1941–44: His Private Conversations*, introd. H. R. Trevor-Roper (1951; English translation, London, 1953), p. 29 (14–15 September 1941).

198 Emil Waxweiler, *Der europäische Krieg. Hat Belgien sein Schicksal verschuldet?* (Zürich, 1915), p. 237 and 246–8; Henri Davignon, *German Posters in Belgium. Their Value as Evidence* (London, 1918), p. 67.

199 The only incident remotely resembling Hitler's remarks was in Goltz's posthumously published memoirs, in which he mentioned the killing of 'many civilians', for 'again' they had fired on German troops south of Ghent (Colmar von der Goltz, *Denkwürdigkeiten* (Berlin, 1929), letter to his wife, 11 October 1914, p. 375).

200 Weinberg, *A World at Arms*, p. 429.

201 Hans Umbreit, *Der Militärbefehlshaber in Frankreich 1940–1944* (Boppard, 1968), p. 123.

202 Ibid., pp. 137–9.

203 Circular from Military Governor, 12 February 1944, cited in ibid., p. 148.

204 Ibid., p. 149.

205 Sarah Farmer, *Martyred Village: Commemorating the 1944 Massacre at Oradour-sur-Glane* (London, 1999), pp. 13–28; Luc Capdevila, *Les Bretons au lendemain de l'occupation. Imaginaire et comportement d'une sortie de guerre 1944–1945* (Rennes, 1999), ch. 2.

206 According to Gerhard Schreiber, *Deutsche Kriegsverbrechen in Italien. Täter, Opfer, Strafverfolgung* (Munich, 1996), 9,000 Italian civilians perished between 1943 and 1945. See also Michael Geyer, '"Es muß daher mit schnellen und drakonischen Maßnahmen durchgegriffen werden"', in Hannes Heer and Klaus Naumann (eds), *Vernichtungskrieg. Verbrechen der Wehrmacht 1941–1944* (1995; new edn, Frankfurt, 1997), pp. 208–38.

207 Mark Mazower, *Inside Hitler's Greece: The Experience of Occupation 1941–1944* (New Haven, 1993), p. 157.

208 Hannes Heer, 'Die Logik des Vernichtungskrieges. Wehrmacht und Partisanenkampf', in Heer and Naumann (eds), *Vernichtungskrieg*, pp. 104–38.

209 John Horne, 'Defining the Enemy: War, Law and the *levée en masse* from 1870 to 1945', in Daniel Moran and Arthur Waldron (eds), *The People in Arms: Military Myth and Political Legitimacy since the French Revolution* (Cambridge, forthcoming).

210 The poster was put up by the Francs-Tireurs et Partisans and the Front National (*Images de la France de Vichy* (Paris, 1988), p. 243). On the inspiration of 1870 for the naming of Franc-Tireur, see Jean-Pierre Lévy (with the collaboration of Dominique Veillon), *Mémoires d'un franc-tireur. Itinéraire d'un résistant (1940–1944)* (Brussels, 1998), p. 51. On Republicanism and the Resistance, see Harry Roderick Kedward,

Resistance in Vichy France: A Study of Ideas and Motivation in the Southern Zone, 1940–1942 (Oxford, 1978), pp. 150–84. On military mythology and the Resistance, see Sergio Luzzatto, *L'Impôt du sang. La gauche française à l'épreuve de la guerre mondiale, 1900–1945* (Lyon, 1996), pp. 151–7.

211 Jean-Louis Crémieux-Brilhac, *La France Libre. De l'appel du 18 juin à la Libération* (Paris, 1996), pp. 772–95.

212 Ibid., pp. 328, 784–7, 859–61; Capdevila, *Les Bretons*, pp. 19–27.

213 Originally in *Tribune*, 31 March 1944, reproduced in Sonia Orwell and Ian Angus (eds), *The Collected Essays, Journalism and Letters of George Orwell* (4 vols, London, 1968), vol. 3, *As I Please 1943–1945* (new edn, Harmondsworth, 1978), pp. 140–1.

214 Victor Gollancz, *'Let My People Go': Some Practical Proposals for Dealing with Hitler's Massacre of the Jews* (London, 1943), p. 10.

215 John Fox, 'The Jewish Factor in British War Crimes Policy in 1942', *English Historical Review*, 362 (1977), pp. 87–8; Walter Laqueur, *The Terrible Secret: Suppression of the Truth about Hitler's 'Final Solution'* (1980; new edn, Harmondsworth, 1982), pp. 8–9, 91, 219, 237.

216 Inter-Allied Information Committee, *Punishment for War Crimes: The Inter-Allied Declaration Signed at St. James's Palace, London, on 13th January 1942 and Relative Documents* (2 vols, London, 1942), vol. 1, pp. 3–4, cited in Michael R. Marrus, *The Nuremberg War Crimes Trial 1945–46: A Documentary History* (Boston and New York, 1997), p. 19.

217 James F. Willis, *Prologue to Nuremberg: The Politics and Diplomacy of Punishing War Criminals of the First World War* (Westport, Conn., and London, 1982), pp. 173–5; Marrus, *The Nuremberg War Crimes Trial*, p. 12.

218 The United Nations War Crimes Commission, *History of the United Nations War Crimes Commission and the Development of the Laws of War* (London, 1948), p. 477.

219 A minority historiography has continued to deal sympathetically with the necessity of the war and with the efforts of the British military to win. It is perhaps significant that the firmest attempt to distinguish between atrocity propaganda and the nature of the German invasion should have come from one of the foremost representatives of this tradition, John Terraine, 'The Smoke and the Fire: Atrocities and Reprisals', in Terraine, *The Smoke and the Fire: Myths and Anti-Myths of War 1861–1945* (London, 1980), pp. 22–54. The popular American historian, Barbara Tuchman, also emphasized the substance, as opposed to the myth, of the German atrocities, in *August 1914* (1962; new edn, London, 1993), pp. 306–15.

220 Henry Rousso, *The Vichy Syndrome: History and Memory in France since 1944* (1987; English translation, Cambridge, Mass., 1991), ch. 2.

221 A rather diffident history of the 'martyrology' of French Lorraine in 1914–18, which was published in Nancy in 1958, sought to keep alive the atrocities of 1914 in view of 'the passage of time and the difficulties of comparing the deportation camps of William II with the horrors of the modern convict camps of Hitlerism' (Marcel Savart, *Occupation 1914–1918. Quarante ans après. Martyrologie de la zone envahie. Massacres et déportations* (Nancy, 1958), p. xi). The keynote of subsequent local histories has been rescuing the events of 1914 from oblivion (e.g. R. Szymanski, *Les Ardennes, terre de France oubliée en 1914–1918* (private pub., 1984)).

222 Wieland, *Belgien 1914*, p. 393, citing *Deutschland-Belgien 1830–1945. Empfehlungen der belgisch-deutschen Historikerkonferenz Braunschweig 1954*. Reprint from the *Jahrbuch für Geschichtsunterricht*, 1955, pp. 39–40.

223 Fernand Mayence, 'La Falsification des sources relatives à la question des prétendus Francs-Tireurs à Louvain, en août 1914', *Bulletin de l'Académie Royale de Belgique* (1955), pp. 155–71.

224 Karl Ditt, 'Die Kulturraumforschung zwischen Wissenschaft und Politik. Das Beispiel Franz Petri (1903–1993)', *Westfälische Forschungen*, 46 (1996), pp. 153–8.

225 Van der Essen was professor of history at the University of Louvain, de Sturler at Brussels, Rothfels at Tübingen, and Conze at Heidelberg.

226 Schöller papers, Petri to Conze, 13 November 1956.

227 Schöller papers, Schöller to Conze, 5 October 1957; Conze to Schöller, 1 October 1957. A Dr Kosthorst was to have worked on Dinant.

228 Peter Schöller, *Der Fall Löwen und das Weißbuch. Eine kritische Untersuchung der deutschen Dokumentation über die Vorgänge in Löwen vom 25. bis 28. August 1914* (Cologne and Graz, 1958).

229 Schöller papers, Conze to Schöller, 18 April 1957. See chapters 1 and 6 above.

230 Schöller papers, Conze to Schöller, 1 October 1957.

231 Cf. Imanuel Geiss, 'Die Kriegsschuldfrage. Das Ende eines nationalen Tabus', in Geiss (ed), *Das Deutsche Reich und die Vorgeschichte des Ersten Weltkriegs* (Munich and Vienna, 1978), pp. 204–29, and vom Bruch and Müller, *Historikerlexikon*, pp. 266–8.

232 Schöller, *Der Fall Löwen*, pp. 5 and 13.

233 Wieland, *Belgien 1914*, pp. 394–5.

234 The main exception was a review in the *Historische Zeitschrift*, one of Germany's leading historical journals. Eberhard Kessel argued that Schöller's methodology was mistaken, for he had not disproved all the assertions in the White Book. He conceded that the German thesis of a planned ambush in Louvain could be doubted, that German troops may have fired at each other, and that there may well have been 'innocent victims'. However, he insisted that the cause of the incident was 'some kind of Belgian attack'. See *Historische Zeitschrift*, 191 (1960), pp. 385–90. Schöller and Petri defended themselves against their critics in an essay, 'Zur Bereinigung des Franktireurproblems vom August 1914', *Vierteljahrshefte für Zeitgeschichte*, 9 (1961), pp. 234–48.

235 E.g. *Frankfurter Neue Presse*, 9 May 1958; *Frankfurter Allgemeine Zeitung*, 17 May 1958; Schöller papers, manuscript of broadcast by Dr Hans Becker on Radio Frankfurt, 9 May 1958; ibid., manuscript of broadcast on Bavarian Radio by Dr Heinrich Uhlig, 'Haben wir genügend Abstand?', 18 March 1959.

236 Schöller papers, Adenauer to Petri and Schöller, 1 July 1958; Brentano to Petri and Schöller, 20 June 1958.

237 *La Libre Belgique*, 7 May 1958.

238 Schöller papers, Mayence to Schöller, 15 May 1958.

239 In their subsequent response to their critics, Petri and Schöller did present evidence they had unearthed relating to Andenne, where there was clear evidence of an order to kill all men capable of bearing arms ('Zur Bereinigung des Franktireurproblems').

240 Schöller, *Der Fall Löwen*, p. 10.

241 Gerhard Ritter, *The Sword and the Sceptre: The Problem of Militarism in Germany* (4 vols, 1954–68; English translation, 1972–3), vol. 3, *The Tragedy of Statesmanship: Bethmann Hollweg as War Chancellor (1914–1917)* (1968; English translation, London, 1973), p. 35, n. 57, in which Ritter refers the reader to Schöller's 'conciliatory pamphlet' as 'hopefully the last in the long series of polemics on the alleged Louvain atrocities'. In fact, Ritter was surrounded by evidence for a different evaluation. The

footnote relates to a quotation from Bethmann Hollweg in 1914 referring to 'the many precipitate and brutal "reprisals"' carried out by the German army in Belgium. In his first volume, Ritter had criticized Bismarck for urging the German army on to harsh reactions against Gambetta's 'people's war' in 1870, observing that such harshness only serves to strengthen resistance. Ritter referred to Allied bombing of German civilians in the Second World War to prove (and relativize) the point. The significance of German military behaviour in 1914 for his argument entirely escaped him (Ritter, *The Sword and the Sceptre*, vol. 1, *The Prussian Tradition 1740–1890* (1954; English translation, London, 1972), pp. 221–2).

242   Fritz Fischer in interview with Alan Kramer, 25 November 1991; confirmed in letter, 11 April 1999.

243   The exceptions are notably Wieland, *Belgien 1914*, and Schivelbusch, *Die Bibliothek von Löwen*.

244   Wieland, *Belgien 1914*, p. 398.

245   Thomas Nipperdey, *Deutsche Geschichte 1866–1918* (2 vols, 2nd edn, Munich, 1993), vol. 2, *Machtstaat vor der Demokratie*, p. 760.

246   Schöller papers, Schöller to Conze, 29 July 1958.

247   Schöller papers, 'Braun' (probably pseudonym), Berlin, to Schöller, 20 June 1958.

248   Schöller papers, Johann Kühl to Schöller, 14 June and 10 August 1958, and 16 April 1959; *Kieler Nachrichten*, 24 May 1958 (veterans' letters protesting at the account of the ceremony in Louvain on 6 May, reported in the paper on 8 May 1958).

249   Schöller papers, *Lübeckesche Blätter*, 118 (14 September 1958), pp. 161–4. The author, Walter Weber, called on veterans to send in their letters and reports on Louvain to the Lübeck city archive.

250   Wilhelm Hahn and Johann Kühl (eds), *Der Fall Löwen 1914 und was dort wirklich geschah. Eine kriegsgeschichtliche Antwort deutscher Soldaten auf die Beschuldigungen von Dr. Peter Schöller* (Plön am See, 1963). Kühl's denunciation of Schöller was to the latter's academic institution (Schöller papers, Kühl to Provinzialinstitut Münster, 8 June 1958).

251   Jozef De Vroey, *Aarschot op Woensdag 19 augustus 1914* (Aarschot, n.d., but 1964). According to Father De Vroey, he originally proposed the inscription for the chapel as: 'We have *not* pardoned the guilty', but was overridden by his superiors.

252   C. Himmer and Antoine Herbecq, *A Dinant, quelques homélies en souvenir du 23 août 1914 et du 11 novembre 1918* (Dinant, 1992), and typescript texts of the homilies for 1994 and 1995 delivered by Father Herbecq. See also Antoine Herbecq and Eugène Herbecq, *À Dinant le 23 août 1914 dans le quartier Saint Nicolas* (private edn, Dinant, 1977). The authors would like to record their gratitude to both Father Antoine Herbecq and Father Eugène Herbecq for the interview given to John Horne on 4 May 1996, in which they confirmed (among many other things) that in their view there had been no act of atonement by any German for the events of 1914, with the exception of Moenius, whose visit in 1929 was still remembered.

Conclusion and perspectives

1   Walter Laqueur, *Guerrilla: A Historical Study* (London, 1977), p. 85.

2   John Horne, 'Defining the Enemy: War, Law and the *levée en masse* from 1870 to 1945', in Daniel Moran and Arthur Waldron (eds), *The People in Arms: Military Myth and Political Legitimacy since the French Revolution* (Cambridge, forthcoming).

3   Klaus-Dietmar Henke, *Die amerikanische Besetzung Deutschlands* (2nd edn, Munich, 1996), pp. 943–65.

4   See chapter 9 above.

5   Michael Fellman, *Inside War: The Guerrilla Conflict in Missouri during the American Civil War* (New York, 1989), pp. 112–31.

6   James McPherson, *Battle Cry Freedom: The Civil War Era* (New York, 1988), pp. 774–830.

7   Bill Nasson, *The South African War* (London, 1999), pp. 281, 283. About 28,000 Boer civilians and at least 16,000 black civilians perished in the camps in 1901–2.

8   During the Russian Civil War, the victims of the Cheka and its troops in the Red Terror amounted to several hundred thousand in a two-year period. It is increasingly clear that White Terror was more concerted than previously thought and not much less lethal. Jewish victims may have numbered upwards of 150,000 (Orlando Figes, *A People's Tragedy: A History of the Russian Revolution* (London, 1997), pp. 649, 679). In the Spanish Civil War, more than 200,000 on the Republican side were killed by Nationalist soldiers, and perhaps 55,000 civilians were killed by Republican soldiers and militias, mainly at the beginning of the conflict. The figures, especially for Nationalist atrocities, are highly approximate and remain the subject of investigation (Paul Preston, *A Concise History of the Spanish Civil War* (London, 1996), pp. 146–7, 168–9).

9   Cf. chapter 4 above. There were 250,000 to 300,000 deaths caused by the punitive famine with which the Germans suppressed the Maji-Maji rebellion in German East Africa in 1905–6 (Thomas Pakenham, *The Scramble for Africa* (London, 1991), p. 622). Ibid, pp. 539–56 (Sudan) and 650–3 (Nigeria).

10 Historians now advance the figure of about 20,000 Aboriginal Australians massacred from the late eighteenth to the early twentieth century (Henry Reynolds, *The Other Side of the Frontier: Aboriginal Resistance to the European Invasion of Australia* (Ringwood, 1982), p. 122).

11 Sigmund Freud, 'Thoughts for the Times on War and Death' (1915), in *The Penguin Freud Library*, vol. 12, *Civilization, Society and Religion* (London, 1991), p. 62.

12 Geoffrey Best, in an excellent brief discussion of German behaviour towards civilians during the invasion, both refers to factors which constitute a particular 'cultural and psychological explanation' of the phenomenon and states that: 'It must not be thought that the Germans' handling of [. . .] guerrilla resistance was more savage than would have been that of any other major military power' (*Humanity in Warfare: The Modern History of the International Law of Armed Conflicts* (London, 1980, new edn, 1983), pp. 226, 237). Werner Conze expressed the same view to Peter Schöller in 1957: 'In a similar situation the British or the French would have acted similarly' (Schöller papers, Conze to Schöller, 1 October 1957).

13 Clausewitz himself took a characteristically dispassionate view of the question: Carl von Clausewitz, *On War*, ed. and trans. Michael Howard and Peter Paret (Princeton, 1976; new edn, 1989), pp. 479–83.

14 Pierre Vidal-Naquet, *Les Crimes de l'armée française* (Paris, 1975); Alistair Horne, *A Savage War of Peace: Algeria 1954–1962* (London, 1977), pp. 197–207.

15 For a fine discussion of these difficulties, which nonetheless upholds the importance of making rules of war, see Michael Walzer, *Just and Unjust Wars. A Moral Argument with Historical Illustrations* (1977; 2nd edn, New York, 1992), pp. 176–96.

16   United Nations War Crimes Commission, *History of the United Nations War Crimes Commission and the Development of the Laws of War* (London, 1948); Best, *Humanity in Warfare*, pp. 290–301; Priscilla Dale-Jones, 'Nazi Atrocities against Allied Airmen: Stalag Luft IV and the End of British War Crimes Trials', *Historical Journal*, 41/2 (1998), pp. 543–65.

17   Adam Roberts and Richard Guelff (eds), *Documents on the Laws of War* (Oxford, 1989), pp. 271–337; Best, *Humanity in Warfare*, pp. 295, 298.

18   Indicated by the number of countries signing the 1977 Additional Protocols to the Geneva Conventions of 1949 (102) compared to the Hague Convention of 1907 (44) (Best, *Humanity in Warfare*, p. 287). Article 44 of the first of the 1977 Additional Protocols afforded civilians more protection than ever before. For a discussion of the post-1949 phase of the law of war, see Best, *Humanity in Warfare*, pp. 315–30, and for the 1977 Additional Protocols, Roberts and Guelff, *Laws of War*, pp. 387–470.

19   Peter Gay, *The Bourgeois Experience: Victoria to Freud* (5 vols, London and New York, 1984–8), vol. 3, *The Cultivation of Hatred* (1993), for the general case. For the case in terms of intellectuals and artists, H. Stuart Hughes, *Consciousness and Society: The Reorientation of European Social Thought, 1890–1930* (1958; new edn, Brighton, 1979), ch. 2. For the arts, see Modris Eksteins, *Rites of Spring: The Great War and the Birth of the Modern Age* (London, 1989), pp. 9–94.

20   Neil J. Smelser, *Theory of Collective Behaviour* (London, 1962), ch. 5.

21   For the best statement of the wars as 'total' conflicts in this sense, see Eric Hobsbawm, *Age of Extremes: The Short Twentieth Century* (London, 1994).

22   The cultural processes by which the Nazis constructed a demonized and dehumanized world-view in which their victims were cast as guilty of the worst atrocities, all-threatening and therefore only safe when annihilated, constitute a crucial issue which goes beyond the debate between 'intentionalists' and 'functionalists'. A recent study which has engaged with this dimension of the Third Reich is Michael Burleigh and Wolfgang Wippermann, *The Racial State: Germany 1933–1945* (Cambridge, 1991). For a (rare) consideration of the links between the cultural and ideological dimension of the Great War and the Nazi genocide of the Jews, see Omer Bartov, 'The European Imagination in the Age of Total War', in his *Murder in Our Midst: The Holocaust, Industrial Killing, and Representation* (New York, 1996), pp. 33–50. There are, needless to say, many other episodes in twentieth-century European history, including the Cold War and the ethnic civil war in former Yugoslavia, to which such an analysis could be applied.

23   On the limitations of journalistic reporting of atrocities in Bosnia, Michael Ignatieff, *The Warrior's Honor: Ethnic War and the Modern Conscience* (London, 1998), pp. 136–7, and John Simpson, *Strange Places, Questionable People* (London, 1998), pp. 440–9.

24   See in particular, Antoine Prost, *Les Anciens Combattants et la société française 1914–1939* (3 vols, Paris, 1977), vol. 3, *Mentalités et idéologies*; George Mosse, *Fallen Soldiers: Reshaping the Memory of the World Wars* (New York, 1990), pp. 70–106; Michael Jeismann and Rolf Westheider, 'Wofür stirbt der Bürger? Nationaler Totenkult und Staatsbürgertum in Deutschland und Frankreich seit der Französischen Revolution', in Reinhart Koselleck and Michael Jeismann (eds), *Der politische Totenkult. Kriegerdenkmäler in der Moderne* (Munich, 1994), pp. 24–50; Adrian Gregory, *The Silence of Memory: Armistice Day 1914–1946* (Oxford and Providence, 1994); Jay Winter, *Sites of Memory, Sites of Mourning: The Great War in*

European Cultural History (Cambridge, 1995).

25   There appears to be almost no historical work on the concept and terminology of war crimes and atrocities – that is, taking as its subject the culturally and historically constructed nature of the phenomenon. The closest is Walzer, *Just and Unjust Wars*.

26   For some first historical approaches to this central aspect of twentieth-century moral sensibility, see Ignatieff, *The Warrior's Honor* (esp. pp. 64–71) on the emergence of a new, post-Cold War moral universalism in relation to war crimes and atrocities, and Eric Hobsbawm, 'Barbarism: A User's Guide', in Hobsbawm, *On History* (London, 1997), pp. 334–50.

27   For the German case, see Mosse, *Fallen Soldiers*, pp. 159–81.

Appendix 1 German atrocities in 1914: incidents with ten or more civilians killed

1   For Belgium, see First Commission and Second Commission reports; on France, see French Commission reports. Cf. chapter 6.

2   See Bibliography for the departmental archive listings.

3   Jean Schmitz and Norbert Nieuwland, *Documents pour servir à l'histoire de l'invasion allemande dans les provinces de Namur et de Luxembourg* (7 vols, Brussels and Paris, 1919–24).

4   M. Majoros, 'Collection de documents relatifs à la guerre de 1914–1918 rassemblés par le chanoine Jean Schmitz' (Archives de l'État à Namur, Namur, 1991 (typescript)). Some of the original archives of this inquiry, notably the papers of Jean Schmitz and the replies to the questionnaire, remain in the state archive in Namur, although Nieuwland's papers appear to have been seized by the German army in 1940.

5   AGR, Brussels, CE III 374 B1; AN, Paris, AJ4, Commission instituée en vue de constater les actes commis par l'ennemi en violation du droit des gens.

6   Auswärtiges Amt, *Die völkerrechtswidrige Führung des belgischen Volkskriegs* (Berlin, 1915).

7   Reichsarchiv, *Der Weltkrieg 1914 bis 1918. Die militärischen Operationen zu Lande* (14 vols, Berlin, 1925–44), vols 1, 3 and 5.

8   See chapter 1, n. 2.

Bibliography

I Archive Sources

1 National archives

i Belgium

Archives Générales du Royaume, Brussels [AGR]

CE III 374 B1 (Commission d'enquête): 12, 20, 21, 26, 32, 34, 49, 54, 81a, 81b
Archives de la guerre: T 179
Papiers de Broqueville: 442, 443, 478–84

ii Britain

Public Record Office, London [PRO]

Foreign Office: FO 370/587, FO 372/495, 496, FO 608/245
Home Office: HO 45, 11061/266503
Treasury: T 102/20

iii France

Archives Nationales, Paris [AN]

Series AJ4, Commission Instituée en Vue de Constater les Actes Commis par l'Ennemi en Violation du
    Droit des Gens, 1–52 [French Commission]
BB 18 Ministère de la Justice: Correspondance Générale de la Division Criminelle, 25682, 25684
96 AP 1, diary of Félix Trépont
F7, 12840–1 (gardes civils), 12930–943 prefects' reports, 1914
F1C III, 1138, 1142, 1176, 1188, 1190, prefects' reports, 1940

Ministère des Affaires Étrangères, Paris [MAE]

Correspondance politique et commerciale, 1914–40
Série Y Affaires internationales, 1918–40

93–102 violations du droit international public
Série Z Europe, Allemagne 1918–29
    571–90 sanctions aux violations du droit des gens: punition des coupables
microfilm P1463, vol. 1098

Service Historique de l'Armée de Terre, Vincennes [SHA]

16N 1587
16N 1603, vol. A III: Q.G.A
22N 297
26N 735, 736

iv Germany

Bundesarchiv, Berlin [BA]

07.01 (Reichskanzlei) 2463, 2465/3
R 1501 (Reichsministerium des Innern) 12276, 25810, 25811
R 3003 (Reichsgericht) Generalia/ 51, 52, 56, 59
R 3003 ORA/RG (Oberreichsanwalt beim Reichsgericht):
    bJ 594/20, Akte des ORA in der Strafsache gegen Obersten Bronsart v. Schellendorf (wegen
        Erschießung von Zivilisten in Andenne)
    bJ 198/20, Strafsache gegen Vitzthum von Eckstädt, 2 vols
    bJ 304/20, Strafsache gegen Kielmannsegg, Graf, Generalmaj. a.D. … wegen Greueltaten in
        Dinant
    bJ 307/20, Strafsache gegen Meister, Johann, Generallt., 3 vols
R 43 (Reichskanzlei) II, 676
NL90 Ge 4/1 Gebsattel

Bundesarchiv, Potsdam [BA] (now in BA Berlin)

Reichskanzlei 2401/2
92: Sachthematische Sammlung, 267

Bundesarchiv-Militärarchiv, Potsdam [BM-MA] (now in BA-MA Freiburg)

PH2 (Kriegsministerium) 466
Kartei Militärgeschichte, microfilms WF-03/32772, WF-10/20966

Bundesarchiv-Militärarchiv, Freiburg [BA-MA]

Msg (Militärgeschichtliche Sammlung) 2/3112 Aufzeichnungen Karl Gruber
Nachlaß 30 Beseler, 52
Nachlaß 266 August von Cramon, 69
Nachlaß 324 Karl von Einem gen. von Rothmaler, 26, 36
PH2 (Preußisches Heer, Kriegsministerium) 35
PHD 3 (Preußisches Heer, Kriegsministerium, Drucksachen) 217
PHD 6 (Preußisches Heer, Kriegsministerium, Druckvorschriften) 145

Bundesarchiv, Koblenz [BA]

Nachlaß 15 Bernhard Schwertfeger, 58, 97, 180, 402

Politisches Archiv des Auswärtigen Amts, Bonn [PAAA] (now Berlin)

R 19881, R 20880-20891, R 22383, R 22386, R 26279, R 26432, R 26578, R 29138, R 29140

v Other

Centre for the Preservation of Historical Documentary Collections, Moscow [CPHDC]

1256 (Chef der Heeresarchive) 1–13, 1–58, 5–47
1275 (Archivalien des ehemaligen Heeresarchivs) 5–62, 5–63
1415 (Generalgouverneur in Belgien, Brüssel) 1–51, 1–54, 1–55
1467 (Reichswehrministerium/Reichskriegsministerium) 1–11, 1–12

National Archives, Washington, D.C.

State Department
  Series M 367 World War I and its Termination
    763 72116 Illegal and Inhumane Warfare

Vatican Archive, Rome

Affari Ecclesiastici Straordinari, Belgio, 1907–14
  116; 199, fasc. 101; 200–02, fasc. 102; 204; 211, fasc. 114; 217
Brussels Nunciature 'Durante la Guerra', Box 93
Segretaria di Stato
  244 A1a; 244 A1b; 244 D1 61; 244 D5; 244 D7

2 Provincial, local, and other archives

i Belgium

Musée Royal de l'Armée, Brussels [MRA]

'Rapport … Joseph Knapen'

ii Britain

Imperial War Museum, Department of Documents, London

Diary of Miss M. B. Peterkin

iii France

Archives Départementales, Ardennes, Charleville-Mézières

12J 1 (Émile Marlier, 'Les Ardennes envahies', part 1, 'La Guerre de 1914–18 dans les Ardennes'; part 2, 'L'Arrivée des allemands' [manuscript, 1937 and 1933 respectively])

Archives Départementales, Meurthe-et-Moselle, Nancy

8R 172, 8R 200, 86J4 2, 86J5, 86J 7, 86J 12, 1M 670, 2R 147bis
WO/1683

Archives Départementales, Nord, Lille

M145a
9R11, 9R 12, 9R 15, 9R 17, 9R 20, 9R 22

Archives Départementales, Pas-de-Calais, Arras

R 587, R 857

iv Germany

Bayerisches Hauptstaatsarchiv, Abteilung IV Kriegsarchiv, Munich [KA]

HS 1592 Handakten Graf Harrach
HS 2234 Bertold Schenk von Stauffenberg
HS 2259 Handakten Friedrich Hurt
HS 2301 Eugen von Frauenholz
HS 2358 Joseph Müller
HS 2373 Die Schlacht bei Weiler am 18.8.1914 …
HS 2643 Konrad Krafft von Dellmensingen
HS 2677 Otto Freiherr von Berchem
HS 2694 Georg Rosentreter
HS 2696 Joseph von Tannstein gen. Fleischmann
HS 2740 Albert Ritter von Beckh
HS 2762 Josef Clement
HS 3372 Leonhard Eisenbeiß
HS 3393 Hans Ritter von Seißer
HS 3411/1 Eugen Clauß
MKr (Kriegsministerium) 13390
IR 1

Badisches Generallandesarchiv, Karlsruhe [GLA]

456 F1 (Armee-Oberkommando 7) 205; 456 F2 7414

Sächsisches Hauptstaatsarchiv, Dresden [HStA]

26882, 40164, 40434, 40442, 40870, 40949
Zeitgeschichtliche Sammlung 73, 75, 78

Württembergisches Hauptstaatsarchiv-Militärarchiv, Stuttgart [HStA-MA]

M1/7 (Kriegsministerium – Justiz-Abteilung) 20
M79/11b
M660
  Nachlaß Berrer
  Nachlaß Ebbinghaus
  Nachlaß Max Flammer
  Nachlaß Gerold von Gleich
  Nachlaß Hans von Pezold
  Nachlaß Adolf Spemann

3 Libraries

Bibliothek für Zeitgeschichte, Stuttgart [BfZ]

NL Klitzing
'A la mémoire des habitants de Rossignol', brochure produced for the inauguration of the monument,
  1925

Bodleian Library, Department of Western Manuscripts, Oxford

MSS Asquith; 7, 87
MSS Bryce; 147, 239, 247
MSS Simon; 50

Columbia University Library, New York

Nicholas Murray Butler papers

Trinity College Library, Dublin

Papyrus 16, 53, 54, 55 (war posters)

4 Private collections

Papers of Professor Dr Peter Schöller in possession of Frau Dr H. Ditt, Münster
Papers of Ernst Rump, in possession of Dr K. Rump, Hamburg

II Published Primary Sources

1 Newspapers and periodicals

Publications to which only single references have been made are not included.

i Belgium

L'Indépendance belge
La Libre Belgique
Le Peuple
Revue belge des livres, documents et archives de la guerre 1914–1918 [RBLDAG]
Le Soir
Le XXe Siècle

ii Britain

Daily Mail
The Nation
New Statesman
Punch
The Times

iii France

Bulletin des Armées de la République
Bulletin de la Ligue Souvenez-Vous
Le Charivari
La Clarté
La Croix
L'Est républicain
L'Evolution
L'Excelsior
La Guerre sociale
L'Humanité
L'Illustration
Le Journal du Droit International
Le Matin
Le Populaire
La Revue des Deux Mondes
Le Rire rouge
Le Temps

iv Germany

Freiheit
Die Gartenlaube
Hamburger Echo
Illustrirte Zeitung
Jugend
Kölnische Volkszeitung
Kölnische Zeitung
Die Kunst

Die Menschheit
Norddeutsche Allgemeine Zeitung
Schwäbischer Merkur
Simplicissimus
Vorwärts
Der Weg zur Freiheit
Die Weltbühne

v Other

De Telegraaf (Amsterdam)
New York Times
The Fatherland (New York)

2 Official publications

i Belgium

La Guerre de 1914. L'Action de l'armée belge pour la défense du pays et le respect de sa neutralité. Rapport du commandement de l'armée. Période du 31 juillet au 31 décembre 1914 (Paris, 1915)
War Crimes committed during the Invasion of the National Territory May 1940 – The Destruction of the Library of the University of Louvain (Liège, 1946)

Bureau Documentaire Belge, *Cahiers Documentaires. Recueil méthodique de documents sur la guerre européenne rassemblés et publiés avec le concours du Bureau Documentaire Belge* (Le Havre, 1914–18)
Chambre des Représentants, *Rapport présenté aux Chambres Législatives par M. le Ministre des Affaires Étrangères sur certaines affirmations de la Commission d'Enquête du Reichstag au sujet d'une prétendue guerre de francs-tireurs en Belgique* (Brussels, 1927); English translation, *Report Made by the Minister of Foreign Affairs Dealing with Certain Assertions of the Reichstag Commission of Inquiry, Concerning a So-called Francs-Tireurs War in Belgium* (Brussels, 1927)
Commission des Crimes de Guerre, *Les Crimes de guerre commis lors de l'invasion du territoire national, mai 1940. Les massacres de Vinkt* (Liège, 1948)
Commission d'enquête sur la violation des règles du droit des gens, des lois et des coutumes de la guerre, *Rapports sur la violation du droit des gens en Belgique*, 2 vols (Paris, 1915); English translation, *Reports on the Violation of the Laws and Customs of War in Belgium*, 2 vols (London, 1915–16) [Belgian First Commission]
Commission d'enquête sur les violations des règles du droit des gens, des lois et des coutumes de la guerre (4 vols), vol. 1, parts 1 and 2, *Rapports sur les attentats commis par les troupes allemandes pendant l'invasion et l'occupation de la Belgique* (Brussels and Liège, 1922); vol. 2, *Rapports sur les déportations des ouvriers belges et sur les traitements infligés aux prisonniers de guerre et aux prisonniers civils belges* (1923) [Belgian Second Commission]
Ministère de la Justice et Ministère des Affaires Étrangères, *Réponse au Livre blanc allemand du 10 mai 1915* (Paris, 1916); English translation, *Reply to the German White Book of the 10th May 1915* (London, 1918)
Rolin, Baron Alberic, *Les Allemands en Belgique, 1914–1918. Conclusions de l'enquête officielle belge* (Liège, 1925)

ii Britain

Committee on Alleged German Outrages. Appendix: Evidence and Documents laid before the Committee on Alleged German Outrages (Cd 7895, London, 1915)

Documents on British Foreign Policy 1919–1939, ed. Ernest L. Woodward, Rohan Butler et al. First Series: 1919–25, 27 vols (London, 1947–86), vols 1, 2, 6, 7, 8, 9, 15, 20; Series 1A: 1925–29, 7 vols (London, 1966–75), vol. 3

First Report of the Departmental Committee appointed [...] in connection with the Reception and Employment of the Belgian Refugees in this Country (Cd 7750, London, 1914)

German Atrocities and Breaches of the Rules of War in Africa (Cd 8306, London, 1916)

Parliamentary Papers (Commons) *1921*, vol. 12, *German War Trials: Report* (Cmd 1450)

Report of the Committee on Alleged German Outrages Appointed by His Britannic Majesty's Government and Presided over by the Right Hon. Viscount Bryce, O.M. (Cd 7894, London, 1915)

Reports on Treatment by the Germans of British Prisoners and Natives in German East Africa 1917–18 (Cd 8689, London, 1918)

iii France

Les Atrocités allemandes pendant la guerre 1914–1918. Rapports officiels. Die deutschen Greueltaten während des Weltkrieges 1914–1918. Nach den amtlichen Berichten (Paris, n.d., but 1919)

Le Livre rouge allemand. Un document écrasant. Les atrocités allemandes. Texte complet du rapport officiel de la commission instituée en vue de constater les actes commis par l'ennemi en violation du droit des gens (Paris, 1915)

Rapports et procès-verbaux d'enquête de la commission instituée en vue de constater les actes commis par l'ennemi en violation du droit des gens (décret du 23 septembre 1914), 12 vols (Paris, 1915–19).

Ministère des Affaires Étrangères, *Les Violations des lois de la guerre par l'Allemagne* (Paris, 1915); English translation, *Germany's Violations of the Laws of War, 1914–1915. Compiled under the Auspices of the French Ministry of Foreign Affairs* (London, 1915)

Ministère de la Guerre, *Les Armées françaises dans la grande guerre* 103 vols (Paris, 1922–37), vol. 1, *La Bataille des frontières jusqu'au 23 août 1914* (1936)

Ministère de l'Instruction Publique et des Beaux-Arts, *Documents officiels. Les allemands destructeurs de cathédrales et de trésors du passé. Mémoire relatif aux bombardements de Reims, Arras, Senlis, Louvain, Soissons etc. ... accompagné de photographies et de pièces justificatives* (Paris, 1915)

Ministère de l'Intérieur, *Mesures d'assistance à l'égard des femmes qui ont été victimes des violences de l'ennemi. Circulaires du Ministère de l'Intérieur en date du 24 mars 1915* (Paris, 1915)

iv Germany

Akten zur Deutschen Auswärtigen Politik 1918–1945, series A: 1918–25, 14 vols (Göttingen, 1984–95), vols 1, 2, 3, 5, 6, 16; series B: 1925–33, 21 vols (Göttingen, 1966–83), vols 1, 6, 10, 13, 16, 20 [*ADA P*]

Felddienstordnung (Berlin, 1908; rev. edn 1911)

Kriegsbrauch im Landkriege (Berlin, 1902) (*Kriegsgeschichtliche Einzelschriften*, 31); English translation, *The German War Book: Being 'The Usages of War on Land' issued by the Great General Staff of the German Army*, with a critical introduction by J. H. Morgan (London, 1915)

Verhandlungen des Deutschen Reichstags. Stenographische Berichte, 13th legislative period, 2nd session, vol. 306 (1914–16)

Verhandlungen der Verfassunggebenden Deutschen Nationalversammlung. Stenographische Berichte, vol. 332 (January–March 1920)

Das Werk des Untersuchungsausschusses der Verfassunggebenden Deutschen Nationalversammlung und des Deutschen Reichstags 1919–1928 (ed. Johannes Bell, Walter Schücking and B. Widmann), 3rd series, *Völkerrecht im Weltkrieg*, 4 vols in 5 parts; vol. 2, *Der belgische Volkskrieg* (Berlin, 1927)

Abramowski, Günter (ed.), *Akten der Reichskanzlei. Weimarer Republik. Die Kabinette Marx III und IV. 17. Mai 1926 bis 29. Januar 1927. 29. Januar 1927 bis 29. Juni 1928*, vol. 1 (Boppard, 1988)

Auswärtiges Amt, *Über die Verletzung der Genfer Konvention vom 6. Juli 1906 durch französische Truppen und Freischärler* (Berlin, 1914); English translation, *Violation of the Geneva Convention of July 6th 1906 by French Troops and Francs-Tireurs* (Berlin, 1914)

——*Denkschrift über die Behandlung der deutschen Konsuln in Rußland und die Zerstörung der deutschen Botschaft in Petersburg* (Berlin, 1915); English translation, *Memorandum Concerning the Treatment of German Consuls in Russia and the Destruction of the German Embassy in St. Petersburg* (Berlin, 1915)

——*Greueltaten russischer Truppen gegen deutsche Zivilpersonen und deutsche Kriegsgefangene* (Berlin,1915). English language summary, *Memorial on Atrocities Committed by Russian Troops upon German Inhabitants and Prisoners of War* (Berlin, 1915)

——*Die völkerrechtswidrige Führung des belgischen Volkskriegs* (Berlin, 1915); abbreviated English translation, *The Belgian People's War, a Violation of International Law. Translations from the Official German White Book, Published by the Imperial Foreign Office* (New York, 1915)

——*Völkerrechtswidrige Verwendung farbiger Truppen auf dem europäischen Kriegsschauplatz durch England und Frankreich* (Berlin, 1915); English translation, *Employment contrary to International Law of Colored Troops upon the European Arena of War by England and France* (Berlin, n.d.)

——*Der Baralong-Fall* (Berlin, 1916)

——*Documents Relative to Polish Atrocities* (1940; English translation, Berlin, 1940)

——*The Polish Atrocities against the German Minority in Poland* (1940; English translation, Berlin, 1940)

——*Bolschewistische Verbrechen gegen Kriegsrecht und Menschlichkeit: Dokumente zusammengestellt vom Auswärtigen Amt* (Berlin, 1942)

Auswärtiges Amt and Militäruntersuchungsstelle für Verletzungen des Kriegsrechts, *Widerlegung der von der französischen Regierung erhobenen Anschuldigungen* (Berlin, 1915)

Generalstab des Heeres, 7. (kriegswissenschaftliche) Abteilung (ed.), *Der Handstreich gegen Lüttich vom 3. bis 7. August 1914* (Berlin, 1939)

Kriegsministerium and Oberste Heeresleitung, *Die deutsche Kriegführung und das Völkerrecht. Beiträge zur Schuldfrage* (Berlin, 1919); French translation, *Le Commandement en chef allemand pendant la guerre et le droit des gens. Étude sur la question des culpabilités* (Berlin, 1919)

Reichsarchiv, *Der Weltkrieg 1914 bis 1918. Die militärischen Operationen zu Lande*, 14 vols (Berlin, 1925–44), vol. 1, *Die Grenzschlachten im Westen* (1925); vol. 3, *Der Marne-Feldzug. Von der Sambre zur Marne* (1926); vol. 5, *Der Herbst-Feldzug 1914* (1929)

Reichswehrministerium, *Sanitätsbericht über das deutsche Heer (Deutsches Feld- und Besatzungsheer) im Weltkriege 1914/1918*, 3 vols (Berlin, 1934–8)

v Other

A la Douma d'Empire. Rapport présenté par M-R. E. P. Kovalevsky, député, sur les travaux de la commission extraordinaire d'enquête chargée de constater les cas de violation des lois et des coutumes de guerre par l'ennemi (Petrograd, n.d., but 1915)

Infractions aux lois de la guerre commises par les troupes allemandes et austro-hongroises en Russie. Mémoire adressé par le gouvernement impérial de Russie aux puissances neutres (Petrograd, 1915)

Mémoire officiel russe sur les atrocités commises en 1914 par les armées des Empires centraux sur le front russe (n.pl, n.d., but 1915)

Papers Relating to the Foreign Relations of the United States. The Paris Peace Conference 1919, vol. 6 (Washington, D.C., 1946)

Trial of the Major War Criminals before the International Military Tribunal. Nuremberg 14 November

1945–1 October 1946, 42 vols (Nuremberg, 1947–9), vol. 6 (1947), vol. 27 (1948)

K.U.K. Ministerium des Äußern, *Sammlung von Nachweisen für die Verletzungen des Völkerrechtes durch die mit Österreich-Ungarn kriegführenden Staaten*, 31 January 1915 (Vienna, 1915)

——*Sammlung von Nachweisen für die Verletzungen des Völkerrechtes durch die mit Österreich-Ungarn kriegführenden Staaten*, 1st supplement, 30 April 1915 (Vienna, 1915)

——*Sammlung von Nachweisen für die Verletzungen des Völkerrechtes durch die mit Österreich-Ungarn kriegführenden Staaten*, 2nd supplement, 30 November 1915 (Vienna, 1916)

Temperley, Harold W. V. (ed.), *A History of the Peace Conference of Paris*, 6 vols (London, 1920–4), vol. 3, *Chronology, Notes and Documents* (1920)

United Nations War Crimes Commission, *History of the United Nations War Crimes Commission and the Development of the Laws of War* (London, 1948)

United States Army, Intelligence Section, *Histories of Two Hundred and Fifty-One Divisions of the German Army which Participated in the War (1914–1918). Compiled from the Records of Intelligence Section of the General Staff, American Expeditionary Forces, at General Headquarters* (Washington, D.C., 1920; reprint London, 1989)

3 Books, pamphlets, and articles

1914. Enquêtes à Dinant, Andenne, Tamines et Luxembourg belge (n.pl., n.d.)

Les Affiches de guerre à Roubaix, à Tourcoing, à Lille, en Belgique. Avis, appels, proclamations, sentences, et documents divers des autorités françaises et allemandes. Août à fin décembre 1914 (Roubaix, 1915)

Les Alsaciens-Lorrains en France pendant la guerre (Paris, 1915)

Anklage und Widerlegung. Taschenbuch zur Kriegsschuldfrage (n.pl., n.d. [1928])

Appel aux consciences. Vers la paix. Avec un avant-propos de Victor Margueritte (Paris, 1925)

Les Atrocités allemandes à Lille. Trois témoignages de députés socialistes (Paris, 1919)

Au long de la voie sanglante. Les étapes douloureuses (Dinant, n.d.)

La Belgique et la guerre (Brussels, 1921–8), 4 vols; vol. 2, Jacques Cuvelier, *L'Invasion allemande* (1921); vol. 3, Maurice Tasnier and R. van Overstraeten, *Les Opérations militaires* (1926)

La Belgique martyre. Les atrocités allemandes dans les environs de Verviers (Verviers, n.d., but post-war)

Les Boches à Surice. Les Huns en Belgique (n.pl., n.d.)

Collection 'le cri des martyrs'. Enquêtes officieuses sur les brigandages allemands en Belgique, lors de l'invasion d'août 1914. Publication hebdomadaire (Dinant, n.d., but 1919–20)

Le Combat d'Arsimont. Les 21 et 22 août 1914 à la 19e Division (Nancy, Paris, Strasbourg, 1926)

Culture. Les crimes allemands. Kultur. Die deutschen Verbrechen (Paris, Nancy, Strasbourg, 1919)

'Die Einnahme von Janinu durch die Griechen', *Vierteljahrshefte für Truppenführung und Heereskunde* 10/4 (1913), pp. 783–90

L'Esprit français. Les caricaturistes (Paris, 1916)

Der Franktireurkrieg in Belgien. Geständnisse der belgischen Presse (Stuttgart and Berlin, 1915)

La Guerre européenne de 1914–1915. L'invasion allemande en France et en Belgique. La fin des barbares. Les atrocités commises par les allemands (Paris, n.d., but 1915)

Historique de 273e régiment d'infanterie pendant la guerre 1914–1918 (Nancy, Paris, Strasbourg, n.d.)

Historique du 277e régiment d'infanterie (Angers, n.d.)

Historique du 325e régiment d'infanterie (Paris, n.d.)

Das Königin Elisabeth Garde-Grenadier-Regiment Nr. 3, 1914–1918 (Oldenburg and Berlin, 1921)

Kriegsfahrten deutscher Maler. Selbsterlebtes im Weltkrieg 1914–1915 (Bielefeld and Leipzig, n.d., but 1916)

Die Legende von den abgehackten Kinderhänden (n.pl., 1926)

Lettres des évêques de Namur et de Liège concernant les atrocités allemandes dans leurs diocèse (Rome, 1916)

Louvain: 1914. Enquêtes à Dinant, Andenne, Tamines et Luxembourg belge (n.pl., n.d.)

Le Martyre de Dinant (5th edn, Dinant, 1920)

Nécrologie Dinantais: La vérité sur les massacres de Dinant (Dinant, n.d., but 1914)

Pages du livre de douleurs de la Belgique (n.pl., n.d.; a clandestine wartime Belgian publication)

Le Parti Socialiste belge et la guerre (n.pl., 1917)

Souvenez-vous! Ligue pour perpétuer le souvenir des crimes allemands. Statuts (Paris, 1916)

Transfeldts Dienstunterricht für Kriegsrekruten der deutschen Infanterie, 54th edn: war edn 1918–19 (Berlin, 1918)

The Truth about German Atrocities: Founded on the Report of the Committee on Alleged German Outrages (London, 1915) [Published by the Parliamentary Recruiting Committee]

Violations of the Laws and Customs of War: Report of the Majority and Dissenting Reports of the American and Japanese Members of the Commission on Responsibilities at the Conference of Paris, 1919 (Oxford, 1919)

Why We Are at War: Great Britain's Case (Oxford, 1914) [Published by the Oxford History School]

Andler, Charles, and Lavisse, Ernest, *Pratique et doctrine allemandes de la guerre* (Paris, 1915)

Arsène, Alexandre, and Ginisty, Paul, *Le Livre du souvenir. Guide du voyageur dans la France envahie en 1914* (Paris, 1916)

Asquith, Herbert, *The War, its Causes and its Message: Speeches delivered by the Prime Minister August–October 1914* (London, 1914)

Badel, Émile, *Lunéville (août–septembre 1914)* (Nancy, 1915)

Badel, Émile et al., *Gerbéviller-la-martyre. Documentaire, historique anecdotique* (Nancy, n.d., but 1915)

Bainville, Jacques, *Les Conséquences politiques de la paix* (Paris, 1920)

Baudrillart, Alfred, *Les Carnets du Cardinal Alfred Baudrillart. 1er août 1914–31 décembre 1918*, ed. Paul Christophe (Paris, 1994)

Beauchamp, Octave, *Les Cités meurtries. Les champs de bataille 1914–1915* (Paris, n.d., but 1915 or 1916)

Bédier, Joseph, *Comment l'Allemagne essaye de justifier ses crimes* (Paris, 1915); English translation, *How Germany Seeks to Justify her Atrocities* (Paris, 1915)

——*Les Crimes allemands d'après des témoignages allemands* (Paris, 1915); English translation, *German Atrocities from German Evidence* (Paris, 1915)

Bennett, Arnold, *The Journals of Arnold Bennett*, vol. 2, *1911–1921* (London, 1932)

Bennett, Ernest N. (ed. and trans.), *The German Army in Belgium: The White Book of May 1915. With a Foreword on Military Reprisals in Belgium and Ireland* (London, 1921)

Berlet, Charles, *Réméréville. Un village lorrain pendant les mois d'août et septembre 1914* (Paris, 1918)

Bernhardi, Friedrich von, *Reiterdienst. Kritische Betrachtungen über Kriegstätigkeit, Taktik, Ausbildung und Organisation unserer Kavallerie* (Berlin, 1910)

——*Deutschland und der nächste Krieg* (Stuttgart and Berlin, 1912); English translation, *Germany and the Next War* (London, 1912)

Bertroz, Loup, *Senlis pendant l'invasion allemande, 1914, d'après le carnet de notes d'un senlisien* (Senlis, n.d., but 1915)

Bloch, Ivan, *The Future of War in its Technical, Economic, and Political Relations* (1898; English translation, London, 1900)

Bloem, Walter, *Volk wider Volk* (Leipzig, 1912)

Böhme, Klaus (ed.), *Aufrufe und Reden deutscher Professoren im Ersten Weltkrieg* (Stuttgart, 1975)

Borries, Major von, 'Die Bevölkerung in belagerten Festungen', *Vierteljahrshefte für Truppenführung und Heereskunde*, 8/1 (1911), pp. 51–79

Breton, W., *Un Régiment belge en campagne (1er août–1er janvier 1915). Quelques fastes du 2e chasseurs à pied* (Paris and Nancy, 1916)

Brock, M. and Brock, E. (eds), *H. H. Asquith: Letters to Venetia Stanley* (Oxford, 1985)

Bryce, Viscount [James], *The Attitude of Great Britain in the Present War* (London, 1916)

Bülow, Kurt Ernst Gottfried von, *Preußischer Militarismus zur Zeit Wilhelms II. Aus meiner Dienstzeit im Heer* (Schweidnitz, 1930)

Carnegie Endowment for International Peace, *Report of the International Commission to Inquire into the Causes and Conduct of the Balkan Wars* (London, 1914)

Chambry, René, *La Vérité sur Louvain* (Paris, 1915); English translation, *The Truth about Louvain* (London, 1915)

Champcommunal, M. J., *Les Lois de la guerre (guerre sur terre). Leur violation systématique par l'Allemagne. Réparations et sanctions. Conférence donnée le samedi 27 novembre 1915 dans la grande salle de l'Hôtel-de-Ville de Limoges* (Paris, 1915)

Chot, Jean, *La Furie allemande dans l'entre-Sambre-et-Meuse (journées des 23, 24, 25 et 26 août 1914)* (Charleroi, 1919)

Church, S. H., *The American Verdict on the War* (Baltimore, 1915)

Clark, Andrew, *Echoes of the Great War: The Diary of the Reverend Andrew Clark, 1914–1919* (Oxford, 1985)

Clausewitz, Carl von, *On War*, ed. and trans. Michael Howard and Peter Paret (Princeton, 1976)

Clemenceau, Georges, *Discours de paix* (Paris, 1938)

Clunet, Edouard, 'Les Criminels de guerre devant le Reichsgericht à Leipzig', *Journal du Droit International*, 48 (1921), pp. 440–7

Cobb, Irvin S., *The Red Glutton: With the German Army at the Front* (London, 1915)

Colin, L., *Les Barbares à la trouée des Vosges. Récits des témoins* (Paris, 1915)

Comité Catholique de Propagande Française à l'Étranger, *La Guerre allemande et le catholicisme* (Paris, 1915)

Cook, Theodore, *Kaiser, Krupp and Kultur* (London, 1915)

——*Kultur and Catastrophe* (London, 1915)

Creel, George, *How We Advertised America* (New York, 1920)

Cuvelier, Jacques, *L'Invasion allemande* (Brussels, 1921), vol. 2 of *La Belgique et la guerre* (above)

Dampierre, Jacques de, *Carnets de route de combattants allemands: traduction intégrale* (Paris, 1916)

Dauzat, Albert, *Légendes, prophéties et superstitions de la guerre* (Paris, n.d.)

Davignon, Henri, *Les Procédés de guerre des allemands en Belgique* (Paris, 1915)

——*La Conduite des armées allemandes en Belgique et en France d'après l'enquête anglaise* (Paris, 1915)

——*Belgium and Germany. Texts and Documents* (London, 1915)

——*Affiches allemandes en Belgique. Leur valeur d'aveu. Nouveaux textes et documents précédés d'un avertissement au lecteur* (Paris: 1916); English translation, *German Posters in Belgium: Their Value as Evidence.* (London, 1918)

——*Souvenirs d'un écrivain belge, 1879–1945* (Paris, 1954)

Davis, Richard Harding, *With the Allies* (London, 1915)

de Soete, Pierre, *Furore teutonico, 1914–1929* (Brussels, n.d., but 1929)

Delbrück, Joachim (ed.), *Der deutsche Krieg in Feldpostbriefen*, 10 vols (Munich, 1915–17), vol. 1, *Lüttich/Namur/Antwerpen* (1915)

Demartial, Georges, *La Mobilisation des consciences. La guerre de 1914* (Paris, 1922; enlarged edn, 1927)

Destrée, Jules, *Le Atrocità tedesche. Documenti ufficiali pubblicati da Giulio Destrée, Deputato di Charleroy* (Milan, 1914)

——*En Italie avant la guerre, 1914–1915* (Brussels and Paris, 1915)

——*Les Socialistes et la guerre européenne 1914–1915* (Paris, 1916)

Deuringer, Karl (for the Bayerisches Kriegsarchiv), *Die Schlacht in Lothringen und in den Vogesen 1914. Die Feuertaufe der Bayerischen Armee*, 2 vols (Munich, 1929)

Dimier, Louis, *L'Appel des intellectuels allemands* (Paris, 1915)

Docquois, G., *La Chair innocente. L'enfant du viol boche* (Paris, n.d., but 1917)

Dromart, Marie-Louise, *Sur le chemin du calvaire* (Paris, 1920)

Duhr, Bernhard, S.J., *Der Lügengeist im Völkerkrieg. Kriegs-Märchen* (Munich and Regensburg, 1915)

Dumas, Jacques, *Les Sanctions pénales des crimes allemands* (Paris, 1916)

Dumoulin, Michel (ed.), *Jules Destrée. Souvenirs des temps de guerre* (Louvain, 1980)

Durkheim, Émile, *L'Allemagne au dessus de tout* (Paris, 1915)

Einem, Generaloberst [Karl] von, *Erinnerungen eines Soldaten 1853–1933* (Leipzig, 1933)

——*Ein Armeeführer erlebt den Weltkrieg. Persönliche Aufzeichnungen des Generalobersten v. Einem*, ed. Junius Alter (Leipzig, 1938)

Ernst, Carl, *Der Große Krieg in Belgien. Beobachtungen, seinen ehemaligen hannoverschen Landsleuten gewidmet* (Gembloux, 1930)

Erzberger, Matthias, *Erlebnisse im Weltkrieg* (Stuttgart and Berlin, 1920)

Escudier, J. and Richepin, J., *Le Livre rouge des atrocités allemandes d'après les rapports officiels des gouvernements français, anglais et belges par l'image [...] 40 estampes hors texte [...] par J.-G. Domergue* (Paris, n.d.)

Essen, Léon van der, *The Invasion and the War in Belgium from Liège to the Yser* (London, 1917)

Fischer-Baling, Eugen, 'Der Untersuchungsausschuß für die Schuldfragen des ersten Weltkrieges', in Alfred Herrmann (ed.), *Aus Geschichte und Politik. Festschrift zum 70. Geburtstag von Ludwig Bergstraesser* (Düsseldorf, 1954)

Fließ, Otto and Dittmar, Kurt, *5. Hannoversches Infanterie-Regiment Nr. 165 im Weltkriege* (Oldenburg and Berlin, 1927)

Foerster, Friedrich Wilhelm, *Zur Beurteilung der deutschen Kriegsführung* (Berlin, 1921)

Fonck, Alfons, *Schrotschüsse in Belgien* (Berlin, 1931)

Franciscus, *'Gott mit uns!' Dieu avec nous!* (Paris, 1916)

Freud, Sigmund, 'Thoughts for the Times on War and Death' (1915), in *The Penguin Freud Library*, vol. 12, *Civilization, Society and Religion* (London, 1991), pp. 61–89

Freycinet, Charles de, *La Guerre en province pendant le siège de Paris, 1870–71* (Paris, 1871)

Fröhlich, Elke (ed.), *Die Tagebücher von Joseph Goebbels. Sämtliche Fragmente*, part 1: *Aufzeichnungen 1924–1941*, vol. 4, *1.1.1940–8.7.1941* (Munich, New York, London, Paris, 1987)

Frymann, Daniel (i.e. Heinrich Claß), *Wenn ich der Kaiser wär. Politische Wahrheiten und Notwendigkeiten* (Leipzig, 1912)

Fuglister, A., *A Neutral Description of the Sack of Louvain* (Concord, N.H., 1929)

Gallinger, August, *Gegenrechnung. Verbrechen an kriegsgefangenen Deutschen* (Leipzig and Munich, 1921); English translation, *The Countercharge: The Matter of War Criminals from the German Side* (Munich, 1922)

Galtier-Boissière, Jean, *Histoire de la guerre*, part 1, *Le Crapouillot*, August 1932

Geffroy, Gustave (ed.), *La Grande Guerre par les artistes* (Paris, n.d., but 1915)

Gérard, Edouard, *La Mort de Dinant. Histoire d'un crime (21, 23, 24 et 25 août 1914)* (Dinant, 1919); English translation, *The War in Belgium, 1914–1918: The Atrocities at Dinant* (Brussels, 1919)

Gerard, James W., *My Four Years in Germany* (New York, 1917)

Gerstäcker, Friedrich, *Die Franctireurs. Erzählung aus dem deutsch-französischen Kriege* (Jena, n.d., but c.1871)

——*Kriegsbilder eines Nachzüglers aus dem deutsch-französischen Kriege* (Jena, n.d., but c.1871)

Gibbs, Philip, *The Soul of the War* (London, 1915)

——*Realities of War* (London, 1929)

Gibson, Hugh, *A Diplomatic Diary* (London, 1917)

Gide, André, *Journal d'André Gide, 1889–1939* (Paris, 1951)

Gollancz, Victor, *'Let My People Go': Some Practical Proposals for Dealing with Hitler's Massacre of the Jews* (London, 1943)

Goltz, Colmar Freiherr von der, *Léon Gambetta und seine Armeen* (Berlin, 1877); French translation, *Gambetta et ses armées* (Paris, 1877)

——*Das Volk in Waffen. Ein Buch über Heerwesen und Kriegführung unserer Zeit* (1883; 6th edn, revised 'on the basis of the experiences of the World War', Berlin, 1925); English translation, *The Nation in Arms: A Treatise on Modern Military Systems and the Conduct of War* (London, 1906)

——*Denkwürdigkeiten*, ed. Friedrich Freiherr von der Goltz and Wolfgang Foerster (Berlin, 1929)

Görlitz, Walter (ed.), *Regierte der Kaiser? Kriegstagebücher, Aufzeichnungen und Briefe des Chefs des Marine-Kabinetts Admiral Georg Alexander von Müller 1914–1918* (Göttingen, Berlin, Frankfurt, 1959)

Grasset, A., *Vingt jours de guerre aux temps héroïques. Carnet de route d'un commandant de compagnie.*

(Août 1914) (Paris and Nancy, 1918)

Graßhoff, Richard, *Belgiens Schuld. Zugleich eine Antwort an Prof. Waxweiler* (Berlin, 1915); English translation, *The Tragedy of Belgium: An Answer to Professor Waxweiler* (New York, 1915)

Graux, Lucien, *Les Fausses Nouvelles de la grande guerre*, 7 vols (Paris, 1918–20)

Graves, Robert, *Goodbye to All That* (1929; new edn, Oxford and Providence, 1995)

Graves, Robert with Alan Hodge, *The Long Week-End: A Social History of Great Britain 1918–1939* (London, 1940)

Grimauty, F.-H., *Six Mois de guerre en Belgique par un soldat belge. Août 1914–février 1915* (Paris, 1915)

Grimme, Hubert, *Ein böswilliger Sprachstümper über 'deutsche Kriegsgreuel'. Entgegnung auf 'Les Crimes Allemands par Joseph Bédier'* (Münster, 1915)

Griselle, Eugène, *Le Martyre du clergé français* (Paris, 1915)

Gromaire, Georges, *L'Occupation allemande en France (1914–1918)* (Paris, 1925)

Grondijs, L. H., *Les Allemands en Belgique (Louvain et Aarschot). Notes d'un témoin hollandais* (Paris and Nancy, 1915); English translation, *The Germans in Belgium* (New York, 1916)

Guillet, L., *Souvenez-vous! La barbarie allemande* (Paris, 1917)

Hankey, Maurice, *The Supreme Control: At the Paris Peace Conference 1919* (London, 1963)

Hauptmann, Gerhart, *Tagebücher 1914 bis 1918*, ed. Peter Sprengel (Berlin, 1997)

[Hausen] *Des Generalobersten Frhrn. v. Hausen Erinnerungen an den Marnefeldzug 1914. Mit einer einleitenden kritischen Studie*, ed. Fr. Max Kircheisen (1920; 2nd edn, Leipzig, 1922)

Hazard, Paul, *Un examen de conscience de l'Allemagne. D'après les papiers de prisonniers de guerre allemands* (Paris, 1915)

Hillis, Newell D., *German Atrocities: Their Nature and Philosophy* (New York, 1918)

Hindenburg, Paul von, *Aus meinem Leben* (Leipzig, 1920)

Hitler, Adolf, *Mein Kampf* (1925–6; English translation, London, 1969)

——*Hitler's Table Talk 1941–44: His Private Conversations*, introd. H. R. Trevor-Roper (1951; English translation, London, 1953)

Höcker, Paul Oskar, *An der Spitze meiner Kompagnie. Drei Monate Kriegserlebnisse* (Berlin, 1914)

Hoffmann, Max, *Die Aufzeichnungen des Generalmajors Max Hoffmann*, 2 vols (Berlin, 1928)

Houtte, P. van, *The Pan-Germanic Crime: Impressions and Investigations in Belgium during the German Occupation* (London, 1915)

Hubert, Joseph and Neujean, Joseph, *Rossignol. Les drames de l'invasion allemande dans le Luxembourg belge* (1922; new edn, Tamines, 1938)

Huch, Gregor, 'Die belgische Schande. Ein Briefwechsel aus Kriegszeit und ein Nachwort', *Der Deutsche*, 1/1 (1919) 'Kommission Schücking' in *Der Deutsche* 1/1 (1919)

Hymans, Paul, *Mémoires*, 2 vols (Brussels, 1958)

Immanuel, Friedrich, *Handbuch der Taktik*, 2 vols (Berlin, 1910)

——*Taktische Aufgaben für Übungen und Kriegsspiel in Verbänden aller Art bis zum Armeekorps einschließlich* (4th edn, Berlin, 1914)

Jacobsen, Hans-Adolf (ed.), *Dokumente zur Vorgeschichte des Westfeldzugs 1939–1940* (Göttingen, 1956)

Jacobson, Wojcieck, *Z Armja Klucka na Paryz: Pammielnik lekarza – Polaka* (Torun, 1934); French translation, *En marche sur Paris avec l'armée prussienne du Général von Kluck* (Brussels, 1937)

Jacomet, R., *Les Lois de la guerre continentale* (Paris, 1913)

Jannasch, Lilli, *Untaten des preußisch-deutschen Militarismus* (Wiesbaden, 1924); English translation, *German Militarism at Work: A Collection of Documents* (London, 1926)

Janson, August von, *Der junge Infanterieoffizier und seine taktische Ausbildung* (Berlin, 1900)

Kautsky, Karl, *Wie der Weltkrieg entstand. Dargestellt nach dem Aktenmaterial des Deutschen Auswärtigen Amts* (Berlin, 1919)

Keim, August, *Erlebtes und Erstrebtes: Lebenserinnerungen von Generalleutnant Keim* (Hanover, 1925)

Kennedy, J. M., *The Campaign round Liège* (London, 1914)

Keynes, John Maynard, *The Economic Consequences of the Peace* (London, 1919)

Klotz, Louis-Lucien, *De la Guerre à la paix. Souvenirs et documents* (Paris, 1924)

Kluck, Alexander von, *Der Marsch auf Paris und die Marneschlacht 1914* (Berlin, 1920); English translation, *The March on Paris and the Battle of the Marne, 1914* (London, 1920)

Knox, Alfred, *With the Russian Army 1914–1917*, 2 vols (London, 1921)

Koester, Adolph and Noske, Gustav, *Kriegsfahrten durch Belgien und Nordfrankreich 1914* (Berlin, n.d., but 1915)

Krafft, Karl, *Handbuch für die Vorbereitung zur Kriegsakademie. Zugleich ein Ratgeber für die wissenschaftliche Beschäftigung jüngerer Offiziere* (Berlin, 1903)

Krause, Paul R., 'Franktireure', *Die Gartenlaube. Illustriertes Familienblatt*, 36 (1914), pp. 764–6

Kretschman, Hans von, *Kriegsbriefe aus den Jahren 1870/71*, ed. Lily Braun (12th edn, Berlin, 1911)

Kurth, Godefroid, *Le Guet-apens prussien en Belgique* (Paris and Brussels, 1919)

Kuttner, Max, *Deutsche Verbrechen? Wider Joseph Bédier, 'Les Crimes allemands': Zugleich eine Antwort aus französischen Dokumenten* (Bielefeld and Leipzig, 1915)

Labour Party, *Report of the Labour Commission to Ireland* (London, 1921)

Lacassagne, A., *Vacher, l'éventreur et les crimes sadiques* (Lyon, 1899)

Ladeuze, P., *Le Crime allemand contre l'université de Louvain. Les leçons de la guerre. (Discours prononcé […] à Louvain, le 21 janvier 1919, pour l'ouverture solennelle des cours de l'université de Louvain, après la grande guerre)* (Louvain, 1919)

Langenhove, Fernand van, *Comment naît un cycle de légendes. Francs-tireurs et atrocités en Belgique* (Lausanne and Paris, 1916); English translation, *The Growth of a Legend: A Study Based upon the German Accounts of Francs-Tireurs and 'Atrocities' in Belgium* (London, 1916); German translation, *Wie Legenden entstehen! Franktireurkrieg und Greueltaten in Belgien* (Zürich, 1917)

Langlois, Gabriel, *Le Clergé, les catholiques et la guerre* (Paris, 1915)

Lapradelle, Albert de (ed.), *La Paix de Versailles* (Paris, 1929–39), 14 vols, vol. 3, *Responsabilités des auteurs de la guerre et sanctions* (1930)

Lapradelle, Albert de with Frédéric Larnaude, *Examen de la responsabilité pénale de l'Empereur Guillaume II* (Paris, 1918)

Larcher, M., *Le 1er Corps à Dinant, Charleroi, Guise (août 1914)* (Paris, 1932)

Larsen, K., *Professor Bédier und die Tagebücher deutscher Soldaten. Von Prof. Karl Larsen* (Berlin, 1915); French translation, *Le Professeur Bédier et les carnets de soldats allemands. Par le Professeur Charles Larsen de Copenhague* (Berne, 1916)

Laudy, Lucien, 'La Garde Civique non active en 1914', *Carnet de la Fourragère*, 1/3 (1925), pp. 73–7

Lavisse, Ernest, *L'Invasion dans le département de l'Aisne* (Laon, 1872)

——(ed.), *L'Allemagne et la guerre de 1914–15* (Paris, 1915)

Le Queux, William, *German Atrocities: A Record of Shameless Deeds* (London, 1914)

Lebert, F., *Varredes. Le martyre des otages* (2nd edn, Paris, 1917)

Lehmann, Konrad and Estorff, [Eggert] von, *Dienstunterricht des Offiziers. Anleitung zur Erteilung des Mannschaftsunterrichts in Beispielen* (Berlin, 1908)

Leitzen, Hans (ed.), *Der große Krieg 1914–15 in Feldpostbriefen. Neue Folge* (Wolfenbüttel, 1915)

Lemaire, A., *La Tragédie de Tamines (21, 22 et 23 août 1914)* (Tamines, 1919)

——*La Controverse des 'francs-tireurs'. Lettre ouverte à M. le Dr. R. P. Oszwald, conseiller supérieur d'archives et membre des archives du Reich* (Brussels, 1932)

Link, Arthur S. (ed.), *The Papers of Woodrow Wilson*, (69 vols, Princeton, 1966–94), vol. 32, *January 1–April 16 1915* (1980)

London, Géo, *Ils ont détruit sans nécessité militaire* (Paris, n.d., but 1918)

Lorimer, James, *The Institutes of the Law of Nations*, 2 vols (Edinburgh, 1883–4)

Loßberg, Fritz von, *Meine Tätigkeit im Weltkriege 1914–1918* (Berlin, 1939)

Loti, Pierre, *La Grande Barbarie (fragments)* (Paris, 1918)

Ludendorff, Erich, *Meine Kriegserinnerungen 1914–1918* (Berlin, 1919); English translation, *My War Memories, 1914–1918*, 2 vols (London, 1920)

Maccas, Léon, *Les Cruautés allemandes. Réquisitoire d'un neutre* (Paris,1915); English translation, *German Barbarism: A Neutral's Indictment* (London, 1916)

MacDonagh, Michael, *In London during the Great War: The Diary of a Journalist* (London, 1935)

Mack, Louise, *A Woman's Experiences in the Great War* (London, 1915)

Magnette, Charles, *Correspondance du grand maître de la maçonnerie belge, le frère Charles Magnette, avec les grands loges de la maçonnerie allemande* (Paris, 1915)

Mailler, A., *De la distinction entre les combattants et les non-combattants comme base du droit de guerre* (Paris, 1916)

Mantoux, Paul (ed.), *Les Délibérations du Conseil des quatre (24 mars–28 juin 1919)*, 2 vols (Paris, 1955)

Marchant, H., *Historique des troupes territoriales en Belgique en 1914. Groupement Clooten: Gardes Civiques, Gendarmerie, Corps de Volontaires* (Ixelles, 1938)

Marès, Roland de, *La Belgique envahie* (Paris, 1915)

Maricourt, André de, *Le Drame de Senlis. Journal d'un témoin. Avant, pendant, après août–septembre 1914* (Paris, 1916)

Martin-Ginouvrier, F., *Le Martyre du curé de Varreddes* (Barcelona and Paris, 1918)

Maser, Werner, *Hitler's Letters and Notes* (1973; English translation, London, 1976)

Massart, Jean, *Comment les belges résistent à la domination allemande. Contribution au livre des douleurs de la Belgique* (Paris and Lausanne, 1916); English translation, *Belgians under the German Eagle* (London, 1916)

——*Les Intellectuels allemands et la recherche de la vérité* (Paris, 1918)

——*La Presse clandestine dans la Belgique occupée* (Paris, 1917); English translation, *The Secret Press in Belgium* (London, 1918)

Matthias, Erich and Miller, Susanne (eds), *Das Kriegstagebuch des Reichstagsabgeordneten Eduard David 1914 bis 1918* (Düsseldorf, 1966)

Mayence, Fernand, 'The Belgian Rejoinder', *Current History* (New York) (July 1928), pp. 566–71

——*La Légende des francs-tireurs de Louvain. Réponse au mémoire de M. le Professeur Meurer de l'Université de Würzburg* (Louvain, 1928); German translation, *Die Legende der Franktireurs von Löwen. Antwort auf das Gutachten des H. Professors Meurer von der Universität Würzburg* (Louvain, 1928)

Mélot, Auguste, *L'Invasione tedesca nel Belgio. Discorso pronunciato da M. Mélot, deputato di Namur al Gabinetto Cattolico di Milano il 23 novembre del 1914* (Milan, n.d. but 1914)

——*Le Martyre du clergé belge* (Paris, 1915)

Mercier, Désiré, *Patriotisme et endurance. Lettre pastorale de Son Eminence le Cardinal Mercier, Archévêque de Malines, noël 1914* (Paris, 1915)

——*The Voice of Belgium: Being the Wartime Utterances of Cardinal Mercier* (London, 1917)

——*La Correspondance de S. E. le Cardinal Mercier avec le gouvernement général allemand pendant l'occupation 1914–1918* (Brussels and Paris, 1919); English translation, *Cardinal Mercier's own Story*, ed. Fernand Mayence (London, 1920)

Mercier, Désiré et al., *Les Évêques de Belgique aux évêques d'Allemagne et d'Autriche-Hongrie* (n.pl., n.d., but November 1915)

Mérignhac, Alexandre and Lémonon, E., *Le Droit des gens et la guerre de 1914–1918*, 2 vols (Paris, 1921)

Meurer, Christian, *Die Haager Friedenskonferenz*, 2 vols (Munich, 1907)

——'The Case for the Germans', *Current History* (New York) (July 1928), pp. 556–66

Meyer, Eduard (ed.), *Für Ehre, Wahrheit und Recht. Erklärung deutscher Hochschullehrer zur Auslieferungsfrage* (Berlin, 1919)

Mirman, Léon, *Sur la tombe des martyrs. Sur la tombe des héros* (Nancy, n.d., but 1916)

Mirman, Léon, with G. Simon and G. Keller, *Leurs Crimes* (Nancy, 1916); English translation, *Their Crimes* (London, 1917)

Mokveld, L., *De Overweldiging van België* (Rotterdam, 1916); English translation, *The German Fury in Belgium* (London, 1917)

Moltke, Helmuth von, *Geschichte des deutsch-französischen Krieges von 1870–71* (Berlin, 1891)

——*Moltkes Militärische Korrespondenz. Aus den Dienstschriften des Krieges 1870/71*, ed. Großer Generalstab (Berlin, 1897)

——*Moltke in seinen Briefen. Mit einem Lebens- und Charakterbild des Verewigten* (Berlin, 1902)

Montague, C. E., *Disenchantment* (London, 1922; new edn, 1940)

Mordacq, Jean-Jules, *Le Ministère Clemenceau. Journal d'un témoin*, 4 vols (Paris, 1930–1)

Morgan, John H., *German Atrocities: An Official Investigation* (London, 1916)

——(ed.), *The German War Book: Being 'The Usages of War on Land' (Kriegsbrauch im Landkrieg) issued by the Great General Staff of the German Army* (London, 1915)

Moser, Otto von, *Die Führung des Armeekorps im Feldkriege* (Berlin, 1910)

Mott, Thomas B., *Myron T. Herrick, Friend of France: An Autobiographical Biography* (New York, 1929)

Mullins, Claud, *The Leipzig Trials* (London, 1921)

Munro, Dana (ed.), *German War Practices* (Washington, D.C., 1918)

Münsterberg, Hugo, *The War and America* (New York, 1914)

Nau, Wilhelm, *Beiträge zur Geschichte des Regiments Hamburg*, 5 vols (Hamburg, 1924–6), vol. 1, *Der Marsch auf Paris* (1924)

Nieuwland, Norbert, and Tschoffen, Maurice, *La Légende des francs-tireurs de Dinant. Réponse au mémoire de M. le professeur Meurer de l'université de Wurzbourg* (Gembloux, 1928); German translation, *Das Märchen von den Franctireurs von Dinant. Antwort auf das Gutachten von Professor Meurer von der Universität Würzburg* (Gembloux, 1928)

Noiht, C., *Les Barbares modernes. Les atrocités et cruautés exercées par les allemands en Belgique, en Alsace-Lorraine et en France pendant la guerre de 1914*, 2 vols (Paris, 1914)

Normand, Lucien, *Le Châtiment des crimes allemands* (Paris, 1919)

Oehme, Walter (ed.), *Ein Bekenntnis deutscher Schuld. Beiträge zur deutschen Kriegsführung* (Berlin, 1920)

d'Orcines, Henry, *Leurs exploits* (Étampes, n.d. but 1919)

Orwell, Sonia and Angus, Ian (eds), *The Collected Essays, Journalism and Letters of George Orwell*, 4 vols (London, 1968), vol. 3, *As I Please, 1943–1945* (new edn, Harmondsworth, 1978)

d'Ostoya, Georges, *Le Livre des atrocités allemandes d'après les rapports officiels* (Paris, 1920)

Oszwald, Robert Paul, *Der Streit um den belgischen Franktireurkrieg. Eine kritische Untersuchung der Ereignisse in den Augusttagen 1914 und der darüber bis 1930 erschienenen Literatur unter Benutzung bisher nicht veröffentlichten Materials* (Cologne, 1931)

Otto, Helmut and Schmiedel, Karl (eds), *Der erste Weltkrieg. Dokumente* (1st edn 1977; Berlin (DDR), 1983)

Paléologue, Maurice, *La Russie des Tsars pendant la Grande Guerre*, 3 vols (Paris, 1921–2), vol. 2, *3 juin 1915–18 août 1916* (1922)

Passelecq, Fernand, *La Légende de la guerre de francs-tireurs en Belgique d'après un pamphlet allemand et le 'Livre Blanc' du 10 mai 1915* (Le Havre, 1915); English translation, *The Legend of the Francs-Tireurs Warfare in Belgium* (Le Havre, 1915)

——*La Réponse du gouvernement belge au Livre blanc allemand du 10 mai 1915. Etude analytique de la publication officielle du gouvernement belge* (Paris, 1916), English translation; *Truth and Travesty. An Analytical Study of the Reply of the Belgian Government to the German White Book* (London, 1916)

——*Francs-tireurs et atrocités belges. Un cycle de légendes allemandes* (Le Havre, n.d., but 1916)

Paxson, Frederic L., *Pre-War Years, 1913–1917* (Boston, 1936)

Paxson, Frederic L. et al., *War Cyclopedia: A Handbook for Ready Reference on the Great War* (Washington D.C., 1918)

Pingaud, A., 'Impressions de guerre allemandes en 1870', *Revue des Deux Mondes*, 15 September 1915, pp. 371–95

Pittard, Hélène, (under pseudonym N. Roger), *Le Passage des évacués à travers la Suisse*, 2 vols (Paris and Neuchâtel, n.d., but 1915 or 1916), vol. 1, *Les Evacués à Genève*

——*Le Cortège des victimes; les rapatriés d'Allemagne, 1914–1916* (Paris, 1917); English translation, *The Victims' Return: With an Historical Note by Eugène Pittard* (London, 1917)

Ponsonby, Arthur, *Now is the Time: An Appeal for Peace* (London, 1925)

——*Falsehood in Wartime: Containing an Assortment of Lies Circulated Throughout the Nations During the Great War* (London, 1928)

Powell, E. Alexander, *Fighting in Flanders* (London, 1914)

Powys, John Cowper, *The Menace of German Culture: A Reply to Professor Münsterberg* (London, 1915)

Rabier, P., *La Loi du mâle. A propos de l'enfant du barbare* (Paris, 1915)

Raemaekers, Louis, *The Great War: A Neutral's Indictment. One Hundred Cartoons by Louis Raemaekers* (London, 1916)

——*The 'Land and Water' Edition of Raemaekers' Cartoons* (London, 1916)

——*Raemaekers' Cartoon History of the War*, ed. J. Murray Allison (London, 1919)

Redier, Antoine, *Les Allemands dans nos maisons* (1938; 2nd edn, Paris, 1945)

Reiss, R.A., *Comment les Austro-hongrois ont fait la guerre en Serbie. Observations directes d'un neutre* (Paris, 1915); English translation, *How Austria-Hungary Waged War in Serbia: Personal Investigation by a Neutral* (Paris, 1915)

——*Report upon the Atrocities Committed by the Austro-Hungarian Army during the First Invasion of Serbia. Submitted to the Serbian Government* (London, 1916)

——*Réponses aux accusations austro-hongroises contre les serbes* (Lausanne and Paris, 1918)

——*Rapport sur les atrocités commises en 1914 par les troupes austro-hongroises pendant la première invasion de la Serbie, présenté au gouvernement serbe par le Dr R. A. Reiss* (Paris, 1919)

Renn, Ludwig, *Krieg* (Frankfurt, 1929); English translation, *War* (London, 1929)

Rezanoff, A.S., *Les Atrocités allemandes du côté russe* (Petrograd, 1915)

Richert, Dominik, *Beste Gelegenheit zum Sterben. Meine Erlebnisse im Kriege 1914–1918*, ed. Angelika Tramitz and Bernd Ulrich (Munich, 1989)

[Riddell, George], *Lord Riddell's War Diary, 1914–1918* (London, 1933)

Roberts, Adam and Guelff, Richard (eds), *Documents on the Laws of War* (Oxford, 1989)

Rolin, L., 'La Bataille de Nomény (20 août 1914)', *Le Pays lorrain* (August 1933), pp. 349–65

Rolland, Romain, *Au-dessus de la mêlée* (1914; new edn, Paris, 1915); English translation, *Above the Battlefield* (Cambridge, 1914)

——*Journal des années de guerre 1914–1919* (Paris, 1952)

Rolland, Romain with Stefan Zweig, *Romain Rolland, Stefan Zweig, Briefwechsel, 1910–1940*, 2 vols (Berlin, 1987)

Rosenberg, A. J., *Der deutsche Krieg und der Katholizismus* (Paderborn, 1915); English translation, *The German War and Catholicism: German Defense against French Attacks* (St Paul, Minn., 1916)

Roubille, Auguste, *La Marseillaise* (n.pl., n.d., but 1915)

Royer, Emile, *German Socialists and Belgium* (London, n.d., but 1915)

Salomon, H., *Les Allemands peints par eux-mêmes* (Dunkirk, 1921)

Santo, Jean, *Les Crimes allemands et leur châtiment* (Paris, n.d., but 1916)

Sarolea, Charles, *The Murder of Nurse Cavell* (London, 1915)

Scharfenort, Louis von, *L'interprète militaire. Zum Gebrauch in Feindesland, sowie behufs Vorbereitung für die Dolmetscherprüfung mit den Lösungen der schwierigeren Texte aus '225 deutsche Aufgaben'* (Berlin, 1906)

[Schlieffen] Großer Generalstab (ed.), *Alfred von Schlieffen: Gesammelte Schriften*, 2 vols (Berlin, 1913)

Schmitz, Jean and Nieuwland, Norbert, *Documents pour servir à l'histoire de l'invasion allemande dans les provinces de Namur et de Luxembourg*, 7 vols (Brussels and Paris, 1919–24)

Schücking, Lothar Engelbert, 'War der Franktireurkrieg verboten?', *Die Weltbühne*, (13 September 1927), pp. 396–400

Schwertfeger, Bernhard, *Belgische Landesverteidigung und Bürgerwacht (garde civique) 1914. Im amtlichen Auftrag bearbeitet* (Berlin, 1920); republished as *Die Grundlagen des belgischen Franktireurkrieges 1914. Das deutsche amtliche Material* (Berlin, n.d., but 1920)

Scott, George W. and Garner, James W., *The German War Code Contrasted with the War Manuals of the United States, Great Britain and France* (Washington, D.C., 1918)

Scott, James B. (ed.), *Texts of the Peace Conferences at the Hague, 1899 and 1907* (Boston and London, 1908)

——(ed.), *The Hague Peace Conferences of 1899 and 1907* (New York, 1909)

——(ed.), *The Proceedings of the Hague Peace Conferences: Translation of the Official Texts*, 5 vols

(New York, 1920–1)

——'The Trial of the Kaiser', in Edward M. House and Charles Seymour (eds), *What Really Happened at Paris* (New York, 1921), pp. 231–58

Seestern (pseudonym for Ferdinand Grautoff), *1906. Der Zusammenbruch der alten Welt* (Leipzig, n.d., 2nd edn [1907])

Selbie, W. B., *The War and Theology* (London, 1915)

Shaw, George Bernard, 'Common Sense about the War' (1914), in *The Works of Bernard Shaw*, vol. 21, *What I Really Wrote About the War* (London, 1930), pp. 23–115

——*Bernard Shaw: Collected Letters*, 4 vols (London, 1965–88), vol. 3, *1911–1925*, ed. Dan H. Laurence (London, 1985)

Shirer, William L., *Berlin Diary: The Journal of a Foreign Correspondent 1934–1941* (London, 1941)

Simonin, J., *De Verdun à Mannheim. Ethe et Goméry (22, 23, 24 août 1914)*, (Paris, 1917)

Skopkiansky, M. D., *Les Atrocités serbes, d'après les témoignages américains, anglais, français, italiens, russes, serbes, suisses* (Lausanne, 1919)

Sombart, Werner, *Händler und Helden: Patriotische Besinnungen* (Leipzig and Munich, 1915)

Somville, Gustave, *Vers Liège. Le chemin du crime. Août 1914* (Paris, 1915); English translation, *The Road to Liège: The Path of Crime, August 1914* (London, 1916)

Sparr, Hermann (ed.), *Feldpostbriefe 1914. Berichte und Stimmungsbilder von Mitkämpfern und Miterlebern* (Leipzig, 1915)

Stresemann, Gustav, *Gustav Stresemann: His Diaries, Letters and Papers*, 3 vols (1933; English translation, London, 1940)

Struycken, A. A. H., *The German White Book and the War in Belgium: A Commentary by Professor A. A. H. Struycken* (London and New York, 1916)

Stühmke, Reinhold, *Das Infanterie-Regiment 'Kaiser Friedrich, König von Preußen' (7. Württ.) Nr. 125 im Weltkrieg 1914–1918* (Stuttgart, 1923)

Stülpnagel, Otto von, *Die Wahrheit über die deutschen Kriegsverbrechen. Die Anklagen der Verbandsmächte in Gegenüberstellung zu ihren eigenen Taten* (Berlin, 1920; 4th edn, 1921)

Tasnier, Maurice and van Overstraeten, R., *Les Opérations Militaires* (Brussels, 1926), vol. 3 of *La Belgique et la guerre* (above)

The Times History of the War, 21 vols (London, 1914–20), vols 1 (1914) and 2 (1915)

Toynbee, Arnold, *Armenian Atrocities: The Murder of a Nation* (London, 1915)

Trochon, P., *Lille avant et pendant l'occupation allemande* (Tourcoing, 1922)

Tschischwitz, Erich von der (ed.), *General von der Marwitz. Weltkriegsbriefe* (Berlin, 1940)

Tschoffen, Maurice, *Le Sac de Dinant et les légendes du Livre blanc allemand du 10 mai 1915* (Leiden, 1917)

Valéry, J., *Les Crimes de la population belge. Réplique à un plaidoyer pour le gouvernement allemand* (Paris, 1916)

Vandaele, F., 'Une offensive de mensonges. Les historiques des régiments allemands', *Revue Générale* (Brussels) (15 July 1932), pp. 31–50

Vandervelde, Émile, *La Belgique envahie et le socialisme international* (Paris, 1917)

Variot, G., *Les Lois de l'hérédité et les femmes violentées pendant la guerre, extrait des Bulletins et mémoires de la Société d'Anthropologie de Paris, séance du 18 février 1915* (Paris, 1915)

Viereck, George S., *Spreading Germs of Hate* (London, 1931)

Viriot, André, *Les Allemands à Nomény (août 1914)* (Nancy, 1916)

Vliegen, F., *La Tragédie de Visé et la captivité des civils en Allemagne* (Liège, n.d., but 1919)

Vuille, C., *L'Affaire Raemaekers. Compte-rendu du procès intenté à Me Charles Vuille devant la Haute Cour Pénale Fédérale* (Neuchâtel, n.d., but 1918)

Waxweiler, Émile, *La Guerre de 1914. La Belgique neutre et loyale* (Paris and Lausanne, 1915); German translation, *Der europäische Krieg. Hat Belgien sein Schicksal verschuldet?* (Zürich, 1915)

Wehberg, Hans, *Wider den Aufruf der 93! Das Ergebnis einer Rundfrage an die 93 Intellektuellen über die Kriegsschuld* (n.pl., 1920)

Whitehouse, J. H., *Belgium at War: A Record of Personal Experiences*, introd. Lloyd George (Cambridge, 1915)

Whitlock, Brand, *Belgium under the German Occupation: A Personal Narrative*, 2 vols (London, 1919)

Wilamowitz-Moellendorf, Ulrich von, *My Recollections 1848–1914* (1929; English translation, London, 1930)

Wolff, Theodor, *Tagebücher 1914–1919. Der Erste Weltkrieg und die Entstehung der Weimarer Republik in Tagebüchern, Leitartikeln und Briefen des Chefredakteurs am 'Berliner Tageblatt' und Mitbegründers der 'Deutschen Demokratischen Partei'*, ed. Bernd Sösemann, part 1 (Boppard, 1984)

Zimmermann, Oberst von, 'Milizheere (Schluß). Die Heere der französischen Republik im Kriege 1870/71', *Vierteljahrshefte für Truppenführung und Heereskunde*, 10/4 (1913), pp. 694–731

Zweig, Stefan, *The World of Yesterday* (London, 1943)

III Secondary Literature (selected)

1 Books and articles

Afflerbach, Holger, *Falkenhayn. Politisches Denken und Handeln im Kaiserreich* (Munich, 1994)

Anderson, Margaret Lavinia, 'Windhorsts Erben: Konfessionalität und Interkonfessionalismus im politischen Katholizismus 1890–1918', in Winfried Becker and Rudolf Morsey (eds), *Christliche Demokratie in Europa: Grundlagen und Entwicklungen seit dem 19. Jahrhundert* (Cologne and Vienna, 1988), pp. 69–90

Audoin-Rouzeau, Stéphane, *1870. La France dans la guerre* (Paris, 1989)

——*La Guerre des enfants 1914–1918: Essai d'histoire culturelle* (Paris, 1993)

——*L'Enfant de l'ennemi (1914–1918). Viol, avortement, infanticide pendant la grande guerre* (Paris, 1995)

Audoin-Rouzeau, Stéphane and Becker, Annette, 'Violence et consentement. La "culture de guerre" du premier conflit mondial', in Jean-Pierre Rioux and Jean-François Sirinelli (eds), *Pour une histoire culturelle* (Paris, 1997), pp. 251–71

——*14–18. Retrouver la guerre* (Paris, 2000)

Augé, Marc, *Le Sens des autres. Actualité de l'anthropologie* (Paris, 1994)

Ballaer, Canon van, *Benoit XV et la Belgique pendant les premiers mois de son pontificat* (Louvain, 1922)

Bartov, Omer, *Hitler's Army: Soldiers, Nazis, and War in the Third Reich* (New York, 1992)

Baumeister, Martin, *Parität und katholische Inferiorität. Untersuchungen zur Stellung des Katholizismus im Deutschen Kaiserreich* (Paderborn, 1987)

Becker, Annette, *Les Monuments aux morts. Mémoire de la grande guerre* (Paris, 1988)

——'Mémoire et commémoration. Les "atrocités" allemandes de la première guerre mondiale dans le nord de la France', *Revue du Nord*, 295 (1992), pp. 339–53

——'D'une guerre à l'autre. Mémoire de l'occupation et de la résistance: 1914–1945', *Revue du Nord*, 306 (1994), pp. 453–65

——'L'Étranger au temps de la guerre de 1870–1871', in Jean-Pierre Jessenne (ed.), *L'Image de l'autre dans l'Europe du nord-ouest à travers l'histoire* (Lille, 1996), pp. 123–32

——*War and Faith: The Religious Imagination in France 1914–1930* (1994; English translation, Oxford, 1998)

——*Oubliés de la grande guerre. Humanitaire et culture de guerre 1914–1918. Populations occupées, déportés civils, prisonniers de guerre* (Paris, 1998)

Becker, Jean-Jacques, *1914: Comment les français sont entrés dans la guerre* (Paris, 1977)

——*The Great War and the French People* (1980; English translation, Leamington Spa, 1985)

——'Le Procès de Leipzig', in Annette Wieviorka (ed.), *Les Procès de Nuremberg et de Tokyo* (Brussels, 1996), pp. 51–60

Becker, Jean-Jacques et al. (eds), *Guerre et cultures 1914–1918* (Paris, 1994)

Becker, Jean-Jacques with Stéphane Audoin-Rouzeau (eds), *Les Sociétés européennes et la guerre de 1914–1918* (Paris, 1990)

Becker, Jean-Jacques with Serge Berstein, *Histoire de l'anticommunisme en France*, 2 vols Paris, 1987) vol. 1, *1917–1940*

——*Nouvelle Histoire de la France contemporaine*, vol. 12, *Victoire et frustration, 1914–1929* (Paris, 1990)

Bénéton, Pierre, *Histoire des mots. Culture et civilisation* (Paris, 1975)

Bercé, Yves-Marie, 'Rumeurs des siècles modernes', in Jean-Pierre Rioux and Jean-François Sirinelli (eds), *Pour une histoire culturelle* (Paris, 1997), pp. 185–92

Berlau, Abraham, *The German Social Democratic Party 1914–1921* (1949; new edn, New York, 1975)

Bessel, Richard, *Germany after the First World War* (Oxford, 1993)

Best, Geoffrey, 'Restraints on War by Land before 1945', in Michael Howard (ed.), *Restraints on War: Studies in the Limitation of Armed Conflict* (Oxford, 1979), pp. 17–37

——*Humanity in Warfare: The Modern History of the International Law of Armed Conflicts* (London, 1980; new edn, 1983)

Bloch, Marc, 'Réflexions d'un historien sur les fausses nouvelles de la guerre', in Bloch, *Écrits de guerre, 1914–1918*, ed. Étienne Bloch, introd. Stéphane Audoin-Rouzeau, (Paris, 1997), pp. 169–84, originally published in the *Revue de Synthèse*, 1921

Bonnefous, Edouard and Bonnefous, Georges, *Histoire politique de la troisième république*, 8 vols (Paris, 1965–86); vol. 3, *L'après-guerre (1919–1924)*, (Paris, 1968); vol. 4, *Cartel des gauches et union nationale (1924–1929)* (Paris, 1973)

Bourke, Joanna, *An Intimate History of Killing: Face-to-Face Killing in Twentieth-Century Warfare* (London, 1999)

Brenet, Amédée, *La France et l'Allemagne devant le droit international pendant les opérations militaires de la guerre de 1870–71* (Paris, 1902)

Brocke, Bernhard vom, '"Wissenschaft und Militarismus." Der Aufruf der 93 "An die Kulturwelt!" und der Zusammenbruch der internationalen Gelehrtenrepublik im Ersten Weltkrieg' in William M. Calder III, Helmut Flashar, and Theodor Lindken (eds), *Wilamowitz nach 50 Jahren* (Darmstadt, 1985), pp. 649–719

Brownlow, Kevin, *The War, the West and the Wilderness* (London, 1979)

Bucholz, Arden, *Moltke, Schlieffen, and Prussian War Planning* (Providence and Oxford, 1991)

Cahalan, Peter, *Belgian Refugee Relief in England during the Great War* (New York, 1932)

Campbell, Craig W., *Reel America and World War I: A Comprehensive Filmography and History of Motion Pictures in the United States, 1914–1920* (Jefferson, N.C., and London, 1985)

Capdevila, Luc, *Les Bretons au lendemain de l'occupation. Imaginaire et comportement d'une sortie de guerre 1944–1945* (Rennes, 1999)

Carrias, E., *La Pensée militaire allemande* (Paris, 1948)

Ceadel, Martin, *Pacifism in Britain 1914–1945: The Defining of a Faith* (Oxford, 1980)

Chauvaud, Frédéric, *De Pierre Rivière à Landru. La violence apprivoisée au XIXe siècle* (Brussels, 1991)

Chickering, Roger, *Imperial Germany and a World without War: The Peace Movement and German Society, 1892–1914* (Princeton, 1975)

——*We Men who Feel most German: A Cultural Study of the Pan-German League, 1886–1914* (Boston, London, Sydney, 1984)

——'Die Alldeutschen erwarten den Krieg', in Jost Dülffer and Karl Holl (eds), *Bereit zum Krieg. Kriegsmentalität im wilhelminischen Deutschland 1890–1914. Beiträge zur historischen Friedensforschung* (Göttingen, 1986), pp. 20–32

Chickering, Roger with Stig Förster (eds), *Great War, Total War: Combat and Mobilization on the Western Front, 1914–1918* (Cambridge, 2000)

Claeys-Boovaert, L. and van Humbeeck, J., 'Les Discours de la propagande belge en Italie: 1914–1918', *Risorgimento. Bulletin semestrial publié par le Comité belge de l'Istituto per la Storia del Risorgimento Italiano*, 21 (1979), pp. 23–46

Clarke, Ignatius F., *Voices Prophesying War: Future Wars, 1763–3749* (1966; 2nd edn, Oxford, 1992)

Clemente, Steven E., *For King and Kaiser! The Making of the Prussian Army Officer, 1860–1914* (New York, Westport, London, 1992)

Cochet, François, *1914–1918: Rémois en guerre. L'héroïsation au quotidien* (Nancy, 1993)

Coetzee, Marilyn Shevin, *The German Army League: Popular Nationalism in Wilhelmine Germany* (New York and Oxford, 1990)

Coles, Alan, *Slaughter at Sea: The Truth behind a Naval War Crime* (London, 1986)

Conze, Werner, *Polnische Nation und deutsche Politik im Ersten Weltkrieg* (Cologne and Graz, 1958)

Cooper, Sandi E., *Patriotic Pacifism: Waging War on War in Europe 1815–1914* (New York and Oxford, 1991)

Craig, Gordon A., *The Politics of the Prussian Army 1640–1945* (1955; new edn, Oxford, 1964)

Crémieux-Brilhac, Jean-Louis, *La France Libre. De l'appel du 18 juin à la Libération* (Paris, 1996)

Creusat, Robert, *La Victoire oubliée. Gerbéviller-Rozelieures, août–septembre 1914* (Lunéville, 1986)

Crozier, Emmet, *American Reporters on the Western Front 1914–1918* (New York, 1959)

Cru, Jean Norton, *Témoins. Essai d'analyse et de critique des souvenirs de combattants édités en français de 1915 à 1928* (Paris, 1929)

Dauzat, Albert, *Légendes, prophéties et superstitions de guerre* (Paris, n.d.)

De Vroey, Jozef, *Aarschot op Woensdag 19 augustus 1914* (Aarschot, n.d., but 1964)

DeBauche, Leslie Midkiff, 'Mary Pickford's Public on the Home Front', in Karel Dibbets and Bert Hogenkamp (eds), *Film and the First World War* (Amsterdam, 1995), pp. 149–59

Delooz, P., 'Towards a Sociological Study of Canonized Sainthood in the Catholic Church', in Stephen Wilson (ed.), *Saints and their Cults. Studies in Religious Sociology, Folklore and History* (Cambridge, 1983), pp. 189–216

Demm, Eberhard, 'Propaganda and Caricature in the First World War', *Journal of Contemporary History*, 28 (1993), pp. 163–92

Deperchin-Gouillard, Annie, 'Responsabilité et violation du droit des gens pendant la première guerre mondiale. Volonté politique et impuissance juridique', in Annette Wieviorka (ed.), *Les Procès de Nuremberg et de Tokyo* (Brussels, 1996), pp. 25–49

Digeon, Claude, *La Crise allemande de la pensée française (1870–1914)* (Paris, 1959)

Ditt, Karl, 'Die Kulturraumforschung zwischen Wissenschaft und Politik. Das Beispiel Franz Petri (1903–1993)', *Westfälische Forschungen*, 46 (1996), pp. 73–176

Doerries, Reinhard R., 'Promoting *Kaiser* and *Reich*: Imperial German Propaganda in the United States during World War I', in Hans-Jürgen Schröder (ed.), *Confrontation and Cooperation: Germany and the United States in the Era of World War I, 1900–1924* (Providence and Oxford, 1993), pp. 135–65

Dollinger, Philippe (ed.), *L'Alsace de 1900 à nos jours* (Toulouse, 1979)

Douglas, R., 'Voluntary Enlistment in the First World War and the PRC', *Journal of Modern History*, 42 (1970), pp. 564–85

Draux, E., *Nouvelle Histoire d'Orchies* (Lille, 1980)

Dreyer, Michael and Lembcke, Oliver, *Die deutsche Diskussion um die Kriegsschuldfrage 1918/19* (Berlin, 1993)

Dülffer, Jost, *Regeln gegen den Krieg? Die Haager Friedens-Konferenzen 1899 und 1907 in der internationalen Politik* (Berlin, 1980)

Dumoulin, Michel, 'La Propagande belge en Italie au début de la première guerre mondiale (août–décembre 1914)', *Bulletin de l'Institut Historique Belge de Rome*, 46–7 (1976–7), pp. 335–67

——'La Propagande belge dans les pays neutres au début de la première guerre mondiale (août 1914–février 1915)', *Revue Belge d'Histoire Militaire*, 22 (1977), pp. 246–59

Eksteins, Modris, *Rites of Spring: The Great War and the Birth of the Modern Age* (London, 1989)

Eley, Geoff, *Reshaping the German Right: Radical Nationalism and Political Change after Bismarck* (New Haven and London, 1980)

Ellis, John, *The Social History of the Machine Gun* (1976; new edn, London, 1993)

Epstein, Klaus, *Matthias Erzberger and the Dilemma of German Democracy* (1959; new edn, New York, 1971)

Erger, Johannes, *Der Kapp-Lüttwitz-Putsch. Ein Beitrag zur deutschen Innenpolitik 1919/20* (Düsseldorf, 1967)

Evans, Ellen and Baylen, Joseph, 'History as Propaganda: The German Foreign Ministry and the

"Enlightenment" of American Historians on the War-Guilt Question, 1930–1935', in Keith Wilson (ed.), *Forging the Collective Memory: Government and International Historians through Two World Wars* (Oxford and Providence, 1996), pp. 151–77

Evans, Richard J., *Kneipengespräche im Kaiserreich. Stimmungsberichte der Hamburger Politischen Polizei 1892–1914* (Reinbek bei Hamburg, 1989)

——*Rituals of Retribution: Capital Punishment in Germany, 1600–1987* (London, 1996)

——'In Search of German Social Darwinism: The History and Historiography of a Concept', in Manfred Berg and Geoffrey Cocks (eds), *Medicine and Modernity: Public Health and Medical Care in Nineteenth- and Twentieth-Century Germany* (Washington, D.C., and Cambridge, 1997), pp. 55–80

Eyck, Erich, *A History of the Weimar Republic*, 2 vols (1954–6; English translation, Cambridge, Mass., 1962–7)

Farge, Arlette and Revel, Jacques, *The Rules of Rebellion: Child Abductions in Paris in 1750* (1988; English translation, Cambridge, 1990)

Farmer, Sarah, *Martyred Village: Commemorating the 1944 Massacre at Oradour-sur-Glane* (London, 1999)

Farrar, Marjorie, *Principled Pragmatist: The Political Career of Alexandre Millerand* (New York and Oxford, 1991)

Fellman, Michael, *Inside War: The Guerrilla Conflict in Missouri during the American Civil War* (New York, 1989)

Fink, Carole, *Marc Bloch: A Life in History* (Cambridge, 1989)

Fischer, Fritz, *Germany's Aims in the First World War* (1961; English translation, London, 1967)

——*War of Illusions: German Policies from 1911 to 1914* (1969; English translation, London, 1975)

——'Exzesse der Autokratie. Das Hale-Interview Wilhelms II. vom 19. Juli 1908', in Fischer (ed.), *Hitler war kein Betriebsunfall. Aufsätze* (Munich, 1992), pp. 104–35

Fisher, H. A. L., *James Bryce*, 2 vols (London, 1927)

Fitzpatrick, David, 'The Logic of Collective Sacrifice: Ireland and the British Army, 1914–1918', *Historical Journal*, 38/4 (1995), pp. 1017–30

——*The Two Irelands, 1912–1939* (Oxford, 1998)

——(ed.), *Ireland and the First World War* (Dublin, 1986)

Fontana, Jacques, *Les Catholiques français pendant la grande guerre* (Paris, 1990)

Förster, Stig, *Der doppelte Militarismus. Die deutsche Heeresrüstungspolitik zwischen Status-Quo-Sicherung und Aggression 1890–1913* (Stuttgart, 1985)

——'Der deutsche Generalstab und die Illusion des kurzen Krieges 1871–1914. Metakritik eines Mythos', *Militärgeschichtliche Mitteilungen*, 54 (1995), pp. 61–95

Fox, John, 'The Jewish Factor in British War Crimes Policy in 1942', *English Historical Review*, 362 (1977), pp. 82–106

French, David, 'Spy Fever in Britain, 1900–15', *Historical Journal*, 21/2 (1978), pp. 355–70

Friedeburg, Robert von, 'Konservatismus und Reichskolonialrecht. Konservatives Weltbild und kolonialer Gedanke in England und Deutschland vom späten 19. Jahrhundert bis zum Ersten Weltkrieg', *Historische Zeitschrift*, 263 (1996), pp. 345–93

Fussell, Paul, *The Great War and Modern Memory* (New York and London, 1975)

Gay, Peter, *The Bourgeois Experience: Victoria to Freud* 5 vols (London and New York, 1984–98), vol. 3, *The Cultivation of Hatred* (1993)

Geiss, Imanuel, 'Die Kosaken kommen! Ostpreußen im August 1914', in Geiss (ed.), *Das Deutsche Reich und der Erste Weltkrieg* (1978; 2nd edn, Munich, 1985)

——'Die Kriegsschuldfrage. Das Ende eines nationalen Tabus', in Geiss (ed.), *Das Deutsche Reich und die Vorgeschichte des Ersten Weltkriegs* (Munich and Vienna, 1978), pp. 204–29

Gérard-Libois, J. and Gotovitch, José, *L'An 40. La Belgique occupée* (Brussels, 1971)

Girardet, Raoul, *Mythes et mythologies politiques* (Paris, 1986)

Giuliano, Gérard, 'L'Exode des populations ardennaises en mai–juin 1940', in Maurice Vaïsse (ed.), *Ardennes 1940* (Paris, 1991)

Giuliano, Gérard, with Jacques Lambert and Valérie Rostowsky, *Les Ardennais dans la tourmente. De la mobilisation à l'évacuation* (Charleville-Mézières, 1990)

Gombin, Richard, *Les Socialistes et la guerre. La S.F.I.O. et la politique étrangère française entre les deux guerres mondiales* (Paris and The Hague, 1970)

Graux, Lucien, *Les Fausses Nouvelles de la grande guerre*, 7 vols (Paris, 1918–20)

Gregory, Adrian, *The Silence of Memory: Armistice Day 1914–1946* (Oxford and Providence, 1994)

Grossmann, Atina, 'A Question of Silence: The Rape of German Women by Occupation Soldiers', *October 72* (Spring 1995), pp. 43–63

Grueber, Carol S., *Mars and Minerva: World War I and the Uses of the Higher Learning in America* (Baton Rouge, La., 1975)

Gullace, Nicoletta, 'Sexual Violence and Family Honor: British Propaganda and International Law during the First World War', *American Historical Review*, 102/3 (1997), pp. 714–47

Habermas, Jürgen, *The Structural Transformation of the Public Sphere* (1962; English translation, Cambridge, Mass., 1989)

Hagen, Mark von, 'The Great War and the Mobilization of Ethnicity in the Russian Empire', in Barnett Rubin and Jack L. Snyder (eds), *Post-Soviet Political Order: Conflict and State Building* (London, 1998)

Hahn, Eric, 'The German Foreign Ministry and the Question of War Guilt in 1918–1919', in Carole Fink, Isabel Hull, and MacGregor Knox (eds), *German Nationalism and the European Response, 1890–1945* (London, 1985), pp. 43–70

Hahn, Wilhelm and Kühl, Johann (eds), *Der Fall Löwen 1914 und was dort wirklich geschah. Eine kriegsgeschichtliche Antwort deutscher Soldaten auf die Beschuldigungen von Dr. Peter Schöller* (Plön am See, 1963)

Halttunen, Karen, 'Humanitarianism and the Pornography of Pain in Anglo-American Culture', *American Historical Review*, 100/2 (1995), pp. 303–34

Hanna, Martha, *The Mobilization of Intellect: French Scholars and Writers during the Great War* (Cambridge, Mass., 1996)

Harris, Ruth, 'The "Child of the Barbarian": Rape, Race and Nationalism in France during the First World War', *Past and Present*, 141 (1993), pp. 170–206

Hauser, Markus, *Der Kampf Irregulärer im Kriegsrecht (Artikel 1 und 2 der Landkriegsordnung 1907)* (Bad Ragaz, 1937)

Hautecler, Georges (ed.), *Le Rapport du général Leman sur la défense de Liège en août 1914* (Brussels, 1960)

Heinemann, Ulrich, *Die verdrängte Niederlage. Politische Öffentlichkeit und Kriegsschuldfrage in der Weimarer Republik* (Göttingen, 1983)

Herbecq, Antoine and Herbecq, Eugène, *A Dinant le 23 août 1914 dans le quartier Saint Nicolas* (Dinant, 1977)

Herwig, Holger, 'Clio Deceived: Patriotic Self-Censorship in Germany after the Great War', in Keith Wilson (ed.), *Forging the Collective Memory: Government and International Historians through Two World Wars* (Oxford and Providence, 1996), pp. 87–127

——*The First World War: Germany and Austria-Hungary 1914–1918* (London, 1997)

Hiley, Nicholas, 'The News Media and British Propaganda 1914–18', in Jean-Jacques Becker with Stéphane Audoin-Rouzeau (eds), *Les Sociétés européennes et la guerre de 1914–1918* (Paris, 1990), pp. 175–81

Himmer, C. and Herbecq, Antoine, *A Dinant, quelques homélies en souvenir du 23 août 1914 et du 11 novembre 1918* (Dinant, 1992)

Hirschfeld, Gerhard and Krumeich, Gerd, with Irina Renz (eds), *Keiner fühlt sich hier mehr als Mensch ... Erlebnis und Wirkung des Ersten Weltkriegs* (Essen, 1993)

Hobsbawm, Eric, 'Barbarism: A User's Guide', in Hobsbawm, *On History* (London, 1997), pp. 334–50

Holl, Karl and Wette, Wolfram (eds), *Pazifismus in der Weimarer Republik. Beiträge zur historischen Friedensforschung* (Paderborn, 1981)

Holroyd, Michael, *Bernard Shaw*, 5 vols (London, 1988–92), vol. 2, *1898–1918: The Pursuit of Power* (London, 1989)

Holt, Richard, *Sport and Society in Modern France* (London, 1981)

Hoover, Arlie J., *God, Germany and Britain in the Great War: A Study in Clerical Nationalism* (New York, Westport, London, 1989)

Horne, John, 'Les Mains coupées: "atrocités allemandes" et opinion française en 1914', in Jean-Jacques Becker et al. (eds), *Guerre et cultures, 1914–1918* (Paris, 1994), pp. 133–46

——'L'Étranger, la guerre, et l'image de l'"autre", 1914–1918', in Jean-Pierre Jessenne (ed.), *L'Image de l'autre dans l'Europe du Nord-Ouest à travers l'histoire* (Lille, 1996)

——'Remobilizing for "Total War": France and Britain, 1917–1918', in Horne (ed.), *State, Society and Mobilization in Europe during the First World War* (Cambridge, 1997), pp. 195–211

——'Corps, lieux et nation. La France et l'invasion de 1914', *Annales: Histoire, Sciences Sociales*, 1 (2000), pp. 73–109

——'Defining the Enemy: War, Law and the *Levée en masse* from 1870 to 1945', in Daniel Moran and Arthur Waldron (eds), *The People in Arms: Military Myth and Political Legitimacy since the French Revolution* (Cambridge, forthcoming)

——(ed.), *State, Society and Mobilization in Europe during the First World War* (Cambridge, 1997)

Horne, John and Alan Kramer, 'German "Atrocities" and Franco-German Opinion, 1914: The Evidence of German Soldiers' Diaries', *Journal of Modern History*, 66/1 (1994), pp. 1–33

——'War between Soldiers and Enemy Civilians, 1914–1915', in Roger Chickering and Stig Förster (eds), *Great War, Total War: Combat and Mobilization on the Western Front, 1914–1918* (Cambridge, 2000), pp. 153–68

Howard, Michael, *The Franco-Prussian War: The German Invasion of France, 1870–1871* (1961; new edn, New York, 1990)

——*War in European History* (Oxford, 1976)

——(ed.), *Restraints on War: Studies in the Limitation of Armed Conflict* (Oxford, 1979)

Huber, Michel, *La Population de la France pendant la guerre* (Paris, 1931)

Hughes, H. Stuart, *Consciousness and Society: The Reorientation of European Social Thought 1890–1930* (1958; new edn, Brighton, 1979)

Hunt, Lynn, *The Family Romance of the French Revolution* (London, 1994)

Hynes, Samuel, *The Edwardian Turn of Mind* (Princeton, 1968)

——*A War Imagined: The First World War and English Culture* (London, 1990)

Ignatieff, Michael, *The Warrior's Honor: Ethnic War and the Modern Conscience* (London, 1998)

Ingram, Norman, *The Politics of Dissent: Pacifism in France, 1919–1939* (Oxford, 1991)

Jacobs, E.-A., 'Les Oubliés. Le rôle de la Garde civique en août 1914', in *Le Roi Albert et ses soldats* (Brussels, 1973), pp. 9–15

——'La Garde Civique de la province de Liège en 1914', in *Fédération des Cercles d'Archéologie et d'Histoire de Belgique, XLIVe Session. Congrès de Huy*, 2 vols (1976), vol. 2, pp. 526–8

Jacobson, Jon, *Locarno Diplomacy: Germany and the West 1925–1929* (Princeton, 1972)

Jäger, Wolfgang, *Historische Forschung und politische Kultur in Deutschland. Die Debatte 1914–1980 über den Ausbruch des Ersten Weltkrieges* (Göttingen, 1984)

Jeismann, Michael *Das Vaterland der Feinde. Studien zum nationalen Feindbegriff und Selbstverständnis in Deutschland und Frankreich 1792–1918* (Stuttgart, 1992)

Jeismann, Michael and Westheider, Rolf, 'Wofür stirbt der Bürger? Nationaler Totenkult und Staatsbürgertum in Deutschland und Frankreich seit der Französischen Revolution', in Reinhart Koselleck and Michael Jeismann (eds), *Der politische Totenkult. Kriegerdenkmäler in der Moderne* (Munich 1994), pp. 25–50

Jeřábek, Rudolf, *Potiorek. General im Schatten von Sarajevo* (Graz, Vienna, Cologne, 1991)

Keegan, John, *Opening Moves: August 1914* (London, 1971)

Keiger, John, *Raymond Poincaré* (Cambridge, 1997)

Kennedy, David, *Over Here: The First World War and American Society* (New York, 1980)

Kennedy, Paul M., *The Rise of the Anglo-German Antagonism, 1860–1914* (London, 1980)

Knightley, Philip, *The First Casualty: The War Correspondent as Hero, Propagandist and Myth Maker* (London, 1982)

Koeltz, Louis, *La Guerre de 1914–1918. Les opérations militaires* (Paris, 1966)

Koszyk, Kurt, *Deutsche Pressepolitik im Ersten Weltkrieg* (Düsseldorf, 1968)

Kramer, Alan, '"Greueltaten". Zum Problem der deutschen Kriegsverbrechen in Belgien und Frankreich 1914', in Gerhard Hirschfeld and Gerd Krumeich, with Irina Renz (eds), *Keiner fühlt sich hier mehr als Mensch …* (Essen, 1993), pp. 85–114

——'Les "Atrocités allemandes": mythologie populaire, propagande et manipulations dans l'armée allemande', in Jean-Jacques Becker et al. (eds), *Guerre et cultures, 1914–1918* (Paris, 1994), pp. 147–64

——'*Wackes* at War: Alsace-Lorraine and the Failure of German National Mobilization, 1914–1918', in John Horne (ed.), *State, Society and Mobilization in Europe during the First World War* (Cambridge, 1997), pp. 105–21

——'Der Umgang mit der Schuld. Die "Schuld im Kriege" und die Republik von Weimar', in Dietrich Papenfuß and Wolfgang Schieder (eds), *Deutsche Umbrüche im 20. Jahrhundert* (Cologne and Weimar, 2000), pp. 75–94

Kramer, Alan and John Horne, 'German "Atrocities" and Franco-German Opinion 1914: The Evidence of German Soldiers' Diaries', *Journal of Modern History*, 66/1 (1994), pp. 1–33

——'War between Soldiers and Enemy Civilians, 1914–1915', in Roger Chickering with Stig Förster (eds), *Great War, Total War. Combat and Mobilization on the Weatern Front, 1914–1918* (Cambridge, 2000), pp. 153–68

Krumeich, Gerd, 'L'Entrée en guerre en Allemagne', in Jean-Jacques Becker and Stéphane Audoin-Rouzeau, *Les Sociétés européennes et la guerre, 1914–1918* (Paris, 1990), pp. 65–74

——'Ernst Lavisse und die Kritik an der deutschen "Kultur", 1914–1918', in Wolfgang Mommsen (ed.), *Kultur und Krieg* (Munich, 1996), pp. 143–54

——'The Myth of Gambetta and the "People's War" in Germany and France, 1871–1914', in Stig Förster and Jörg Nagler (eds), *On the Road to Total War: The American Civil War and the German Wars of Unification, 1861–1871* (Cambridge, 1997), pp. 641–55

Kruse, Wolfgang, *Krieg und nationale Integration. Eine Neuinterpretation des sozialdemokratischen Burgfriedensschlusses 1914–15* (Essen, 1993)

Lange, Karl, *Marneschlacht und deutsche Öffentlichkeit 1914–1939. Eine verdrängte Niederlage und ihre Folgen* (Düsseldorf, 1974)

Laqueur, Walter, *Guerrilla: A Historical Study* (London, 1977)

——*The Terrible Secret: Suppression of the Truth about Hitler's 'Final Solution'* (1980; new edn, Harmondsworth, 1982)

Lasswell, Harold D., *Propaganda Technique in World War I* (1927; new edn, Cambridge, Mass., 1971)

Latour, Francis, *La Papauté et les problèmes de la paix pendant la grande guerre* (Paris, 1996)

Le Goff, Jacques, 'Reims, City of Coronation', in Pierre Nora (ed.), *Realms of Memory*, vol. 3, *Symbols* (English translation, New York, 1998), pp. 193–251

Lefebvre, Georges, *The Great Fear of 1789: Rural Panic in Revolutionary France* (1932; English translation, London, 1973)

Levene, Mark, 'Frontiers of Genocide: Jews in the Eastern War Zones', in Panikos Panayi (ed.), *Minorities in Wartime: National and Racial Groupings in Europe, North America and Australia during the Two World Wars* (Oxford, 1993), pp. 83–117

Lévy, Jean-Pierre (with the collaboration of Dominique Veillon), *Mémoires d'un franc-tireur. Itinéraire d'un résistant (1940–1944)* (Brussels, 1998)

Liulevicius, Vejas G., *War Land on the Eastern Front: Culture, National Identity, and German Occupation in World War I* (Cambridge, 2000)

Loftus, Elizabeth F., *Eyewitness Testimony* (Cambridge, Mass., 1978)

Luckau, Alma, *The German Delegation at the Paris Peace Conference* (New York, 1941)

Luebke, Frederick C., *Bonds of Loyalty: German Americans and World War I* (De Kalb, Ill., 1974)

Lukes, Stephen, *Émile Durkheim: His Life and Work* (London, 1973)

Luzzatto, Sergio, *L'Impôt du sang. La gauche française à l'épreuve de la guerre mondiale, 1900–1945* (Lyon, 1996)

Lyon, Bryce, *Henri Pirenne: A Biographical and Intellectual Study* (Ghent, 1974)

McMillan, James, 'French Catholics: *Rumeurs Infâmes* and the *Union Sacrée*, 1914–1918', in Frans Coetzee and Marilyn Shevin-Coetzee (eds), *Authority, Identity and the Social History of the Great*

War (Oxford and Providence, 1995), pp. 113–32

Marby, Jean-Pierre, 'Les Monuments aux morts ardennais de la grande guerre', *Revue historique ardennaise*, 22 (1987), pp. 137–53

Marrus, Michael R., *The Nuremberg War Crimes Trial 1945–46: A Documentary History* (Boston and New York, 1997)

Masterman, Lucy, *C. F. G. Masterman* (London, 1939)

Maurin, Jules, *Armée, guerre, société. Soldats languedociens (1889–1919)* (Paris, 1982)

Mayence, Fernand, 'La Falsification des sources relatives à la question des prétendus Francs-Tireurs à Louvain, en août 1914', *Bulletin de l'Académie Royale de Belgique* (1955), pp. 155–71

Mazower, Mark, *Inside Hitler's Greece: The Experience of Occupation 1941–1944* (New Haven, 1993)

Meseberg-Haubold, Ilse, *Der Widerstand Kardinal Merciers gegen die deutsche Besetzung Belgiens 1914–1918. Ein Beitrag zur politischen Rolle des Katholizismus im ersten Weltkrieg* (Frankfurt and Berne, 1982)

Messinger, Gary S., *British Propaganda and the State in the First World War* (Manchester, 1992)

Miller, Jane Kathryn, *Belgian Foreign Policy between the Two Wars, 1919–1940* (New York, 1951)

Miquel, Pierre, *La Paix de Versailles et l'opinion publique française* (Paris, 1972)

Mock, James R. and Larson, Cedric, *Words that Won the War: The Story of the Committee on Public Information* (Princeton, 1939)

Molis, Robert, *Les Francs-Tireurs et les Garibaldi. Soldats de la République. 1870–1871 en Bourgogne* (Paris, 1995)

Mommsen, Wolfgang J., 'Public Opinion and Foreign Policy in Wilhelmine Germany, 1897–1914', in Mommsen (ed.), *Imperial Germany 1867–1918: Politics, Culture, and Society in an Authoritarian Empire* (1990; English translation, London, 1995), pp. 189–204

——'Culture and Politics in the German Empire', in Mommsen, *Imperial Germany 1867–1918* (1990; English translation, London, 1995), pp. 119–40

——'The Prussian Conception of the State and the German Idea of Empire: Prussia and the German Empire in Recent German History', in Mommsen, *Imperial Germany 1867–1918* (1990; English translation, London, 1995), pp. 41–56

——*Großmachtstellung und Weltpolitik 1870–1914. Die Außenpolitik des Deutschen Reiches* (Frankfurt and Berlin, 1993)

——*Bürgerliche Kultur und künstlerische Avantgarde 1870 bis 1918. Kultur und Politik im deutschen Kaiserreich* (Frankfurt and Berlin, 1994)

——(ed.) *Kultur und Krieg: Die Rolle der Intellektuellen, Künstler und Schriftsteller im Ersten Weltkrieg* (Munich, 1996)

——'German Artists, Writers, and Intellectuals and the Meaning of War, 1914–1918', in John Horne (ed.), *State, Society and Mobilization in Europe during the First World War* (Cambridge, 1997), pp. 21–38

Moncure, John, *Forging the King's Sword: Military Education between Tradition and Modernization, The Case of the Royal Prussian Cadet Corps, 1871–1918* (New York and Frankfurt, 1993)

Monticone, Alberto, *La Germania e la neutralità italiana* (Bologna, 1971)

Morgan, Kenneth O., *Consensus and Disunity: The Lloyd George Coalition Government, 1918–1922* (Oxford, 1979)

Morin, Edgar, *Rumour in Orléans* (1969; English translation, London, 1971)

Morris, A. J. A., *The Scaremongers: The Advocacy of War and Rearmament 1896–1914* (London, 1984)

Mosse, George, *Fallen Soldiers: Reshaping the Memory of the World Wars* (New York, 1990)

Naquet, Emmanuel, 'La Société d'études documentaires et critiques sur la guerre. Ou la naissance d'une minorité pacifiste au sein de la Ligue des Droits de l'Homme', in 'S'Engager pour la paix dans la France de l'entre-deux-guerres', *Matériaux pour l'histoire de notre temps*, 30 (1993), pp. 6–10

Nelson, Keith, 'The "Black Horror on the Rhine": Race as a Factor in Post-World War I Diplomacy', *Journal of Modern History*, 42/4 (1970), pp. 606–27

Néré, Jacques, *The Foreign Policy of France from 1914 to 1945* (1974; English translation, London, 1975)

Nipperdey, Thomas, *Deutsche Geschichte 1866–1918*, 2 vols (Munich, 1990–2), vol. 2, *Machtstaat vor der Demokratie* (2nd edn, Munich, 1993)

Nora, Pierre, 'Lavisse, instituteur national', in Nora (ed.), *Les Lieux de mémoire*, vol. 1 (new edn, Paris, 1997), pp. 239–75

——(ed.), *Les Lieux de mémoire. La République, la Nation, les France* (Paris, 1984–92; new edn, 3 vols, 1997). Abbreviated English translation, *Realms of Memory: Rethinking the French Past*, 3 vols (New York, 1996–8)

Novick, Peter, *That Noble Dream: The 'Objectivity Question' and the American Historical Profession* (New York, 1988)

Otto, Ernst, *Schlieffen und der Generalstab. Der preußisch-deutsche Generalstab unter Leitung des Generals von Schlieffen 1891–1905* (Berlin [DDR], 1966)

Panayi, Panikos, *The Enemy in our Midst: Germans in Britain during the First World War* (New York and Oxford, 1991)

——(ed.) *Minorities in Wartime: National and Racial Groupings in Europe, North America and Australia during the Two World Wars* (Oxford, 1993)

Paret, Peter, *Clausewitz and the State: The Man, his Theories, and his Times* (1976; new edn, Princeton, 1985)

——'Conscription and the End of the Ancien Regime in France and Prussia', in Paret, *Understanding War: Essays on Clausewitz and the History of Military Power* (Princeton, 1992), pp. 53–74

Peemans, F., 'Tensions dans les relations belgo-vaticanes en 1914–1918. La conciliation difficile des nationalismes et des intérêts catholiques en Europe', *Risorgimento*, 21 (1979), pp. 173–94

Petri, Franz and Schöller, Peter, 'Zur Bereinigung des Franktireurproblems vom August 1914', *Vierteljahrshefte für Zeitgeschichte*, 9 (1961), pp. 234–48

Peukert, Detlev, *The Weimar Republic: The Crisis of Classical Modernity* (1987; English translation, London, 1991)

Pflanze, Otto, *Bismarck: der Reichsgründer* (Munich, 1997)

Pirenne, Henri, *La Belgique et la guerre mondiale* (Paris, 1928)

Playne, Caroline, *Britain Holds On, 1917–18* (London, 1933)

Pogge von Strandmann, Hartmut, 'The Role of British and German Historians in Mobilizing Public Opinion in 1914', in Benedikt Stuchtey and Peter Wende (eds), *British and German Historiography 1750–1950: Traditions, Perceptions, and Transfers* (Oxford, 2000), pp. 335–71

Prochasson, Christophe, *Les Intellectuels, le socialisme et la guerre 1900–1938* (Paris, 1993)

Prochasson, Christophe and Rasmussen, Anne, *Au nom de la patrie. Les intellectuels et la première guerre mondiale* (Paris, 1996)

Prost, Antoine, *Les Anciens Combattants et la société française 1914–1939*, 3 vols (Paris, 1977), vol. 3, *Mentalités et idéologies*

——(ed.), *Les Anciens Combattants 1914–1940* (Paris, 1977)

Ranitz, Ariane de, *'Met een Pen en een Potlood als Wapen!' Louis Raemaekers (1869–1956). Schets van een Politiek Tekenaar* (n.pl., 1989)

Read, James M., *Atrocity Propaganda 1914–1919* (New Haven, 1941)

Reemtsma, Jan Philipp, 'Die Idee des Vernichtungskrieges. Clausewitz – Ludendorff – Hitler', in Hannes Heer and Klaus Naumann (eds), *Vernichtungskrieg. Verbrechen der Wehrmacht 1941–1944* (1995; new edn, Frankfurt, 1997), pp. 377–401

Reeves, Nicholas, *Official British Film Propaganda during the First World War* (London, 1986)

Renouvin, Pierre, 'L'Opinion publique et la guerre en 1917', *Revue d'histoire moderne et contemporaine*, 15/1 (1968), pp. 4–23

Reshef, Oriel, *Guerres, mythes et caricature. Au berceau d'une mentalité française* (Paris, 1984)

Ringer, Fritz, *The Decline of the German Mandarins: The German Academic Community 1890–1933* (1969; new edn, Hanover and London, 1990)

Ritter, Gerhard, *The Sword and the Sceptre: The Problem of Militarism in Germany*, 4 vols (1954–68; English translation, 1972–3); vol. 1, *The Prussian Tradition 1740–1890* (1954; English translation, London, 1972); vol. 3, *The Tragedy of Statesmanship: Bethmann Hollweg as War Chancellor (1914–1917)* (1968; English translation, London, 1973)

——*The Schlieffen Plan: Critique of a Myth* (1956: English translation, New York, 1958)

Robbins, Keith, 'History and Politics: The Career of James Bryce', in Robbins (ed.), *Politicians, Diplomacy and War in Modern British History* (London, 1994), pp. 189–214

Rohrkrämer, Thomas, *Der Militarismus der 'kleinen Leute'. Die Kriegervereine im Deutschen Kaiserreich 1871–1914* (Munich, 1990)

Rossé, J. et al. (eds) on behalf of the friends of Abbé Dr Haegy, *Das Elsaß von 1870–1932*, 4 vols (Colmar, n.d., but 1936), vol. 1, *Politische Geschichte*

Roth, François, *La Guerre de 70* (Paris, 1990)

——'Lorraine annexée et Lorraine occupée, 1914–1918', in Jean-Jacques Becker and Stéphane Audoin-Rouzeau (eds), *Les Sociétés européennes et la guerre de 1914–1918* (Paris, 1990), pp. 289–309

Rürup, Reinhard, 'Der "Geist von 1914" in Deutschland. Kriegsbegeisterung und Ideologisierung des Krieges im Ersten Weltkrieg', in Bernd Hüppauf (ed.), *Ansichten vom Krieg. Vergleichende Studien zum Ersten Weltkrieg in Literatur und Gesellschaft* (Königstein/Ts, 1984), pp. 1–30

Sanders, Michael L. and Taylor, Philip M., *British Propaganda during the First World War* (London, 1982)

Savart, Marcel, *Occupation 1914–1918. Quarante ans après. Martyrologie de la zone envahie. Massacres et déportations* (Nancy, 1958)

Sayer, Derek, 'British Reaction to the Amritsar Massacre, 1919–1920', *Past and Present*, 131 (1991), pp. 130–64

Schaepdrijver, Sophie de, *De Groote Oorlog. Het koninkrijk België tijdens de Eerste Wereldoorlog* (Amsterdam, 1997)

——'Occupation, Propaganda, and the Idea of Belgium', in Aviel Roshwald and Richard Stites (eds), *European Culture in the Great War: The Arts, Entertainment, and Propaganda, 1914–1918* (Cambridge, 1999), pp. 267–94

Scheidgen, Hermann-Josef, *Deutsche Bischöfe im Ersten Weltkrieg. Die Mitglieder der Fuldaer Bischofskonferenz und ihre Ordinariate 1914–1918* (Cologne, Weimar, Vienna, 1991)

Schivelbusch, Wolfgang, *Die Bibliothek von Löwen. Eine Episode aus der Zeit der Weltkriege* (Munich and Vienna, 1988)

Schoenbaum, David, *Zabern 1913: Consensus Politics in Imperial Germany* (London, 1982)

Schöller, Peter, *Der Fall Löwen und das Weißbuch. Eine kritische Untersuchung der deutschen Dokumentation über die Vorgänge in Löwen vom 25. bis 28. August 1914* (Cologne and Graz, 1958); French translation, *Le Cas de Louvain et le Livre Blanc allemand* (Louvain and Paris, 1958)

Schreiber, Gerhard, *Deutsche Kriegsverbrechen in Italien: Täter, Opfer, Strafverfolgung* (Munich, 1996)

Schulte, Bernd F., *Die deutsche Armee 1900–1914. Zwischen Beharren und Verändern* (Düsseldorf, 1977)

——*Europäische Krise und Erster Weltkrieg: Beiträge zur Militärpolitik des Kaiserreichs, 1871–1914*, (Frankfurt, 1983)

Schumann, Andreas, '"Der Künstler an die Krieger". Zur Kriegsliteratur kanonisierter Autoren', in Wolfgang J. Mommsen (ed.), *Kultur und Krieg* (Munich, 1996), pp. 221–33

Schwengler, Walter, *Völkerrecht, Versailler Vertrag und Auslieferungsfrage. Die Strafverfolgung wegen Kriegsverbrechen als Problem des Friedensschlusses 1919/20* (Stuttgart, 1982)

Showalter, Denis, *Tannenberg: Clash of Empires* (Hamden, Conn., 1991)

Simkins, Peter, *Kitchener's Army: The Raising of the New Armies, 1914–1916* (Manchester, 1988)

Skidelsky, Robert, *John Maynard Keynes: Hopes Betrayed 1883–1920* (London, 1983; new edn, 1992)

Smelser, Neil J., *Theory of Collective Behavior* (London, 1962)

Soboul, Albert, 'Religious Feeling and Popular Cults during the French Revolution: "Patriot Saints" and Martyrs for Liberty', in Stephen Wilson (ed.), *Saints and their Cults: Studies in Religious Sociology, Folklore and History* (Cambridge, 1983), pp. 217–32

Speitkamp, Winfried, '"Ein dauerndes und ehrenvolles Denkmal deutscher Kulturtätigkeit". Denkmalpflege im Kaiserreich 1871–1918', *Die Alte Stadt. Vierteljahreszeitschrift für Stadtgeschichte, Stadtsoziologie und Denkmalpflege*, 18/2 (1991), pp. 173–97

Spence, Donald F., *Narrative Truth and Historical Truth: Meaning and Interpretation in Psychoanalysis* (New York, 1982)

Sproule, J. Michael, *Propaganda and Democracy: The American Experience of Media and Mass*

Persuasion (Cambridge, 1997)

Squires, James D., *British Propaganda at Home and in the United States from 1914 to 1917* (Cambridge, 1935)

Stargardt, Nicholas, *The German Idea of Militarism: Radical and Socialist Critics 1866–1914* (Cambridge, 1994)

Steinberg, Jonathan, 'The Copenhagen Complex', *Journal of Contemporary History*, 3 (1966), pp. 23–46

Stengers, Jean, 'Notice sur Fernand Vanlangenhove', *Académie Royale de Belgique. Annuaire 1984* (Brussels, 1984), pp. 135–225

——*Congo. Mythes et réalités* (Louvain-la-Neuve, 1989)

——'L'Entrée en guerre de la Belgique', *Guerres Mondiales et Conflits Contemporains*, 179 (1995), pp. 13–33

Stern, Fritz, *Dreams and Delusions: The Drama of German History* (London, 1988)

Stevenson, David, *French War Aims against Germany 1914–1919* (Oxford, 1982)

Stibbe, Matthew, *German Anglophobia and the Great War 1914–1918* (Cambridge, 2001)

Stone, Norman, *The Eastern Front 1914–1917* (London, 1975)

Storz, Dieter, *Kriegsbild und Rüstung vor 1914. Europäische Landstreitkräfte vor dem Ersten Weltkrieg* (Herford, Berlin, Bonn, 1992)

Strachan, Hew, 'Clausewitz and the Rise of Prussian Hegemony', in Strachan, *European Armies and the Conduct of War* (London, 1983), pp. 90–107

Strazhas, Abba, *Deutsche Ostpolitik im Ersten Weltkrieg. Der Fall Ober Ost 1915–1917* (Wiesbaden, 1993)

Stromberg, Roland, *Redemption by War: The Intellectuals and 1914* (Lawrence, Kans., 1982)

Swartz, Marvin, *The Union of Democratic Control in British Politics during the First World War* (Oxford, 1971)

Szymanski, R., *Les Ardennes, terre de France oubliée en 1914–1918* (n.pl. [private publication], 1984)

Taghon, P., *Mai 40. La campagne de dix-huit jours* (Paris and Louvain-la-Neuve, 1989)

Tassier, Suzanne, *La Belgique et l'entrée en guerre des États-Unis (1914–1917)* (Brussels, 1951)

Ternon, Yves, *Les Arméniens. Histoire d'un génocide* (Paris, 1977; new edn, 1996)

Terraine, John, *The Smoke and the Fire: Myths and Anti-Myths of War 1861–1945* (London, 1980)

Thielemans, M. R. and Vandewoude, E. (eds), *Le Roi Albert à travers ses lettres inédites, 1882–1916* (Brussels, 1982)

Tierney, Mark, Bowen, Paul and Fitzpatrick, David, 'Recruiting Posters', in Fitzpatrick (ed.), *Ireland and the First World War* (Dublin, 1986), pp. 47–58

Townshend, Charles, *The British Campaign in Ireland, 1919–1921: The Development of Political and Military Policies* (Oxford, 1978)

Travers, Tim, *The Killing Ground: The British Army, the Western Front and the Emergence of Modern Warfare, 1900–1918* (London, 1987)

Umbreit, Hans, *Der Militärbefehlshaber in Frankreich 1940–1944* (Boppard, 1968)

——'Les Projets allemands et les premières semaines d'occupation', in Maurice Vaïssé (ed.), *Ardennes 1940* (Paris, 1991), pp. 235–46

Ungern-Sternberg, Jürgen von and Ungern-Sternberg, Wolfgang von, *Der Aufruf 'An die Kulturwelt!'. Das Manifest der 93 und die Anfänge der Kriegspropaganda im Ersten Weltkrieg* (Stuttgart, 1996)

Verhey, Jeffrey, *The Spirit of 1914: Militarism, Myth, and Mobilization in Germany* (Cambridge, 2000)

Vidalenc, Jean, *L'Exode de mai–juin 1940* (Paris, 1957)

Villepin, Patrick de, 'La Revue *Évolution* et le pacifisme révisionniste (1926–1933)', in 'S'Engager pour la paix dans la France de l'entre-deux-guerres', *Matériaux pour l'histoire de notre temps*, 30 (1993), pp. 11–13

Vos, Luc de, *Het effectief van de Belgische Krijgsmacht en de Militiewetgeving, 1830–1940* (Brussels, 1985)

Vovelle, Michel, 'La Marseillaise: War or Peace', in Pierre Nora (ed.), *Realms of Memory*, vol. 3, *Symbols* (English translation, New York, 1998), pp. 29–74

Wallace, Stuart, *War and the Image of Germany: British Academics 1914–1918* (Edinburgh, 1988)

Walzer, Michael, *Just and Unjust Wars. A Moral Argument with Historical Illustrations* (1977; 2nd edn, New York, 1992)

Watson, David, *Georges Clemenceau: A Political Biography* (London, 1974)

Wehler, Hans-Ulrich, 'Symbol des halbabsolutistischen Herrschaftssystems: Der Fall Zabern von 1913/14 als Verfassungskrise des Wilhelminischen Kaiserreichs', in Wehler, ed., *Krisenherde des Kaiserreichs 1871–1918. Studien zur deutschen Sozial- und Verfassungsgeschichte* (Göttingen, 1970), pp. 65–84

——'Unfähig zur Verfassungsreform: Das 'Reichsland' Elsaß-Lothringen von 1870 bis 1918', in Wehler (ed.), *Krisenherde des Kaiserreichs 1871–1918* (Göttingen, 1970), pp. 30–51

——*Deutsche Gesellschaftsgeschichte*, 3 vols (Munich, 1987–95), vol. 3, *Von der 'Deutschen Doppelrevolution' bis zum Beginn des Ersten Weltkrieges 1849–1914* (1995)

Weigel, Hans et al., *Jeder Schuss ein Russ. Jeder Stoss ein Franzos. Literarische und graphische Kriegspropaganda in Deutschland und Österreich 1914–1918* (Vienna, 1983)

Wieland, Lothar, *Belgien 1914. Die Frage des belgischen 'Franktireurkrieges' und die deutsche öffentliche Meinung von 1914 bis 1936* (Frankfurt, Berne, New York, 1984)

Wieviorka, Annette (ed.), *Les Procès de Nuremberg et de Tokyo* (Brussels, 1996)

Willis, Irene Cooper, *England's Holy War: A Study of English Liberal Idealism during the Great War* (New York, 1928)

Willis, James F., *Prologue to Nuremberg: The Politics and Diplomacy of Punishing War Criminals of the First World War* (Westport, Conn., and London, 1982)

Wilson, Keith (ed.), *Forging the Collective Memory: Government and International Historians through Two World Wars* (Oxford and Providence, 1996)

Wilson, Trevor, 'Lord Bryce's Investigation into Alleged German Atrocities in Belgium 1914–15', *Journal of Contemporary History*, 14/3 (1979), pp. 369–83

——*The Myriad Faces of War: Britain and the Great War, 1914–1918* (Cambridge, 1986)

Winter, Jay, *Sites of Memory, Sites of Mourning: The Great War in European Cultural History* (Cambridge, 1995)

Wishnia, Judith, 'Natalisme et nationalisme pendant la première guerre mondiale', *Vingtième siècle*, 45 (1995), pp. 30–9

Wohl, Robert, *The Generation of 1914* (Cambridge, Mass., 1979)

Wolf, Karin, *Sir Roger Casement und die deutsch-irischen Beziehungen* (Berlin, 1972)

Ypersele, Laurence van, *Le Roi Albert. Histoire d'un mythe* (Ottignies, 1995)

Ziemann, Benjamin, *Front und Heimat. Ländliche Kriegserfahrungen im südlichen Bayern 1914–1923* (Essen, 1997)

2 Theses and dissertations

Eck, Jean-François, 'Louis Marin et la Lorraine, 1905–1914. Le pouvoir local d'un parlementaire sous la IIIe République', Doctorat de Troisième Cycle, Institut d'Études Politiques, Paris, 1980

Montant, Jean-Claude, 'La Propagande extérieure de la France pendant la première guerre mondiale: l'exemple de quelques neutres européens', Doctoral thesis, Université de Paris I, 1988

Ribeiro de Meneses, Filipe, 'The Failure of the Portuguese First Republic: An Analysis of Wartime Political Mobilization', Ph.D. thesis, Trinity College Dublin, 1996

Stoneman, Mark, 'The Bavarian Army and French Civilians in the War of 1870–71', Master's dissertation, University of Augsburg, 1994

Thiers, Eric, 'Intellectuels et culture de guerre 1914–1918. L'exemple du Comité d'Études et de Documents sur la Guerre', D.E.A. dissertation, École des Hautes Études en Sciences Sociales, Paris, 1996

Tixhon, Axel, 'Le Souvenir des massacres du 23 août 1914 à Dinant. Étude des commémorations organisées durant l'entre-deux-guerres', Licence dissertation, Université Catholique de Louvain-la-Neuve, 1995

Index